'A town tormented by the sea': GALWAY, 1790–1914

John Cunningham

GEOGRAPHY PUBLICATIONS

I set out with the intention of providing as rounded as possible a picture of 19th century Galway life. The principal focus throughout is on the majority of the population — the men, women, and children who had to struggle in order to make ends meet — but there are glimpses also of the lives and outlooks of the resident elite.

A few words on the structure of the book may be considered necessary. The short first chapter provides a snapshot of the town towards the end of the period — there will be no surprise ending therefore. The first section, which follows, considers economic, social, and political developments up to and including the Famine of the late 1840s; the middle section takes up that story for the post-Famine period. The final section treats, broadly speaking, of cultural life during the long century — subjects including popular amusements, religious faith, education, literacy and language that did not fit easily into a pre-Famine / post-Famine schema.

Starting with the late 18th century, the book takes up Galway's story at the point where James Hardiman's classic *History of Galway* left it in 1820. Hardiman was a useful source for the early chapters, but the historical concerns of the present are rather different to those of his world. I have been influenced, however, by Hardiman's unsentimental approach to his subject.

Published in Ireland by
Geography Publications,
Kennington Road,
Templeogue, Dublin 6w.

ISBN 0 906602 32 7

Design and typesetting by Keystrokes, Dublin.
Printed by The Leinster Leader, Naas, Co. Kildare.

Contents

Acknowledgements   viii

1.   The whole place is practically a ruin…':   1

Economy, Politics, Society, *c*.1790-1850

2.   ECONOMY, ADMINISTRATION, &
     INFRASTRUCTURE, 1800-45   13
     Administrative structures and failings
     The economy
     Administrative change: impulse and impact

3.   CHARITY & WELFARE, 1790-1845   43
     The Galway Mendicity Institute
     A 'chain of charities'
     The Poor Law
     The Galway workhouse, 1842-46

4.   SOCIAL PROTEST, 1810-45   73
     Labour
     The fishermen
     Food rioters

5.   ELECTIONS & POLITICS, 1793-1845   103
     1793-1832
     1832-c.1850

6.   FAMINE, 1846-49   125
     'Up Galwaymen, at them!'
     Let them eat pop-corn
     '… somewhat more generous measures'
     '… protecting the trade in provisions.'
     '… perfect incubi on society…'
     '… the conflicting opinions of the Guardians…'
     '… divested of every feeling of home and humanity.'
     '… the revival of former days…'

Economy, Politics, Society, 1850-1914

7. ECONOMY & INFRASTRUCTURE, 1850-1914   165
    Routes of hope and glory?
    The economy
    Contemplating stubborn realities: a view from the
    late 19th century

8. WELFARE & CHARITY, 1850-1914   193
    The Poor Law after the Famine
    Charity and voluntary relief in the poor law era

9. ELECTIONS & POLITICS, 1850-1914   205
    Electoral corruption: the 1857 Commission
    Elections, c.1868-1914

10. LABOUR & SOCIAL PROTEST, 1850-1914   229
    'But there's no law for the poor now'
    Trade unionism

Culture & Society, c.1790-1914

11. RELIGION: 1790-1914   247
    Churches, chapels and meeting-houses
    The end of the wardenship
    Worship
    Desecrating the Sabbath
    Catholics and Protestants

12. LEISURE & ENTERTAINMENT   279
    Feast days and festivals
    Theatre and performance
    Sport and play
    Races and regattas

13. LEARNING AND LITERACY   317
    Free Schools
    Towards a National Education system
    National schools
    National Schools during and after the Famine
    Primary education in the late 19th century
    Education of the middle-class
    Mechanics' Institute
    '… every article in the stationery and bookselling way'

Epilogue
    A 'most interesting encampment…'   365
    Bibliography   369
    Index   389

Figures and tables

2.1	Percentage of families in each class of accommodation in four Irish towns	18
6.1	Workhouse mortality in the Galway Union	138
8.1	Age and sex of adults in Galway workhouse	200
8.2	Marital status of adult workhouse inmates	200
10.1	Numbers engaged in selected trades	237
13.1	Male literacy, 1780s-1820s	318
13.2	Female literacy, 1780s-1820s	319
13.3	Spoken language(s), 1800-1850	321
13.4	Literacy in three age groups, 1891	338

Illustrations

1.	Distress Committee Time-book	6
2.	The Tholsel	20
3.	County Courthouse	21
4.	Boys of the Claddagh	25
5.	The 'Four Corners'	32
6.	Shop sign	33
7.	View from the Claddagh	37
8.	1818 map	50
9.	1846 map	51
10.	County Infirmary	55
11.	Wanted poster	77
12.	Making a fishing net	82
13.	'Bread or blood', notice	88
14.	Food riot, 1842	90
15.	Anti-export cartoon	94
16.	Market women	96
17.	Election scene	105
18.	View from Wood Quay	114
19.	Election poster	119
20.	Turf Market	148
21.	Emigration advertisements	153
22.	'Poor house from Galway'	155
23.	1898 map	162

24. Browne Doorway   166
25. Opening of Eglinton Canal   168
26. Eglinton reception   170
27. John Orrell Lever   174
28. Fr Peter Daly meets Lord Palmerston   175
29. Persse's Distillery   184
30. 'The Antient Mansion of the Browne's'   186
31. Market Day   188
32. Group on Courthouse steps   195
33. 'The general state of affairs'   198
34. Election scene, 1906   223
35. Fishery notice   230
36. Blessing of the bay   234
37. Fish market scene   235
38. Battle of the placards   238
39. Catholic pro-Cathedral   249
40. Collegiate Church   253
41. Worshipping at a well   258
42. Commerce at every corner   263
43. Galway piper   288
44. Menlo Castle   290
45. Theatre handbill   293
46. Theatre advertisement   298
47. Heading for the Galway Races   309
48. Queen's College Galway   344
49. Two periodicals   355
50. 'Martin Blake and Ireland For Ever'   357

Plates in block between pages

1. Rag day outside the workhouse
2. Aerial view of the workhouse
3. Day out at Menlo Castle
4. Galway Woollen Mills banner
5. Military band in Eyre Square
6. Salthill tram at the Square
7. Sisters of Mercy with their pupils
8. The Jes Sports
9. Working at Cloherty and Semple's timber yard
10. The Iodine Works
11. Eglinton-street RIC barracks
12. The sock market
13. Wash day at the Eglinton Canal
14. Outside a pub
15. Colonial Building and Eglinton Buildings
16. View of Shop-street
17. Sheltering from the storm
18. Sailing ships at the docks
19. Proposed new harbour
20. Máirtín Mór McDonogh
21. Padge King with Mrs King
22. Passing the railway station
23. At market, Collegiate Church
24. Shambles barracks
25. Wooden bridge
26. Piscatorial school
27. Claddagh houses
28. Mechanics Institute
29. James Hardiman
30. Paul O'Connor
31. Eviction scene
32. Fr Peter Daly
33. Fr John Roche
34. Resting in Salthill
35. Salthill cyclist

Acknowledgements

It has been ten years since I began work on this book, and the end result is rather different from what was envisaged in 1994. For their help in bringing the work to its present state, I am obliged to many people, most of all those mentioned below.

My greatest obligation is to Professor Gearóid Ó Tuathaigh, who supervised the dissertation on which the book is based. He was always a generous and perceptive mentor. Alf MacLochlainn read later drafts, and I am grateful for his suggestions — as I have been on previous occasions. Mary Cunningham also read various drafts, drawing attention to shortcomings, and providing encouragement when appropriate. The work benefited greatly also from the suggestions of Professors David Dickson and Nicholas Canny.

Des Kenny of Kenny's bookshop advised on how the original dissertation might best be transformed into a book that would appeal to his customers. The advice is appreciated, as is that of other pre-publication readers, Niall Farrell and Brian Hanney.

As far as the illustrations are concerned, my greatest debt is to Thomas Kenny, who placed both his expertise and his picture collection at my disposal. Jim Higgins of Galway City Council was also very helpful in this regard, as were Timothy Collins and Brendan Glynn.

Over the past ten years, there were many who drew source material to my attention, or provided useful nuggets of information. I thank in particular, Mary Clancy, Frank Canavan, Niall O Ciosain, Caitriona Clear, Martin Feely, Aidan Hynes Maurice Laheen, Dick Lyng, Richard McMahon, Gerard Moran, Tony Varley,

The staff members at the libraries and archives where I conducted my research were courteous, knowledgeable and helpful. At least, 90% of the research was carried out between the James Hardiman Library at NUI, Galway, and the Galway County Library at Island House. I am indebted to all of the staff in both institutions, but in particular to Maureen Moran and Mary Kavanagh at Island House, and to Marie Boran, Margaret Hughes and Kieran Hoare at NUI, Galway. I would also like to acknowledge the assistance of staff at the National Library and at the National Archive. I am grateful also to Tom Maye at the Galway Diocesan Office, to Rev. Patrick Towers and Ann Walton at St Nicholas Collegiate Church, and to Rev. David Kelly of the Augustinian Fathers in Ballyboden, Dublin for facilitating my research on papers in their care. For their hospitality (and for their good company) during research trips in Dublin, I thank Emmet Farrell, Denise Diver, Breda McHugh and Tommie McHugh, Aidan Hynes and Barbara Hynes.

In having offered my work to Geography Publications, I consider myself fortunate — Willie and Teresa Nolan have been accommodating and enthusiastic publishers. And I would like to acknowledge the work of Vincent Canning who designed the website which gave prospective readers a flavour of the book.

The entire process was greatly assisted by the decision of the Heritage Council to grant-aid the publication. I also wish to thank Galway City Council for its generous subvention.

Finally, I must acknowledge the contribution to my life and work of Katie Cunningham and Liam Cunningham.

John Cunningham
September 2004

I ndíl-chuimhne ar Tom Glynn

CHAPTER 1

'The whole place is practically a ruin…'

I know a town tormented by the sea
And there time goes slow
That the people see it flow
And watch it drowsily
And growing older, hour by hour, they say.
'Please God to-morrow!
Then we will work and play'
And their tall houses crumble away.
This town is eaten through with memory
Of pride and thick Spanish gold and wine
And of the great come and go…

> Mary Devenport O'Neill, from 'Galway',
> *Prometheus,* London 1929

Galway entered the 20th century at a low ebb, its population falling, its economy declining, its buildings collapsing. The 'Citie of the Tribes' was no longer officially a city and its so-called tribes, with their fortunes and influence, were thoroughly dispersed. For those few who had been striving to reverse Galway's decline, the publication of the Census of 1911 brought further bad news. It showed that the urban population had decreased for the sixth successive decade, to a mere 13,255. The city had incontrovertibly become a town — it might yet be a village.

In the week that the 1911 census was taken, witnesses were examined at a sworn inquiry into housing conditions in the area around Henry-street known as 'the West'. 'The whole place is practically a ruin', stated one urban councillor. 'Over 100 houses have fallen in, while those still standing are not fit for human habitation'. The description of the chairman of the Board of Guardians was even more graphic:

> I know of instances in which nine or ten live in one little room —
> a kitchen — and that is not more than fourteen feet wide. There

1

are people even living in houses where one would not allow pigs. About a fortnight ago, one of these houses tumbled down, and a family of seven or eight escaped with their lives About five or six years ago fever broke out in Munster-lane, and it took very nearly twelve months to get rid of it … The marvel is that there is not fever now; these tenants have not any sanitary accommodation, and all the slops are thrown out the front door.[1]

The inhabitants of these houses were the sinew and muscle of Galway's economic life. The men of 'the West', according to other witnesses at the inquiry, were working on the docks, in the various mills, and at the building of the new Catholic diocesan college. Later in 1911, they would establish the Galway Workers and General Labourers Union, in an attempt to improve their working conditions.[2]

In centuries past, Galway had been among Ireland's leading ports, its maritime location the key to its prosperity. In their penury, Galwegians retained exalted notions about their place. From the tone of their discourse, it is apparent that its civic leaders regarded Galway as a great city that was going through a bad patch — even if that bad patch was of several centuries duration. And it was natural that those who hoped for a revival in Galway's fortunes in the 19th and early 20th centuries should have looked seawards, to the abundant fishery, to the exceptionally sheltered harbour. The Atlantic tantalised them, rebuking them for their failure to exploit its riches, an ever-present reminder that they were incapable of seizing opportunity in the way that their forefathers had done

By the late 19th century, Galway handled only about 0.6% of Ireland's sea-borne trade. That its imports were coal, building materials, flour, animal feed and fertiliser shows that the local economy was not a particularly diverse or bustling one. But the list of its exports during the census month of April 1911 presented an even bleaker picture. Nine cargoes left the port: one for Preston, eight for Liverpool. Of these, four were timber, two were 'rags and bones', one was 'gut and bones', one was moss, and one was 'bales of waste' from the Galway Woollen Mill. Without doubt, the rags and the other waste would have been left to decay alongside the scrap iron and oat hulls that were sent out in subsequent months, had not Liverpool coal-boats been available to take them away cheaply.[3]

The list of exports for April 1911 was characteristic, but not fully representative. At other times of the year, there were some agricultural exports — eggs, wool, bacon. And small quantities of fish were sent to Liverpool on three occasions during 1911. Locally-quarried limestone and marble were other occasional exports.

Building materials were carried in both directions, but it is noteworthy that it was the primary products — stone and timber — that were leaving the town, while it was the manufactured articles — bricks, tiles, galvanised sheets, cement

— that were being brought in. Galway did have one manufactured export — seven consignments of whiskey were sent out during 1911. Persse's bonded warehouse would continue to do a steady trade in ten-year-old whiskey, but the family's distillery on Nun's Island had closed in 1908, 'with a loss of forty to fifty jobs and five or six excise officers'.[4]

Galway's manufacturing sector supplied a local market. In 1911, it comprised two woollen mills, two saw mills, a flour mill, a brush factory, a foundry, a stone-polishing works, and a mineral water plant. Except for the Woollen Mill, all were small enterprises; most had originated in the previous two decades.[5]

A significant addition to local industry was the fertiliser plant — 'on a scale of stupendous magnitude' — that was opened by leading local merchants, Thomas McDonogh & Sons, in 1912. That firm's director, Máirtín Mór McDonogh, was Galway's 'merchant prince', according to an announcement of his venture, the only man in the town with the 'courage or the "war chest" for such an enterprise'.[6] Until a dispute arose with his suppliers, Máirtín Mór had imported his fertilisers. Then, according to his friend Stephen Gwynn, sometime MP for Galway, he was contemplating his difficulty with the 'ring' of combined fertiliser manufacturers, when:

> Looking around him, [he] saw water power running to waste in Galway, then full of derelict mills'. Knowing 'enough chemistry to appreciate the problem', and with one of the swift decisions that were characteristic of him, he decided to manufacture and fight the 'ring'.[7]

Máirtín Mór's was an overwhelming presence. He was 'pre-eminently a strong man' according to one profile, 'firm and unyielding when once a conviction has entered his mind'.[8] According to Stephen Gwynn, he 'gave the impression of elephantine strength, and not always of a very approachable elephant'. Gruff, overbearing and arrogant, Máirtín Mór dominated the town's economic life, and directed its civic affairs, through his membership of the Urban Council, of the Harbour Board, of the Galway Races Committee. His was very much the public face of the town.

The McDonogh family business developed in the post-Famine decades, distributing imports which were rendered inexpensive by the development of steam shipping and rail — the same cheap imports which pushed indigenous industry into bankruptcy. The firm's progress, part of local folklore, was thus recounted by Gwynn:

> It was the typical Irish shop and dealt in everything: its customers, as usual, often preferred to pay in kind, and young beasts had to be accepted for a bill. Therefore, there had to be land where they could be grazed, and then the land had to be fully stocked.[9]

The novelist Liam O'Flaherty had a less benign view of the relationship between Máirtín Mór and his customers:

> Within a radius of twenty miles … he has the people within his power … He can charge whatever price he likes, and as the people are always in his debt, he pays what he likes for their produce, as they have to sell to him, since, as I said before, they are in his debt.[10]

O'Flaherty was a socialist republican — and sometime communist — so in his fictional recasting of Máirtín Mór as capitalist ogre, one may suppose that he took certain liberties. Following O'Flaherty, several writers have represented McDonogh as the archetypal 'gombeenman' — a parasitic manipulator of credit relationships, at once the self-appointed spokesman and the principal exploiter of the community.[11] But regardless of the ethical basis of its accumulation, it is undeniable that his firm's 'war-chest' enabled Máirtín Mór to diversify into almost every sector of the local economy.[12] And that his resources and his personality made him almost impervious to challenge.

Notwithstanding the civic honours that were piled upon him, Máirtín Mór's first loyalty was to Thomas McDonogh & Sons. He might have given a lead in establishing a Chamber of Commerce — one could not have succeeded without him — but Galway was without such a body until 1923. Máirtín Mór did, however, initiate an Employers Federation in 1911, when the interests of Thomas McDonogh & Sons necessitated that all employers be marshalled to resist workers' wage demands.[13] More long-sighted initiatives directed at urban development, however, came from others. The Galway Development Association of 1906-10 was the most ambitious of such undertakings in the decade before the Great War, and its experience merits a detailed examination. The Development Association was a component of the Irish Industrial Development Association (IIDA) which had been founded in Cork in 1903. To the fore in its Galway affairs from March 1906 were five men: Captain John Shawe-Taylor, landlord in the county, originator of the national land conference of 1903, and close relative of the Persses; Fr Dennis Travers, Augustinian prior, amateur dramatics enthusiast, and scion of a Cork business family; Wilbraham Fitz-John Trench, Professor of History, English Literature and Mental Science at the Queen's College, sometime chairman of the Galway Granite Company, and staunch Unionist; Philip O'Gorman, owner of a printing works, prominent local activist, and antiquarian; Patrick J. Hannon, sometime chairman of the Galway Woollen Mills, magistrate, and brother-in-law of Máirtín Mór McDonogh. The first tasks of the provisional committee were to conduct an industrial census and to visit manufacturers.* This work

---

* The following enterprises were visited: Beatty's Ironfoundry; Connaught Brush Factory; Lydon's Woollen Mill; Galway Woollen Mill; Galway Hosiery; Michael Curran, nailmaker; Palmer's Flour Mills; Cloran's Flour Mills; Young's Mineral Water Manufactory; Hynes's Clay Pipe Manufactory; Hughes's Carriage Works; Clare's Sculpture Works; Dennis's Sculpturing Works; Garrett's Harness Manufactory; Galway Granite Works; Galway Biscuit Factory.

completed, a 'monster meeting' was called for the Town Hall on the evening of Tuesday, 15 May 1906. The Mechanics' Institute was invited to lead a procession of the various trades to the meeting, where the speakers would include Mr O'Riordan, Cork-based IIDA General Secretary.[14]

That the early efforts of the Development Association aroused enthusiasm was shown by the attendance at this meeting, where many had to listen from outside to the 'enthusiastic proceedings'. One of the eight speakers, Fr Travers, issued a call to arms:

> Of all cities of our country, the ruthless hand of decay has pressed most heavily on Galway. It has become a mere skeleton of its former self. Its houses are in ruin. Poverty is our best possession. We seem to stand on the verge of extinction. Our position seems more hopeless, our prospects more dismal than ever before. We must strike upon some plan that will stay the hand of decay, and bring about the resurrection of Galway.[15]

High railway charges had already been identified as an obstacle to industrial expansion, and suggestions that might assist in the formulation of a 'plan' for development had been sought from business people. But those received were unimaginative, and reflected what was known of IIDA policy — 'by inducing people to support home manufactures'; 'by local merchants stocking and pushing our home goods'; 'by copying the Cork people'.[16] Fr Travers laid out the approach of the movement in more tangible terms:

> The Association is to have for its object the betterment of trade and industry in our city, our county, and our country, by encouraging the support of Galway goods before Irish goods, Irish goods before foreign goods, and where foreign goods must be got by getting them through Galway traders.[17]

After the meeting, the provisional council was wound up and a committee was elected. It was a large committee, and one subject to conflicts of various kinds — personal, political and religious. The first task was to restore relations with Fr Peter Dooley, sulking since being excluded from the list of speakers at the 'monster meeting'. And other committee members proved equally quarrelsome and petulant. Moreover, far too many of them were Catholic priests. This imbalance was perceived to be a problem — it was why Fr Dooley had been omitted in the first place — but it was not one that could be resolved without giving offence. At the same time, steps that might have altered the balance were not taken. A proposal that trade unions — only shop assistants, bakers and tailors were unionised at that point — be given representation on the committee was thrown out, on the grounds that the committee was already large enough. And the establishment of a Ladies sub-committee, something that was constantly talked about, was never acted upon. The situation of Association president, Shawe-Taylor, also posed problems. His role in the land conference of 1903 had made him a prominent public figure, an asset to any cause identified with him, but he had political ambitions, something that became evident when he reminded those attending the May 'monster meeting' that his great-grandfather had been mayor of Galway. And a political opportunity arose earlier than he might have expected. When the Galway town constituency fell vacant in October 1906, Shawe-Taylor* was nominated as an Independent 'devolutionist' — he was regarded as a Unionist — and although defeated by the Nationalist Stephen Gwynn, he polled a creditable 36% of the total vote.[18] However, its president's prominence on the minority side in a bruising campaign was hardly advantageous to Galway's Development Association.

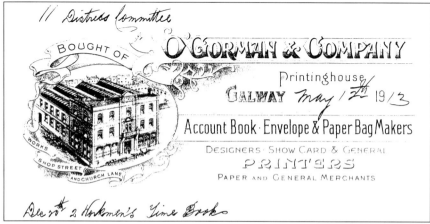

Distress Committee time books, supplied by Philip O'Gorman' printing business, 1913 (courtesy of Tom Kenny).

The main concern of the Association during the remainder of 1906 was to encourage Galway participation in the IIDA's Munster-Connacht Exhibition in Limerick: local businesses were urged to exhibit; shopkeepers were approached to close for a 'general holiday' to enable themselves and Galway people generally to travel; the railway company was lobbied to offer concessionary tickets for the duration. During 1907, the Association succeeded in holding another 'great public meeting' in the Town Hall, but the tone of proceedings was very different to the previous gathering. Captain Shaw-Taylor, in the chair, faced heckling, while secretary, Philip O'Gorman, was first defended and then extenuated on charges that his business had repeatedly supplied the Association with imported stationery. After eighteen months of effort, it was asserted that 'a good start' had been made, but it had to be acknowledged that there were yet no 'signs of activity and industry as there ought to be' in Galway.[19]

---

* Reminiscing in his poem 'Coole Park, 1929', Yeats joined Shawe-Taylor in a trinity of visitors to Lady Gregory's home: 'That meditative man, John Synge, and those / Impetuous men, Shaw Taylor and Hugh Lane / Found pride established in humility, / A scene well set and excellent company'.

The Galway Development Association's finest moment came in September 1908, when it hosted the IIDA annual conference and the associated 'Great Galway Exhibition'. For four days, visiting dignitaries of all sorts — legislators, bureaucrats, diplomats, magnates, ecclesiastics — conferred with delegates, and mingled with visiting country people at the industrial exhibition and at the concurrent Galway Horse Show. Prominent local business people, Máirtín Mór McDonogh among them, joined in the organisational work and took prominent parts in the proceedings. There was satisfaction at the extent of local participation, in particular that twelve Galway exhibitors won medals for excellence — including O'Gorman's for ledgers and account books; Thomas McDonogh & Sons for their 'very substantial' carts, wheelbarrows and trucks; and Beatty Bros for spades and shovels 'of excellent workmanship'. A substantial amount of business was done: several shopkeepers later announced that they had prize-winning articles from all over Ireland in stock, while the Brush Company, Thomas McDonogh's, and Hughes's Carriage Works were reported to have received substantial orders. A talking point, incidentally, at the conference and afterwards, was the discovery of potassium in Conamara, and of the possibilities which it opened up for an Irish fertilizer industry.[20]

Unfortunately, the Development Association's finest moment also proved to be one of its last. At the 3rd — and final — AGM in the Town Hall in November 1909, the chairman, Professor Trench, regretted that the Association's efforts had not been sufficient to 'keep industries established in Galway' or to 'have some new industries set up'. For his part, the keynote speaker, Bishop O'Dea, admitted to possessing only 'general knowledge of the industrial problem', but, in the course of his remarks, he directed his audience's attention towards the sea. In commending the re-emerging opportunity of developing Galway as a trans-Atlantic port, his lordship was passing a metaphorical baton from the Irish self-reliance model of the IIDA, to the Empire-dependent All-Red Route* proposals, as a panacea for Galway's ills.[21]

Three years of vainly fostering local industry was enough for Galway's city fathers — both lay and clerical. In a way, it was understandable that 'public men' would have found the process of securing the All-Red Route for Galway — preparing parliamentary bills, lobbying governments, discussing great engineering projects — to be more congenial than trying to persuade their neighbours to buy locally-produced wheelbarrows and yardbrushes. In any case, the Development Association was abandoned, and all economic hopes between 1909 and the outbreak of the Great War invested instead in the in the age-old dream of developing Galway — through a proposed new port at Bearna — as the 'Liverpool of Ireland'.[22]

---

* The All-Red Route was a shorter, northerly, trans-Atlantic shipping route, the subject of the North Atlantic Agreement of 1908. Galway and Halifax in Nova Scotia, their advocates argued, were 800 miles closer together than Liverpool and New York, and were best-positioned to be the ports for the new route. Not only could goods be moved more quickly between them, but ships on the route would require less coal, leaving more space for cargo.

That the Development Association at its demise had little to show for its efforts, even in its own terms, is unsurprising. While it had enjoyed public approval, it was representative neither of the community at large nor of local business. And its attempts to encourage the purchase of locally-manufactured articles might have been better served if its committee had agreed to give representation to unions representing shop assistants, whose members were in a position to influence directly what people bought. Moreover, if the repeatedly-shelved Ladies sub-committee had been activated, it might have encouraged women shoppers to seek out actively Irish and local produce. But the narrow focus on publicising and commending Irish and local manufacturers was itself limiting. If, in addition, the Association could have persuaded the local authorities to avail of low-interest government loans to replace the hundreds of sub-standard homes in the town with new artisans' and labourers' cottages, the stimulus to local enterprise would have been considerable. The greatest deficiencies of the Association, however, were of expertise and of capital. And the leading local merchants, who might have supplied these, remained mostly on the sidelines — perhaps with good reason. For some of them, the challenge of making an impression on the Association's platitudinous, quarrelsome and priest-ridden committee would have seemed too great. Others would have felt that they were already doing their bit for the town through their investment in the Galway Woollen Company. Finally, since the wealthiest of the merchants were themselves substantial importers, there was a potential conflict between the aspiration to develop local industry and the reality that trading in foreign goods was a key source of profits.

NOTES

1. *Connacht Tribune,* 8 April 1911.
2. John Cunningham, *Labour in the West of Ireland, 1890-1914,* Belfast 1995, pp. 150-72.
3. Galway Harbour Commissioners: Tonnage & Imports dues book, 1882-1914; Export dues book, 1882-1914, returns for 1911; *Thom's official directory ... for the year 1889* . Galway Harbour Commissioners:
4. *Galway Observer,* 4 April 1908.
5. N. P. T. O'Donnellan, 'Manufacturing Industry in Galway, 1911-1957', M.A. thesis, UCG 1979, pp. 44-47.
6. *Connacht Tribune,* 26 October 1911.
7. Stephen Gwynn, 'A Galway Merchant', in *Memories of Enjoyment,* Tralee 1948, pp. 96-99.
8. *Connacht Tribune,* 28 January 1911.
9. Gwynn, *Merchant,* p. 97.
10. Liam O'Flaherty, *The House of Gold,* London 1939, p. 153. In O'Flaherty's novel, the anti-hero, Ramon Mór, represents Máirtín Mór; the town of Barra is Galway.
11. Patrick Sheeran, *The Novels of Liam O'Flaherty: a Study in Romantic Realism,* Dublin 1976, pp. 40-41, 126-29; M. D. Higgins, 'The "Gombeenman" in fact and fiction' in *Etudes Irlandaises,* 10, 1985, pp. 31-52.
12. Breathnach & Ní Mhurchú,'Máirtín MacDonnchadha' in *1882-1982: Beathaisnéis 3,* Seán Spellissy, 'Thomas McDonogh & Sons' in *The History of Galway: City & County,* Limerick 1999, pp. 113-15.
13. Kieran Woodman, *Tribes to Tiger: A History of Galway Chamber of Commerce & Industry,* Galway 2001, pp 137-51; Cunningham, *Labour,* pp. 152-53.
14. Woodman, *Tigers,* pp 139-44; *Galway Observer,* 24 March, 5, 12 May 1906
15. *Galway Observer,* 19 May 1906.

16. ibid., 12 May 1906.
17. ibid.
18. ibid., 6, 27 October, 10 November 1906.
19. ibid., 26 May, 2 June, 13 October 1906, 24 August 1907.
20. ibid., 19, 26 September 1908.
21. ibid., 27 November 1909; Woodman, *Tigers,* pp. 143-44
22. Woodman, *Annals,* pp 172-74; Timothy Collins, 'The Galway Line in Context', pt.1, in *JGAHS* 46, 1994, pp. 65, 74n.

Economy, Politics, Society
1790-1850

CHAPTER 2

'...almost proverbial for uncleanliness & inconvenience'

ECONOMY, ADMINISTRATION, AND INFRASTRUCTURE, 1800-45

> Not Foynes nor Cove of Cork, by Jove,
> Not Mersey, Thames or Solway,
> Can ever dare, e'en to compare,
> With our fine bay of Galway.
> From 'The Old Packet Station', McCall Ballad Collection, NLI.

i) Administrative structures and failings

Given the neglected appearance of their town, its greatly diminished trade, and the domination of its affairs by a powerful oligarch, it is not surprising that the civic pride of early 20th century Galwegians was very much bound up with the past. Galway was once a great maritime city, went the dictum, it could be great again. But were things very different a century earlier? Not according to James Hardiman's account of an 1811 protest at the unopposed return of an MP for the town. The election was orchestrated by James Daly of Dunsandle, a cunning political operator prepared to employ any means to maintain his hereditary authority. In one unguarded moment, he was alleged to have boasted that he could cause grass to grow in Galway's streets if he wished.[1] There were times when that threat seemed close to fulfilment.

As far as the self-styled 'Galway Independents' of 1811 were concerned, Daly was personally responsible for the town's manifest misfortunes:

> that their prisons were crowded with debtors and malefactors, their quays left without shipping, their store-houses empty, their poor without employment; and, in fine, that the town itself had become almost proverbial for uncleanliness and inconvenience, without either trade, manufactories, or business of any description.[2]

Other contemporaries confirmed the description. An English radical — with no local axe to grind — who passed through the town a few years later, declared himself 'pleased with its situation', but 'disappointed with its appearance':

We saw some ships, particularly American ones, but the trade of this place has greatly decreased of late times, and is now little ... There is much wretchedness in the cabins, and other miserable houses of the poor ... In short, though Galway is a considerable town, it is in no manner a pleasing sight, from its bad construction and want of cleanliness.[3]

They were not unanimous about the causes, but the opinions of tourists, Independents, and Dalyites concurred on the condition of early 19th century Galway. For Independents, the restoration of Galway to its place among the cities of Europe could not begin until the Daly stranglehold was loosened, and they fought on several fronts over several decades to achieve this. An outline account of Galway's administrative and political system will give the background to the struggle.

Galway's affairs in 1800 were overseen by a complex patchwork of interlocking and overlapping agencies. There was the town itself, which extended about two miles in all landward directions from the centre, but there was also a so-called 'county of the town' — extending about four Irish miles from the centre. And, although it was not part of it, the town was also the administrative centre for the much larger county of Galway. The county and the county of the town each had their own grand juries which met in the town, and each returned its own members of parliament at elections that were held in the town, but according to different sets of electoral rules.

The town had a venerable corporation which by the time James Hardiman described it in 1820, was 'little more than a name'. He went on: 'the ancient state and insignia of that proud and opulent body have been entirely laid aside; the old and creditable offices ... have fallen into disuse, and its possessions have been alienated'.[4] But even in its reduced condition, the corporation was important, not least in that it was the key to Daly authority. Control of the corporation gave considerable patronage: it appointed dozens of officials to undemanding positions, from the warden of the Collegiate church, through the port surveyor, to the bearers of sword and mace.

Also corporation appointees were the two town sheriffs who had vitally important responsibilities. Firstly, they selected the grand jury that met twice yearly to exercise some judicial functions, and to consider presentments for public works and for the support of public institutions. Secondly, they were responsible for the running of elections.[5] Having gained mastery over the corporation, therefore, the Daly connection was enabled to keep control. Its sheriffs decided on the list of 'freemen' — the group from which membership of the corporation was drawn and which, along with property-qualified freeholders, formed the parliamentary electorate. Control of the corporation, therefore, brought with it control of the grand jury and a potentially-decisive influence over parliamentary representation. Only by quarrelling among themselves could the Dalys have lost control, but they did not allow disagreement to threaten their power base. So, although Denis Bowes Daly, M.P. and St George Daly, M.P. disagreed in the Act of Union debate, their branches of the family were able to agree on a rotation when, following the Union, the representation of the county of the town was reduced from two M.Ps to one.[6]

Some freemen from the preceding Eyre/Blake hegemony continued to hold the franchise, but the significant latent threat to Daly control of parliamentary representation was from those electors whose vote derived from small property interests — the twenty-shilling (later forty-shilling) freeholders. When Catholics were granted the right to vote in 1793, the freemen might have been overwhelmed by freeholders, but the corporation was quick to create hundreds of additional Catholic freemen. For those excluded from influence — as for those conscious of Galway's civic dignity — it was a grievance that few of the new freemen had any connection with the town, being Daly tenants and clients from the Loughrea district. It did not prove necessary, however, to convey the Loughrea freemen to vote in Galway until 1812, when the mobilisation of the Independents provided an opponent for the Daly/corporation nominee, in the person of Valentine Blake of Menlo Castle.

Through Valentine Blake and others, the Independents had connections with the long-excluded Blake/Eyre faction in borough politics. But this was a minor element in the new alliance that was dominated by merchants, and driven by their economic frustration. Having been the second port in Ireland after Dublin 150 years earlier, Galway lagged in 15th position in the early 1800s, behind even Youghal and Kinsale.[7] For James Daly, Galway's decline had two causes: 'the decay of public spirit in the merchants and wealthy inhabitants, and the habitual idleness and want of industry so prevalent and conspicuous among the lower orders'.[8] As far as the merchants were concerned, this was audacious nonsense from one who had monopolised all instruments of public-spiritedness, and neglected all channels of industry. The condition of the harbour was regarded as being particularly reprehensible, its ruinous state ensuring that any prudent sea-captain who docked there would never return. Moreover, cargoes that were successfully landed were vulnerable to pilferage due to the absence of watchmen and lighting.[9]

Equally neglected were the streets, unpaved and littered with detritus. When some citizens complained about this in the late 18th century, they were advised by Mayor Richard Daly to 'individually pave before their doors, as each person is the best overseer to superintend what concerns him'.[10] But the corporation levied tolls and customs for the maintenance of the streets and the town walls. The long-ruinous town walls were levelled in the years around 1800, but this did not result in improved conditions on the streets.

The situation was considered to be doubly scandalous, since the right to collect tolls and customs was farmed out by the corporation to speculators, who maximised their own revenue by exacting tolls capriciously and often illegally from those who came to do business in Galway. The exactions of toll farmers were regarded as a serious discouragement to commerce, and those paying them did not even have the consolation of decently-maintained streets, since the revenue was misappropriated for the corporation's purposes.[11]

The objections to the Dalys, therefore, might be summed up as follows: that they were outsiders, whose only interest in the town was as a base for extending their family's influence; that through their control of corporation and grand jury they prevented others from addressing Galway's inadequacies; that they levied unjust and economically harmful taxation, and alienated the proceeds; that those they sent to represent Galway in parliament had not interceded effectively to promote her interests.

Cushioned by the support of the Loughrea freemen, the Daly nominee won the 1812 general election comfortably. The Independents, however, did not let matters rest, and backed by the resources of Galway's mercantile sector, they petitioned the House of Commons to overturn the result. On a technicality, the Independents won their case, when the non-resident voters were excluded on the grounds that they had not been properly registered. Valentine Blake took his seat in 1813, and the following years were marked by procedural manoeuvres and legal challenges. Local sensitivities in the overwhelmingly Catholic town were roused when the Dalys employed the anti-Catholic clauses of the 1717 Galway Act to protect their position, something that proved counter-productive, for it mobilised the Catholic clergy on the Independent side in the 1818 election. And, in a context where the destination of every vote was publicly known, clerical influence could be decisive in determining how it was cast. The Independents, therefore, were able to hold their seat in 1818, only to lose it in 1820 after the non-resident freemen were readmitted. There were further legal setbacks for the Independents after the election. Thus, after a decade of campaigning, of petitioning, of litigating, that had left the Independents with their finances and their determination exhausted, the Daly interest remained in control.[12]

ii) The economy
But were the Independents correct in attributing Galway's decay to maladministration and to the venality of its governors? There was certainly circumstantial evidence in favour of their view: the conspicuous neglect of the harbour; high port charges; the advance of rival ports to the south and north. A flaw in the Independent diagnosis was that Galway's decline was a protracted process, with roots in the pre-Daly era. No one was more aware of that than James Hardiman, whose explanation indirectly supported Daly's accusation that indigenous inertia lay at the root of Galway's problems. For the town's historian, the decline of its port was due, firstly, to 'numberless' British restrictions on Irish trade generally, and on Galway trade specifically, and secondly, to the resulting demoralisation of the people of Galway.[13]

Hardiman's was an expedient analysis: it did not unduly offend either of the conflicting factions in the town, and it conformed to a widely-accepted Irish nationalist critique inherited from late 18th century 'patriots' and volunteers. But it is no less persuasive for that. Would-be exporters were disadvantaged by 17th and early 18th century embargoes and discrimatory tariffs, and this made it difficult to maintain a share of the expanding commerce of the period. Galway, with its prosperity contingent on free commercial intercourse with the European continent, was more disadvantaged than most ports. One economic historian has argued, however, that there were larger reasons for Galway's decline, relating to its poor hinterland and to its unsuitable location in changed economic circumstances.[14]

To appreciate the nature and full extent of Galway's 18th century decline, it is necessary to consider the broader context. Despite restrictions, the period saw a great expansion in trade. The value of Irish exports was five times greater in 1800 than it had been in 1700; the value of imports eight times greater. But to this immense expansion in commerce, Galway was virtually irrelevant. In fact, the volume of cargo through the port was roughly the same in 1800 as it had been in 1700. What had altered was that the balance of trade had become markedly unfavourable and that British ports had replaced European ports as Galway's main trading partners.

Galway had a significant trade with France in the early 18th century. It exported provisions — mainly butter and beef — and imported wine for the west of Ireland market. Some merchants ran a profitable sideline in smuggling highly-taxed luxuries into Galway — brandy, tea, and tobacco — while wool was surreptitiously sent in the opposite direction. For reasons that will be explored below, Galway's provisions trade was virtually non-existent by the mid-18th century. In the second half of the century, due to the growing population and to rising living standards, there was an increased demand for luxury items in Connacht. Some of these came through Galway, and although they did not necessarily originate there, most of them came from Britain.[15]

While not disputing that trade restrictions hindered Galway's trade, or that its affairs might have been better managed, Louis Cullen has shown that these factors only partially explain the port's decline. Galway, he has argued, was poorly located to take advantage of the burgeoning provisions trade. Cork and Waterford were much closer to the continent, and consequently more convenient for European merchants. Likewise for British ships bound for the Atlantic colonies. With this advantage — and more favourably-circumstanced agricultural hinterlands — it was possible for Cork and Waterford to consolidate their position by specialising in the provisions trade. In response, much of Ireland's commercial agriculture oriented itself towards the South.

Associated with the development of commerce in the 18th century were increases in the average size of transactions, and in the average capacity of ships. Spancelled by a poor hinterland, and by unevenly developed inland transport connections, Galway-based merchants could not consistently trade on the larger scale required and several of them moved their operations to other ports, in Ireland and elsewhere. Those of Galway's tribal families, therefore, who continued to thrive in commerce did so in the French Atlantic ports, in the West Indies, in London and in Dublin.[16]

Meanwhile, as far as the growing maritime trade with Britain was concerned, Galway was also at a disadvantage. Sligo and Limerick were closer, respectively, to Scottish and English ports and their trade grew as Galway's stagnated. But, in a sense, it was Dublin that provided the greatest competition, as her merchants distributed their imported commodities over an ever-wider area, and bought up the agricultural surplus for the British market.[17] This reality was already very clear by the early 19th century.

The generally bleak economic picture was frustrating for merchants and for would-be-capitalists, but it was worse than that for the majority of the townspeople, who laboured to feed, clothe and shelter themselves in ordinary times, and faced destitution during the frequent subsistence crises of the early 19th century. The recurring hunger-driven popular disturbances (see Chapter Four), and the despairing appeals of charitable agencies (see Chapter Three), indicate that economic stagnation remained the norm in Galway right up to the Famine.

Evidence of stagnation was provided too by early 19th century censuses. A census of 1812 returned a population of 24,484 for the county of the town (which included a substantial rural hinterland), but Hardiman considered this to be an underestimate. In 1821, there was a return of 28,445, and this increased to 33,120 in 1831, before falling to 32,511 in 1841. As far as the urban area proper was concerned, it would seem that there was a fall in population during both the 1820s and 1830s, for the increase of the 1820s occurred in the rural districts of the county of the town. For its part, the parish of St Nicholas — most of the urban area — fell by 568 to 16,392 during the 1820s and by 857 to 15,535 in 1841. The total urban area had 17,232 in 1841.[18]

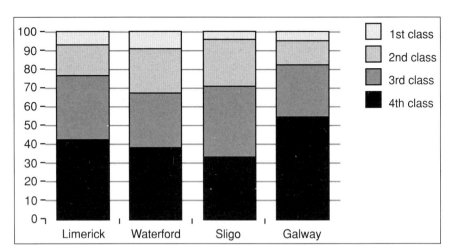

FIGURE 2.1: % of families in each class of accommodation in four towns, 1841. *Source:* 1841 Census.

And if it showed a declining population, the 1841 census also went some way towards confirming the impression that Galway was a place of incomparable poverty. The condition of housing is one key indicator, and by this criterion a high percentage of Galwegians were in distress. Over 55% of families lived in accommodation classified as 4th class. This compared to 43% in Limerick, 38% in Waterford, and 33% in Sligo [See Figure 2.1].

Clearly, the 'evident misery of the lower class' of Galway's inhabitants, which was commented upon by the Misses Blake of Renvyle in the 1820s, had not been alleviated.[19] And travellers' descriptions suggest that this misery was shared by the rural tenantry surrounding the town. Jonathan Binns, a Sussex farmer and a commissioner of the Irish Poor Inquiry, spent a few hours in the village of Tonabrucky, Rahoon* in 1835:

> Tornabrucky is comprised of small thatched cabins on the side of the steep hill of Crookanabrucky, and is a curious village. The street is exceedingly abrupt, and serves the double purpose of a road and the bed of a riotous torrent. The inclosures on the mountainside contain each only a few perches, and are fenced by the industry of the inhabitants at their own expense. The walls are five or six feet high, and notwithstanding their great extent, considerable numbers of stones which previously encumbered the ground are unappropriated, and are piled in tall heaps in the little paddocks. At a short distance, the village and the surrounding enclosures resemble a honeycomb, nor is there a tree, hedge, or shrub visible in the neighbourhood.[20]

For Binns, their poverty was visible in the clothing and demeanour of the women:

> The women wear red petticoats and vests and a short blue cloak that covers part of the head — a dress that is peculiar to the female peasantry of Galway. Few of them wear stockings. The prevailing colours, red and blue, are dull and dirty looking, very different to the bright colours so greatly admired and so much in vogue in most parts of Ireland. A large proportion of the drudgery falls upon the countrywomen, who (probably in consequence) are generally short, square and inelegant.[21]

---

* Another 'curious' village — Menlo — was described as follows in 1845: 'There is no church or chapel in the village; no schoolmaster or doctor, and no magistrate, though the population is as large as that of many an English town. The way through the village is the most crooked, as well as the most narrow and dirty lane that can be conceived. There is no row of houses, or any thing approaching to a row, but each cottage is stuck independently by itself, and always at an acute, obtuse, or right angle, to the next cottage as the case may be. The irregularity is curious; there are no two cottages in a line, or of the same size, dimension, or build. The Irish mind has here, without obstruction or instruction, fully developed itself. As this is the largest village I ever saw, so it is the poorest, the worst built, the most strangely irregular, and the most completely without head or centre, or market or church, or school, of any village I ever was in. It is an overgrown democracy. No man is better or richer than his neighbour in it. It is, in fact, an Irish rundale village.' (Thomas C. Foster, *Letters on the Condition of the People of Ireland*, London 1846, pp 292-93).

It would be wrong, however, to conclude that the first half of the 19th century was a period of unrelieved decline. There were enough examples of enterprise and of town improvement to permit one commentator to reflect positively on Galway's condition. For the agronomist Hely Dutton, writing just after Hardiman in the early 1820s, Galway's 'great decay' was an historical fact, but a revival was under way. It began, he stated, 'at the period of the union':

> At this time Dominick-street was built; also houses about Meyrick's Square, some near the infirmary, and in other places, began to appear, and gave an air of improvement to the town. The old useless town wall was nearly demolished, to make room for extensive stores and other buildings…[22]

The Tholsel, Galway's administrative and judicial building until it was replaced by the Town Hall in the early 1820s (from Hardiman Collection, courtesy of Galway County Library).

In 1800, and the years following, several improvements were carried out on the initiative of the resident military commander, General Meyrick. The only bridge in the town, at Mainguard-street, was widened, while Meyrick Square was enclosed as a parade ground and as 'a walk for the beau monde'. And, in an effort to reduce disorder, the general launched a subscription for a fish market in 1800. Only by regulating the fish-sellers, subscribers were persuaded, could the 'filthy practices of heading and gutting their fish in the streets' be ended. In 1802, a meat market opened in Williamsgate-street, but force had to be employed to persuade butchers — accustomed to keeping their meat 'hanging in the most disgusting manner against the walls of houses in the different parts of town' — to use it.* Emboldened by his successes, Meyrick planned to clean, pave and light the streets, but his proposal met opposition and was abandoned. Whether the opposition came from a corporation resisting a trespass on its functions, or from toll-paying citizens reluctant to pay twice over for the same work, Hely Dutton did not reveal.[23]

A view of the County Courthouse completed in 1815, with the gaols (1810) and the new bridge (1819) in the background (Hardiman, *Galway*).

An important development too was the late 18th century 'new town' — Newtownsmith — built outside the town wall on the northern side. The project was undertaken by the governors of the Erasmus Smith estate. In this suburb, a county court-house was erected between 1812 and 1815, and a town courthouse during 1824.† Galway's second bridge, completed in 1819, connected Newtownsmith and the courthouses with the new county and town jails on Nuns Island, which had been completed in 1810.[24]

These developments were no doubt welcomed by the building tradesmen and labourers, for whom employment was almost always elusive. That many were dependent on construction for their livelihoods is indicated by the 1831 Census which returned 111 carpenters and 68 masons, among other trades. Numbers in the building trades increased in the next decade or so, but work for most remained irregular. Of Galway's carpenters in 1845 it was reported that 'not more than 20 [are] permanently employed'; of her stonemasons that that they were 'half the year idle and not fully employed the other half'.[25]

---

* By 1823, Meyrick's meat market had deteriorated, being considered 'a sink of filth… perfectly offensive to the senses'. In that year, William Murphy erected a new meat market, for 'butchers of the higher class' at Bridge-street. In 1826, however, complaints were voiced about the new facility, in particular that 'at this warm season… the butchers dogs with slaver and froth about their mouth [are] licking every bit of meat that is exposed for sale' (*Pigot's Directory*, 1824, p.205; *Connaught Journal*, 21 April, 1 May 1823; 12 June 1826).
† In 1823, it was objected that there were several suitable sites for a town courthouse 'immediately in the town' and that it was 'quite idle to lay the foundations in Newtownsmith, or in any part of the suburb (*Connaught Journal*, 10 April 1823).

By Dutton's account, Galway's industry in the early 1820s consisted of twenty-three flour mills, six oat mills, two malt mills, four tuck mills, a bleach mill, a tobacco-pipe factory, a paper mill, and three quarries specialising in 'black marble chimney pieces' at Angliham and Merlin Park. Obviously, this picture was constantly changing, as reference to brewing and distilling sectors will indicate. Dutton recorded that there was no working distillery in the town,* but that there were several breweries, including 'a very extensive one at Newcastle where an imitation of pale English ale is brewed'.[26] Three advertisements in the same issue of the *Connaught Journal* in 1823 showed that a considerable shake-up occurred in that sector soon afterwards: Richard Adams announced that he was removing his 'Ale and Porter Brewery Establishment' from Newcastle to Madiera Island; Messrs Joyce offered for lease their 'extensive distillery concerns' at Newtownsmith; Burton Persse sought to let his brewery which, he stated, 'could at a very moderate expense be converted to an excellent distillery'. The latter advertisement revealed something of the operation of the brewing trade:

> The extensive brewery and concerns at Newcastle, Galway, situated on the banks of a river by which corn, fuels, &c., are brought to the stores, from whence the boats in return take malt liqueurs up said river to the extent of 40 miles, supplying several intermediate towns. It has at present a considerable and advantageous trade, which could be much increased by a person understanding the business, with a command of capital.[27]

This flurry of activity suggests that the drink trade was facing difficulties, and it would not be surprising if the concurrent subsistence crisis reduced alcohol consumption. The marble export business too was declining for want, it was said, of 'spirit and judgement'. And the long-established kelp trade, which supplied the Ulster linen industry, had collapsed, because of the poor quality of the local product.† Market prices fell from £13 a ton to £4 between 1808 and 1820, allegedly because the Scottish-produced article was found superior to the often deliberately adulterated Conamara kelp.[28] (More pertinent, arguably, to the decline were post-Napoleonic wars competition and the discovery of alternatives to kelp.)

---

* According to E.B. McGuire, there were two extremely small licenced distilleries in Galway in the early 1820s. This had increased to four a decade later, as the Distillery Act of 1823 impacted on illegal distilling (*Irish Whiskey: A History of Distilling in Ireland*, pp 359-60, 420-21).

† Stones and sand, it was stated, were mixed with the kelp to increase its weight at market. But there were also more legitimate attempts to increase profits: James Morris announced the opening of the Galway Blue Manufactory —'the first ever attempted in this town, and the only one in the province of Connaught'— alongside his 'old established flour mill and starch manufactory' in Dominick-street. Retailers were advised that due to the 'superior style of perfection' of his works, he could supply detergent more cheaply than any other establishment in Ireland (*Connaught Journal*, 3 November 1823).

Each area of business faced its own particular difficulties and challenges, but common to most of them was the need for adequate banking facilities. The two principal local banks, Ffrench of Tuam and Joyce & Lynch of Galway, had failed in the years before 1820, leaving distraught investors and a region bereft of financial services. There were two discount bank offices in the early 1820s — Oliver Clayton in High-street, Patrick & James Lynch in Shop-street — but these did not meet the needs of the town. Hely Dutton noted that in the absence of gold coin, 'minor concerns are transacted by Bank of Ireland tokens of different value', but that people 'under the necessity of taking bills, find a considerable difficulty in discounting them'.[29] Nonetheless, an editorial comment of 1824 indicates that there may have been exaggerated hopes about the effect that the opening of a bank would have on the local economy:

> It would give a stimulus to trade, it would enhance the value of the produce of the agriculturist and enable him to pay his rent, it would be the means of giving permanent and lucrative employment to the artisan, for it is evident that the want of the free circulation of money, together with other grievances, has retarded and impaired our commercial pursuits and rendered Galway one of the most insignificant instead of being one of the most opulent towns in Ireland.[30]

When the Provincial Bank opened a Galway branch in 1826, local sensitivities were offended that it was the second Connacht branch, after Sligo. Moreover, local experience was not such as to engender confidence in banking, and a 'run' on the new branch forced it to close for a time early in 1828. The opening of a Galway branch of the Bank of Ireland in 1830 was also followed by a 'run' on that establishment. But these were temporary setbacks, unlike the earlier misfortunes of the local banks. The National Bank arrived in Galway in 1836.[31]

As regards Galway's business personnel, the many failures led to a significant turnover in the early 19th century. If we consider the business elite — as represented in lists of merchants, millers, brewers and distillers in trade directories from 1824 and 1846 — this is very apparent. To give one example, only fourteen individuals from these categories in 1846 shared a surname with the forty-four listed in 1824. Indicative of change also was the decline in the numbers bearing the names of Galway's formerly illustrious tribes: ten members of 1824's business elite bore 'tribal' surnames, but only three of 1846's.* Of the newcomers, some were of local origin, others were recent arrivals. The entry into Galway's merchant class of the dynamic Munster man, Thomas Appleyard, was achieved by means of a business partnership (and a marriage alliance) with a long-established tribe family, the Joyces of Merview. Others who became

---

* The fourteen families of mainly Norman origin who emerged as a merchant oligarchy during the 16th century were: Athy, Blake, Bodkin, Browne, d'Arcy, Deane, ffont, ffrench, Joyce, Kirwan, Lynch, Martin, Morris, Skerrett.

prominent in the life of the town were the brothers Ireland who arrived in the early 1820s from England in the early 1820s — and were 'then in an humble sphere', according to one source. The brothers' plan was to exploit a newly-discovered seam of black marble (in fact it was high-quality limestone) at Angliham, near Menlo. The Irelands' subsequent 'rise in the world' was attributed to their success in exporting the faux marble to their native country.[32]

The Appleyard and Ireland stories were hardly typical of pre-Famine enterprise in Galway, but they were not utterly exceptional either. That there was progress in some areas — even if it seemed tentative and liable to be reversed — is shown by the following outlines of developments in five key sectors: a) flour and grain; b) the fisheries; c) textiles; d) tourism; e) retailing.

a) *Flour and grain*
Dublin, as has been shown, was a competitor of Galway port, but the growing population of that city also represented a significant market for food. Before its abolition, the Irish parliament paid subsidies to those supplying flour and grain to the capital, something that was a great stimulus to flour-milling . Galway was relatively late in entering this market, but, between 1786 and 1790, eight mills were erected in the town.[33] By 1820 (when bounties were no longer payable), twenty-three mills were turning out 12,000 tons of flour annually, some for local consumption, with the rest being sent by road, or by road and canal, to Dublin. (The Royal Canal reached west to Athlone and, after 1828, to Ballinasloe.) It was this sector that supported the relative recovery in Galway's affairs detected by Hely Dutton, and that spearheaded the Independents' campaign to weaken the grip over the Dalys on local affairs.

For Hely Dutton, the growth of milling was a stimulus to commercial agriculture in the county. Competition among millers ensured that good prices were paid but, nonetheless, the organisation of the trade left much to be desired. There was no market house, for example, so bargains had to be struck in a cellar in Market-street and, after 1810, in a former coach-house off the Square.[34]

The importance of milling was not fully appreciated by Hardiman, who was more occupied with the civic dignity of the town than with rural prosperity. One mill in Nun's Island, however, was so extensive that he described it in detail:

> Mr Regan's mill was commenced on 4th May 1813; it is a large double building, 80 feet long and 41 broad in the clear, erected on five arches… It receives light through 100 glass windows. The machinery is entirely of metal and was prepared according to the plan and under the inspection of Mr John Mackie, an ingenious Scotch engineer and mill-wright… The entire building it is said cost upwards of £10,000.[35]

Ancillary to milling, Galway developed a trade in undressed grain. Merchant Thomas Appleyard began exporting around 1804, and others took up the trade in the favourable conditions of war-time. The end of the war in 1815 was a setback, but exports continued at about 6,000 tons a year. In the 1820s, despite the condition of the harbour, grain exports increased steadily, reaching 13,000 tons by 1829.[36] The trade in grain did not always enjoy public approval (during times of scarcity, there was resentment that it forced up food prices), but it significantly boosted Galway's port which had recovered to be tenth in Ireland by 1835. The total value of cargoes leaving the port in that year was £252,000, 86% of which was accounted for by corn, meal and flour, 12% by provisions, and 1% each by tallow, and by 'various other articles'.[37]

b) *The Fisheries*
The salmon fishery on the river, owned by the Eyre family, was 'one of the most valuable in the kingdom', according to Hardiman, and had recently become even more valuable to its owners as a result of a legal case that gave them exclusive rights to fish on the river. Fresh salmon, most of which was consumed locally, was always available since it was transferred alive from the nets into large river-side tanks.[38]

Boys of the Claddagh from *Illustrated London News* (Brendan Laurence Glynn Collection).

The salmon fishery was a source of profits and of employment for a few, but the sea fishery was of much greater economic significance. Herrings were by far the most important of the two dozen species that were fished in the bay, and which gave a living to the several thousand inhabitants of the Claddagh, a self-contained Irish-speaking community, located only a half-mile from the town centre, but considered by many townspeople to be a place apart. Contemporaries understood that the economic benefits of fishing extended throughout the urban area: 'it is well known' wrote one commentator in 1844, that 'the greater part of the business of the shopkeepers and tradesmen of Galway depends upon the unfortunate Claddaghmen'.[39] Accepting that fishing was important to Galway, it was nonetheless an exaggeration to state that the 'greater part' of local prosperity was dependent upon it.

Exaggeration and ignorance, it seems, were commonplace in discussions about fishing. Hardiman estimated that there were 2,500 'hands' engaged in fishing 'the inner bay alone'. There was perhaps a third as many, if fishermen from the part-time fishing communities at Renville/Ardfry and at Bearna/Na Forbacha were added to the total from the Claddagh. Only 559 in Galway town were returned as fishermen in the 1841 Census, and it is unlikely that numbers had declined greatly in the previous two decades. But Hardiman's estimates were closer to the mark than those of expert witnesses who persuaded the Fisheries Commission in the mid-1830s that 85 million herrings were sold in Galway annually — and none of them for export. This would have represented an average annual consumption of eleven Galway herrings by every Irish woman, man, and child. But given that fish consumption was limited to one day a week over most of the island, that it was rarely available in many inland areas, that other species were eaten, that there were ports with larger catches, it seems unlikely that a fraction of that number was sold out of Galway.

Galway's fish was sold widely enough, however. In the early decades of the 19th century, Scottish and English vessels followed the fleet so as to buy herrings as they were caught for immediate salting aboard ship. It would appear too that Claddagh boats landed occasional cargoes in Limerick, Sligo and Westport.[40] But the fishermen did not handle the sale of the fish that reached Galway:

> …Their return is hailed with great joy by their families, [they are] ushered into the whiskey shops by their wives, and in a state of intoxication, put to bed. The boat is then unladen, and the fish carried to market by the women, who exclusively take possession of it, the husbands never interfering, and it is sold to hawkers and women who keep standings in the market.* The women pay for everything, having complete control of the purse.[41]

Although Scottish-cured herrings were sold in Galway, little curing took place locally before 1820. For Hely Dutton, this showed a lack of 'a spirit of proper enterprise'. However, government aid for the industry (and the lifting of the tax on salt) facilitated the development of herring curing during the 1820s. Within

---

* The marketing of fish was only one aspect of the Claddagh women's role in the industry: 490 females were returned as 'netmakers' in the 1841 census, while Hardiman stated that women and children spent the days before each fishing expedition digging for bait in the strands.

a decade there were a dozen local curing operators. But most Galway curing was 'in pile' rather than in barrels, since this process required less salt, less labour, and no coopering. It was a low-grade product, however, that was bought only by 'the poorer description of the population of the country'.[42]

At the same time as curing was opening up new outlets, improvements in transport were extending the market for fresh Galway-caught herrings. Buyers supplying urban markets throughout Ireland came to do business, negotiating, like the curers, with the fishermen themselves, rather than with their womenfolk. The Claddagh women, meanwhile, continued to supply the female dealers in the fishmarket and those fishmongers from the inland towns and villages of Connacht and Clare who came to purchase small amounts.[43]

But if there were more outlets for fish, the impression is that the supply was extremely erratic, something that must have hindered attempts to consolidate processing and marketing functions. In 1824, it was stated that herrings were rotting on the quays for want of salt, while people throughout the county were dying of starvation; in 1828, that the herring fishery had failed for three seasons past; in 1831, that the scarcity of fish was causing 'great distress' in the Claddagh; in 1835, that no fish had been landed for three months, causing the Claddagh men to have 'altogether relinquished their fishing pursuits and embraced the avocation of transporting seaweed'. In 1844, the total 'failure' of the fishery was again recorded.[44]

The frustration of commercial interests at the erratic supply was reflected in denunciations of the Claddagh people. Because of their fecklessness, their obduracy, their primitive disposition, went the accusations, a regional resource was being squandered to give a subsistence-level existence to a few thousand people.[45] (Agricultural 'improvers' made similar observations about those utilising land for subsistence). The prevailing view was that the fruits of the sea were limitless; that nature's bounty could be harvested if modern methods were diligently applied. Claddagh people did not share this view.

Two major criticisms were levelled at the Claddagh fishermen: that they did not fish often enough, and that they were hidebound by tradition when they did. But there were reasons why fishermen would have restricted fishing, not least a reluctance to cause a price-collapsing glut. Moreover, there were times when fish were scarce, and if Hardiman was correct in stating that the Claddagh men had 'unerring prognostics' regarding when fish were present, they probably also knew when they were not. There were ecological reasons too for limiting fishing. The Claddagh men permitted only autumn and winter herring fisheries in the bay, and would not countenance a summer fishery, resulting in what, for some, was the farcical position of 'Scottish herrings being brought in to feed the working classes — including the very fishermen who won't fish for them here'.[46] As far as one sceptic was concerned: 'they pretend to be nursing the fish to promote their increase'.[47] However, given the number of occasions that the herring fishery failed in the 1820s, 1830s and 1840s, there were good reasons for yielding to the wisdom of generations of fishermen in the matter. As for fishing practices, there were suggestions that larger vessels would enable the fishermen to seek fish in the open seas when there were none in the bay, and that the adoption of trawling would maximise catches. By all accounts, the Claddagh people were already better-equipped and more highly-skilled than any others on the coast, and it is difficult to imagine how they might have acquired bigger boats. As for trawling, the Claddagh people contended that it would disturb spawning grounds, so they refused to adopt the practice — even when offered free equipment — and resisted the efforts of successive fishing 'companies' established by local merchants and outside speculators.[48] Partly because of the response of the Claddagh community, 'commercial' fishing interests had made negligible headway in the Galway area by the 1840s. It would seem too that the uncertainty of supply of fish and the withdrawal of government support in the 1830s had combined to kill off the nascent fish-curing industry by that point.[49]

c) *Textiles*

Coquebert de Montbret's impression in the 1790s was that textile manufacturing was Galway's leading industry. Cloth 'suitable for household sheets' was produced, as was 'rather good cloth of pure Connemara wool'. There was certainly the raw material for a woollen industry, with several observers remarking on the extensiveness of 'sheep walks' near the town, but the indications are that the sector was declining by 1820, probably because of falling demand for military uniforms in the post-Napoleonic wars period. Hardiman stated that 'vast quantities' of wool were sent 'in its raw state' to Britain and to other parts of Ireland, but that this was of little local benefit, because neither the port of Galway nor the craftsmanship of her citizens were utilised.[50] Nevertheless, a lively local market in coarse home-spun articles continued into the 1830s, according to Lewis, in flannels, blankets, and woollen stockings. These were sold on market-days, but not it would seem to the well-to-do, for the fashionable 'London & Leeds Woollen-Hall' in William-street announced in 1830 that it specialised in 'West of England cloths'.[51]

Another sector that faced difficulty was the linen industry. In the late 18th century, it had been considered a panacea for the economic health of the region. Most Galway linen was produced and marketed in the north and east of the county, but there were attempts after 1760 to promote the town of Galway as a centre of the trade. These efforts met with some success, but it was no longer 'a favorite branch of industry' by 1820, according to Hardiman, when the linen hall had 'long since gone into decay'. It is likely that the falling demand for sailcloth, post-1815, that damaged Cork's linen industry, also affected Galway's. Nevertheless, a bleach green was maintained at Earl's Island, and there were occasional efforts to renew interest in linen.[52] Both a Gentlemens' Committee and a Ladies' Association interested themselves in the question in the 1820s, but the response to the latter's efforts to revive the Saturday linen market in the Square in 1823 was poor, prompting the suggestion that it be moved to the old linen hall in the 'west suburbs' instead.[53] Efforts to revive the linen market may not have succeeded, but they were worthwhile. Not all such efforts were, however, and one half-baked initiative is worth describing for the insight it offers into the contemporary philanthropic mindset. Having concluded that the decay of the linen industry was due to the underdeveloped skills of local spinners, a group of ladies resolved to correct this by organising trials of skill in 'the art of spinning, pretty much in the style of the ploughing matches'. The first match was held during May 1824 in the gardens of Mrs Lushington Reilly, wife of the port collector. For one observer, the thirty competitors who spun for four hours and thirteen minutes, until the fastest of them had completed her half pound of yarn, were a picturesque sight: 'under the shade of almost every tree in the shrubbery was seated a busy competitor dressed in her holiday clothes and striving her best for one of the premiums'. Whilst spinning, the young women sang to one another, enabling the hostess to discover why they were so much slower at their work than their contemporaries in Ulster. It was so clearly their repertoire of 'doleful ditties' that delayed them — so different to the 'enlivening airs' of the North — that she summoned a fiddler and two pipers to speed things up. To the winner, Kitty O'Neill, 'a native of Newry', was presented a new spinning wheel. Runners-up received other useful articles. Afterwards there was a celebration:

> When the prizes were distributed, they were borne off by the elated winners, in joyful triumph through the streets of the West Suburb, where the several candidates principally reside, and amidst the cheerful acclamations of all present. The evening was afterwards spent in partaking of some slight refreshments, and in the merry dance, the fair victors of the day being always sure of the best partners in the group...[54]

Such efforts could achieve little in the face of the mechanisation of spinning and the contraction of the industry to its northern heartlands. In 1830, the 'general distress' of those engaged in linen production in the Galway region was being reported. Some evidently continued in the trade, for, according to the census returns of 1841, there were 28 flax-spinners and 8 flax-weavers resident in the town. And that was almost certainly an under-representation of the position, for in addition to 23 spinners of wool, there were 65 'unspecified' spinners and 49 'unspecified' weavers.[55]

d) *Tourism*

Galway became a holiday resort in the late 18th century, at a time when the seaside was replacing the spa well as the favoured health restorative of the elite. During the 1790s, a French visitor remarked that people came 'from all parts of the province under pretence of sea bathing', adding a graphic detail: 'young damsels, packed five or six on a car, legs dangling, go to refresh their charms in the sea about two miles from the city'. Another visitor noted in 1812 that the 'ladies of the province frequent Galway as a bathing place.[56]

Tourism evidently grew greatly during the 1820s, for in 1828 it was remarked that 'a vast number of strangers' had visited the town during the summer, and that houses near the sea had commanded high rents. This was encouraging others to erect bathing lodges in Salthill, something that was commended as 'a good speculation'. By the following summer, it was expected that there would be up to fifty such lodges available to 'country families', where there had been just two or three a few years earlier.[57]

Bathing lodges varied greatly, from substantial houses on their own grounds, like Merville and Blackrock House* — in both of which the prominent young Catholic clergyman, Fr Peter Daly, had an interest — to modest cottages. Of the latter it was observed that they were 'reasonably set ... as in all bathing places'. Best was 'one range of cottages, on the right as you leave the town, leaving the beach open, and the refreshing breezes of the ocean unbroken and unobstructed'. An alternative to the bathing lodges, the Montpellier Hotel, advised the public of 'the salubrity of its air' during 1831.[58] Henry Inglis, who visited in 1834, remarked on the 'great many houses' that had been built to accommodate 'strangers'. He commented however, that Salthill had 'nothing to recommend it but the sea', and that the western side of Galway generally was 'as ugly, as flatness, sterility, and want of wood, can make it'. Another 1830s observer remarked on the 'several very good houses and sundry neat cottages on the shores of the bay, for the accommodation of visitors.[59]

Sea bathing, according to the medical wisdom of the period, benefited the young and healthy, but might be detrimental to the unfit. Yet, according to one physician, the beaches at Salthill during the summer were 'crowded like the brinks of the Bethesda with the infirm and the unsound, seeking to be relieved of misery and disease' —people who would find safer relief in 'artificial' bathing.[60] And such was available from 1831 at the 'New Baths' on the Salthill Road. Patrons could choose from a variety of baths — hot, cold, 'plain', 'medicated' — but the greatest benefits of all were from the vapour bath:

> In internal inflammations, as of the liver, lungs, kidneys, &c., and from its power of promoting perspiration, it is highly and deservedly recommended for removing the dropsical effusions — there is no bath more in repute for removing the effects of mercury from the constitution; and scrofulous swellings, ulcers, and obstinate diseases of the skin in general...[61]

---

* An advertisement for one of the properties read — Desirable Bathing Residence to be let, from the 25th instant, for such terms as may be agreed on: Black-Rock House (lately built by the Rev. Peter Daly) together with 4 or 8 acres of land, beautifully situated, convenient to the best part of the shore for bathing, and within one mile and a half from the town of Galway. The house which is finished in the best manner, and fit for the immediate reception of a family, consists of a dining room, parlour, drawing room and study, 6 bedrooms, a large kitchen, servants' hall, 4 servants' bedrooms, cellars, dairy, &c., with coach house and stable for 4 horses (*Connaught Journal*, 16 May 1831).

With its artificial baths, its bathing lodges and hotels; with its round of public amusements — 'regattas races, theatrical exhibitions, concerts, balls, &c'. — Galway and Salthill held many attractions for the 1830s tourist. There was one thing lacking, however, according to an observer, and that was 'bathing accommodation'. The 'accommodation' in question was that afforded by 'bathing machines', which protected the modesty of demure swimmers in other early 19th century resorts.[62]

But some were lacking in modesty, something that had been a source of complaint for 'many years':

> Along all that part of Salthill shore which is open to the road, may at most hours of the day, be counted hundreds of ignorant country-fellows from various quarters, careless of all circumstances, bathing within a few yards of the road.* In consequence of this most offensive practice, all visitors are driven from the delightful and beautiful promenade, while those whose distant residence, or whose business may compel them to pass, cannot avoid being disgusted by an exposure so indecent and intolerable.[63]

e) *Retailing*

The chroniclers of early 19th century Galway gave detailed descriptions of the markets of the town, hardly referring at all to shops. This showed the importance of the markets, which supplied most of the needs of most of the people. Fish, meat, vegetables, butter and turf were sold in separate designated areas, and, reflecting the importance of their supply, they were subject to by-laws against a range of speculative practices. These, however, were enforced by the market jury only when disgruntled shoppers threatened to take the law into their own hands.[64] Of greater concern to the authorities was the tendency of markets to spill over into adjacent areas, causing congestion and general 'nuisance'. New markets were set out in the years around 1800 but their limits were constantly breached, fish-sellers being the most frequent offenders, but not the only ones. Of the 'public highways' of Lombard-street, Mainguard-street, and the lower end of Shop-street, it was pointed out in 1831 that they had 'for a long time been converted into an *arena* for the sale of cabbages'.[65] Market days (Wednesdays and Saturdays during most of the early 19th century) were especially busy, creating a boisterous atmosphere in the streets. A visitor of 1817 tried to convey what he saw:

> The market in Galway is very plentiful and good, and affords an excellent opportunity of hearing the country people, who are well-dressed, speak Irish, which gives one a strong idea of the Welsh…

---

* Nude bathing in the rivers of the town was also regarded as a 'nuisance' (Galway Patriot, 7 June 1837). Such indelicacy on the part of the 'lower orders' was also a cause of concern in the resort of Kilkee (Ignatius Murphy, *Before the Famine Struck*, p.82) and further afield (Walvin, *Seaside*, pp. 23-24, 69-71).

Butter, fish, eggs, potatoes, mutton and beef were in great plenty in the market and very good. There was much turf in it; also coarse linen, yarn, and webs, and woollen-cloths. The mixture on market day of cattle, country people, soldiery, &c., &c., produced a lively effect.[66]

Twenty-five years later, Thackeray commented on the number of pigs in the streets — 'the whole town shrieks with them', he wrote — and on the multitudes 'humming and swarming in and out of dark, ruinous old houses' and 'congregated around numberless apple stalls, nail-stalls, bottle-stalls, pigs' foot stalls.[67] But even more boisterous than market days were fair days, twice yearly in May and September in the pre-Famine decades. In September 1830, it was considered noteworthy that there were no disturbances at the fair of Fairhill. This happenstance was attributed to the efforts of Fr Fahy of the Dominican priory who spent the day on the green, so that he could 'use his influence with his parishioners in the prevention of rioting should any occur'.[68]

Also subject to the market jury was the bread supply, which one expert considered to be of excellent quality — a credit to the millers who had only 'very inferior' locally-grown wheat to work with.[69] But not everybody agreed, and there were frequent calls for punishment of purveyors of 'adulterated' or underweight loaves.[70] It took a considerable number of bakers to feed Galway's population: an 1824 directory listed sixteen bakeries, while there were forty bakers in the town in 1831, according to the census.[71]

View of 'The Four Corners' including Lynch's Castle by Bartlett, 1840.

Specialist tradesmen, many of them operating in small workshops or in their homes, clothed the people. There were 156 shoemakers and 115 tailors in 1831, but only a few such businesses were substantial enough to be listed in trade directories. Incidental purchases and occasional luxuries were available from 49 'hucksters, hawkers, peddlars and duffers', or from 15 shopkeepers stocking 'sundry necessary articles, such as are sold in a village shop'.[72]

For one English visitor of the early 1830s, Galway's shops were 'very indifferent', but, in another opinion, they were 'plentifully stored with those articles which vanity requires or necessity demands'. Neither were referring to the small shops selling 'sundry necessary articles' to the working class and peasantry, but to the larger stores catering to the upper and upper-middle classes.[73] Cosmopolitan visitors were accustomed to greater specialisation than could be offered by merchants in a small and impoverished west of Ireland town, and while there was a market for blended teas and delicate wines, for crafted silverware and furniture, for fine clothes and toiletries, it was limited, and apparently incongruous articles had to be sought in the same premises.* For example, during 1832, John Clayton's High-street shop stocked the following: jewellery, cutlery, hosiery, perfumes, petty sessions' books, Cuban cigars, travelling bags and trunks, musical instruments ranging from pianofortes to flageolets, fishing rods, tea and coffee urns, mahogany backgammon tables, Italian bird cages, and 'an immense variety of other new and useful articles in the various branches of his trade'.[74] Given the range of his goods, it is unlikely that Clayton offered his customers a choice with regard to specific items, so it is not surprising that some strangers were disappointed.

Developments in shopkeeping in the pre-Famine decades are difficult to measure with certainty. Directories provide lists of traders and merchants but they are not always helpful, or even reliable. Clayton's, for example, was listed as 'booksellers' in 1821 and 1824, and as 'booksellers (and general fancy repository)' in 1846, but these descriptions hardly did justice to the shop.[75] Changes in the nature and the extent of advertising by shopkeepers, however, show that shopkeeping was itself changing. Retailers' advertisements in the *Connaught Journal* in the 1790s and in 1817 were simply announcements — either that the advertiser had moved premises or had received a fresh cargo. The impression is that shops had limited and ever-changing stock. By the 1820s, advertising was more strategic and more extensive, especially during the summer and Christmas seasons. The following advertisement from 1824 might be considered

Galway shop sign sketched by Thackeray, 1840s (courtesy of James Hardiman Library, NUI, Galway).

---

* Of the same phenomenon, Xenophon (428-354 BC) wrote: 'In small towns, the same man makes couches, doors, ploughs, tables, and often he even builds houses… In large cities, one man makes shoes for men, another for women, there are even places where one man makes a living just by mending shoes, another by cutting them out'.

typical of the new type of advertising, insofar as it emphasised that the availability of 'every article' was guaranteed, but also that it was connected with a prestigious Dublin establishment:

> P. K. MARTIN & CO. beg leave to announce to the Nobility and Gentry, their friends and the public that they propose opening in a few days, their house in the New Buildings, Shop-street, Galway (opposite the Castle), where every article in the GROCERY, TEA, WINE AND SPIRIT line shall constantly be found, and at the most moderate prices of the day, being themselves the importers of most of the articles, and having the opportunity of being daily supplied from one of the first establishments of the kingdom, viz, that of CHARLES SMYTH, 30 Upper Sackville-street... R. K. MARTIN begs further to state that from many years experience in the aforesaid establishment of CHARLES SMYTH which has given such unprecedented satisfaction to the public at large, he trusts, combined with his own judgement, in securing every article in their line of the best quality...[76]

*

Around 1800, according to Robert McDowell, 'the main function of all Irish urban centres was to be a market town for the surrounding agricultural population, and, if a seaport, to be an outlet for Irish exports'. Urban centres, of course, also had administrative functions, that would grow in the course of the 19th century with the expansion of the role of the state and with the increase in employment in the public service generally. Public officials in Galway town in 1841, to give an example, included 53 excise men and 23 policemen. More important than either of these services, however, was the British army, whose strength in Ireland fluctuated between 15,000 and 30,000.[77] In Galway, there were three army barracks in the early 19th century, and while numbers varied, there were normally at least two hundred soldiers in the town — and often many more — with each regiment typically remaining for a relatively short length of time. Expenditure on the provisioning of several hundred men must have been a significant prop of the local economy, as must the recreational spending of soldiers. In this last regard, there is ample evidence that army officers moved easily in elite circles in Irish towns, but rather less to indicate how the rank-and-file mingled in the broader community. There were certainly times when relations were strained: for one thing, the army's role in supporting the civil power occasionally brought it into conflict with townspeople; for another, sectarian tensions arose between the people and certain regiments; for yet another, there were those who resented the army's political role. On the other hand, there is evidence of good relations between soldiery and citizenry — in reports of popular appreciation for regimental bands and, most of all, in the significant number of marriages between transient soldiers and local women.[78]

iii) Administrative change: impulse and impact

The achievement of Catholic emancipation in 1829 changed the political landscape, and the decade that followed was one of administrative innovation in Ireland. Among the most significant legacies of the era were a centralised police force, a 'national' system of education, and a poor law system. Government also addressed a number of festering grievances — tithe collection was reformed; vestry cess was abolished; a measure of accountability was introduced into the operation of the grand jury system.

In the changed atmosphere, the Daly stranglehold over parliamentary representation in Galway was no longer tenable, and it was decisively ended by the Galway Enfranchisement Act of 1831. Moreover, local initiatives combined with legislative changes to gradually dilute the family's control of municipal government to a point where it too was eliminated.

A key figure in the changing Galway of the period was Rev. John d'Arcy, the Anglican vicar since his ordination in 1820, and an advocate of political economy who had tried to reform charitable bodies in the town in the 1820s.[79]

Municipal reform was a burning topic of the 1830s. That corporations were corrupt, incompetent and unrepresentative was undeniable, and both Whigs and O'Connellites were keen to reform them. But for Tories, corporations were bastions of Protestant influence in hostile territory, and their opposition delayed substantial reform until the passage of the 1840 Municipal Reform Act. But already some of the neglected functions of corporations were being carried out by town commissioners. Under legislation of 1828, property-owners in boroughs where basic services were lacking were empowered to elect commissioners to take charge of lighting, cleaning and paving.[80]

In Galway, a decade of improvement began in June 1830 with the passage through parliament of the Galway Docks and Canal Bill. It was the outcome of several years of agitation — and of lobbying against Daly counter-proposals — by merchants grouped in the Galway Chamber of Commerce. The legislation established a Board of Harbour Commissioners, that was charged with the maintenance and improvement of docks and quay, and with opening navigation between Lough Corrib and the port. The 63 commissioners were substantial property owners — only those with personal worth over £3000 were eligible — and it was a source of satisfaction to them that those using the port finally controlled it. Rev. d'Arcy was appointed secretary and the Board set to business. The greatest need was for new docks and quays, so plans were drawn up and an application prepared for a government loan to finance the engineering works. Both plans and loan were approved by the Board of Works, on the understanding that repayments would come from port revenue.

A £17,000 loan was authorised by the Treasury in June 1832. During an otherwise dreadful month in Galway's history — cholera was raging — the news was welcome, but the harbour commissioners received no further good news for some time. From the beginning, their project was plagued by problems. First, their contractor's illness caused delays, then his death meant that he had

S.W. view of the town of Galway, 1820 (Hardiman, *Galway*).

to be replaced. The passage of time and the alteration of plans increased costs, while falling port revenues in the early 1830s made it difficult to service loan commitments. Geological obstacles and a skilled labour shortage delayed things further, and autumn storms damaged the new pier in 1838. The combination of events gave an impression of incompetence, and the Board of Works announced the appointment of a receiver, in 'the public interest', to take charge of port revenues and to ensure that loans were repaid. The new receiver was the Board's secretary, Rev. d'Arcy, causing other commissioners to feel that their competence was being questioned. In practical terms, d'Arcy's dual role made him governor of the harbour. The commissioners were left without authority, but they were not relieved of the anxiety resulting from legal proceedings taken by their contractor — or of responsibility in the public mind for the condition of the harbour.[81]

The Board of Harbour Commissioners was the first of three representative public bodies formed in Galway during the 1830s. Last, in 1839, was the Board of Poor Law Guardians, the origins of which will be considered in Chapter Three. The other was the Board of Town Commissioners, which was charged with 'regulating and improving Galway'. These were properly the tasks of the corporation, tasks that it refused to accept, despite pressure. Finally, on foot of an 1829 ruling by the lord chancellor, the corporation was deprived of the tolls and customs, its only remaining sources of revenue.[82] Far from expediting matters, however, the lord chancellor's decision only delayed them further. A proposal in 1830 that commissioners be elected under the 1828 act to clean, pave, police and light the town was narrowly defeated at a public meeting, the majority choosing to wait until the House of Lords made an order regarding the proper application of tolls and customs.[83] For several further years, pedestrians were 'left to grope [their] way through narrow decayed streets, in danger of falling into cellars, or tumbling over heaps of mud and every other nuisance collected in the streets'.[84]

The Galway Improvements Bill establishing a Board of Town Commissioners and giving it control over tolls and customs was passed in parliament in June 1836. Some of the commissioners' work had been anticipated by a committee under Rev. John d'Arcy that began to pave some of the streets, having prepared a 'Plan of Specification' for that purpose. d'Arcy was appointed secretary to the town commissioners and his preparatory work enabled the new body to begin work immediately. By mid-July 1836, it was reported that Cross-street was being paved 'under the direction of a master-paviour from Dublin', and that several of the other streets were macadamised.[85] After years of neglect, there was satisfaction with the rate of progress and with the results:

> The repairs and other works effected in all or many of our streets
> within the last nine months have already given much comfort to
> the inhabitants, as well as to strangers, with whom the uncleanliness
> of our town was formerly the subject of a proverb.[86]

But not everything about the town commissioners' affairs gave full satisfaction. In 1838 and 1839, allegations of jobbery prompted comparisons between their behaviour and that of the corporation.[87] Especial concern centred on the relationship between commissioners and the Gas Company.

The Town of Galway 1840, viewed from the Claddagh by Bartlett.

The provision of gas lighting was one of the principal objectives of the Board of Town Commissioners on its establishment. Tenders were sought unsuccessfully during July 1836 from existing gas companies and, following that, a sub-committee of commissioners was formed to expedite matters. In December 1836, a Mr Lyddle of Glasgow (who was engaged in the lighting of Armagh) was invited to survey the town.[88] At an ensuing public meeting in the Town Hall, Lyddle recommended the establishment of a Galway Gas Company. Investors in such a company, he predicted, would be joining 'a most lucrative speculation'. His advice was taken. Almost inevitably, Rev d'Arcy emerged as company secretary, and from the spring of 1837, things moved quickly. Shares were snapped up (though there were complaints that they were beyond the means of the 'ordinary householder'), an agreement was concluded between the company and the town commission, and gas works were erected near the new docks. Lamps, lamp-posts and braziers were manufactured at Stephens's Foundry, Back-street. Work in the streets proceeded quickly through the summer and autumn, until the night of 30 November 1837, when the lights were switched on amidst great 'bustle' — and to 'the enthusiasm of the inhabitants in every quarter'.[89]

But the enthusiasm was short-lived, for the following winter it was observed that the lights were 'quite dim, not half as brilliant as last year'. It was surmised that the company was adding to its profitability by saving on gas. And if the Gas Company proved to be lucrative for its shareholders, this provoked 'jealousy', and allegations of a clash of interest against those who were shareholders and, at the same time, members of the local authority that agreed to pay the allegedly excessive charges of the company. Rev. d'Arcy, secretary to both bodies, defended the arrangement against the criticism of 'ignorant people': arguing that 'no town in the Empire was better lighted'; pointing out that because of the different 'quantity of consumption', the cost per light was inevitably greater in Galway than in Belfast; stating that only a minority of town commissioners were connected with the gas company; insisting that the 9% per annum earned by shareholders was not excessive, being little more than they could have got on deposit.[90] d'Arcy's stout defence did not quell the controversy, nor did it dissuade 'the rather unreflecting portion of the public' from electing in 1842 'a party of the Board' strongly opposed to the Gas Company.[91] One consequence of the election was that the streets of Galway were again plunged into darkness during the winter of 1842-43. A compromise allowed the lights to be switched on again, but the settlement was not permanent and there was intermittent friction and litigation between the local authority and the gas company during the remainder of the century.[92]

The reform of Galway's local government, then, was a difficult process. Rather than local acclaim, those involved faced criticism and ridicule, not to mention allegations of incompetence and dishonesty. Arguably, however, most of the inadequacies of the nascent local authorities of the 1830s were attributable to inexperience — both collective and individual. The appointment of Rev d'Arcy as secretary to all of the new bodies was both a symptom and a consequence of this. But the teething difficulties of Harbour Board, Town Commission, and Gas Company should not obscure their achievements. Galway streets were far cleaner, far better paved, far better lit and — because of developments at national level — far better policed in the early 1840s than they had been a decade earlier. And although they were not satisfactorily finished, Galway also had new quays and a new harbour.

The corporation, which continued in existence during the 1830s, was marginal to these developments. The only notable departure in its affairs was the election in 1830 of Galway's first Catholic mayor in 150 years. Lieutenant Colonel John Blake's accession was celebrated, but it was merely a Dalyite sop to Catholic sentiment.[93] When the long-awaited municipal reform measures were passed in 1840, there was disappointment. Galway's was not one of the ten reformed corporations provided for in the legislation; its corporation was simply abolished. This was seen to considerably diminish Galway's status, but protests — including the parliamentary objections of Daniel O'Connell — had no effect. Galway entered the 1840s therefore with an administrative apparatus appropriate to its size rather than to its traditions — being clearly classified as a town, and not as a city.

NOTES

1. James Kelly, 'The Politics of Protestant Ascendancy', in G. Moran, ed., *Galway: History & Society*, Dublin 1996, pp. 259-65; J. N. Dillon, 'The Lords of Dunsandle' in *Kiltullagh/Killimordaly: a History from 1500 to 1900*, Kiltullagh 2000, pp. 49-51.
2. James Hardiman, *The History of the Town and County of the Town of Galway*, Dublin 1820, p. 192.
3. John B. Trotter, *Walks through Ireland in the years 1812, 1814, and 1817*, London 1819, pp. 402-07.
4. Hardiman, *Galway*, p. 285.
5. ibid., Thomas Murtagh, 'Power and Politics in Galway, 1770-1830', M.A. thesis, UCG 1982, pp. 116-20; Virginia Crossman, *Local Government in Nineteenth-century Ireland*, Belfast 1994, pp. 75-79.
6. Murtagh, 'Power', pp. 151-53; Padraic Flynn, 'A Study of Local Government in Galway in the early 19th Century', M.A. thesis, UCG 1981, pp. 201-02.
7. Woodman, *Annals*, pp. 4-6.
8. Hardiman, *Galway*, p. 194.
9. Woodman, *Annals*, p. 6.
10. Cited in Woodman, *Tribes*, p. 40.
11. Flynn, 'Local Government', pp. 216-20; Paul Walsh, 'The Topography of Medieval and Early Modern Galway' in Moran, *Galway*, pp. 64-66.
12. Murtagh, 'Power', pp. 158-68
13. Hardiman, *Galway*, pp. 174-75.
14. Lughaidh Ó Cuileáin, 'Tráchtáil is Baincéaracht i nGaillimh san 18ú Céad' in *Galvia*, v, 1958, pp. 49-52.
15 . ibid.
16. Louis M. Cullen, 'Galway Merchants and the Outside World, 1650-1800' in D. Ó Cearbhaill, ed., *Galway,: Town & Gown*, 1484-1984, 1984, pp. 62-89.
17. Ó Cuileáin, 'Baincéaracht', pp.43-55; 'Tráchtáil idir Iarthar na hÉireann is an Fhrainc, 1660-1800', in *Galvia* iv, 1957, pp. 27-48.
18. Hardiman's *Galway*, p. 192; 1831 Census, 1833 xxxix, p. 37; 1841 Census, 1843 xxiv, pp. 368-69.
19. [The Misses Blake], *Letters from the Irish Highlands of Cunnemara by a Family Party*, London 1825, p. 356.
20. Jonathan Binns, *The Miseries and Beauties of Ireland*, London 1837, vol. i, pp. 404-06.
21. ibid.

22. Hely Dutton, *A Statistical and Agricultural Survey of the County of Galway*, Dublin 1824, p. 197.

23. Dutton, *Galway*, pp. 201-03.

24. Walsh, 'Topography', pp. 45-48; Hardiman, *Galway*, pp. 297-303.

25. 1831 Census, 1833, xxxix, p. 308; Greagóir Ó Dúill, 'Galway in the First Famine Winter' in *Saothar* 1, 1975, pp. 65-67.

26. Dutton, *Galway*, pp. 367, 430-32.

27. *Connaught Journal*, 1 September 1823.

28. Hardiman, *Galway*, pp. 288-89.

29. Dutton, *Galway*, p. 418.

30. *Connaught Journal*, 29 April 1824.

31. Lewis, *Topographical Dictionary*, p. 634; *Connaught Journal*, 10 April 1826, 28 February, 3 March, 7 April 1828, 31 January 1831.

32. Hugh W. L. Weir, *Houses of Clare*, p. 71; Hall's *Ireland*, vol. iii.

33. L. M. Cullen, 'Eighteenth Century Flour Milling in Ireland', in *IESHJ* iv, 1977, pp. 5-25.

34. Dutton, *Galway*, pp. 95-96, 361-62.

35. Hardiman, *Galway*, p. 289n.

36. ibid., p. 287; *Connaught Journal*, 28 January 1830.

37. Lewis, *Dictionary*, p. 634; *2nd Report of the Railway Commissioners*, 1837-8 xxxv, p. 90.

38. Hardiman, *Galway*, pp. 291-92.

39. *Galway Vindicator*, 20 March 1844.

40. Hardiman, *Galway*, pp. 292-97; Dutton, *Galway*, p. 396.

41. Dutton, *Galway*, pp. 199-200.

42. Columba Leahy, 'The Galway Sea Fishing Industry from the Union to the Famine', MA thesis, UCG 1964, pp. 377-79.

43. ibid., pp. 351-65.

44. *Connaught Journal*, 2 February 1824, 21 February 1828, 24 February 1831, 2 July 1835, *Galway Vindicator*, 2 March, 4 May 1844.

45. See, for example, Hardiman, *Galway*, pp. 293-96 and *Connaught Journal*, 16 October 1823.

46. *Connaught Journal*, 28 May 1829 (see also ibid., 17 July 1826).

47. ibid., 29 August 1833.

48. These attempts are detailed in Chapters Four and Ten.

49. Leahy, 'Fishing Industry', p. 375.

50. Síle Ní Chinnéide, 'Coquebert de Montbret's Impressions of Galway City and County in the Year 1791', in *JGAHS* xxv, 1952, pp. 1-14; Dutton, *Galway*, p. 104, Curwen's *Observations*, vol. ii, pp. 339-41; Lewis, *Dictionary*, pp. 627-28; Andy Bielenberg, *Cork's Industrial Revolution*, 1780-1880, Cork 1991, pp. 34-35; Hardiman, *Galway*, p. 290n.

51. Lewis, Dictionary, p.630; Connaught Journal, 5 April 1830.

52. Arthur Young, *Tour in Ireland*, passim; Hardiman, *Galway*, p. 290; Bielenberg, *Cork*, pp. 16-17; *Connaught Journal*, 20 December 1824.

53. *Connaught Journal*, 2 October 1823.

54. ibid.

55. ibid., 12 April 1830; 1841 Census, 1843 xxiv, p. 372.

56. John Towner, *An Historical Geography of Recreation & Tourism in the Western World*, 1540-1940, Chichester 1996, pp. 167-71; James Walvin, *Beside the Seaside*, London 1978, pp. 13-22; de Latocnaye & Stevenson, *A Frenchman's Walk through Ireland*, 1796-97, pp. 149-50; Gilbert Wakefield, *An Account of Ireland, Statistical and Political*, London 1812, vol. 2, p. 759.

57. *Connaught Journal*, 18 December 1828.

58. ibid., 2 June 1831; 18 August 1836.

59. Henry Inglis, *A Journey throughout Ireland during the Spring, Summer, and Autumn of 1834*, London 1838, p. 217; *The Angler in Ireland, or an Englishman's ramble through Connaught & Munster during the Summer of 1833*, London, 1834. vol. i, pp. 81-82).

60. *Connaught Journal*, 20 July 1835.

61. ibid., 5 May 1831.

62. ibid., 18 August 1836.

63. *Galway Vindicator*, 24 July 1841 (see also ibid., 23 July 1842).

64. Hardiman, *Galway*, pp. 308-10; Hely Dutton, Galway, pp. 201-03.

65. *Connaught Journal*, 27 January 1831.

66. Trotter, *Walks*, p. 401.

67. W. M. Thackeray, *The Irish Sketchbook*, 1990 edn, p. 179.

68. *Connaught Journal*, 6 September 1830; Lewis's *Dictionary*, p. 634.

69. Hely Dutton, *Galway*, pp. 361-62.

70. For example: *Connaught Journal*, 16 July 1792, 16 March 1829; *Galway Advertiser*, 18 August 1838, 13 February 1841; *Galway Vindicator*, 3 September 1842.

71. *1831 Census: Abstract of Answers and Returns, County of the Town of Galway*, 1833 xxxix, p. 308; Pigot's *City of Dublin & Hibernian Provincial Directory*, 1824, p. 205.

72. *1831 Census: Abstract of Answers and Returns, County of the Town of Galway*, 1833 xxxix, p. 308.

73. *The Angler*, p. 71; Pigot, *City of Dublin & Hibernian Provincial Directory*, 1824, p. 205. See also Inglis, *Journey*, p. 216.

74. *Connaught Journal*, 22 March 1832.

75. See Cormac Ó Gráda, *Ireland: a new Economic History, 1780-1939*, Oxford 1994, pp. 265-70; Michael Winstanley, *The Shopkeeper's World*, 1830-1914, Manchester 1983, pp. 2-16; Pigot's *Directory*, 1821, 1824; Slater's *Directory*, 1846.

76. *Connaught Journal*, 13 December 1824.

77. R. B. McDowell, 'Ireland in 1800' in Moody & Vaughan, *A New History of Ireland, IV: Eighteenth Century Ireland*, Oxford 1986, pp. 666-67; Gearóid Ó Tuathaigh, 'Galway in the Modern Period: Survival and Revival', in Howard B. Clarke, ed., *Irish Cities*, Cork 1995, pp. 140-41; Virginia Crossman, 'The Army and Law and Order in the Nineteenth Century' in Bartlett & Jeffrey, eds, *A Military History of Ireland*, Cambridge 1996, pp. 358-59.

78. Crossman, 'The Army', pp. 358-78; Anne M. A. Mannion, 'The Social Geography of the British Army in Nineteenth Century Ireland with Specific Reference to Galway', Unpublished M.A. thesis, University College Galway, 1994, pp. 77-96, 103-13.

79. See Chapter Three, and D'Arcy obituary, *Galway Express*, 4 September 1873.

80. Crossman, *Local Government*, pp. 65-85; Ó Tuathaigh, *Ireland*, pp. 80-86; Oliver McDonagh, 'Ideas and Institutions, 1830-45' in Vaughan, *A New History of Ireland, v: Ireland Under the Union*, 1, pp. 193-217.

81. Woodman, *Annals*, pp. 16-37.

82. Lewis, *Dictionary*, p. 634; Flynn, 'Local Government', pp. 234-35; Murtagh, 'Power', p. 173.

83. *Connaught Journal*, 19 April 1830, 16 July 1835.

84. ibid., 10 September 1835.

85. ibid., 22 October 1835, 16 June, 21 July 1836.

86. *Galway Patriot*, 2 September 1837.

87. Flynn, 'Local Government', p. 248; *Galway Advertiser*, 15 December 1838, 14 September 1839.

88. *Galway Vindicator*, 27 May 1843.

89. *Connaught Journal*, 15 December 1836, *Galway Patriot*, 7 January, 18 February, 22 April, 16 August, 2 December 1837.

90. *Galway Advertiser*, 15 December 1838; *Galway Vindicator*, 9 July 1842.

91. *Galway Vindicator*, 27 May 1843.

92. ibid., 10, 27 May 1843, 28 February 1874; *Galway Packet*, 18 May 1853; *Galway Express*, 20 January, 2 November 1872, 8 January 1876.

93. Flynn, 'Local Government', p. 237.

CHAPTER 3

'The very name of the Mendicity frightens them'

CHARITY & WELFARE, 1790-1845

Your hardy peasants, your dependent poor
Goaded by want now clamour at your door;
Whilst the pale widow and the orphans moan
Their secret woes; in anguish and alone.
For these, Hibernia shall never plead in vain,
For these, though rude and artless be my strain,
Shall genuine pity every breast expand,
And liberal heart shall join with liberal hand.

Prologue to charity show for Galway's
'indigent house-keepers', 1817.[1]

Due to the growing population, to sporadically-adverse weather, and to a series of economic set-backs, the thirty years between the Napoleonic wars and the Famine was a period of exceptional poverty in Ireland. In towns, according to one writer, it was a time of 'chronic distress', marked by widespread unemployment, high food prices and epidemic diseases.[2]

During these years, visitors familiar with other towns found Galway's poverty to be particularly striking. J.C. Curwen, described people occupying 'low mean cabins', and 'living apparently in great poverty'; Maria Edgeworth, thought it 'the dirtiest town' she ever saw, 'and the most desolate and idle-looking'; John Bernard Trotter was appalled that there was so 'much wretchedness in the cabins and other miserable houses of the poor'.[3]

If the effects of idleness, hunger and disease were felt acutely by Ireland's urban working class, the associated symptoms — begging, food riots, contagion — brought them forcibly to the attention of the other classes. Consequently, there was a proliferation of philanthropic societies and welfare institutions in the years before the Famine. Orphans, mendicants, so-called 'magdalens' and 'lunatics', were among the categories for whom dedicated facilities were provided; the temporarily indisposed were catered for in a network of dispensaries and fever hospitals; those worst affected by the intermittent subsistence crises were assisted by stopgap 'funds' and relief committees. Since Ireland was almost a *tabula rasa* as far as formal social provision was concerned, there was room for initiative and for experiment, at least until the mid-1830s, when the imminence of a Poor Law system began to discourage philanthropic effort in this regard.

Prior to the 1838 legislation, the Irish poor law system was piecemeal and patchy, especially when compared with England's long-established country-wide, parish-based system. Parish vestries of the Church of Ireland had certain responsibilities, but fulfilling them could only be attempted where that Church had a presence. The Church of Ireland did have a profile in the town of Galway, and its vestry records from the early 19th century show regular but modest expenditure on welfare and public health, charged to vestry cess, a levy on urban property equivalent to the controversial tithes. This included outgoings on the care of foundlings and 'parish children', on the employment of a 'head nurse', on pauper burials, on graveyard maintenance (including of several 'intrusted' to Catholic religious orders), on the provision of badges for 'deserving' local beggars (to distinguish them from outsiders). In addition, 'officers of health' were appointed by the vestry during epidemics.[4]

There was some state intervention in the welfare/public health arena. A decree of the Irish parliament in 1765 that public infirmaries be established in each county and borough was generally followed, but not the 1772 legislation providing for the erection by local authorities of Houses of Industry — consisting of 'an asylum for the aged, infirm, and industrious, and a bridewell for the profligate, idle, and refractory'. Only nine such institutions were established on foot of this legislation, none of them in Connacht or Ulster.[5]

In the decades between the enactment of the Houses of Industry legislation and the adoption of the Poor Law, fierce debates took place about the correct approach to provision for the poor. The intellectual champions of rising capitalism scrutinised the long-standing assumptions of the mercantilist era, while the French revolution raised questions of its own: how was social stability best maintained? would a poor law distort the labour market? was all social provision futile? With its very slender public relief system, Ireland was not an ideal laboratory for discovering solutions to these questions, but the country's notorious poverty ensured that its experience — imagined or actual — was utilised for illustrative purposes by social thinkers as divergent as Robert Malthus and Robert Owen.[6]

The traditional view on provision for the poor was predicated on an assumption that the majority of the working population needed occasional assistance — at certain times of the year, or at certain times of life. 'Everyone but an idiot', wrote Arthur Young, 'knows that the lower classes must be kept poor, or they will never be industrious'.[7] If working people were necessarily poor, it followed that they might sometimes fall into destitution, and need help. The emerging view in the early 19th century — which found expression in the English Poor Law of 1834 and in its Irish offshoot of 1838 — distinguished between the labouring poor, who were capable of supporting themselves, and a small minority of dependent poor, who needed to be supported. The support provided would act as a safety net for the genuinely helpless, but it should be offered on unattractive terms so as to deter the wilfully indolent, and to remind the labouring poor of the awful alternatives to thrift and toil.[8] Both views had their adherents in early 19th century Ireland, but there were also other views. If there were those who thought that there was no such category as the 'deserving', there were others — pious Catholics in particular — who were guided by traditional Christian theology, and unconditionally gave alms and assistance.[9] There was something of this attitude in the *Connaught Journal*'s advice in 1791:

> The severity of the season … will be afflicting to the poor in general, while to the rich it affords an opportunity of showing their gratitude to the donor of the blessings they enjoy by sharing what to them is superfluous with those in want.[10]

If public and private bodies were taking an increasing interest in the welfare of the poor, it would seem, nevertheless, that most of the assistance received by the poverty-stricken came from other relatively poor people. According to an estimate from the 1830s, Irish farmers gave a million pounds worth of potatoes annually in alms.[11] The calculation may have been a wild guess, but it testifies to the presence of strong bonds of solidarity in rural Ireland, bonds which evidently existed also in towns. Fr Peter Daly told the Poor Inquiry that 'very few' of his poor parishioners would be 'thrown on the benevolence of the public, if their friends who are able and willing to work could procure employment, for the lower orders would generally support their poor and aged friends'.[12] And if neither family nor friends were in a position to help, there was the pawn shop. Nine licensed pawnbrokers were trading in Galway in the 1830s, catering mainly to the families of tradesmen and labourers, although many of the latter, it was said, were 'too poor to possess any article worth pawning'. For those who had something of value — and their blankets were often the only security of the poorest — the transaction could be expensive. By one account, the full value of smaller items would have been due in interest charges at the end of fifteen months, at which point unredeemed articles were auctioned off.[13]

It is not surprising that people preferred to rely on pawnbrokers and neighbours than on charitable institutions. Pure altruism was rarely the motivation of the promoters of charities — when their objective was not to transform society, they wished at least to transform the individual pauper. Moreover, procedures designed to deter the work-shy and the fraudulent, also deterred the people whom institutions existed to serve. 'The uses of charity', it has been argued, 'were different from its purposes', and the needs it met were not those that the poor themselves would have identified.[14]

The 'purposes' of poor relief and of charity are briefly discussed above, but what were the purposes of the charitable? It has been shown that those associated with particular causes gained status, perhaps even political connections, through their work. And, as patrons, they also acquired the right to recommend 'worthy objects' for assistance[15] No doubt, empathy, altruism, and Christian solidarity sustained many in their fund-raising, motives that also prompted the well-to-do to give subscriptions. The reality, however, was that giving was rarely an entirely voluntary matter. Sometimes, people gave indirectly to institutions through county or vestry cess. Otherwise, the charitable gave because they wished to remove a persistent beggar from their path or their doorstep; because they were embarrassed by the appeals of an acquaintant fund-raiser; because they feared disorder in times of distress; because they were alarmed lest diseases rampant among the poor might, if unchecked, infect their own households. Not always voluntary either were the occasional gifts of the poor themselves to charities. The 'peculiar satisfaction' felt by the Galway Mendicity Institute's Committee at the donation in 1824 of half-a-crown each by forty-six of 'the weavers of the town', is seen in a different light, when it is discovered that all were employed in 'the Hall of this town', where they were subject to a committee whose membership overlapped with the Mendicity's.[16]

The publication of details of the weavers' mite was intended to embarrass affluent citizens into contributing to the charity. This was always a function of subscription lists, even if their ostensible purpose was to acknowledge donations and to render committees accountable. Such lists sustained communities of donors; they reminded tardy contributors to pay up; they testified to the *bona fides* of a cause by giving precedence to contributions from the eminent. A comparison of subscription lists shows that different charities drew on the same relatively small group of people.[17] Charitable amateur theatricals — like those 'in aid of the poor' in 1817 — must have drawn their attendances from the same social set. Likewise with charity sermons, in both Protestant and Catholic churches, which, it has been shown, were the mainstays of many early 19th century charities in Ireland.[18]

The big institutions, with their powerful patrons, their subscription lists, their published annual reports, loom large in accounts of poor relief and charity. But it may be that in the pre-Poor Law period, more actual relief was provided by those who responded spontaneously to daily and weekly calamities. For example, in November 1817, a doctor and a priest sought 'the smallest benefactions' to clothe a woman, who had been burnt and reduced to 'a state of nakedness' by an explosion in a house near the quays. In the following month, it was the turn of 'a poor man ... with a long young family' whose legs had been amputated, to be assisted to 'get into some small little business'.[19] But evidently the response to such appeals was sometimes disappointing for, in January 1827, a bereaved woman complained that many of 'those gentlemen' who had listed themselves as subscribers to an appeal for her support had failed to pay.[20] Mrs Sullivan had discovered something well-known to the treasurers of Galway's charities — that it was easier to extract a promise than a cash amount from many highly-regarded citizens.

The Galway Mendicity Institute

On 8 November 1824, the Galway Mendicity Institute opened in Woodquay. For the *Galway Advertiser*, this meant that 'the chain of charities is now complete':

> There is now no institution for the relief of the poor, to be found in any city, town or village in the Kingdom, that does not exist here. We have an Infirmary, a Fever Hospital and Dispensary, schools Protestant and Roman Catholic, Foundling Hospitals, Orphans' School, Magdalen Asylum, a magnificent Asylum for old people on College-road … and now a Mendicity Institute which opened on Monday providing food and work at Woodquay for as many of the town beggars as thought proper to attend.[21]

On the face of it, the catalogue of facilities was impressive, and we shall return to it later in the chapter. As for the Mendicity Institute itself, it filled a need that was long-felt. In 1772, local authorities had been enabled to establish workhouses in their own jurisdictions but, unlike Limerick and Ennis where Houses of Industry were set up, Galway did not avail of the grant-aid provided by the exchequer.[22]

One motive of those supporting such establishments was the wish to curtail the movement of beggars, who, it was believed, spread diseases by carrying them from town to town.[23] During periods of distress in particular, when both mendicancy and disease were rampant, the clamour against beggars was most intense. According to an investigation into the fever epidemic in Co. Galway in 1817-18:

> It was carried from place to place by the beggars; hence it spread more rapidly in the suburbs of the towns and villages where the mendicants were usually lodged; and this extension of febrile contagion ceased when measures were taken to exclude these hordes of strangers from sojourning in the towns.[24]

Steps were taken at such times to discourage strolling beggars. In 1821, the mayor brought the full rigour of the law to bear upon them, going so far, it was said, as to 'take them up with his own hands'. And in 1822 his successor had erected on the outskirts large painted placards 'cautioning poor strangers against coming into town'. So that outsiders could be easily distinguished in the streets, both by magistrates and the charitable public, it was the practice to issue badges and licences to 'deserving' local beggars'.[25]

In ordinary times, institutions 'for the relief of the poor', fulfilled the social function of saving the affluent from meeting face-to-face with the poor. A year before the doors opened in Woodquay, the editor of the *Connaught Journal* admitted as much in urging the establishment of a Mendicity Institute. For a 'trifling sum annually from each house-keeper', he promised, his readers would be relieved of receiving beggars at their doors, and of dealing with daily 'importunities' on the street. Moreover, with native beggars locked away, it would be easy to detect newcomers, who could be quickly despatched 'to the places where they belonged'.[26]

Until such a facility was provided, the editor continued, 'the chain is incomplete' and, consequently, 'the attempt to introduce better habits among the poor can never succeed'. Merchants, he anticipated, 'whose shops are beset, and whose profits must be considerably diminished by the droves of beggars that haunt every part of this Town, would contribute largely to the support of such an establishment'.[27] As a ready-made model for its management, he drew attention to the strict rules of the Sligo Mendicity Association, which catered only to the 'deserving' resident poor:

> No person is admitted to the Institution who has not been resident in the town for at least three years prior to its commencement, or who is able to obtain subsistence other than by begging.
>
> All persons admitted shall attend at the house from April 1st to October 1st, at six o'clock in the morning and continue there till six in the evening. From October 1st till April 1st, attendance is required from eight till half past four. The inmates are employed breaking stones, making nets, spinning coarse yarn and wool, knitting, plaiting straw, picking oakum, making baskets…
>
> A pint of oatmeal made into stirabout and a pint and a half of buttermilk, or three pounds of potatoes and a pint and a half of buttermilk or soup, is allowed to each individual at each meal. The soup is made from broken meat collected through the town. Each adult is allowed 8d per week to provide lodging, clothing and other necessities not furnished by the Institute.[28]

Unlike institutions established under the 1772 legislation, there was not to be compulsory incarceration in the Galway Mendicity. Nevertheless, it is unlikely that its establishment — or, indeed the news that 'the chain of charities' was complete — was hailed by the intended beneficiaries. Indeed, the remarks of the principals at the founding meeting of the Institute show that their philanthropy was circumscribed by their desire to control or to expose beggars.* Proposing the founding resolutions, Rev. John d'Arcy stated that 'in the garb of the beggar, every description of impostor was to be found, and that in the tone of misery by which our ears were assailed, the voice of feigned distress was heard much more frequently than that of real want'. Port collector and churchwarden, John Lushington Reilly (Rev. d'Arcy's future father-in-law), agreed:

---

* The equivalent society in Dublin, founded in 1818, was explicit too about its objectives — it was called 'The Association for the Prevention and Suppression of Mendicity in Dublin' (Woods, *Mendicity*, p. 12). A more indulgent view was held by James Hardiman. Commenting on proposals to establish a 'workhouse or general asylum', he predicted that such an institution 'would have the effect of clearing the streets for a time', but 'as long as the principal cause, viz. the poverty of the peasantry, continues, so long numbers of the mendicant poor may reasonably be expected' (*Galway*, p. 307).

In comparison with other towns, the number of real objects to be found in Galway were remarkably few, and therefore it was the more necessary to make a distinction between them and the impostor — to the success of whose trade falsehood was essential, which was accompanied by chicanery and fraud, and which necessarily engendered idleness, dissoluteness, and profligacy.[29]

For his part, 'Humanity' Dick Martin was keen to see that charity be 'properly applied' and that 'genuine distress' be relieved.

Clergymen of both denominations joined the committee formed in July 1824 to secure premises and finance. When the Institute opened, it was claimed that many were eager to avail of the 'substantial dinner of soup and meat', and of the 'advantage of being enabled to earn a few pence in the day there, to defray the expense of their bed'. As for the incorrigible and the ineligible, a 'large squadron immediately left town'. Citizens were reminded repeatedly that the success of the undertaking was in their own hands. They should contribute financially to the Institute, but more importantly, they should not give any alms whatsoever. The genuinely needy were catered for; only 'impostors' were still at large.[30]

The efforts of Fr Mark Fynn, notwithstanding, many Catholics were suspicious of the motives of committee members, and withheld their support for a time.[31] On the anniversary of the establishment of the Galway Mendicity Association, however, those attending the body's Annual General Meeting were in self-congratulatory mood. The reasons for their satisfaction were summed up by the *Journal:*

Who would have believed a few years ago that anything but the point of a bayonet could rid our town of the hordes of mendicants who infected it…? Before the establishment of this Institution, Galway was legendary for mendicity. There was scarce a corner or shop door which they did not block up. Now they have totally disappeared from our streets. They who were hitherto idle are forced in their own defence to work for the necessaries of life, and many to whom the begging system was an easy and profitable practice, have been constrained to go to service. As for strange beggars we now have no such persons amongst us. The very name of the Mendicity frightens them to a different route when they are bending their way towards Galway; and the poor people fed at the Mendicity are supplied with sound and wholesome food, the effects of which are visible in their improved appearance.[32]

But the Institute soon fell into financial difficulties. Subscriptions, supplemented by the proceeds of occasional charity sermons and balls, proved insufficient to the needs of an average of 172 paupers, and severe economies were implemented early in 1827.[33] The problem was that too few of the twelve-member committee took a sufficiently active interest. One of the few who did, Rev. John d'Arcy, complained about this in January 1828, on his return from Dublin after an absence of six weeks:

> While I was absent no collection was made for the Mendicity, but the institution was not closed. During the whole time, its door was opened wide as ever. All the expenses were paid, and everything necessary for the institution was provided with the same, or greater, liberality, than if I had been at home. I found the institution on my return in the most perfect order — I found the number of persons in it was greater than when I went away and yet *I found the streets crowded with beggars.* How can this be accounted for? Is it not manifest that it is to be ascribed to the absence of the Collectors of the institution? If they had been at the doors of the inhabitants, pressing up on them the wants of the institution, and imploring

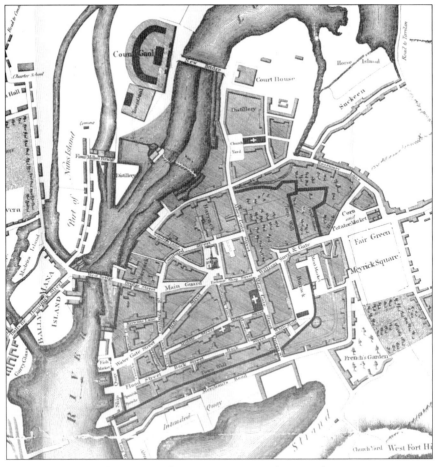

Galway in 1818 from Logan's map (Hardiman, *Galway*).

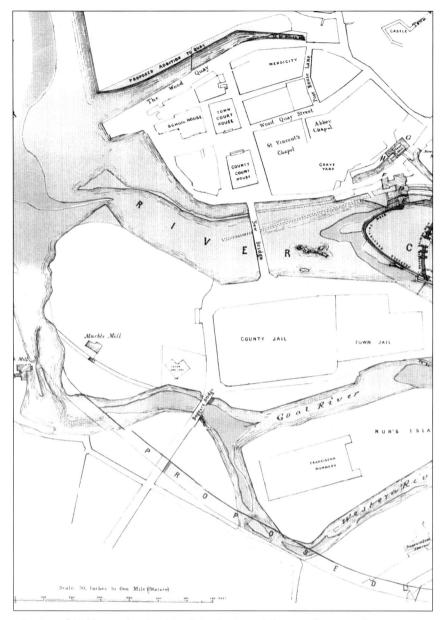

Section of 1846 map showing Mendicity Institute, jails, court houses and waterways
(including part of proposed canal).

their alms — if they had obtained these alms, there would have
been nothing for the common beggar, and the common beggar
would have shunned the place. No Sir, the Mendicity is not a
house for the reception of any number of paupers to be supported
by any number of affluent persons. It is a combination of the
inhabitants of any place to put down mendicity in that place, and

it must be sustained and supported by maintaining and supporting
a lively interest in the public mind.[34] *

Notwithstanding d'Arcy's commitment, the Mendicity never fully recovered
and, from 1828 until its final closure in 1837, it staggered from one financial
crisis to the next. The key problem was that, unlike comparable institutions in
Waterford, Clonmel and Limerick, which received an average of £1800 a year
each in Grand Jury presentments,[35] the public subsidy for the Galway
Mendicity was modest. Its other sources of income — subscriptions, the
proceeds of fund-raising events, the labour of inmates — were uncertain, being
vulnerable to the economic climate, and to competition from other causes. The
accounts for 1835 show that 38% of total income (£284.12.3), was granted by
the Grand Jury; that 35% was collected by seventeen pairs of Association
collectors; that 17% was earned by paupers breaking stones for paving and
collecting animal droppings for sale as manure; that 7% came from a charity
performance of a play.[36] A shortfall in any one area could cause problems. In
1828, it was the negligence of the voluntary collectors that angered Revd
d'Arcy, but in 1829 it was the financial embarrassment of the Corporation and
its consequent inability to pay a debt for stone-breaking that caused the closure
of the Asylum, and 'the throwing out of nearly two hundred miserable people
on our streets'.[37]

Following the 1829 closure, there were 'many meetings' of those committed
to the revival of the Mendicity. To overcome still-lingering suspicions, efforts
were made to involve the Catholic clergy to a greater extent, and when it was
announced in April 1830 that the facility was reopening, the joint treasurers
were both priests. Again, the people were scolded for persisting in almsgiving.
If they gave all alms to the Mendicity, it was pointed out, rather than to
'importunate street beggars', there would no additional expense, but a
persistent social problem could be eliminated.[38]

The 'backwardness' of subscribers in 1834 resulted in indebtedness, raising
fears that the Mendicity would have to close again. Matters continued to
worsen and, in the spring of 1835, a meeting was held 'to take into
consideration' the future of the institution. Again, the public was reminded of
its duty to the indigent and to the 'credit and comfort of the town'. And, in the
aftermath of the cholera epidemic of 1832, they were also reminded that
unconfined paupers carried disease:

> … the Mendicity deserves support because it gathers together in
> one receptacle, where cleanliness is observed, a great number of

---

* Intentionally or not, d'Arcy paraphrased Adam Smith in the final section above: 'Laws and governments may be considered
in this and indeed in every case as a combination of the rich to oppress the poor, and preserve to themselves the inequality
of the goods which would otherwise be soon destroyed by the attacks of the poor, who if not hindered by the government
would soon reduce the others to an equality with themselves by open violence (Adam Smith, *Lectures on Jurisprudence*,
Oxford, 1978).

those, who, if left unnoticed, might themselves become the victims, and impart to others the contagion of that desolating social affliction which has recently carried death, orphanage, and broken hearts, into many a home which had previously been happy.[39]

A two-week-closure in March 1835 stimulated some subscribers into honouring their commitments, but the respite was short-lived, and the threat of closure loomed again in July and September. The institution struggled on, surviving only by making the 'greatest economies consistent with the comforts of the inmates'.[40] Over-dependence on income from the labour of paupers was one cause of difficulty. Stone-breaking required capital outlay on horses, carts and tools, and it could only be done by relatively strong men. Moreover, Galway's corporation was not always in a position to pay for paving the streets. For these reasons, it was discontinued it in 1836. The problems raised by the collection of animal-droppings were different:

> In consequence of the many poor people in all parts of the town engaged in the collection of manure as their only source of livelihood; the committee considered if they interfered or endeavoured to prevent those persons that they would reduce them to a state of pauperism, and consequently increase the numbers in the Mendicity.[41]

In light of the enquiries of government-appointed Commissioners, Galway's Mendicity committee looked forward to a time when the landed interest would be made to share the cost of poverty as part of 'a modified system of Poor Laws, which would equalise the burthens, that press too heavy on the industrious classes, and place a portion of them on those who are well able to bear it, but always unwilling to contribute'.[42] In the meantime, the committee continued to publicise its financial difficulties, seeking to harness public opinion in support of its petition for increased funding from the Grand Jury. But, to a request for £400 at the Summer Assizes of 1837, the Grand Jury responded with a presentment of £300. This provoked the immediate resignation of the committee, leading to the final closure of the Mendiciry in July 1837. Two months later, the furniture and fittings of the house in Woodquay were placed at auction, in order that debts might be met.[43]

The survival of the Mendicity Institute for thirteen troubled years was more remarkable than its eventual failure. It was an ideological project, that was sustained so long only because of the commitment of advocates like the Anglican Rev. John d'Arcy and the Catholic Rev. Mark Fynn. But despite their efforts, the people of Galway were never fully convinced that its objectives were either realisable or desirable. Suspicions were aroused by the prominence of Protestants on early committees — including the unpopular Archbishop of Tuam — and even the involvement of priests could not transform the

Mendicity into as 'Catholic' a charity as the Magdalen Asylum or the Widows' and Orphans' Institute. In the circumstances, the support of public bodies was crucial, but such support was either grudging or erratic. The institution was dependent, in particular, on income from stone-breaking but such contracts were not always available from Galway's crisis-stricken Corporation and its emergent replacements. Moreover, involvement in road-maintenance caused confusion regarding the Mendicity's function. With its network of collectors and its paupers employed on the streets, it came to be regarded almost as a local authority itself. Consequently, when public bodies were unable to pay for its services, the Mendicity was blamed for the state of the streets and to the loss in contract income was added a loss from declining subscriptions.

But the support of 'deserving' paupers was only part of the Mendicity's mission. Statements emphasised that its larger objective was to stamp out mendicancy, which it saw as being sustained by a gullible public. The constancy of this theme in the Association's propaganda indicates that many people were not persuaded.

Although it was a petulant gesture of resignation which ended its decade-long struggle against public indifference, the Mendicity Association would have been redundant in any case. Members of the Grand Jury may have been surprised that their offer of increased funding was spurned, but all parties knew that the imminent Poor Law system was about to take responsibility for the mendicant and the pauper.

A 'chain of charities'

Of the other links on the *Galway Advertiser's* 'chain of charities' of 1824, the free schools will be considered in Chapter Thirteen, so it remains to examine (a) the infirmary, (b) dispensary and fever hospital, (c) benefit funds and savings banks, (d) lying-in hospitals, (e) foundling facilities, (f) widows' and orphans' asylum, and (g) Magdalen asylum.

a) *County Infirmary*

Dating from the late 17th century, the County Infirmary was the oldest of the institutions. On foot of 1765 legislation, the Corporation resolved to establish a complementary infirmary to serve the town. To facilitate this, the Erasmus Smith foundation donated two acres, but, as with urban improvement generally during the period of Daly hegemony, little progress was made. When John Howard came to investigate public institutions in 1788, he found 'a large house not finished' in Prospect Hill and, in Abbeygate-street, a 'Mansion of Misery', housing five patients:

> There is neither pallias nor any sort of thing between the bodies of two patients and the boarded-bottomed bedsteads; under the three others was a little straw; there was not a single sheet in the house, and the few blankets which cover the wretched people were old

County Infirmary, c.1820 (from Hardiman Collection, Galway County Library).

and filthy. The floors were uncommonly dirty, and the walls abominably so, besmeared with repeated foul spittings. There was no sort of convenience in the house, not even to warm whey, except an old broken pot.[44]

Howard complained before the Assizes about the state of things, but the 'spacious and elegant three storey building' in Prospect Hill did not open until 1802. When it did open, the new facility replaced the old County Infirmary, and was not under Corporation auspices as originally envisaged.[45]

By 1820, the infirmary was admitting seven to eight hundred resident patients annually, in addition to treating 'numerous' external patients.[46] Apparently, its affairs were better managed in Prospect Hill than they had been in Abbeygate-street. Hardiman recorded the dietary regime there:

The inmates receive daily for breakfast one quart of fresh stirabout, composed of the best meal and pure water, with a pint of new, or a quart of sour milk; and for dinner twenty ounces of loaf bread; with a quart of new milk four days a week; and for the other three days, three quarters of a pound of boiled beef each day, a quarter of a stone of potatoes, with as much broth and vegetables as they can use; for drink they get gruel and whey, and according to the nature of each individual case, are supplied with wine and other restoratives.[47]

Hardiman was satisfied that the infirmary was in 'no way inferior to any other establishment of the kind in Ireland', an opinion that was supported by Elizabeth Fry a few years later. Indeed, after speaking with both male and female patients, the Quaker philanthropist was reported to have asked for a copy of the rules and regulations of the institution, so that 'she might point them out to others'.[48] Fry, however, may have been unaware of restrictions on the utility of the institution. The most pressing of these, as discovered by the Poor Inquiry, was that this county facility was not open to townspeople, unless they acquired a recommendation from one of the voluntary subscribers, most of whom lived in rural parts. If the Corporation or town grand jury had agreed to contribute to the running of the infirmary, this problem would have been solved, but they refused (and continued to refuse). The Poor Inquiry also showed that the infirmary gave poor value for money. 232 resident patients were treated during 1833 — far fewer evidently than in 1820 — but at a cost that was three times greater per patient than in the fever hospital.[49] Perhaps reflecting the high expenditure, mortality was low — less than half that of equivalent institutions in Dublin and Cork.[50] It would seem, however, that resident surgeons — Dr James Veitch until 1833, Dr Andrew James Veitch from 1833 to 1858 — enjoyed more lifestyle advantages than the patients:

> The surgeon occupies three-sevenths of the whole house … The ground in front of the house is in the occupation of the surgeon (about three quarters of an acre) partly as a potato field, partly as a kitchen garden … Five pigs are now kept in a stye in the hospital yard, but there is no space that we could observe laid out for the recreation of the convalescents … The patients cannot appear in front of the house, for there are the surgeon's windows and his family, they cannot enjoy the grounds in the rear for there are the surgeon's gardens and his farmyard, they must therefore, and do generally, remain all day in their wards, whatever be the state of their convalescence or the weather.[51]

Privileges such as those enjoyed by the elder Veitch were common in Ireland, though not 'in any other nation in Europe' that the Poor Inquiry inspectors were acquainted with. They ended in 1838 when a surgeon's residence was built, and the number of hospital beds increased from 30 to 80.

b) *Public health: the Fever Hospital and Dispensary*

The fever hospital and dispensary were closely associated. Both were founded during the 1817 typhus epidemic, when panic-induced over-subscription to the dispensary permitted the establishment of the hospital.[52] In 1818, the hospital was established permanently on Earls' Island, but the dispensary closed until another health crisis in 1822. Then, in line with the dispensary legislation of 1805, it too was placed on a permanent footing under the fever hospital's physician, Stephen Burke.[53] Both became dependent upon neglectful subscribers and grudging grand jurors. During a period of especial financial adversity in 1828, the merger of hospital, dispensary and Mendicity Institute was considered, on the grounds that all had the same primary objective — curtailment of the spread of disease.[54]

Curtailing the spread of disease, indeed, was an ever-present concern. In the late 18th century, those advocating the demolition of the town walls argued that their removal would 'clear the town of contagious disorders'.[55] But the levelling of the walls was not a panacea, as was shown by the remarks of a medical expert two decades later:

> When an epidemic constitution prevailed, Galway is well circumstanced to favour its extension: the streets are narrow and dirty; dung-hills and stagnant pools are frequently met with ... add to this, that the cellars are filled with poor of the lowest order, and of the most negligent and filthy habits.[56]

Both dispensary and fever hospital were set up to cater for those who could not afford to pay for treatment and, insofar as one was strictly for out-patients, and the other had no out-patient facilities, they were complementary institutions. Living conditions ensured that illness, including febrile illness, was pervasive, so medical assistance was always in demand. But what was available was not always what was needed. The dispensary, for example, was not equipped to treat accidents. Moreover, because it was almost impossible for townspeople to gain admission to the infirmary, many 'fever' patients during non-epidemic periods were, in reality, suffering from mundane afflictions, but were given diagnoses qualifying them for intern treatment. For public health reasons, admission to the fever hospital was a simple matter — the prospective patient presented before the physician — but those seeking dispensary treatment had to first get a recommendation from a subscriber. One incidental effect of this was that the dispensary continued to attract voluntary subscriptions from would-be-patrons of poor acquaintances and clients, while the fever hospital ultimately became totally dependent on grand jury presentments.[57]

The 1817 typhus epidemic — midwife to both dispensary and hospital —was long-anticipated and, when it hit nearby towns, precautions were taken in Galway. Citizens were advised to prepare: 'inhabitants' to ensure the cleanliness of their homes; magistrates to have dung-hills and other 'mounds of filth' removed; 'the lower orders' to be 'particular in the admission of strange beggars to their houses'.[58] But it was not until the fever had begun to circulate 'indiscriminately amongst the rich and poor' that the dispensary and fever hospital opened.[59] Inevitably in the circumstances, both were makeshift, as one appeal for medicine indicates:

> The situation of the patients in the Fever Hospital is such as to require wine, which the funds are unable to procure. It is therefore hoped that this necessary medicine may be supplied by contributions

from those families who are in the habit of using it for gratification … Any quantity left for the use of the hospital at Mr Doyle's, the apothecary to the Institution, will be thankfully received.[60]

The typhus epidemic lasted two years, reaching a peak in March 1818, whereupon disease was reported to have lessened to 'ordinary proportion'. The respite was short, however, and a more severe typhus epidemic struck in 1822. During that summer, the addition of temporary sheds and tents increased accommodation in the Fever Hospital from 60 to 120. At first, most of those admitted were country people, but the spread of infection in the town was inevitable. Among those who died was Dr Burke of the dispensary and fever hospital.[61] More than in any other crisis, substantial amounts of money were available in 1822-23 (notably from the London Tavern Committee).[62] Fever patients, therefore, could be nourished as well as treated, and for that reason mortality was relatively low. In December 1822, for example, there were 144 admissions to the fever hospital, but only four deaths.[63] By early summer, 1823, the worst was over. Potential visitors were advised of the fact:

> Bathers and persons desirous of spending the summer months in town may remove their fears on the subject of fever. It is now completely gone. There are only a few patients in the hospital, which is always the case and we do not hear of *any out-patients*.[64]

But fever was not long absent and, in the winter of 1826-27, an outbreak of dysentery caused alarm. Dr O'Maley, medical superintendent, reported in February that it was under control, but resources had been stretched beyond breaking point and, for want of an additional grant from the Grand Jury, the fever hospital closed. It took another fever outbreak in the following winter to secure the funds to reopen it.[65]

The arrival in Europe of the cholera pandemic in 1830 guaranteed the fever hospital's survival. All over the continent, there was apprehension. In October 1831, the *Connaught Journal* reprinted the following from the *Dublin Evening Post*: 'It is ascertained that the cholera rages at Hamburg … It is coming round through Egypt and Palestine by the Mediterranean. In short, the greater part of the continent of Europe is likely to be affected …'[66] A week later, families were advised to purchase ingredients to treat the disease: 'One pint of spirits of wine and camphor, one or two pounds of mustard and linseed powder; two ounces of sal volatile; one ounce of essential oil of peppermint, cloves, or cajeput'.[67] It must have been reassuring for Galwegians that they had in their midst Dr Thomas O'Maley, author of a 'scientific and well-written treatise', on cholera morbus, published in Dublin in January 1832. Reportedly, the book had a 'rapid sale' in his native town.[68]

Deaths from cholera — first in Belfast, then in Dublin — were reported from mid-March 1832.[69] The progress of the disease was followed with fearful fascination until, at 3 p.m. on Sunday 13 May, the first case was diagnosed in Galway. Within 24 hours, there were six cases including three deaths; within a week, there were 54 cases including 26 deaths. Belatedly, a Galway Board of Health was formed, with Rev John d'Arcy as secretary. The establishment of the Board was a responsibility of the Church of Ireland vestry, and it was indicative of the seriousness of the situation that the relevant meeting was attended by two Catholic priests.[70] The new Board requisitioned the Fever Hospital — a step resisted by its committee on the grounds that the needs of non-cholera febrile patients should continue to be met. Through June, the disease raged, and by mid July, when the number of deaths reached 400, there was concern that it showed no sign of abating. In other towns, complained one observer, cholera was 'gradually subsiding', but not in Galway. This state of affairs, he urged, was directly attributable to obtuse behaviour:

> Whilst the poor are permitted to attend wakes and funerals, and suffered to convey the remains of the dead upon their shoulders to the grave, we may naturally expect a continuance of the disease, for it must inevitably be generated by close contact.[71]

In the autumn of 1834 — more than two years after the start of the outbreak — it was reported that many of those who had fled to the countryside to escape infection were coming back to Galway. Meanwhile, doctors assured the doubtful that it was perfectly safe to return. The crisis had been an overwhelmingly urban one: 80% of the estimated 25,000 deaths occurred in towns. And Galway was worse affected than most. Over a thousand cholera deaths in a population of some 20,000 meant that most extended families had lost one or more members to the disease.

Special government loans were welcome at the height of the epidemic, but repaying these became a cause of resentment. The costs of cholera were borne overwhelmingly by urban authorities, but town grand juries felt that they should not have to carry the burden alone, since the 1832-34 crisis was a national one. In Galway, where a debt of £3200 had been incurred, and where country people had been admitted to the only fever hospital for fifty miles, the resentment of the town grand jury caused it to cease funding the fever hospital. The institution would have folded in 1837, but for the county grand jury's support.[72]

In the aftermath of the cholera epidemic, Galway's dispensary and fever hospital were among the institutions examined by the Poor Inquiry. The hospital, it was observed, was 'a well-built, strong stone building, divided internally into four wards' and was adequately managed by a 26-year-old Edinburgh medical graduate. The building, however, was considered far too small and poorly equipped. Of its governors, moreover, only Dr Whistler had displayed any interest in its affairs since its foundation. This circumstance, surely, accounts for its perpetually precarious financial position. The dispensary in Abbeygate-street was considered 'very central' with 'a good shop and waiting room'.[73] The medical officer was a 27-year-old licentiate of the Royal College of Surgeons in Ireland, and also possessed of midwifery certificates. He was a busy man with a private practice, but he had attended 747 public patients during the previous three weeks. While it was remarked that the young physician did not approve of inoculation with small pox, and that leeches were 'not afforded', the results of the examination were generally positive. The satisfactory condition of things was novel, however, for the 'institution has been but lately rescued and thoroughly regenerated from a state of great confusion and abuse into which it had fallen during the administration of the late apothecary'.[74] But if the condition of the dispensary had improved considerably, it remained grievously under-resourced. Returns for 1839 show that Galway Town was considerably below the average of the counties and towns in Ireland, as far as the funding of dispensaries was concerned, and above average in the size of the population catered for (only Limerick City fared worse on both sets of criteria).[75]

Dispensary administration was taken over by the poor law guardians, following legislation of 1851. The Fever Hospital struggled on until 1863, when financial difficulties forced it too to join the poor law system.[76]

c) *Benefit funds and savings banks*

The periods when fever was prevalent were also periods of general scarcity. At such times, the fever hospital and dispensary could only address one aspect of the problem, and their efforts were complemented by municipal intervention to reduce food prices, and by the voluntary distribution of provisions. But circumstances were such during a dysentery outbreak of 1827 that the dispensary itself had to intervene with a 'timely supply of food to the wretched inhabitants of Bohermore'.[77]

During several crises, local efforts were augmented by those of outside bodies, most extensively in 1822, when the government provided funds for public works, and voluntary bodies raised subscriptions to relieve destitution in the west of Ireland. Of the latter, the London Tavern Committee and the (Dublin) Mansion House Committee assisted Galway institutions. Later appeals met with a diminished response, as the British public became immunised to Ireland's poverty, and exasperated by the apparent ingratitude of her representatives.[78]

Locally, each crisis mobilised its own caucuses, most members of which resumed regular routines when the worst had passed. But, inevitably, some were profoundly affected by their contact with the poor, and were moved to reflect upon the causes of poverty. The commonest conclusion was that it was the improvidence of the poor themselves that led to distress. It followed that if thrift could be encouraged, people would be better equipped to face future adversity. Thus should be understood the ambitions of a Ladies' Association of 1823 'to encourage, foresight, punctuality and order' among the poor, 'by affording them a facility of obtaining materials for work, both for domestic purposes and for easy manufactories'.[79]

The general dependence of the poor on pawnbrokers was considered to be a particular evil, and the establishment of a 'Tradesmen's Fund' in 1823, making available 'small loans on good security, was intended to provide an alternative'.[80] In the same year, a Savings Bank was established for 'the poor and industrious tradesman, mechanics, agriculturalists, servants, &c.' Evidently, saving was not regarded as an entirely voluntary matter, for employers were urged to open accounts on behalf of their workers, and to deposit all wages in them. Deposits were accepted each Friday between noon and two o'clock, and were withdrawable at a week's notice.[81] The wisdom of these arrangements was definitively established several years later:

> Some time since, a sailor after a voyage deposited £20, wishing to provide 'while the sun shone' against future squalls. But his common sense having lacked in less than an hour, Jack returned with jolly drinking friends for the money and was informed that he should give a week's notice to draw it. Jack put to sea, and after a long voyage his money was safe for his wife and family at his return'.[82]

By the mid-1830s, the Savings Bank was closed. Replying to a Poor Inquiry questionnaire, future bishop Laurence O'Donnell stated that 'there is nothing to save: the people are in a state of nudity and starvation'. The only functioning benefit fund at that time was that run by the Galway Mortality Society, and its sphere was limited to relieving relatives of deceased tradesmen who had paid contributions during their lifetimes — its funds were derived from such contributions, together with occasional donations from 'candidates at elections'.[83] Subsequently, the efforts of Fr Peter Daly and Rev. John d'Arcy to establish a Charitable Pawn Office were sparked by the parliamentary committee on pawnbroking, which collected evidence in Galway in May 1838.[84]

Other initiatives of the late 1830s were associated with the Temperance movement, which had a self-evident interest in promoting outlets for the spare cash of pledge-takers. A Deposit Fund established in 1837 announced that it would facilitate the non-temperate section of the community also. Temperance-connected too was the Galway Loan Fund of 1839 which offered 6% on deposits in 1843. Its goal was to facilitate tradesmen, in accumulating 'capital of their own to engage in business'.[85]

d) *Lying-in Hospitals*

In the 18th and early 19th centuries, it was common for medical practitioners to offer some services free to the poor. This raised the caring profile of the ambitious young doctor, but it also provided useful experience. Such motivation might be inferred in the case of Surgeon Robert Gray — a graduate of the Royal College of Surgeons in Ireland — who published a notice* in May

---

* On the subject of medical advertising, an ingenious notice appeared in the *Connaught Journal* of 25 June 1835. Placed (but hardly paid for) by Thomas Barnicle, Baker — most probably Nora Barnacle's great-grandfather— the notice was a paean of praise to a Doctor Moran of Nuns' Island who, Thomas claimed, had rescued him 'from an early grave' The letter went on: 'Having been afflicted some time since with a severe attack of the liver complaint, or bile on the liver, and drooping under it in the most excruciating torture, my friends were most necessarily obliged to have recourse to medical aid for my preservation... At length hearing of the celebrity of Dr Moran, my friends solicited his advice: that gentleman promptly responded to their call — and after a period of of six weeks during which time he was incessant in his attention, both day and night: and having had to perform a most dangerous operation with the lancet, he succeeded in effecting a radical cure of my disease'.

1824 advising that he was moving from Middle-street to Flood-street, that he was planning to deliver a course of lectures 'On the Anatomy of the Human Skeleton', and that he 'would attend any poor women gratis in their confinement, who are unable to pay for medical attendance'.[86]

Gray was associated with several other obstetric and pædiatric initiatives. In 1825, when a committee under Mrs Georgina Blake of Merlin-park opened a Lying-in Hospital — for poor women 'recommended' by any subscriber of a guinea or more — he praised their efforts, and volunteered his services. The six-bed hospital would be a great boon, he contended, to the poor expectant mother who spent her confinement in the 'care of an ignorant woman who injures her far more than assists her, and is eventually obliged to ask some charitable *accoucheur* to relieve her from her torments'.[87] The alleged shortcomings of untrained midwives were again highlighted in 1826, when a Menlo woman, 'had a narrow escape from death through the ignorance of old women', being saved only by 'an awful operation, termed foetiotomy'.[88] In 1828, Surgeon Gray was to able 'to give up a few hours each morning' to attend a dispensary at his house in Dominick-street 'for the benefit of the poor children of Galway'. In this instance, no recommendation was required, only that patients satisfy him that they were 'unable to purchase medicines'.[89]

Perhaps because poor women thought more highly of midwives than did medical professionals, perhaps because the committee was unable to support it financially, Mrs Blake's Lying-in Hospital did not survive long, and its activities had faded from memory by 1836, when a new maternity hospital opened. Again, a committee of ladies took the initiative, appointing Mrs Latty, certified by the Dublin Lying-in Hospital, as 'Matron and Head Nurse-Tender', and Doctor Blake as 'Assistant Medical Attendant'. (Incidentally, Latty's midwifery training in Dublin was paid for by the town grand jury in 1831 — 'for the benefit of the town of Galway and its neighbourhood'.[90]) Twelve beds were provided in 'a commodious house' — possibly located in Mill-street — ten for women admitted free on the recommendation of a subscriber, two for those who could pay 'a moderate sum'.[91] According to one source this hospital operated until 1842, when its functions were taken over by the workhouse hospital. But it would seem that Matron Latty and Doctor Blake were not overwhelmed by patients. In its first year, fifty women were admitted, utilising between them perhaps 10% of the facility's capacity.[92]

e) *Foundlings*

Certain welfare functions, as has been pointed out, were a responsibility of the select vestry of the established church, and a portion of the vestry cess — an unpopular local tax, mainly applied to the upkeep of church infrastructure — was allocated to the care of foundlings, to the clothing of 'parish-children', and to the burial of paupers. Foundlings accounted for the bulk of such expenditure, often more than £100 year.[93] By law, the established church had responsibility for abandoned infants, being obliged to baptise and care for them. The opportunity to increase their numbers was welcomed by zealous Protestants. In 18th century Dublin, poor Catholics were encouraged to place their infants in the Foundling Hospital, and a 'cradle' was placed outside the institution so that they might anonymously abandon them.* It is possible that the 'public cradle', on which Galway's select vestry spent £10 in 1814, had a similar function.[94]

Occasionally, Galway foundlings were sent to the Dublin institution, as indicated by the following note in the vestry records explaining the expenditure of £24 — 'to reimburse Church Wardens for sending 9 children to the Foundling Hospital and rejected there'. According to the Poor Inquiry of the mid-1830s, there was also a 'small Hospital for Foundlings' in Galway, financed by vestry cess of £68.† That institution existed in 1823, when it was described as 'The Foundlings Asylum' in the vestry records.[95] However, there had been no admissions in the seven years before the Poor Inquiry report. Did the expenditure support children over the age of seven in school or in apprenticeship, or did it provide sinecures for officials of a vacant 'hospital'? There was certainly an impression among Galwegians that the cess levied for foundlings was wasted, and when the vestry sought to make economies, the proposition that such infants be no longer supported excited less opposition than a proposal that paupers be buried coffinless.[96]

But the apparent redundancy of the foundling hospital in the years before 1834 did not signify that no infants were abandoned. Rather, it is likely that foundlings were accommodated in the Widows' and Orphans' Asylum which opened under Catholic auspices in 1824. With religious tensions sharpening, it is unlikely that abandoned infants — in Galway, almost certainly the illegitimate children of Catholics — would have been surrendered into the hands of Protestants. By 1836, according to one official, 'the churchwardens no longer took responsibility for such cases'. And in the absence of a 'public cradle', unwanted infants were placed in the doorways of the houses of the charitable.

In general, evidence on the incidence of illegitimacy, abandonment, and infanticide is fragmented and contradictory. One visitor interviewed separately a police constable, a sergeant, and a sub-inspector about sexual mores in the town in 1851. The two longest-serving men were dimly aware of one instance of illegitimate birth a decade earlier — 'they had *heard* that a servant girl has had one' — but all three strongly asserted that the Galway girls were singularly chaste.[97]

On the other hand, there is evidence that many infants were abandoned. In 1823, the Church of Ireland vestry voted to expend £25 'for the purpose of

---

* According to a Dr Corrigan: 'To facilitate the easy abandonment of infants, the famous cradle at the gate was built, a revolving door with basket attached in which the child was placed. A bell was then rung and the gate porter turned a wheel inside, receiving the child, whilst being unable to observe the person abandoning it.

† Observing that these institutions were considered 'utterly indefensible in principle', the Commissioners reported on the other two such hospitals in Ireland at that time: 'There have been no admissions into the Dublin Foundling Hospital for some time past, with the exception of one child, whose mother died in the Lying-in Hospital and who was (under the existing law) transferred to the care of the Governors; …Cork Foundling Hospital is still continued, though under a somewhat restricted system of management.' (*2nd Report of Poor Inquiry*, 1837, vol. xxxi, p. 6).

preventing the increase of foundlings by offering rewards for the discovery of their parents, and adopting such other measures as may be conducive to the that end'. And during 1836, to give another example, Dublin Castle was advised of six instances of infant abandonment or infanticide in Galway — most likely of illegitimate babies — and the impression given by the accompanying reports is that they represented the tip of an iceberg. In April 1836, reporting that a male infant had been left at a hall-door in Dominick-street, Major Warburton noted that this was 'a practice rather persistent in this town'. It was fortunate, he went on, that there were 'persons possessed of so much humanity' as to 'take charge of such children without any hope of reward'. Shortly afterwards, a female infant was left at the door of a Catholic priest in Nuns' Island, in the hope, presumably, that he would arrange her admission to the orphanage. In this instance, Major Warburton despaired of discovering who the mother might be. 'The inhabitants appear to feel very little for such occurrences', he commented.[98]

f) *Widows' and Orphans' Asylum*

Fr Mark Fynn, parish priest of Bohermore, founded the Widows and Orphans' Asylum at College Road in 1824. By June 1826, after two years of efforts 'to furnish the house and to render it habitable', it was home to twenty-six widows and thirty-four orphans. Most of the widows were elderly and several of them 'had known better days, and had once enjoyed the comforts, and even the luxuries of life'.[99]

Finn's report for the annual meeting of 1826 shows that the asylum was not merely a refuge; it also had a reforming mission. In expressing satisfaction with the institution's achievements, the priest paid tribute to the efforts of the superintendent, Mrs Hurd. And, with the voluntary assistance of 'some young ladies of the town', he said, the children had made 'really astonishing' progress in spelling, reading, and catechistical instruction. Also 'astonishing' was 'the 'alteration … effected in the temper of some of the widows … who had entered with a violent temper, but who had become remarkable for their peaceable conduct and gentle demeanour'. They had become 'remarkable for their conscientious adherence to rule, as well as for their scrupulous anxiety to edify and to instruct by their good example'. And they were displaying an 'increased anxiety for employment' and a 'punctuality and neatness in the execution of needlework'. That humane methods were employed in promoting order, is indicated by the tone of an appeal for voluntary assistance:

> The poor orphan is cheered and encouraged by the smiles and commendations of its more fortunate fellow creature; and it is incredible what good a young lady might effect in fixing the character or improving the morals of a young and destitute orphan, simply by showing an interest in its progress, and by bestowing a little praise or a little censure when deserved. All this might be

effected by a casual visit, which would not interfere with other domestic occupations.[100]

Supported by subscriptions, balls, raffles, and by the 'zealous exertions' of Fr Fynn, the asylum continued to cater for about sixty people — admitting new residents as widows died, or as orphans took up positions as servants.[101] Expenditure, about £2 per resident per year, was modest and foreseeable, circumstances that explain the apparent absence of financial crises in its affairs.

g) *The Magdalen Asylum*

The Magdalen Asylum opened in Lombard-street in November 1824, within weeks of the Mendicity Institute and the Widows' and Orphans' Asylum. Like the Widows and Orphans', the Magdalen was a specifically Catholic charity, and like both of the others, it was the pet project of a particular clergyman, in this instance Fr Peter Daly. Daly, with Miss Lynch of Dooras and Mrs Lynch of Blackrock, established their charity in 1821, so it is likely that its eventual opening was expedited by the example of the other two.[102]

The evidence suggests that the Lynch women were related — either mother-and-daughter or sisters-in-law — and that it was they who directed the institution on its foundation.* Fundraising and overall management was undertaken by a committee of ladies — 'The St Magdalen Society' — which admitted to membership 'every lady contributing by annual subscription'. The subscriptions were augmented by the efforts of Fr Daly, who persuaded the London Tavern Committee — active in the area during the subsistence crisis of 1822-23 — to give £100.[103]

An excerpt from the rules indicates that it was not easy for a would-be-penitent to gain admission to the asylum. First she had to show that her wish to 'return to the bosom of society' was genuine and strongly-felt:

> That no female shall be received until she has been three months reclaimed from the crimes — that it is absolutely necessary that she shall have been under the care of some clergyman during that period — and that, after having given such proof of her sincerity, that she obtains a certificate of same from such clergyman, & that such certificate be only granted *not on hearsay,* but accurate observation — that during such time of probation, that the penitent must not have been seen ever in one instance to have held intercourse with her former companions; and that she shall have lodged in the house, and under the consideration of, some unobjectionable and honest housekeeper, who may give testimony

---

* An 1824 list of supporters of the Magdalen included a Mrs Lynch, a Miss Lynch, and a Miss M. Lynch, all of Lombard-street, while its first rules designated a 'Miss Lynch of Nantz' as the responsible official. (In Chapter Thirteen, it will be seen that 'the Misses Lynch of Nantes' ran Galway's first Catholic charity school for girls.)

of her mildness, repentance, sobriety, and regularity as to hours, and strict propriety — that during such period of probation, such extern penitent receive her daily support of the simplest kind from Miss Lynch, at the hour she should come to receive instruction; as also that she be supplied with some materials of industry, the produce of which to go towards defraying the expenses of her lodging.[104]

From the moment of admission — always on Friday, the day on which Christ suffered and died to save sinners such as they — inmates were never permitted to forget their 'Penitent' status. But, as the objective of the charity was the reform of the individual, some sensitivity was necessary. Accordingly, it was decreed:

> As it may be of essential benefit to the reclaimed females … to be totally unknown, that the *internal management* of the Asylum be confided in Miss Lynch of Nantz, as far as relates to all intercourse with the penitents; and that therefore, the *enclosures* of the Asylum be never opened to any visitor whatsoever.[105]

The Magdalen was relatively small — it had ten residents in 1826. Its financial needs were modest, therefore, and most of them were met from the proceeds of an annual charity sermon.[106] Women stayed for a term of years, during which they were instructed in 'useful and practical industry', and, when it was felt that they had acquired 'regular and pious habits', they were placed in jobs as servants.[107] Miss Lynch remained in charge for two decades, before she 'bequeathed' the Asylum to the Mercy Sisters. They took over in 1845.[108]

The Poor Law

George Nicholls was despatched to Ireland in August 1836 to ascertain whether the 'new' English poor law of 1834 could usefully be extended to the country. There are indications that his political masters had already decided upon the outcome of the investigation and, within months, Nicholls reported that, yes indeed, a poor law would benefit Ireland. Before the end of 1836, the government had adopted his report and had instructed him to prepare appropriate legislation.

The background to Nicholls's mission was one of growing unease about Irish poverty, and his was one in a series of investigations of the phenomenon. As recently as March 1836, the Whately Commission had concluded almost three years of hearings and deliberations. Whately, however, had rejected the 'new Poor Law' model on the grounds that the Irish poor were far too numerous to be accommodated in workhouses and proposed instead an integrated plan for economic improvement. Viscount Melbourne's administration was reform-minded, but it was not prepared to consider going as far as Whately recommended. From the government's perspective, the evidence of the 1,590 Whately witnesses might well be useful and interesting, but their

Commissioners had drawn inappropriate conclusions. Nicholls's task was to recommend a more palatable course of action.[109]

Nicholls proposed a system catering for 80,000 people — 1% of the Irish population — who would be accommodated in 130 workhouses, one in each of 130 Poor Law Unions. Owners and occupiers of property within each Union would pay poor law rates for the maintenance of their local workhouse, and elect three quarters of the members of supervisory Boards of Guardians. The Boards of Guardians would report to the Poor Law Commissioners in Dublin.[110]

Following English precedent, the Irish poor law rested on two key deterrent concepts — the so-called 'workhouse test' and the principle of 'lesser eligibility'. 'Lesser eligibility' — meaning that pauper rations should be less attractive than those purchasable with a labourer's wage — was difficult to enforce in Ireland because the diet of many labouring families was utterly monotonous and barely adequate. The more pertinent 'workhouse test' of destitution prescribed that relief be only available to those prepared to endure incarceration in spartan and rigidly-segregated institutions. Under no circumstances was 'outdoor' relief to be given to those of the poor who remained in their own homes. Only the genuinely destitute, it was anticipated, would seek assistance under these conditions.

When the somewhat amended Nicholls scheme passed into law in July 1838, Irish reaction was mixed. Landlords, suspicious of any development tending to raise taxation, generally opposed the measures, and there was apprehension too that poor rates might bear heavily on tenant farmers. Daniel O'Connell was sceptical, but, under pressure from religious associates, he voted in favour of an Irish poor law on several occasions. However, he was one of the minority of Irish M.Ps who opposed the final stage of the Poor Law bill in the Commons.[111]

Perhaps because of low expectations of government intervention in general, the local reaction to the new system was muted. There were, however, expressions of opposition from several sources. From Tuam, Archbishop MacHale condemned the workhouses as, at once, inadequate and demoralising to the poor, and oppressive of the impoverished peasantry who were partly liable for their upkeep. MacHale's attitude, it was believed, contributed to the difficulty in collecting poor rates throughout Co. Galway.[112] Other churchmen shared MacHale's reservations. In 1835, Alexis de Tocqueville heard a Protestant clergyman preach against any form of poor law. Charity was a sacred duty, never a legal obligation, he argued, and state intervention would break 'the greatest bond in society', that between rich and poor.[113]

The first elections for guardians, held in June 1839, stimulated some interest, but the coincidental efforts of a Galway Relief Committee loomed larger in the public consciousness. Five of the twelve electoral divisions in the Galway Union were urban; each was entitled to elect three guardians. In 1839 and 1840, nominated candidates arranged among themselves — by drawing lots and otherwise — to fill positions without putting the Union to the cost of an election. The heightened political tensions of subsequent years saw Repealers and others openly fight for seats.[114] But there was little for early boards to do, since the Poor Law Commissioners were responsible for erecting the workhouse, and the guardians did not arrange rate collection until after the building opened on 2 March 1842.

Although the original plan was for 800, the Galway workhouse was built to accommodate 1,000 people. Located behind high walls on an eight-acre site on the Newcastle-road, it followed the 'General Plan for Union Workhouses' prepared for Nicholls in 1838. The entrance lodge contained a meeting room, administrative office, porter's lodge, a waiting area, and probationary wards for the destitute. The workhouse proper was H-shaped, with chapel and dining-room located in the low connecting section. In the rear leg of the H were the hospital facilities, infirmary, maternity wards, and wards for the mentally-ill and the mentally-impaired — so-called lunatics and idiots. The middle of the complex, the front-leg of the H, was three storeys high. To the left were the female wards, to the right the male — they were divided at the centre by the master's and matron's quarters. Wards on the ground floor were for the old and infirm; upstairs was for the able-bodied. The layout allowed for five segregated yards — for men, for boys, for women, for girls, and for infirmary patients. As elsewhere, inmates wore rough institutional clothing and slept in dormitories on straw mats placed side-by-side on a long wooden platform.[115]

The Galway workhouse, 1842-46

An account of the early experience of the new system in Galway was given by Richard Mark Lynch, Guardians' vice-chairman, before a Select Committee in March 1846. Despite the recent outbreak of potato blight, neither he nor his questioners displayed any premonition that they were meeting on the eve of a catastrophe. Rather, their discussion centred on teething problems encountered, and on how the system might be adapted to better serve the ratepayers' interests.[116]

Since it opened four years earlier, the workhouse had catered, generally, for only one third of its 1,000 capacity. Exceptionally, there been more than 500 inmates during an 1842 fever epidemic, when the workhouse accommodated the surplus from the fever hospital. At that time, according to Lynch, pauper numbers had been boosted by applications from 'a class which would not have applied for relief except for their illness'. About 500, in any case, was the maximum that could be accommodated because, despite provision of 1,000 sleeping places, the day rooms had space for only half that number.

Low numbers notwithstanding, the Union was in a bad financial state. This, Lynch stated, was because the workhouse had opened before any rates were collected. In the circumstances — for which the Poor Law Commissioners bore responsibility — he felt that the guardians should be relieved of their debt. Another financial injustice — this time to the urban ratepayers that Lynch represented — arose from the manner in which electoral divisions within the Union were rated according to the addresses given by workhouse inmates. Beggars, most of whom originated in rural districts, invariably 'resided' in towns, so town ratepayers were liable for their upkeep. Lynch felt that the burden should be shared by all divisions.

One of the objectives of the poor law was to reduce mendicancy, and Lynch was questioned on the extent to which this had been achieved in Galway:

> I think it has relieved the town of those I may call the country beggars, but we still have a class of sturdy town beggars who annoy people just as much as before; they are a class of people who find they can live better by begging than they could in the workhouse…
> At a certain hour of the day, you find the same set about the post office, and when the coaches start, the same people go there, and then to the chapels and other places of resort.[117]

Evidently, the Galway guardians were extremely concerned that the ratepayers' largesse should not be abused. Applicants were frequently refused, in particular 'women of notoriously bad character' and 'persons who have frequently come in and gone out again without any good reason'. The guardians were rigorous in enforcing the regulation denying 'parts of a family' admission to the workhouse. Sometimes husbands or wives applied as individuals, and it had been noted that people 'frequently send their children and make them pretend to be orphans and practice deceit upon the Board'. It was also the practice to refuse relief to those considered to have 'no claim' on the Union, although such a refusal was contrary to poor law regulations in Ireland. This policy, remarkably, was prompted by concerns that the workhouse might be overwhelmed by improvident tourists. Lynch instanced the case of a Roscommon family 'who came for benefit of sea-bathing'. While in Galway, the father died, and the remaining family members sought admission to the workhouse. Unwilling to set a precedent, the guardians refused, but they did hold a collection for a car-fare to Roscommon among themselves.

That there were administrative shortcomings, Lynch acknowledged. For one thing, many guardians missed meetings, attending only to vote for their favourites when there were 'situations' to be filled. Then there was the workhouse visiting committee, 'an irresponsible party' that visited only in the half-hour before meetings, and never unexpectedly. Lynch thought that this committee's role should be undertaken by 'some paid functionary'.

But shortcomings notwithstanding, the Galway Board was keen to expand its jurisdiction. It had passed resolutions urging that responsibility for dispensaries and fever hospitals be transferred to poor law unions, and that power to establish new medical facilities be vested in them. Another resolution sought authority to pay for apprenticeships for pauper boys and girls. According to Lynch: 'It costs us £4 or £5 in the year to support one of those boys. But if we had the power of laying out that sum, we could get rid of him altogether'.[118] Several 'promising young lads' had received training in the workhouse in cobbling and tailoring, but existing restrictions prevented their being placed 'in the way of gaining a respectable livelihood'. Because there was no fee involved, it had been possible to apprentice boys to ship-owners as sailors, but nothing could be done for the majority as things stood.

NOTES

1. *Connaught Journal,* 24 February 1817.
2. Timothy O'Neill, 'Poverty in Ireland, 1815-45' in *Folk Life* xi, 1973, pp. 22-33.
3. J. C. Curwen, *Observations on the state of Ireland,* London 1818, vol. 2 , p. 343; Maria Edgeworth, *Tour in Connemara, and the Martins of Ballinahinch,* (edited by H. Edgeworth Butler), London 1950, pp. 14-15; John B. Trotter, *Walks through Ireland in the years, 1812, 1814 and 1817,* London 1819, pp. 404-05.
4. David Dickson, 'In Search of the Old Irish Poor Law' in Mitchenson & Roebuck, eds, *Economy and Society in Scotland and Ireland, 1500-1939,* Edinburgh 1988, pp. 149-59; St Nicholas Collegiate Church, vestry records book, 1805-1909 — see, for example, record for 1816.
5. F. W. Powell, *The Politics of Irish Social Policy, 1600-1990.* Lewiston 1992, pp.35-39
6. ibid., pp. 53-69; Angus McIntyre, *The Liberator: Daniel O'Connell and the Irish Party, 1830-1847,* London 1965, pp. 201-09.
7. Cited by David Englander, *Poverty and Poor Law Reform in 19th Century Britain, 1834-1914.* London 1998, p. 5.
8. Lis & Soly, *Poverty and Capitalism in Pre-Industrial Europe,* Brighton, 1979, pp. 116-29, 194-214.
9. Timothy P. O'Neill, 'The Catholic Church and the Relief of the Poor, 1815-45' in *Archivium Hibernicum* xxxi, 1973, pp. 132-45.
10. *Connaught Journal,* 15 December 1791.
11. O'Neill, 'Poverty', p. 23.
12. *Supplement to Appendix C (Part 1) to report of Commissioners on Poorer Classes,* 1836 xxx, p. 4.
13. ibid., p. 7; *Minutes of Evidence of Select Committee on Pawnbroking in Ireland,* 1837-8 xvii, pp. 81-84.
14. P. Mandler, 'Poverty and Charity in the Nineteenth Century Metropolis', in Mandler, ed., *The Uses of Charity,* Philadelphia, 1990, pp. 1-37.
15. Marco H. D. van Leeuwen, 'Logic of charity: Poor relief in Preindustrial Europe', *Journal of Interdisciplinary History,* xxiv: 4, 1994, pp. 589-613.
16. *Connaught Journal,* 20 December 1824.
17. See subscription lists for Mendicity Association, Fever Hospital, and Magdalen Asylum — ibid., 2, 20 December 1824, 6 June 1825, 6 March 1826.
18. O'Neill, 'The Catholic Church', pp. 139-40.
19. *Connaught Journal,* 6 November, 29 December 1817.
20. ibid., 29 January 1827. Jeremiah Sullivan was shot by one of a party of 'gentlemen' during election rioting (ibid., 29 June 1826). The support of his family, therefore, had a political complexion.
21. Cited by J. P. Murray, *Galway: A Medico-Social History,* pp. 54-55.
22. F. W. Powell, *The Politics of Irish Social Policy,* pp. 35-39; P. B. Lysaght, 'The House of Industry: a register, 1774-1793' in *North Munster Antiquarian Journal,* xxx, 1990, pp. 70-74; Audrey Woods, *Dublin Outsiders: a History of the Mendicity Institution, 1818-1998,* Dublin 1998, pp. 1-11.
23. Joseph Robins, *The Miasma: Epidemic and Panic in Nineteenth Century Ireland,* Dublin 1995, pp. 42-43.
24. *Appendix to the 1st Report from the Select Committee on the State of Disease and Condition of the Labouring Poor in Ireland,* 1819 vii, p. 44.
25. *Connaught Journal,* 20 March, 10 April 1823; St Nicholas Vestry Records for 1820.
26. ibid., 23 October 1823.
27. *Connaught Journal,* 6 October 1823.
28. ibid., 1 July 1824; P. J. Henry, *Sligo: Medical Care in the Past, 1800-1965,* Sligo 1995, pp. 27-30.
29. ibid., 19 July 1824.
30. *Connaught Journal,* 15 November 2 December 1824.
31. ibid., 22 August, 7 November 1825.
32. ibid., 22 August 1825.
33. ibid., 26 January, 2 February, 27 March 1826, 8, 26 January, 8 February 1827, 8 March 1828.
34. ibid., 24 January 1828.

35. *Appendix to 2nd Report on Poor Laws in Ireland*, 1837-8, xxxviii, pp. 54-55.
36. *Connaught Journal*, 24 March 1836. A portion of the money from the Grand Jury was income from presentments for roads.
37. ibid., 9 November 1829. Other such facilities faced similar problems. In 1827, the Dublin Mendicity closed due, allegedly, to the 'apathy' of Dubliners (ibid., 16 December 1827).
38. ibid., 7, 18 January, 12 April 1830.
39. ibid., 26 February 1835.
40. ibid., 5, 12, 19 March, 2 July, 10 September 1835.
41. ibid., 24 March 1836
42. ibid.
43. *Galway Patriot*, 4 October 1837.
44. Murray, *Medico-social history*, pp. 60-61, 248
45. ibid., pp. 60-61.
46. Hardiman, *Galway*, p. 304.
47. ibid., p. 305n.
48. *Connaught Journal*, 2 April 1827.
49. *Appendix to 1st Report of Poor Inquiry*, 1835 xxxii pt.2, pp. 13-14.
50. Murray, *Medico-social history*, p. 66.
51. *Appendix to 1st Report of Poor Inquiry*, 1835 xxxii pt.2, p. 13.
52. *Connaught Journal*, 2, 20 October, 20, 24 November 1817.
53. Murray, *Medico-social history*, pp. 48-50.
54. *Connaught Journal*, 14 January 1828.
55. Hely Dutton, *Survey*, p. 197.
56. *Appendix to 1st Report from Select Committee on the State of Disease, and Condition of the Labouring Poor, in Ireland*, H. of C., 1819 viii, p. 41.
57. *Appendix B to 1st Report of Poor Inquiry*, 1835 xxxii, pp. 13-15, 268-70.
58. *Connaught Journal*, 15 September 1817.
59. ibid., 18 September, 2 October 1817.
60. ibid., 4 December 1817.
61. Murray, *Medico-social history*, pp.51-53.
62. Timothy P. O'Neill, 'Minor famines and relief in County Galway, 1815-1925' in G. Moran, ed., *Galway: History & Society*, pp. 445-85
63. *Connaught Journal*, 27 January 1823.
64. ibid., 29 May 1823.
65. ibid., 8 January, 2, 26 February, 8 March, 23 April, 13 December 1827, 3, 24 January, 7 February 1828.
66. ibid., 27 October 1831.
67. ibid., 3 November 1831.
68. ibid., 26, 30 January 1832.
69. Joseph Robins, *The Miasma: Epidemic and Panic in Nineteenth Century Ireland*, Dublin 1995, pp. 68-76; S. J. Connolly, 'The "blessed turf": cholera and popular panic in Ireland, June 1832', in *Irish Historical Studies*, xxiii, May 1983, pp. 215-31.
70. St Nicholas vestry records for 1832.
71. *Connaught Journal*, 19 July 1832.
72. *Galway Patriot*, 5, 8 April 1837; Patrick J. Kennedy, 'The County of the Town of Galway' in *JGAHS* 30, nos. i & ii, 1963, p. 99.
73. *Appendix B to 1st Report of Poor Inquiry*, 1835 xxxii, pp. 268-70
74. ibid., pp. 13-15.
75. *Appendix to Report of Poor Law Commissioners on Medical Charities, Ireland*, 1841 xi, p. 22.
76. Murray, *Medico-social history*, pp. 48-50.
77. *Connaught Journal*, 21 January 1828.
78. Timothy P. O'Neill, 'Minor famines and relief in County Galway, 1815-1925' in G. Moran, ed., *Galway: History & Society*, pp. 445-85.
79. *Connaught Journal*, 19 May 1823.
80. ibid., 25 August 1823.
81. ibid. See also 24 July 1823, 12, 16 August 1824, 2 January 1826, 8 March 1827
82. ibid., 10 December 1827.
83. *Supplement to Appendix C (Part 1) to Report of Poor Inquiry*, 1836 xxx, pp. 4-8.

84. *Connaught Journal,* 10 November 1836; *Galway Advertiser,* 23 June 1838; *Evidence before Select Committee on Pawnbroking in Ireland,* 1837-8 xvii, pp. 81-84.
85. *Galway Patriot,* 20 December 1837; *Galway Vindicator,* 15 April 1843.
86. *Connaught Journal,* 3 May 1824.
87. ibid., 7 April 1825. See also 10, 14 , 21 March, and 4, 14 April 1825.
88. ibid., 23 February 1826.
89. ibid., 20 October 1828.
90. Kennedy, 'County of the Town', p. 98.
91. ibid., 10 November, 5 December 1836. Murray mentioned a small Lying-in hospital in 'Mill Street at Madeira Island' (*Medico-social history*, p. 55).
92. Murray, *Medico-social history,* p. 55; *Galway Patriot,* 6 December 1837.
93. Berry, *St Nicholas,* pp. 46-47.
94. Helen Burke, *The People and the Poor Law in 19th Century Ireland,* Littlehampton 1987, pp. 54-61; Berry, *St Nicholas,* pp. 46-47.
95. St Nicholas vestry records for 1823 and 1824
96. *Connaught Journal,* 12, 15 22 May, 5, 12 June 1823.
97. Sir Francis Head, *A fortnight in Ireland,* pp. 227-30.
98. St Nicholas vestry records for 1823; Outrage papers, Galway - letter from Major Warburton, 15 April 1836.
99. *Connaught Journal,* 22 June 1826.
100. ibid., 28 September 1826.
101. ibid., 18 June 1827, 1 August 1833, 7 August 1834, *Galway Press,* 7 January 1837, *Galway Vindicator,* 4 October 1843; *Appendix to Report of Poor Inquiry,* 1836 xxx, p. 7.
102. J. Mitchell, 'Fr Peter Daly', pp. 28-30.
103. ibid., pp. 29-30.
104. *Connaught Journal,* 2 December 1824.
105. ibid.
106. ibid., 28 December 1826, 4 June 1829, 3 June 1830, 16 May 1831, 4 June 1835, 26 May 1836.
107. ibid., 31 May 1827
108. M. P. Cryan, 'The Sisters of Mercy in Connaught, 1840-70', unpublished M.A., UCG 1963, p. 48.
109. Gerard O'Brien, 'The Establishment of Poor-Law Unions in Ireland, 1838-43', in *IHS* xxiii, no. 90, November 1982, pp. 1-24; Burke, *Poor Law,* pp. 17-44; Virginia Crossman, *Local Government in Nineteenth-century Ireland,* Belfast 1994, pp. 44-46; Christine Kinealy, *This Great Calamity,* Dublin 1994, pp. 18-26; Powell, *Irish Social Policy,* pp. 76-92; Gearóid Ó Tuathaigh, *Ireland before the Famine,* Dublin 1990 edn, pp. 108-14.
110. Crossman, *Local Government,* pp. 44-47; O'Brien, 'Establishment', pp. 3-9; Kinealy, *Calamity,* pp. 24-25.
111. McIntyre, *Liberator,* pp. 217-22; Powell, *Social Policy,* pp. 92-94; Ó Tuathaigh, *Ireland,* pp. 110-13.
112. Tadhg P. Ó Néill, 'Seán Mac Héil agus bochtaineacht and Iarthair' in Ní Cheanáin, ed., *Leon an Iarthair,* Dublin 1983, pp.31-32; *Select Committee on the Laws relating to relief of the Destitute Poor,* 1846 xi, pt.1, pp. 597-98.
113. Larkin, *de Tocqueville's Journey,* pp. 100-01.
114. *Galway Advertiser,* 8 June 1839, 10 April 1841; *Galway Vindicator, 12 March 1845; Select Committee on the Laws relating to relief of the Destitute Poor in Ireland,* 1846 xi, pt.1, evidence of R. M. Lynch, p. 287.
115. Murray, *Medico-social history,* pp. 72-74.
116. *Select Committee on the Laws relating to relief of the Destitute Poor in Ireland,* 1846 xi, pt.1: evidence of R. M. Lynch, pp. 285-95.
117. ibid., p. 287.
118. ibid., p. 293.

CHAPTER 4

'Be true to the cause or you will starve'

SOCIAL PROTEST, 1810-45

So to conclude and make an end
Unto those verses I have penned,
That the Almighty may befriend
His suffering poor in Galway
The time will come boys, never fear,
Keep up your hearts, be of good cheer;
Although provisions now are dear,
They'll soon be cheap in Galway.

'The Galway Subsidy', 1850s ballad.[1]

The governors of pre-Famine Ireland were preoccupied with 'Whiteboyism', a rural phenomenon that occasionally reached the outskirts of towns.* Urban rebellion or protest caused less alarm, because its motivation was well understood and because the cleavage between governors and governed was less pronounced in towns than in the countryside. Moreover, urban protestors drew on municipal by-laws in their appeals to custom and tradition, by which means they sometimes succeeded in arousing sympathy in those to whom they were appealing.

Social protest in pre-Famine Galway fell into three broad categories: labour struggle by artisans; defence of fishing rights by Claddagh fishermen; food rioting by the broader proletarian community. Generally, protestors asserted what they saw as their traditional rights as town dwellers: artisans defended restrictive practices they associated with medieval guilds; fishermen enforced 16th century by-laws; food-rioters derived their sense of legitimacy from ancient laws anathematising forestallers and regraters. Frequently several different types of protest coincided. This is not surprising, for traditional rights

---

* For example, the killing of William le Poer Trench's cow just outside the town and the removal of the carcase led 107 individuals to subscribe almost £500 in June 1817 for information leading to the detection of the 'evil disposed persons' concerned. (*Connaught Journal*, 30 June 1817). And during the 'Ribbon' turbulence of 1819, the sheriff of Galway was disturbed to learn of 'nightly meetings' of two to five hundred people on the 'borders of the town..., on Rahoon roads..., near the woods of Barna..., on the East suburbs' (NA, State of the Country papers 1819, 2071/14-15).

came under threat during periods of economic hardship, as the various sections of the community sought to maximise their share of limited resources.

Nor is it surprising that the same people were involved in different types of protest. At times when the Claddagh people were mobilising against anti-social fishing practices, for instance, it was to be expected that they would also participate in protests against anti-social food marketing.

This study of early 19th century social protest will examine the more significant episodes. In doing so, it will uncover aspects of the social organisation of the working class community, and give insights into that community's mentality — the assumption being that the demands around which rioters mobilised, and their behaviour when mobilised, were indicators of popular values and attitudes. Arguably also, the consequences of a riot or a strike were felt long after the incident itself ended. For protest affected the attitude of those in authority. If people had previously rebelled, they were liable to do so again, and those wishing to avert conflict were encouraged to address grievances before they reached boiling point.

Labour

Galway's trades had a long tradition of organisation. Late 17th century charters confirmed the rights of guilds representing eighteen occupations. According to an 1830s investigation, some of these bodies were 'kept up in some form', continuing to 'elect masters and wardens, admit freemen' and 'make rules for the regulation of the trade as to apprentices, wages, &c'. The guilds, according to the same report, maintained wage levels by preventing non-members from under-cutting qualified men, but they had not 'lately' used violence to further their objectives.[2]

The history of Galway's guilds and combinations had an important political aspect, which will be considered in Chapter Five. It will be shown that guilds were 'revived' in the early 19th century, with middle-class encouragement, to secure the vote for Catholic artisans, and to enlist them in the merchants' struggle against the Daly interest. This undoubtedly contributed to the development of an *esprit de corps* among Galway artisans and must also have helped to stimulate consciousness regarding the archaic vocational role of the guilds.

Trades guilds had existed in Irish towns since medieval times, products of the Anglo-Norman system of urban administration. Historically, an artisan was admitted to his guild on completing his apprenticeship, thereby becoming eligible for 'freeman' status of his town. The guild itself regulated relationships within the trade — setting wages, restricting apprentice numbers — and also between the trade and the community. Guilds were closed to Catholics following the Williamite triumph of the 1690s; Protestant journeymen were also increasingly excluded as guilds shed their vocational functions. During the 18th century, excluded journeymen formed their own combinations, mostly of a temporary character. These combinations defended wages and asserted the ancient privileges of journeymen as defined by the guilds — limiting the number apprenticed annually, ensuring that 'handymen' not be employed at tasks normally carried out by artisans, insisting that local artisans be preferred to outsiders. It was only by limiting numbers that craft wages could be maintained at a level at least two-and-a-half times that of labourers.* For similar reasons, artisans opposed technical innovations in their craft. And such opposition could be violent, as with the Galway bakers of the late 18th century who took exception to new milling technology and burnt down an offending premises.[3]

Workers 'combinations' were illegal under Combination Acts of the 18th and early 19th centuries. Nonetheless, the customary rights of artisans were widely respected, and there are indications that Galway employers were sensitive to criticism that they exploited their tradesmen. A 1792 advertisement in a local paper, placed by Thomas Nuttall, master shoemaker of Mainguard-street, and addressed to 'his friends and the public', offered a reward for information identifying those who had complained to the journeymen's union (almost certainly an illegal combination) that he paid less than the going wage. The source of the complaint, he suspected, was another shoemaker who wished 'merely to hurt him in his trade'. Keen to protect his reputation, Nuttall offered to 'produce the journeymen to whom he paid 18d per pair for men's shoes and 3s 9d for boots', at the time of a shoemakers' strike two years previously.[4]

In circumstances where the customary rights of artisans were recognised, their enforcement did not necessarily require the permanent organisation of journeymen. Indeed, the response to grievance was often spontaneous and short-lived. In many Irish towns, friendly societies provided the cloak under which the illegal business of journeymen's combinations was conducted. Trade unions became legal with the repeal of the Combination Acts in 1824, but legislation restricted them to dealing with wage rates and working hours. Prohibition, in any case, had not prevented labour organisation. In the opinion of lawmakers in 1824, it had merely driven it underground and forced it into behaving violently.[5]

That things did not change immediately on the repeal of the Combination Acts is indicated by the conduct of the first reported labour dispute in Galway under the new dispensation. It broke out in September 1825, and involved journeyman nailors who, it was reported, 'almost without an exception *turned out* for an advance in wages far beyond all reason', and when their demand was not acceded to, 'they commenced in the real Dublin *style*'. In the course of the dispute, Mr Davis, described as 'an industrious master nailor', was brutally assaulted by a group of strikers, as were some journeymen who refused to join with their fellows. One strike leader, Thomas Walsh, was arrested, whereupon the others left Galway. Following the circulation of their descriptions, however, three of them were captured in Gort and one in Headford.[6] Other such

---

* In Galway in 1845, labourers' wages varied between 10*d* and a shilling a day; the lowest paid artisans were wheelwrights who earned 2*s* (24*d*) to 2*s* 6*d* per day, while the highest paid artisans were bakers who were paid 3*s* to 4*s* 6*d* (54*d*) per day (Greagóir Ó Dúghaill, 'Galway in the first famine winter' in *Saothar* 1, 1975, pp. 63-67).

'combinations' in the pre-Famine period also involved journeymen rather than unskilled workers.

In 1823 was reported a 'regular procession' of 200 tradesmen, each wearing a scarf and hatband, for the funeral of one Mr Traynor. All of Galway's trades were represented, marshalled by a Union of Trades, a body 'of late institution', which was established, it was stated, 'not for any illegal combination, but to contribute a small sum against contingencies of sickness, old age and death'. This Union was more than a benefit society, however, for two months later its 'insignia' were carried in a political demonstration.[7] And, given that its inception coincided with a sawyers' strike, it is likely that the Union of Trades also took an interest in vocational matters. The sawyers' strike of August 1823 was a bitter one, during which John Rochford, Stephen Connolly and Thomas Burke were convicted of having 'as combinators, entered the yard of some of their fellow-tradesmen, whose saws they broke'. The likelihood is that the three received assistance from the broad community of artisans, since they were able to afford a 'truly respectable' attorney for their unsuccessful appeal.[8]

In 1829, during a period of turmoil that also saw an episode of food rioting, there was more general labour unrest. Galway tradesmen 'turned out, ceasing to work for their employers', but the *Connaught Journal* writer was 'unable to discover yet the cause of this foolish proceeding', There was little sympathy either from the 'respectable gentlemen' of the Loan Fund committee who announced that no loans were to be given to strikers. And the Mortality Society felt obliged to deny that it was giving financial succour to those involved, even amending its rules to castigate specifically 'the system of combination so ruinous to the Tradesmen'.[9] The dispute involved several trades, indicating that the 1823 'Union of Trades' had either survived or been revived.

In the mid-1830s, the general body of trades was reportedly organised as 'the *Trades Union*'. In 1836 it came to the assistance of 'the sons of St Crispan', whose own resources were exhausted after a month-long strike. Financial assistance from their 'new ally' enabled the shoemakers to hold out for full victory, a result that was marked by 'the merry tolling' of the bells of St Nicholas and by the illumination of the strike headquarters, Laffey's pub in Cross-street.[10] The agreement then concluded was still being observed a decade later.

If there existed a continuous body co-ordinating the affairs of the trades — and the evidence is persuasive — Galway was exceptional in the Irish context during the 1820s and 1830s.[11] In the circumstances, it is likely that it was their political aspirations that bound the trades together, that the Union of Trades existed primarily to secure the right to vote for its members, but that it occasionally intervened to represent their vocational grievances.

In general, it would seem that employers continued to accept craft rules, and that breaches caused indignation, as they did during the construction of the workhouse in 1841. With respect to that project, Thomas MacDonagh and Thomas Cusack protested on behalf of their fellow carpenters before the Board of Guardians about a piece-work system which limited earnings to eight shillings a week. Qualified carpenters refused to work under such conditions, leaving only 'boys without masters' and box makers. This, the two insisted, was 'contrary to specifications'.[12]

£10

REWARD.

WHEREAS a Rockite Letter signed " *Galway Bakers* " was recently left at the residence of M *Patrick Hughes*, of this Town, Miller, threatening him should he discharge a Baker named *Kennedy*:

I HEREBY OFFER A REWARD OF

TEN POUNDS

To any Person who shall, within Six Months from the date hereof, give such information as shall lead to the discovery and prosecution to conviction of the Person concerned in writing or delivering the Letter in question.

S. JONES,

Resident Magistrate.

Galway, 29th September, 1842.

25,834—G

Notice posted on instruction of magistrate during bakers' strike of 1842.

1842 was a year of social conflict, of food riots and strikes. In January, the trades took the part of merchant, Mr Stephens, in a Town Commission by-election. They were acting out of hostility to Commission secretary, Revd John d'Arcy, who had been insensitive to the concerns of the trades in awarding contracts: Stephens's opponent, Denis Kirwan, was acknowledged to be a 'proper person' to fill the vacancy, but he was perceived to be d'Arcy's protégé. The right of d'Arcy's artisan opponents to speak for all tradesmen, however, was challenged on that occasion by the secretary of 'another body of the Trades', the Mechanics' Institute.[13]

Further complaints against the Town Commission were raised by stone masons in June. The masons, incidentally were a well-organised body who had become 'federated' in the late 1830s when, with their colleagues in seven other Irish towns, they had joined the Birmingham-based amalgamated body for their trade. Their grievance against the Town Commission arose from the employment on a public contract of allegedly incompetent 'dry-wall masons'.[14] There was anger also when the contract for the manufacture and erection of the new Eyre Square railings was awarded to one Fogarty, a Limerick contractor. Fogarty received a 'Rockite' letter signed 'JRR' threatening to obstruct the works. The letter was judged to represent the feelings of 'a portion of the inhabitants of the town, 1200 to 1400 people, quite distinct from the trades'.[15] Sawyers, meanwhile, protested at the threat to their employment from machinery introduced by Mr Franklin, an English entrepreneur. And compositors gathered to denounce the ill-treatment of their fellows in a newly established Protestant newspaper 'yclept the *Galway Standard*'.[16]

The bitterest labour conflict of 1842 was that of the operative bakers, led by Michael Barnacle.* In August, a resolution of Galway bakers lauded efforts by their colleagues in Dublin to abolish night-work. Shortly afterwards, the Galway master bakers conceded to their employees demands on the matter.[17] But the agreement was soon broken, something that the bakers blamed on one of their number. This blackleg received a threatening notice and two journeymen, Michael and John Kennedy, and an apprentice, were seen posting placards throughout the town:

> Fellow tradesmen, the bakers of Ireland have come to the resolution of quitting night work. Even the bakers of Galway have followed their example. Now we are obliged to resume our former night slavery in consequence of one of our members going to work in opposition to us and the bakers of Ireland in general — the rascal's name in Andrew O'Halloran.[18]

---

* The Barnacle family was notable among Galway's journeymen bakers during the 19th century, something which has not been adequately acknowledged by Nora Barnacle's biographers. Referring to the difficult working life of his subject's baker father, one of them remarked that 'there was no difficulty from unions, as the unions were not then developed' (Padraic O Laoi, *Nora Barnacle Joyce: a Portrait*, p. 3). If they were not it was hardly the fault of the Barnacles, for Nora's grand-uncle, Michael, was chairman of the Galway Operative Bakers during their 1842 dispute. And half a century later, one M. Barnacle — possibly Nora's uncle — was prominent in the Galway branch of the Bakers' Society (*Galway Observer*, 24 October 1896).

The consequence was that one of the Kennedys was sacked, whereupon a threatening letter, signed 'The Galway Bakers' was despatched to his employer. This 'Rockite letter' was considered to be a sufficiently serious matter for the resident magistrate to offer a £10 reward for the discovery of its author.[19]

Remarkably, trades organisation was maintained even during the Famine. In April 1846, master tailors yielded to their employees' wage demands, 'in consideration of the high price of provisions'. Six months later, shoemakers declared a 'turn out' to protest at the hiring of an apprentice by a master who already had one. The shoemakers insisted that this breached their 1836 agreement,* and that any new indenture had to be postponed until after the old one was completed.[20]

A similar case brought officials of the masons' guild to court in September 1848, and masons' representatives were diligent generally in the Famine years. In June 1847, the general body of the trades sought to arbitrate between them and contractors working on the Claddagh pier and at the Queen's College, who, allegedly, had employed 'strangers' while Galway masons were idle. An agreement was concluded with Brady, the College contractor, when he accepted the masons' rules and excluded outsiders from working on the project.[21]

Carpenters met resistance when they similarly challenged Samuel Roberts, Board of Works engineer on the Corrib/Mask drainage. Only twelve of sixty-one carpenters employed on the canal works in Galway, they insisted, were *bona fide* Galwaymen, and all those given responsible positions were outsiders, some of them incompetent outsiders. Roberts contested the claims: all his craftsmen were local; his supervisors were experienced and trustworthy; the carpenters' grudge originated with dismissals for incompetence and insubordination.[22] Patt Sweeney, secretary of the Carpenters' Guild replied in newspaper advertisements, in which he criticised the quality of engineering and carpentry on the canal, asserting that craftsmen who had made similar points had been dismissed for insubordination.[23] The outcome of the controversy is unknown but, evidently, harmony was restored, for Roberts was guest of honour at a Mechanics Institute 'soirée' to mark the completion of the works. In his speech, he remarked that he had never met 'more zealous or efficient workmen ... than the tradesmen of Galway'.[24]

The carpenters' grievances on the canal works followed an established pattern but in February 1849, the contractor had to deal with a phenomenon which had been relatively unusual in the pre-famine period—a labourers' strike. The grievance was piece-work, something that was causing unrest on famine works elsewhere. In this instance, the men claimed that the rate per cubic yard for excavation allowed the average worker to earn only 4d to 8d a day after deductions. The works superintendent dismissed the complaint. The strikers' real objective, he said, was to 'get employed by the day not by the piece'.[25]

---

* There was an identical regulation on apprenticeship in Cork's shoemaking trade (Cronin, *Class or Craft*, p. 37).

The fishermen

The sea fishermens' guild was one of Galway's oldest.[26] Associated with the Claddagh and recognised as a corporate body by 16th century municipal statutes, fishermen continued to assert their collective rights into the 19th century.* By then, their civic traditions and pretensions were misconstrued as superstitions, although their craft status was occasionally acknowledged, such as when the entire body was briefly entered in the electoral roll (as freemen) in 1841.[27]

By statute and tradition, Claddagh fishermen were guardians of Galway Bay, a responsibility they exercised by limiting the duration of fishing seasons and by defending their resource against those threatening its fruitfulness. Historically, the major ecological threat had come from part-time fishermen around the bay. Claddaghmen had no objection to sharing the bay, as long as their by-laws were observed. And while these by-laws, like those of other guilds, were entered in the Corporation statute book, the fishermen themselves were left to enforce them.

As the largest fishing community on the coast and the community equipped with the best sailing craft, the Claddagh had the capacity to enforce their regulations.[28] Moreover, it was the only full-time fishing community; other western fishermen were part-time farmers.† The fact that they were completely dependent on the fruits of the bay accounts for the zeal with which the men — and sometimes the women — of the Claddagh exercised their guardianship The by-laws most often infringed were those regulating the date of the fishing season. In the early 19th century, for instance, the autumn herring fishery could not begin before 1 August. But straitened rural coastal communities were not always willing to wait. For the Claddaghmen, the only course open to them in enforcing their laws was the punishment of miscreants who broke them. Thus, people were physically prevented from fishing out of season or, alternatively, exemplary punishment was meted out after the fact. In February 1824, 'Cunnemaramen' had their nets and catch destroyed; during March 1825, in 'one of a thousand instances ... the inhuman pirates' of Claddagh destroyed nets of both Aran and Conamara fishermen; four months later, during a 'great appearance' of herrings, the New Quay fisherman were afraid to bring their catch to the Galway market because of the Claddaghmen's unfortunate 'prejudice in favour of old regulations'.[29]

Other by-laws prohibited fishing on Sunday or on any of the many designated 'holy days'. According to one commentator in 1820:

---

* Galway may not have been the only Irish town to have a fishermen's guild which survived to a late date. The imagery on a 19th century Boyne fishermen's banner indicates earlier guild organisation in their case also (Timothy O'Neill, 'Irish Trade Banners' in C. Ó Danchair, ed., *Folk and Farm*, Dublin 1976, pp. 185-87). And the ancient rights claimed by the Abbey fishermen of Limerick 'to fish all the waters round the city', together with the restrictive practices enforced by them, suggest by-law recognition at some point (Robert Herbert, 'The Lax Weir and Fishers Stent of Limerick, *North Munster Antiquarian Journal*, vol. v, nos. 2 & 3, 1946-47, p. 57.

† The Claddagh men, evidently, were prohibited by 16th century by-law from engaging in agriculture: "That no ... fisherman, do take in hande either the plowghe, spade, or teithe, that would barr them from fyshinge, bothe to serve themselves and the comon wealthe with fyshe ..." (Hardiman, p. 210).

Exclusively of fifty-two days in the year held as the Sabbath of Christians, there are about sixty *saints days* observed by the half-starved fishermen of Ireland. No nation could bear such a waste of time … The Galway fishermen will not catch the fish themselves, nor will they allow any others to do it; no, they destroy the nets and assault the crews of the boats which come from other quarters to fish in the bay, as if they had an exclusive privilege to the produce of the ocean.[30]

Thus, a Knocknacarra boat was overturned and several others were damaged on a December Sunday in 1836. The occupants gave no information about their attackers, 'partly from fear, and partly from an impression that they were wrong to fish on Sunday'.[31]

If coastal communities reluctantly acquiesced in guild legislation, there was resentment at the often whimsical attitude of the Claddaghmen. The Claddagh fleet would not take to sea until all boats were ready, so the season might be delayed to allow a few individuals to repair boats or to negotiate the release of pawned equipment.[32] During 1833, there were complaints that the bay had been full of fish for two months but, in accordance with 'ancient practice', nobody might catch them until 1 August. Three weeks into August, the fish remained unmolested because some Claddagh boats were 'not yet ready'. The remainder mustered as 'guard boats, armed to watch the bay; and deal deadly blows upon all who dare to go out to fish till the Lords of the Claddagh pleased to give permission'.[33] Eventually, the Ballynacourty fishermen lost patience and, armed by their landlord Lord Wallscourt, fired at their tormentors. The Claddaghmen hurriedly declared the start of the season. The *Connaught Journal* praised Wallscourt and urged other landlords to come to their tenants' assistance against any 'ruffian' who prevented them fishing.[34]

In 1836, Wallscourt again supported his tenants who were fishing out of season by the Claddagh calendar. His petition brought the Dublin Coastguard's revenue cutter to the Bay.[35]

On occasion, there were fully-fledged naval encounters in the bay. When Captain Morris brought the *Townshend* revenue cutter to protect 'such industrious persons as may be disposed to fish for herrings' before the start of winter fishery of 1810, his craft was followed by hundreds from the Claddagh. The captain and his crew were threatened 'in a most alarming manner', provoking them to discharge 'many shots'. And the few who were encouraged to fish by the cutter's presence were surprised by the Claddaghmen, who half-drowned them and destroyed their catch. In its captain's absence, even the *Townshend* itself was boarded and its crew attacked. Eventually, with military assistance, Captain Morris managed to capture three he designated 'ringleaders' and proceeded to lead them to the gaol.[36] At the bottom of Dominick-street, however, their escort was challenged 'by a phalanx of Amazonian heroines from four to six hundred strong'. According to one report, the women having … laid aside the oratorical weapon of women's warfare which, though it often wounds, seldom kills, so beset the party with lapidious bullets that they conceived it prudent to march in double quick time until their retreat was luckily covered by the guard at the West Bridge, who turned out for the purpose.[37]

Thus, the three were incarcerated to await the quarter sessions, but not before Captain Morris and the soldiers acquired 'severe contusions'. As this and other incidents show, the women of the Claddagh were as involved in the defence of the traditional rights of their community as they were in its economic life. The participation of women in rioting generally is dealt with in greater detail below. The 'illegal combination' continued to operate even during the famine: William Todhunter referred to a 'dispute between fishermen' in the bay in the autumn of 1847. A few years later, the sheriff and J.Ps. of the town memorialised the under secretary regarding intimidation which forced the 'inhabitant fishermen' along the coast to ignore the abundant waters rather than face the 'certainty of their being injured and their nets destroyed by the Claddaghmen'.[38]

In protecting the fisheries, the Claddagh people were acting as responsible citizens in their own minds. In the eyes of others, however, they were regarded as irrational, — as 'piratical banditti' in the words of a hostile commentator.[39] Frank bewilderment greeted their attachment to so-called 'ancient practice',

Making a fishing net in the Claddagh (1880), (from *Illustrated London News*).

which was dismissed as mere laziness by some. One writer commented that it was bad enough that the Claddaghmen should fish in the vicinities of other communities, but that it was outrageous that they should purport to instruct those communities on how and when to fish, even destroying their nets if they refused to comply with directives.[40]

If the attachment to 'ancient practice' provoked derision in some quarters, it attracted interest in others. Early 19th century literary travellers were eager to record the exotic; when they found it within ten minutes of a reasonably comfortable hotel, they were sure to give it a thorough, if sometimes fanciful, examination. Thus it was that the Claddagh came to have a king.

One authority attributes the origin of the 'king of the Claddagh' myth to the Halls' 1843 account. There was no such official in the Claddagh tradition, although, following guild practice, a leader with the civic title of 'mayor' or 'admiral' was elected annually. The coincidence of the Claddagh's leading fisherman being surnamed King, Columba Leahy surmised, confused the Halls and led them to invent a king.[41] What confused them, however, may have been the local joke based on the same coincidence which was current in the few years before their arrival.[42]

The surviving account of an election in the Claddagh is from 1846, by which date the post of Claddagh's admiral had lost most of its cachet. Moreover, the election may not have been typical, since it took place during a period of acute crisis and demoralisation in the community. Since it would appear that Dominican priests played a key role in organising the 1846 contest, it is possible that they stepped in to kick-start the fishing season. But, even if this was so, they would probably have had to observe at least some of the traditional forms of Claddagh elections

The election took place on a Sunday evening in August, when the bellman was sent to summon voters to the newly-built but as-yet-unopened Piscatory School. Supervised by several Dominicans and a solicitor, the process took two-and-a-half hours, but, reportedly, many of those eligible failed to attend for want of respectable clothing. By prevailing standards, procedures were extremely democratic: all males over 18 were allowed to vote and there was evidently a secret ballot, since only one was admitted at a time. During the poll, participants were entertained outside by a piper, and afterwards a bonfire was lit outside the Dominican friary but rain curtailed other planned amusements. Bartley Hynes emerged as admiral, Owen Jones as vice-admiral, while the other contenders formed a 'council'. On the following morning, Fr Rush blessed the bay from the new admiral's boat.[43]

If the quest for the exotic gave the Claddagh a king, it also caused many of its civic traditions to be misinterpreted. There were obvious guild parallels with practices such as the blessing of the bay and the annual fishermen's march through the town on St John's Day. Moreover, the fact that this procession passed around the whole town shows that the fishermen's guild was *of* the town and not merely of the Claddagh.* The likely urban provenance of Claddagh's tradition, however, was passed over in favour of explanations drawing on the primeval or the aboriginal. And ethnographers with micrometers, measuring faces for their Iberian and Celtic affinities or for a 'tinge of the Dane or the Saxon', were not far behind.†

If the 19th century brought travellers escaping from the bustle of industrial life to the Claddagh, it also brought elements of that industrial life itself. Commercial fishing, synonymous with trawling, was hailed by those who saw it as a means to restore Galway's prosperity. It was stoutly opposed, however, by the Claddagh community. As early as 1811, Claddaghmen, 'aided by those whose education should have placed them on a higher ground', petitioned the Lord Lieutenant to restrain Captain Morris of the *Townshend* revenue cutter who, with 'several other gentlemen', had begun trawling for turbot.[44] A decade later, local merchant Lachlan MacLachlan equipped a boat for trawling in the bay. The coastguard provided a vessel to protect it from the hostility of the Claddaghmen, who protested that trawling would destroy spawn and disturb herrings, causing them to leave the bay.[45] MacLachlann's boat, however, soon went aground on the rocks. In 1825, a National Coast and Deep-Sea Fishery Company published a prospectus in the local press.[46] Although its initiative was welcomed, it had no apparent local impact. More ominously in 1831, the Dominican, Fr Patrick Hughes, was 'busy collecting for a thrawl for the distressed fishermen of the Claddagh'. and using his influence to persuade them to abandon 'their ancient prejudice against that species of angling'.[47] Two years later, the trawl was purchased and a trial arranged. The trial, which was conducted while Fr Hughes was absent from Galway, was violently interrupted by the Claddagh fleet. No further attempt was made and the trawl was left to rot on the quay.[48]

Incidentally, the Claddaghmen's opposition to trawling — 'a peculiar mode of fishing which is practised in most bays of Great Britain and Ireland, and found highly productive' — was among the delinquent activities denounced in an 1839 memorial to the Lord Lieutenant from the 'nobility, gentry and clergy of the county of Galway'.[49]

---

* Hardiman's description (*Galway*, p. 295): '...their mayor, whose orders are decisive, adjusts the rank, order and precedence of this curious procession. They then set out, headed by a band of music, and march with loud and continued huzzas and acclamations of joy, accompanied by crowds of people, through the principal streets and suburbs of the town: the young men all uniformly arrayed in short white jackets, with silken sashes, their hats ornamented with ribbons and flowers, and upwards of sixty or seventy of the number bearing long poles and standards with suitable devices which are in general emblematic of their profession. To heighten the merriment of this festive scene, two of the stoutest disguised in masks, and entirely covered in party-coloured rags, as "merrymen," with many antic tricks and gambols, make way for the remainder.' Thomas Carlyle, who visited the Claddagh in 1849, wrote that 'they had lately a revered senior they called their "admiral" (a kind of real king) among them...' (*Reminiscences of my Irish Journey in 1849*, London 1882, p. 192).

† In his 'Ethnological sketches. — No.1: The fishermen of the Claddagh, at Galway' (*Ulster Journal of Archaeology*, 1854, Vol. 2, pp. 160-67), J. McE. concluded that the customs of the Claddagh people showed that they were 'representatives of society two thousand years ago.' More recently, Peadar O'Dowd's *Down by the Claddagh* (Galway 1993, p. 32) argued that the powers of Claddagh's 'king' were of 'ancient origin, perhaps touching on a time when Ireland was divided into tuatha, or kingdoms, each ruled by a rí or king, and each obeying the Brehon laws'.

The next attempt to convert the Claddagh to trawling came in 1848-49, when the community was designated by the Society of Friends as a beneficiary of its famine relief efforts. The Quakers realised that to be effective they would first have to win the co-operation of the admiral — 'a common fisherman of the Claddagh who takes the lead in council and in action amongst this unworkable body of men' — and also of the Dominican friars who had the confidence of the community.[50]

In the period before the Quaker intervention, there was frustration that the Claddagh people, who could have been adding to the local food supply, were dependent on gratuitous soup, and occupying scarce places on relief schemes, being unable to follow their vocation because they could not afford to release their fishing gear from pawn.[51] Arthur Chard, the fishing captain sent to oversee the project, therefore, greatly improved his standing when he paid the pawnbrokers.* A local committee — consisting of the Anglican Rev. John d'Arcy, the Dominican Fr Rush, and Robert Fisher, bank manager — assisted Chard but proved reluctant to take on long-term commitments. As far as Chard was concerned, the long-term needs of the Claddagh were for a fish-curing station and for improved fishing methods.

Public finance was available for a fish-curing station, and the Claddagh people had no objection. The civic authorities, however, refused to provide a suitable site, and the local committee was reluctant to accept more responsibilities. But these difficulties were overcome and, when the facility opened, Quaker philanthropy further commended itself, as the Claddagh people were promptly and honestly paid for their fish, something to which they were unaccustomed.

'Improving' fishing methods was another story. Chard did succeed in persuading the fishermen to take to sea on All Saints Day, a traditional religious holiday, but he was unable to overcome resistance to trawling. Following a committee decision, however, a trawler was purchased in August 1849 and outfitted in England. The Claddaghmen were persuaded to allow it a trial, provided no trawling was done in the bay itself. The trial was not a success: there were technical difficulties with equipment intended for sheltered English waters, and there were communication difficulties between English crew members and the Irish-speaking Claddaghmen. The arrangement broke down in threats against the crew, leaving the Quakers to decide whether there was any 'possibility of bringing them to reason, either thro their bishop, or their parish priest, or the piscatorial school?' The question was answered in the negative, the trawler was sold, and the attempt abandoned. It was pointless, the Quakers realised, trying to 'improve' people against their wishes.[52]

---

* Of those who held the Claddagh fishing tackle, W. E. Foster observed: 'These pawnbrokers, who were the most prosperous-looking I had seen on my journey, were, however, full of complaints against the times'. (*Transactions of the Central Relief Committee of the Society of Friends*, Dublin 1852, p. 159).

Food rioters

The earliest food riot of which there is a full account broke out on 23 March 1812. On that day, there was a concerted attack on the grain stores by a large crowd, the ships on the quays had their sails removed, lest they carry 'grain, oatmeal and salted provisions' from the town, and Mr Appleyard, merchant, was stoned and 'maltreated'. The cause of the commotion, according to the military commander, Major-General Brereton, was 'an alledged scarcity of provisions'.[53]

In fact, actual scarcity was general throughout Ireland following a 'partial failure of the crops' in 1811.[54] The *Freeman's Journal* reported 'dearth in many districts', noting that potatoes were four times their normal price and that bread was 'becoming equally extravagant and inaccessible to the poor'. Widespread apprehension among the comfortable classes was heightened by the coincidence of the shortages with the high-point of English Luddism and, to reduce the possibility of unrest, the government was urged to intervene with a ban on distilling which was calculated to be 'consuming the subsistence of 100,000 weekly'.[55]

But the Galway outbreak was short-lived. Resident troops restored order and reinforcements from the cavalry of the Enniskillen regiment arrived to protect ships. Within days the guard was withdrawn and the authorities declared that normal trade could be resumed. Repression, however, had been tempered by concession. A meeting of the 'principal inhabitants', was attended by some rioters who were scolded for their disorderly conduct. With that out of the way, 'liberal subscriptions' were used to purchase oatmeal for distribution among the people.[56]

What occurred was an example of 'collective bargaining by riot', a ritualised confrontation to which all parties knew the rules. Popular grievances were expressed through limited violence, whereupon the crowd had dispersed rather than come into conflict with troops. Had they chosen, the people could have scattered the small garrison and claimed the contents of the foodstores. But that was not their purpose. Like town crowds elsewhere, they knew from experience that if protest was kept within limits, local notables would respond to their distress.[57]

Food rioting, evidently, was traditional in Galway. In 1812, Major-General Brereton observed that Holy Week was a period when riots had been 'very prevalent', in the town. There is no more direct evidence than that, but the remark indicates that there was unrest on at least a few occasions in the previous decade or so. (Much earlier, during the catastrophic 1740s famine, an anti-export riot was dispersed by troops.)[58]

1817 was a year of particular distress. The previous harvest had been 'so constantly cold and rainy, as to destroy the sown crops and rising crops, to a degree that led to famine and pestilence in Ireland'.[59] On 9 January, unrest broke out in Galway. A 'mob' broke windows at the home of 'a respectable merchant who was shipping oatmeal contrary to their wish', before destroying his carts and throwing his scales into the river. Later, windows of flour mills and stores were smashed. Merchants complained about the impossibility of doing business; Dublin Castle officials responded by pressurising the authorities to restore order, threatening to place the town under the Peace Preservation Act — equivalent to martial law — if they did not.

The political position in the town was sensitive. A new mayor had been elected — excise officer Parnell Gale, representing the Daly interest. Normally, mayors were 'qualified both by *consanguinity* and by *name*', but in December 1816 no Daly was eligible under residency rules. The prospect that an opposition 'Independent' might fill the post was briefly raised, so when a 'man of straw' was chosen, there were protests, including one from John Moore, the oatmeal exporter targeted by the rioters.[60] Clearly, Gale's stewardship would be closely and critically scrutinised.

Mayor Gale called a meeting to protest at exaggerated accounts of disturbance that had reached Dublin. A resolution of the meeting professed 'astonishment' that:

> A clandestine Memorial has been forwarded by a few individuals … erroneously representing the population of the town of Galway as being actuated by a spirit of hostility to the laws of the land, and of riotous insubordination, subversive of the peace of the country; and therefore praying His Majesty's Government to suspend the ordinary course of law in this town, and to substitute in its place the rigorous and coercive operation of the *Peace Preservation Act.*[61]

Other parts of the resolution emphasised that the authorities were in control and that the magistrates were 'fully able at all times to rectify any error into which the populace may be betrayed by their wants or their passions'.

'What had occurred', the resolution went on, was a 'solitary and exaggerated instance of insubordination' from 'an insulated quarter of our suburbs'. The implication, was that the Independent faction had maliciously circulated lies in order to undermine the mayor, who had been 'at his post at all times'. For his part, Gale stressed that he had been willing to act on behalf of complaining merchants, but they themselves had voluntarily surrendered their rights by submitting to the 'mob'. In the circumstances, there was little, the mayor said, that he could do.

It would seem, therefore, that the crowd prevented the export of provisions. Moreover, the protest prompted the establishment of a fund for the purchase of food, whose availability at moderate prices from a 'public store' in Back-street was guaranteed until September. In announcing this, magistrates issued a warning to those who would 'in any manner, obstruct, the corn, flour, meal, or potato trade'.[62] There were also other, more modest, efforts to appease the poor. 'Worthy gentlemen' of Dominick-street dispensed daily soup to their favourite objects, while 'young gentlemen' put on charity performances in the Theatre.[63]

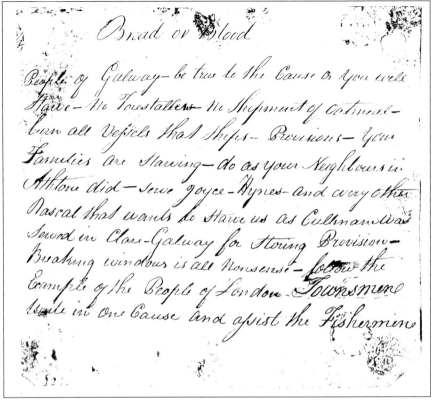

'Bread or Blood'! Notice posted on Tholsel Gate during food riots of 1817 (NAI).

But this benevolence did not end unrest. By 3 March, six weeks after the first outbreak, the mayor was no longer confident about maintaining order. In a letter to Dublin Castle, describing 'outrages' on stores, merchants' houses and ships, he requested that cavalry be sent, since mounted troops might more effectively pursue rioters.

Among the manifestations of unrest was a notice posted on the Tholsel gate, ominously entitled 'Bread or blood':

> People of Galway — be true to the Cause or you will Starve — no Forestallers — no shipments of oatmeal — burn all vessels that ships provisions — your Families are starving — do as your neighbours in Athlone did — serve Joyce-Hynes-and every other Rascal that wants to starve us as Cullinane was served in Clare-Galway for storing Provisions — Breaking windows is all nonsense — follow the example of the people of London. TOWNSMEN unite in one cause and assist the fishermen.[64]

The references in the notice to Athlone and London show that both the writer and his audience were aware of events elsewhere. Athlone had its own food riot during February, as had other towns in the northern half of the country, notably Belfast, Enniskillen, Strabane, Tullamore, Moate, Athlone, Mullingar and Ballina.[65] Closer to home, 'Cullinane' was William Cullinane, of Rock Park, Claregalway who was murdered near his home on the night of 21 February 1817.[66] The text seems to argue that that time-worn tactics — breaking windows and removing sails — were ineffective, but the fact that the notice was placed on the Tholsel gate suggests that the writer was trying to frighten those with the capacity to relieve poverty rather than to incite the crowd to greater destruction.

If so, it had the desired effect, for fund-raising for relief provisions continued. As a precaution, however, the mayor swore in special constables.[67] There was renewed apprehension in June, a month of widespread food rioting in Munster towns.[68] The authorities in Dublin Castle became so alarmed at the scarcity that they issued a proclamation asking the prosperous to refrain from consuming potatoes and from feeding scarce oats to their horses.[69]

A Galway merchant, James King, wrote in early June, that he feared an attack by the 'mob' on ships exporting meal. Later in June, there were rumours of a 'contemplated rising' on the Saturday after St John's Eve.[70] Nothing happened, but the rumours gave a boost to fund-raising. The fund opened in March reached £529 by the end of June, at which point Mayor Gale appealed to the Lord Lieutenant, claiming that the fund was exhausted, and that there was 'no hope of replenishing it by further subscriptions'. It would appear, nevertheless, that there was some loose change lying about, for £482 was subscribed a week later for information on those who killed William Le Poer Trench's cow on the outskirts of the town.[71]

It took a good harvest and a falling market to bring the disturbances of 1817 to an end.* With the exception of the early Famine period, it was the year of most sustained food rioting in 19th century Galway. There were actual riots in January and March, and preparations for others, at least among merchants and the town administration, throughout June. In a year of particular distress, the objective of the rioters was to prevent the export of food, something they believed to be immoral during a period of scarcity. As the placard makes clear, there was an awareness among the rioters of events elsewhere, whether of the punishment meted out to an alleged hoarder of food in nearby Claregalway, or of the behaviour of crowds in faraway Athlone or London. But if the distress was the principal catalyst of popular unrest in 1817, undoubtedly local political tensions contributed to the excitement.

In the following years there were further food disturbances: in July 1824, women and children attacked a convoy of relief provisions bound for Moycullen; in August 1829, a large crowd imposed *taxation populaire* when

---

* The Irish crisis of 1817 was part of a Europe-wide phenomenon which arose, in part at least, from unusual meteorological conditions, sparked off by volcanic activity. The 'Bread or blood' slogan appeared on a banner in East Anglia in May 1816 (John Dexter Post, *The Last Great Subsistence Crisis*, Baltimore 1977, pp. xi-xv, 69-70).

Galway food riots of 1842, as depicted in the *Illustrated London News.*

they attacked the potato market and compelled the potato-sellers to reduce their prices;[72] in June 1840, there were rumours of an imminent attack on the stores. On the latter occasion, additional forces were sought by the magistrates, and considerable funds were collected to provide potatoes at reduced prices.[73] But these measures had only a temporary effect. In mid-August 1840, the measuring baskets of stall holders were seized following a march through the town to 'put down the forestallers'. On the following day, the authorities' attempts to prevent a similar display were thwarted by the Claddagh people who left their suburb in ones and twos and assembled in town before going through the market, overturning stalls as they went. Even the victims of this protest, incidentally, wouldn't inform the police as to the culprits.[74]

Galway's best-known food riot occurred on 13 June 1842. It would appear to have been a somewhat less restrained affair than earlier outbreaks. The *Illustrated London News* reported on 'The Galway starvation riots'* as follows:

---

* It is interesting to compare this account with an equally sympathetic description from John Wesley (generally a more primly fastidious observer) of an earlier West of Ireland food riot that he happened upon at Jamestown, Co. Leitrim, in May 1758: 'they had been in motion all day; but their business was only with the forestallers of the market who had bought up all the corn far and wide, to starve the poor, and load a Dutch ship, which lay at the quay; but the mob brought it all out into the market, and sold it for the owners for the common price. And they did this with all the calmness and composure imaginable, and without striking or hurting anyone.'

During the entire day, the town was in the hands of a fierce and ungovernable mob, led on apparently by women and children, but having an imposing reserve in the rear, of the Claddagh fishermen. The Sheriff, with a strong force of police and the depot of the 30th Regiment, which constitutes the garrison, vainly attempted to restrain them. They assailed him and his armed bands with showers of stones, which wounded the commanding officer of the military party in the head, and hurt several of the men. But with singular forbearance and humanity, the gallant thirtieth held their fire, and as it was impossible to disperse such a mob without firing into them, the millers were induced to promise that meal should be retailed on the following day at 15*d* a stone. The discontent of the sufferers has been aggravated by the unfeeling, and, there was some reason to suspect, the dishonest artifices of those who had food to sell. Farmers known to have abundant supplies of potatoes, had not only refused to part with any portion of them at the present high prices, but had actually sent into the markets and made purchases in order to augment the scarcity. Numbers of dealers, also, speculating on a rise, had stored quantities of provisions which they refused to give out at a fair profit, and in several instances these persons had cleared out the markets the instant they were opened, and left the poor famishing housekeepers, with their money in their hands, in the midst of apparent plenty, unable to procure even the supply of a single day.[75]

In the evening, to celebrate the popular triumph, the verger of St Nicholas was forced to ring *Joybells*, whereupon the crowd marched through the town and insisted that citizens illuminate their houses, breaking the windows of those who refused.[76]

On the following day, a meeting was held in the Royal Galway Institute rooms to consider approaches to relief. One prominent citizen, John Ireland J.P., who had taken the initiative in purchasing 2,000 stones of potatoes and had commenced selling them at less than half the market price, was complimented for his prompt and humanitarian response. There was general agreement at the meeting that, while the prevailing market price was not exceptionally high, the lack of employment in the town meant that people could not afford to purchase food. Rev. John d'Arcy expressed regrets that relief measures had not been considered sooner and asserted that 'the people had behaved on the whole more peaceably than might have been expected' in the circumstances.[77] A 'Committee of Thirteen' was established which included the Catholic bishop, the episcopalian warden, the high sheriff, the chairman of the town commission and the infirmary doctor. They set to work and a few days later it was being reported that a 'large sum has been collected, and a considerable quantity of provisions purchased, which are now being retailed at reduced prices, and the distress has been alleviated to a considerable extent'.[78] There were different views on the seriousness of the disturbance. Locally, the tendency was to downplay its gravity. The *Vindicator* was critical of 'the tissue of gross misrepresentation' being printed elsewhere while a magistrate wrote to Dublin Castle expressing surprise at the intervention of the troops. 'So little riot was there', he wrote, 'that I perceived some ladies in carriages and cars driving quietly through the streets without the slightest apprehension'. There was no real disorder, he went on, merely 'a crowd following soldiers'. Although the potato stores were broken open, those involved were merely 'women and half-grown boys' who believed that their contents were the property of forestallers; the minor transgressions of the evening were committed by 'boys, led by a fiddler'. It is difficult to reconcile this account with the official report detailing ten cases of housebreaking, twenty cases of other damage to property, and most seriously, the robbery of firearms.[79] Clearly, like their predecessors in 1817, those in authority were sensitive to the reflection on their competence consequent to 'the disgrace of popular commotion'.

Food disturbances invariably occurred during periods of scarcity and high prices. But, as Edward Thompson pointed out, to deduce merely that people rioted when they were hungry is to 'conclude investigation at the exact point at which it becomes of serious sociological or cultural interest'. Each act of the crowd, he argued, had at its root, some 'legitimising notion'.[80] In this context, it is worth considering Major-General Brereton's observation that rioting had been 'very prevalent' during Holy Week in Galway before 1812. Of course, this might be due to the time of year, when the fruits of the previous harvest were close to exhaustion. But the timing of Easter could vary by up to five weeks, so there may well have been a deeper meaning to such a coincidence between the high-point of the religious calendar and the expression of popular outrage.

And if riots broke out during periods of scarcity, they did not break out during all such periods. Nor did people simply riot against scarcity or high prices, but against the practices and the people that they held responsible for their difficulties. Grain exporters were the villains in Galway in 1812 and 1817; in 1829, 1840 and 1842 it was the forestallers of potatoes. To resort to rioting was both to attempt to enforce natural justice and to appeal to the authorities to apply archaic legislation. If the authorities did not acquiesce, the solvent citizenry could usually be depended upon to intervene with a subscription.

In earlier centuries, for reasons of stability, it was considered important that urban populations be well and cheaply fed. Accordingly, by-laws protected the poor from such villains of the marketplace as engrossers, forestallers and regraters. For instance, one early 16th century Galway by-law reads: 'That no butter be sold above a peny a pound and no dearer on payn to lose 12*d* and his body to be put in prison that doth the contrary'.[81] If there is no indication that people were routinely imprisoned for overcharging for butter, there were occasional appeals and official attempts to enforce the assize of bread in the early 19th century.[82]

Protectionist tendencies came under pressure with the development of trade in the early 18th century, but they proved resilient until rather late in the century. By then the ideas of people like Adam Smith were becoming influential among the elite, in particular the assertion that merchants, traders and producers were justified in behaving more or less as they saw fit in seeking to maximise profits. Increased price was only a rationing mechanism, this theory held, encouraging the poor to husband scarce resources; government or civic interference with the market's rationing mechanism could only postpone the moment of truth and in postponing it cause it to be more terrible when it came. The ascendancy of a new orthodoxy was confirmed with the repeal of the statutes forbidding forestalling and regrating in 1791, although common law and by-law interdictions could still be invoked.

The old — and not long discredited — notions on the responsibilities that went with power and affluence, however, still lingered. They were held most strongly among the poor who were dependent on market regulation during times of scarcity, but traditional ideas also survived among people who were not personally greatly concerned about the cost of basic foodstuffs. James Hardiman was one such. He lamented in 1820 that 'the iniquitous practice of regrating or forestalling (was) not unknown' in the Galway potato market,[83] and it can be assumed that the same general attitude was widely held within the local elite.* According to such a traditional mindset, it was immoral to profit in food, the staff of life itself; the producer should be the seller, and there should be no intermediary making profits between the producer and the consumer.

Well into to the 19th century, Galway's local authorities took a great interest in the operations of local markets. A market jury was appointed each year, with responsibility for ensuring that by-laws and regulations were observed, but civic interest did not end there. There are reports from three successive Saturdays in July 1792 of the mayor, Richard Daly, and the other magistrates visiting the markets, probably in response to complaints. On two of the occasions, breaches of regulations were discovered: bread was deficient in weight, and meat was found to be blown. In each case, the offending product was seized for distribution 'among prisoners and other indigent objects'.[84]

So who was involved in the food rioting? To answer the question, we have to consider the composition of the urban 'mob' or crowd. And sources are sometimes unhelpful, since they do not always state what would have been obvious to their readers. In considering the 'classical' mob of the pre-industrial European city, Eric Hobsbawm cautioned against taking the prejudiced and ill-informed accounts of contemporaries at face value and proceeding to represent the 'mob' as being composed of vagrants and other lumpenproletarians.[85]

* To forestall was to hold back supplies in order to force prices up, to regrate was to buy food in order to resell at a profit; to engross was to monopolise. Incidentally, a pragmatic reason for adhering to the traditional view was advanced by Lord Chief Justice Kenyon in 1800: 'When the people knew there was a law to resort to, it composed their minds' thereby removing the threat of 'insurrection' (Thompson, 'Moral economy reviewed', p. 270).

'The Orangeman of Galway': anti-export cartoon published in *The Looking Glass* during shortages of 1831.

While there can be no doubt but that such folk often took opportunistic advantage of the activities of the larger crowd, they rarely accounted for more than its fringe. Hobsbawm's 'mob' was composed of

> wage earners, small property owners and the unclassifiable urban poor … porters … dockers … apprentices and journeymen of the lower trades and crafts … the mass of hawkers and unclassifiable small dealers and people making ends meet which filled pre-industrial cities.[86]

If we add the families of these people, Galway offers no contradiction to the above list. Women and children, at any rate, were active participants in Galway food-rioting. This fact is directly referred to in accounts of the 1824 and 1842 disturbances and, as we shall see in Chapter Six, a female food rioter was killed in 1846. On other occasions, the involvement of women may have been considered too commonplace to be worth commenting upon. It has already been shown that Galway women were involved in Claddagh fishery disturbances, and they participated too in election riots. Elsewhere, also, women were prominent as rioters.[87] Several reasons have been advanced for this. On the one hand it has been suggested that, as the principal market customers, women were sensitive to price movements and also had the experience to detect short-falls in quality or quantity. A spontaneous vocal protest in such a situation might escalate into a minor riot. On other occasions women's involvement was strategic, based on the assumption that women were less likely to suffer at the hands of police and troops and that, if arrested, they would be treated more leniently than men. So women placed themselves at the forefront of a riot in order to protect the riot.[88]

The other people who crop up repeatedly in connection with food rioting were the Claddagh fishermen. Claddagh people are mentioned specifically in relation to the 1840 incident, 'the fishermen' are mentioned in the threatening notice of March 1817 and are also referred to in reports of events of 1842 and 1845. Rioters in January 1817 are reported as coming from 'an insulated quarter of our suburbs'. This almost certainly means the Claddagh. So it is clear that Claddagh people, men and women, were regularly involved. Indeed the accounts would suggest that not alone was the Claddagh involved, but that it provided the leadership of food riots.

It has been established that food rioting was not generally a spontaneous and unrestrained affair. One historian, indeed, has questioned whether the word 'riot' is appropriately employed in connection with such an ordered form of protest.[89] The gathering together of the crowd, the enforcement of *taxation populaire*, the observance of 'the protocol of riot', — and the orderly dispersal of participants — required a disciplined leadership, a 'directing intelligence', in Bohstedt's phrase. Such a leadership has been identified in other places as emanating from the best-organised section of the proletarian community — miners in some areas, weavers in others.[90] In Galway in the early 19th century, as has been established above, the best-organised proletarians were the Claddagh fishermen. And although it goes somewhat against the grain to appoint the Claddagh people as leaders of the Galway crowd, since this detracts from their attested 'singularity' and detachment, the evidence indicates that they were indeed leaders.

Considering that the Claddagh fishermen were already organised to defend their livelihood, it was natural that they deploy their organisational capacity in defence of the food supply, both on their own behalf and on behalf of the other poor of the town. There is confirmation of their leading role in attempting to regulate the market in an 1841 polemic in the *Galway Advertiser*:

> We had hoped that the King of the Claddagh had laid prostrate his sceptre before the Majesty of the Law, but we were deceived, his Majesty of the Fishermen is still Legislating in this Town. The late Proclamation was levelled against the Potatoe Market which is nearly annihilated. No man dare buy a potato in this town except an inhabitant of the town itself. In former years the Connemara people brought in their Sea Weed and in return brought home potatoes. Our market then was immense, now it is reduced nine-tenths — Kinvarra, Tyrone, and the different villages along the coast are the markets whither they go with the produce of the soil — sure of protection — in Galway they have none. A few days ago,

a gentleman's servant, his horse and car, were well nigh thrown over the Quay for daring to sell Potatoes to a Mountaineer. What are the Magistrates about? What are the Police doing.[91]

One does not have to accept the writer's physiocratic analysis of the reasons for the decline of Galway's potato market, but his strictures do establish that popular militancy was a significant factor in the market-place and that the Claddagh people were a significant factor in that militancy.

Galway's poor continued to draw on their food rioting tradition during the 1845-47 period. Although famine unrest will not be considered here but in Chapter Six, it might be appropriate to note that this form of protest all but disappeared during 1847, with subsequent disorder taking the form of robbery by small groups and individuals. It has been argued that people were too worn out and demoralised to protest after this point, but one writer has suggested a connection between the end of food rioting and the change in the form in which relief was offered. Public works were closed and replaced by soup kitchens; people became supplicants rather than workers and lost their sense of personal dignity. Beggars, he concludes, do not engage in collective protest.[92]

By the post-Famine period, the era of the food riot had virtually come to an end. Among those hit hardest in the disaster itself were the communities that made up the urban crowd; the consequent dislocation bore heavily on traditional cultural practices. The Poor Law must also be counted as having contributed to change. In the early 1840s, workhouses opened their doors to the destitute. Thereafter, those paying for the facility through poor rates

'Market women at the Old Booths, Galway', (from *Illustrated London News*), 1879.

became less inclined to subscribe to relief funds than to direct the afflicted to the workhouse. Other developments were also altering the nature of the bonds between governors and governed on which the existence of a phenomenon like food rioting depended. The centralisation of power towards national government widened the gulf of sympathy, while the increasing effectiveness of the forces of law and order meant that crowds could be taken on and defeated. Moreover, as we have seen, food rioting was an affront to the economic orthodoxy of the mid-19th century: political economy had non-interference in the market as a central principle; such interference was the very purpose of the food riot.

But was food-rioting an effective strategy? This is difficult to establish one way or the other, since it is impossible to measure the long-term consequences of such popular action. Certainly it must have inhibited would-be forestallers and would-be exporters of food. But in forbidding all but the retailing of potatoes in the market — with the threat of disorder, presumably, backing him up — did Claddagh's mayor reduce Galway's total supply in the years around 1841? The *Advertiser* commentator certainly thought so and he would find support for his view among latter-day historians.[93] In terms of immediate results, however, food rioting was clearly an effective strategy in pre-Famine Galway. It would appear indeed, to have been more effective in Galway than in other places, perhaps due to the town's relative isolation. Since it took such a long time for military reinforcements to reach the town, it may have been considered safer to appease rioters than to disperse them by violent means. In several instances, as we have seen, merchants and dealers conceded the crowd's demand, but in almost every instance before the Famine local worthies intervened in the market with cheap food purchased by subscription.

As an epilogue to the above, there was a further episode on 25 April 1857. On that morning, a large crowd gathered and attacked the potato stores, while others concentrated on the smack, *Vixen,* which was being loaded with potatoes for export. Several people, identified as Claddagh fishermen, boarded the vessel, and warned the captain and crew that the sails and cargo would be removed if any more potatoes were loaded. On the following day, several men returned to caution the crew against attempting to sail, threatening that the vessel would be attacked in the bay if there was an attempt to remove potatoes. No public subscription was initiated on this occasion and the authorities' response came in the form of two additional companies of infantry in the town and the admiralty steamer *Advice* in the bay.[94] A few years later, in December 1861, there was alarm about the likelihood of provisions rioting. Nine magistrates wrote to the police inspector, advising him of the great distress in the town and warning that 'an outbreak on the part of the unemployed may occur at any time'. As people were being advised by 'agitators' that 'they should not allow themselves to die of cold and hunger', the police force was considered inadequate if food riots broke out. The magistrates' alarm was communicated to Dublin Castle, but no outbreak took place.[95]

Writing in 1991, Edward Thompson commented on the lack of 'a tradition of food rioting in Ireland'. While suggesting that the case might not be clear-cut, and citing a number of exceptional examples, he bowed to the received wisdom* and attempted to account for the ostensibly 'divergent national traditions'. He posited the shortage of 'political space' for such activity in Ireland, surmising that an early 18th century food rioting tradition had been smothered by the lack of positive results.[96] The Galway experience of 1812-1861, however, shows that there was a vibrant food rioting tradition in the town, one that was not quite killed off by the 1840s famine. There are indications too that the Galway experience was not unique, since in almost every instance, Galway food riots coincided with outbreaks elsewhere in Ireland. Generally speaking, rioters in different towns were responding to the same economic stimuli, but it is clear, especially in 1817, that people outraged by the insensitivity of merchants and traders mimicked the response of crowds in neighbouring towns. The divergence, therefore, is not a matter of traditions, but of historiography. Urban food riots have been generally ignored by Irish historians and, when they have not been ignored, they have been sometimes misinterpreted. In Jordan's study of Mayo, for example, apparent urban food riots in 1817 and 1831 have been credited to agrarian secret societies.[97] There are some indications, however, that the Irish food riot is in the process of being rediscovered.[98]

---

* The received wisdom was expressed in definitive fashion by Thomas Bartlett: 'Irish violence was however different: the food riot, common in England, was almost unknown in Ireland' ('An end to moral economy: the Irish militia disturbances of 1793' in *Past and Present* 99, 1983, pp. 41-64). Desmond McCabe has argued that 'no exact counterpart to the English food riots can be identified in Ireland, since English crowds seem to have been composed of the waged poor pitted against the farmer and the miller' ('Social order & the ghost of moral economy in pre-Famine Mayo', in *A various country: essays in Mayo history, 1500-1900*, Gillespie and Moran, eds., Westport 1987, p. 93). While allowing that there were 'somewhat similar activities' to food rioting in Ireland', Samuel Clarke took the same view (*Social origins of the Irish land war*, Princeton 1979, p. 67).

NOTES

1. National Library of Ireland, MacLochlainn Collection, 'The Galway Subsidy', c.1860.
2. *Municipal Corporations' Commissioners,* 1835 xxvii, p. 319.
3. Hely Dutton, *A Statistical and Agricultural Survey of the County of Galway,* Dublin 1824, p. 433.
4. John Boyle, *The Irish Labour Movement in the Nineteenth Century,* Washington 1988, pp. 7-25; *Connaught Journal,* 27 December 1792
5. Emmet O'Connor, *A Labour History of Ireland, 1824-1960,* Dublin 1992, pp. 1-6.
6. *Connaught Journal,* 15, 19, 22, 26 September 1825. Dublin artisans were notoriously violent defenders of their interests.
7. ibid., 20 November 1823, 22 January 1824.
8. ibid., 1 September 1823.
9. ibid., 15, 18 October 1829.
10. ibid., 20 October 1836.
11. See Boyle, *Irish Labor Movement,* Maura Cronin, *Country, Class or Craft? The Politicisation of the Skilled Artisan in Nineteenth-Century Cork,* Cork 1994; Emmet O'Connor, *A Labour History of Waterford,* Waterford 1989, all passim.
12. *Galway Advertiser,* 29 May 1841.
13. *Galway Vindicator,* 5 January 1842.
14. ibid., 22 June 1842; Cronin, *Class or Craft,* p. 37.
15. National Archives, Outrage papers 1842, 11/8459.

16. *Galway Vindicator,* 9 July, 16 November 1842.
17. ibid., 17 August, 14 September 1842.
18. National Archives, Outrage papers 1842, 11/19675.
19. ibid.
20. *Galway Vindicator,* 22 April 1846, 21 October 1846.
21. ibid., 26 June 1847; *Galway Mercury,* 16 September 1848.
22. *Galway Mercury,* 20, 27 October 1849.
23. ibid., 1, 8 December 1849.
24. ibid., 24 May 1851.
25. ibid., 10 February 1849. For Famine 'piece-work' disturbances, see Andrés Eiríksson, 'Food supply and food riots' in *Famine 150: Commemorative Lecture Series,* Cormac Ó Gráda, ed., Dublin 1997, pp. 67-94 and Christina Kinealy's *This Great Calamity: the Irish Famine, 1845-52,* Dublin 1994, pp. 92-95.
26. Colomba R. D. Leahy, 'The social and political structure of the Galway sea fishing industry from the Union to the Famine' unpublished M.A. thesis, UCG 1964, pp. 16-17.
27. *Report of the commissioners appointed to investigate into the existence of corrupt practices in elections of members to serve in parliament for the county of the town of Galway,* H. of C. 1857-8, vol.XXVI, p. viii. During the 1812 election, when Galway's 'guilds' mustered in support of Valentine Blake, the popular candidate, the procession was headed by 'a fisherman with a flag, motto: "A long pull, a strong pull, and a pull all together", followed by three hundred of his profession'. (Hardiman, *Galway,* p. 195).
28. Richard J. Scott, *The Galway Hookers,* Dublin 1983, pp.43-52.
29. *Connaught Journal,* 12 February 1824, 7 March, 17 July 1825.
30. Comment from *Faulkner's Journal,* cited in Dutton, *Galway,* p.400.
31. National Archives, Outrage papers 1836, 11/4580.
32. *First Report of the Commissioners of Inquiry into the State of the Irish Fisheries,* 1836 xxii, p. 105.
33. *Connaught Journal,* 19 August 1833
34. ibid., 29 August 1833.
35. National Archives, Outrage papers, 1836 11/4580.
36. *Galway Chronicle,* 10 October 1810 (enclosure in State of the Country papers, 1810, 1278/2).
37. ibid.
38. Leahy, 'Sea Fishing', Chapter Six; National Archives, Outrage papers 1850, 11/285.
39. *Galway Chronicle,* 10 October 1810.
40. *Connaught Journal,* 12 February 1824.
41. Leahy, 'Sea fishing', p. 123.
42. See *Galway Advertiser,* 31 August, 17 September 1839, 10 October 1841.
43. *Galway Vindicator,* 2 September 1846.
44. Dutton, *Galway,* p. 398.
45. *First Fisheries Report,* p. 107. Comparable resistance to innovative fishing practices led to the formation of the St Peter's Society by the Barrow, Nore and Suir fishermen in 1835 (Fidelma Maddock, 'The cot fishermen of the River Nore' in Nolan & Whelan, eds., *Kilkenny, History and Society,* Dublin 1990, pp. 543-44.
46. *Connaught Journal,* 19 May 1825.
47. ibid., 27 June 1831.
48. *First fisheries report,* p. 107.
49. *Copy of a memorial submitted to the Lord Lieutenant of Ireland in the month of December 1839, respecting the present state of the fisheries in the Bay of Galway; with the reply of the Lord Lieutenant,* H.of C. 1840. There are indications, also, of sporadic clashes between the Claddagh fleet and trawlermen during the mid-1840s (Leahy, 'Sea Fishing' pp. 191-2).
50. Helen E.Hatton, *The largest amount of good: Quaker relief in Ireland, 1654-1921,* Montreal, 1993, pp. 216-7.
51. Leahy, 'Sea fishing', pp. 180-85.
52. Hatton, *Quaker Relief,* pp. 217-222.
53. National Archives, State of the Country papers 1812, 1408/3. Thomas Appleyard was the merchant who initiated Galway's grain export trade, 'about 1804' (Dutton, *Galway,* p. 95).
54. (William Wilde), *The Census of Ireland for the year 1851. Part V. Tables of Deaths. Vol.1. Containing the report, tables of pestilences, and analysis of the tables of deaths,* H. of C., 1856, vol. XXIX, p. 171.
55. *Freeman's Journal,* 24 March, 9 April 1812.
56. National Archives, State of the Country papers 1812, 1408/4-5; *Freemans Journal,* 2 April 1812.

57. For pre-industrial crowds, see George Rudé, *The Crowd in History*, 1995 edn, London, and Eric Hobsbawm, *Primitive rebels: studies in archaic forms of social movements in the 19th and 20th centuries*, 1978 edn, Manchester. The most useful study of the 'mob' or crowd remains E.P. Thompson's 1971 *Past & Present* article, 'The Moral Economy of the English Crowd in the Eighteenth Century' reprinted in Thompson's *Customs in Common*, London 1991, pp. 185-258. The book also includes the author's 'comment on his commentators':'The Moral Economy Reviewed', pp. 259-351.

58. National Archives, State of the Country papers 1812, 1408/4; Thompson, 'Moral Economy Reviewed', p. 295; David Dickson, *Arctic Ireland*, Dublin 1997, p. 29. Much earlier still, there were food disturbances in Galway in 1511 (Philip O'Gorman, 'The Labour Court is Not New', in *The Galway Reader*, vol. 2, nos. 1 & 2, 1949-50, pp. 100-101). In the absence of a description of a pre-1812 food riot in Galway, there is an account of a successful 1801 riot nearby in *The Corporation Book of Ennis*, B.Ó Dálaigh, ed., Dublin 1990, pp. 286-87.

59. Wilde, *Tables*, p. 177.

60. *Freemans Journal,* 10 January 1817.

61. *Connaught Journal,* 23 January 1817.

62. ibid., 23 January, 6 February 1817.

63. *Connaught Journal*, 13, 24 February 1817.

64. National Archives, State of the Country papers 1817, 1833/4.

65. *Freeman's Journal,* 11, 15 February 1817; *Connaught Journal*, 3 March 1817.

66. *Connaught Journal*, 6 March 1817.

67. ibid., 3, 6, 20 March 1817.

68. O'Connor, *Waterford*, p. 18.

69. *Freemans Journal,* 12 June 1817.

70. State of the Country papers 1817, 1833/5-6.

71. *Connaught Journal,* 23, 30 June 1817.

72. National Archives, State of the Country papers 1824, 2624/17; *Connaught Journal,* 20 August 1829.

73. National Archives, Outrage papers 1840, 11/12179.

74. ibid., 11/14745.

75. *Illustrated London News,* 25 June 1842.

76. National Archives, Outrage papers 1842, 11/11045.

77. *Galway Vindicator.*, 15 June 1842.

78. ibid., 18 June 1842.

79. ibid., National Archives, Outrage papers 1842, 11/11045, 11/729.

80. Thompson, 'Moral Economy of the English Crowd', 185-89.

81. Hardiman, *Galway*, p.200. Such local legislation was supplemented by statute during the Tudor period.

82. *Connaught Journal,* 16 March 1829; *Galway Advertiser,* 18 August 1838; *Galway Vindicator,* 3 September 1842

83. Hardiman, *Galway*, p. 310.

84. *Connaught Journal,* 9, 16, 23 July 1792. The mayor was complying with a Corporation by-law of 1685, which ordered that 'all meat blown in the shambles should be seised, and disposed of to the prisoners and the poor.' (Hardiman, *Galway*, p. 219).

85. Eric Hobsbawm, 'The City Mob' in *Primitive rebels*, pp.108-25. See also John Bohstedt, *Riots and Community Politics in England and Wales, 1790-1910,* Harvard 1983, p. 38.

86. ibid., p. 111.

87. For discussion on women's involvement in food rioting, see John Bohstedt, 'Gender, Household and Community Politics: Women in English Riots 1790-1810' in *Past and Present* 120, 1988, pp. 88-122; Thompson, 'Moral economy reviewed', pp. 305-36; Manfred Gailus, 'Food riots in Germany in the late 1840s' *Past and Present*, 145, 1994, pp. 174-75.

88. Thompson, 'The Moral Economy of the English Crowd,' pp. 233-35, and 'Moral economy reviewed,' pp. 305-36.

89. Thompson, 'The moral economy of the crowd,' p. 185-87

90. ibid., p. 224; Bohstedt, *Riots and Community Politics in England and Wales,* p. 46.

91. *Galway Advertiser,* 10 April 1841.

92. Eiríksson, 'Food supply', pp. 67-91.

93. See A.W. Coats, 'Contrary moralities: plebs, paternalists and political economists' in *Past & Present* 54, 1972, pp. 130-33.

94. CSORP 1857-58/5511.

95. CSORP 1860-61/10052.

96. Thompson, 'Moral economy reviewed', pp. 295-96.

97. Donald E. Jordan, *Land and popular politics in Ireland: County Mayo from the Plantation to the Land War,* Cambridge 1994, pp. 94-96. Attempts to enforce *taxation populaire* in the Thurles area in 1800 are outlined by Thomas P. Power in *Land, Politics and Society in Eighteenth Century Tipperary,* Oxford 1993, pp. 193-94.

98. Eiríksson, 'Food supply' and Roger Wells 'The Irish Famine of 1799-1801: Market Culture, Moral Economies and Social Protest' in Randall & Charlesworth, *Markets, Market Culture, and Popular Protest in 18th Century Britain and Ireland,* Liverpool 1996, pp. 163-93. Eoin Magennis, 'In Search of the "Moral Economy": Food Scarcity in 1856-57 and the Crowd' in Peter Jupp and Eoin Maginnis *Crowds in Ireland, c.1720-1920,* London 2000, pp. 189-211.

CHAPTER 5
'The Man for Galway'

ELECTIONS & POLITICS, 1793-1845

Oh! Did you hear the glorious news which fills the Vindicator,
O'Connell comes, then who'll refuse to cheer the Liberator.
He comes to lead us to Repeal, to teach us freedom always,
He comes to burst our bonds of steel, and right the men of Galway.

Then heed no weather, but come together, from Corrib to the Solway,
With heart and voice, rejoice, rejoice, and welcome Dan to Galway.[1]

In the aftermath of a disorderly by-election for the town in November 1906, the *Irish People* published a cartoon under the heading 'Galway Election'. It depicted a bewildered candidate being guarded by a detachment of police, and protected by an umbrella from a shower of missiles —fish, rotten vegetables, and small animals (see p.223). The cartoon was an illustration of a topical news item, but it was also a stereotypical representation of electoral excesses in Galway. For almost a century, Galway elections had been notorious: for their extreme violence, for their corruption, for the extent of popular participation in them. And some of that notoriety derived from actual events. However, perceptions of Galway elections were substantially shaped by a passage from an popular novel of 1841, *Charles O'Malley*, by Charles Lever:

Each [candidate] went forth like a general to battle surrounded by a numerous and well-chosen staff; one party of friends acting as a commissariat, attending to the victualling of the voters, that they obtained a due — or rather undue — allowance of liquor, and came properly drunk to the poll; others again broke into skirmishing parties, and cut off the enemy's supplies, breaking down their post-chaises, upsetting their jaunting-cars, stealing their poll-books, and kidnapping their agents. Then, there were secret service people, bribing the enemy and enticing them to desert; and lastly there was a species of sapper-and-miner force, who invented false documents, denied the identity of the opposite parties' people, and, when hard-pushed, provided persons who took bribes from the enemy, and gave evidence afterwards on a petition.[2]

103

Lever's fictional election only mildly exaggerated tactics that were commonplace in Irish elections during the period of enfranchisement of the Catholic forty-shilling freeholders. Such tactics were employed in Galway, but they were not specific to Galway. What was specific to Galway in the novel was the figure of Godfrey O'Malley, who was modelled on Richard Martin (1754-1834), an MP during six decades, and a key figure in Galway politics for most of his life.* O'Malley was the blustering and audacious 'Man for Galway', whose proclivities were the ones outlined in a ballad included in the novel:

> To drink a toast, a proctor roast,
> Or bailiff, as the case is,
> To kiss your wife, or take your life
> At ten or fifteen paces
> To keep gamecocks, to hunt the fox,
> To drink in punch the Solway,
> With debts galore, but fun far more
> Oh! That's the man for Galway.[3]

Richard Martin, founder of the RSPCA, did not keep gamecocks, or hunt the fox, but otherwise the delineation was faithful. As for the ballad, it gained a wide currency, to the extent that life came to imitate art. A successful candidate for the borough was invariably described as 'the man for Galway',† and no election was complete without the composition of at least one parody of the ballad.[4] In the circumstances, it is possible that the behaviour and expectations of Galwegians were shaped to some extent by Lever's work.

Lever's 'man for Galway' represented the county but the sobriquet came to be applied to the member for the borough, a transposition that was understandable because, for much of their history, the two constituencies were closely bound together. The Daly connection, which dominated the town in the late 18th and early 19th centuries, also had a significant presence in the county, so representation in each constituency was a subject of trade-offs in the other. Moreover, the borough was surrounded by the county constituency, and until the 1850s county elections were held in the town. Indeed, because they were objectively more exciting — at least until franchise changes in the 1830s — county elections were generally of greater interest, even to townspeople, than borough elections. County contests had a larger electorate and their outcome was less predictable. And, because freeholders had to be conveyed up to 50 miles to vote, they went on for much longer — one county election of 1783 lasted 52 days, another of 1790 lasted 32 days.[5] The enfranchisement of Catholics greatly widened the appeal of county elections. Adding to the interest

---

* Martin's exploits were fictionalised also in novels by Lady Morgan and by his daughter, Harriet Martin.

† Incidentally, the expression 'the man for Galway' meaning 'the most suitable person for the position' was used throughout the Anglophone world in the later 19th century.

A Galway election scene as depicted in Lever's *Charles O'Malley* (1841).

was the fact that many of the non-voting citizens of the town had walk-on parts in county contests — just as described by Lever.

Two distinct periods in electoral politics can be identified in Galway during the period under consideration: before and after the radical overhaul in franchise eligibility in 1829-32. In this chapter, we will consider developments during each of these two periods.

1793-1832

Between 1793 and 1801, there were major changes in the system of parliamentary representation. The pool of potential voters was greatly increased when Catholics were enfranchised in 1793, while the number of Irish MPs was greatly reduced by the Act of Union. The Galway borough constituency had its representation cut from two to one in 1801 but, like other county constituencies, County Galway continued to elect two members.[6] As for the changes in the franchise, a period elapsed before they had any effect in practice. Only just enough candidates to fill the available county seats came forward in 1797, 1800, and 1802, so Catholics had to await an 1805 by-election for their electoral initiation. But not many new freeholders actually cast votes in 1805 —votes which, in any case, were considered to be at the disposal of their landlords. Twelve years after the electoral concession to Catholics, fewer than 2,000 voted for Denis Bowes Daly and Giles Eyre (almost 1,000 had voted in 1783).[7] Catholics resident in the town of Galway had to wait even longer for their own enfranchisement.

The electoral rules for boroughs were different from those for counties. Counties had a property-based freeholder franchise; the parliamentary boroughs that survived the Act of Union had mixed freeholder/freeman franchises. Moreover, borough elections were governed by legislation — such as the Galway Act of 1717 — that was often specific to the individual borough. In several major towns and cities, power-brokers were able to exclude Catholics from the electoral rolls until the 1830s.[8] As it was for power-brokers in other boroughs, Catholic enfranchisement was a threat to Daly hegemony in Galway. But the Dalys faced this threat decisively in September 1793 when they had more than 300 Catholic freemen admitted to the corporation. The new freemen, however, were not townsmen, but rural tenants of Daly families in the county, who were expected to vote as instructed. These new Catholic freemen were in no way free, being enfranchised only to counter-balance the independent tendencies of Catholic and Protestant freeholders in the borough. By Galway Catholics, and, in particular, by the artisans who sought enfranchisement themselves, the Daly manoeuvre was regarded as anti-Catholic and unjust. For their own parts, the rural freemen were not required to travel to Galway until the Daly position came under challenge from the Galway Independents in 1811 and 1812.[8]

The revolutionary politics of the 1790s, historians have concluded, had little immediate impact in Galway.[10] It was certainly true that the Catholic leadership had close ties with *ancien regime* France — mediated through the clerical and mercantile connections of the 'tribe' families — and that both Louis XVI and Marie Antoinette were scrupulously mourned when news of their executions reached the town.* James Hardiman offered evidence that the local population remained anti-revolutionary in the stormy years that followed. According to the historian, Galway's merchants presented the resident military commander with 1,500 guineas to equip his forces for a march on Killala on hearing that the French had landed. And the authorities were confident enough about the loyalty of the inhabitants to remove both regiment and yeomanry to Mayo. In their absence, according to Hardiman, 'the Catholic clergy were

---

* Reports emphasised that the clergy from all the Galway convents were in attendance. With regard to the 'solemn funeral service' for the king, it was stated that 'the congregation was most numerous and respectable on the awful occasion'. (*Connaught Journal*, 7 February, 14 November 1793).

indefatigable in their exertions to preserve the public peace', enabling magistrates 'to swear in the population as a loyal guard'. Other contemporary references support Hardiman's account.[11]

But, if the letter of a senior military officer is to be believed, this was not the whole story. Reporting the arrival in Galway of 'another united man' in March 1799, the correspondent mentioned the earlier arrest of a Mr and Mrs Fallon, who ran a tavern near the churchyard. The two were sentenced to transportation, but 'thru some interests' were released. It was in the Fallons' tavern, the letter continued, that the mayor of Galway, the Collector, and 'many others' had held 'treasonable meetings' during May 1798. For the officer, immediate action against these individuals was advisable — 'the greatest advantage for the Government being a detection as general as possible of all the people of rank concerned in this conspiracy'. The writer raises the intriguing possibility that individuals within Galway's ruling coterie had United Irishmen connections, and that these continued until the moment of rebellion in Leinster and Ulster. Members of Galway's Catholic elite also had revolutionary connections. Captain Francis Kirwan, an officer of the Annaghdown yeomanry, and 'a principal instigator of rebellion' in the district, who was executed in Galway in June 1799, belonged to a prominent Galway merchant family, and was a relative of the late Catholic warden.[12]

Even if individual Dalys were implicated in the events of 1798, the parliamentary connection survived. The key leaders of the alliance, James Daly of Dunsandle and Denis Bowes Daly of Dalyston, differed politically on the Act of Union but they agreed to rotate the town's solitary Westminster seat between them. As has been shown in Chapter Two, the arrangement, and the consequences that were perceived to flow from it, led to dissatisfaction among Galway's merchants, who were frustrated, in particular, by the neglect of the town and harbour. It was this frustration which galvanised the so-called 'Independent' opposition (Opponents of the Daly connection had previously mobilised under the 'Independent' banner in the 1780s and 1790s[13]). But it would seem that the impetus for the revival of the faction came from Richard Martin, a key figure in Galway politics since he first contested the county constituency in 1776. In 1811-12, Martin was marginalised in county politics, so he decided not to contest the general election. He was available, therefore, to intervene in the politics of the town.

It was in the aftermath of the 1811 by-election that the Independents protested at the manipulation of the representative apparatus, which had enabled the Dalys to avoid a contest. The citizenry was mobilised in a series of indignation meetings. By the general election of the following year, the Independents were alert and in a position to nominate Valentine Blake of Menlo Castle, whose estate was within the county of the town.[14]

Much was at stake in September 1812. There was prestige certainly, but issues of power and authority were also involved, not least the national position of the Daly interest. The two main wings of the family, — represented by James

Daly and by Denis Bowes Daly — were supporters of different parties in Westminster. By 1811, James Daly was a supporter of the government, but it was Bowes Daly's turn to claim the Galway seat, and his nominee was his relative, Frederick Ponsonby, scion of the family that had given its name to a faction in the College Green parliament. Ponsonby was put forward again in 1812. For the Independents, prosperity was bound up with the election, and it would seem that they were able to persuade most townspeople that their very future was dependent on the result.[15]

Details of the election are obscure but, given the depth of animosity between the parties, given the tone of the language that Hardiman attributed to the Independents, and given what is known about subsequent elections, it would be surprising if there was no violence. Certainly, the arrival in the town, as voters, for the first time of several hundred of the anathemised 'bare-footed gentry of Dunsandle' can hardly have passed without incident.

The outcome of the election was clear-cut: Ponsonby got 311 votes; Blake got 159. But the Independents lodged a petition against the participation of non-resident freemen. The petition was successful, but only to the extent that the non-residents were found to be improperly registered. The larger question — whether they were eligible in the first place — remained to be decided. So, as Valentine Blake took his Commons seat in 1813, his supporters were considering how to consolidate their position. They could not be certain of reducing the Daly constituency, but could they increase their own?[16]

An answer to the question was found in the charters and statutes governing admission to the freedom of the town. Galway's administration, like that of other boroughs, had evolved over the centuries, but the principles of urban government remained rooted in a mediaeval concept of the town. Historically, urban independence was protected by royal charter from interference by powerful local lords, and authority vested instead in corporations representing economic interests within the town. Corporations, notionally, were composed of guilds, each one representing an occupational group. The guilds regulated affairs within the respective trades, as well as between the trade and the community, and with the other guilds conducted urban business. Membership of a guild, accordingly, conferred the freedom of the town on the tradesman. And freedom brought with it the right to vote in parliamentary elections.[17] As in other early 19th century towns, the practice in Galway was different from the ideal. A local lord — not for the first time — was in control of its affairs and the granting of freedom and other privileges was in his gift.

According to a Galway statute of the Stuart period, 'all artificers and artisans residing in the said town shall be to all intents and purposes freemen', but the Galway Act of 1717 had restricted the privilege to Protestants. Following Catholic enfranchisement, the restriction seemed anomalous, and the demand that latter-day Catholic 'artificers and artisans' be made freemen was taken up by the Independents. Indeed, from 1813, the enfranchisement of the trades became central to the Independents' pursuit of their objective.[18]

The trades were marshalled into 17 distinct companies with an aggregate membership of 519 men. In September 1813, each of the companies submitted a demand for freedom on behalf of its own members to the mayor, Hyacinth Daly.[19] Daly admitted the few Protestant applicants under the 1717 Act but refused the Catholics on the grounds that the companies to which they belonged were 'for the first time heard of by the council'. The move strengthened the Dalys' position, but their use of a 'penal law', dented their credibility as friends to the Catholic cause.

When a legal ruling re-admitted non-resident freemen, two free Protestant tradesmen lodged an Independent-funded appeal to the King's Bench. For the next election, that of 1818, there was a great increase in the number of freeholders, but freeman numbers were restricted by the continued exclusion of Catholics and by the appeal against the non-resident franchise. Opposed by the Catholic clergy, because of his patron's recourse to the Galway Act, the Dalyite performed poorly, and Valentine Blake retained the seat.

The electoral landscape changed later in 1818, when the non-resident case was decided in favour of the Dalys. The Independents responded with a legal challenge to the exclusion of Catholic tradesmen, but that issue had not been decided before the 1820 general election, and the augmented electorate returned the Dalyite with a majority of 434. Even had the artisan vote been available, an Independent victory would have been difficult to achieve, for Blake had become unpopular because it was believed that he had sought an agreement with James Daly disfranchising both Catholic tradesmen and non-resident freemen. The circulation of an Independent resolution testifying to his principled conduct in the negotiations did not restore confidence in him.[20]

In 1821, the King's Bench ruled that the Catholic relief measures did not oblige the corporation to admit Catholics as freemen.[21] It was a setback for the Independents, and a disappointment for the tradesmen. But, after a decade of agitation for their enfranchisement, the trades were emerging as a distinct constituency in their own right. One indication of this was their establishment in 1823 of a 'Union of Trades'.[22] Another was their rejection of a corporation proposal to bestow freedom on the most 'respectable' of them.[23] And if the trades were becoming more assertive, the following complaint from Moll Doyle suggests that the agitation was awakening another unenfranchised element — the women of Galway — to a sense of their own rights:

> I remember to have heard my great-grandfather say that in ancient times, the *daughters* of freemen in Galway were entitled to confer the freedom of the Corporation of Galway upon their husbands. If this be so, Sir, I request to know why I should be restrained from helping to lash the monster who has plundered me of my fortune. I am the daughter of an honest old tradesman of Galway — my poverty and not my will has been the means of obliging me to lead a single life. At first I was not aware of the extent to which I was

defrauded; but now I believe that if my inheritance was not taken away and given to bare-footed gentry of Dunsandle — instead of brooding over my misfortunes, I would be now the mother of a numerous family. Upon inquiry, I find this right is, and has been, from time immemorial, exercised in Bristol. There, a contested election is the certain signal for all the young maids to get married. A freeman there has no occasion for money to portion his daughters ... I hear that these privileges, so delightfully enjoyed by the citizens of Bristol, were conferred by Queen Bess on our Galway lasses. I pray you, Sir, to look to the Charter, and if it be so, only let me be certain of the fact, and no power on earth shall deter me from scourging the cruel monster with my own hands who dares to vindicate the robbery and to uphold the system which dooms the men of Galway to slavery and the women (who like myself have no money) to a life of celibacy ... Be united my boys and I shall have two husbands yet.[24]

The disillusionment in Valentine Blake, the defeat of 1820, the adverse legal rulings, demoralised the Independents and factionalism emerged among them. Responding to an 1823 rumour that 'three or four gentlemen' had offered themselves as Independent candidates, the *Connaught Journal* commented that James Staunton Lambert had displayed a 'willingness to support the intolerant Orange faction, and to throw barriers across the road to Emancipation' and that, while Richard Martin had been a friend to 'the brute creation', his 'county is not indebted to him as yet, for any favour, unless, indeed, it can be called a favour to deprive her of her parliament, and reduce her to the degraded level of a province'.[25]

Valentine Blake was keen to remain the Independent candidate, but he was marginalised, and not toasted, for example, at an August 1823 banquet for Daniel O'Connell. One who was toasted on that occasion was the Earl of Clanricarde, and the Independents devoted considerable energy to courting his support between then and the 1826 general election. The trades too joined in the flattery, presenting an address to the nobleman in January 1824 which hailed him as their 'true patron and deliverer'. According to a report:

On Monday at 2 o'clock, the various guilds of trades assembled at the Square, and marched in procession with a band of music before them playing *All the Way to Galway*, *Patrick's Day*, and other appropriate tunes, and the masters and the wardens with white wands, insignia of the Union of Trades, &c., to Dominick-street, accompanied by an immense crowd.[26]

In Dominick-street, Clanricarde addressed the trades from an open window, returning the compliments and stressing his interest in Galway's prosperity.

The search for a candidate continued until Clanricarde intervened in September 1825 with a letter to the Independents promising to recommend 'a candidate for the town representation who will possess all of the qualifications necessary', and who would 'relieve them from the grievances which now oppress the tradesmen'.[27·] Clanricarde's position in the 1826 general election, however, would disappoint those who had placed their hopes in him.

The general election of 1826 saw a significant intervention by O'Connell's Catholic Association, which detached voters in several county constituencies from their landlords. In Galway, there was strong support for emancipation, but the impression is that it was not effectively marshalled. In February 1825, a meeting of the 'Catholic inhabitants' in the Augustinian Chapel — including, perched in the galleries and organ loft, 'an assemblage of the beauty and fashion of this town and vicinage' — had expressed 'warm confidence in the Catholic Association' and protested against moves to proscribe it. Later in 1825, O'Connell himself was welcomed 'by a large concourse of persons who took the horse from his carriage, which they drew through the principal streets'. Notwithstanding these demonstrations of support for O'Connell's cause, the clergy were slow to collect the 'new Catholic rent' in 1826. In fact, the struggle for the enfranchisement of Catholic tradesmen loomed larger in Galway consciousness than emancipation, the tradesmen's demands being regarded as a component of the broader campaign for Catholic rights. In time, the Catholic Association recognised them to be such.[28]

Certainly, local factors were to the fore in Galway constituencies in 1826, and there was little evidence that the altered political atmosphere nationally had a major impact.[29] There was, however intense excitement in Galway, and several weeks of riotous electoral disorder, during which three men lost their lives.

The riots were sponsored by associates of the gentlemen contestants, but triggered in part by elaborate pre-election intrigues. Because the alliances of major power-brokers had entangled the affairs of town and county, it was townspeople who dominated the disturbances during the closely-fought county election. Feelings ran high also in the town election, and the violent outbreaks which occurred during that contest might have been worse, if it had not been for the overwhelming weight of sentiment on one side.[30]

The principal link between the two constituencies was James Daly. He was a candidate for one of the county seats, and, to secure the votes of the Clanricarde interest, he pledged the corporation's support to the Clanricarde-sponsored Dudley Persse in the town election. Due to internal friction and possibly to depleted resources, there was no Independent candidate as such. But because of Perrse's association with Daly, the Independents threw their weight behind his opponent, James O'Hara, a corporation official recently estranged from James Daly. The trades and the town crowd followed their lead. But it would seem that the wily Daly had anticipated this reaction.

During the election, the crowd was active on behalf of O'Hara: corporation property and officials were attacked; even James Daly himself was assaulted.

More seriously, Persse supporters were prevented from voting, with the result that the candidate received only four votes. The celebrations of the O'Hara victory, however, were overshadowed by the suspicion that his estrangement from James Daly was one of convenience only.[31] But before the suspicions were confirmed, the trades organised the 'chairing' of the victorious candidate through the streets. It was a colourful demonstration, headed by the Claddagh fishermen, 'two and two, preceded by music, dressed in white jackets and velveteen small cloths, their hats decorated by a profusion of flowers'. Following behind were 'neatly-dressed' O'Hara tenants, Corrib boatmen, and the trades with their own banners: tailors, smiths, bakers, carpenters, tanners, shoemakers, slaters, sawyers, nailers, shipwrights, bricklayers and millers.[32]

James Daly's challengers in the county constituency were Richard Martin and James Staunton Lambert. In fact, neither could match Daly, and the actual struggle was between Martin and Lambert for the second seat. Each voter had two votes, but by the time the election was called, Daly had secured one of the two from the landlords of almost all freeholders. The Catholic Association urged voters to support Martin and Lambert, despite the latter's poor record in relation to Catholic claims. This intervention had little effect, there being no indication that tenants defied their landlords. Daly polled more than 6,000 votes out of a maximum possible of about 7,000, while Martin and Lambert employed every imaginable method to secure people's second votes. Martin represented himself as the 'Catholic' candidate, while Catholic Association backing did not save Lambert from being denounced as an ultra-Protestant.[33]

Martin won the second seat but because of the tactics employed and the close outcome, Lambert petitioned the House of Commons to overturn the result. His petition was successful. Before awarding Lambert the seat, the select committee charged with inquiring into the election conducted a thorough examination of witnesses and of relevant documents. Their report, together with the testimony of those involved in the election, is a valuable source of information about Galway's electoral culture in the four decades between the enfranchisement of Catholics and the disfranchisement of the forty shilling freeholders, and merits detailed consideration.

The election lasted 15 days. During this time, 7,000 rural electors arrived in groups to cast their votes in Galway, each group chaperoned by an agent or relative of their landlord. Polling booths were located throughout the town — one booth per barony. Each landlord arranged for the accommodation of his tenantry, while the associates of candidates took care of their entertainment. Innkeeper John Morisey, for example, presented a bill for £159 to Lambert for 'refreshments' enjoyed by his voters during the second week of the election.[34]

From the beginning of the election, so-called 'mobs' roamed the streets. The largest of these, 600 to 800 strong, was the 'town mob'. Witnesses differed as to the loyalties of the town mob, with pro-Martin witnesses indicating that it was interested originally only in the urban election, and the Lambert side that it was controlled by Martin from the beginning.[35] But, having mobilised for

O'Hara, the crowd was hardly likely to stand down while there was still a contest in progress. And given Martin's Independent background and his long association with the town, the town crowd was supportive of him in any case. Whatever about the town mob, it is clear that there were also distinct Martin and Lambert mobs, which were recruited and paid by individuals associated with the candidates. The town mob, as has been already stated, prevented Persse's voters from reaching the booths in the short town election, but Martin and Lambert mobs were also busy from the start. There were demonstrations and attacks on committee rooms and on boarding houses, while rural voters were prevented from reaching the polling booths (and even from entering the town). One witness described Martin's followers:

> It was not exactly a mob such as the meaning of the word generally implies, but it appeared to me it was more a species of guerrilla force, if I may use that term, regularly organised for the purpose of organising freeholders …, all acting in concert and generally under the command of leaders.[36]

Martin's mob included some of his own Iar-Chonnacht tenants. There was also a strong urban element, which included the butchers of the town. A number of urban artisans were employed by Martin's campaign for the so-called 'dressing' of rural votes — equipping them with documentation for voting and for personation, and advising those who did not understand English on how to conduct themselves. It would not be surprising if the same individuals were the leaders of Martin's 'guerrilla force', the members of which, allegedly, were promised '£60 and a farm' for doing their disorderly best. (Incidentally, one of these leaders, linen weaver Michael O'Connor, was cross-examined in London about his fine clothing by a member of the select committee: the neckerchief, the socks and the shoes, he said, were his own; the great coat, the undercoat, the waistcoat and the hat were supplied by political friends.[37]) But, alleged payments and promises to rioters aside, little evidence of bribery was raised before the select committee. There was testimony that Martin freeholders from Rosmuc were promised oatmeal, but for personating absent neighbours rather than for casting their own votes.[38]

The evidence concerning Lambert's mob was contradictory, but it would seem that it did not have a rural element. One prominent supporter, Robert Brown, stated that there was no Lambert mob at all, adding that new MP, James O'Hara, advised him to 'employ mob against mob'. Apart from the niceties involved, Brown considered this would have been 'quite ineffectual', — 'because we could not get any mob to compete with Mr Martin's mob'.[39] As things transpired that proved to be the case, for the Lambertists were soundly trounced in the latter stages of the campaign. But it was also the case that Martin's committee rooms were 'broken' by a Lambert mob at the beginning of the election, a mob led by so-called 'bludgeon men' based in Morisey's inn,

A view of Wood Quay and the bridge around 1820 (Hardiman, *Galway*).

a premises where hospitality was provided for Lambert voters.

The bludgeon men — analogous, perhaps, to Dublin's 'Liberty boys' — were ordinarily Corrib boatmen and were each paid 5s a day for their trouble, and they mobilised the entire Woodquay community, including womenfolk, for rioting. Their auxiliaries were Blake tenants from Menlo, led, allegedly, by two sons of Valentine Blake, himself a Lambert partisan.

Intimidation and a degree of violence were regular features of elections, however, and their extent during the first days of the 1826 county election of, caused little alarm.* 'We could have carried on our own elections very well', declared one witness, 'but being interfered with by the town, we could not'.[40] It is probable that the interference of the urban crowd was sparked by an incident on Sunday evening, 25 June.

No demonstrations were anticipated for Sunday, because it was not a polling day. According to the officer in charge of the police, Major George Warburton:

> Sunday being an idle day, not interfering in any part of the transaction, I thought it right to take the men out a mile or two to bathe and clean themselves, and to get a little fresh air to fit them for the next week; we went off at four and returned at half-past-nine...[41]

At half-past-nine, they were too late. By 8 o'clock, the Martinites — described as a 'mob of rather a better description of persons' — had assembled outside the large thatched house in Eyre Square that was being used to accommodate 200 tenants of John d'Arcy of Clifden. d'Arcy was a cousin of Richard Martin, and it was a cause of irritation in the Martin camp that he switched his support to Lambert. Banners with the slogan 'Martin and O'Hara, and no treachery' expressed the disappointment of this rather exclusive mob, and at the same

---

* Of 19th century elections, Theodore Hoppen remarked that many were 'quiet enough, but the surprised tone in which such news was usually reported reveals that it was the absence rather than the presence of violence which seems to have been thought worthy of comment and explanation' (*Elections*, p.390).

time associated their cause with that of the urban populace. In the course of the demonstration, the windows of the house were smashed and the building set alight. One d'Arcy freeholder was trapped and lost his life.[42]

In the days following, there was continuous tumult, as polling booths were besieged and freeholders terrorised. Then, on the Wednesday evening, a Martin crowd gathered outside Kilroy's Hotel, the Lambert headquarters. Members of a party returning to the hotel took fright and opened fire. Among them was the candidate's brother, Thomas Lambert, who shot and killed a young father of three, Jeremiah O'Sullivan. Thomas Lambert was arrested, but he was subsequently acquitted of murder on the grounds that he had acted in self-defence. The pro-Martin *Connaught Journal* commented:

> Heaven knows it had been more reasonable for gentlemen to remain in their hotels, than to intermix with those with whom they are not favourites, and to take from them and their little families that which God alone can give.[43]

Dennis O'Sullivan of Eyre Square, a brother of the dead man, who was present on the evening of the killing, was a witness before the select committee in London. He stated that he was employed by Martin as a poll clerk, and it would seem that he was a rioter also, for he was charged with setting fire to the d'Arcy accommodation. He further stated that he had accepted half-crowns on several occasions from John Blake of Menlo Castle to bludgeon for Lambert, but without any intention of delivering on his side of the bargain. In relation to the election rioting, O'Sullivan testified that the mobs, numbering about 300 each, were evenly matched until the killing of his brother, but that after this incident, 'the whole town got in an uproar against Mr Lambert'.[44] (Nor did the subsequent killing of a butcher by a policeman help to mollify the people.) O'Sullivan was partisan, and his assertion that the intimidation in favour of Martin towards the end of the election was spontaneous, bolstered his employer's case. But there is other evidence that it was after O'Sullivan's death that the crowd took control of the streets. It was an element of Lambert's case before the select committee that he was leading the poll until the later stages, and that it was from this point that the intimidation of his voters — together with large-scale personation — enabled Martin to take a narrow lead. The town crowd were decisive in both respects. They blocked access to polling booths for those baronies where Lambert was strong, and they intimidated those who might challenge multiple voters.

Major George Warburton blamed 'the constituted authorities' for the uncontrolled rioting, in this instance the county high sheriff and the town magistrates, without whose authority the 200 police in the town, the 400 soldiers, and the troop of 30 hussars could not be deployed. It was Warburton's opinion that the force of police, by itself, was not sufficient to have controlled the crowd, but that with the assistance of troops, it might easily have done so.

There were several reasons, he implied, for the failure of the authorities to act as they should have done, including incompetence, favouritism towards Richard Martin, and jurisdictional jealousies.

The evidence was overwhelmingly in Lambert's favour, and the select committee did not hesitate to award him the seat. For Richard Martin, it was a humiliating end to a long political career. Having lost parliamentary immunity from his creditors, he spent the remaining seven years of his life in Boulogne.[45]

The parliament of 1826-30 — dissolved at the death of George IV — witnessed the climax of the great popular movement that won Catholic Emancipation. However, local affairs loomed larger in Galway, and the period saw a number of developments specific to the town. The corporation was deprived of its toll revenues by a November 1828 ruling, greatly undermined its authority, while the Galway Harbour and Canal Act of 1830 set up a new elected board.

Between 1826 and 1830, James O'Hara MP tried to show that he was independent of James Daly. By articulating the popular view on artisan enfranchisement, and through his association with the harbour legislation, O'Hara won over some Independents, but the extent of his own independence remained suspect. For the trades, O'Hara's deviousness was illustrated by the way he went about delivering on his promise to enfranchise them. As recorder of the town, he had ordered the town clerk to enrol all guild members as freemen, but he resigned the recordership before the order was carried out. The new recorder — O'Hara'a own father — let the matter sit.[46]

Valentine Blake's efforts on behalf of the trades were more persuasive. It was he who authored the Galway Enfranchisement Bill, introduced late in 1829 by Thomas Spring Rice, MP for Limerick and a champion of the Limerick trades. Having been outflanked by his rival, James O'Hara declared himself a supporter of the measure, which successfully passed through the Commons. However, James Daly had it sabotaged in the Lords by means of an amendment annulling the 1717 Galway Act, thereby disenfranchising both Protestant and Catholic artisans. The King died before signing the bill into law, but this did not save Daly from opprobrium. His opposition to Catholic emancipation had antagonised many in the county; his subversion of the Galway Enfranchisement Bill deepened the antagonism. As a result, he lost his county seat in 1830. The outgoing Lambert was returned, and Daly was replaced by Sir John Burke, uncle of Clanricarde. One great landed interest was, therefore, replaced by another. Daly unsuccessfully petitioned the House of Commons to overturn the result, on the grounds that a Catholic mob had prevented his voters reaching the polling booths.[47]

If the 1830 election was less exciting than the preceding one, this was largely due to the post-Emancipation disfranchisement of forty-shilling freeholders. The poll was only 17% of the 1826 poll. The Reform Act somewhat restored the county electorate, however, and the 1832 poll was 34% of the 1826.[48]

Valentine Blake's identification with the original Galway Enfranchisement

Bill, meanwhile, won him political kudos. In March 1830, he was made a freeman of the bakers' the shoemakers', the broguemakers' and the sawyers' guilds,[49] and entered the town election against the sitting O'Hara as the popular champion and as the favourite of Daniel O'Connell. A witness described the scenes which followed the nomination procedure in the Town Hall:

> The friends of Mr O'Hara, in a close and compact body, then proceeded from the Court-house towards his Committee-room in Back-street, having occasionally met with slight interruption from the vast concourse of the lower orders and the tenantry of Mr Blake. We witnessed at the onset every manifestation to riot and tumult, but these infatuated and misguided people did not proceed to open violence and hostility until they got into Abbeygate-street, when they simultaneously commenced the attack and assailed, without provocation, Mr O'Hara and his numerous friends in the most infuriated and brutal manner, almost every one of the combatants having been provided with the most desperate bludgeons, calculated to kill and maim their unoffending victims.[50]

Popular feeling may have been on the side of Blake but, from the evidence of 1826, it seems unlikely that the crowd's behaviour was spontaneous. Blake's bludgeon-men and their followers were following a preconceived strategy. Over the four days of the election, the disturbances were such that O'Hara's associates, 'in defence of their lives and persons', felt 'constrained to arm themselves'. On this occasion, the authorities zealously protected voters, and the streets were constantly patrolled by detachments with fixed bayonets. Thus, according to the *Connaught Journal,* 'plans for intimidation' were frustrated, and voters were enabled to reach the polling booth.[51] And rumour notwithstanding, O'Hara did not need to convey non-resident freemen from Loughrea to win by 381 votes to 306. Prominent Catholics, evidently, including priests, ignored O'Connell's advice, and voted against Blake.[52]

The Reform crisis brought the 1830 parliament to an early end, and fresh elections were held in April 1831. Neither O'Hara nor Blake entered the contest for the town, and two new candidates, Andrew Lynch and John Bodkin, came forward. However, when Blake declared for Bodkin, Lynch withdrew and there was no contest. Bodkin was duly 'chaired through several of our streets by an immense crowd of *the People* as the 'bells of St Nicholas pealed merrily at intervals'. For the county, James Daly declined to enter the race, and the outgoing Burke and Lambert were likewise returned unopposed.

1832-*c.*1850

The Galway Enfranchisement Bill was reintroduced early in the following parliament, and passed into law. After two decades of struggle, Galway's Catholic artisans could finally vote. But no sooner had the right been won than it was threatened by the Irish Reform bill of 1832. O'Connell intervened, however, with a clause protecting borough freemen.[53] Two significant provisions affecting the Galway borough constituency remained: non-resident freemen were excluded, and the second parliamentary seat was restored.

The post-1832 arrangements, whereby resident tradesmen were automatically entitled to freedom by virtue of their calling, were 'peculiar to the town of Galway', according to one parliamentary enquiry. Exceptionally, the status could not be transmitted by either birth or marriage — despite the hopes of women such as Moll Doyle. Conformity with the spirit of the charter and the statute demanded that the free artisan be in good standing with the guild of his occupation, and the Municipal Corporations Commissioners reported in 1835 that 'companies of trades' established under 17th and early 18th century charters were still 'kept up' in the town.[54] But, given that they were dominated by Catholics, it seems likely that these guilds were only two decades old, and that they owed their existence to the researches of early 19th century lawyers, seeking to enfranchise a portion of the Galway Independents' constituency.

The formation of a Galway Trades Political Union in November 1831 reflected the sense of anticipation among Galway tradesmen. Befitting the respectability of its recently-emancipated members, the Union's first resolution was to enter into communication with Daniel O'Connell, 'for the purpose of procuring from him such instructions as may enable us to carry out the proceedings of our Body, without violating the existing laws of the Realm'. The political purpose of the fawning resolution was to distance Galway tradesmen from the Dublin Trades Political Union, which had been reprimanded by O'Connell for taking a hardline position in favour of Repeal. There is no record of O'Connell's reply, but there are indications of an early split, with the formation of the Valentine Blake-supporting Galway Liberal Trades Club, a body denounced by the leadership of the Trades Political Union.[55]

The number of voters that these organisations sought to influence was substantial. 688 artisans were made freemen of Galway in September 1832, roughly a third of the electorate in the December 1832 general election.

Three candidates presented themselves, all as Repealers. Townsmen Andrew Lynch and Lachlann MacLachlann were elected with the support of the trades but, on petition, the latter was unseated in favour of the third-placed candidate, Catholic landlord, Martin J. Blake. Blake, who sat for the constituency until 1857, later admitted spending £5,000 on the election (half of it on the petition), and remembered it as 'the most expensive' election of his career. Extensive 'bribing and treating', he said, were the principal causes of the great expense, but corruption, in this instance, was not the cause of MacLachlann's removal. Rather, it was the disqualification of the 688 new freemen that gave the seat to Blake. It was a technical disqualification — six months had not elapsed between the granting of the freedom and the election — and it would not affect the future rights of the men concerned.[56]

If the town was solid for Repeal, things were otherwise in the county. James

GALWAY REFORM ASSOCIATION.

The Members of this PATRIOTIC SOCIETY (comprising the Trades of Galway, and a great Majority of other ELECTORS) are requested to meet

This Morning at Ten o'Clock,

ON THE

GREAT SPACE,

OPPOSITE TO THE ASSOCIATION ROOMS, Eyre Square,

For the purpose of Exhibiting the Power of Moral Opinion in Opposition to

Tory Despotism, Tithes, and Corporation Monopoly.

From thence to march in Procession to the Court House.---Our Motto is

Blake and Lynch,

Reform all Public Abuses.

NO TORY, NO TITHES, NO BLOOD, NO CORPORATIONIST.

Signed on behalf of the Galway Reform Association,

DOMINICK DOYLE, Secretary.

Poster for election meeting, 1835 (courtesy of NAI).

Daly was returned for the last time in 1832, alongside Thomas Martin, son of Richard, who would represent County Galway until his death in 1847. Daly stood as a Conservative, and Martin as a Liberal, but they co-operated against the outgoing Liberal uncle of Clanricarde, Sir John Burke, and the Conservative, Colonel Blake, to take the seats. The victors engaged in widespread 'treating', and it was reported that James Daly appointed agents 'solely for the purpose of giving orders for drink'. 'Booth agents have long been known at elections,' commented the *Connaught Journal,* 'but the merit of introducing *Boozing* agents must, we think, be yielded to Mr Daly'.[57] Daly was a late withdrawal in 1835, by which time O'Connell's forces were better organised. Branches of the Anti-Tory Association — broadening the political base of O'Connell's alliance with the Whigs and providing ideological justification for it — were established throughout Galway in the months before the election, and the Liberal candidates, Thomas Martin, and John J. Bodkin, were welcomed into the anti-Tory fold. Their Conservative opponent, John d'Arcy of Clifden, polled only 12 votes in a low-key contest. After 1835, there was no contested county election until 1857, by which time the rules governing the location of polling stations had been reformed. The 1835 contest, therefore, was the last county election to be held entirely in the town.[58]

The trades were reconciled with Martin J. Blake before the 1835 election. By resolution of the shoemakers guild, for example, both he and the outgoing Lynch were deemed 'fit and proper representatives', mainly on the grounds that they had the approval of O'Connell. And the mood in favour of unity among the popular forces in the town was strong enough to force the withdrawal of Valentine Blake. Reflecting 'anti-Tory' feelings also was a so-called Galway Reform Association — 'comprising the Trades of Galway and a great majority of other Electors' — which in the course of the election, printed a placard denouncing 'Tory Despotism, Tithes, and Corporation Monopoly'.[59] The roles of Tory despot and corporation monopolist were combined in the person of Conservative candidate, Denis Daly, son of James. National issues, in this instance, had a strong local resonance. Something of the political atmosphere — especially its strongly sectarian aspect — was expressed in an election ballad entitled 'Martin Blake and Ireland for ever':

> *Since Luther deserted, like slaves we're kept under*
> *Till the man of the people our chains rent asunder*
> *And the true sons of Grannia once more are in clover*
> *And the Boyne water bloodhounds are fairly done o'er...*
> *The vengeance of Heaven I am sure will prevail*
> *On any apostate that will turn tail*
> *To join those priest hunters who are sworn to grind you*
> *So vote for Martin Blake and Sheela na Guire.*[60]

Buoyed by such sentiments, Blake and Lynch were returned. The 1835 election, as things turned out, marked the end of the Daly dynasty in Galway parliamentary politics.

Valentine Blake still retained political ambitions, and his opportunity came in 1838 when Andrew Lynch was obliged to fight a by-election on being appointed a master in chancery. At the announcement of the vacancy, the trades issued a proclamation denouncing Lynch's relationship with the government and calling on Valentine Blake to enter the fray:

We who are electors of the town … do, in the face of the United Empire, protest against any servant of the Crown representing us in parliament, and do denounce the policy of any man, or set of men, who, from sinister motives, would propose, support, or encourage any individual to sport with the independence of our town. For although we admit that the present Government is *comparatively speaking,* the best for Ireland that has ever been … we think it more wise to be represented by a man who will pledge himself, and can pledge himself to support the people … Wherefore, we call on, invite, and beseech Sir Valentine Blake of Menlo Castle, to come forward and stand for the town, he having the highest claim on our support.[61]

There was then formed a Galway Enfranchisement Association, to 'which the tradesmen in general were admitted'. The Association defended the earlier statement, and adopted a number of resolutions:

That as Mr Lynch, whose services we admit, has been returned for the third time to Parliament, and has now been favoured with a situation returning him three thousand pounds per annum, we feel ourselves bound in gratitude and justice not to forget the services of Sir Valentine Blake, who has been up to the present period without his reward … That Sir Valentine Blake, Bart., Deputy Lieutenant, is entitled to our gratitude for the vast services he has rendered to the town of Galway …[62]

Little gratitude towards Valentine Blake was revealed at the polling booths, and Lynch won comfortably. Eventually, after a gap of 21 years, Blake was returned for his third parliamentary term in the uncontested election of 1841. He held the seat at his death in 1847.[63]

The precise role of tradesmen in the nomination of Blake in 1838 was a matter of controversy. Stung by the accusation that they stood to gain financially from a contest, the Galway Enfranchisement Association posted a placard to 'repudiate the calumny which would say that the sole object of the tradesmen is to provoke a contest for their own benefit…' In the few years since their enfranchisement, the trades had declared their high principles through a variety of *ad hoc* groupings, but evidently there was a widely-held view that many of the new voters were already corrupt in 1838. This would remain a matter of speculation until 1857, when the existence of an organised system of bribery, and of electoral abuse generally, was confirmed by a commission of inquiry. It was the opinion of the commissioners that this state of affairs had existed since 1832, although they were precluded by the terms of their appointment from conducting detailed inquiries into the pre-1847 period.[64]

The availability of electoral 'inducements' to freemen was by no means peculiar to Galway. Freemen, generally, were the poorest voters in borough constituencies, and vote-buying was easily-organised before the Secret Ballot Act of 1872. Peculiar to the constituency, however, was the electoral weight of this element, and the fact that it was composed entirely of Catholic tradesmen. The tradesmen voters formed a third of the electorate in 1832 and there were times during the following decades when they formed a majority.[65] This was partly due to the particular mechanism employed to enfranchise them, and partly to the liberal regime operated by the responsible officials.

Patrick Mark Lynch — a 'merchant of respectability with landed property in the county of the town' — was the official charged with the admission of freemen after the abolition of the corporation. Describing his *modus operandi*, he stated that whenever a 'reasonable number' of applications for freedom reached his desk, he called a special court, giving notice in the local newspapers and by handbill. Sometimes from personal knowledge, sometimes from consultation with 'competent persons', and sometimes from the appearance of the individual, he decided whether any claim should be allowed. But most frequently, he relied on the opinion of those in the court. This was the best indicator of the status of the applicant, since 'tradesmen are unwilling to share their privileges with unqualified persons'. It was noted, moreover, that Lynch — and evidently the tradesmen who attended his court — did not insist that a freeman should have served an apprenticeship to his trade.

The achievement of freeman status was the first of a two-stage process in gaining the right to vote. The next, registration by the Assistant Barrister, was usually automatic, but on one notable occasion that official rejected 396 Claddagh fishermen who, on the advice of the Crown's law officers, had been judged artisans by Patrick Mark Lynch.[66] The Assistant Barrister's decision, in this instance, was not controversial, for this extension of democracy was not welcomed by some of the most ostensibly democratic elements in the town. As far as the *Galway Vindicator* was concerned, it was all a Tory plot:

> The people of the Claddagh and other suburban districts were supposed to possess less political information, less combined energy, and less means of resisting the control of aristocratic influences. To crush the political power of the town, it seemed desirable to the Tory party to throw open, by some means, the franchise to the suburban districts — hence their support of the claims of fishermen, of gardeners, and other such persons, not strictly coming under the designation — and hence the opposition offered by the *bona fide* tradesmen to the admission of the former.[67]

The vaunted independence of the '*bona fide* tradesmen' was compromised, but it is noteworthy that more odium was heaped upon the relatively poor tradesmen for accepting payment for their votes, than upon the relatively wealthy individuals who provided the payments. Indeed, it was the liberality of the latter that had so corrupted Galway politics that an accusation that 'the sole object of the tradesmen is to provoke a contest' was credible in 1838.

1. *Galway Vindicator*, 21 June 1843.
2. Charles Lever, *Charles O'Malley*, pp. 47-48.
3. ibid., p. 27.
4. See, for example, *Galway Express,* 14 November 1885; *Galway Observer,* 16 November 1901.
5. Hardiman, *Galway*, p. 190n.
6. Peter Jupp, 'Urban Politics in Ireland' in Harkness & O'Dowd, eds, *The Town in Ireland*. Belfast 1981, pp. 103-04; Thomas Murtagh, 'Power and Politics in Galway, 1770-1830, unpublished M.A. thesis, UCG 1982, pp. 152, 212-14.
7. ibid., pp. 91-97; Thomas Bartlett, 'A Galway Election Squib of 1783, in *JGAHS* 37, 1979-80, pp. 85-89.
8. Jupp, 'Urban Politics', pp. 104-11.
9. Murtagh, 'Power and Politics, pp. 152-55;
10. See Rev. Patrick K. Egan, 'Progress and Suppression of the United Irishmen in the Western Counties, 1798-99' in *JGAHS* 25, *1953-54,* pp. 104-34, and P.M. Hogan, 'Civil Unrest in the Province of Connacht, 1793-98, unpublished M.Ed. thesis (minor), UCG 1976, passim.
11. Hardiman, *Galway*, p. 191; J. Connolly, *The Galviad*, Galway 1825, pp. 3-4; National Archives, State of the Country Papers, 1817, 1833/3; 1823, 2501/30.
12. National Archives, Rebellion Papers, 620/7/74/17 and 620/9/96/21; Egan, 'Progress', pp. 126; (John Cunningham &) Seán Mac Giollarnáth, 'Frank Ó Ciardhubháin as Cluain Lionnáin' in *Béaloideas* 17, nos. i & ii, 1947; pp. 116-18; Martin Cunningham, 'Dabhach Cuana' in *Kilcoona Grapevine,* Kilcoona 1997, p. 24.
13. Bartlett, 'Election squib'; *Connaught Journal,* 2, 9, 16, 19 November, 1795.
14. Murtagh, 'Power', pp. 155-56.
15. ibid., pp. 157-59.
16. ibid., pp. 160-61.
17. See Jacqueline Hill, 'Corporatist Ideology and Practice in Ireland', in S.J. Connolly, ed., *Political Ideas in Eighteenth Century Ireland,* Dublin 2000, pp. 64-82, and K. Theodore Hoppen's *Elections, Politics and Society in Ireland, 1832-1885,* Oxford 1984, pp. 86-88, 436-46.
18. *Reports from the Commissioners on Municipal Corporations in Ireland,* 1835 xxvii, pp. 318-21; Murtagh, 'Power', pp. 162, 167-68.
19. Hardiman Library, NUI, Galway, Galway Corporation Papers, 'Names of trademen who were sworn in before Mr Blake in the Year 1828'.
20. The text of the resolution passed at a meeting chaired by Martin J. Blake of Ballyglunin (future M.P. for the town) was published in the *Connaught Journal,* 1 February 1819 and again on 23 October 1823: 'That we have at the request of Valentine Blake, Esq., our representative in Parliament, investigated his conduct at the last general election and subsequently, and we are decidedly of the opinion that he has not in any manner, surrendered or compromised the rights of the inhabitants of the town and county of the town of Galway'. See also letters from Valentine Blake, *Connaught Journal,* 8 September, 2 October 1823.
21. *Municipal Corporations Commissioners*, 1835, p. 322.
22. *Connaught Journal,* 20 November 1823.
23. *Municipal Corporations Commissioners*, 1835, p. 323.
24. *Connaught Journal,* 20 February 1823.
25. ibid., 16 August 1824; 8 September 1823.
26. ibid., 22 January 1824.
27. ibid., 15 September 1825.
28. Oliver McDonagh, *O'Connell: the Life of Daniel O'Connell, 1775-1847,* London 1991, pp. 222-31; *Connaught Journal,* 17 February, 4 August 1825, 10 August 1826; James Kelly, 'The Politics of "Protestant Ascendancy": County Galway, 1650-1832' in Moran's *Galway: History & Society,* Dublin 1996, p. 262-63.
29. *Connaught Journal,* 17 February, 4 August 1825, 10 August 1826; Murtagh, 'Power', pp. 106-09.
30. Kelly, 'Politics', p. 262.
31. Murtagh, 'Power', pp. 169-73.
32. *Connaught Journal,* 10 July 1826.
33. Kelly, 'Protestant Ascendancy', p. 261; *Report from the Select Committee on the Galway Election. together with the Special Report from the said Committee, and also the Minutes of Evidence taken before them,* 1826-27, iv, p. 15. A total of 13, 641 votes were cast in the election: 6,206 for Daly; 3,719 for Martin; 3,635 for Lambert. 81 votes went to the Martin-supporting John Kirwan of Castlehackett, who sought to boost the chances of his favourite by entering the election himself towards the end of polling. Since each voter was entitled to vote for two candidates, there were rather more than 6,820 voters.

34. *1826 Election Petition*, pp. 15-16, 56-57, 108-09, 116-18.
35. ibid., p. 35.
36. ibid., p. 23.
37. ibid., p. 48.
38. ibid.
39. ibid., pp. 25, 31.
40. ibid., p. 36.
41. ibid., p. 37.
42. National Archives, State of the Country Papers, 1826, 2766/4.
43. *Connaught Journal,* 29 June 1826.
44. *1826 Election Petition,* p. 105.
45. Lynam, *Humanity Dick,* pp. 265-83.
46. *Connaught Journal,* 15 December 1828.
47. Kelly, 'Politics', p. 263.
48. Brian M. Walker, *Parliamentary Election Results in Ireland, 1801-1922,* Dublin 1978, pp. 218-19, 283. There were 13,641 votes cast in 1826, 2,337 in 1830, and 4,662 in 1832; each voter had two votes, but not everybody used both of them.
49. ibid., 22, 29 March 1830.
50. *Connaught Journal,* 2 August 1830.
51. ibid., 5 August 1830.
52. ibid., 12 August 1830.
53. Hoppen, *Elections,* pp. 3-4.
54. *Municipal Corporations' Commissioners,* 1835 xxvii, p. 319; *Report of the Commissioners Appointed to Investigate into the Existence of Corrupt Practices in Elections of Members to Serve in Parliament for the County of the Town of Galway,* 1857-58 xxvi, pp. vi-viii.
55. *Connaught Journal,* 21 November 1831, 3 December 1832; Emmet O'Connor, *A Labour History of Ireland, 1824-1860,* Dublin 1992, pp. 20-25; Fergus d'Arcy, 'The Artisans of Dublin and Daniel O'Connell: an Unquiet Liaison', in *Irish Historical Studies,* xvii, pp. 221-43; McDonagh, *O'Connell,* pp. 340.
56. *Municipal Corporations' Commissioners,* p. 320; *Corrupt Practices Commissioners,* 1857-58, p. viii.
57. *Connaught Journal,* 6 November 1834.
58. ibid, 11 December 1834, 22 January 1835; Walker, *Election Results,* Dublin 1978, pp. 283.
59. *Connaught Journal.*
60. ibid. There were similar sentiments in a number of other contemporary ballads cited by Gearóid Ó Tuathaigh in 'Gaelic Ireland, Popular Politics, and Daniel O'Connell', *JGAHS,* vol. 34, 1974-75, pp. 30-31.
61. National Archives, Outrage reports, 1838, 11/39.
62. ibid.
63. Walker, *Elections,* p. 282.
64. National Archives, Outrage reports, 1838, 11/39; *Corrupt Practices Commissioners,* 1857-58, pp. viii-ix.
65. Hoppen, *Elections,* pp. 75-77, 436-56.
66. *Corrupt Pracrices Commissioners,* pp. 3-4.
67. *Galway Vindicator,* 30 October 1841. Generally, however, it would appear that Liberals were more inclined than Conservatives to support the admission to the franchise of the doubtfully qualified (Hoppen, *Elections,* pp. 9-10).

CHAPTER 6

'...our children starving and staring us in the face'

FAMINE, 1846-49

Is a Johnny Seoighe tuig mo ghlór
Is mé ag teacht le dóchas faoi do dhéin
Mar is tú an réalt eolais is breátha glóir
Ós mo chomhair ag teampail Dé
Is tú bláth na hóige is gile lóchrann
A dhearc mo shúil ó rugadh mé
Is as ucht Chríost tabhair dom relief
Nó go gcaitear oíche Nollaig féin.
'Johnny Seoighe', traditional song from Carna, Co. Galway.*

That the rural dimension of the Famine crisis has dominated historical studies is not surprising. After all, 80% of the Irish population was rural and the immediate cause of distress was potato failure. But the famine had important urban aspects; townspeople suffered great distress; towns attracted the indigent from the countryside; towns were centres for the administration of relief; towns were embarkation points for those fleeing the island.[1]

Potato blight was first reported in Ireland in early September 1845. Already, there was apprehension at reports of potato failure elsewhere in Europe. Ireland, however, was more vulnerable than other countries — three million of her people were totally dependent on the root for their food. While townspeople were less dependent on potatoes than the rural poor, any scarcity of the staple could only force up the cost of foodstuffs generally.

It was not until October, when the main crop was harvested, that the extent of the problem became clear. Early reports indicated that half the crop might be lost. Throughout Ireland, representative bodies expressed alarm about the threatened crisis, most notably the Mansion House Committee, formed in Dublin at the end of October to protest at apparent government inaction.[2]

---

* One translation reads: 'Oh Johnny Seoighe, heed my voice, / As I come to you full of hope, / For you are the star of knowledge, the brightest beacon /My eye has encountered in the House of God./ You are the flower of youth of the finest talk /That my eye has seen since I was born, / For the love of Christ, grant me relief /At least until Christmas Eve is over (*Between the Jigs and the Reels* programme, Town Hall Theatre, Galway, Summer 1997).

In Galway, public bodies expressed the same type of alarm expressed by equivalent bodies elsewhere. When a memorial, sent in late October, elicited no response from the Lords of the Treasury, the Galway town commissioners assumed that their missive had 'miscarried', so they asked their former M.P., A.H. Lynch — a 'respectable gentleman' residing in London — to present the memorial in person. The requests of the memorialists were typical of many then arriving in London: the stopping of distillation; the banning of provisions' export from Ireland; the opening of Irish ports to foreign produce.[3]

The administration was already preoccupied with the blight. Police throughout the country were instructed in mid-September to collect data on the extent of crop failure. Within weeks, the scale of losses was apparent and the Prime Minister, Robert Peel, appointed a Scientific Commission to investigate the blight's causes and to suggest how to deal with it. Unfortunately, neither its diagnoses nor its remedies proved useful.

In formulating his response, Peel — a former Irish Chief Secretary — had the experience of previous Irish subsistence crises to draw upon. Although the new poor law system was operative — Galway's Workhouse had opened in 1842 — the system was aimed at 'ordinary' distress and was not deemed capable of relieving people on the scale anticipated.

Following precedent, Peel decided that relief works should be initiated in distressed areas to enable people to buy food. It was believed that providing earning opportunities was less demoralising to poor people than doling out free supplies. A special commission was established to oversee the administration of relief measures, with a network of subordinate local relief committees to address distress in their own areas. Local committees, it was felt, would better direct aid where it was needed, and be more adept than public officials at preventing fraud. But, so that central expenditure might be minimised and voluntary effort stimulated, schemes were to begin only when the crisis became acute.

Of importance also was the consideration that food prices be kept stable during the period of want. To this end, a quantity of maize was purchased secretly by the government to be released onto the market when prices became too high.[4]

Phase I: 'Up Galwaymen, at them!'

The demand that food exports be prohibited — now being raised by committees of the respectable — had a resonance among Galway's poor. Food rioters, after all, had threatened to burn export-bearing ships during previous crises.

According to a persistent rumour of early November, a dramatic initiative on the part of the 'humbler classes' was imminent. And, in the middle of that month, the resident magistrate was advised of a threat to four ships loading with corn for Liverpool and London. He approached the Dominican friars to ask for help. Having established that they had been approached by 'emissaries from the town' to prevent ships from sailing, Fr Folan warned the fishermen of the 'inevitable consequences' of such piracy and persuaded them not to get involved. The priest's advice was similar to that being offered by his colleagues elsewhere.[5]

Merchants, however, remained worried about their cornstores. They feared a 'sudden rising of the mob' and lobbied the authorities to send additional military force. All that stood between potential rioters and the food, they pointed out, were twenty-eight policemen and sixty soldiers. Agreeing with the merchants, one magistrate estimated that 500 extra troops were required to 'aid the civic authority in the event of rioting by a town mob of several thousand' which might ally itself with the estimated 1,500 seamen of the Claddagh.[6] Rumour continued to disturb the town. Following representations from 'the Trades and other respectable inhabitants' a public meeting was called for 1 pm on Thursday, 20 November.[7]

The meeting — held in the Courthouse and chaired by the High Sheriff — took place in an atmosphere of tremendous excitement and was 'densely crowded, especially with the humbler classes'. The main speaker was Fr B. J. Roche, who proposed a series of resolutions. Urging that there be no breaches of the peace, he reiterated the necessity of ceasing food exports, praised those 'prudent and humane landlords' who were encouraging tenants to retain their grain unthreshed, stressed the need for a programme of public works, and called for the establishment of food depots. A committee of twenty-one was formed to monitor the situation, and it was suggested that Fr Roche's resolutions should be reformulated as a deferential address to the Queen.

The proceedings failed to pacify the people. When a town commissioner emphasised the necessity of government intervention, he was shouted down. A heckler summed up the popular mood: 'We don't care about the government, but we must keep the corn at home'. Others asserted that it was preferable to die fighting to retain food in the town, rather than to die later of starvation. Seeing that the meeting was having the opposite effect to that intended, the organisers hurriedly put the resolutions to the assembly. Fr Roche urged the people 'not to give way to angry feelings'; Fr George Commons did the same in the Irish language. With the people 'still labouring under the greatest excitement', the meeting dispersed. The entire proceedings had taken just over half an hour.[8]

The local press continued to monitor the potato crop. City fathers, meanwhile, exploited the anticipated crisis to expedite a number of infrastructural projects in the region. Particular attention was paid to the employment potential of a Corrib/Mask drainage and navigation scheme. Town commissioners and MPs lobbied Board of Works and government to press ahead with the project.[9]

Food prices continued to spiral, the *Galway Mercury* reporting in March that potatoes 'can't be secured, even at exorbitant prices'. Popular anxiety found expression in 'Rockite' notices and anonymous letters. Demanding that town commissioners stop food exports, one threatened: 'in spite of priests and bishops that we will break and smash all the cellars in the town and rob and steal both day and night, hour and minute that we can'.[10] Another, headed 'Food! Food Food', appealed sardonically to the author's 'Fellow townsmen':

> We have been supplied, thanks be to government, with a quantity of food until next harvest. What, think is it bullets, bayonets and sabres washed down with hot steam. O Lord, did anyone hear of such nourishment, nearly as good as the Cantbridge gally grass and seaweed. We will not stand it if twice the number of troops come to town for to see our children starving and staring us in the face. It is better to die by the sword than to die of starvation. Up Galwaymen, at them.[11]

There were no serious outbreaks, yet magistrates remained concerned. Late in January, John Kernan, R.M. protested at the withdrawal of the admiralty steamer, warning that '… in consequence of the present state of things … it will take a very large military force to keep the Galway people in order'. Citing the wisdom of his predecessor, one Jones, who had 'experience of the mob in many places, but never has he had to contend with such a mob as the mob of Galway', Kernan pleaded that the imminent 'evil' could only be 'warded off by giving employment to the people. 'Otherwise', he went on, 'place in the hands of magistrates such a force as will overcome the mob'.[12]

The return of the admiralty steamer and the arrival of two regiments placated Kernan. He reported in February that the town was 'perfectly quiet' despite the provocative presence of eleven ships 'taking in large cargoes of corn for the English market'. In April, however, magistrates sought further reinforcements. There were fears also that the locally-raised 88th regiment — the Connaught Rangers — might not be reliable in a confrontation with the citizenry, and they were removed from the town. Fairly specific intelligence from a Catholic clergyman that there was a plan to 'storm the town of Galway with a view to plunder' — starting with the Comerford's stores — led to requests for the provision of a force of cavalry. These were refused by the military authorities.[13]

Phase II: Let them eat pop-corn

Parliament passed several statutes in March 1846 providing the framework for relief schemes. Because it was labour-intensive, road-building would be the principal expedient: Board of Works schemes were repayable by grand jury cess-payers; other schemes could be undertaken by grand juries themselves, with government bearing half the cost. In Galway in late February, magistrates had held a cess-payers' meeting to consider works schemes. Weeks later, a Galway Relief Committee was formed. Chaired by John Ireland, the committee took responsibility for the town and the county of the town.[14]

Meanwhile, the Galway master tailors and Messrs Rush & Palmer, flour millers, responded with wage increases to their employees' insistence that they could no longer afford to buy food. The latter firm also announced that it had imported a cargo of 'superior oats' from Russia with a view to reducing local market prices.[15]

The relief committee considered proposals for public works schemes, lobbied Board of Works and Drainage Commissioners to have them carried out, and sent circulars to 137 of the 'nobility, gentry, merchants' seeking the local contributions which were required to attract matching funds from the government. The committee itself was lobbied by the Mechanics' Institute to alleviate the 'alarming state of the mechanics and the labouring population'.[16] According to one observer:

> masons, slaters, stone-cutters and carpenters are to be seen every moment in the streets wandering about in batches, while hundreds of the labouring classes have no better occupation than standing with their backs to the walls communing with each other on their afflictions.[17]

A London *Morning Chronicle* correspondent estimated that a quarter of the town's population was in a state of absolute pauperism, 'either reduced to that condition by the present disease of the potato, or such is their normal state':

> Galway, the capital of the west of Ireland, seems to be pre-eminently the city of the poor. Huts and hovels and mean dwellings are not here, as elsewhere, mere *addenda*, the flying of the poor for relief and refuge to the habitations of the rich — they are the town itself'.[18]

One task facing the relief committee was the distribution of the maize or Indian corn, which arrived from the government stores in April. In establishing a depot to receive and sell the corn, the agent of the Commissariat was assisted by four representatives of the committee. Already, the local press was advising the poor of how to prepare the novel food, and recipes for a variety of dishes were published. Most of these, it should be said, required resources unavailable in the typical proletarian household. Detailed instructions for the preparation of Mush, Suppawn and Hasty Pudding, Hominy, Graham Bread and Johnny Cake — dishes from the American slave dietary — were copied from official circulars. Included also was the aboriginal American method 'on which the Indians will travel long journeys without fatigue' — the corn should be 'dropped on a hot frying pan or hot stones, when it bursts and becomes beautifully white'.[19]

When the maize was finally made available for sale in the courthouse in late April, crowds thronged to buy it. Obliged to charge the cost price, but finding that many could not afford this 'excellent and palatable food', the committee reduced the price. A provisions committee of the town commissioners, meanwhile, attempted to curb speculation by buying potatoes for re-sale in the market. These measures had a prompt effect. Grain prices fell and 'forestallers' released their stores of potatoes, bringing a significant reduction in their cost also.[20]

As well as purchasing maize from the government, the relief committee bought meal from local merchants. However, there were regular consumer complaints about the fare supplied. Much of it was mouldy; oatmeal, allegedly, was diluted with barley; wholemeal was 'nearly all bran'. On investigation, members of the committee and 'experts' disagreed about the quality of samples.[21]

The committee's work was hampered also by lack of funds. When subscriptions to the initial appeal to local notables dried up, it was decided to call on non-subscribers. There was anger when some of these refused outright and others undertook only to 'consider the matter'. On the advice of the Relief Commissioners, it was decided to publish a list of donors in order to embarrass

> men of extensive property in the town and County of the town [who], with few, very few exceptions, indeed, have most shamefully failed in contributing as liberally as they ought to have done to relieve the necessities of the people — some of them have not subscribed at all.[22]

Local contributions totaling £729 were subscribed to relief committee funds between May and August 1846, £35 was sent by the Calcutta Relief Committee, while the government gave £370. With this money, eighty-nine tons of oatmeal were purchased, seventy-two of wholemeal, and twenty-five of Indian meal. After the first few weeks, all meal was sold at a loss, costing the committee £490.[23]

Relief works, which would have enabled more people to purchase food, were delayed by bickering at relief committee meetings. Committee members — eager to place their own favourites in supervisory roles on the works — provoked the temporary resignation of Mr Clements the county surveyor. Some work did begin in mid-May, when the Board of Works hired 175 to build a road linking Dangan with Salthill. But a new sea front road between Seapoint and Blackrock was delayed due to the difficulty of hiring carts to move stones. Those hired included army pensioners — not the most destitute of the people.[24]

The destitute presented their own problems. Of Bartholomew Keedy, who was sacked because his inertia gave bad example, it was later asserted that he had got 'weak on his spade' due to hunger. And malnutrition rather than drink was found to explain the shambling gait of another would-be worker. Responding to such reports, the committee ordered that meal be made immediately available to destitute workers, with the cost to be deducted on pay-day.

Before being hired, people had to present a ticket from the relief committee — a regulation that might have been useful if the number of tickets issued equaled the number of jobs. But committee members blithely issued tickets to their own tenants and clients and, by June, there were 1500 ticket holders, but only 250 jobs.[25]

Holders of useless work tickets responded in predictable fashion. A large crowd of destitute people threatened stewards on the scheme at Thonabrucky, attacking the overseer, Mr Thomas. The surveyor responded by discharging workers 'in order to give an opportunity to others'. Elsewhere, there was a serious affray at Coolough when sixteen ticket-holders — 'with a leader' — forced themselves onto the works there. Captain Ainslie, Board of Works inspector, protested that the relief committee was encouraging such incidents by issuing too many tickets. At Menlo, where tenants threatened to obstruct work unless employed themselves, their landlord, Thomas Blake, denied reports that they were acting on his advice. Responding to complaints, and to the crowds seeking employment outside every meeting, the committee resolved that work should be rotated on all schemes so that more people might have the opportunity of earning some money.[26]

The growing frustration of the people was reflected in a number of so-called 'outrages', directed at food convoys. In late June, 200 people attacked five cartloads of wholemeal and Indian meal, dispatched by the relief committee to Oranmore. The cargo was saved by the Head Constable — without, however, 'any assistance from the car-men'.[27] In another incident, relief workers on the outskirts of the town robbed a cartload of flour bound for Ballindine. Four men and a woman were arrested and charged, but acquitted by a lenient magistrate. Like the car-men and the magistrate, the *Galway Vindicator* sympathised with the actions of men 'maddened by hunger, and the sad condition of their wretched families'. The paper urged greater exertion on the public authorities, arguing that otherwise 'it will be impossible to preserve the peace, or protect private property'.[28] The principal targets of the newspaper's remarks were the town commissioners — who were meeting only intermittently due to the difficulty in mustering a quorum — and those relief committee members with poor attendance records.[29]

Those members of the relief committee who were active continued to badger the Board of Works to extend relief schemes, and the number of schemes and of workers increased gradually until a total of 873 were employed in mid-July. By then, supervisors were complaining that works were overcrowded.[30]

All classes in the town, meanwhile, looked forward to the day when work might begin on a number of long-mooted projects: an army barracks at Renmore, the Queen's College, the new docks, the Claddagh bridge, the Corrib-Mask canal. Each of these would provide much-needed work for tradesmen as well as labourers.

Their parlous state did not drive many to the workhouse. In the week ending 21 March 1846, there were 383 inmates, 30% more than the same week in 1845, but far short of the institution's 1,000 capacity. Nor did the promise of a full stomach incline many towards military service. The

Connaught Rangers, who conducted a recruitment campaign in the town during April, stimulated 'little interest'.[31]

Phase III: '… somewhat more generous measures'

In June 1846, Peel's administration fell. Throughout Ireland, there were hopes that Lord John Russell's Whigs would prove less parsimonious in addressing Irish distress. In Galway, there was satisfaction when Thomas Redington, chairman of the Galway Guardians, was appointed Under-Secretary for Ireland in the new administration. Few doubted but that 'the present government will adopt, so far at least as the poor of Galway and its vicinity are concerned, somewhat more generous measures of relief than those of their predecessors'.[32]

Phase IV: '… protecting the trade in provisions'

The expectations in Ireland of the incoming government were based on a perception that the Whigs were 'friends of Ireland'. This arose principally from the co-operation between them and O'Connell's parliamentary contingent during the 1830s, co-operation that was based less on principle than on a coincidence of interest between the parties — in the removal of religious disabilities, in municipal reform — and in their shared antipathy towards Irish landlords. In the Famine crisis, however, Whig policy would fall far short of Irish expectations.

No one was certain in the summer of 1846 that the potato would fail again but, as things turned out, only large-scale state intervention could have averted mass starvation. This, however, was unthinkable for adherents of political economy.

Political economy was the doctrine of the rising capitalist element in British society, who, as the most cost-efficient producers, favoured free trade and *laissez faire*. They believed that 'artificial' barriers inhibiting trade should be removed; that tariffs, restrictive practices, 'superstition', should not be allowed to stand in the way of progress. And political economists had a mystical faith in the market, arguing that its free operation discouraged waste, having the effect of rationing scarce resources. If central or local authorities assisted the poor to buy food in a season of scarcity, their argument went, the poor — being improvident — would gorge themselves, and suffer the greater scarcity which would inevitably follow.

No party — from O'Connell's to the Tories — was immune to political economy, but none was more under its influence than the nascent Liberal Party. And while there were leading Whigs willing to do whatever was necessary to relieve the Irish people, their position was weak in 1846, and it would become weaker.

Before the Famine, there was agreement that Ireland's agriculture needed radical restructuring, that smallholding stood in the way of commercial agriculture, that there was a need for more labourers and fewer tenant farmers and cottiers. For some, not least the influential permanent assistant secretary to the Treasury, Charles Trevelyan, the Famine presented an opportunity to bring this about. The immediate needs of individuals (many of whom had no real future anyway), he believed, should be made subservient to long-term economic objectives.

The position of Trevelyan was greatly strengthened by the change of government in 1846. Incoming ministers, unsure of their briefs, sought his advice, and as often as not, acted upon it. Trevelyan's influence on policy, accordingly, was much greater than it had been under Peel. And, with the consolidation of a bloc of like-minded ministers around Sir Charles Wood, the secretary at the Treasury, Trevelyan established himself as the unchallenged expert on Irish famine relief. Moreover, in their hard line against Irish demands, the Treasury secretary and his assistant were supported by British opinion, which was convinced that vast sums were squandered in Ireland in the last year of Tory rule.[33]

The view of the new administration was expressed by Lord John Russell in a letter to the Lord Lieutenant. Criticising his predecessor's policy, he insisted: 'It must be thoroughly understood that we cannot feed the people. It was a cruel delusion to pretend to do so'.[34]

The new government acted quickly. An edict of 21 July 1846 ordered that all 'emergency' relief works should end as soon as possible — 15 August was set as the date when food depots should be closed. During July and August alarming reports were circulating about the new potato crop but, by then, in line with instructions, the Galway Relief Committee was winding up its operations.[35] An unspent £600 — receipts from the sale of foodstuffs — was left in the care of three trustees, John Ireland, Fr Peter Daly and the Anglican Warden Daly.[36]

By September, it was clear that there was a total potato failure and that disaster on an unprecedented scale lay ahead. The government's honeymoon came to an abrupt end. Just two months after it assumed office it was being argued that if

> Sir Robert Peel, rather than the Whigs, was in office, the poor would not be thus dealt with, nor impoverished, ruined and plundered Ireland be required to bear the entire weight of the present awful calamity, to save the pockets of a people the misgovernment of whose rulers has precipitated this country into its present depth of misery and wretchedness.[37]

At a public meeting called to promote 'the employment of the people', which was attended by thousands of the poor, government parsimony was criticised by Thomas Stephens, secretary of the defunct relief committee. £10,000 had been sanctioned for relief works, yet only £3,000 had yet been allocated. Mr Aylwood, 'an old inhabitant', directed his fire at the town commissioners who were failing to thwart forestallers at the markets. Before the meeting ended, a 'labouring man' in the body of the hall was permitted to speak on behalf of his fellows. He urged that the government not 'take advantage of their necessities by requiring them to labour for ten pence per day, which was little enough to provide food for an individual, not to speak of the family he would have to support'.[38]

The feelings of the poor were also expressed in direct fashion. In early October, sustained rioting took place. The officer-in-charge of the coastguard — alarmed by a great assembly seeking to prevent the export of meal — deployed armed boats as had been done the previous November, in order to 'protect the River between the Claddagh and the Shipping so as to prevent their crossing in the Hookers … in case the Claddagh men should be persuaded to join the townspeople'.[39]

The people then turned their attention to the meal leaving by road for the interior. Carts bearing food were turned back at the outskirts of town, raising concern about the consequences to 'the people of Tuam and other localities'.[40]

Responding to the blockade, the town commissioners held an emergency meeting and decided to borrow £500 'on the security of the tolls' for Indian meal 'to be retailed to the poor in small quantities under cost price, and prevent, if possible, a recurrence to violence and outrage'. The meal was purchased from Rush & Palmer, who were able to supply cheaper than the Commissary-General. Meanwhile, the editor of the *Vindicator* sought to counsel the people — 'if in the midst of their suffering, our friendly advice can reach them'. Arguing that it was short-sighted to prevent food leaving the town, he pointed to the smallness of the Saturday market as evidence that no farmer would bring grain to town if he might be prevented from taking it away again. Employees in mills and kilns would suffer, while importers of grain* would become 'insecure' and avoid the place. The result of disturbances would be greater shortages and higher prices.[41]

One observer detected a marked shift in popular attitudes 'in relation to individual right in property' as a result of deprivation, noting that 'the women are even more frantic than the men in this respect'. The general foolhardiness being displayed on the streets, he thought, arose from the fact that people looked upon 'a violent death from collision with the authorities as far preferable to that which starvation, though more lingeringly, is certain to bring'.[42]

The authorities were not inclined to provide the merciful ending which so many allegedly sought. Magistrates were fearful of the consequences of calling out the military, and it was left to some private citizens to take an initiative. Fr John Roche was persuaded to lead an escort of his parishioners, to protect grain leaving the town. The co-operation of the car-men was secured and 40 carts set out for Tuam on Thursday, 8 October. At Boherbeg, however, three carts were surrounded by a crowd of women and children. One woman, Bridget Kelly, was

---

* Importers of grain were few in any case, the general direction of such cargo being outwards. Three Galway merchants, however, began to import on a small scale. One of these, having bought 1,000 tons of barley and a quantity of Egyptian beans in the Mediterranean, thought that it would 'probably be more advantageous … to send these supplies to the continent than to land them here (*Distress Correspondence, July 1846–January 1847, Commissariat series*, H. of C. 1847, Vol. LI, p.479 — extract from letter of Commissariat official Trimmer).

killed in the meleê. An inquest heard that she was the sole support of her 100-year-old mother and that neither had eaten a morsel in the previous 24 hours.[43]

Further attacks prompted Kernan to provide bi-weekly military escorts.[44]

Messrs Rush & Palmer wrote to Under Secretary Redington detailing 'the deplorable state of the town'. Magistrates had attempted to restore order, but according to the merchants, they had done so 'without either promptitude or firmness', and their pusillanimity had only 'increased the spirit of resistance'. The people were forcibly administering oaths to the car-drivers, binding them not to remove food from the town. Another merchant organised sixteen of the drivers — 'poor industrious men' — to memorialise the Lord Lieutenant in protest at the lack of protection afforded them by Mr Kernan. Kernan's efficacy was also questioned by other merchants. The military authorities responded by despatching the 6th Dragoons 'for the purpose of protecting the trade in provisions'. The merchants were still not satisfied, but Kernan was adamant that arrangements were adequate. He insisted that he provided escorts on two days a week, and that if merchants confined their trade with the interior to those days, they had nothing to fear. Addressing the causes of popular discontent, he chided merchants and millers for mixing barley with wholemeal and 'selling it as pure', and lobbied the Board of Works to increase employment, in particular to employ the Claddagh fishermen. Otherwise, he would be unable to keep the peace 'without resorting to such measures as must end in the loss of many lives'.[45]

In the following weeks, Menlo villagers plundered three laden meal vessels bound for Cong. In the town itself, 'organised bands of plunderers' patrolled the thoroughfares, confiscating whatever supplies came their way.[46]

Locally, it was believed that government policy was responsible for the food shortage and the high prices. The guarantee of non-interference in the provisions market was believed to have encouraged forestalling and to account for 'the utter impossibility of inducing farmers to part with their stock for love or money'.[47]

In mid-October, a meeting was held to establish a new relief committee. Bearna landlord, Nicholas Lynch, emerged as chairman. The Board of Works released funds for work on a new road between Blackrock and Bearna and another between Nile Lodge and Newcastle. By early November, 3,000 were employed on new works. Many more than 3,000 work tickets had been issued by members of the new committee, however, and several overseers were attacked by unsuccessful applicants. Unsurprisingly, in these circumstances, an attempted boycott of the works failed. The protest was in reaction to the new policy of paying piece-rates rather than day-rates, enabling overseers to 'rate task-work so low that it is impossible to earn more than 8d to 10d a day'. Facing difficulty on all sides, the Board of Works official responsible for liaising with the relief committee in issuing work tickets, shot himself through the head on Monday 2 November 1846. He survived, but was subsequently considered to be 'quite out of his mind'.[48]

A feeling persisted that not all those on schemes were particularly needy. This suspicion was given substance when one Faherty, a tenant of relief committee chairman, Nicholas Lynch, was arrested for leading a riot and for assaulting a surveyor. The rioters had demanded that they be hired on a scheme and that Faherty be their ganger. At the barracks, £25 was found in Faherty's pocket, together with a letter from Lynch recommending that he be hired at the works.[49]

Prompted by the incident, the *Vindicator* accused Nicholas Lynch of issuing work tickets to 'comfortable tenantry upon his own property to enable them to pay rents to him with more facility, [while he] had withheld them from squatters and other needy persons on his estate'. Lynch responded indignantly,[50] but the relief committee investigated the *Vindicator* allegations to establish whether '200 people in comfortable circumstances, such as meal-mongers, money-lenders, pensioners, and owners of bathing-lodges were employed on the Salthill road'. Lynch's defence was not convincing:

> It is said, indeed, that I issued tickets to my tenants who had corn in their haggards and were possessed of cows, etc. But I would say that though I even did, such parties ought not be denied them, when that corn was not theirs but mine and when their cattle were not, perhaps, their own but were got from me on credit, and for which the parties are indebted to me … I did not wish, in order to compel them to pay me, to dispose of the corn they had for seed, and to pay their rent, and is it because of my forbearance in this respect that I am to have my character impeached.[51]

One member of the committee charged that Lynch was not looking after his tenants' interests, but his own. By enabling tenants to hoard grain, he was contributing to the general scarcity, and causing food prices to rise further. At a time when the destitute were unable to get on relief works, their chairman was anticipating a further rise in food prices so that his tenants would be able to pay rent and other debts to himself. When a vote was called on the substance of the allegations, Lynch failed to get any support, and he resigned immediately.[52]

Clearly, there were difficulties in directing relief towards the most needy. Since it was hardly the daily wages of 8-10*d* that were attracting money-lenders, mealmongers and others with means, it would appear that existing exploitative networks were being incorporated into the relief schemes.

Necessity was overcoming people's reluctance to enter the workhouse, where numbers increased gradually through the spring and summer: there were 383 inmates in late March, 489 in early October, 641 by late October, 725 by mid-November and over 900 by early December, when people had to be turned away. Although the house had not yet reached its capacity of a thousand, there were large numbers of sick inmates, and many more women than men seeking admission, compelling the Board of Guardians to place a ceiling of 900 on admissions. There was a striking increase, moreover, in the rate of mortality in the workhouse during the same months. In the three months September-November, 1846, twenty-five people died in the house, but sixty-five succumbed, in the month of December (see Figure 4.1) The guardians pointed out that the majority of those dying were recently admitted and were already weakened by starvation or illness; long-term inmates remained healthy.[53]

Famine deaths, which had loomed in anticipation for more than a year, assumed a terrible reality in late 1846, presenting new problems for those with responsibility for relief. Frustration at their relative powerlessness became evident in the remarks of relief committee members. According to John Ireland:

> nothing could exceed the perpetual applications from morning till night at my door, by persons intreating of me to procure them employment. My mind is completely harassed in listening to the weeping and wailing of the crowds that come to me, old men and young, women, boys and girls crying for work. I do not know what is to be done.[54]

In the same vein, Rev. John d'Arcy spoke of one Grimes whom he had unsuccessfully tried to place on the works, whereupon the man died of starvation. He then described another case:

> not less deplorable, that of a family, the head of which being returned for employment, but when he applied being refused to be taken into work, took ill of fever with some more of his family. They were sent to the Fever Hospital and I endeavoured to get the remainder employed by Mr Tallon at the paper mill but could not. They had then to seek for admission to the poor-house but were not received and the result was that these unfortunate creatures were starving for want of any relief.[55]

Disposing of the remains of the deceased also presented problems. In the workhouse, men removing bodies had to walk on corpses, while some of those expiring outside the workhouse, 'in the lanes, alleys and confined places of the town, where no relief reached, and where death is doing its awful work', were buried uncoffined 'like carrion', the 'means of the Clergy exhausted in buying coffins' and the relief committee not being permitted to expend money on the already dead.[56] Many of the dying were recent arrivals from rural parts, but the traffic was not in one direction only. Folklore sources indicate that farmers in Annaghdown were pestered by townspeople stealing from fields at night.[57]

In some respects, and for some people, life proceeded as normal. There were assizes balls and race meetings, and, in October 1846, Wombwell's Royal National Menagerie and Zoological School of Intuition exhibited at Eyre Square, showing 'lions, tigers and four hyenas ... Mrs King, the Lion Queen and The Great Gemian Marmont or Savage of Ethiopia'. The theatre was open, though many performances were charity fund-raisers. One charitable comedy performance in October 1846, was insensitively entitled 'How to Pay the Rent'!* while a fund-raising raffle rather melodramatically offered as first prize, a painting of 'The Aran Fisherman's Drowned Child'.[58]

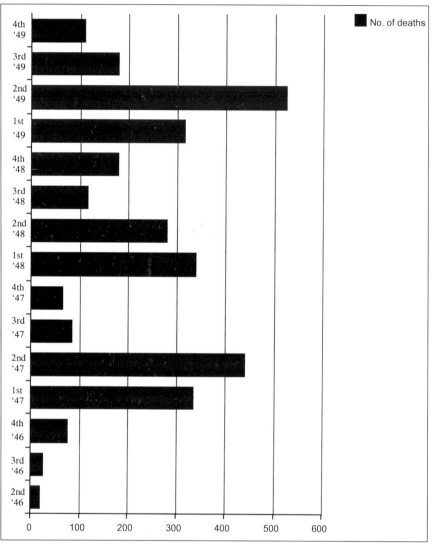

FIGURE 6.1: Workhouse Mortality in the Galway Union, April 1846 — December 1849.
Source: Galway Poor Law Minute Books, 1846-49.

---

* One is reminded of Canon O'Rourke's comment on the behaviour of the 'humane, proper-thinking "gentlemen"' of Galway during the 1741 famine who removed their races, balls and plays to Tuam in order to avoid the fever raging in the county town (*The History of the Great Irish Famine of 1847*, 3rd edn. Dublin 1902, pp. 22-23).

To general consternation, the Galway shoemakers went on strike in October 1846, not for wages, but for an organisational principle. Normality intervened also in the town by-election of February, 1847 and, for a few weeks, the condition of the people was largely ignored in the newspapers. In a close contest, government supporter, J. H. Monahan, defeated Repealer Anthony O'Flaherty. Despite blandishments, the trades and the town-dwellers generally 'rallied to Repeal' but were outvoted by 'the ignorant, wretched and intimidated serfs of the rural districts'. There was some half-hearted rioting during the campaign, but a magistrate reported: 'never was known so quiet an election in Galway'. His assessment was premature, however, being dispatched as the government-supporting verger of the Collegiate Church was celebrating the Monahan victory, but some hours before that gentleman locked himself in his belfry and proceeded to ring *Joybells*. An O'Flaherty mob gathered, which dispersed only when the intoxicated verger ceased his ringing. When he resumed, the 'mob became outrageous', breaking windows and causing the 'respectable inhabitants' to fear for their cornstores.[59]

Later, the *Vindicator* noted that even amidst the political excitement it had been 'impossible to overlook the wretched and emaciated appearance of the poor'. Rural electors — not the poorest of country people — had 'haggard and pinched features', while the tradesmen had mustered in 'tattered garb and wasted forms'.[60]

Phase V: '… perfect incubi on society …'

In early 1847, the government reconsidered its relief policy. Public works were absorbing enormous sums, their rapid expansion had created administrative gridlock in the Board of Works, yet people were succumbing to starvation and disease in unprecedented numbers. In addition, it was felt that those employed on relief schemes would, of necessity, neglect their ordinary agricultural work during the coming season, thereby exacerbating the spiral of dependency.

The government, therefore, swallowed a cherished principle of political economy and permitted the distribution of gratuitous relief, a policy shift that was heralded by the Temporary Relief Act of February, 1847. Relief schemes were to be wound down and cooked food was to be supplied from soup kitchens throughout the country. In taking this step, the government was encouraged by the economical results already achieved by charities, and by its own desire to eliminate abuses: soup would only be claimed as a last resort by the extremely destitute; unlike relief work, it didn't require elaborate administrative machinery; and, it couldn't as easily be traded for whiskey as raw food.

But in turning the system of relief inside out, policy makers did not forget their larger objectives. Soup kitchens were regarded as a short-term expedient, and, while the initial expense of establishing facilities and dispensing food were borne by the exchequer, the cost was recoverable from the poor law union in which the expenditure took place. The government was therefore ensuring that Irish property-owners — and landlords in particular — would bear the cost of a disaster for which, according to Whig wisdom, they were principally responsible.[61]

In Galway, some soup kitchens were already operating. At the relief committee in December 1846, Rev. John d'Arcy proposed that soup be sold to the poor rather than meal, but, to facilitate those who 'would rather die than apply for soup', that meal should not be entirely withdrawn. Soup kitchens, he argued, should also offer instruction 'in the art of making up good substantial dishes of wholesome and savoury food at the smallest cost — an art deficient in this country'.[62]

Charities such as the Patrician Brothers' Breakfast Institute had extended their operations as the poor became more numerous, while the Mercy Sisters established a soup kitchen in December, 1846, that fed 100 children a daily dinner of '12 ozs of bread and sufficient soup with vegetables, rice and oatmeal'. Shortly afterwards, a soup kitchen opened at the Dominican Priory in the Claddagh to feed a people who, having been prevented by storms from fishing, had pawned their nets and were unable to redeem them. Immediately, 'hundreds of poor creatures' rushed with their mugs for sustenance. These kitchens were aided by the relief committee which also ran its own facility at Back-street.[63]

Relief was interrupted in March with the winding up of the relief committee. The Temporary Relief Act — in line with the policy of forcing the poor law to take responsibility for relief — required that relief committees take charge of an entire poor law union. Membership of the new committee was announced by Captain Hellard, inspecting officer, 'in accordance with the direction of the Lord Lieutenant'. It was composed of eleven magistrates, fifteen guardians, twelve clergymen, eight recommended by the inspecting officer, and the inspecting officer himself, ex-officio. Lachlann Maclachlann continued as chairman.[64]

The forty-seven member committee was required to implement a completely new system, but was delayed by bureaucratic preparations from dispensing the free soup. Members protested about the 'tedious routine' and 'absurd… descriptions' demanded. The forms were 'so intricate' that it was considered almost impossible to complete them correctly.[65] The *Vindicator* had no sympathy with these complaints, accusing the relief committee of sharing culpability with the government for the delay in providing food. Three weeks was spent in compiling lists of those eligible for relief, a task that could have been completed in days if those responsible had shown 'greater attention to duty'.[66]

In mid-April, a journalist watched from his window as a man with a cart-load of beans was attacked by a group of women. In the fracas, beans were scattered over the road. All the while, the bean-owner was abused and pelted with stones, and was only saved from injury by the intervention of public works' labourers. The journalist noted that such attacks were becoming common, especially around the docks and in Quay-street. Plunder on a larger scale also persisted. Galway labourers were arrested at Lackagh, when they seized the contents of thirteen Roscommon-bound provision carts, having followed the convoy for ten miles.[67]

Those worried about 'life and property' were concerned that the drying up of relief would provoke the people into concerted and uncontrollable action. In early May, rumours circulated of a plan to plunder the foodstores and shops. And when hundreds of labourers assembled on the morning of 4 May, these rumours seemed to be confirmed. However, the protesters dispersed after marching through the streets, behind a white banner with the legend 'We are Starving: Bread or Employment',[68] 'Respectable opinion' was reassured, especially as the marchers, with 'their emaciated countenances and haggard looks, their tattered raiment and tottering steps', seemed almost too pathetic to riot. Consequently, there was no alarm when they assembled on the following day, and again on the day after, each time dispersing outside the relief committee meeting.

By the precepts of their moral economy, the protestors believed that 'having peaceably represented their grievances for three days without relief', they were justified in taking violent action. A deputation of protestors met the colonel commanding the 49th Regiment, asking 'in compassion for their suffering', that his men refrain from firing if called out by magistrates. Crowds then assembled outside Comerford's store in Merchants Road, but they were driven back by troops.[69]

If the would-be rioters did not succeed in suborning the military, they succeeded in expediting the work of the relief committee, whose lists were declared 'complete' in the aftermath of the protest. Within weeks, most of the planned soup kitchens were open for business and by the end of July, more than 50,000 people were receiving free soup daily in the Galway Poor Law Union.[70]

There was no great enthusiasm for the new system. The *Vindicator,* which had previously criticised the dilatoriness of the relief committee, now advised it to be 'zealously attentive to guard the interests of the (ratepaying) public'. That public was also wary. At a county election meeting in May, speakers ignored the crisis but hecklers interrupted: 'Down with the Whigs and their soup system'.[71] One 'not educated in the science of Political Economy', Fr Kavanagh of St Nicholas East, expressed the reservations of many about the soup kitchens:

> … under the system of outdoor relief, men, women and children are idle … waiting their turn to receive their 'noggin of soup' or 'little lock' of Indian corn or pea-meal; and when they receive it, dissatisfied, murmuring, envious of their neighbours' better success at getting more, or a superior quantity, planning how they themselves might better succeed the next time, and on this account becoming liars and backbiters, perfect incubi on society; returning nothing to supply the constant drain that must go on by taxes and poor rates for their support, and by this, dragging with themselves

into the one deep, universal and inevitable gulph of bankruptcy and want respectable tradesmen, shopkeepers, householders, nay, even the holders of landed estates …'.[72]

Fr Kavanagh prayed that God would intervene to help the suffering, and 'send them sudden relief by touching the hearts of the benevolent in their favour'.

Phase VI: '… the conflicting opinions of the Guardians …'

Views similar to Fr Kavanagh's were held at the highest levels, and they emerged strengthened from the May 1847 election. Russell's Whigs were returned but the balance of forces within the party changed, with the more flexible grandees losing further ground to the rigid commercial element. The shift was reflected in the enhanced influence of Sir Charles Wood, at the Exchequer, and, through him, of Charles Trevelyan.[73] And although Trevelyan's diagnosis of the problem was similar to Fr Kavanagh's, his remedy was going to be much more rigorous.

The Poor Law was the mechanism chosen by the Treasury to apply the orthodoxies of political economy to Ireland. The intermediary relief committees and their soup kitchens were to be dismantled; local rates were to fund future relief — and to repay past loans. But as things stood, the Poor Law was capable of dealing only with 'ordinary' destitution. Thus, the Poor Law Amendment which came into effect in August 1847, ending the various expedients of the previous years. Henceforth, relief was to be a local responsibility.

The Amendment provided for so-called 'outdoor' relief for the non able-bodied. Old, sick and widowed paupers might receive food — preferably cooked, to prevent them selling it — without being admitted to the workhouse, which was to give preference to able-bodied paupers. The Amendment's notorious Gregory Clause — named after its progenitor, Sir William Gregory*: member for Dublin; also south Galway landlord and future husband of Lady Augusta — required guardians to refuse relief to holders of more than a quarter acre of land.

In effect, the Galway Poor Law Union, like others in distressed areas, was being asked to assume the responsibilities of the relief committee in addition to its own. This aroused no enthusiasm among the guardians, who, prompted by difficulty of collecting rates, had considered in July the alternatives of mass resignation or closing the workhouse.[74]

In the same month, scandalous allegations against workhouse master, Pat Coghlan, and his staff entered the public domain. It was bad enough that charges of drunkenness against Coghlan were 'completely established', that Mrs Coghlan, matron, was found to have 'conducted herself most irregularly'

---

* Gregory's notoriety was immediate as the following excerpt from a ballad (*Galway Vindicator*, 27 January 1849) entitled 'Gregory's Quarter Acre' indicates:
Mercy will point to regions hot / For those who will forsake her,
Ye Gods! to Gregory grant that spot / As his own quarter acre.

and that a wardmaster was deemed 'totally unfit for the situation he holds', but there was worse. It was discovered that that only 595 inmates were present during the week ending 18 June, when 728 had been returned. In Pat Coghlan's defence, it was claimed that he did not benefit from the fraud, but that he had boosted the rations of the smaller number and dispensed occasional relief at the workhouse gate. He avoided dismissal by persuading a majority of the guardians that he was not a thoroughgoing rogue. Instead, his resignation and that of Mrs Coghlan was accepted by the guardians.[75] How long the deceit had continued is unknown but workhouse returns must be presumed unreliable prior to mid-1847.

The soup kitchens closed in September and the relief committee was wound up,[76] but the difficulty of persuading Galway's property to support Galway's poverty remained, and would remain for as long as Galway's property was allowed to oversee the transaction.

Indeed, it was clear that many of the eminently respectable, were less likely to relieve distress than to cause it. In December 1847, Christopher St George. M.P., cleared tenants from two townlands, Gortrevagh and Clush, near Oughterard, and served notice on the inhabitants of Pouleeny, Furbo. His example was quickly followed by Patrick Blake, who levelled the townland of Gortnamona, near Inverin, allegedly without any legal authority to do so. Those evicted became beggars in the streets of Galway. It was estimated that there were 3,000 beggars in the town, including children — 'mere animated skeletons ... screaming for food'.[77]

Even landlords who had better relationships with their own tenantry were disinclined to relieve poverty throughout the Poor Law Union to the extent required. In July 1847, before the new policy came into effect, the Union was already £5000 in debt, with a like sum outstanding from ratepayers. Among the defaulters was Nicholas Lynch of Bearna who had the largest valuation in the county of the town. Lynch, the discredited ex-chairman of the relief committee, was a guardian himself, but nonetheless disputed his assessment in October 1847. Scorning the appeals procedure, he simply refused to pay. Moreover, when seven of his cattle were distrained by the poor rate collector, they were violently rescued at Knocknacarra by 'a large number of persons ... with sticks and stones', — Lynch's tenants. The loss of the revenue was bad enough but the 'bad example to his tenants' was of more concern. And the effects of Lynch's example soon became evident, when other attempts at distraint were thwarted by rioting tenantry.[78]

Other solidarities also manifested themselves. Lay magistrates were reluctant to find against their peers, and absented themselves from Petty Sessions whenever distraining orders against landlords were sought by the guardians.[79]

Like magistrates, the Galway guardians were sensitive to the interests of their own class. Thus, they deliberately misinterpreted a Poor Law Commissioners' circular in order to set a low rate, and were generally less than diligent in collecting the rates. Only £550, a fraction of the amount due, was collected during September, October and November — the months most 'favorable for the collection', And, aware of the cost of large-scale outdoor relief, the majority of the guardians sabotaged attempts to introduce it. They postponed the appointment of relieving officers and members of the revising sub-committee repeatedly failed to attend meetings, thereby denying applicants admission to the workhouse.[80]

The guardians' ineffectiveness was also evident within the workhouse. There, the regime was extremely lax, with inmates inadequately clothed and not required to bathe even on admission. A fever outbreak in November was attributed to 'the imprudent removal of blankets that had been used in the fever hospital, to the body of the house, without being previously washed.'[81] Moreover, the guardians' reluctance to issue outdoor relief meant that there was no room for new applicants. All 209 who sought admission on 15 December were turned away, but two days later 92 of them were arrested for begging. They had deliberately contravened the new Vagrancy Act so as to gain relief in the town gaol. John Kernan RM obliged, sentencing them to one month in prison. In taking the humane course, Kernan may have been influenced by the fate of Anthony Carty who had appeared before him a fortnight earlier charged with attempted window-breaking. Recognising that the man was only interested in the prison rations, Kernan discharged him. Three days later, Carty died.[82]

But the respite offered by imprisonment was limited. There was severe overcrowding, and only minimal resources for the 903 prisoners and 34 children in a county jail intended for 110 persons. There were no blankets, and inmates had to sleep in their inadequate rags on bare flags. An average of 35 people a week died in the institution in early 1848 — some of cold, others of fever — with 115 succumbing in the fortnight beginning 20 February. Most prisoners were incarcerated for 'starvation crimes'. One Galway town commissioner alleged that landlords were 'committing their dependents in shoals to Galway prison for petty offences and larcenies, &c., and thus clearing their grounds of so many wretched people'.[83]

To a dutiful public servant, the guardians' incompetence was frustrating, and the impatience of Captain Hellard, poor law inspector, was increasingly evident. Reporting on a December meeting in 1847, he complained that the guardians

> as usual talked away the entire day, leaving the house in the same state as last week … The conflicting opinions of the Guardians, as well as their want of attention, completely upsetting that routine of business which is so absolutely necessary in conducting minor establishments, much less one of this importance to so large a proportion of society.[84]

But Hellard wasn't the only frustrated one. Lord Wallscourt, the short-tempered chairman of the Guardians and a sincere humanitarian, proposed the dissolution of his board on several occasions, asking that it be replaced by paid guardians. He argued that since most members had shown themselves 'little disposed to transact the business for the discharge of which they were elected', his time would be better spent in relieving distress on his own property at Ardfry, than in travelling to interminable meetings.[85]

Eventually, on 28 December 1847, the Poor Law Commissioners dissolved the Galway Board, citing its refusal to prepare for the provision of outdoor relief and its failure to collect rates. The Board was one of forty-two dissolved in 1847-8, but unlike several of the others, the Galway guardians had not lost their status because of any generosity to the distressed.[86]

Phase VII: '… divested of every feeling of home and humanity'
Two paid Vice-Guardians took responsibility for the relief of Galway's poor in January 1848. With Captain Hellard, they examined the claims of applicants and offered outdoor relief to those eligible, but they found the able-bodied reluctant to take up the workhouse places offered. Captain Hellard's 'unremitting exertions' ended, however, when he died of fever on 28 January. A tribute to the naval officer in the *Galway Mercury* attributed his demise to his dedication to duty —which 'broke down a naturally strong constitution' The paper acknowledged that the captain's 'firm and straightforward conduct, united to a scrupulous impartiality in the execution of his duties and a general urbanity of manners and benevolence of disposition, procured for him the respect of all parties'.[87]

Hellard's replacement, Major Patrick McKie, served for seventeen months before succumbing to 'malignant fever' that he contracted in the workhouse. The *Mercury's* comments were rather different in this instance:

> … we may be permitted to express the hope that officers of his caste and age will not in future be foisted upon us; let men graduate once in India and with very few exceptions they will be found to have divested themselves of every feeling of home and humanity. Petty tyrants seldom bring fine feelings into display in their treatment of the humbler classes …[88]

McKie's reports to his superiors do not show him to be bereft of humanity, but the tasks he was required to carry out were not such as to win him popularity. Each ratepayer, whether landed, urban, or tenant farmer, had to be squeezed to the last penny; each claimant had to be assessed and, if judged able-bodied, admitted to the workhouse or put stone-breaking; each minor official had to be pressurised to meet impossible targets.

For the new poor law officials, rate collection remained the issue 'of first importance'. Some progress was made: the average weekly amount collected during January-February — £435 — more than matched expenditure during those months. The improvement was achieved by deploying police and military in support of the rate collectors, although the decision to take landlords to the higher courts rather than to Petty Sessions where 'feelings of delicacy' were making magistrates reluctant to issue distraining orders also contributed. Exemplary seizures of hay from tenant farmers had the desired effect — it was harder for the poor law officials to transport and dispose of hay, but it was not as easily hidden by farmers as livestock.[89] Collectors, who had previously been lobbied by guardians 'not to press particular parties' were now instructed to extract the maximum amount possible, leaving them with an unenviable choice. The diligence of Galway area collector, Mr Martyn, caused him and his assistant to be badly beaten by country people on the streets of the town, while the more lackadaisical approach of Walter Amos in the Moycullen area, led Major McKie to approve his dismissal, 'as an example to the remaining collectors'.[90]

But the improvement in rates collection was short-lived. Small tenants were abandoning their holdings in order to claim relief, while those remaining were encouraged to withhold payment by a rumour that 'rates are to be forgiven for three years'.[91] And the Vice-Guardians could not be too rigorous. During their travels through the Union on 13 March, they were pleased to see tenant farmers busy at work, so they gave directions that this class not be troubled for rates lest it 'have the effect of paralyzing the exertions very generally making to get a crop into the land'. With their ranks so depleted it was difficult for the ratepayers to bear their ever-increasing burden. In mid-March, McKie solicited assistance from the British Relief Association to pay for Union services. Coincidentally, the Association had just acquired some local notoriety for its other activities.

The British Relief Association was nominally independent, but it lacked a distributive network. Because it depended on official agencies to distribute its relief, the charity was often regarded as an arm of government. During 1847-8, it distributed food to schoolchildren, with the one condition that beneficiaries attend school (See Chapter Thirteen). In Galway, one zealous Association representative went somewhat further, causing a Presentation nun to complain to Archbishop Murray in March 1848 that pupils were 'being prepared by proselytising agents in the national school in Rahoon'.* Fr B. J. Roche also showed concern when he asked that the Association 'dissolve any connexion between their body and those who try to pervert, not convert, the children…'[92] And the *Galway Mercury* asked: 'was it for Protestant proselytism that the Sultan, for instance, contributed' to Association funds?[93]

If revenue had to be found to pay for outdoor relief, the workhouse itself also needed attention. No member of the Board of Guardians had set foot in the institution since March 1847 and the new functionaries appointed on the resignation of the Coghlans were less than dynamic. The Vice-Guardians

---

* Another letter from a Galway Presentation nun, Sr Mary De Pazzi, referred to the activities of 'the most wild set of mad false preachers that ever visited an unhappy island.' She confessed: 'We are much more alarmed for them [the children] than when suffering the horrors of famine or yet during the terrors of the cholera, for the present plague [of proselytisers] is far more dreadful.' (Sr M. Colombiere Scully, PhD, 'The Great Famine and the role of the Presentation sisters' in *City Tribune*, 31 May 1991).

sought to improve cleanliness, to introduce order into the lives of the inmates and to regularise book-keeping, but their efforts were thwarted by the master and by the matron who was described as 'dirty in her person and negligent in her general duty'. When both were dismissed in March, it was discovered that there were forty-one fewer inmates than claimed.

There were other changes. It was decided, for instance, to hold meetings in 'distant parts of the Union', rather than always in the workhouse as had been the practice. Thus, congestion in the town might be eased and the suffering of those compelled to come long distances to apply for relief alleviated somewhat.[94]

Also serving to alleviate pressure in the town was the growing amount of employment. Engineering projects were absorbing the labour force, especially the skilled part of it. In early 1848, it was expected that the canal works would soon occupy 'most or all of the able bodied in the town'. Meanwhile, work was continuing on the Queen's College and on the Claddagh basin.[95]

But in the union as a whole, demand for relief was growing inexorably. In line with official policy, non-able-bodied inmates were sent from the workhouse and placed on outdoor relief. Some refused to leave. A small number who had relinquished their homes were given rent and fuel allowances.[96] Children were also removed from the workhouse and taken to a new facility accomodating 600 at Dangan, where it was envisaged that the attached farm would be utilised as 'an industrial agricultural school, instead of a workhouse retreat for idleness, which when once embarked in by youth is seldom, or never, shaken off...'[97]

In the circumstances, the establishment of a totally new system of outdoor relief was not an easy task. Apart altogether from the financial challenges facing them, the paid guardians and the poor law inspector had to satisfy the Poor Law Commissioners (and behind them, Treasury officials), that they were acting in a frugal and ideologically acceptable fashion. And where economy and ideology clashed, ideology triumphed. One instance was the dispute between the Galway officials and their superiors over the form of outdoor relief, with the former arguing that individual portions of meal would be easier to dispense, — and 25% cheaper — than cooked food. The Commissioners refused to entertain the idea.[98]

Outdoor relief also required the employment of a layer of local officials — relieving officers. It was difficult to find suitable candidates for these positions, especially since the wages offered did not take account of the heavy workload, not to mention the risk from contagion.* The result, according to Major McKie, was that men who were 'not intelligent, or fitted to their office' had to be employed.[99]

Candidates for outdoor relief ideally had to face the 'workhouse test' — to show that they were so bereft that they were prepared to enter the workhouse.

---

* It is easy to forget that these officials, referred to with utter contempt in the official correspondence, were regarded as minor gods by the destitute who depended upon their favourable decisions. The traditional song, Johnny Seoighe, quoted at beginning of this chapter, was almost a prayer to the eponymous relieving officer.

This was not very practical in 1848, so a 'labour test' was substituted, requiring able-bodied males to work for their food. The provision of such work, usually stonebreaking — the only task which was 'as repulsive as possible consistent with humanity' and at the same time did not interfere with the free market in labour — occupied much of Major McKie's time and energy. Applicants sometimes refused to submit themselves to either test, but what this indicates is open to question. For example, McKie reported on two work groups in the town in February 1848. In the course of a week, there were six deserters from a gang of 103 stone breakers in Taylor's Hill, but only half of a gang of 20 street sweepers completed their first day. Since street sweeping was hardly more arduous than stone breaking, it can be assumed that it was the public humiliation of scavenging that caused those so deployed to leave their employment.[100]

Despite obstacles, the number on outdoor relief rose rapidly: 4,087 in the first week of February 1848; 16,096 in the first week of March; 32,191 in July. By then, the population of the Union must have been considerably less than the 88,973 enumerated in 1841. Thereafter, the number of claimants declined as the harvest advanced.[101]

But the news of the harvest was not encouraging. The disease-free crop of 1847 had encouraged tenants to resume potato culture. Blight returned, however, and half of the crop in the Galway Union was lost. The only potato crop that escaped blight was that grown by the agriculturalist, Thomas Skilling, who managed Lord Wallscourt's various utopian schemes at Ardfry. To make matters worse, the grain crop was adversely affected by summer rain, and the turnip-fly had been very active.[102]

'Turf Market', Spanish Parade, early twentieth century.

In the circumstances, the local officials anticipated a level of demand equal to the previous year. In January 1849, McKie estimated that an average of 3000 workhouse inmates would have to be catered for, along with an average of 15,000 outdoor relief claimants. £21,000 would be required between January and September, but the most optimistic calculation was that 10% of that sum could be collected locally. The means of most ratepayers were exhausted. Landed proprietors, although 'struggling to keep up an appearance that their changed circumstances will not justify' had received little rent in three years, while having to pay much increased rates. Some were encouraging their tenants to avoid rates in order to pay rent, while others were distraining for rent, leaving nothing for the rates. Solvent tenants were 'secreting what little property they have, disposing of their stock, and running away, leaving long arrears of rents and rates unpaid'. Many poorer tenant ratepayers had become paupers themselves and were hardly likely to pay the amount levied upon them.[103]

Cholera reached Belfast late in 1848. Shortly afterwards, Boards of Guardians were warned that the spread of the epidemic was inevitable, and advised precautionary measures. By early March 1849, there was no sign of the disease reaching Galway, but the Town Grand Jury asked Martin Blake, M.P., owner of the fever sheds at Straw Lodge, to leave them standing as they might be needed for 'a dreadful calamity'. According to the *Mercury,* the streets of the town were filthy in late March and there were no apparent preparations for the inevitable, despite the fact that the cholera was 'already on the southern shores of our own bay'.[104]

If there was apparent resignation in the face of disaster, it was not Major McKie's fault. With his record of service in India, he knew what had to be done. However, his order, under Diseases Prevention legislation, that dung-heaps be removed and that drains be cleaned, was not much observed. 'Able-bodied' paupers were engaged to do some of the work of nuisance-removal.[105]

The first cholera case was diagnosed on 7 April; a few days later, the Fever Hospital was declared to be a cholera hospital. Additional facilities became available when Straw Lodge was requisitioned and when the Workhouse's 'idiot' ward was temporarily cleared of people with learning disabilities. Despite all of this, the *Mercury* condemned 'rumours and false reports of cholera' on 14 April. A week later, however, there was no denying the outbreak. By late April, there had been 560 admissions to the cholera hospitals, and 240 fatalities. Others died in their homes. Fr Kavanagh attended 79 cases in 8 days. Of those, he estimated that only seven or eight were admitted to hospital. Many 'pined in their cold, desolate cabins without drink or food, without medical aid, without fire or clothing, without anything of comfort, unless what the priest could bring them'.

The estimate of the census commissioners, a few years later, was that 611 people died of cholera in the town. Among them were two Mercy Sisters who were stricken while tending the sick and Lachlann MacLachlann, merchant, who had been chairman of the Galway Relief Committee during 1847 and, briefly, MP for the town in the 1830s.[106]

Phase VIII. '… the revival of former days …'

The cholera hospital closed on 1 June 1849, bringing the epidemic to an official end. In the same week came the announcement that the railway was to be extended to Galway, news that was greeted by the ringing of *Joybells* and by the illumination of the town. The next day thousands gathered at the coach station to cheer Fr Peter Daly, who was credited with securing the railway. In the excitement, according to a local paper, 'poverty seemed to be entirely forgotten'.[107]

For the same writer, this was no bad thing and in the following weeks he coaxed Galwegians out of their torpor. The fact that all the bathing lodges in Salthill were occupied during July he interpreted as a 'strong indication that the good old times are coming' and good old times were evident again in the full and fashionable attendance at the Galway Races. Several balls went off successfully, notably the Grand Military Ball in mid-August which was attended by 360 people. For the *Mercury* this was nothing less than 'the revival of former days after the long and dreary ones we had for the preceding years of famine and affliction, and proves that this is only a prelude to those that are yet in store for Galway'.[108]

But it was not only among the elite that there were signs of optimism and recovery. During July and August, the Magdalen asylum reopened, the Augustinian community purchased a new church organ, the Mechanics' Institute ran a series of popular lectures on 'Universal History', and the guild of stonemasons held a 'splendid soirée' for Anthony O'Flaherty MP, acknowledging his role in securing the railway. The soirée was attended by the masons' wives and children who danced till dawn to an orchestra and were deemed remarkable for their 'elegance of dress and refinement of manners'.[109]

On Monday 27 August 1849, the first ceremonial sod was turned for the railway station. By 6 a.m., all the trades were 'marshalled' at the Mechanics' Institute, waiting for the band of the 68th Regiment. At 6.30 a.m., on a signal from the St Nicholas bells, the procession moved off. Later, participants heard a speech from Fr Peter Daly and were treated to a 'sumptuous breakfast' by the carpenters and masons' guilds. All day, to the chiming of bells, 'the Trades were assembled in various and joyful groups … [with] not an ill-tempered expression' to be seen.[110]

That the trades were able to celebrate so lavishly was due to the unprecedented amount of construction work then in progress. While the various projects could never fully occupy the almost infinite number of labourers in the town and vicinity, their relative scarcity (and the campaigning described in Chapter Four) ensured full employment for artisans. Artisans' high daily wages acknowledged that work was only fitfully available to them; constant work with overtime, consequently, made them quite prosperous, prosperity which was shared by others, including those responsible for the 'elegance of dress' of artisan families.

But Galway was celebrating more than the end of three years of gloom. Rather, the news was regarded as a vote of confidence after decades of disappointment. More than that, the railway was seen as the key to the future, when Galway's location on the far west of the United Kingdom would make it the obvious station for mail between America and Europe. It was only a matter of time, or so many believed, before Galway replaced Liverpool as the major transAtlantic port.

Arguably, the celebrations of Monday, 27 August 1849 marked the end of Famine in Galway. A good harvest, moreover, ensured that optimism of the type displayed in the western capital was felt elsewhere in the country, although the blight persisted in parts of Munster, bringing the Famine into the new decade.[111]

But the air of optimism did not bring prosperity to everyone, although the prosperity did attract some who wished to share in it, like the starving would-be labourers from Clare who swamped the railway works. There was widespread dislocation: numbers in the workhouse remained high, as did workhouse mortality; beggars continued to irritate the citizens; while gangs of vagrant youths were believed responsible for a wave of petty crime. The survival instinct drove people into taking desperate measures as J. B. Keane, R.M., discovered when a 'half naked creature' walked into his petty sessions court and threw a stone at him. The 'heartless ruffian' then demanded that he be sent to jail.[112]

An English philanthropist, the Honourable Sidney Godolphin Osborne, who visited early in 1850, described the scene in the town as follows:

> I can only suppose that the opportunity of begging of the many men earning good wages, and the cheapness of food in the shape of coarse fish, has drawn hither the masses of nearly naked women and children who by day choke up every thoroughfare: where they sleep at night no one could tell me. I saw them again and again seeking food, even in the offal of the fish-market.[113]

Osborne's impressions were published in a book dedicated to Clarendon, the Lord Lieutenant. Inevitably, the work attracted significant attention, and the forthright criticism of practices Osborne witnessed in the west of Ireland's poor law institutions prompted a Poor Law Commission investigation. Although his observations on Galway's institutions were not entirely negative — he praised the Union's agricultural training facility for boys at Dangan — Jonathan Hall, poor law inspector, felt obliged to reply in detail to the criticisms. Osborne, he argued, had failed to acknowledge that his visit took place at 'a period of the year when the greatest destitution, and consequently the greatest pressure on the workhouse occurs'. In the circumstances, Hall argued that the feeding of inmates took priority and that if a minority had to spend a few days in their own clothes or on improvised bedding, it was of no great significance, especially as they were kept separate from the others.[114] These relatively minor deviations, he continued, took place against a background of resistance to the rules by a portion of the paupers:

> I have seen many take their discharge in preference to putting on the Union clothing; I have seen others go away, sooner than submit to be washed. Being deprived of the free use of tobacco has caused the departure of several; and some leave the house in consequence of being obliged to go to bed and get up at a regular hour. The most obnoxious regulation, however, is that which requires the able-bodied to be kept at work. To recent admissions, and more particularly among the adult males, anything like labour is objectionable.*

And if the men were incorrigible, the women were worse:

> The sole object of some women who come into the workhouse seems to be to oppose every effort which is made to maintain order, regularity and discipline. They cannot be made to work and they plead ignorance of the most ordinary domestic occupations. They watch every opportunity of abstracting food, in which they carry on a traffic.[115]

It may have presented difficulties for the administration, but it would seem from these remarks that many of Galway's poor had retained some sense of personal dignity through the vicissitudes of the previous years, and still resisted attempts to institutionalise them. Other evidence shows that resistance was stronger among men (women's commitment to their children, arguably, was stronger than their aversion to the poor law). Of 3911 workhouse inmates in Galway on 28 February 1850, 1,885 (48%) were under 15 years of age, 1446 (37%) were females over 15, while only 580 (15%) were males over 15. The difference in their relative capacities to survive independently in the mid-19th century world explains why more women than men took shelter in the workhouse. Only incapacitated or institutionalised men were availing of Galway's poor law system by February 1850 — 91.5% of the remaining adult male inmates had been inside for more than twelve months; the equivalent percentile for females was 51%. By then the workhouse was catering for virtually all claimants, only 11% of paupers remained on the outdoor relief lists, most of them aged people.[116]

---

* Another visitor's impressions of Galway Workhouse, published in the same year, were far more positive than Godolphin Osborne's: 'The workhouse here was on the best plan of any I had seen; the master and matron had been indefatigable in placing everything in its true position, and appeared to feel that their station was a responsible one, and that the poor were a sacred trust belonging still to the order of human beings'. (Asenath Nicholson, *Lights and Shades in Ireland*, London 1850, pp. 367-8).

Reflecting the return to normality, the Board of Guardians resumed responsibility for the Galway Union on 1 November 1849 simultaneously with 25 other Unions, leaving only four in the hands of paid guardians. Unlike some others, Galway's guardians paid tribute to the vice-guardians for the way they had 'conducted the affairs of the Union during seasons of very great distress and difficulty'.[117] All difficulty was not an end, however, for ratepayers were still attempting, by various means, to reduce their liabilities. Jonathan Hall reported that the 'impunity which has almost invariably heretofore attended the opposition of the ratepayers in some parts of the union' was still evident, necessitating the deployment of troops in support of rate collectors. Most serious was Nicholas Lynch's attempt to 'mulct the town' by having his estate on the west of the town removed from the Galway electoral division, leaving urban dwellers to 'support the nest of paupers who had first been allowed to squat upon the Barna property and who were soon after cleared away from these lands'.[118]

The tone of public discourse indicates that there was little empathy between the majority of healthy, law-abiding Galwegians on the one hand and the 'nests of paupers', and 'vagrant youths' — surviving victims of Famine — on the other. When Miss Hayes, 'the queen of song, our Irish prima donna' appeared in the theatre in November 1849, there was a place in the hierarchy of seating for almost everyone, everyone that is except the outcast and the indigent:

> The dress circle alone with its array of beauty, rank, fashion…, the second circle with its crowds of wealthy citizens and the fair and gifted members of their families…, the second gallery with its

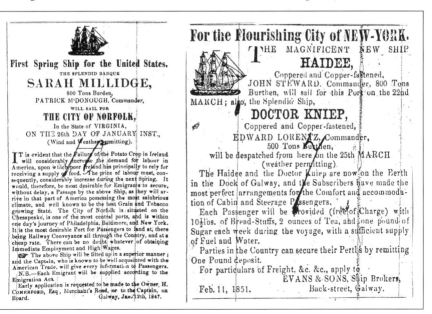

Changing the message: advertisements directed at would-be emigrants, 1847 and 1851.

distinct crowd of bachelors and belles…, the pit with its distinct crowd of critics and music fanatics and though last, not least, the upper gallery of the gods with its rows and roisterers.[119]

The conclusion to a local Famine study is necessarily tentative. The raw figures — for excess mortality, for population decline, for emigration from particular ports — tells much about national and regional patterns, but they can mislead also, since they shed little light on localised population movements.*

For example, County Galway lost 125,026 people, 30% of population, between 1841 and 1851. The average annual excess mortality rate in the county was among the highest on the island, with only Mayo and Sligo being worse affected. In the same period, the Galway Poor Law Union registered a decline of 16% in population, although rural parishes adjoining the town showed a more grievous decline: that part of Annaghdown in the Galway Union fell by 46%, Lackagh by 44%; Oranmore by 43%.[120] The population of the town of Galway, meanwhile, grew by 6,512 (38%). This was not unusual: other Irish towns and cities also registered significant population increases. The destitute were attracted by the opportunities to beg or to claim assistance available in urban areas, while the operation of the Gregory Clause meant that many of those attracted had no place to return to. An examination of the Galway town population in 1851 illustrates the point. 3,610 people, 15% of the total, were institutionalised, either in the workhouses or the gaols. Undoubtedly, a large part of the workhouse population came from elsewhere in the poor law union, while the prison population was drawn from the entire county. Likewise, the increase in the non-institutionalised part of the population can be accounted for by newcomers. Even mortality figures tell us little. The census estimate for excess mortality in the town of Galway of 3,592 cannot be considered either reliable or meaningful, when much of the evidence about the scale and timing of the influx is impressionistic or propagandist.

The level of emigration from the town is equally difficult to ascertain. It can be established that 8,675 or 1.3% of the 651,931 Irish people who landed in New York between 1846 and 1851 sailed from Galway, but this, unfortunately, is not a very revealing statistic. In the first place, we don't know where those people came from. What proportion hailed from the Galway poor law union, or from elsewhere in the west of Ireland? Not all emigrants, moreover, went to New York. Some ships sailed from Galway to St. Johns, to Quebec and to New Orleans. And many Galway emigrants sailed from other ports: from Liverpool, for example, which handled three-quarters of Irish emigration to North America during the period.[121] For what it's worth and for what it may say about

---

* . The 1851 Census did attempt to measure such movement (*General report*, 1856 xxxi, p. liii), but the results for Galway town are quite useless, showing, compared with 1841, a small drop in the percentage 'not born within the localities in which they then dwelt.' Limerick and Waterford cities, by contrast, show up to a quarter of their populations in this category. Urban Galway and Cork had hinterlands which were entirely in their own counties, so the influx in their cases was not measured in any meaningful way.

earlier patterns, 11.69% of the population of county Galway emigrated during the years 1851-55. This conformed almost exactly to the national average, but was markedly different to the adjoining counties of Mayo (7.72%) and Clare (17.59%).[122]

Like that of other ports, Galway's passenger trade was hastily improvised to meet demand. Only two ships carrying 185 people left Galway for New York in 1846, while 2,108 left on 16 ships during 1849.[123] The early emigrants travelled on perfunctorily adapted and inadequately provisioned cargo craft, which condescended to take passengers rather than ballast on their return journey Among them was Galway merchant Henry Comerford's *Sarah Milledge*.

High mortality among passengers, and the terrible tales of survivors gave birth to the 'coffin ship' legend. Before regulatory legislation was enacted, ship-owners tried to reassure a wary public. One strategy was to place accounts of successfully completed voyages in the local press — editors would not refuse 'news' from such regular advertisers. In June 1846, the *Vindicator* advised of six ships that had arrived in North America, all 'emigrants and hands quite well' after passages of between 30 and 40 days. The paper was particularly insistent on contradicting the 'painful but unfounded rumours put into circulation relative to the

That Galway became a by-word for poverty and destitution in the US in the post-famine period is indicated by this *Harper's Weekly* (1883) cartoon entitled 'Poor House from Galway'.

passengers in the *Sarah Milledge*.[124] A year later, the *Galway Mercury* announced that six ships had all reached America 'after an excellent passage', from whence they would soon return 'laden with corn from the fertile plains of the new world'. In the same issue appeared an 'unprompted' letter from passengers Michael Burke and John Geoghegan to Captain Stitt of the brig *Midas*:

> At the request of our fellow passengers, in all 190 souls, we beg to return you our sincere and heart-felt thanks for your kind and fatherly attention to all our wants and comforts during the voyage, in giving us all full share of provisions and plenty of water, and medicine late and early when required, and your constant attention on all occasions for which we shall be ever grateful and an account of which we have written to our friends in poor old Ireland.[125]

The news was not always good. In June 1848, for example, the *Commerce*, with 68 passengers, went down at Port Manton Island, Nova Scotia. Those drowned were 'Mary Burke and infant; Mrs Coyne and infant; Pat Corcoran, 24; a boy named Fogarty, 8; an infant named Cummings, 1; and a lad named John Leyden'.[126] And there was an even worse disaster in October 1849, when Henry Comerford's vessel, the St John, capsized at Cohasset, Massachussets, with the loss of ninety-nine Galway and Clare people. On this occasion, the fact that the brig had more passengers than she was licensed to carry attracted attention, as did the fact that Captain Oliver and the majority of his crew survived, but only eight of their passengers.[127]

Attempts to address the concerns of passengers and their families can be detected in advertisements placed by ship-owners. During 1846-47, the emphasis was on reassuring them about economic opportunities abroad. Henry Comerford argued:

> … the failure of the potato crop in Ireland will considerably increase the demand for labour in America, upon which poor Ireland has principally to rely for receiving a supply of food … There can be no doubt, whatever, of obtaining immediate employment and high wages.[128]

A few years later, there was no need to convince people of the advantages of emigration, but there were worries about the passage. Advertisements, consequently, drew attention to passenger amenities:

> … the subscribers have made the most perfect arrangements for the comfort and accommodation of cabin and steerage passengers. Each passenger will be provided (free of charge) with 10 lbs of breadstuffs, 2 ozs of tea, and 1 lb of sugar each week during the voyage, with a sufficient supply of fuel and water.[129]

The owners of the *Haidee* were making a virtue of necessity since the Passenger Acts, enacted due to public outcry, required them to properly provision the ship.

Incidentally, despite the relatively small numbers who sailed directly from its port, Galway was notorious in the New World. A caricature in *Harper's Weekly* depicting a coffin ship importing the disease-bearing denizens of the 'Poor House from Galway' indicates that Galway became a by-word for destitution.[130]

But if Galway immigrants were anathemised abroad, migrants were not welcome in Galway either. Prompted by the fear that 'strolling beggars' were carrying disease and that the Gregory Clause would increase their number, there was an attempt to expel mendicant non-citizens from the town in mid-1847. The failure of the attempt did not discourage those who wished to repeat it.[131]

The attitude towards indigent outsiders typified the contradictory nature of much of contemporary discourse. Denunciations of those believed responsible for starvation were combined with disdain for the starving; the insistence that Galway would 'look after its own' (to the exclusion of outsiders) was expressed by a community seeking public funding for projects of regional importance. Thus, Galway artisans demanded preference on all works, while the average 'decent person', weary of being approached by beggars, insisted that a particular landlord or the ratepayers of another union be made accountable for the beggars' upkeep.

The solvent citizen's fear of infection, the ratepayer's interest in a low rate, defined the attitude of the prosperous towards those in distress. Empathy was weak, class antagonism strong. At its mildest, this antagonism was expressed as suspicion: that every beggar was bogus; that every claimant had hidden resources. But occasionally, suspicion boiled over into violence against the poor. One instance was described by Fr John Roche, who gave the last rites to a dying child, Mary Coombe, at Renmore in July 1847. Finding her and her ailing parents lying in the ruins of their home, he established that the Coombes' house had been 'thrown down' by tenant neighbours of this labouring family as punishment for their having trampled 'a little corn' while gathering wild herbs for food. A few months later, when Christopher St George evicted cottiers and squatters from his Conamara estate, he claimed that he had only done so at the insistence — and with the assistance — of his tenantry.[132]

The antagonism and suspicion was reciprocal. It is difficult to establish, particularly from local evidence, whether the Famine resulted from an absolute shortage of food or from the fact that sections of the community were unable to establish their 'entitlement' to food.* But there is no doubt that the Galway crowd thought that sufficient food was available and that scarcity was being artificially created by exporters and farmers. The attacks on foodstores, the blockading of the roads and the port, all point to this. And if these

---

* It has been argued that adequate food has been available during the majority of famines, and that it is their lack of entitlement to a share of the food that causes people to starve. (See Amartya Sen, *Poverty and famines: an essay on entitlement and deprivation*, Oxford 1982 edn, pp. 1-8).

demonstrations, arguably, had little overall effect, they did expedite relief provision on at least two occasions.

After active collective protest ended in mid-1847, popular resistance was expressed in other ways: in the refusal of outdoor relief recipients to accept cooked food, to act as 'scavengers', or to enter the workhouse; in the resistance of inmates to the workhouse regime; in the opposition to piece-work on public works schemes. Such assertions of personal dignity were interpreted as proof that paupers were not needy after all, an interpretation which was supported by an official policy that insisted on paying starving workers on the basis of their performance, that refused to supply uncooked food lest it be traded for drink, and that wasted the time of its officials in devising projects for a 'labour test'.

NOTES

1. Mary Daly, *The Famine in Ireland,* Dundalk 1986, p. 124; Raymond Crotty, *Irish Agricultural Production: Its Volume and Structure,* Cork 1966, pp. 46-51, 66-68. Christine Kinealy, *This Great Calamity: the Irish Famine, 1845-52,* Dublin 1994, pp. xv-xxi.

2. J. S. Donnelly, 'Famine and the Government Response, 1845-46' in Vaughan, *New History,* pp. 273-78.

3. ibid.; *Galway Vindicator,* 8 November 1845; Kevin P. Nowlan, 'The Political Background' in Edwards and Williams, eds., *The Great Famine: studies in Irish history, 1845-52,* 1994 edn Dublin, p. 133-38.; Donald E. Jordan, *Land and Popular Politics in Ireland: County Mayo from the Plantation to the Famine,* Cambridge 1994, p. 105.

4. Mary E. Daly, 'The Operations of Famine Relief, 1845-47' in *The Great Irish Famine,* Cathal Póirtéar, ed., 1995, pp. 123-25; Nowlan, 'Political Background', pp. 133-36.

5. Outrage Papers 1845, 11/22865; Donal Kerr, *The Catholic Church and the Famine,* Dublin 1996, pp. 11-12.

6. Outrage Papers 1845, 11/22865. The figure for the Claddagh was an exaggeration.

7. *Galway Vindictor,* 5, 22 November 1845.

8. ibid., 22 November 1845.

9. *Galway Mercury,* 21, 28 February,

10. ibid., 24 January, 7 March 1846; National Archives, Outrage papers 1846, 11/1933.

11. *Galway Mercury,* 14 February 1846; see also *Galway Vindicator,* 11 February 1846.

12. Outrage papers 1846, 11/1933.

13. ibid 1846, 11/2541, 11/9415, 11/9623, 11/12273.

14. Kinealy, *Calamity,* pp. 54-60; *Galway Mercury,* 28 February 1846; *Galway Vindicator* 8 April 1846.

15. *Galway Vindicator,* 7 March, 15, 22 April 1846.

16. ibid., 8, 15, 18 April, 2 May 1846.

17. ibid., 1 April 1846.

18. ibid., 13 May 1846

19. ibid., 1, 15, 18 April 1846.

20. ibid., 6, 9, 13 May 1846

21. ibid., 16, 23 May

22. ibid., 17 June 1846.

23. ibid., 5 September 1846. The accounts of the Galway Relief Committee were published in the local press. During the same period, incidentally, the Cork committee raised £2300 locally (Kinealy, *Calamity,* p. 46).

24. *Galway Vindicator,* 29 April, 27 May 1846.

25. ibid., 27, 30 May, 3 June 1846.

26. ibid., 1, 7 July 1846. For similar disturbances elsewhere, see Andrés Eiríksson, 'Food Supply and Food Riots' in Cormac Ó Gráda, ed., *Famine 150: Commemorative Lecture Series,* Dublin 1997, pp. 67-93).

27. National Archives, Outrage papers 1846, 11/19291.

28. *Galway Vindicator,* 1 July, 5 August 1846.

29. ibid., 10, 27 June, 4 July 1846.

30. ibid., 30 May, 24 June, 4, 25 July 1846.
31. Galway Board of Guardians Minute Books; *Galway Vindicator*, 22 April 1846.
32. *Galway Vindicator*, 19 August 1846.
33. Peter Gray, *Famine, Land and Politics, British Government and Irish Society, 1843, 1850*, Dublin 1999, pp. 227-39; James S. Donnelly, 'The Administration of Relief' in Vaughan, *New History*, pp. 294-96; F. Darrell Munsell, 'Charles Edward Trevelyan and the Peelite Irish Famine Policy, 1845-1846' in *Societas — a Review of Social History*, I, iv, 1971, pp. 299-315.
34. Kinealy, *Calamity*, pp. 74-5.
35. ibid., pp.59-60, 71-3; *Galway Vindicator*, 1, 15, 22 July, 8, 19 August 1846.
36. *Galway Vindicator*, 19, 26 August, 9 September 1846.
37. ibid., 9 September 1846.
38. ibid., 12 September 1846.
39. Outrage papers 1846, 11/27341.
40. *Galway Vindicator*, 10 October 1846.
41. ibid., 7 October 1846.
42. *Galway Vindicator*, 10 October 1846
43. ibid., 10, 14 October 1846
44. Outrage papers 1846, 11/27635.
45. Outrage papers 1846, 11/26995, 11/27163, 11/27635, 11/27731, 11/30871; 1847, 11/15; *Galway Vindicator*, 10 October 1846.
46. *Galway Vindicator*, 4, 7 November 1846. See also Tomás de Bhaldraithe *Seanchas Thomáis Laighléis*, Dublin 1977, p. 20-21.
47. *Galway Vindicator*, 24 October 1846.
48. ibid, 21, 28, October, 7 November 1846; *Distress Correspondence*, July 1846-January 1847, Board of Works series, 1847 l, Galway Relief Committee to Walker, 2 November 1846; Captain Wynne to Lieut.-Colonel Jones, 5 November 1846.
49. *Galway Vindicator*, 7 November 1846.
50. ibid., 7, 10, 14 November 1846.
51. ibid., 17 November 1846.
52. ibid.
53. Galway Board of Guardians minutes, 14 February-26 December 1846; *Galway Vindicator*, 19, 23 December 1846, 2 January 1847. The workhouse returns may have been unreliable, as shall be seen later in this chapter.
54. *Galway Vindicator*, 27 February 1847.
55. ibid.
56. ibid., 9 January 1847.
57. Roinn Bhéaloideas Éireann, Iml. 1073, l.76-85.
58. See *Galway Vindicator* 15 April, 3, 14, 17 October 1846.
59. ibid., 23 January, 3, 20 February 1847; National Archives, Outrage papers 1847, 11/216, 11/240.
60. *Galway Vindicator*, 20 February 1847.
61. Thomas P. O'Neill 'The Organisation and Administration of Relief, 1845-52' in Edwards & Williams, *The Great Famine*, 235-38; Kinealy, *Calamity*, pp. 136-39; James S. Donnelly Jr., 'Irish Property Must Pay for Irish Poverty: British Public Opinion and the Great Irish Famine' in Morash & Hayes, eds, *Fearful Realities: New Perspectives on the Famine*, Dublin 1996, pp. 60-76.
62. *Galway Vindicator*, 16 December 1846.
63. ibid., 23 December 1846, 2 January 1847; James P. Murray, *Galway: a Medico-social history*, pp. 89-90.
64. *Galway Vindicator*, 24 March 1847.
65. ibid., 7, 14 April 1847.
66. ibid., 8 May 1847.
67. ibid., 21 April 1847, 12 May 1847
68. ibid., 5 May 1847. For other protests during the transition from public works to soup kitchen, see Eiríksson, 'Food Supply', pp. 84-88.
69. *Galway Vindicator*, 8 May 1847.
70. ibid., 8, 29 May 1847; *Appendix to the 5th Report of the Relief Commissioners*, H. of C. 1847-8, vol.?, p. 7.
71. *Galway Vindicator*, 19 May 1847.
72. ibid., 23 June 1847.

73. Peter Gray, 'Ideology and the Famine' in Póirtéir's *Irish Famine,* pp. 96-101.
74. *Galway Mercury,* 3 July 1847.
75. Galway Board of Guardian minutes, 10 July 1847, 'Report of the committee to inquire into the conduct of the master and other officers of the workhouse' and 'Report of Galway workhouse visiting committee, 27 July 1847.
76. *Galway Mercury,* 25 September 1847.
77. *Distress papers,* 5th series, 1847-48 lv, Hellard to Commissioners, 30 December 1847; 4, 23 January 1848; Cecil Woodham Smith, *The Great Hunger,* Sevenoaks, 1977 edn, p. 333.
78. National Archives, Outrage papers 1848, 11/922; *Distress papers,* 4th series, Hellard to Commissioners, 11, 15 November 1847 (enclosures); Commissioners to Hellard, 12, 13 November 1847.
79. ibid., 10 January 1848.
80. ibid., Hellard to Commissioners, 12 November 1847; 5th series, Hellard to Commissioners, 22 November, 16, 23 December 1847: Commissioners to Guardians, 28 December 1847.
81. ibid., Hellard to Commissioners, 12 November 1847; 5th series, Hellard to Commissioners, 18 November 1847, 29 January 1848.
82. ibid., 5th series, 16, 19 December 1847
83. *The Nation* 10 March 1848.
84. *Distress papers,* 5th series, Hellard to Commissioners, 23 December 1847.
85. ibid., *Galway Mercury,* 4 December 1847, 4 January 1848.
86. *Distress papers, 5th series,* Commissioners to Guardians, 28 December 1847; Thomas P. O'Neill, 'Relief', p. 247; Kinealy, *Calamity,* 210-16.
87. *Galway Mercury,* 15 January, 5 February 1848.
88. ibid., 23 June 1849.
89. National Archives, Outrage papers 1848, 11/111; *Distress papers,* 6th series, 1847-48 lvi, Vice Guardians to Commissioners, 5, 19 February 1848.
90. *Distress papers, 6th series,* Vice-Guardians to Commissioners, 6 March 1848; Commissioners to Vice-Guardians, 21 March 1848; McKie to the Commissioners, 23 March 1848.
91. National Archives, Outrage papers 1848, 11/347.
92. Irene Whelan, 'The stigma of souperism' in Póirtéir's *Famine,* p. 148; *Galway Mercury,* 26 February 1848.
93. Kerr, *Catholic Church,* pp. 83-89, *Galway Mercury,* 3 June, 29 July 1848.
94. *Distress papers,* 5th series, Bourke to Commissioners, 27 January 1848; Commissioners to Bourke, 29 January 1848.
95. ibid., 6th series, McKie to Commissioners, 6 March 1848; *Galway Mercury,* 15 April 1848.
96. *Distress papers,* 6th series, Vice-Guardians to Commissioners, 6 March 1848; Woodham Smith's, *Great Hunger,* p. 314.
97. ibid, 5th series, Hellard to Commissioners, 4 December 1847; 6th series, Vice Guardians, to Commissioners, 26 February, 11 March 1848.
98. ibid., 6th series, McKie to Commissioners, 17 February 1848; Commissioners to McKie, 22 February 1848; Vice-Guardians to Commissioners, 19 February 1848; Commissioners to Vice-Guardians, 22 February 1848.
99. ibid., McKie to Commissioners, 10 February 1848
100. *Distress papers,* 6th series, McKie to Commissioners, 24 February 1848; Vice Guardians to Commissioners, 26 February 1848.
101. ibid., p. 1030-31; 7th series, 1847-48 liv, p. 237; Appendix to 8th series, 1849 xlviii, pp. cv-cvi.
102. ibid., 7th series, McKie to Commissioners, 13 August 1849.
103. ibid., 8th series, McKie to Commissioners, 23 January 1849, Vice Guardians to Commissioners, 23 January 1849.
104. *Galway Mercury,* 17, 24 March 1849.
105. ibid., 31 March, 7 April 1849.
106. Murray, *Medico-social history,* pp. 96-99; *Galway Mercury,* 14, 21, 28 April, 5 May 1849.
107. *Galway Mercury,* 2 June 1849.
108. ibid., 14 July, 4, 18 August 1849.
109. ibid., 21 July, 11, 18 August 1849.
110. ibid., 2 September 1849.
111. See Kinealy, *Calamity,* pp. 265-68.
112. *Galway Mercury,* 29 September, 13 October, 17, 24 November, 29 December 1849

113. Hon. & Rev. S. Godolphin Osborne, *Gleanings in the West of Ireland*, London, 1850, pp. 49-50.

114. *Copies of the Correspondence between the Poor Law Commissioners of Ireland and their inspectors, relative to the statements contained in an extract from a book, entitled 'Gleanings in the West of Ireland'*, 1851, xlix, p. 5.

115. ibid., 1851, xlix, p. 5.

116. *Returns of the numbers of persons who were receiving relief on the last day of February 1850, distinguishing the unions, the in-door from the out-door paupers, the males from the females; and, with regard to in-door relief, the children under fifteen years old from the rest*, 1850 l, p. 2.

117. *A return showing the financial state of each union in Ireland where paid guardians have been appointed ... and copies of all reports and resolutions made by Boards of Guardians ... in those Unions ...* 1850 l, pp. 4-7, 14-15.

118. National Archives, Outrage papers 1849, 11/680, 30 November 1849; *Galway Mercury*, 6 October 1849.

119. ibid., 17 November 1849.

120. *1851 Census, area population and number of houses*, 1852-53 xcii, Co. Galway, pp. 81-2; *1851 Census, tables of deaths*, 1856, xxx, pp. 588, 598; Joel Mokyr, *Why Ireland starved*, London 1983, table 9.2. N.B. Calculations take account of the fact that the Galway PLU ceded territory to the newly-created Oughterard PLU in 1849.

121. Glazier & Tepper, eds., *The Famine Immigrants: lists of Irish immigrants arriving at the port of New York, 1846-1851*, Baltimore, 1986, vol. VII, pp. vii-ix. Only four Irish ports handled more of the New York emigration than Galway: Belfast, 3%; Dublin 2.2%; Cork 2.1%; Limerick 2.1%.

122. 1851 Census, *General Report*, 1856, xxxi, p. liv.

123. Glazier & Tepper, *Immigrants*, Table 1.

124. *Galway Vindicator*, 17 June 1846.

125. *Galway Mercury*, 5 June 1847.

126. ibid., 24 June, 1 July 1848.

127. *Boston Evening Herald*, 8 October 1849; *Boston Daily Times*, 10 October 1849; *Boston Pilot*, 13, 20 October 1849. Henry David Thoreau, *Cape Cod*, 1998 edn, Princeton, pp. 3-14.

128. *Galway Mercury*, 16 January 1847.

129. ibid., 1 March 1851.

130. Peter Gray, *The Irish Famine*, London, 1995, p. 94.

131. *Galway Vindicator*, 2, 5, 19 June 1847; 9 August 1848; *Galway Mercury*, 17 February 1849.

132. *Galway Mercury*, 10 July 1847; *Distress papers*, 6th series, St George to Redington, 28 March 1848.

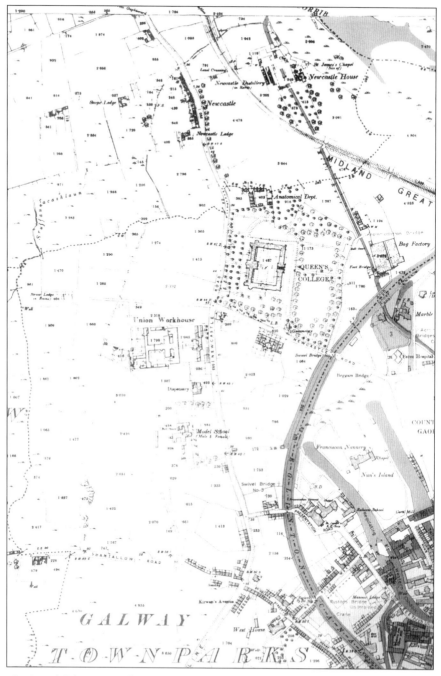

Section of Galway map of 1898 showing university, workhouse, model school, bag factory, Eglinton Canal and Galway-Clifden railway.

Economy, Politics, Society, 1850-1914

CHAPTER 7

'...commingled barbarianism and civilisation'

ECONOMY & INFRASTRUCTURE, 1850-1914

A Custom House with pillars and tower
Would rise where the Claddagh hovels cower,
Great chimes should ring and searchlights out-flash,
And liners the waves out there would thrash.
I'd make it Europe's first port of call...

Séamas O'Kelly, from 'The Lazy Wall'
Ranns and Ballads, 1918.

i) Routes of hope and glory?

Galway emerged from the Famine with its highest ever population, and with a civic tone that was uncharacteristically optimistic. Population increase* — accounted for by displaced country people — was experienced by most Irish towns during the crisis of those years, but Galway's optimism was not generally shared. The key factor in raising morale was the news in June 1849 that the railway was to be immediately extended to Galway.

For almost twenty years, there had been interest in developing a rail link between Galway and the east. A Galway Rail Committee was formed in 1831 — before the first railway sleeper was laid in Ireland — and during 1835 its secretary (Rev. John d'Arcy) had joined in discussions with the British and American Intercourse Company about improving communications between London and the new world. A packet station on Ireland's west coast, it was believed, linked by rail to Dublin and by steamship and rail to London, would significantly shorten the time and reduce the danger of the transAtlantic journey.[1] From a Galway perspective, the objective was to convince promoters that its port was better circumstanced than any other on the coast for their project. The celebrations of 1849 therefore were prompted by more than the promise of a rail link with Dublin — the railway would restore Galway's fortunes by giving her a share in transAtlantic trade.

---

* The urban population, as recorded in 1851, was 23,744, an increase of 6,518, or 38%, over 1841. But 3,610 (c.15%) of the people were in institutions in 1851.

165

The Browne Doorway, mid-19th century. It was moved to Eyre Square in the early 20th century. Note the boy posting a placard advertising 'excursion tickets' (courtesy of Irish Architectural Archive).

The announcement of June 1849 came at the end of a decade of 'railway mania'. There were only 31 miles of rail in Ireland in 1842, but this had risen to 700, either completed or under construction by 1850. Galway's claims, despite early local interest, had not won priority.

Credit for persuading the government and the railway company to extend the line from Mullingar to Galway was shared by Anthony O'Flaherty, MP, and the parish priest of Rahoon and St Nicholas North, Fr Peter Daly. Daly, a stubborn, abrasive, guileful and egotistical populist, would emerge as the dominant public figure in Galway during the 1850s; the railway celebrations marked the beginning of his ascendancy. Daly was a contemporary of Rev.

John d'Arcy and, in his own way, had been equally prominent, but hitherto his efforts had been mainly in the religious field. In the three decades since his ordination, he had been involved in inter-church controversies, implicated in intra-Catholic strife, and associated with efforts to improve the Catholic religious infrastructure. He had also accumulated personal wealth — sometimes in publicly unpopular circumstances. Daly's ambition to be bishop of Galway was frustrated in 1844 and, soon afterwards, he had himself co-opted onto the Town Commission. Thereafter, he devoted his energy to public affairs. Soon after his co-option, he was recognised by his fellow commissioners as one of their 'most competent members', and was chosen to present an address to the queen on their behalf. During 1849, he was elected chairman of the Gas Company, and co-opted onto the Harbour Board. In 1850, his standing was confirmed when he chaired a joint meeting of town and harbour commissioners called to memorialise the government for a commission of enquiry to determine the most suitable Irish port for a packet station.[2] Such an enquiry, locals felt, would confirm Galway's claims.

Less than two years elapsed between the turning of the sod for the Galway station on 27 August 1849 and the arrival of the first train on 21 July 1851.* All stages of the process, from the announcement to the official opening were thoroughly celebrated, and not even the destruction of the station roof in a gale a week before the first train was due dampened the anticipation.[3]

The first train to arrive averaged 30 miles an hour from Athlone, a significant improvement on the road transport speed. Travelling times had halved in the previous half-century, due to improved roads and to better-sprung carriages, but coaches still struggled to average ten miles an hour.[4] Although the ordinary fares were expensive —at 4s, a 3rd class trip to Athlone cost half a labourer's weekly wage — the introduction of cheap excursions enabled many who could not otherwise have afforded it to experience train travel before 1851 was out.[5]

Some were apprehensive about the railway age, not least local car-men, who expected to lose business. They hoped, however, that the loss would be offset by new opportunities in a context of increasing travel and trade. But they were disappointed, for the station manager made an arrangement with a Dublin contractor which had the effect of excluding them, and the car-men — 'poor industrious men', according to their statement — were 'crushed by the combination of those in office'.[6]

The expectation that the railway would bring visitors was fulfilled and, under the heading: 'Fashionable arrivals', one journal reported in August 1851

---

* It took some time, but the railway eventually brought an end to 'Galway time', and local clocks were put forward by 11.5 minutes, to bring them into line with the 'Dublin time' of the railway timetable. During 1870, a complaint was raised: 'Railway time is in advance of our old town clock, and, in consequence, a number of soldiers today, on forlough and intending to spend Christmas at home in England, were late for the train and had to return to barracks… Dublin time is the standard in every other town in Ireland' (*Galway Express*, 8 January 1870). A few years later, the town clock had been brought into conformity, but publicans persisted in serving drink beyond official closing time, pleading with magistrates that they were keeping 'Galway time' (National Archives, CSORP 1877/11751).

Official opening of Eglinton Canal by the Earl of Eglinton, Lord Lieutenant, 28 August 1852
(from *Illustrated London News* courtesy of Timothy Collins).

that, already, 'a large number of strangers have availed themselves of the opportunity offered by the railway to visit our town'. The development was welcomed in 'fashionable circles', where, since the opening of the railway, people had been 'had been enjoying an almost uninterrupted series of balls'. For some visitors, Galway was a staging post to more exotic destinations and, in 1852, it was remarked that 'the wild and magnificent scenery' of Conamara, was gaining 'a widespread celebrity'. In the circumstances, it was anticipated that Galway was well-positioned to become 'the most fashionable resort … not alone in the kingdom, but in Europe'.[7]

There was an increase, too, in the numbers frequenting Salthill, raising expectations that it could become the premier seaside destination on 'the Great Western route'. But the resort was not benefiting to the extent that it might. Because there were many deep holes near the shore — a 'reprehensible practice' of the peasantry was blamed — it was dangerous for swimmers. And rocks and stones marred the most accessible beach, the one near Seapoint House. Moreover, bathing facilities were as meagre as they had been in the 1830s, with no provision for men, and the 'few miserable' bathing boxes for ladies considered inadequate. Most serious, however, was the accommodation shortage, which caused hundreds to cut short their visits during 1852.[8]

But there were indications of imminent improvements. A Mr Barton had purchased, in the Encumbered Estates court, a large tract between Salthill village and Blackrock, and was examining ways of transforming it into 'one of the most scenic places in Ireland'. He intended to erect villas and bathing lodges, laid out in 'model villages'. A *Galway Packet* writer had a better idea: 'If Mr Barton's property were divided into small lots or terraces, like Kingston, Killiney, Dalkey etc., it would offer accommodation to the multitude eager to frequent Galway'. And in welcoming the eviction of forty tenants on the adjoining estate of Lord Clanmorris, the paper anticipated that the vacant tenements would be demolished and the property 'laid out like Mr Barton's'. Barton himself proceeded quickly and by the following spring 130 men and 12 horses were employed in building piers and a sea-wall to make the shoreline suitable for bathing.[9]

Others followed Barton's example in providing tourist facilities, and in coming to live in Salthill. In 1860, one commentator marvelled at the development of the suburb:

> Some few years ago, none of the neat cottages which now present themselves to the eye were in existence at this favourite watering place. The ground beyond Seapoint was a mere waste … We have had for the past few years much pleasure in observing the remarkable progress which has been made in this locality, where small cabins are giving way to buildings of more modern construction. Some beautiful residences of modern architecture for gentlemen preferring to reside beyond the smoke and dust of the town were raised by Mr Rutledge … Certainly, this year at all events, the proprietors, &c., of land in that direction would appear to have simultaneously decided upon erecting houses and cottages for the reception of those persons who seek in summer the sea-side, to enjoy the exhilarating breezes, and to participate in the health-restoring benefits of sea-bathing. But the most astonishing thing of all, perhaps, is the erection of a splendid and commodious hotel [the Eglinton] on a spot where, a few years ago, seagulls had sole possession of the swamp.[10]

Elsewhere in the town, a number of other projects had been completed. The new Queen's College had enrolled its first cohort of 68 students on 30 October 1849, although the building would not be completed for another year. The delay was attributed to the shortage in the town of skilled building workers. Indeed, the period 1848-52 was one of almost unprecedented prosperity for Galway's tradesmen, as their services were sought by rival contractors on several projects, and their trade unions consequently enabled to regulate working conditions and to win excellent wages.[11]

Following the completion of the railway, the railway company continued to employ building workers in the erection of a prestigious hotel, which opened in the summer of 1852. The Railway Hotel — 'a chief ornament to our ancient town' — boasted '69 bedrooms; a saloon 50 feet by 24; 4 dining rooms; 2 spacious coffee rooms, 36 feet by 22; corridors and galleries, with grand staircase in centre hall', and had 100 lamps which were lit by the Gas

Company.[12] A telegraph line, erected on poles 68 yards apart along the railway, also came into operation in 1852, bringing Galway 'within a few minutes speaking distance of the capital of the kingdom'.[13]

Another undertaking which was completed in the summer of 1852 was the canal linking Galway port with Lough Corrib. Work on this project — which was suggested by the engineer Alexander Nimmo in the early 1820s and was part of the harbour commissioners' brief in the 1830s — was begun by the Board of Works in March 1848. But the canal was only one element of a scheme to improve drainage, navigation and millpower, it being also envisaged that Ballinrobe and Castlebar would be linked with Galway by canals between Loughs Corrib, Mask and Carra. Considerable work was carried out on the 4-mile Corrib/Mask canal, but it was left incomplete, due to engineering difficulties, to a post-Famine labour shortage, and to the realisation that inland navigation would be of only marginal utility in the railway age.[14] But that was all in the future on Friday 20 August 1852, when the Earl of Eglinton, Lord Lieutenant of Ireland, performed the official opening of the Galway canal. Thousands gathered for a ceremony, the highlights of which were a gun salute from a ship in the bay, — 'to the delight of the Galwegians, unaccustomed to these things' — and a flotilla led by the Eglinton party aboard the steamer *O'Connell,* and followed by 'a long procession ... of fishing hookers and other boats belonging to the Claddagh, with those of the Board of Works, and private parties'.[15]

It was not the sort of reception that the *Galway Packet* would have organised. Advising Galwegians to receive Eglinton 'courteously as a foreign visitor', it

Reception for the Earl of Eglinton at Queen's College Galway, August 1852
(from *Illustrated London News*).

urged them not to 'wallow before him as the representative of an alien foreign government'.[16]

During his visit, the Lord Lieutenant presided over the Royal Irish Agricultural Society's prestigious cattle show, held for the first time in Galway, and attended by visitors from 'every quarter of the Kingdom'. The event took place in the Grammar School fields, where three acres were covered by temporary sheds, erected in the shape of a crescent. Galway farmers were advised to be 'prepared to receive beneficial hints' about cattle raising, in light of the recent salutary lesson on the 'dangerous dependency on potatoes'.[17] It soon became apparent that this lesson was well-learned. And ultimately, contrary to expectations in 1852, the cattle show proved to be a better signpost to the west of Ireland's future than the Eglinton Canal.

As for the Earl of Eglinton, the people of Galway and their representatives would 'wallow' before him, to a greater extent than they had before any equivalent public figure. Through his relationship with Fr Daly and others, all hopes for economic well-being came to be vested in him, and a veritable litany of developments were named in his honour. As well as the Eglinton Canal, there were the Eglinton Hotel, the Eglinton Cricket Club, the Eglinton Racquet Court and the Eglinton Baths in Salthill. For her part, Lady Eglinton bestowed her name upon a Corrib steamer. There was also Eglinton-street, connecting Newtownsmith and Woodquay with the main shopping area along the line of a section of the town wall.[18] On Eglinton-street were located two shopping emporia, each almost as impressive as the Railway Hotel — the Colonial Buildings operated by Killian & Co., and the Eglinton Buildings operated by Farquarson & Moon.[19]

An English visitor of the early 1850s remarked on the appearance of Galway, with its 'commingled barbarianism and civilisation'. There was 'great preparation for the future', she wrote — telegraph, railway, 'monster hotel', docks, canal, were complete — but there was 'no manufactures yet, no traffic, no shipping, and the people asleep'.[20] All of this, meanwhile, had left its mark on the streets. The canal works in particular had wrought havoc, with Mill-street being frequently impassable. And the canal itself was without barriers, so people frequently fell in. By 1853 — five years after digging commenced — 30 people had already drowned and, but for the efforts of one Georgy Ward, the tally would have been higher. In July 1854, it was reported that 'a boy named King, under influence of intoxication', had found himself in the canal near New Road, but was rescued by Ward. In commending the young man, a journalist pointed out that King was the eighth person he had rescued from the canal. But the story had a tragic denouement, for in October 1854 it was reported that Georgy himself had been fished from the canal, having attempted suicide. Another guardian of drunks was Patrick McArdle. During 1855, after he pulled a 'respectable-looking' countryman from the water he informed readers of a local paper that this was the third time that he had rescued that particular individual. Such episodes bolstered the arguments of those demanding barriers, but there were navigational and financial reasons for not erecting them. Two decades passed, during which the number of drownings reached 85, before the authorities moved to provide the long-demanded railings.[21]

Visitors might have been bemused by 'great preparation for the future' side-by-side with neglect of the present, but Galwegians saw no contradiction. As far as one leader writer was aware, 'the eyes of all intelligent persons at home and abroad, in Europe and America, are fixed upon Galway'.[22] The rail link to Dublin had conferred 'important advantages' on the place, but it was the imminent developments that were capturing international attention:

> By means of this splendid Canal ... upwards of sixty miles of internal navigation will be opened up through a fertile and once densely populated country — the products of which, as through a great artery, will thereby be poured into this seaport. Galway will then drain the exports of a larger basin than any other port in the kingdom ... A most material augmentation may also be anticipated from the projected railway connecting Belfast with Galway, which twelve months more will see, in all human probability, an accomplished feat. This line would open to Galway the traffic of Scotland and the North, and, joined with steam communication with America, would operate in a few brief years to elevate the 'ancient citie' to a position of commercial greatness to which the most sanguine amongst us would not now dare to look forward.[23]

The mixture of hyperbole, anticipation and fantasy was typical of discourse in Galway during the 1850s. That this was so was due in large measure to Fr Peter Daly. He was a man for whom understatement — of ambition or intention — was never the preferred register.

But Fr Daly was not just a day-dreamer and a braggart. He might be more accurately seen as a man of action who, in seeking to motivate was inclined to overstep the mark and raise false expectations. In 1849, with the rail link secured, he set about demonstrating Galway's suitability as a packet station. Locally-raised funds, backed by contributions from an American investor and from the Midland & Great Western Railway (MGWR), enabled him to charter the *Viceroy*. It only remained to browbeat the Postmaster General into bestowing quasi-official status on the paddle-steamer's transAtlantic voyage from Galway by permitting it to carry a token amount of mail.

Fr Daly watched the *Viceroy* leave Galway on 1 June 1850. Its objective was to reach Nova Scotia in six days, one day less than the journey from Liverpool. But storms and fog ensured that the voyage took eleven days, and that the short leg from Halifax to New York took another four. On its return voyage, the *Viceroy* fared even worse: two days out of port she was lost. Further disappointments for those interested in Galway's development followed. In 1851, the American promoters of a 'New York & Galway Steamship Company' abandoned their project and during September 1852, the Steam Packet Commissioners reported unfavourably on Galway. That several of the commissioners had vested interests in Liverpool's retention of the mail contract was but a small consolation in the circumstances.[24]

The commissioners' report was a setback. A mail contract would have guaranteed regular sailings between Galway and America, and its revenue would have subsidised passenger and cargo services. Given this boost, or so proponents of the project insisted, Galway could become the conduit through which would pass all Irish traffic to the new world. In the absence of packet station status, however, there remained an opportunity to develop passenger services. There was certainly demand: 12% of Co Galway's population, for example, and 8% of Mayo's, left the island between 1851 and 1855. And most of those going to America went first to Liverpool. But to win a share of this business in an era of ever-larger ships and of intense competition, Galway port needed considerable improvement. Ship-owners would not risk running aground in a west of Ireland harbour lacking even repair facilities. In the 1850s, the harbour commissioners began to consider how a new pier, breakwater, and dry dock might be provided, but were restricted by their own regulations. New legislation removing some of the obstacles, however, came into effect in autumn 1853. The Harbour Board became a legal corporation with 21 elected members, something that did not happen without intrigue, as Fr Daly and a party of his opponents sought to gain advantage. The same pattern was apparent in efforts to reform the Town Commission, the subject of another parliamentary bill of 1853.[25] And if the improvements to the town and to the harbour canvassed during the reform process were not effected quickly, the strengths and weaknesses of the contending factions were immediately apparent. Fr Daly became chairman — and undisputed master — of the town commissioners, while his critics gained the upper hand among the harbour commissioners.

Disappointed expectations were responsible for the recriminatory tone of public discourse in Galway in the middle 1850s. Railway, canal and hotel were all completed, while Fr Daly claimed to be on familiar terms with the Empire's most powerful figures, yet there were few signs of the promised benefits. It would take the intervention of an outsider to restore the sense of optimism that had been evident in the immediate post-Famine period.

John Orrel Lever, a Manchester businessman, had grown rich by leasing ships to the British government during the Crimean war, and was looking around for fresh opportunities. Through trading contacts with the west of Ireland, he was persuaded of Galway's potential and with the backing of the MGWR, he formed a transAtlantic steamship company with himself and Fr Daly as co-directors. The company chartered a number of ships, and began operations of 1858. But the misfortunes of the Galway Line — according to its historian, Timothy Collins, 'one of the most unfortunate shipping lines ever registered' — began almost immediately. As the *Indian Empire* entered Galway Bay for the first time, to receive passengers and cargo for the Galway Line's first

John Orrell Lever, sometime MP for Galway (courtesy of Timothy Collins).

transAtlantic voyage, it ran aground. It was symptomatic of the state of public opinion that, on reaching shore, both pilots were arrested on suspicion of having been bribed by 'certain Liverpool interests' to scupper the Galway Line. Repairs were carried out, but fresh misfortunes presented themselves in mid-Atlantic and the *Indian Empire* eventually limped into Halifax, a disappointing twelve days after she left Galway.

In the first six months, Galway Line ships had other mishaps, but if these were attributed to teething problems — and a modicum of bad luck — the promoters were justified in feeling satisfaction as they faced into 1859. And satisfaction soon gave way to euphoria when it was announced that the Line had been awarded the postal contract. The award — in the gift of the government — was controversial, being the result of the parliamentary arithmetic at Westminster. Irish M.Ps held the balance of power, and they had been marshalled in Galway's cause, principally by Fr Daly.

The arrangement with the post office was for a fortnightly sailing from Galway to Boston/New York, via Halifax, with a subsidy of £3,000 for each return journey completed. There were penalty clauses however: a fine being deductible, for example if a ship took longer than eleven days and two hours to get from Galway to New York in summer-time. In the circumstances — transAtlantic steam-shipping was still at an experimental stage — accidents were inevitable.[26]

In the re-structuring of the company to meet its new circumstances, it was given a new name: the Atlantic Royal Mail Steam Navigation Company. However, it continued to be known generally as the Galway Line. Finance was raised through a share issue of 5000 shares at £10 each, but only two-thirds of this amount was subscribed, and the company was seriously under-capitalised. Evidently, Galway provided a significant portion of its capital, for, according to one list of shareholders, 65 had addresses in the town and county. Notable among them were town-based merchants and clergymen.[27]

The contract came into effect in June 1859 but before that there were two elections, a February by-election and a May general election. The candidacy, in the Conservative interest, of John Orrell Lever was strongly promoted by his

PUNCH, OR THE LONDON CHARIVARI.—June 15, 1861.

THE MAN FOR GALWAY.

Pam (loq). "OHO! FATHER DALY! NOW I THINK I UNDERSTAND YOU."

Press cartoon showing Fr Peter Daly persuading Prime Minister Palmerstown to award postal subsidy to Galway, *Punch*, 15 June 1861 (courtesy of Timothy Collins).

business partner Fr Daly. In February, after Sir Thomas Redington was intimidated into withdrawing, Lever was returned unopposed. In May, Lever headed the poll, benefiting, according to one sceptic from 'Galway gratitude' — a 'lively sense of favours to come'.[28] In the excitement of the campaigns, it seemed that Galway's prospects knew no bounds. For his part, John Orrell Lever had a very specific vision of a prosperous Galway:

> I want to see every man, woman and child in Galway well-fed, well-clad, and well-housed; their children well-educated; bonnets on the heads of working men's wives; good boots and stockings on their feet, and a twelve pound leg of mutton in their kitchen ranges every Sunday and Thursday, with all the appropriate accompaniments.[29]

Rhetoric, however, did not float ships, and the Galway Line's vessels continued to encounter difficulties. The sinking of the *Connaught* in October 1860 — in the wake of the loss of the *Argo* — was an especially serious setback. The consequent financial problems and loss of confidence were bad enough, but even worse was the effect on the Line's capacity to fulfil existing commitments. It was indicative of the extent of local disappointment that sabotage by 'Liverpool interests' was again investigated.

There were competitors who took advantage of the Line's embarrassment to lobby against her, and in January 1861, the post office announced the temporary suspension of the contract. Because there was little sign by May that the company had seaworthy vessels sufficient to resume, the temporary suspension was made permanent. Only 17 of the previous year's 45 contracted voyages had been completed, it emerged, and of these only three had been within the terms of the contract.[30] Soon afterwards, the Galway Line's services ceased. There was to be an epilogue to the saga, however.

The struggle of Galway and its shipping line to establish a packet station had enough romantic ingredients for a 19th century novel — an aged priest fighting to save his community, the adventure of ocean travel, the latest in steam technology, the race to establish record transAtlantic speeds — and it was little wonder that it captured the public imagination. It seemed, moreover, that the enhanced opportunities for trade that it promised could only stimulate industry and agriculture. In Galway, where fortunes and futures were more immediately at stake, hopes lingered that the line could be revived and the mail contract restored. Indeed, in the economic environment of the early 1860s, there was little choice but to hope.[31]

Then, in 1863, the balance of parliamentary forces again worked to Galway's advantage. This time it was the turn of the Whigs to succumb to pressure from Irish MPs, and to announce that the postal subsidy would be restored if the Galway Line could show that it had sufficient seaworthy ships. But the company that took up the offer was rather different to the one that had lost the contract two years earlier. Financial problems had forced the directors to seek new investors, and the Galway influence in its affairs was very much diluted. When services resumed in August 1863, Liverpool was the port of embarkation and Galway merely a port of call. One thing did not change, however, and that was the undercapitalised state of the company. It was not in a position to weather even minor adversity, and within months it was in difficulty. In February 1864, the last of the Galway Line's ships was withdrawn from service, and in June, the company was wound up.[32]

In 1865, John Orrel Lever failed in his bid to be re-elected for Galway; in 1867, he was declared bankrupt. Fr Peter Daly died in 1868, in his 80th year.

ii) The economy
In 1850, the harbour commissioners received a query on Galway's economy and infrastructure from an Irish-American business organisation. The response emphasised the town's great potential, but revealed that little of that potential was being exploited. Only six locally-produced articles — marble, wool, stockings, hides, brushes, and whiskey — were identified as being suitable for export to the United States.[33] It is evident that economic activity generally was severely retarded in the Famine's aftermath and that the few signs of local prosperity detected by observers in the early 1850s derived from the short-term employment available on the various infrastructural projects in the town and vicinity.[34]

It may have been a collective response to the trauma of Famine that those charged with directing Galway's affairs became fixated on the grandiose rather than on the workaday (the neglect of the harbour being a case in point). A number of factors affected the fortunes of Galway port: the local economy, the disposition of government, competition from other ports. But a safe and navigable harbour was a prerequisite for a port seeking a share of transAtlantic trade. And this was something that Galway lacked. A major reason for this was a dispute over a few thousand pounds between the harbour commissioners and their contractor in the late 1830s. One effect of the dispute, which was not resolved until the late 1860s, was to give the contractor a mortgage on the harbour, restricting the commissioners' capacity to complete the 1830s scheme, and impeding further improvement. And even after that problem was resolved, the impression is that Galway harbour development continued to lag behind developments in shipping.[35]

Away from the spotlight, routine economic activity resumed (or continued) in the post-Famine period, and there was a trickle of outside investment, perhaps attracted by Galway's prospects in the age of steam. Tourism in Salthill, it has already been shown, benefited from the efforts of parvenu, Mr Barton. There were changes too in the long-established paper-making industry. Low grade paper had been produced in Galway since the late 18th century but, in the early 1850s, a Mr Tatton began to turn out a better quality product that could be used by the local newspapers.[36]

The important milling industry was grievously affected by the Famine, and circumstances made recovery difficult. In 1851, a visitor remarked on Galway's many empty warehouses, and late in the following year, millers were prominent among the traders and merchants who addressed a memorial to the MGWR. The cost of transporting was too high, contended the petitioners; would the directors consider reducing freight charges? But the directors would not. For the millers, the response was so disappointing that they contemplated establishing their own steamer service to compete with the rail monopoly.[37] But broader changes in agriculture in the post-Famine period also affected milling. Due to the repeal of the corn laws and to greater demand for meat, farmers turned away from tillage, and towards cattle and sheep-rearing. Increasingly, the raw material for Galway's milling industry came from the American plains rather than from the fields of Connacht.[38]

For some, the growing numbers of livestock represented a business opportunity and, in 1854, Messrs Beard and Partridge established a Horse, Cattle and Carriage Repository at Merchants Rd (Beard also operated a Coach Factory in Abbeygate-street; Partridge was a fellow of the London Veterinary Medical Association). Auctions were held in the Merchants Road premises on the last Saturday of each month, where 5% commission was payable on sales of horses and carriages, and half as much on cattle.[39]

The sea-fishing community emerged demoralised from the Famine. Many of the younger men joined the Navy; others emigrated, including some that continued fishing in Baltimore, Maryland.[40] And of those who could not afford to emigrate, fifteen stowaways were discovered on the New York-bound *Adriatic* in 1861.[41] The fishing industry was among those that attracted outside investment during the 1850s. Several enterprises put trawlers in the bay, but their efforts — fully detailed in Chapter Ten — elicited mixed reactions. Business interests and public bodies were generally welcoming, but the fishermen bitterly resisted. Moreover, the fishermen's arguments — which were given weight by their conspicuous poverty — were occasionally echoed outside their own ranks, as in a press comment on the London & West of Ireland Fishing & Fish Manure Company:

> The Fishing Company are sweeping the seas of all kinds of fish, which they are exporting in large quantities. Fish and lobsters are being sent off to Holyhead for the English market; whilst there is scarcely a thought bestowed upon the necessity of leaving anything like a supply for the home market ... In the midst of all this, what has been done by the company to improve the condition of the poor Claddagh men?[42]

While it is unlikely that that the 'condition of the poor Claddagh men' had a high priority with the owners of the Fishing & Fish Manure Company, local prosperity was a declared objective of several enterprises established in the post-Famine period. Most of them generated more expectations than riches, but all provided some employment. The three most significant — (a) the Linen and

Muslin industry, (b) the Irish Iodine & Marine Salts Company, and (c) the Bag Factory — merit individual examination.

a) *Linen and muslin*

For some advocates of Galway, improvements in transport raised the possibility of making profitable connections with Ulster's textile industries. And when the directors of the Ulster Railway Company considered opening a direct line to the west, their arguments were strengthened.[43]

At a Galway meeting in December 1851 of the Irish Manufacture Movement — according to a report 'self-reliance' was the movement's 'invaluable talisman' — speakers commended flax-growing as a starting-point for the development of manufacturing. A few months later, two local businessmen were satisfied enough with the amount of the crop planted locally to announce the opening of the Eglinton Scutch Mill. And in the following year, Belfast merchants established a flax market on the banks of the canal, next to the scutch mill. To celebrate, the Royal Galway Institute — whose main business was the organisation of public lectures and the maintenance of a library — held a banquet for the principal Belfast flax-buyers.[44]

Belfast investors also provided the capital for Mr Overend's new factory in Whitehall. The factory, on three floors, employed 33 weavers — 'who had preserved their looms against all vicissitudes'. They were earning 8s to 10s per week for making checked muslin and coloured calico, but this was expected to rise to £1 when they had accustomed themselves to the fly-shuttle.[45] With muslin being manufactured locally, other possibilities suggested themselves and, in March 1853, the Royal Galway Institute invited a Mr McCaul of Belfast to lecture on the sewed muslin trade. The Dominican, Fr Thomas Rush, was persuaded and he established a Sewed Muslin School in the Claddagh. By May 1853, 130 girls were receiving instruction there, and it was anticipated that 'all Catholic female children of the town' could be occupied in the trade, when work was given out to the houses of those trained. Competent workers would earn 2s 6d to 3s a week. The industry was hardly established, however, when it was hit by a Crimean war-related downturn in maritime trade. Belfast merchants were urged to ensure that Galway's infant industry survived the crisis and not to reduce wage rates, already far lower than in Ulster. But no heed was paid to the appeals, for, in 1854, it was reported that poor girls were being 'defrauded of a great portion of their wages' in a 'manufactory for muslin sewing in this town purporting to have been established for the purpose of encouraging female industrial labour'. Fr Rush was said to be busy in setting up a less exploitative alternative. Manifestly, the muslin sewing industry did not fulfil expectations, but it survived in a small way, at least until the departure from the town of northern businessman, Mr Andrews, in 1862.[46]

b) *Irish Iodine & Marine Salts Company*

A success story of the post-Famine period was McArdle & Bullock's iodine factory on Long Walk, which utilised locally-harvested seaweed. The only such factory in Ireland in the early 1850s, it exported to Britain, the United States, and several European countries. Local residents, however, objected to emissions of a 'deadly poisonous vapour' from the plant and, in 1855, they lobbied the local authorities to suppress activity 'calculated to bring on the town cholera and typhus fever'.[47] One of the firm's principals, James Smith McArdle of Co. Monaghan, was a chemist and, in 1851 it was reported that he was conducting experiments with a view to extracting other compounds from seaweed. By 1862, he had registered a new patent for iodine.[48]

McArdle had not sufficient capital to exploit his discovery, and in 1863 he announced the formation of the Irish Iodine & Marine Salts Company, based in Galway but financed by investors from further afield. Lord George Hill became chairman of the company, Sir James Dombrain, vice-chairman, and Thomas H. Thompson, a land agent on Árainn, was also prominent in its affairs. McArdle was company manager and chemist.

The new company erected a depot for the collection of seaweed on Árainn, and a factory for the extraction of 'an extraordinary number of substances' in Galway. The factory on Long Walk consisted of a number of sheds, floored with perforated flags, under which were situated large tanks. As the raw seaweed decomposed, liquid matter flowed into the tanks. The liquid was next reduced by distillation to 'a charred substance'. From this substance was extracted Iodine, Magnesium Salts and other compounds. Barges brought the decomposed seaweed by canal and river to an auxiliary factory building which was erected on the property of Lord Clanricarde at Terryland — presumably so as not to upset the Long Walk residents. There, the waste material was rendered into fertiliser.[49]

McArdle's connection with the Marine Salts Company did not last long and, in 1865, a new manager, Mr Glassford, announced changes in the company's operations. Drying sheds and a large kiln were erected on Árainn, and the preliminary processing was carried out there. Changes followed too in the Galway plant: the working environment in the Long Walk factory was reported to have become much cleaner, and it would appear that activity at Terryland ceased. In 1866, the Galway factory was extended when a property was leased from the Harbour Commissioners.[50] These heavy investments stretched the company's resources — 'keeping it down, paralysing its energies, and retarding its progress' — but it was reported in 1868 that the burden was being 'gradually removed'. In that year also, the first Galway-based director, James Campbell, J.P., was appointed to the board. It was anticipated that his availability would be advantageous to Glassford, but it would seem, rather, that Campbell replaced him as manager. In 1872, the company was 'vigorous' under Campbell, but within a few years it had gone out of business. By September 1876, a Mr Irvine had taken over the Long Walk premises, where he was manufacturing sulphuric acid. A few years later still, a witness before the Select Committee on Irish Industries stated that the Iodine company had collapsed because it became uncompetitive, 'owing to the discovery in

Germany of nitrate of soda in the mines near Magdeburg' and 'discoveries in Peru of certain salts that produced iodine'.[51]

c) *The Bag Factory*

Two industries — the Bag Factory and the Clog Factory — were established on adjoining sites in Earl's Island in the mid-1860s. The former, a locally-owned enterprise which imported its raw material, was a significant employer for almost three decades; the latter, a subsidiary of the Lancashire Clog Sole Manufacturing Company Limited which used Mountbellew-grown timber, was short-lived. The problems of the Clog Factory, which traded successfully for a few years after 1867, were said to have resulted from the introduction of an expensive new chemical process in the early 1870s.[52]

The origins of the Galway Jute Spinning Company — which operated the Bag Factory — went back to 1865, when a sub-committee of the town commissioners examined the feasibility of such an industry. (It would seem that the commissioners — taking their cue from Fr Peter Daly — considered that they had responsibility for industrial development as well as for urban administration). From the beginning, the fortunes of the factory were tied to those of the flour-milling trade. Indeed, it was the realisation that hundreds of thousands of flour sacks annually were brought in from Dublin and elsewhere that attracted the town commissioners' interest. As anticipated, the sub-committee reported favourably, and recommended the idle former bleach mill near the Queen's College as suitable premises. A limited liability company was formed, shares were offered, the directors took possession of the vacant mill, and alterations commenced during July 1866.[53] Some years later, one of the original shareholders, Colonel James O'Hara, won control of the company. His account of its early history was as follows:

> The Company was got up for the purpose of developing the industrial resources of the west of Ireland ... We got a great number of philanthropic people together who took a certain number of shares, and it worked with great success for a number of years. I then, to give myself a sufficient interest to enable me to work the concern without charging them a salary for my services, in a weak moment, bought up the greater part of the shares, more than half the shares at all events, and I have been working it ever since for myself and the shareholders.[54]

O'Hara was Galway's leading citizen in the later decades of the 19th century, the inheritor of Fr Peter Daly's mantle. A landed proprietor at Lenaboy and a member of a prominent Galway family,* he became chairman of the Harbour

---

* James O'Hara of Lenaboy, sometime associate of James Daly, was MP for Galway, 1826-31. Colonel James O'Hara was an unsuccessful Conservative candidate for the town in 1868.

Board in 1865, a position he would hold for thirty years. He was also a long-time chairman of the town commissioners.

Over two days in June 1885, O'Hara was examined by the Select Committee on Industries (Ireland). As a leading local politician and public official, he was well-acquainted with economic circumstances in the west. Of particular interest to the committee, however, was his experience as chairman of one of the leading industries in Connacht.

The Bag Factory entered a period of difficulty in the mid-1870s, soon after O'Hara took control, due mainly to competition in flour-milling. Large-scale rolling technology enabled American flour exporters to supply Ireland at a low cost. Flour merchants in Limerick, Cork, and Dublin survived by adopting the new technology, a strategy not open to under-resourced Galway millers. The Galway Bag Factory had supplied over a million bags a year in the mid-1870s; by the early 1880s, this had fallen to 435,000.[55]

The company had two to three hundred workers in 1885. The vast majority were women, some of them outworkers who were able to 'add to the value of otherwise empty hours, without the disadvantage of leaving their homes all day for the factories'.[56]

O'Hara'a evidence would indicate that the relationship between Galway's leading industrialist and his workers was not harmonious. However, 1885 was a difficult year — a wage cut in March provoked a strike, while financial problems temporarily closed the factory later in the summer[57] — and this may have prejudiced his outlook. The impression is that the colonel was puzzled and frustrated by his fellow Galwegians' approach to their work.

One of the factory's greatest difficulties was in finding suitable workers. This difficulty, Colonel O'Hara attributed to the schools, which he said neglected technical education, leaving pupils with a preference for 'head work'. Farmers' sons were constantly applying to him for positions as clerks but would not consider offers of apprenticeships, while girls, having learned to read and write, only wanted to become teachers themselves.[58]

And it was difficult to retain workers. Boys starting at 14 earned 4*s* and girls 3*s* 6*d*. O'Hara considered that after five years a boy would have completed an informal apprenticeship, and be entitled to the wages of a skilled worker. He must have been remiss in communicating this however, for no boy had ever stayed that long. Consequently, all skilled male workers since the foundation of the factory had been brought in from Scotland. To attract them, it was necessary to pay £2 a week, considerably more than they would have earned at home. And, of the hundreds of Galway people who had worked in the factory, only one had briefly won promotion to overseer. This information led one committee member to ask rhetorically: 'Whatever may be the cause of it, the spectacle of men from other countries occupying all the higher posts is not one particularly calculated to excite ambition and steadiness in the lower ranks of labour, is it?'

Adult women in the factory were employed on a piece-work basis, and some of them were capable of earning 18*s* a week (adult male labourers in the factory got 14*s*). Rarely, however, did any of the women take home 18*s*. Once she had earned 5*s*, according to her employer, the typical female took the rest of the week off.

When the factory closed later in 1885, an appeal for investment, backed by the Catholic bishop, raised enough capital to enable it to open again, and the factory struggled on for a few more years. Colonel O'Hara continued to blame the 'unpunctual and careless' workforce for all difficulties, and in order to improve matters, he offered incentives. And when incentives failed, fines were introduced, causing employees to complain that 'a good part of our wages are being stopped for trivial offences'.[59]

The final closure of the factory in 1893 was a great loss to the town. And for the newly unemployed, it was no consolation that the reason given for the closure was not their indolence, but the failure of the jute crop in Asia.[60]

iii) Contemplating stubborn realities: a view from the late 19th century

Despite efforts to transform her into a city of commerce and industry, Galway remained at the end of the 19th century what she had been at the beginning — a relatively small market town and an administrative centre. The administrative/public sector had expanded — almost 15% of the adult males who spent the census night of 1881 in Galway were employees (or pensioners) of local government or central government — but commerce was generally stagnant. In this, Galway's experience was not too different from towns over five-sixths of Ireland.[61] The reason for her atrophy, indeed, broadly reflected the reasons for the relative decline of Ireland as a whole —political distance from the centres of power, lack of natural resources for industry, and geographical disadvantages in the age of steam. Only by increasing the volume of added-value exports could Galway's — no less than Ireland's — situation have been improved.[62] And the zealous but vainglorious efforts of Galway interests to make connections with North America and with Belfast in the 1850s and 1860s, show that this economic imperative was understood, even if efforts to act upon the understanding left something to be desired.

Only one Galway industry was performing well in the 1880s, O'Hara told the Select Committee on Industry, and that was Persse's Distillery. The family was long established in the business, having run one of two distilleries in the town in the 1820s. Nun's Island distillery which produced whiskey until 1908, was formerly operated by Persse's business rival, Patrick Joyce, but was purchased in the Encumbered Estates Court by Thomas Moore Persse, and refurbished in the post-Famine period. At the time of the Colonel's statement, it was producing 400,000 proof gallons of whiskey a year.[63]

As for the difficulties of other enterprises, there were specific local reasons for them, according to O'Hara, not least the monopoly of the MGWR. Freight charges, he claimed, were exceptionally high, and they were also levied unfairly, the reason being that the directors of the railway favoured Dublin port. They

Persse's Distillery, 1860s (courtesy of Tom Kenny).

had contrived, therefore to charge lower rates to transport goods between inland towns and Dublin than between those towns and other ports. The development of light rail in the west of Ireland, O'Hara felt, would make transport more competitive. He himself was a director of a company interested in establishing a light railway between Mountbellew and Woodlawn, and he advocated state funding for a line between Galway and Clifden. (A Galway-Clifden link was first proposed in the early 1870s, but when it was finally built — with state assistance — during the early 1890s, it did not challenge the MGWR, for it was operated by that company.)[64]

The shallowness of the approaches to Galway port continued to be a cause for complaint. 'Our having to pay 5s a ton for lightening our vessels in Galway', O'Hara said, 'enables the Dublin merchant to send his grain, and corn, and flour, further down the Midland line in competition with us'.[65]

Another disadvantage for those doing business in the west, according to O'Hara, was the lending policy of the banks. With branches only of the Bank of Ireland, the National Bank and the Provincial Bank, Galway's financial facilities were the same as they had been fifty years earlier. And none of them was considered by O'Hara to be a commercial bank with a proper sympathy for the needs of business. Consequently, they would not advance money on bills of lading, or on goods in stock, as was usual elsewhere. The Ulster Bank was more amenable, but it had no branch in Galway, and its Tuam branch was not 'a commercial bank' either, rather a farmers' bank.[66]

O'Hara's experience had made him pessimistic about Galway's position and prospects, and there are indications that his attitude was widely shared.

However, one anonymous contemporary — 'M' — painted a more cheerful picture. During the winter of 1887-88, M visited Galway's various enterprises, and contributed a series entitled 'What Galway can do' to the *Galway Express*. If his purpose was to reassure and to inspire his fellow citizens — and his tone would indicate that this was so — M can hardly have succeeded. Of those premises he visited, only the Bag Factory gave significant employment, and it was in constant difficulty, while his accounts of the clay pipe manufactory, marble works, Salthill Industrial School, brush factory and straw bottle envelope industry reveal that they had inconsequential workforces and primitive working methods. The description of the latter enterprise in Market-street — 'started by some very noble ladies early this year as a means of providing employment' — shows the low condition of Galway 'industry' in the late 19th century:

> The office, a bare room really, is full of bundles of straw covers or envelopes, piled up to the ceiling, and the little dark room at the back is also full. The manager tells us trade is not very brisk … At the present time there are twenty-seven girls employed, whose ages range from about 14 to 18 or 20 … In the summertime, the work hours are from 7 a.m. to 6 p.m., but in winter work begins at 8 a.m. and ends at 4 p.m., the reason being that no lights could be permitted in a workroom so full of straw as they must of need be … It takes but a very few days for the novice to learn the trade, and of course she will grow expert with daily practice. Twelve or fourteen dozen covers are made by the quicker fingered damsels, but even fifteen dozen have been accomplished. In the long summer days many of them will work up to eighteen or even twenty dozen. The girls are all on piece-work, receiving one penny a dozen … The girls all look healthy and they are certainly active enough, but their dress shows all too plainly their poverty …[67]

If M's painstaking reports of industrial endeavour in Galway only succeeded in demonstrating its acute limitations, his account of the vibrant atmosphere at the Saturday market indicated that the place retained some commercial life, even if the scene had changed little in centuries:

> The streets are about two inches deep in the whitish mud … and the country carts passing through them splash up the thick soup-like water on our clothes, and into our faces … The women are nearly all clad in the characteristic red flannel petticoat of the country, short as regards length, and allowing the whole of a pair of strong hob-nailed boots to be visible. Over their heads they wear the universal black cloak, with its heavy webbings, the cape of which is fastened up behind with a rosette. The cloak has a very odd

appearance behind, as underneath it is always carried the basket, slung from the shoulder, in which the market women carry their wares … Toward Lough Corrib, and close to it, at the end of Corrib Terrace, we come upon the potato market. The market is held in the open air (there is no covered market in all Galway), quite close to a little boat dock, in which lies two or three row-boats.[68]

'The Antient Mansion of the Brownes': deriliction in Lower Abbeygate Street
(from *The Architect*, July, 1879).

From Corrib terrace, M walked through Woodquay, passing the sally market, the turnip and mangold market, and the home-spun flannel market. Turning into Francis-street, he came upon a line of women seated on the ground selling home-knitted socks and stockings. From there, he walked through Lombard-street and Market-street, the location of busy fowl and butter markets. The entire of Eyre Square, he found, was taken over by hay and straw markets, while there was a busy pig market in the docks.

Saturday remained the only busy day for most of Galway's resident traders. According to a 1908 trade directory, the town's streets were generally 'almost deserted'. That 71 of the 175 Galway traders listed in the same directory were 'spirit dealers' or publicans indicates the extent to which Galway's business life depended on serving refreshments to country people coming to market. Evidently, however, there were some new opportunities in retailing in 1908, for five traders competed in the sale and service of bicycles.[69]

But among the traders and merchants of 1908 were Galway's most prosperous citizens, a few who had risen to local eminence by distributing imports throughout the region. Foremost among them was Máirtín Mór McDonogh of Thomas McDonogh & Sons, who was introduced in Chapter One. McDonogh was 'Mr Galway', in the words of one admirer, the successor to figures like James Daly, Rev. John d'Arcy, Rev. Peter Daly, and Colonel James O'Hara, who had dominated the town for intervals during the 19th century. Máirtín Mór's reputation as an astute and calculating businessman was earned, but his generation of McDonogh's had inherited a thriving business in 1902 from their father, Thomas McDonogh, the founder of the dynasty. A brief outline of the early history of the business will give a flavour of the entrepreneurial context of the period.

Thomas McDonogh arrived in Galway from the Ceantar na nOileáin district of Conamara in the 1860s. His story, however, was not exactly the rags-to-riches ascent of legend, for the McDonoghs had already won prominence in their native place as successful smugglers, as substantial middlemen tenants, and as dealers. Their position was sustained by the connection they established with the Comerford family, Galway merchants and Ceantar na nOileáin landlords. That the McDonoghs had risen by the 1850s from being tenants and trusted employees of the Comerfords to become their social equals was indicated by the marriage of Thomas's brother, Michael, to Marie Comerford.

Not long after his arrival in Galway in the 1860s, Thomas McDonogh himself climbed into the Comerford nest when he took a position as foreman/manager in the family sawmills. Soon, he was made a partner in the firm; by the early 1870s, the business was trading as McDonogh & Comerford; before the decade was out, the name over the door was Thomas McDonogh & Sons. Thomas's wife Honoria, meanwhile, had established a successful provisions and grocery business at High-street. A key factor in the early success of the nascent empire was the commercial connection maintained with McDonogh relatives in Conamara, in particular with Thomas's sister, Monica

Mór, owner of several shops and of a small fleet of hookers. The Conamara connection was continued by Thomas's sons — Máirtín Mór in particular — who guided the business into the 20th century by anticipating the needs of the local agricultural economy and by single-mindedly expanding the firm's share of a stagnant local market.[70]

There can be no doubt that it was commerce and handicrafts, rather than industry, that sustained the majority of Galwegians. But, notwithstanding its small contribution to Galway's economic life, the continuance of industry was considered vitally important. The loss of the Bag Factory in 1893, therefore,

Market Day, St. Nicholas Church, *c.*1880, with a view of Shop Street market booths known as the 'standings' (courtesy of Tom Kenny).

was regarded as a tragedy and there were immediate efforts to establish a replacement industry. The replacement came in 1895 in the form of the Woollen Mills in Newtownsmith. The origins of that industry were similar to those of the Bag Factory 30 years earlier, insofar as it was set up to provide employment, for young women in particular, rather than to generate profits. The difference was that the initiative, on this occasion, came from the local Catholic Church, rather than from the local authority. Bishop McCormack was prominent among those who appealed for local investment in the Galway Woollen Manufacturing Company in 1895, but it was the energy of McCormack's administrator which was responsible for the consolidation of the company, a fact which was acknowledged by the citizens of the town who continued to call the enterprise 'Fr Dooley's Mill' for many years after the man died in 1911.[71]

Fr Dooley's efforts, and indeed those of Fr Travers and his clerical colleagues in the Galway Development Association a few years later, invite comparison with those of Fr Peter Daly. Yet they were quite different in character: Daly was self-consciously an entrepreneur; Dooley and Travers were not. Indeed, the intervention of priests in Galway's business life in the decades before the first world war was an extension of their charitable work rather than anything else. Fr Dooley was also the promoter of an artisan's dwellings scheme,[72] and his success in providing decent housing and employment for some of his working-class parishioners was a testament to his energy and his commitment. And it might also be regarded as a rebuke to Galway's politicians and businessmen.

NOTES
1. *Connaught Journal,* 4 April, 12, 16, 31, May 1831, 18 June, 15 October, 10 December 1835.
2. James Mitchell, 'Father Peter Daly' in *JGAHS* 39, 1983-84, pp. 48-55.
3. *Galway Mercury,* 24 May, 19 July, 2, 9 August 1851.
4. ibid., 26 July 1851; *Appendix to 2nd report of Railway Commissioners (Ireland),* 1837-8, xxxv, p. 38; Patrick Wallace, 'The Organisation of pre-Railway Public Transport in Counties Limerick and Clare' in *North Munster Antiquarian Journal,* vol. xv, 1972, pp. 34-58.
5. *Returns Relating to the Galway Extension Railway,* 1864, liii, pp. 2-3; *Galway Mercury,* 27 September 1851.
6. *Galway Mercury,* 31 January 1851. See also ibid., 14 January, 4 March 1854.
7. ibid., 16 August 1851; *Galway Packet,* 4 September 1852.
8. *Galway Packet,* 25 August, 11 September 1852.
9. ibid., 11, 18 September 1852, 12 February 1853.
10. *Galway Express,* 3 March 1860. The hotel was the Eglinton.
11. James Mitchell, 'Queen's College Galway, 1845-58: From Site to Structure' in *JGAHS* 50, 1998, pp. 49-89.
12. *Galway Packet,* 8 May 1852.
13. ibid., 28 April, 2 June 1852.
14. Maurice Semple, *Reflections on Lough Corrib,* 2nd edn, Galway 1989, pp. 7-19, and *By the Corribside,* 2nd edn, Galway 1984, pp. 61-65, 129-44.
15. *Illustrated London News,* 28 August 1852.
16. *Galway Packet,* 14 August 1852.
17. ibid., 14, 18, 21 August 1852.
18. *Galway Mercury,* 15 February 1851, *Galway Express,* 23 June 1860, Semple, *Reflections,* p. 43.
19. Walsh, 'Topography', p. 67; *Galway Mercury,* 15 February, 27 December 1851; *Galway Express,* 18 April 1858.

20. *Galway Packet,* 8 September 1852.

21. *Galway Mercury,* 8 July, 7 October 1854, 27 October 1855; *Galway Express,* 28 January 1873, 5 July 1879.

22. *Galway Mercury,* 6 December 1851.

23. ibid.

24. Collins, 'Galway Line', pt. 1, pp. 5-8; Walter S. Sanderlin, 'Galway as a Trans-Atlantic Port in the Nineteenth Century' in *Éire-Ireland* 5, 1970, no. iii, p. 26.

25. Mitchell, 'Daly', pp. 59-65. The Galway legislation was distinct from the Towns Improvement (Ireland) Act of 1854.

26. Collin, 'Galway Line', pt. 1, pp. 11-21.

27. 'Galway Line: List of Shareholders in the Atlantic Royal Mail Steam Navigation Company'. I am grateful to Tim Collins for providing me with a copy of this document.

28. *Galway Express,* 30 April 1859.

29. Cited in Mitchell, 'Fr Daly', p. 76.

30. Collins, 'Galway Line', pt. 2, pp. 36-42.

31. There were severe econonomic recessions in Ireland in 1861-64, and again in 1866-67 (Mary E. Daly: *Dublin, the Deposed Capital. 1860-1914,* Cork 1984, pp.55-57.

32. ibid., pp. 52-62.

33. Woodman, *Annals,* pp. 53-54.

34. Osborne, *Gleanings,* pp. 49-50; *Galway Packet,* 12 October 1853.

35. Woodman, *Annals,* pp. 104-10; *Report from the Select Committee on Industries (Ireland),* 1884-5, vol. ix, p. 293.

36. Hardiman, *Galway,* p. 290, Dutton, *Galway,* p. 430; *Galway Packet,* 5 June 1852.

37. Sir Francis Head, *A fortnight in Ireland,* London 1852, p. 217; *Galway Packet,* 1 January 1853.

38. Raymond Crotty, *Irish Agricultural Production: its Volume and Structure,* Cork 1966, pp. 66-68; *Select Committee on Industries (Ireland),* 1884-85, pp. 296-97.

39. *Galway Mercury,* 11 March 1854.

40. *Appendix to the Report of the Fishery Commissioners, Ireland, for 1868,* 1868-9, vol. xv, p. 9.

41. Collins, 'Galway Line', pt. 2, p. 42.

42. *Galway Mercury,* 27 June 1857.

43. *Galway Mercury,* 6 December 1851; *Galway Packet,* 2 April 1853.

44. *Galway Packet*, 3 January, 1 May 1852, 18, 26 January, 8 February 1853.

45. ibid., 19 February 1853.

46. ibid., 28 September 1853; *Galway Mercury,* 8 April 1854; *Galway Express,* 8 November 1862.

47. *Galway Mercury,* 7 July 1855.

48. ibid., 27 September 1851; Toby Joyce, 'The *Galway American,* 1862-63', pt. 2, in *JGAHS* 48, 1996, n. 26.

49. *Galway Express,* 12 September, 19 December 1863.

50. ibid., 26 September 1865. The efforts of the company on Árainn are described by Tim Robinson in *Stones of Aran: Pilgrimage,* Mullingar 1986, pp. 182-85.

51. *Galway Express,* 5 February 1868; 18 May 1872, 16 September 1876; *Select Committee on Industries,* p. 300.

52. Re Clog Factory: *Galway Express,* 12 January, 2 March, 12 October, 9 November, 7 December 1867, 24 June 1871; *Committee on Industries,* pp. 297, 310.

53. *Galway Express,* 9 December 1865, 3, 24 February, 9 June, 28 July 1866.

54. *Committee on Industries (Ireland),* p. 296.

55. Mary E. Daly, *Social and Economic History of Ireland since 1800,* Dublin 1981, pp. 71-72; Ó Gráda, *New Economic History,* p. 304-05; *Select Committee on Industries,* p. 296.

56. Helen Blackburn, *Handy Book of Reference for Irishwomen,* London 1888, p. 7.

57. Cunningham, *Labour in the West,* pp. 79-80.

58. *Select Committee on Industries,* pp. 298, 302.

59. Cunningham, *Labour in the West,* pp. 79-80.

60. ibid.

61. 1881 Census, 1882 lxxix, Co of Town of Galway, Table xxi; S. A. Royle, 'Industrialisation, Urbanisation and Urban Society in Post-Famine Ireland, *c.*1850-1921' in Graham & Proudfoot, eds, *An Historical Geography of Ireland,* London 1993, pp. 258-92.

62. See Ó Gráda, *New Economic History,* pp. 306-13, 347-48.

63. E. B. McGuire, *Irish Whiskey: a History of Irish Distilling,* Dublin 1973, pp. 359-60; J. L. Pethica & J. C. Roy, *Henry Stratford Persse's Letters from Galway to America, 1821-1832,* pp. 15-16, 57-58. In 1887, Power's Distillery of Dublin produced 900,000 gallons, and John Jameson's, also of Dublin, a million gallons).

64. *Select Committee on Industries,* p. 299-300, 305, 318, 329; Kathleen Villiers-Tuthill, *Beyond the Twelve Bens: A History of Clifden and District,* Galway 1986, pp. 89-101; Semple, *Reflections,* pp. 161-63.

65. *Select Committee on Industries,* p. 298.

66. ibid., p. 321.

67. *Galway Express,* 24 December 1887.

68. ibid, 17 December 1887.

69. *Porter's Guide to the Manufacturers and Shippers of Ireland, Containing the Names and Addresses of Persons Interested in the Make or Sale of Irish manufactures or Products,* Belfast 1908, pp. 311-16.

70. Peadar O'Dowd, *In from the West — the McDonogh Dynasty,* Galway 2002, pp. 13-32; Tim Robinson, *Connemara, Part 1: Introduction and Gazetteer,* Roundstone 1990, p. 125; Patrick Sheeran, *The Novels of Liam O'Flaherty: a Study in Romantic Realism,* Dublin 1976, p. 126-29.

71. Cunningham, *Labour in the West,* pp. 80-81.

72. T. P. Boland, *Thomas Carr: Archbishop of Melbourne,* Melbourne 1997, p. 89.

CHAPTER 8

'...the most clamorous and importunate supplicants'

WELFARE & CHARITY, 1850-1914

Next morning our new cares began,
Each one proposing her own plan —
All different taste.
What some approved some deemed bad,
But all agreed that we now had
No time to waste.

> Catherine McAuley, on her arrival in Galway
> in 1840 to establish a Mercy convent and school.
> (M.A. Carroll), *Leaves from the annals of the
> Sisters of Mercy in Ireland*, 1998 edn,

The Poor Law after the Famine

The Famine and the government response to it pushed the incipient poor law system to its limits and beyond, and it was a considerably altered system that emerged into the 1850s. One important change was that out-door relief was no longer forbidden, although its extent was severely restricted by the Poor Law Commissioners.[1] Of more significance, however, was the poor law's growing domination of public health functions.

From the moment of its opening in March 1842, the workhouse was a successor to several of the links in the 'chain of charities' outlined in Chapter Three. As well as replacing the Mendicity Institute, it provided for widows and orphans, and for foundlings. It had obstetric facilities — never in great demand — replacing those that had been fitfully available in Galway's Lying-in hospitals since 1825. And it had an infirmary where, unlike in the county infirmary, poor townspeople could claim treatment as of right. Wards for 'lunatics' and for 'imbeciles', meanwhile, sheltered groups that had not heretofore been specifically catered for in the town.*

But, if it began with significant public health responsibilities, the scope of the poor law was extended considerably by the Medical Dispensaries Act of

---

* Some people with psychiatric illnesses and learning disabilities had been accommodated in county infirmaries and houses of industry. From the mid-1820s, insane asylums were built throughout the country, including the Connaught Lunatic Asylum at Ballinasloe, which opened in 1833.

1851. The unevenness and general inadequacy of dispensary provision had been exposed during the Famine; the new legislation sought to extend coverage and standards. Under its provisions, the country was divided into dispensary districts, with a qualified medical officer responsible for each. And, although costs were paid from poor rates, dispensaries were not located in workhouses, lessening the social stigma that would otherwise have attached to them.[2] Disagreement, unfortunately, marked the new arrangements in Galway. The now-redundant dispensary committee refused to transfer to the Board of Guardians its substantial resources — investments made with the proceeds of public appeals and other donations in 1822-23 — and it was not until 1862 that the matter was eventually settled, enabling the Board of Guardians to build a new dispensary. To their credit, the Galway guardians sought to have their lying-in wards transferred from the workhouse to the new dispensary, but their efforts in this regard were stymied by the Poor Law Commissioners. During the construction of the new dispensary, the Guardians also took charge of the fever hospital, after a scandal revealed the incompetence of the institution's governors. By 1863, therefore, only the County Infirmary and a number of minor institutions in Galway remained outside the control of the poor law.[3]

Other legislation further extended the poor law's boundaries. Registration of births, marriages and deaths became compulsory in 1863, with dispensary doctors acting as local registrars. In 1864, smallpox vaccination was made compulsory with, again, the dispensary doctor being the responsible officer.[4]

But if the authority of Boards of Guardians and their officials extended into new areas, it was workhouse administration that had the highest profile. During the 1850s, administrative shortcomings in the institution were reported in scandalous terms — the sexual adventures of inmates in 1853; the burning to death of a child and the embezzling of provisions in 1858; the sacking of the Catholic chaplain for his unapproved baptism of a foundling in 1859; the ragged and filthy condition of pauper children in 1860.[5] In the circumstances, guardians must have been glad to give publicity to the opinion of Bishop MacEvilly who testified to the 'very edifying knowledge of the Christian Doctrine' displayed by pauper confirmation candidates and to 'the spirit of order and regularity which seemed to pervade the entire of this workhouse'.[6]

Formerly the superior of a boarding school, MacEvilly was a connoisseur of 'order and regularity', but these attributes of the workhouse did not appeal to everybody. In particular, the 'sturdy town beggars' retained their attachment to free movement, and they continued to practice their trade. One who signed himself 'A Tourist' described his reception in 1865:

> I have travelled all through the North without being molested, and it
> was only when I set foot in Galway that I was besieged, molested and
> set upon … I went to visit the far-famed Claddagh, where I gave a
> copper to a miserable-looking child. I had scarcely bestowed my
> charity, when I was surrounded by such a mob of certainly miserable-

looking creatures demanding charity, that I had to make off as fast as I could without attaining my object … If the poor can be provided for in other places, and begging stopped, why not in Galway.[7]

The impression of a local resident, 'Civis', was similar: 'Go where you will' he contended, 'you cannot pass a single street without being assailed by groups of the most clamorous and importunate supplicants'. For 'Civis', the magistrates were responsible for the overwhelming extent of the problem, and more particularly for permitting dangerous mendicants to remain at large. He instanced 'Butcher Egan', also known as 'mad Egan':

Group on courthouse steps sketched for *Illustrated London News* (1880) and captioned
'Some disconsolate groups outside the door of the offices where the local relief committee is
deliberating on the grants it can afford to bestow on so many poor applicants for public bounty'
(Brendan Laurence Glynn Collection).

He was about the middle of Shop-street when he attracted my notice, and was saluting with shouts and grimaces all that passed him, the more respectable coming in for the greatest share of his most troublesome attentions. At length a Protestant clergyman appeared in the distance. This seemed to give additional life to the performance. It was not a moment till Egan was in front of this gentleman standing close rank, and face-to-face, staring most wildly at him, then grinning and gesticulating in a style the most grotesque and unnatural. In this way he figured through the entire length of Shop-street, and failing to evoke any opposition, he became more violent, and had not the police stepped forward, and laid an interdict on his proceeding. I cannot tell what might have been the result. There were large knives in the open windows of the butchers' shops, as there always are, and what was to hinder this man, in his frenzy, from taking up one of these weapons, and using it in a way that is unpleasant even to think of? Surely this is a case for magisterial interference.[8]

The effrontery of beggars — although not always as compelling as that of Butcher Egan — was a perennial source of complaint, and the failure of the workhouse to solve the problem a cause of mystification.[9]

The number of workhouse inmates — which had declined during the 1850s to the pre-Famine level of 300 or so — passed 600 on several occasions during the first half of the 1860s. Relief committees were again established to distribute fuel and food, and stories began to circulate of deaths from actual starvation. The condition of the poor, as described by those charged with disbursing charity, was terrible.[10] The example was given of the family of 'a poor man who has been a labourer over 20 years':

A short time since he took a pain in his hip, incapacitating him for work, and in endeavouring to cure himself he had spent all his means. I visited the house that evening and found the husband, the wife, and four children sitting in the corner of a room fourteen feet by ten, while the half of a farthing candle was all the light in the apartment. A little straw lay in the corner, but there was neither rug nor blanket … He had boiled a turnip for the breakfast of himself and his family, and he showed me a turnip which they were going to eat before going to bed.[11]

By all accounts, the position of the able-bodied was not much better with, according to one report, many 'labourers and mechanics reduced to a state of destitution as bad as in the famine years'. In 1863, a relief committee decided to stop providing gratuitous assistance, and to instead offer employment — 'the proper mode of dispensing charity to able-bodied men'.[12] But it was not possible to provide adequate work, and pauperisation became a real prospect for the unemployed. An episode of 1865 sheds light on the expectations of impoverished men in this situation, and on the roles and mutual relationships of poor law guardians, poor law officials, and the commissioners in Dublin.

On Friday 20 January 1865, police sub-inspector O'Reilly reported that 'a number of the labouring poor' had sent out the bell-man to announce a public meeting for noon in Eyre Square. He watched 200 men and boys assemble behind a white flag, edged in black and inscribed 'Peace & Tranquility — Employment for the Labourers of Galway'. The labourers marched to the workhouse, where a deputation was admitted to the guardians' meeting. Replying to a request for special 'measures', Anthony O'Flaherty, guardians' chairman, expressed his sympathy, and his admiration for the labourers' 'orderly conduct'. If they 'persevered' in their moderate course, he said, they would secure public support. He regretted that the guardians could not help, because they were precluded from giving out-door relief to the able-bodied unless the workhouse was full, or disease was present in it.[13]

Dr Brodie, poor law inspector, interpreted these events for his superiors. There was extensive distress in Galway, he allowed, and the unemployed were seeking relief as they had done in previous years. He suspected, however, that they were 'probably incited to urge their demands with clamour by some of the local petty agitators among the mechanics'. Brodie advised that it was 'not practical' to implement 'extraordinary measures year after year' and, in general, that it was 'better to leave them to the operation of the relief in force than to hold out to them the hope of being relieved whenever employment fails'. Brodie approved of Anthony O'Flaherty's remarks, and regretted that things were not left at that. However, following a request to the town sheriff, a public meeting was 'got up' in the Town Hall, which was chaired by Bishop MacEvilly. The estimated 500 labourers who turned up passed a resolution asking the Board of Guardians to petition the Poor Law Commissioners 'to extend out-door relief to all classes of the destitute poor'. Kept abreast of developments by the sceptical Brodie, the Poor Law Commissioners merely advised the Galway guardians of their limited powers in this regard.[14]

The 'clamour', however, forced the Town and Harbour Commissioners to take an initiative, and they established a joint committee to improve the sewage system. But, when only £60 was subscribed for the work, John Harrison, a populist guardian, advised the labourers to have nothing to do with such an inadequate scheme. He urged them instead to present themselves, *en masse*, at the workhouse gates to seek admission. The workhouse would be unable to accommodate the sudden influx, and the guardians would be enabled (and obliged) to provide out-door assistance. Brodie immediately acquired extra bedding to undermine this strategy. Meanwhile, Harrison's fellow guardians — with their eyes on the rates — repudiated the suggestion, and the labourers too were unenthusiastic. Enquiries made by one Lee — 'a sort of petty leader among the tradesmen' — indicated that only a hundred workers were prepared to present themselves at the workhouse. Brodie explained why Galway tradesmen would not enter the workhouse — even in protest. All those having 'the name of tradesmen' had the parliamentary franchise, which was both prestigious and lucrative. Their acceptance of relief — either indoor or outdoor — would have the effect of disenfranchising them. A public works scheme, consequently, was the only form of assistance acceptable to tradesmen.

On Saturday 28 January 1865, fifty or sixty men, without their families, sought admission to the workhouse. Their arrival was anticipated and they were directed to the prepared places by a relieving officer. All left quietly.

The promised relief works began on Monday 30 January, but there was consternation when it was discovered that wages were only 10*d* a day, 2*d* less than in 1864, and 4*d* less than in 1863. The low pay was defended on the grounds that prices were exceptionally low, but this failed to satisfy the labourers and a strike was declared. 100 soldiers were immediately despatched. For Brodie, the developments proved that 'destitution to the extent that has been represented does not exist'. By the end of the week, however, poverty had forced the unemployed to swallow their pride, the strike had collapsed, and 230 were working for 10d a day.[15]

The events of January 1865 represented a complex negotiation between the impoverished working class and local agencies about the form relief should take. People petitioned the guardians as a means of drawing attention to their plight, but they were not necessarily seeking poor relief. In several respects, the protest was a successor to the pre-Famine food riots detailed in Chapter Two, and it set the pattern for late 19th century demonstrations by the poor.

In January 1880, 400 'workmen' marched to a guardians' meeting, behind a banner reading 'Work or Hunger'. Significantly, loaves of bread were stuck on the flagpoles — a venerable symbol of distress. On this occasion it was the turn of Pierce Joyce, guardians' chairman, to sympathise — he 'deeply felt for their

'The general state of affairs': some Galwegians sketched in 1880. Note the Distress Fund Committee poster placed on the left (from *Illustrated London News*).

distress' — and to advise that he could do nothing except offer them places in the workhouse.[16] This course, according to report, 'the poor fellows declined', but over the following weeks, a Relief Committee and the Harbour Commissioners were stirred to provide employment.[17] There was a similar sequence of events in 1886, according to James Coleman, relieving officer:

> I may mention that there was a lot of town labourers called here at a meeting of the Board of Guardians, asking for relief and the guardians offered them the house, and they said they would not come in, so they offered them work to break stones at 1s. a day and they refused, and the following Board day they came again in a body, about sixty or seventy, all married people, and the chairman then presiding, Mr Lynch, left them in the hands of the relieving officer.[18]

Coleman visited the individuals concerned, found that they were truly destitute, and again offered them places in the workhouse. When they refused, he took it on himself to issue outdoor relief, a step that did not meet with the full approval of the guardians. But the crisis soon came to an end: 'The following week a lot of ships came in, and they all got work'.[19]

The reports of poor law officials Brodie and Coleman reveal contrasting attitudes to the poor. This might be explained by difference in personality, by difference in rank, or by difference in origin. Coleman's work was at the coal-face of poverty and, given his surname, it is likely that he possessed the empathy for his fellow citizens of a native Galwegian. But changes in the context during the two decades between their reports were also important. The Local Government Board took over from the Poor Law Commissioners in 1872, but even before that, there was a growing tendency to allow out-door relief. In general, social attitudes towards the poor were moderating, and the disposition to respond rigidly and punitively to their plight was diminishing.[20]

Only those 'entirely broken down in energy and constitution', according to Dr Brodie in the 1860s, would consider applying to the Galway workhouse. The evidence supports his statement. Clearly, significant numbers of Galway's poor found mendicancy to be more to their taste than pauperdom. And recurring protests by the unemployed for non-poor law relief or, failing that, for outdoor relief, shows that the workhouse was utterly unacceptable to them. The 1901 census returns enable the researcher to discover something about those who resigned themselves to the workhouse. Data show that the typical pauper was old, unskilled and single. Of those over the age of 20 who spent the night of 1 April 1901, in the Galway workhouse, 134 (54.5%) were female and 112 (45.5%) were male. Two-thirds of the adult males were over 60, and half of the females. Of inmates in their 20s and 30s, many of the women had children, and several of the men had debilitating illnesses. And the indications are that most were alone in the world — only 19% of the men and 11% of the women were returned as being currently married (see Figures 8.1 and 8.2).

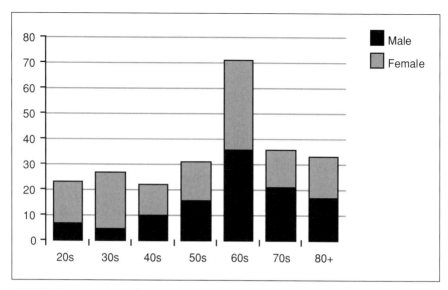

FIGURE 8.1: Age and sex of adults in Galway Workhouse, 1901.

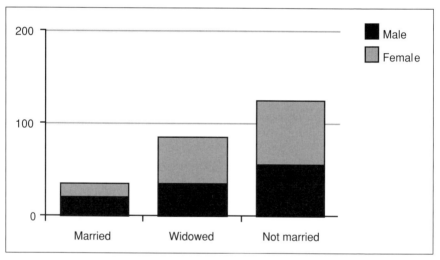

FIGURE 8.2: Marital status of adult workhouse inmates, 1901.

Source: Galway workhouse census schedules, 1901.

The majority of pauper men belonged to 'unskilled' occupational categories, but about 20% had higher status: there were four weavers, three musicians, three grooms, two clerks, two masons, two carpenters, two blacksmiths, a baker, a tailor, a stonecutter, a shipwright, a shopkeeper, a chandler, and a butcher. As for the women, most of those who were listed as having an occupation were domestic servants, but there were two teachers, two confectioners, a dressmaker and a marble carver.

Charity and voluntary relief in the poor law era

As poor law guardians took charge of institutions that had previously been supported by voluntary committees, the nature of charitable effort itself changed. Some of the changes were superficial — many of the people who had sat on the committees of pre-poor law institutions were elected guardians, and they continued on much as before. But there was less scope for voluntary initiative, except at times of exceptional distress. Clergymen were prominent on relief committees during the crises of the 1860s and 1880s, but guardians — because of their 'expert' status — were also strongly represented.

Charity traditionally had a religious aspect but, whatever the reality in particular instances in the pre-poor law era, it was generally emphasised that it was a 'Christian duty' rather than a denominational one. With the major responsibilities removed from the voluntary sphere, even pretence in this regard could be abandoned. Moreover, the religious atmosphere of the mid-19th century — which saw self-regarding Cullenite Catholicism locked in struggle with self-righteous Second Reformation Protestantism — was not conducive to inter-denominational endeavour. Increasingly, the active charitable organisations were subsidiaries of one or other of the churches.

Evangelical Protestants established a range of charities — including branches of the Army Scripture Readers & Soldiers Friend Society and of the Scottish Benevolent Society of St Andrew — but the impression is that these were quite limited in scope.[21] There were also several Protestant charities of a more traditional type. One was the long-established Eyre charity, which survived 19th century vicissitudes including the abolition of the Corporation which formerly administered it and the passage of the Eyre property which formerly sustained it to the Guinness brewing family. By the 1860s it was distributing annually £1.9.10 to each of 12 elderly Protestant men. Another was the Grace Asylum in Nuns Island where a similar number of Protestant women were offered accommodation. That the institution gave priority to the spiritual needs of its inmates is indicated by a typical entry in the journal recording visits by 'lady' volunteers: 'Visited today and read Isa. 25 and part of 26 & 7 to inmates, E. Cuthbert, July 26-7 [1871]'.[22]

For Catholics, there was a branch of the St Vincent de Paul Society, established in 1849 by Fr Peter Daly.* Ten years later, 34 members were striving to give effect to the branch's objectives: visiting poor families in their homes; clothing orphans; providing for homes; establishing religious libraries. The impression is, however, that their efforts were hampered by financial difficulties.[23] For St Vincent de Paul activists, the difficulty lay in convincing the public that subscriptions would not be wasted on people who could claim poor law relief anyway, so it was necessary to explain their procedures:

---

* More than a decade previously, Daly had been involved in establishing a Galway branch of the Ladies of Charity, the women's auxiliary of the St Vincent de Paul Society. Jonathan Binns (*The Miseries and Beauties of Ireland*, 1837, vol. ii, pp. 410-11) was impressed by the work of the members in visiting the sick poor and in providing them with food, medicine and clothing, 'without distinction of sect or creed, and gratuitously.'

> It is decidedly the best form of out-door relief, for the recipient of
> the alms of the Society must be some family in actual need of relief,
> and whose circumstances have been enquired into by visitors,
> members of the Society, who are instructed to be most
> discriminating and particular … If the case was hopeless and an
> application for public assistance from the Board of Guardians,
> either by workhouse or outdoor relief, inevitable, then, although
> alms might be given to relieve present want, the Society would not
> attempt to expend its fund in a vain endeavour.[24]

But the most significant development in Catholic charity during the 19th
century was what amounted to its 'professionalisation' by religious orders.[25]
Chapter Six describes how schools for the poor and associated services —
'Breakfast Institutes' and orphanages — came under the control of Catholic
religious congregations in the early and middle decades of the century. Lay
people with temporal responsibilities were replaced by men and women
prepared to dedicate themselves 365 days a year to their charges. Thus, for
example, the redoubtable 'Misses Lynch of Nantes' were replaced by the
Presentation Sisters in their free school and orphanage in 1815, and succeeded
by the Mercy Sisters in the Magdalen Asylum in 1845.

A new religious congregation entered Galway in 1876, when A.B. Kerins of
the Christian Brothers took charge of the state-funded Salthill Industrial
School. The school was founded five years earlier under the Industrial Schools
Act of 1868, but the early regime of Patrician Brother John Lynch failed to
satisfy the Inspector of Reformatory and Industrial Schools. In time, the
Industrial School grew to become a significant Galway institution. By 1886,
200 boys were in residence there, receiving an education of sorts and being
trained in a variety of vocationally-useful skills. Local tradesmen had occasion
to complain at unfair competition from the school's workshops, but for most
Galwegians, the school band was the only point of contact. In the late 19th and
early 20th centuries, the Industrial School Band was an essential feature of
sports days, regattas and St Patrick's Day parades in the town.[26]

As far as non-educational services were concerned, the Mercy Sisters played
a more important role than any other congregation. Just over a decade after
that order's establishment, a convent was established in Galway in 1840, and
its superiors set about executing the 'design' of founder, Catherine McAuley:

> Each convent on its establishment should have attached to it, as far
> as its means permitted and the circumstances of the place required,
> poor schools for girls, a House of Mercy for destitute young
> women of good character, and a female orphanage, all conducted
> by the Sisters in addition to their main work of the visitation and
> relief of the sick poor.[27]

In addition to this designated work, the sisters quickly found themselves responsible for two of Galway's few remaining non-poor law institutions — the Magdalen Asylum and the Widows' Asylum. The original Magdalen Asylum in Lombard-street was abandoned in 1870 and, with the aid of a legacy, relocated to College-road. Elsewhere, a 'House of Mercy' — for unemployed servants — had opened immediately when the order occupied its new convent in Newtownsmith in 1842. There, thirty young women of 'attested' character were taught needlework, laundry, washing, scouring, cleaning, and basic literacy.[28] Along similar lines, the order opened a Factory Girls' Home in the 1880s — with 'penny dinners' and recreational facilities for non-residents.[29]

Increasingly, too, the Mercy Sisters became indispensable to the poor law system itself. Their first contact with the system was in the course of their 'visitation' of the institutional poor, which began with the opening of the workhouse — they also visited prisoners in the gaols.[30] Such visiting was uncontroversial, but attempts to extend the Sisters' role in workhouses encountered resistance. In Limerick, guardians voted in 1860 to appoint Mercy nurses to the workhouse hospital, and although this threat to the non-denominational character of its institutions was opposed by the Poor Law Commissioners, three nuns took up positions in January 1861. The Limerick affair was considered to have set a precedent, but individual guardians — Protestants mainly — continued to fight such appointments.[31]

The Galway guardians appointed Mercy Sisters as nurses to the Galway workhouse in September 1864. That there was a vacancy was due to the dismissal of the matron, Miss Lambert, when it was discovered that she had a sideline as an egg contractor to the institution. But the suggestion that Lambert be replaced by Mercy nuns caused dissension, resulting in a compromise proposal to re-employ Miss Lambert, but as a nurse rather than as a matron, and under the supervision of a Sister of Mercy.[32] The Protestant *Galway Express* opposed the development — on financial as well as on religious grounds. If the proposal was approved, the editor pointed out, the ratepayers would be paying three women to do the work formerly carried out by one. More forcefully, the religious objections of Protestants were stated as follows:

> They are members of a religious body bound by solemn vows — that their objects are missionary as well as charitable … In sickness, when an unending future begins to dawn on the sufferer, he is more susceptible to religious impressions than at another time, and how great is the temptation to the young lady, believing that the Protestant is altogether lost if he continues in that faith, to whisper to him of another means of obtaining pardon for his sins than that he has been taught to believe. It is an opportunity that the ardent religieuse cannot allow to pass; and, we believe, if she would obey her church, must not.[33]

But all objections were ignored, and four Mercy nuns took charge of the workhouse hospital early in 1865.[34] There the order remained, outlasting even the poor law system itself. Another bastion fell to the Mercy in 1900 when, in the face of opposition from members of the Queen's College medical faculty, it took responsibility for nursing in the County Infirmary (run since 1892 by a board made up of representatives of western poor law unions).[35] The 'chain' of charities and social services of the late 19th and early 20th century might have been overwhelmingly under poor law auspices, but the system had been unable to resist the advances of religious orders. Consequently, by 1900, institutional care in the town of Galway — in both charity and poor law sectors — was delivered almost exclusively by the Sisters of Mercy.

NOTES

1. Helen Burke, *The People and the Poor Law in 19th Century Ireland,* Littlehampton, 1987, pp. 125-55.
2. ibid., pp. 153-55.
3. J. P. Murray, *Galway: A medico-social history,* Galway, n.d., pp. 47-49.
4. Burke, *Poor Law,* pp. 278-81.
5. *Galway Packet,* 13 July 1853; *Galway Express,* 6 November, 11 December 1858, 8 January 1859, 25 February, 19 May 1860.
6. *Minutes of Evidence of Select Committee of Poor Relief (Ireland),* 1861 x, par. 341.
7. *Galway Express,* 19 August 1865.
8. ibid., 10 September 1864.
9. See, for example, ibid., 29 September 1866; 22 June 1867; 20 June 1868; 18 June 1870.
10. *Galway Express,* 19 July 1862, O'Neill, 'Minor Famines', pp. 461-65.
11. *Galway Express,* 30 November 1861.
12. ibid., 24 January 1863.
13. National Archives, CSORP 1865/1141; Galway Board of Guardians Minutes, 20 January 1865.
14. National Archives, CSORP, 1865/1141.
15. ibid.
16. *Galway Express,* 10 January 1880.
17. ibid., 10 January, 7 February 1880.
18. *Minutes of Evidence of Poor Relief (Ireland) Inquiry Commission,* 1887 xxxviii, p. 203.
19. ibid., pp. 203-04.
20. Burke, *Poor Law,* pp.240-41; Powell, *Social Policy,* pp. 115-16.
21. See Chapter Five.
22. St Nicholas Vestry Minutes, 4 April 1864; Journal of the Committee of Ladies Visiting the Grace Asylum, 1867-1900.
23. James Casserly, *An Open Door: A History of the Society of St Vincent de Paul in Galway, 1849-1999,* Galway 1999, pp. 25-28; *Galway Express,* 28 July 1877; 10 January 1880.
24. *Galway Vindicator,* 25 November 1874.
25. Caitríona Clear, *Nuns in Nineteenth Century Ireland,* Dublin 1987, pp. 101-12.
26. Tony Regan, 'The Salthill Industrial School', in MacLochlainn & Regan *Two Galway Schools,* Galway 1993, pp. 21-36; *Centenary Record: St Joseph's Residential Home, Lower Salthill, 1876-1976,* Galway 1976; Burke, *Poor Law,* pp. 227-28.
27. Cryan, 'Sisters of Mercy', p.45.
28. ibid., pp. 47, 208-09.
29. John Cunningham, *Labour in the West of Ireland, 1890-1914,* Belfast 1995, p. 80.
30. Cryan, 'Sisters of Mercy', pp. 46-47, 160.
31. Burke, *Poor Law,* pp. 262-72; Cryan, 'Sisters of Mercy', pp. 207-08.
32. *Galway Express,* 10 September 1864.
33. ibid.
34. Cryan, 'Sisters of Mercy', pp. 208-09.
35. Murray, *Medico-social history,* p. 67.

CHAPTER 9

'I would not do it for all of the seats in the world'

ELECTIONS & POLITICS, 1850-1914

Now a public man I intend to be,
To try and set old Ireland free,
For English laws they don't agree
With man, woman, or child in Galway
From 'Peter McCann from Galway'[1]

The period between the Great Famine and the Great War saw a great transformation in Irish politics. For this, there were a number of inter-linked and over-lapping causes: reforms in the electoral system; a concerted intervention by the Catholic bishops; developments in society and in communications facilitating the emergence of a coherent and disciplined national movement.

But if electoral reforms significantly democratised politics, restrictions remained — notably, that women were still excluded. Moreover, as far as nationalists were concerned, their democratically expressed views on the constitutional relationship between the islands continued to be ignored by successive parliaments.

The Reform Act of 1868 was a modest measure in the national context, but, by reducing the freeholder qualification in borough constituencies, it had a significant effect on urban politics. As for the Secret Ballot Act of 1872, it has been authoritatively argued that it did not have a major impact on Irish politics either. It did not alter the small and unrepresentative character of the electorate, and some of the political changes which contemporaries attributed to secret voting — notably the growing independence from their landlords of tenant freeholders — were already in train before 1872.[2] Nonetheless, the importance of the ballot in breaking up established forms of corruption in Galway and a number of other urban constituencies should not be discounted.

In the mid-1880s, there were three reforming acts, starting with the Corrupt Practices Act (1883), which limited electoral expenditure. The Representation of the People Act (1884) gave the vote to householders, enfranchising labourers and small tenant farmers, and increasing the Irish electorate from a quarter of a million to three-quarters. However, the effect on Galway was not great — the electorate rose from 1,146 in 1881 to 1,655 in 1891. Finally, the Redistribution

Act (1885) equalised constituencies, increased their number from 65 to 101, and allocated them a member each. For Galway town, this meant the loss of an MP.[3]

The changed circumstances would greatly affect Galway's electoral culture. This was regretted by some, for under the new dispensations, elections were less engaging affairs than under the old. Quite how exciting and how sociable election periods were in Galway between the 1830s and the 1870s was revealed by a parliamentary commission of 1857.

Electoral corruption: the 1857 Commission

In Chapter Five, we read of suspicions that Galway's Catholic tradesmen were corrupted within a few years of their gaining the right to vote in 1832. Exactly twenty-five years after the tradesmen's enfranchisement the matter was thoroughly investigated. The wide-ranging investigation into 'the existence of corrupt practices in elections of members to serve in Parliament for the County of the Town of Galway' was held on foot of a petition lodged by the defeated candidate, Colonel French, against the result of the 1857 election in the constituency.

Among the investigating commissioners were some who doubted that working artisans could have an independent political thought — or an independent political interest — of their own. For such men, approaches by trades' representatives to potential candidates, such as to Valentine Blake in 1838 and to Colonel French in 1857, served to confirm allegations of malpractice.[4] But, even allowing that venal motives were not absent, it is plain that Blake's advocacy of their political rights, and French's 'advanced' nationalist views, gave credibility to their candidacies among the trades. The fact was that the generality of those freemen who accepted bribes accepted them only from those they were disposed to vote for anyway. Thus, tradesmen who had supported him in 1847 and 1852 abandoned Anthony O'Flaherty — an associate of the opprobrious Sadlier and Keogh — in 1857, not because he ran out of money but because they considered that he had betrayed a political principle. Patrick Greaney, leather-cutter, declared that most freemen 'would not take a hundred pounds' to vote for O'Flaherty in 1857. For his part, Greaney was opposed to bribery, but it was nuanced opposition: 'I would not consider it bribery if I liked a man and voted for him, if he were to give me money afterwards.[5] Greaney's attitude — tolerant of minor abuses — was widely-held and it provided shelter for the perpetration of major abuses by the unscrupulous.

Candidates' attitudes too were permissive. Martin Blake, MP from 1832 to 1857, was involved in several expensive Galway elections. That he was as opposed to bribery as Greaney was shown by his reply to a question about the 1852 election:

> Q. Am I also to understand from you that, while these expenses were being incurred by the numerous persons that incurred them, you never sanctioned or were aware of them?
> A. Oh! Certainly, to the fullest extent. I never did sanction them, nor was aware of them. I would not do it for all of the seats in the world.[6]

Some months afterwards, however, Blake paid those who spent money securing tradesmen's votes for him. Questioned about one such individual, he responded: 'I was told that there was a certain expenditure, and the party who I thought was responsible for it I would not see lose money on my account, and accordingly I paid him'. The commissioners accepted Blake's explanation, finding that in 1852 there had been 'a considerable extent of treating and distribution of orders for goods, and some direct money payments', but that 'these corrupt practices have entirely occurred without the knowledge or consent of the said Martin Joseph Blake'.[7]

It was an extraordinary judgement. Blake had admitted to paying similar bills for his 'friends' since his first election in 1832, so he was no innocent in these matters.

Martin Blake retired in 1857, but his rivals of 1852, Catholic landlord, Anthony O'Flaherty, and eldest son of Clanricarde, Lord Dunkellin, returned to the fray. Colonel French, scion of a Catholic landed family, joined them in the contest for the two Galway urban seats. The connections of the candidates were at least as important as their affiliations, but it was considered worthy of comment that all three were 'of Liberal politics'. (No Conservative had contested the constituency since Denis Daly's unsuccessful outing in 1837). The 'Liberal' tag, however, concealed important differences. Lord Dunkellin was Protestant, and this was used against him, as was the fact that his privy councillor father had signed the unpopular Ecclesiastical Titles Bill into law. Anthony O'Flaherty was a government supporter, and this was used against him, as was the fact that some of his constituents did not benefit from the patronage which flowed from his association. Colonel French was an 'independent oppositionist', a designation adopted by those seeking to distance themselves from the place-seeking Tenant Leaguers of 1852.[8]

The commission of inquiry was appointed because of suspected irregularities in 1857, but the commissioners were authorised to seek the roots of corruption in earlier contests. However, despite reporting that 'for a long period corrupt practices have prevailed at contested elections', they were precluded from examining witnesses to corruption that occurred before 1847, because they were unable to uncover anything unseemly in the uncontested general election of that year.

Electoral corruption, the commissioners found, was almost completely confined to freemen, who numbered 540 in an electorate of 1,091. Of the 540, 250 were 'proved, either in 1852 or 1857, to have given their votes for a corrupt inducement', but this did not 'by any means include all those who have at the last two elections been corruptly influenced in the exercise of the franchise'.[9] The inference was that electoral corruption was general among freemen and almost totally absent among the propertied. However, it is apparent that the commissioners were operating with a limited definition of what constituted corruption, and that they considered only inducements in cash or in kind. Other pressures on electors were not considered.

One third of the population resided in the rural part of the constituency, so tenant farmers formed a substantial part of the freeholder electorate. The expectation was that such freeholders would vote in accordance with the wishes of their landlords. This gave influence to Lord Clanricarde who had property in the Terryland area, and to other families with paternalistic traditions like the Lynches of Bearna who had earlier been a vital prop of the Daly interest. Despite the efforts of Daniel O'Connell to entice freeholders away from their landlords, even veteran O'Connellites like Martin Blake did not regard such influence as corrupt. Something that was considered corrupt by Blake — the extent of the practice was not investigated by the commissioners — was the trading of their tenants' votes by landlords in exchange for appointments to magistracies and suchlike.[10]

But the influence of property was not confined to rural parts. Many leaseholders in the urban area were also expected to vote in accordance with the wishes of the owners of their properties. For his part, Martin Blake had consolidated his electoral position by acquiring an extensive portfolio of house property in the town.[11]

If the pervasiveness of economic pressure of one sort or another partially absolves Galway's tradesmen of their electoral sins, there is also evidence that freemen were motivated at least as much by political as by financial factors. It was established by the commissioners that the campaign of Colonel French — whose candidacy had been sought by the trades — was by far the least corrupt of the three in 1857, and that only to a very 'small extent' were inducements offered by his supporters. That he came last might be regarded as a consequence of his fastidiousness in this regard, but the picture was more complex than that. Among freemen, French headed the poll, receiving 322 votes, 60% of those on the register. The free-spending campaign of Lord Dunkellin came second with 306 votes, while Anthony O'Flaherty (unseated for his corrupt campaign) received only 184 freemen votes.[12] The pattern would suggest that most freemen used one of their two votes conscientiously, and accepted payment for the other.

The overwhelming impression from the evidence of the 396 witnesses examined by the commission of 1857 is that elections were periods of carnival in Galway. Work ceased for several weeks, public houses were thronged from morning to night, and there was constant commotion on the streets:

> … For a considerable period before an election, a general interruption of industry and employment takes place among the freemen. The more influential convene meetings of those they can, or hope to, influence; make out lists of voters for whom they undertake to answer … And, accordingly, money is given on faith of these lists, and to treat and entertain those listed upon them as combined together. In this way, and by this habit, of acting in bodies in concert, a constant excitement is kept up; and the poorer tradesmen and artisans … abandon their employments for the

treating and other temptations held out to them, and except by obtaining money from the candidates whom they support, have no means of repairing to themselves and their families the pecuniary loss thus occasioned.[13]

'Inducements' to voters, the evidence showed, were several. Most extensively, there was 'treating', hardly regarded as an inducement at all. Free drink, paid for by one or other campaign, was available in a number of public houses. By frequenting a particular pub, voters — and non-voters — identified themselves with a particular candidate. 'Treating' was enjoyed by freeholders as by freemen, and acceptance of drink did not commit the individual to supporting the campaign which paid for it. At most, 'treating' testified to a candidate's liberality, and consolidated his support by bringing voters into close contact with his 'friends', notably the individual publican.

A more pointed 'inducement' was the provision of groceries for the duration of an election, compensating the voter's family for the loss of the society — and the earnings — of the breadwinner. It was also valuable for shopkeeper supporters of candidates who could expect payment for their stock when the election was over.

Another inducement was the employment of influential individuals as booth agents, street agents, door-keepers and clerks. Little work was involved, but such positions gave status to those engaged. They were regarded — and might have regarded themselves — as trusted lieutenants rather than as a foot-soldiers in corruption.

A statement of accounts from Martin Blake's 1852 campaign shows that 'treating', the provision of groceries, and the employment of agents and 'bludgeon men', loomed larger than open bribery:

To the solicitors employed	— 160	10	0
To various shopkeepers and other persons, for goods and entertainment supplied both to electors, on orders or by direction of friends of Mr Blake	— 383	0	6
Cash paid, street agents	— 21	18	6
Cash paid to clerks and door-keepers	— 23	5	2
Paid for securing a mob from the commencement to the termination of the election	— 56	0	0
Amount paid bringing out voters from adjoining counties, &c.	— 25	0	0
Stationery, &c.	— 8	0	0
Paid to meet orders of Thomas Clare on shopkeepers	— 175	0	0
Amount of cash paid to voters	— 13	0	0
To further agents	— 18	14	0
To Patrick Greaney, to pay the butchers	— 96	0	0
Various cash payments	— 11	2	4
Total	£991	10	6[14]

Blake's expenditure in 1852, however, was modest in comparison with Lord Dunkellin's. But the 'extensive system of treating and bribery' in favour of his lordship yielded a total of only 272 votes. And no evidence was found to prove 'participation in such corrupt practices' by Dunkellin himself.[15]

As indicated by the examples of Dunkellin and Blake, candidates were careful to avoid personal involvement in malpractice. Only after an election were they presented with the bills. Even the 'conducting agents' — lawyers who managed the campaign for the various candidates — did their best to remain ignorant of the murkier details.[16] It would seem that the management of corruption was handled, on a nod and wink basis, by trusted individuals who were left to do as they saw fit. Merchant, John Semple, and Queen's College professor of surgery, James Valentine Browne, distributed largesse on behalf of Lord Dunkellin in 1857. Dr Browne, by his own evidence, was a relative innocent in electoral matters:

> I regret the part I took in it, and I never in my life had anything to do with elections before. I am a professional man … Up to that period — up to the very day before the voting — we were all strongly of the opinion that no money should be given, in fact we were very anxious that no money should be given. There were very numerous applications to us for money — there were lists handed in, with, as you heard, the prices appended to those lists; and we avoided all these … Well, on the morning of the polling, the party which was opposed to us came in great force and pulled away our voters — took them away off in cars. Two men were taken off in my own car in front of the tally rooms … dragged off in the car; and then it was that all the friends who met there stated that unless money were given the freemen would not vote.[17]

Having buckled under pressure to the avaricious demands of the freemen, Dr Browne was able to offer some justification for his actions:

> There were a great number of these freemen who were idle for several days pending this election, and their families many of them were in very great want of money, and many of these freemen applied for money as a sort of support for their families during this period. I thought two objects would be attained by giving the money; one was the thing would be given as a sort of payment of expenses; and next their physical force was of very great value at that time … and the money was given as much for that object. Perhaps it was more given for this purpose than for bribery.[18]

Browne did not himself bribe the individual freemen. This was the task of John Oliver, master baker of Mainguard-street, who had received £240 from the doctor. Oliver was one of those considered influential among the freemen and he was an important intermediary, as was Patrick Greaney, master leather-cutter, whose evidence has been already detailed. Another was pawnbroker, John Kirwan, whose economic role gave him considerable political leverage among the poorest freemen.[19] A few trades — notably the butchers and the shoemakers — acted collectively in elections, and their 'inducements' were received through their recognised leaders. Other trades were not as rigorously organised in the 1850s, and their members were marshalled by brokers whose position gave them authority in the daily lives of individual tradesmen — employers, publicans and pawnbrokers.* In cases where craft solidarities were weak, and individual freemen were subject to pressure from several sources, it was difficult to ensure that those who were bought remained bought. Consequently, elaborate mechanisms had to be contrived that would guarantee the bribed voter's compliance, and provide some anonymity for those doing the bribing. John Connor, a working baker, described his experience of voting in 1857. First, his voting ticket was 'sealed' by Dr Browne, testifying that he had voted for Dunkellin; then he was directed to John Oliver's house. He was shown in by Oliver's daughter: 'she brought me and showed me where to put up my hand; I put up my hand and there I got my demand; it was to a partition — there was a hole in it; I put up the ticket; and as I put it up I got two pound notes'.[20] Oliver admitted to 'treating' voters, to paying some for their 'exertions', and to bribing a small number of freemen. However, he denied involvement in the 'pigeon-hole' operation in his own house:

> Were you yourself at the pigeon-hole? — No
> Who was at the pigeon hole? — I cannot tell, I was not looking.
> Do you say you cannot tell who put the man or woman, or whoever it was, inside the pigeon-hole? — I think Dr Browne knows more about it than me.
> Did you go away when you heard of the pigeon-hole? — I was not aware of the pigeon-hole taking place.
> And were your daughters managing it all? — I believe they were told by somebody, not me.
> Then it was the young ladies that managed the matter? I cannot tell. You kept yourself away from it? — I did.
> … Was it not one of your daughters you believe was inside that hole? — I believe it was not; you see I do not know because I did not look.
> But surely you could see as well as anybody? — Well I tell you I did not like to know it.
> But you did know it? — I heard it.

---

* The political influence of the Galway pawnbroker had long been a matter of comment. The Tory *Galway Advertiser*, for example, complained that 'Mr Timothy Murray, the uncircumcised Jew of Abbeygate-street and pawnbroker arrogated to himself the command of the liberal mob...' (15 December 1838).

> Who was it that you heard was inside the pigeon-hole, and whom
> did you believe to have been there? — I heard it was my wife. I did
> not see it at all.[21]

The exposure of the extent of electoral corruption was embarrassing for those implicated and, indeed, for those concerned for Galway's reputation. The *Galway Express* reassured the second group: 'Those having a stake in the town' had been absolved of involvement in malpractice and, anyway: 'There is not 'a town, borough, or city in Ireland that would not produce its freemen as corrupt and as venal as Galway … We contend further that the sinners are an excrescence upon our constituency, not an actual part of it'.[22]

The discovery of the mechanisms of bribery did not put an end to its practice. Sir Rowland Blennerhasset expended £4,000 on bribes in 1865, while Fr Peter Daly gave out £2 'Christmas boxes' to those freemen callers to his house that had voted for John Orrel Lever in the same election.[23]

Elections, c.1868-1914

The popular excitement around elections was a casualty of democratisation, and a political culture based on vocational identification and economic dependency, on 'pigeon-holes' and 'bludgeon men', on distinctions between 'plumpers' and 'split votes', disappeared in a short space of time. As far as this political transformation was concerned — at least in Galway — the introduction of the secret ballot made the greatest difference. If one could not know with certainty how a man voted, it was pointless trying in bribe or intimidate him. And if the progress of an election was shrouded until the boxes were opened, there was no reason for people to gather around polling stations either. In time, there would emerge new electoral rituals, appropriate to the altered context, but as an account of an 1874 Galway town by-election indicates, their colourless character was the most salient feature of electoral proceedings in the immediate aftermath of the Secret Ballot Act:

> Both candidates were in the courthouse from the commencement
> and both were treated with the greatest respect and consideration
> by the people. There was not anything like a popular
> demonstration … and, except in the neighbourhood of the
> courthouse, a stranger would hardly know that so important a
> business as the election of a parliamentary representative was being
> decided. At 5 o'clock, the booths were closed, and the High Sheriff,
> Mr Charles ffrench Blake-Forster, announced that the scrutiny
> should take place next day.[24]

One thing that had not changed was the disposition of defeated candidates to challenge the result, and the by-election described was one necessitated by a successful petition. Frank Hugh O'Donnell — a recent graduate of the Queen's

College and a 'cousin to everybody [in the constituency], from the high sheriff to the blacksmith on the bridge'[25] — had been unseated, on the grounds that the Catholic clergy had exercised undue influence in his cause. It was the contention of the petitioners that Bishop MacEvilly had been engaged as an agent by O'Donnell, a role from which he was precluded because, within the previous seven years, he had been found guilty of corrupt electoral practice. This was on foot of the Keogh judgement in the 1872 county election, which will be discussed below.

MacEvilly supported O'Donnell in 1874, but with mixed feelings, considering that it was a 'dangerous game to send so young and penniless a man to parliament'. The candidate had promised the bishop that he would be a relentless advocate for the hierarchy, but, for many of the clergy, O'Donnell's piety was exposed as fraudulent when he planned victory celebrations for the Lenten period, and when he treated supporters — 'all healthy strong young men' — to a meat supper on a Friday.[26] Nonetheless, his removal was unsatisfactory as far as MacEvilly was concerned.

John MacEvilly was not a notably political bishop, but a conservative man who became a strong ally of Cardinal Cullen's. In relation to the 1857 election, which was held on Holy Thursday and which coincided with his arrival in the Galway diocese, he urged priests only to 'respect the sanctity of the day'. This advice was consistent with Cullen's view of the time that the clergy should remain aloof from public affairs, but circumstances changed and, by the mid-1860s, Cullen's followers were deeply involved in politics. To provide an alternative to Fenianism, a church-sponsored National Association was established in advance of the 1865 general election and, in order to secure Anglican disestablishment, Cullen determined to bolster Gladstone's Liberals. In Galway, MacEvilly loyally followed what amounted to a party line, as he sought to give effect to Cullen's political objectives.

The situation in 1865 was difficult for the bishop. Fr Peter Daly was the principal backer of the Conservative, John Orrel Lever, and rather than see 'priest actively arrayed against priest' in an election, MacEvilly decided to remain aloof.[27] Lever was defeated, but the election of Michael Morris, presented problems of its own.

Morris and his Catholic landed family of Spiddal were popular with the clergy and the people. Galwegians, Morris's son remarked, 'were all strong Nationalists, but they were still stronger Morrisites', recalling that his family's supporters included 'fish-wives' who although they had no vote 'wielded a big influence politically and physically'. The family had been long influential in Galway politics. Michael Morris' father was the first Catholic high-sheriff in the modern period, in which position he was succeeded by his son. Since the 1850s, Michael had used his influence in favour of Lord Dunkellin, but when that nobleman opted for the county constituency in 1865, he decided to seek the seat himself, and was comfortably returned.[28]

Morris's support for the Conservative government put him at odds with the

Catholic bishops, but it won him the Irish attorney generalship and, in 1867, a senior judicial appointment. Morris's brother, George, was the only candidate for the resulting vacancy. For MacEvilly, this did not resolve the problem, and he established a so-called Galway Independent Club to demand that George Morris pledge himself a Liberal. When he refused, the diocesan clergy declared him 'an unfit person to represent this Catholic borough'. Morris withdrew from the 1868 general election, and MacEvilly supported the outgoing Blennerhassett and Lord St Lawrence, a nephew of Clanricarde. A third Liberal, Martin O'Flaherty, declined to be interviewed by the clergy and was denounced by MacEvilly. The denunciation, like his other dramatic interventions in Galway life described in Chapters Twelve and Thirteen, came only because MacEvilly was confident of the outcome. In the aftermath of the election, O'Flaherty challenged the result, but Judge William Keogh found that the bishop and the clergy had acted within their rights.[29] The same judge's verdict in the 1872 County election petition, however, would be rather different.

The 1872 County Galway by-election was one of the pre-Ballot Act contests that most explicitly highlighted the changing political climate. But the decisive victory achieved by Home Ruler, Captain Nolan, over the Conservative landlords' champion, Captain le Poer Trench, was overturned in the Galway courthouse by Judge Keogh on the grounds that 'undue influence' was brought to bear on the electors, in particular by the Catholic clergy. MacHale of Tuam, MacEvilly, and a number of priests were singled out for special mention. For his part, MacEvilly had been an unenthusiastic supporter of Nolan. He considered the Catholic landlord to be too radical and feared that his campaign's emphasis on tenants' rights would raise divisions between wealthy Catholics and poor Catholics.[30]

In his judgement, Keogh recalled an earlier County Galway election that he had witnessed, eccentrically contrasting the honest-to-goodness nature of the arson and slaughter that had characterised it, with the devious and reprehensible interference of the Catholic clergy on the most recent occasion:

> I was not very old at the time, but I well recollect the many stirring scenes. The celebrated Mr Martin — or, as he was popularly known, Dick Martin — an accomplished gentleman, friend of the Regent who was after Sovereign, he was one of the candidates … There was much violence used; houses were burned, and I saw one blazing here which has never been rebuilt, and several persons were killed. Yet, there was no sectarian animosity; there was not a whisper in the whole affair of what is now to be called priestly interference.[31]

The 1872 county contest was aggressively fought, with popular feeling running high in favour of Nolan, not least outside the constituency in Galway itself. Cars carrying Trench supporters to the polling station in the town received military protection, lest they be obstructed by the urban crowd.[32] The unseating of Nolan raised the political temperature and before the official

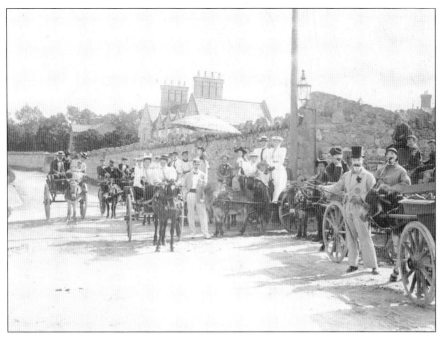

1. Queen's University Galway students posing for a rag day photograph outside the Galway workhouse (courtesy of Tom Kenny).

2. Aerial view of Galway workhouse in the early 1950s shortly before its demolition (courtesy of NLI).

3. A day out at Menlo Castle in the late 19th century. The crowd was gathered either for May Sunday celebrations or for a regatta (courtesy of Tom Kenny).

4. Galway Woollen Mill workers line up with banner for St Patrick's Day parade (courtesy of Tom Kenny).

5. A military band rehearses in Eyre Square. In the background is the Railway Hotel (courtesy of NLI).

6. Salthill tram at the Square, with calf market in the background (courtesy of NLI).

7. Sisters of Mercy with their pupils at Newtownsmith (courtesy of NLI).

8. The 'Jes' Sports — St Ignatius's College boys ready for action at Merlin Park
(courtesy of NLI).

9. Working at Cloherty and Semple's timber yard (courtesy of NLI).

10. The Iodine Works at Long Walk (courtesy of NLI).

11. Friends meet outside Eglinton Street RIC barracks (courtesy of NLI).

12. The sock market — opposite the RIC barracks·(courtesy of NLI).

13. Wash day at the Eglinton Canal (courtesy of NLI).

14. 'Ne'er a wing: ne'er a wet': outside a public house (courtesy of NLI).

15. The Colonial Building and the Eglinton Buildings on the left and 'Dublin Time' at Dillon's Watchmaking and Jewellery Shop on the right. For a note on 'Dublin time' and 'Galway time', see page 167 (courtesy of NLI).

16. View of Shop Street with Salthill tram approaching (courtesy of NLI).

17. Taking shelter from the storm at the docks (courtesy of NLI).

18. Sailing ships at the docks (courtesy of NLI).

19. Fanciful representation of proposed new harbour for trans-Atlantic traffic at Furbo (courtesy of Timothy Collins).

20. Máirtín Mór McDonogh addressing a public meeting.

21. Claddagh's 'mayor' of c.1890, Padge King (see p. 233) with Mrs King (see p. 236), and unidentified youth (courtesy of NLI).

22. Passing by the railway station on the way to market.

23. At market in the shadow of the Collegiate Church.

24. The Shambles barracks, with Mainguard Street and the Collegiate Church in the background (courtesy of NLI).

FISH MARKET. GALWAY. 906. W.L.

25. Wooden bridge connecting the fish market with the Claddagh (courtesy of NLI).

26. The Piscatorial National School building and the Dominican Church at the Claddagh (courtesy of NLI).

27. Claddagh houses (courtesy of Ulster Folk & Transport Museum).

28. The Mechanics' Institute and the Pro-Cathedral, Middle Street.

29. James Hardiman (courtesy of James
Hardiman Library, NUI, Galway).

30. Brother Paul O'Connor.

31. Eviction scene at Nuns Island (courtesy of Tom Kenny).

32. Fr Peter Daly
(courtesy of Galway City Council).

33. Monument in Bushy Park churchyard
'erected by the people of Galway' to
Fr John Roche (1818-47) a casualty of
the Famine.

34. Resting on benches — and on a rock — at Salthill (courtesy of NLI).

35. A cyclist considers the view at Salthill (courtesy of NLI).

'indignation meeting' could be organised, something of the spirit of 1826 manifested itself in an impromptu popular demonstration. The *Galway Express* described the proceedings:

> The West was made the headquarters, and there his lordship [in effigy] was ermined, wigged, and complimented, with the insignia in front 'Norbury Keogh', and behind in large letters 'Judas'. A band hailing from Shell-lane was got into requisition, and soon tin-whistles, home-made tambourines, tattered and torn *dhrums*, clappers, and janglers of all conceivable shape began to 'waste their sweetness on the desert air'. The police seemed on the alert, but yet were outflanked by these geniuses, who, whenever the Royal Irish came into view, lowered the effigy, and again raised it when they became invisible. When they got to the Square, they halted, as if that seemed to be the point to rally. Police were drawn up opposite the [County] Club, but there only being about fifty of them, and the streets crowded with thousands of people, they seemed quite paralysed, and their forbearance appeared almost to savour of perfect inability to grapple with the emergency. After some stump oratory … the effigy was raised, and after very rough handling and anything but prayers and complimentary epithets, was finally blown to atoms with powder.[33]

Later, sections of the crowd broke the windows of Black's Hotel, Trench headquarters during the petition hearings, and those of the County Club, meeting place of the landed elite. However, after the reading of the Riot Act and a police charge during which a number of people were injured, the crowd dispersed.

A popular perspective on these events was given in a ballad, 'Conversation Between Judy From Menlo And Patsy Friday On The Galway Election Petition':

> As Judy from Menlo one evening was walking,
> For sweet recreation along the main street;
> After coming from Salthill on the buss called the Erin,
> A man they call Friday she happened to meet.
> Arra Patsy agra have you any news for me,
> Is the petition over, or is Nolan in?
> I hear then, said she, that he is unseated,
> And for to shed tears, sure, they both did begin
> … Be gob then, says Judy, it's too good to hang him,
> Says Scowogue, we'll hang him and tie him to a car,
> O heaven, says Friday, give me a kick at him,
> And then we will burn him in a barrel of tar.
> He insulted our clergy and likewise our bishop,
> And scoffed at MacHale, the bright star of Mayo,
> All Galway denies him, and Ireland will think on,
> The name of that hero, "So help me God" Keogh.[34]

The labelling of the effigy as 'Judas' was a reference to Keogh's perceived betrayal of his Catholicism. Also guilty of apostasy, by implication, were the Catholic landlords who put their economic interests before their religious identities by supporting Trench rather than Nolan (and in some instances testifying before Keogh about pro-Nolan homilies delivered in their local churches).

By 1874, John MacEvilly was an experienced political operator, a veteran witness at election petitions, and an advocate for Catholic candidates in local government elections.[35] His interventions had not always been successful, however — most recently, George Morris, by then a luke-warm 'Home Ruler', had trounced his favourite, Frank Hugh O'Donnell, in the first post-Ballot Act general election.[36]

In the by-election following the unseating of Frank Hugh O'Donnell, the third election of 1874 in the town of Galway, MacEvilly did not have to raise a finger to secure the election of his favoured candidate. This was O'Donnell's election agent and friend — another recent student of the Queen's College — Dr Michael Ward.[37] Popular indignation at the treatment of O'Donnell by Judge Lawson was such that the young man was overwhelmingly returned. He would serve only one term, however, for reasons that were set out by his successor, another member of O'Donnell's Queen's College set, T. P. O'Connor:

> He was consumed by violent passions, and the curious thing to complete the strange make up was that he had not a particle of sentiment. He would disappear for weeks together, and nobody could trace him … This terrible strain would go on for months at a time, and then would come the breakdown. The glimpse of a barmaid with a V-shaped blouse would be sufficient to light again the fire of his fiery sensuality; and on that same night, and for weeks after he would disappear — it will be easily understood where — and would be lost to everybody … Men given to 'sprees' always choose the worst moment for them. While every constituency was panting for the presence of its candidate, my poor friend went off on his spree in haste, but alone, it need scarcely be said. As usual he left no trace; and the newspapers were not so ubiquitous or so inquisitive as they are nowadays. So far as his constituents, his friends, his family were concerned, he had disappeared as completely as if he were dead.[38]

The disappearance of his friend was O'Connor's opportunity. He was working as a journalist in London, in which capacity he had become acquainted with many leading politicians, including Parnell. By his own account, however, the invitation from Dr Ward's supporters to contest the constituency was prompted by the reputation he had acquired as a student debater in Galway a decade earlier. He was one of three candidates, all describing themselves as Home Rulers, for the two town seats. His rivals were Hugh Tarpey, a Galway-born ex-Mayor of Dublin, and John Orrel Lever. Of the three, O'Connor was regarded as the Parnellite, and he attributed his return to the votes of tenant farmers in the rural part of the constituency. Remarkably, Lever was also returned, something O'Connor attributed to nostalgia for the ephemeral glory of the late 1850s and 1860s. O'Connor did not mention any clerical influence in the election. If it was deployed, and MacEvilly's preoccupations with matters in the Tuam diocese may have meant that it was not, it was most likely in the interests of respectable Catholic businessman Tarpey rather than in that of the Parnellite or the renegade Tory.[39]

O'Connor was the Nationalist candidate for the sole Galway seat in 1885, when he was elected by an overwhelming majority over Loyalist, T. G. P. Hallet. But O'Connor was also returned by Irish emigrant voters in a Liverpool constituency, and he opted to represent them in Westminster, precipitating an extraordinary by-election. According to F. S. L. Lyons:

> The Galway by-election of 1886 has a unique importance in the history of Parnell's leadership of the home rule movement as the only occasion on which prior to the O'Shea divorce, Parnell's private life obtruded onto his public conduct, and his authority within the party was seriously threatened.[40]

Two candidates sought the Nationalist nomination: Michael Lynch, a local activist with a Fenian background, and Captain William O'Shea, ex-member for Clare and husband of Parnell's lover, Katherine. Galway nationalists favoured Lynch, as did those members of the parliamentary party acquainted with O'Shea's character and with the nature of Parnell's connection with him. Parnell was adamant that O'Shea be selected, but Joseph Biggar and Tim Healy arrived in the constituency to block him. Convinced by their backers that the other would withdraw, both men had themselves nominated.[41] The bemused *Galway Express* noted that Lynch's papers were signed by leading local nationalist political and business figures, while O'Shea had to depend on his relative, Fr Joseph O'Shea and a number of men with less-than-prestigious addresses. In the gossip fuelled excitement, it seemed that Lynch was set for an overwhelming victory.[42]

On the day after nominations closed, Parnell himself arrived, accompanied by T. P. O'Connor and William O'Brien. At the railway station, a number of priests protected them from the hostility of a crowd of several thousands. A meeting followed in the Railway Hotel between the priests and the parliamentarians. The priests supported O'Shea — whether because of Lynch's Fenian associations, or because of an instruction from the new bishop, Thomas Carr, to support the recognised leader of the Irish people.[43] There followed a disorderly meeting in the Young Ireland Hall, in the course of which Parnell demanded that he be allowed to lead as he saw fit, and Michael Lynch announced his withdrawal. It was too late however to withdraw Lynch's nomination, and the election scheduled for the following Thursday had to proceed. At the end of the meeting, Parnell promised that he would give an explanation on the following day for his conduct in the affair.

On Wednesday, Parnell spoke from the steps of the Railway Hotel, stating (disingenuously) that he understood that Michael Lynch was not willing to put himself forward. As leader, he then had to decide on a candidate and, on balance, had chosen O'Shea. Having made the decision, it was his duty to implement it:

> Having recommended him in my position, I was bound not to recede one hair's breadth — one jot — but to carry through that recommendation to the bitter end, to test whether the people of Galway and the people of Ireland have that confidence in me which I believed they had …[44]

Only 54 votes were cast for Lynch. Most of those who wished to protest, it would seem, abstained, for O'Shea got just over two-thirds of the vote received by O'Connor a few months earlier. The announcement of the result was received with cheers, and the Labourers' Band was on hand to play *God Save Ireland*.[45]

O'Shea's period as Galway's representative was brought to an early end by the July 1886 general election, itself the consequence of the defeat of the home rule bill. In his five months as MP, he won over the Claddagh people — for initiating an inquiry into the grievances of fisherman — and he was greeted by a large bonfire and a pier 'ornamented with flags, green boughs and bunting' on his arrival to visit that community in April. Unwisely, however, he insulted the still-popular Michael Lynch in the following month, reducing his stock with the generality of Galwegians to the low level of February.[46] John Pinkerton, a Unitarian tenant farmer from Ballymoney who had unsuccessfully contested North Antrim in 1885, was returned unopposed in July 1886, and he would represent the constituency until 1900.

Like O'Shea, Pinkerton was personally selected by Parnell, and recommended by him to the constituency as 'a Protestant gentleman from the North of Ireland'. The 'Irish leader', according to one tactful observer, 'received no local assistance in the matter'. Pinkerton's election, the people of Galway were advised, 'would be a demonstration of toleration that would have a telling effect on the people of Ulster who are opposed to the establishment of an Irish parliament in Dublin'. Galway nationalists were disappointed but, in the aftermath of the February events, not surprised. Locally, the candidacy of Christopher Talbot Redington of Clarinbridge had been canvassed. Redington, son of Thomas Redington, the first Catholic to hold the post of Under-Secretary for Ireland, was a National Education Commissioner and a former president of the Oxford Union. He was also a nationalist, an advocate of tenants' rights — and a socialist, according to one authority. Local sentiment, however, did not influence Parnell, and significant Galway nationalists were informed by telegram a few days before nominations closed of Pinkerton's 'selection'. There was not even the pretence of local democracy on this occasion, for no constituency convention was held. On Pinkerton's arrival, he was guided to the Railway Hotel for a brief 'consultation with some gentlemen'. Then, from the steps of the hotel, he addressed a waiting crowd. The only challenger to party hegemony was the exuberant and eccentric James O'Mara, but such was the derision which greeted his announcement of interest that he declined to lodge his nomination papers. The announcement of Pinkerton's unopposed return generated little excitement, but 'in response to calls', a twice-disappointed Michael Lynch addressed the assembled crowd. Stressing that he bore no ill-will towards the new MP, he declared nonetheless that 'the people of Galway felt that they had not been well-treated either in this or the last election'.[47]

The *Vindicator* commented that, given the neglect of the town, Pinkerton had a 'wide field for the exercise of energy and zeal in the promotion of local interests'. And, for a time, the MP gave no cause for complaint. However, after Parnell's fall, when the party was unable to pay its members, Pinkerton could not afford to attend parliament regularly. Local interests, therefore, remained unpromoted.[48]

Before the 1892 general election Galwegians were reminded of the salacious gossip which had reached the town in 1886, a reminder which must have been embarrassing for Father Peter Dooley and other clergymen who had promoted the O'Shea candidacy. The O'Shea divorce case of 1890, and the 'fall' of Parnell which flowed from it, blew apart the nationalist unity that had been painstakingly built over the previous decade. Several bitter by-elections exposed fault-lines that had been concealed since the early 1880s, between the Catholic clergy on one side, and ideological nationalists and republicans on the other. Galway's representative, Pinkerton, took an extreme anti-Parnell position. The former leader's whole life, he declared, 'had been a tissue of selfish intrigues'. In the heat of the North Sligo by-election of 1891, Parnell returned the compliment, dismissing Pinkerton as an 'Ulster Protestant' and commenting: 'the Protestants of Ireland are capable of looking after their own business, and they do not want any souping Presbyterian to go in among the Catholics and instruct them on that point'.[49]

There was no by-election in Galway in the stormy period between Parnell's 'fall' and his death. There was political division, however, which came into the open when Fr Peter Dooley organised an anti-Parnell rally shortly after the bishops' statement of denunciation. Posters for the event referred to the 'drunken Dublin mob' as the only remaining supporters of the erstwhile Chief. At the beginning of the meeting, an argument developed about the insulting nature of the poster — and its implied attitude to both Parnellites and the working people of Galway — before a scuffle broke out for the chair and the platform. Parnellite town commissioners, Tom Sullivan and Tom Ashe — convivial men who had served prison terms for political causes — won physical control, so Fr Dooley led his supporters to the Temperance Hall. A resolution criticising the poster and defending the characters of Parnellites was passed by acclamation. The crowd that remained consisted mainly of labourers and shop assistants — from the sections of the community which, throughout nationalist Ireland, remained most loyal to Parnell. It is to be supposed that Sullivan, as honorary secretary of the recently-founded Labourers' Society, had influence with the working class, but it was limited, and the controversy opened up divisions in the Society which were partly responsible for its demise.[50]

When Parnell arrived to address a rally in March, he was greeted by the labourers' band and 3,000 people, in defiance of Bishop McCormack's condemnation of the visit as 'a grave scandal, a political blunder, and a social disgrace'.[51]

Among the resolutions of welcome for Parnell was one from the Town Commissioners, which had, been passed amidst acrimony a few days earlier. It was this resolution which led Fr Peter Dooley to attempt to alter the composition of the board. A so-called Ratepayers' Association was launched in August 1891, a few weeks before elections for eight commissioners. A slate of seven candidates — supported by Bishop McCormack and pledged to tackle municipal corruption — presented themselves. The Parnellite *United Irishman* printed a ballad composed by a local wag, mocking the pretensions of the would-be ratepayer representatives:

> *I always thought Tom Sullivan a patriot tried and true*
> *I knew he faced a prison cell, dared Balfour and his crew*
> *And never shirked when duty call, though others quailed with fear*
> *And that ever to his manly heart, old Erin's heart was dear*
> *But Fr. Dooley says I'm wrong, says Tom is low and mean*
> *And if I want a patriot I must take Timothy Kean.*
>
> *It was an old belief of mine that if e'er the foe we'd smash*
> *Twas with a noble vanguard of men like Thomas Ashe*
> *A man who knows what plank beds are and though they aren't down*
> *Would face them twice a hundred times in the interests of the town*
> *But Fr. Dooley says I'm wrong and calls Tom Ashe a traitor*
> *And if I want a soldier brave I must take John N. Sleator.*[52]

The ballad has been cited as one of the few anti-clerical ballads in the Irish tradition. Arguably, however, it is no more anti-clerical than were those of Fr Dooley's clerical colleagues who came into conflict with him over the years.[53] But it did reflect the attitude of many Galwegians. 'The voters', commented a disappointed post-election editorialist, 'are not to be relied upon at any time'.[54] In the general election of 1892, the anti-Parnellites did better. Boosted by support from the rural part of the constituency, Pinkerton held his seat with 644 votes to Parnellite Arthur Lynch's 593. In the 1895 election, the outcome was similar: Pinkerton got 596 votes; Parnellite, Edmund Leamy got 465;

Unionist, Martin Morris, son of the since-ennobled MP of 1865, got 395. Indicative of the intensity of the political competition — and testifying to the durability of Galway's political traditions — selection conventions of the period invited 'delegates' from mostly non-existent trades' organisation. For example, the Parnellite convention of 1892, where Arthur Lynch addressed himself to 'the labour question', was attended by representatives of blacksmiths, brushmakers, carpenters, masons, painters, plasterers, plumbers, shoemakers, slaters and tailors.[55]

Lynch's interest in labour affairs was not opportunistic — his father was a militant of the Eureka Stockade, and he himself would later join the British Labour Party — but it was a precocious interest in the west of Ireland of the early 1890s. Before the decade was out, however, the Local Government Act of 1898 would put the 'labour question' at the centre of politics. The Act created county councils and district councils, gave votes in restricted instances to women, and equalised the local and parliamentary franchise, giving the mass of male labourers the vote in local elections. As was the case with the Galway freemen of the 1830s, it was anticipated that newly-enfranchised labourers would vote *en masse* for candidates promising to represent their interests. Consequently, the majority of candidates in the first elections of the new dispensation, in 1899, adopted labour-friendly policies. And, in most of the significant towns, there were Labour candidates, selected by hastily improvised Labour Electoral Associations or by trade unions. To take the best-organised west of Ireland example, the Ballinasloe Workingmen's Association, led by carriage-trimmer John Brutin, narrowly missed winning a majority on the town's fifteen-member urban council. In Galway, a Labour Electoral Association was formed in December 1898, but, with no coherent trade union input, it came under clerical control. No labour candidates emerged, and the Association satisfied itself with administering a 'labour pledge' to all candidates. The pledge had four clauses: to support 'every proposal for the betterment of the working classes'; to enforce the sanitary laws; to encourage the spread of technical education; to arrange that all council meetings be held at night so that working class representatives could attend if elected.[56] In the election of the following year, under the same clerical guidance, the Labour Electoral Association found itself in the Unionist camp, having been lured by the 'local' and 'Catholic' credentials of Martin Morris.

The end of division between Galway Parnellites and anti-Parnellites was heralded at the inaugural public meeting of the United Irish League branch in November 1898. By one report, it was the largest meeting in Galway since Parnell's day, and 'remarkable' insofar as many of those participating had been 'unable to share a common platform in seven years.[57] Two years later, Parnellite Edmund Leamy was the general election candidate of the united party. Leamy's supporters had reason to be optimistic, as their sole opponent was Unionist Martin Morris, third-placed candidate in 1895. Morris's 27% in 1895, however, was high for a Unionist in a three-way contest — 'Loyalist' Hallet had only managed 11% a decade earlier — showing that the Morris name had a resonance beyond the usual Unionist constituency. 'Local' credentials, moreover, had a particular appeal in the wake of the disappointing incumbency of the stranger Pinkerton.

In the course of the campaign, tradition re-asserted itself, and there was widespread treating. According to one source, Morris's supporters 'were so enthusiastic that fifteen public-houses kept their doors open in his interest, with free drink for all his adherents'. Nationalists responded in like fashion, but they were unable to save the seat. Moreover, their own behaviour in the campaign made it impossible for them to petition the result.[58] A candidate in a subsequent election thought that the Morris-Leamy contest had a long-term effect on Galway's electoral culture:

> Everybody in Galway was convinced that the election laws did not run in that city: and that the occasion of a contest was the occasion of free drinks. There was good encouragement for any enterprising man to assail the seat —since such an assailant could afford to take unusual risks.[59]

What Morris's narrow victory of 1900 showed was that the new-found 'unity' of nationalists did not run very deep. Given the Catholic roots of anti-Parnellism, many of its adherents preferred to transfer their allegiance to a Catholic Unionist rather than to a candidate with a Parnellite past. Certainly, one clerical faction did just that, as did the majority of Claddagh people, and the contest was marked by high feelings and by riotous confrontations.

Within a year, Martin Morris succeeded to the title of Lord Killanin, causing a by-election, for which two remarkable candidates offered themselves. Horace Plunkett, recently rejected by South Dublin Unionists, was convinced that his constructive unionist record on co-operation and agricultural development would prove more popular in Galway. The new Lord Killanin thought otherwise, advising Plunkett that he had held a Morris seat, not a Unionist seat, and adding, cynically, that 'there could not be two less appealing words in the English language to his supporters in Galway than Economics and Co-operation'.[60] The Nationalist candidate was Arthur Lynch, Parnellite candidate in 1892, and since notorious as Colonel of the second pro-Boer Irish Brigade in South Africa — John McBride commanded the first. Australian-born Lynch was a larger than life figure. A polymath, a religious sceptic, and an owner of land at Quilty, Co. Clare, with qualifications in medicine and engineering and an M.A, in Mathematics from Melbourne University, he had written (in English and French) books on psychology, evolution, literature, and other subjects. Lynch's candidacy was suggested by John Redmond, under pressure from pro-Boer sentiment in Irish America, but also from sentiment in Galway where party members wished to nominate General Kruger.* On this occasion,

---

* Support for the Boers was also expressed in the naming of the GAA clubs Tuam Krugers and Athenry De Wets.

the Galway clergy were united behind the revolutionary agnostic, and he took the seat in another violent election.[61] In the circumstances, Plunkett's vote of 27.5% — not to mention the willingness of people to riot on his behalf — was creditable, indicating that the Morris influence had converted many Galway Catholics to Unionism.

Fearing arrest, Lynch fought the election from Paris. But when he travelled to London to claim his seat at war's end, he was arrested, tried for treason, and sentenced to death. Influential friends ensured that the sentence was commuted, but his conviction led to a by-election.[62] Another colonial — a former member of the Canadian parliament — Charles Devlin, was returned unopposed as a Nationalist in March 1903, and likewise in the 1906 general election. Shortly afterwards, however, Devlin was re-elected to the Canadian Commons, and he returned to take up the position of Minister of Colonisation, Mines and Fisheries. Yet another riotous by-election ensued, in which another peripatetic intellectual, Stephen Gwynn, was the Nationalist candidate. A grassroots campaign to select a local man fizzled out when the local leadership bowed to Redmond at the party convention.[63]

A local man emerged from outside the party, however, when John Shawe-Taylor offered himself as an Independent. Shawe-Taylor had a profile as president of the Galway Development Association but, more significantly, he had emerged as a spokesman for conciliationist landlords. Whether accidentally or as a pawn of Chief Secretary Wyndham, he had played an important role in the discussions, which led to the Land Act of 1903. Since

"Victory!—Under Police Protection."

[Mr. Redmond announced that all was lost unless Galway gave the candidate of the Standing Committee an "overwhelming victory." The "overwhelming victory" is depicted above. The Standing Committee and their candidate were indebted to police protection for getting into Galway or out of it with safety.]

The riotous Galway election of 1906, as depicted by an *Irish People* cartoonist.

that time, his association with Lord Dunraven's Irish Reform Association had brought him into contact with William O'Brien, then estranged from Redmond's party. O'Brien, however, did not openly support his candidature. The fact was that although he proclaimed himself a 'devolutionist', Shawe-Taylor was conspicuously a Unionist, and was regarded as one, not least by other Unionists. The Tory *Express,* while professing to disagree with him on many issues, urged that there be 'no hunkersliding same as when Mr Plunkett stood'. Under the heading, 'A warm week in Galway', the same paper reported on clashes between mobs, and alleged 'treating' on the part of Gywnn's supporters. Gwynn himself later described the election:

> The streets filled up with 'batyeen boys' [descendants of the 'bludgeon men' of yore?] carrying sticks and shouting 'Up Taylor' and 'To Hell with Gwynn', or vice versa. There was a good deal of scrimmaging: our meetings were systematically interrupted and, worst of all, no band could be procured. It seemed that nothing could be done without a band and the other side had got one. There was a general air of dismay, much complaint of blackguardism, and recognition of the other side's tactics — which were simply to frighten people away from the poll. One afternoon as I was driving through town with Murphy [a Galway solicitor] we were held up at a narrow corner and some drunken fellow ran out and hit me on the back. With the utmost promptitude Mutrphy stood up, turned in his seat, and gave the staggering creature his whip lash full around the neck and face — and then went on as if it was the most ordinary civility. A little further, as we drove on, three or four carloads of the the batyeen boys (as the stick bearers were called, came galloping behind us with much shouting…)[64]

Enthusiastic support in working class communities, including the West and the Claddagh, enabled Shawe-Taylor to hold his own on the streets, but it was not enough for victory, and he had to be satisfied with 36% of the vote.[65] A coalition of Unionists, of former Morris supporters, of nationalists protesting at insensitivity to local concerns, had presented a significant challenge to the parliamentary party.

Ever since the imposition of Captain O'Shea in 1885, the preferred 'man for Galway' of the mainstream nationalist party had consistently been a stranger. But only in 1900, when a uniquely-qualified alternative was available, did the complaint that Galwegians were being taken for granted lead to the rejection of the party's anointed. Nevertheless, the strong performances of Plunkett and Shawe-Taylor showed that there was a large constituency that was alienated from Redmond's party. This constituency was an obvious target for William O'Brien's conciliationist All For Ireland League, and it supported a Galway newspaper, the *Connaught Champion.* Redmondites responded to the challenge with the *Connacht Tribune* in 1909, driving the *Champion* out of business. Stephen Gwynn held his Galway seat until the 1918 general election. A challenge from J. L. Wanklyn, in 1910 failed to win support outside of the core Unionist constituency.[66]

Redmondism had other Galway critics in the years before the Great War. There was a branch of Sinn Féin from 1907, and members, notably Dr Tom Walsh, were elected onto the Urban Council, and won influence in the emerging labourers' trade union.[67] In 1911, Christabel Pankhurst addressed a crowded public meeting in Galway, inaugurating a campaign for women's suffrage that sought to influence public opinion, and to exert pressure on parliamentary representatives.[68]

Two other organisations established in 1911, and representing a working-class constituency, gave expression to a specifically urban political agenda. The Galway United Trades Council oversaw the extension of trade unionism into almost all employments in the town, lobbied public bodies to endorse 'fair labour' principles, and articulated the grievances and aspirations of its members and affiliates in press statements to the local papers, and in the pages of its short-lived *Advocate*.[69] At the same time, a branch of the Town Tenants League — successor to a short-lived Galway House League of 1886 and a Town Tenants League branch of 1905 — sought the same entitlements for town-dwellers as had been conferred upon farmers by the land acts. The 1911 body had links with the Trades Council, and represented the demands of working-class tenants for public housing, for reduced rents and for security of tenure. These demands featured too on the labour programme for the 1914 local elections, when Galway's first two Trades-Council-nominated Labour councillors were returned.[70]

NOTES

1. National Library of Ireland, McCall Ballad Collection.
2. Michael Hurst, 'Ireland and the Ballot Act of 1872' in Alan O'Day, ed., *Reactions to Irish Nationalism*, London 1987, pp. 33-59; James Loughlin, 'Constructing the Political Spectacle: Parnell, the Press, and National Leadership, 1879-1886', in Boyce & O'Day, eds, *Parnell in Perspective*, London 1991, pp. 221-41; Hoppen, *Elections*, p. 73.
3. Hoppen, *Elections*, pp. 31-32, 87-88; Walker, *Results*, pp. 282-83, 350-51.
4. National Archives, Outrage reports, 1838, 11/39; *Corrupt Practices Commissioners*, 1857-58, pp. 148-49.
5. *Corrupt Practices Commissioners*, 1857-58, p. 46-48.
6. ibid., p. 71-72.
7. ibid., pp. xv, 71-72
8. ibid., pp. viii, 46-50; R. V. Comerford, *The Fenians in Context: Irish Politics and Irish Society, 1848-82*, pp. 26-28.
9. *Corrupt Practices Commissioners*, 1857-58, p. xiv.
10. ibid., pp. 71-75.
11. ibid.
12. ibid., pp. xiv-xvi.
13. ibid., p. xv.
14. ibid., p. 130.
15. ibid., p. xv.

16. ibid., p. 33-35.
17. ibid., pp. 23-27.
18. ibid.
19. *Minutes of Evidence taken before the Select Committee on the Galway Town Election Petitions, with the Proceedings of the Committee,* 1866 x, p. 4.
20. ibid., p. 7.
21. ibid., p. 28.
22. *Galway Express,* 19 December 1857.
23. Hoppen, *Elections,* pp. 77, 84; *Election Petition,* 1866, pp. 30-33.
24. *Galway Vindicator,* 1 July 1874.
25. F. Hugh O'Donnell, *A History of the Irish Parliamentary Party,* vol. i, Port Washington, pp. 95-96.
26. Liam Bane, *The Bishop in Politics: Life and Career of John MacEvilly,* Westport 1993, pp. 30-35.
27. ibid., pp. 14-18
28. Maud Wynne, *An Irishman and his Family: Lord Morris and Killanin,* London 1937, pp. 10, 100-01; *1866 Petition,* pp. 56-59.
29. Bane, *MacEvilly,* pp. 18-24; Emmet Larkin, *The Consolidation of the Roman Catholic Church in Ireland, 1860-1870,* Chapel Hill 1987, pp. 341-93.
30. Bane, *MacEvilly,* pp. 24-30; Gerard Moran, *A Radical Priest in Mayo,* Dublin 1994, pp. 136-41.
31. *Galway Express,* 1 June 1872 (Keogh was nine years of age in 1826).
32. Moran, *Lavelle,* p. 139.
33. *Galway Express,* 1 June 1872.
34. National Library of Ireland, Bradshaw Collection, vol.iv, p. 38. The ballad was printed by Brereton of Dublin.
35. *Galway Express,*
36. Bane, *MacEvilly,* p. 35.
37. ibid.
38. T. P. O'Connor, M.P., *Memoirs of an Old Parliamentarian,* vol. i, London 1929, pp. 22-24.
39. ibid., pp. 23-26, 37-41.
40. F. S. L. Lyons, 'Parnell and the Galway by-election of 1886' in *IHS,* vol. ix, no. 35, March 1955, pp. 319-38.
41. ibid., p. 320-26; Frank Callanan, *T. M. Healy,* Cork 1996, pp. 155-61.
42. *Galway Express,* 13 February 1886
43. ibid., 13, 18 February; Lyons, 'Galway by-election', p. 326.
44. *Galway Express,* 18 February 1886.
45. ibid.
46. ibid., 1 May, 5 June 1886.
47. *Galway Vindicator,* 26, 30 June, 3 July 1886; *Galway Express,* 3 July 1886; Joseph Murphy, *The Redingtons of Clarinbridge: Leading Catholic Landlords in the 19th Century,* Clarinbridge 1999, pp. 251-54.
48. *Galway Vindicator,* 3 July 1886; Michael Ryan, 'Municipal Dignity?: a Controversy in Galway, 1898' in *JGAHS* 43, 1991, p. 143.
49. Frank Callanan in *T. M. Healy,* p. 288, and idem, *The Parnell Split,* p. 114.
50. John Cunningham, *Labour in the West of Ireland, 1890-1914,* pp. 26-27; Maura Murphy, 'Fenianism, Parnellism, and the Cork Trades' in *Saothar* 5, 1979, pp. 27-38.
51. *Galway Vindicator,* 14 February 1891; *Galway Observer,* 21 March 1891.
52. The verses appeared in the *United Irishman,* 19 September 1891.
53. George Dennis Zimmerman, *Songs of Irish Rebellion: Political Street Ballads and Rebel Songs, 1780-1960,* Dublin 1967, p. 64n; Boland, *Carr,* p. 61.
54. *Galway Observer,* 5 September 1891.
55. ibid., 25 June 1892; *Galway Vindicator,* 25 June 1892.
56. Cunningham, *Labour,* pp. 133-38; *Galway Observer,* 7 January 1899.
57. *Galway Observer,* 19 November 1898.
58. Stephen Gwynn, *Experiences of a Literary Man,* London 1926, p. 292-93
59. ibid.
60. Wynn, *Killanin,* p. 101.
61. Patrick Maume, *The Long Gestation: Irish Nationalist Life, 1891-1918,* Dublin 1999, p. 42; Arthur Lynch, *My Life Story,* London 1924, *passim*; Michael Stenton and Stephen Lees, *Who's Who of British Members of Parliament, vol.ii, 1886-1918,* Hassocks 1978, p. 226; Dónal McCracken, *McBride's*

Brigade: Irish Commandos in the Anglo-Boer War, Dublin 1999, pp. 94-101, 157-60; *Galway Express,* 9, 16 November 1901.

62. Pauric Travers, 'Arthur Lynch: An Australian Republican and Ireland's Vital Hour' in *Irish Australian Studies: Papers Delivered at the 9th Irish-Australian Conference, Galway, April 1997,* Foley & Bateman, eds, Galway 2000, pp. 257-72.
63. *Galway Observer,* 14 March 1903, 6 October 1906; Gwynn, *Literary Man,* p. 293.
64. Gwynn, *Literary Man,* p. 298.
65. *Galway Express,* 3 November 1906.
66. Maume, *Gestation,* pp. 70, 116-17
67. *Galway Observer,* 23 March, 27 April 1907; Cunningham's *Labour,* p.155.
68. Mary Clancy, '…it was our joy to keep the flag flying': a Study of the Women's Suffrage Campaign in County Galway' in *U.C.G. Women's Studies Center Review,* vol. iii, 1995, pp. 91-104;
69. Cunningham, *Labour,* pp. 66, 99.
70. ibid., and idem, 'The 'Soviet at Galway' and the Downfall of Dunkellin' in *Cathair na Mart* 10, 1990, pp. 115-33; *Galway Express,* 20 March, 16 October 1886; *Galway Observer,* 6 May, 28 October 1905: Connacht Tribune, 3 June 1911, 6 January 1912. See also B. J. Graham & Susan Hood, 'Town Tenant Protest in Late Nineteenth- and Early Twentieth-Century Ireland' in *IESH* 21, 1994, pp. 39-57, and Gerard Moran, 'The Land War, Urban Destitution, and Town Tenant Protests, 1879-1882', in *Saothar* 20, 1995, pp. 17-30.

CHAPTER 10
'...local petty agitators among the mechanics'

LABOUR & SOCIAL PROTEST, 1850-1914

Scilling bhreise an focal faire!
Ó bhéal na mbocht, ó chlann an duig,
Scilling a dhiúltaigh no toicí móra,
Scilling bhreise san uair do na fir,
'Ne'er a wing, ne'er a wet' ...

Scilling á hiarraidh, beart is daonna
Ná códáin á ríomhadh mar éileamh,
Á ríomhadh an chaoi nach léir dom,
Fios a d'fhionnas ó chlann an duig,
'Ne'er a wing, ne'er a wet'.*

Máirtín Ó Direáin, 'An Stailc'

In Chapter Four, social protest was considered under three headings, food rioting, fisheries disturbances, and labour agitation. One of the three phenomena, food rioting, was almost extinct by the 1850s, although some of its motifs were appropriated by protestors against unemployment in the later 19th century. This chapter will follow the remaining two categories of protest into the post-Famine period, exploring, respectively, the Claddagh community's continuing struggle against trawling, and the fortunes of organised labour.

'But there's no law for the poor now'
If Quaker philanthropists were reluctant to impose modern ways on the Claddagh, commercial interests were less inhibited. Shortly after the departure of the Quakers in 1850, two new trawlers arrived in the bay. The first was owned by one Browne, the other by Árainn-based episcopalian clergyman Alexander Synge and his brother Francis of Ashford, county Wicklow —

---

* Translation of 'An Stailc' (The Strike) courtesy of Alf & Fionnuala MacLochlainn: 'An extra shilling is the slogan / From the mouths of the poor, from the dock-siders / A shilling which the big bosses refused / An extra shilling an hour for the men / Ne'er a wing, ne'er a wet... A shilling is what they ask for, a decenter thing / Than turning their demands into fiddly fractions / Calculating in ways that are beyond me / But the dockers made it clear to me / Ne'er a wing, ne'er a set'. (A 'wing' was a penny; a 'wet' was a drink.)

NOTICE.

HERRING FISHERY IN GALWAY BAY.

Notice is hereby given, that it shall be Lawful to Set Herring Nets in the Bay of Galway, between Sun-Set and Sun-Rise, and any Person or Persons so employed with Legal Boats and Nets, will be protected by the Officers of Her Majesty's Steamer "ADVICE." The Blue, White, and Red Flag will be hoisted at the Main-Top-Mast, or Main-Mast Head of Her Majesty's Steamer "ADVICE," at Sun-Set, before which time, no Herring nets are to be set. The same Flag will be hoisted at Sun Rise, by which time all Herring Nets are to be hauled up.

J. B. KERNAN,
Resident Magistrate.

Galway, September 1, 1853.

GALWAY : PRINTED AT THE " PACKET OFFICE."

Warning from magistrate to Claddagh fishermen that trawlers will have the full protection of the law (courtesy of NAI).

uncles, incidentally, of John Millington. During June 1852, Rev. Alexander protested that his vessel had been attacked by thirty or forty others in the bay, and that all his crew was 'more or less injured by stones'. A few days later, when he was landing fish in Galway, a hundred-strong crowd, armed with stones, sought to extract promises from him that he would cease trawling. Several of his crew were intimidated into leaving his service, and it proved impossible to land the catch. The Synges further complained that they were not properly protected by the forces of order. They demanded that the coastguard captain explain why he didn't facilitate the identification of law-breakers by enforcing the law requiring that sails be clearly marked.

There is a slightly sectarian tone to the Synges' complaint, later in the year, regarding the total withdrawal of their protection. This, they said, was a 'surrender to the Claddagh men and their priests who have defended the view that trawling affects spawning'.[1]

Hostilities intensified during 1853. In April, Browne's trawl was destroyed by the Claddagh fleet at Black Head. Later the same day, twenty boats attacked the Synge craft between there and Inis Oírr.[2] Stones were thrown at first, but when the Claddaghmen produced the axes and spears they used for catching sunfish, the trawlermen responded with gunfire. Eventually, sheer numbers prevailed and the trawler had to cut its nets 'and run for Aran'. A few days later, while foolhardily walking on Claddagh Quay hoping to identify his attackers, Alexander Synge was set upon by a crowd of women and children who tried to throw him into the canal. He ran to get away and, not expecting to reach the wooden bridge to the town before being caught, he decided to ford the river. The river was deeper than he thought and the current stronger, so he had to stand in the water, all the time being pelted with stones. Constables Gillen and Hennessy saved him from further humiliation, and identified Mary O'Dea as well as Maria, Bridget and Michael McNally as prominent stone-throwers.[3]

The most serious injuries were inflicted on Bridget Faherty, a servant who had been sent out with a penny to buy milk. She brought a summons for assault against a policeman, Alexander McDougall, who hit her with the butt of a gun and then 'bayoneted her near the spine'. Finding in favour of McDougall, the magistrates scolded Faherty for dallying near a riot and observed that the police had behaved responsibly and 'moderately' at all times.[4] Later in the day, two Claddagh houses were attacked by the same crowd. One was occupied by Catherine Connor, whose husband was employed on the Browne trawler, the other was the home of an absent trawlerman named Callaghan. Unseen by the attackers, Catherine Connor watched from a distance and saw:

> Mary Fallon at the head of a mob, urging them to pull down the house. Kate Hickey pulled down part of the roof and also urged on the crowd. Biddy Curran was at the head of the crowd but did no damage … Peggy Delaney threw stones.[5]

In early May, the coastguard assembled a force sufficient to intimidate the Claddagh fleet of seventy-two boats, spread over ten miles across the bay. All boats were searched; twenty-five men were arrested and brought to Galway, where a crowd of women and children failed to rescue them. Two of the Árainn men employed on the Synge boat, meanwhile, were persuaded to give evidence but soon regretted their decision. Kernan, the resident magistrate stressed the necessity of removing them from the locality until after the Assizes. They were terrified, he wrote, and would 'be got at' if they remained anywhere near Galway. 'The Claddaghmen,' he observed, 'have hitherto escaped because of the terror they have always struck in the minds of witnesses'.[6]

On this occasion, the Claddaghmen decided that they had lost a battle. All seventy-two boat-owners provided sureties for the prisoners, and indicated that they had 'given up their absurd and illegal opposition to trawling'. Similar assurances were given at the July Assizes, where twenty-eight fishermen pleaded guilty to assault. In view of their 'peaceable demeanour' since April, all defendants were released without penalty.[7]

That the peaceable demeanour was due to coercion became clear a year later during the short absence of the *Advice* steamer. No sooner had the vessel departed for provisioning than violence resumed. Ardfry vessels were attacked because their owners began the autumn fishery before the Claddaghmen were ready. The attackers were identified however and sent from Oranmore Petty Sessions to the following assizes. John Kernan, R.M. was certain that if convictions could be secured, 'the trade in herring fishing will be equally successfully established' as trawling already was. The gathering of evidence proved difficult, however, and was only sufficient for larceny conviction.

In the mid-1850s one investigator wrote: 'A gun brig was sent some years ago to protect strange boats which might enter the bay for the purpose of fishing, but after she had left, the Claddagh fishermen resumed their dominion over its waters'.[8] But this 'dominion' was increasingly precarious.

While opposition to trawling continued, the capacity to resist it was weakening, partly because ever more Claddagh residents were employed on trawlers. There was a sense of desperation about 1861 anti-trawling protests that were conducted entirely on dry land. On the morning of 17 August, crowds assembled 'determined to allow no man to go aboard a trawler this morning'. Houses of trawlermen were surrounded and vessels sheltering in the old dock were disabled. After trawler owner, John Good of Dublin, pleaded for protection of his legitimate business, a vessel was sent 'for the suppression of a disposition to violence that has re-appeared among the Claddagh fishermen'.[9]

In 1863, the fishermen turned away from direct action when they memorialised the Earl of Carlisle, lord lieutenant, outlining the 'miserable condition and daily increasing destitution of the fishermen of Galway caused by the unnatural destruction of their bountiful supplies'. The response was an investigation by the fisheries department of the Board of Works. A hearing in Galway on 3 December 1863 took evidence from the fishermen but the trawling interest was not represented. On Easter Saturday 1864, trawler owners put their case at a special hearing in Dublin, provoking a strong reaction in Galway. A further memorial — from 'clergy, magistrates, and other inhabitants' — complained that the evidence taken in Dublin was 'of a confessedly one-sided, partial, and ex-parte character,' that it was taken at a time and in a place inconvenient to the Claddaghmen, and that the fishery commissioners' procedure implied that 'the administration of justice in that particular was a thing not to be obtained in Galway'.[10]

For a time, the trawler-owners were just as shy about sending their boats into the bay and for several years after 1863 there was no trawling.* Supporters of trawling blamed the violent conduct of the Claddaghmen. The Claddaghmen, for their part, blamed their own lack of prosperity on the depredation wreaked by trawlers in previous years.[11] This belief was forcefully articulated years later by Padge King, one who served as 'admiral':

> Landsfolk cannot always understand why we are so bitter set against the trawlers. They think the sea in beside the land is the same that it is a hundred miles out — all deep, an' the fish all a fair take for large and small craft. But it's no such thing. Here's how it is. Galway Bay is only like a shallow, sandy-bottomed pond. Very well. Us with our wide mesh nets, just caught the fish … the trawlers come into the shallow seas, with nets of big and little meshes kept to the bottom of the bay with great bars that sweeps — sweeps along, and gathers up all before them — fish, old and young, and sand. Now, mind you, the sand is weighted with the spawn for the next year … An', then, there's worse again. The almighty gives great sense to all creatures for their own protection, and fish have a high sense of what is destruction to their own kind. The trawl bars ever an' always disturbing the bottom of the bay, the herrings that used to come in millions, soon began to desert it and turn elsewhere for shelter …[12]

In early 1867, trawling resumed when three boats were sent into the bay by 'some native gentry'. During the year, the numbers increased.[13] At first, they were ignored, but on the night of 6 October 1867, a placard appeared on the pillar of the Claddagh chapel:

> NOTICE: Capt Walker he is after coming from Boston tonight to see his friends and every man in Claddagh both big and little will be slautering on Claddagh Bay. Connemara men will appear too and every man that will let them into their boats will be burned, both boats and houses and any man that won't appear on Monday morning let them look sharp and every man in Claddagh will be killing them and we won't be dying any more with hunger for these Claddagh men will be slautering.[14]

---

* Royal Navy commander, Thomas Edward Symonds, was inaccurate in his assessment of attitudes to trawling in the Claddagh. Writing in 1855, he considered the 'reformation in the character of the Claddagh' to be 'remarkable'. Having resisted trawling 'in the most determined and violent manner' only a few years earlier, he wrote, they had come to tolerate it. And this change was 'effected more by moral and natural causes than by force' (*Observations on the Fisheries of the West Coast of Ireland*, London 1855, p. 16.)

Blessing of the bay: Charles Whymper's 1888 sketch shows the Dominican prior and a much-diminished Claddagh fleet (courtesy of Brendan Laurence Glynn).

Other placards in the same vein threatened crews of certain vessels that their houses would be torched. The authorities wondered whether to take the threats seriously: 'Would they publish it if they intended to take the law into their own hands?' As a precaution, the *Research* and the *Gripe* were despatched to Galway, but there was no attempt to execute the threats that brought them to the Claddagh.[15]

It was not just the action of the authorities and the defection of members of their community to trawling that was weakening the Claddaghmen's 'dominion' over the bay. There was, in addition, a sharp decline in the number of Claddagh boats and fishermen. 549 Galway fishermen were enumerated in the 1841 census, this dropped to 504 in 1851. By 1871 the total was a mere 164.[16] John Brophy, acting for the fishery commissioners, visited the Claddagh in September 1868. His report — not accurate in every detail — described the fishing community and offered reasons for its decline:

> Before the famine of 1846 the Claddagh contained over 3,000 stalwart fishermen; now the number of men is not more than 200, and of these the great majority are old and decripid. In fact it would seem as if there were no intermediate state of existence between youth and old age — but it is a youth haggard and wolfish — an old age wretched and helpless.[17]

This state of affairs he attributed to a number of causes, with the famine having been 'the first blow'. Since then, the people were 'half in and half out of the workhouse'. Their lack of thrift, he went on, made matters worse. During bad weather, they were in the habit of pawning their gear and they had no resources, either savings or access to a loan fund, to fall back on when boat or tackle needed replacing. But that was not all:

To these physical causes, there may, perhaps, be added others of a moral character, such as ineradicable ignorance, strong prejudices against improved modes of fishing, tenacity in adhering to absurd old customs as to time, place, and order of fishing …'[18]

Many of the young had emigrated to the United States and, Brophy was informed, some of these were still engaged in fishing in Baltimore, where they had become prosperous. The evidence was that 'once a beginning was made in that direction, the outgoing tide rapidly increased through the assistance forwarded by the successful'. Not all went to the America; some followed their nautical tradition in the Royal Navy. Movement in both directions, undoubtedly, was facilitated by the Piscatory School (See Chapter Thirteen). Even if the education there was not notably piscatory, it brought the bulk of the Claddagh children to school and equipped them with the English language as well as the literacy and other skills required for successful subsistence in the world outside the Claddagh.[19]

Those who stayed behind remained hostile to trawling and would not be coaxed or cajoled into supporting it. One well-meaning improver who failed to persuade the Claddagh people to fall in with his plans, was told by the *Vindicator* that he had 'made a mistake in negotiating with the poor people' themselves; he should have first made contacts who would 'engage to have gentlemen present at the interview who would act matters to right'.[20] It is unlikely that such 'gentlemen' would have fared much better.

As trawling became more widespread, there were complaints that trawls interfered with the lines of the traditional fishermen, complaints that were found to have a real basis.[21] Notwithstanding this, the single remaining piece of legal protection enjoyed by the Claddaghmen, an order of 1843 prohibiting

Animated scene at the fish market, 1880 (from *Illustrated London News*).

235

trawling in the inner bay, was repealed by the fishery commissioners in 1877, opening even the shallows to trawlers.[22]

A Claddagh perspective on the consequences which flowed from the triumph of trawling was given to Mary Banim in 1891 by Mrs King, a grandmother and the wife of Claddagh's then mayor:

> But there's no law for the poor now. The poor man has few friends. Once the bay as far as the Aran Isles belonged to the fishermen of the Claddagh, of Oran, an' the other people along the coast; but the rich came in and drove the fish away, an' now, I've seen the strong men weak for the want of food, an' the little children white with cold an' hunger. All the young men of the Claddagh have been forced to enter the Navy Reserve, to try an' keep a roof over their people; an' if ever war comes, then God be with us all.[23]

Mrs King was lamenting the passing of a way of life, but she was also recalling a system of values that included an element of 'law for the poor'. And if even in its heyday the efficacy of such law had been dependent on the capacity of the poor themselves to enforce it, at least it offered some redress. Clearly this 'law for the poor' had been recognised to some extent outside the ranks of the poor themselves. Thus food rioters were appeased and not persecuted, while Claddagh's 'pirates' continued to be treated leniently by the courts.

Mrs King's 'law for the poor' sits easily with Edward Thompson's concept of 'moral economy,' a concept which the historian developed originally to describe the political culture which supported food rioting and other popular turbulence calculated to curtail speculation in food. According to Thompson, the moral economy of the poor encompassed 'a consistent traditional view of social norms and obligations, of the proper economic functions of several parties within the community …'[24]

The 'consistent traditional view' of the poor was often given added force by a body of archaic legislation from which a popular collectivity derived its sense of legitimacy. In Galway, several overlapping collectivities were able to appeal to such legislation and if the relevant statutes could not always be confidently cited by those seeking their protection, there is no doubt but that proletarian tradition had adopted them as its own.

The 'law for the poor' came under pressure from the 19th century's ascendant economic forces and their accompanying ideology. The Poor Law of 1838 sounded the death knell of food disturbances, while merchant fishermen eventually ended the hegemony of the Claddagh people in Galway Bay.

Trade unionism

A new departure in labour affairs in the immediate post-Famine period was the inauguration of organisation among shopworkers. Following the appearance in the *Galway Mercury* of a circular from the London-based Early Closing Association, a meeting of drapers' assistants was held in Carr's Hotel. The meeting passed resolutions asking employers to adopt 'the same closing as

Dublin, Belfast, Cork and Limerick' — 7 p.m. in summer and 6 p.m. in winter, with two additional hours on Saturdays. A deputation was elected to bring the resolution to the attention of employers and, in May 1850, the new trading hours were introduced. However, two shopkeepers broke the agreement, and soon others followed their example. The pattern — shopworkers' deputation; agreement with employers; breach of agreement by one or two employers; collapse of agreement — was repeated in the subsequent decades.[25]

Generally, the voice of labour — which had even made itself heard during the Famine — was silent in the 1850s. Labourers at Franklin's quarry in Menlo took opportunistic advantage of the general labour shortage due to 'emigration and other causes' to strike for higher wages in April 1853 and a petition was presented on behalf of the trades four years later, but there was little other evidence of labour activity. An 1857 inquiry into electoral malpractice heard that there was no organisation among the trades.[26]

Emigration and mortality combined to cause a labour shortage — and relatively buoyant wages — in the immediate post-famine period, but this was short-lived and a return to high levels of unemployment undermined labour's bargaining position. Tradesmen constituted 'a good proportion of the unemployed' and their position was made worse by the fact that, unlike many labourers, they were unwilling to accept poor relief since in being rendered paupers they would become ineligible to exercise the franchise that they enjoyed as freemen.[27] The post-Famine demoralisation of the trades is illustrated by Table 10.1. The major trades were declining in numbers, which implied relatively little demand for their services, little bargaining power, and consequently little incentive to organise. The exceptional case of the shoemakers is explained by the fact that the sons of St Crispan were getting younger. Over a quarter were under the age of 21, indicating that the shoemakers were unable to enforce their rule of one apprentice per master, which they had asserted in 1836 and defended in 1846.

TABLE 10.1
Numbers engaged in selected trades, 1851 & 1871

Trade	1851	1871
Bakers	65	60
Masons	113	51
Carpenters	103	86
Sawyers	48	17
Boot- & shoemakers	143	188
Tailors	142	101

Source: Censuses of 1851 and 1871.

The early 1860s saw something of a revival of trade unionism, causing one commentator to wonder if the 'spirit of hostility which has for some time been raging in the great centres of labour in England is beginning to show itself among us'. The writer reminded workers that their employers were suffering also during what was a period of economic difficulty, and advised them that, because of the over-supply of labour in the west of Ireland, they would inevitably be the losers in any conflict. The outcome of a recent dispute at Fenton's coach factory, he continued, was a salutary reminder to the shoemakers and others who had 'of late manifested a similar spirit of insubordination'.[28]

One instance of 'insubordination' had occurred in Williamsgate-street in 1860, when a delegation of shoemakers met with Mr Andrews, the owner of a newly opened shop, and 'requested' that he leave town immediately. The shopkeeper's offence was to stock cheap *gutta percha*-soled shoes, something regarded as a threat to the livelihood of local shoemakers. Not surprisingly, the request was ignored, to the annoyance of the shoemakers who arranged a demonstration outside the premises. Shots were fired by those defending the shop during the riot that followed, but they failed to disperse the shoemakers, who smashed the shop windows and scattered the *gutta percha*-soled shoes in the streets.[29] Other indications of a vibrant labour culture during the first half of the 1860s were few, but it is apparent that the economic hardship of the period provoked a response from several groups. A strike of labourers on relief works (see Chapter Eight), was said to have been fomented by 'local petty agitators among the mechanics'. And it is conceivable that it was the same

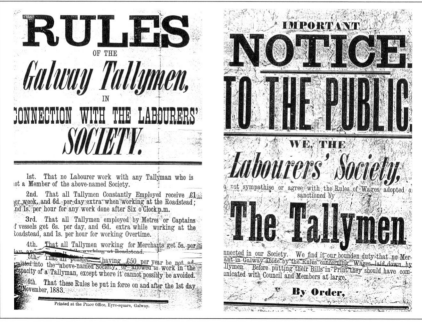

Battle of the placards: notice from unionised tallymen of the Galway docks, and the reply from their labouring comrades (courtesy of Stephen Ball).

agitators who represented the Galway trades at the 1864 Dublin meeting called to establish an All-Ireland Congress of Trades.[30]

For labour in Galway over the next 40 years, economic conditions remained unfavourable, and trade union organisation among artisans was at a low ebb. A few union bodies struggled on, but the impression is that they had few members. Among them were the bakers, who organised during the 1870s, as they had in the 1840s, to oppose night-time working, an issue that mobilised Irish bakers generally. However, a revived County Galway Bakers' Society chose to remain aloof from the Belfast-based Irish National Bakers' Federal Trade Union when invited to affiliate in 1894. Tailors, evidently, were not so parochial, for the Galway branch of the Amalgamated Society of Tailors had a continuous though uneventful existence from the early 1870s. There were unionised printers, too, but they were not numerous enough to sustain their own branch of the Typographical Association, and they enrolled in the Sligo branch. 'Guilds' and unions in the building trades were moribund, but practitioners did not forget their 'ancient rights'. These were asserted by a short-lived Galway Amalgamated Building Trades Society of 1891-92, which lobbied contractors to employ its own properly-qualified members, and, on other occasions, by delegations of carpenters protesting against practices which the trade considered to contravene fair labour principles.[31]

Only dock labourers, whose vital function, particular skill, and uncommon combativeness gave them some bargaining power, made their presence felt on a regular basis. A Galway Labourers' Society, with dock labourers at its core, which was formed in 1880 and 'revived' periodically, led at least seven dock strikes during the following decade.[32] It was also the instigator of a resonant 1884 'monster meeting' at the so-called Repeal Rock in Shantalla — where Daniel O'Connell had addressed tens of thousands forty years earlier. The meeting was called to demand that work commence immediately on the projected Galway to Clifden railway.[33] When work finally began on the railway project almost seven years later, under-employed dockers who were taken on as labourers led a strike for higher wages, that spread along the works all the way to Clifden, and briefly involved up to a thousand men. The unsatisfactory outcome of that dispute, however, together with political divisions in the dockers' ranks sparked by the fall of Parnell, brought an end to the Labourer's Society during 1891. It did not quite bring an end to dock strikes, however, and spontaneous actions were reported in the following decade or so.[34]

Grocers' and drapers' assistants were generally a more deferential group than the dockers but they combined from time to time, sending delegations to their shopkeeper employers to seek holidays and shorter working hours. Unusually, assistants in Galway's leading shop, Alexander Moon's, went on strike in 1891, when a representative they sent to complain about the quality of the food was dismissed. Concessions granted to the shop assistants' delegations were usually short-lived, but this changed for one section of them at least, when they joined the Irish Drapers' Assistants Association in 1902, and were enrolled as that union's first branch outside of Dublin. Significant and lasting improvements in conditions were won in the following years, as the drapers' assistants became the first Galway trade unionists to participate meaningfully in labour affairs at a national level.[35]

The case of the shop assistants excepted, labour in Galway was so demoralised that it seemed incapable of revitalising itself. With some outside encouragement, however, trade unionism was placed on a firm footing during the turbulent years 1911-14. The first to organise were carpenters who established a Galway branch of the Amalgamated Society of Carpenters and Joiners during the summer of 1910, following a visit by a Limerick official of that union. For its part, the organisation of carpenters enabled the Irish Trades Union Congress (Congress) to hold its June 1911 conference in Galway, and to use the occasion for recruitment purposes. A Congress Reception Committee, with representation from the various Galway trades, was set up during February 1911, and it was expected that this would develop into a permanent trades' council. The development was delayed because activists did not take sufficient care to enrol their various trades as branches of the unions recognised by Congress, but matters were sufficiently regularised in August 1911 to permit the formation of the Galway United Trades and Labour Council. In the following years, this council articulated the concerns of its affiliates — not least in exposing breaches of the time-honoured principle that skilled work be carried out by men who were both qualified and local.[36]

A separate but not entirely unconnected development in August 1911 was the formation by dock labourers of the Galway Workers and General Labourers Union (GWGLU), a significant step for a group that had been neither unionised not notably militant for twenty years. According to William O'Halloran, the GWGLU's founding secretary, the new union was formed among the ruins of Cromwell's Fort, by a group of dock labourers who gathered there one evening in their working clothes. O'Halloran and his comrades were roused, in the first instance, by strongly-felt grievances about their working conditions, but these were not new, and it can be assumed that their decision to organise was encouraged by events outside of Galway docks.[37] They knew that their counterparts in Liverpool — Galway port's principal trading partner — and elsewhere had won large wage increases through striking. They were surely aware too that Galway tradesmen had recently become unionised.* And, although they made no personal contact with him, they must have been influenced by the speech delivered in Eyre Square by dockworkers' champion, Jim Larkin, during the Congress week in June.

The dock labourers of the GWGLU soon found allies. They quickly enrolled the workers in the merchants' yards with whom they had regular contact in their work, then they recruited the building labourers and, over a

---

* Reflecting the temper of the times, a number of non-unionised groups engaged in protests during the same period: university students went on strike in response to the disciplining of a few of their number (*Tuam Herald*, 8 April 1911); women workers in the Connacht Laundry struck to demand the dismissal of an over-zealous supervisor; newsboys struck for higher commission (Cunningham, *Labour in the West*, pp. 85-86).

period of months, came to represent almost all of the other male labourers in the town. At the same time, the GWGLU began to play its part in the Trades' Council, representing the interests of unskilled and semi-skilled labour, the majority in fact of Galway workers.

If it found allies, the GWGLU also made powerful enemies. Galway merchants were not accustomed to negotiating with workers' representatives and, like their counterparts elsewhere, had to be forced into doing so. For the self-consciously paternalistic Máirtín Mór McDonogh, the recruitment of his employees into the union was worse than gross interference, it was a personal affront. As the leading merchant and employer in the region, therefore, he mobilised his colleagues and business clients to resist the union demands, through a Galway Employers' Federation.

From January to March 1912, discussions took place between the GWGLU and the employers, until Máirtín Mór's Federation precipitedly posted a 'Schedule of Wages'. This was regarded as prejudicial to negotiations by the union side and its docker-members were instructed not to unload a recently-arrived ship until the document was withdrawn. The Employers' Federation immediately declared a lock-out of all GWGLU members in the twenty-three workplaces that it represented. Five hundred labourers were affected, as well as, indirectly, 80 tradesmen. Mediators intervened, and after a week, they persuaded both sides to accept a compromise. The 'compromise' reached around midnight on Saturday 30/Sunday 31 March 1912 was jubilantly celebrated by the labourers, who marched around the streets in procession through the night. They were marking the concession of a wage increase, of 'wet-time' to building workers, and of a five-and-a-half (rather than a six) day working week to the permanently employed. It was an important dispute, not least because it established in the minds of workers that it was possible to wring concessions from their employers. In the aftermath of the dispute, there was a discernable change in the disposition of Galway's labourers. For one businessman, workers had 'got an insolent manner of late'; for another, it was time that the interests of workers were once again 'made subservient to local prosperity'.[38]

The outcome of the lock-out was far from conclusive. Concessions were won, but not the principle of the 'closed shop', vital as an organisational tool for trade unions. To achieve it, and to secure the resources necessary to weather employer resistance, the GWGLU resolved to merge with a larger union. Among those considered was Jim Larkin's IT&GWU which organised most other Irish ports, but the GWGLU joined instead with the National Union of Dock Labourers (NUDL), which had its headquarters in Liverpool, the port with which Galway dock labourers had greatest contact.

The anticipated rematch between the Employers Federation and the former GWGLU (lately Section 20 of the NUDL) began in March 1913 when discussions about wages broke down. More than a thousand workers went on strike and, for five weeks, Galway's economic life was at a standstill. The atmosphere in the streets had elements of both carnival and warfare, as the whole population joined in the struggle. In the early stages of the dispute, there were minor riots when the wives and children of strikers obstructed 'plucky lady carters' and young men 'in fancy waistcoats' who were endeavouring to move cargo around the town. After two weeks, things took a more serious turn, when Máirtín Mór McDonogh resolved that a strike-bound ship should be unloaded. It was not a task that he or his relatives could attempt, but if the labourers could seek support in Liverpool, then so could the Employers Federation, and the Shipping Federation of Great Britain (a strike-breaking agency) was persuaded to send forty-nine men to unload the cargo. A large crowd gathered for their arrival, but police reinforcements protected all but one of the forty-nine from hostile attention. Only Mary Murray, a young mother and the wife of a striker, was able to get close enough to the strike-breakers to demonstrate the popular indignation with the cast-iron handle of a frying-pan. Less than a week later, having completed assigned task, the Liverpudlians returned home.[39]

Tensions in the town were heightened by the provocative introduction of the strike-breakers, and the consequent growth in hostility between the classes alarmed some observers. Would-be-mediators tried to bring the sides together, and eventually Stephen Gwynn, M.P. for the town, persuaded the Board of Trade to intervene. The outcome of the resulting discussions in early May 1913 was another compromise. The labourers did not get the large wage increase they sought, but they did get a lesser one to add to what had been secured a year previously.

There was widespread relief that the dispute was over. Savings and other resources were long exhausted, and extreme poverty had been experienced by many working-class families. Businesses too had suffered losses. On both sides, there was determination that such a damaging conflict would not be repeated, and a three-year agreement was concluded between the two sides.[40]

By early 1914, when the first Trades Council-nominated Labour councillors were elected onto Galway's local authority, trade unionism seemed firmly established. In little over two years, the overwhelming majority of male workers — tradesmen, shop assistants and labourers — had joined trade unions and nurtured a representative institution to articulate their grievances. Nobody had questioned the right of tradesmen to form unions, but labourers had to struggle to win recognition of their own rights. And if the situation in these respects was no different in Galway from that in other Irish towns in 1914, there were few places where labour's fortunes had been at such a low ebb only a few years earlier.

NOTES

1. National Archives, Outrage papers 1852, 11/353
2. *Galway Mercury,* 16 April 1853
3. National Archives, CSORP 1861/6840.
4. *Galway Mercury,* 23 April 1853.
5. National Archives, CSORP 1861/6480. Evidence sworn on 18 April 1853.

6. ibid.
7. *Galway Packet,* 11 May, 27 July 1853.
8. Anthony Marmion, *The ancient and modern history of the maritime ports of Ireland,* 3rd edn, London 1858, p. 464.
9. National Archives, CSORP 1861 / 6840
10. CSORP 1863-4 / 16344
11. *Report from the Select Committee on the Fisheries (Ireland) Bill; with the proceedings, minutes of evidence, appendix, and index,* H.of C. 1867, Vol. XIV, p. 94.
12. Mary Banim, *Here and there through Ireland,* Vol. 2, 1892, p. 181-2
13. *1867 Fisheries Bill Report,* p.94; *Appendix to Report of the Fishery Commissioners for 1867,* H. of C. 1867-8, vol. XIX, p. 18-21.
14. National Archives, CSORP 1867 / 17950
15. ibid.; *1867 Fishery Commissioners Report,* pp. 18-21
16. Census of Population, 1841, 1851 and 1871. The Claddagh decline mirrored a national decline in the number of sea fishermen: an estimated 93,000 in 1845; 29,860 in 1875 (John de Courcey Ireland, *Ireland's Sea Fisheries: a History,* Dublin 1981, pp. 48-62).
17. *Appendix to the Report of the Fishery Commissioners, Ireland, for 1868,* H. of C. 1868-9 xv, p. 9.
18. ibid.
19. Alf MacLochlainn, 'The Claddagh Piscatory School' in *Two Galway Schools,* Galway 1993, pp. 5-20.
20. O'Dowd, *Claddagh,* p. 92.
21. *Report of the Inspectors of the Sea and Inland Fisheries for Ireland for 1879,* 1880 xiv, p. 4; *Report ... for 1885,* 1886 xv, p. 18.
22. *Appendix to the Report of the Irish Fisheries,* 1882 xvii, p. 51.
23. Mary Banim, *Here and there through Ireland,* Vol. 2, p. 181
24. Thompson, *The moral economy of the crowd,* p. 188.
25. John Cunningham, 'Galway shopworkers and trades unionism — the early years', MANDATE Conference Programme, 2000; John Cunningham, *Labour in the West of Ireland,* pp. 91-99.
26. *Report of the Commissioners appointed to enquire into the existence of corrupt practices in elections of members to serve in Parliament for the county of the town of Galway,* H. of C. 1857-58, vol. XII, pp. vi-vii.
27. National Archives, CSORP, 1865/1141.
28. *Galway Express,* 14 September 1861.
29. ibid., 4 February 1860.
30. National Archives, CSORP 1865/1141; J. D. Clarkson, *Labour and Nationalism in Ireland,* 1970 edn, New York, p. 171.
31. Cunningham, *Labour,* pp. 50-65; Boyle, *Labour,* passim.
32. *Galway Express,* 3 April 1880, 5 March 1881, 27 May 1882, 8 September 1883, 12 January, 1 March 1884, *Galway Observer,* 9 November 1889, 13 September 1890.
33. *Galway Express,* 11 October 1884.
34. John Cunningham, 'Waiting for the Promised Money: Trade Unions in County Galway, 1890-1914', in Moran, ed., *Galway: History & Society,* pp. 522-26, 543.
35. Cunningham, *Labour,* pp. 89-108.
36. ibid., pp. 57-59, 65-66.
37. John Cunningham, 'A Glimpse of the Galway Workers and Labourers' Union, 1913', in *Saothar* 15, 1990, pp. 109-12. See also the text of the William O'Halloran interview in Cunningham's *Labour,* pp. 187-91.
38. Cunningham, *Labour,* pp. 164-69.
39. ibid.
40. ibid.

Culture and Society
1790-1914

CHAPTER 11

'...libelling the faith of the inhabitants...'

RELIGION: 1790-1914

The victory gained, thank Heaven for the same,
The enemies of Galway, they are put down…
The biggots may snarrel, we will plant the laurel,
Around every Chapel, the Cross we'll display
Most high elevated, each house illuminated,
Since our holy Clergy has gained the day…

> From 'Lines written on the glorious victory
> gained by our bishop and Catholick clergy
> in favour of our Liberal members', 1868.
> (NLI, J/LB/39988/V.2(2A))

At 6 o'clock on Christmas morning, 1842, panic swept through the congregation at the early mass in the pro-Cathedral. Fearing that the overcrowded gallery was about to give way, hundreds rushed for the stairs and the doors. In the melee, thirty-seven died, and, according to one report, 'an immense number were dreadfully injured'. The disaster was attributable the building being 'crowded almost to suffocation'.

There was 'no respectable person' among the dead, according to the *Freeman's Journal*. An eyewitness said that the attendance at that hour consisted 'principally of the inhabitants of the adjoining country parts and the working classes'. For that section of the population, the attraction was the sermon in Irish, something rare enough to stir people from their beds.[1]

The ultra-Protestant *Galway Standard* reported that individuals in the congregation were drunk and that the conduct of the crowd before the priest's entrance was 'more appropriate to a theatre than a house of worship'. Moreover, to facilitate a collection for the bishop, the doors were only half-open. For the writer, the lesson to be learned was clear:

> Unfortunately old customs are more strictly preserved in Galway than anywhere else; we believe that except in the far west, the Christmas Night-masses are in every other part of Ireland

247

abandoned, and we hope and trust sincerely that there is an end to them here for ever. Respectable people are not wont to attend them, but the peasantry flock in groups to them, as do almost all the lower classes of tradesmen, servants, &c.[2]

In the following days, an inquest tried to discover the cause of the panic. Witnesses agreed that the sound of breaking timber was followed by a voice warning that the galleries were falling, but they differed on the source of the sounds. Some said that it was caused by the weight of boys on a ladder used to light lamps; others that it came from a handrail broken by the pressure of the crowd. What happened next was not disputed:

> The minute [the warning] was heard the entire mass of the human beings present rushed from their places in the wildest disorder. Some raised up the windows and precipitated themselves into the streets, when their brains were dashed to pieces. Others pressed up to the railings before the altar, leaped into the Sanctuary, and almost killed one another in efforts to escape through the Sacristy … From the highest lobby on either side down to the principal entrance, the entire were wedged together — men of the most athletic frames strangled and suffocated; women dead in the arms of their husbands and relatives; boys whose bones were broken in every part; and men, women and children trampled on, until their bodies could be identified in no other way than by the clothes they wore.[3]

Soon, the clamour gave way to pathos as relatives and friends arrived, 'all endeavouring, by the lurid light of the gas-lamps, to see in the features of the dead … whether those for whom they sought chanced to be among them'.[4]

The scale of the tragedy seemed disproportionate to the cause and rumour sought a scapegoat more substantial than a creaking timber. The most persistent story — and one given credibility by references in both Tory *Standard* and O'Connellite *Vindicator* — was that the panic was instigated by Protestants. Whether as a prank or as a deliberate attempt to cause mayhem, the rumour went, the alarm about the falling gallery was raised by a few Protestants in the congregation, who had attended for that purpose.[5]

John Burke, John Swan, John Bright and Henry Bright, the Protestants to whom the rumours had most firmly attached themselves, were all sworn as witnesses at the inquest. The Brights, it transpired, were not present at all, and John Swan — whose evidence was greeted by groans from members of the public— had attended with Mrs Bright, a Catholic, who had 'called him up that morning to accompany her'. He stated that he often attended services in the pro-Cathedral. John Burke, whose first time it was in the building, 'was induced to go' when he heard that High Mass was to be celebrated and that 'there would be some fine singing'. Burke denied that any of his persuasion had

The Catholic Collegiate Church (later the Pro-Cathedral), which was consecrated in 1820 (Hardiman Collection, Galway Co. Library).

called on him 'to witness a lark in the chapel' and, addressing other rumours, said that he did not see anybody with a rattle, anybody breaking sticks, or anybody setting off detonating balls. The testimony of Swan and Burke was accepted by a jury which found that the deaths were caused by 'the rush of the congregation to gain egress on a cry being raised by some person or persons', adding that 'said alarm was given without any wilful intent'.[6]

In the way of tragic occurrences, the episode provides insights into religious feelings, attitudes and practices in pre-Famine Galway. In their boisterous demeanour, in their attachment to the night-time Christmas Mass, and in their preference for Irish, the common people of Galway differed from their contemporaries in other towns. Clearly, too, there were differences in the religious tastes of the different classes. The early morning preaching in Irish in the pro-Cathedral — and in venues such as the Mechanics' Institute — was a seasonal concession by the clergy to their working class parishioners. And those middle-class Catholics and Protestants who attended did so as observers of the curious rather than as full participants.

But, notwithstanding the attendance at the Christmas Mass of a significant number of Protestants — the *Galway Standard* furnished a full list — the impression left by the episode is one of Catholic distrust of Protestants. This distrust, evidently, was strongest among the poor and the working class, but was not confined to these groups if the recriminatory tone of reports of the tragedy in the *Galway Vindicator* and the *Galway Standard* are indicative. It may be that the people's true feelings were only revealed at moments of crisis. Certainly, the extent of popular antipathy towards Protestants was not apparent to early 19th century visitors. In remarking, only a few years earlier, that Galway had 'a more Popish aspect than any other Irish town', Henry Inglis noted that Catholics and

Protestants lived together 'amicably enough,' a state of affairs 'most commonly observed where there is a great preponderance on either side'.[7] Inglis's estimate was that 'scarcely one in a hundred' of the local population was Protestant. More precise figures show that Protestants accounted for more than 3% of the population: there were 31,204 Roman Catholics in the parishes of St Nicholas and Rahoon, 922 members of the Church of Ireland and 81 Presbyterians.[8] No other denominations were represented in 1834 — Methodists would have been included in the Church of Ireland figures.

Because of the Catholic preponderance in the population and because of the growing political influence of Catholics, members of the various Protestant denominations increasingly shared a common identity. Therefore, one may reduce the number of religious communities over most of Ireland to two.[9] Developments in the relationship between the two major communities in Galway will be considered in this chapter, but first the developments in religious infrastructure and administration will be outlined.

Churches, chapels and meeting-houses

The most significant pre-Famine development in the facilities for worship was the erection, at the junction of Lower Abbeygate-street and Middle-street, of the Catholic Church of St Nicholas — re-christened the pro-Cathedral when Galway became a diocese in 1831. It replaced the parish chapel that had stood on the site since 1752. The foundation stone was laid on 1 July 1816, following a procession from the temporary chapel of the 'principal gentlemen of the town, two and two, linked arm and arm, without distinction of Protestant or Catholic, Methodist or Dissenter, Tribe or Non-Tribe':

> It was an unusual but gratifying sight to behold on the first of July. Protestant and Catholics, the Civil and Ecclesiastical Corporations, the secular and regular clergy, all clothed in their robes of office, preceded by their various insignia, and marching in solemn procession through the principal streets of the town — not for the purpose of reminding the Catholic of the galling degradation under which he labours … no — to lay the foundation stone of an edifice, which being dedicated to the supreme worship of deity, will at the same time be a monument to succeeding generations of the unanimity, concord and harmony which exists between those of every religious persuasion in the loyal and extensive county. On arriving at the site on which the chapel is to be erected, the warden handed a silver trowel to our liberal and worthy Mayor, who laid the foundation stone, with the accustomed ceremonies, amidst the acclamations of upwards of 10,000 delighted spectators.[10]

Celebrations continued into the evening when the population gathered around 'an amazing large bonfire', outside the Mayor's house.

The ceremonial and the display of religious tolerance proved easier to arrange than the completion of the building. Much remained to be done even after the consecration of the building in 1820. According to the *Connaught Journal*:

> More than three years have elapsed since its consecration during which period it has remained in its present unfinished and uncomfortable state. Such indifference manifested towards the only Parish Chapel of so populous a town would afford no small grounds to the inquiry of a stranger to judge favorably of our principle as Catholics, or our respectability as a community.[11]

A levy of a penny per household per week was instituted to pay for the remaining work, this amount being 'the only one the poverty of the lower orders has rendered practicable'. But the response to the levy was insufficient and, more than eight years after the laying of the foundation stone, a worshipper made an ironic suggestion:

> It would be doing an act of justice to the ladies who attend at Mass in the Parochial Chapel, to recommend to the Very Rev. Warden the propriety of purchasing a temporary shed of some description for their protection from the torrents of rain falling in upon the congregation through the roof of that *elegant structure*.[12]

Evidently, Warden Ffrench was stung by this complaint and, a few days later, he announced that he had called his priests together to expedite matters. Work on the church resumed immediately, with the warden reminding Galway Catholics that it was 'primarily incumbent on them to attend to the decency, comfort and improvement of their own parish chapel, …the mother and mistress of all other churches in the parish'. The absence of further complaints would indicate that the church was soon completed to a satisfactory standard, with subsequent adornment being funded by the proceeds from occasional lectures on religious and moral topics.[13]

Other improvements in the Catholic infrastructure followed. College House, a central residence for the clergy of the town, was completed in 1827. Work began on St Patrick's at Bohermore and a Franciscan chapel during 1836, while a church at Bushypark was consecrated in 1838. The fundraising campaign for the new Augustinian chapel, which began in 1852, introduced several novel elements, most notably the despatching of a member of the community to the United States to collect money from the Irish emigrant community there.[14] The early 19th century also saw the introduction of several new religious orders to the town to work among the poor: Presentation Sisters in 1815; Patrician Brothers in 1826; Mercy Sisters in 1840.

The 'ladies' who worshipped in the Anglican Collegiate Church were no more comfortable in the early 1820s than their Catholic sisters. In 1824, it was ascertained that the roof of the building was in 'ruinous condition', and that unless £2000 was expended immediately, it 'might break down and do much mischief'.[15] The news was of interest beyond the small Anglican community, since Catholics, too, were liable for vestry cess for the maintenance of the buildings of the state church. To general relief, the members of the vestry committee decided to spend a lesser sum — which they had in hand — on repairs to the roof and spire, rather than on their replacement. Further repairs and redecoration were undertaken in 1829 and in 1832. The results of these efforts were not pleasing to the visitor who observed that the Collegiate church was 'a large building kept in extremely bad repair, both internally and externally, and the very small congregation therein assembled appeared as nothing in the middle of its spacious but gloomy aisles'. Another agreed that the church was badly maintained: 'The paving stones are disjointed; one would say they have difficulty in preventing the grass from growing there. The walls are dirty and have the appearance of being half-repaired'.[16]

Further alterations were effected in 1838 and 1839, but whether these were 'improvements' is questionable. According to one source, 'inartistic and unsightly' walls were constructed between the pillars in an effort to retain heat and to improve acoustics. However, the effect was that the 'voice was lost through these many apertures, and went echoing round the Church as if chasing the perpetual draughts also caused by them'.[17] In the 1870s, the Ecclesiastical Commissioners contributed several thousand pounds to an attempt to free St Nicholas's 'from the pollution of bad taste, which has white-washed its cut-stone pillars, lath-and-plastered its open-worked ceilings, and walled up the spaces between columns of nave and aisle'.[18] A new stone pulpit, a lectern and a prayer desk were installed, nave and chancel were restored to their original design, and floors were cemented and tiled. The new central heating system was an improvement on the forty-year-old stoves, but, in 1879, it was the cause of a serious fire in the building.[19]

The smaller Protestant congregations, meanwhile, were not idle. A foundation stone for a Presbyterian meeting-house was laid at Nun's Island on 15 September 1834 in the presence of Church dignitaries from Dublin and Ulster. That evening, the building workers were treated to dinner, a course, the committee considered to be 'more proper on such an occasion than the distribution of a sum of money to be expended on intemperance'. On 8 May 1838, a similar ceremony was conducted for the Wesleyan Methodists by the celebrated preacher — and Galwayman — Gideon Ouseley*, to mark the inauguration of work, near Eyre Square, on a replacement for Methodists'

---

* Born into an Anglican gentry family in Dunmore, Co. Galway, Gideon Ouseley (1762-1839) spent much of his childhood in the cabins of peasant neighbours. Later, during a wild youth, he lost an eye in a tavern brawl, a loss which reputedly left him with a frightening appearance. In 1791, Ouseley left his wild ways behind when he was converted to Methodism by English soldiers stationed in Dunmore. Setting out, in turn, to convert and reform others, his knowledge of the Irish language and of peasant mores — not to mention his eccentric street preaching astride a white horse — won him renown as Methodism's 'apostle to the Irish'.

The Anglican Collegiate Church of St. Nicholas in the early 19th century (Hardiman, *Galway*).

existing 'incommodious and inconvenient structure'.[20] In 1860, a Congregational Church — usually described as the Scotch Church — was built at Sea Road, to cater principally for individuals who had arrived in the post-Famine period: university staff, business people and public officials. Local residents present at the laying of the foundation stone included Alexander Melville, Professor of Natural History; Alexander Moon, merchant; Mr & Mrs MacDougall of the Tory *Galway Express*, and John Miller of the Galway fishery. A year later, Methodists built a second church at Salthill, while evangelical Anglicans opened a small chapel at Taylor's Hill in 1863.[21]

The end of the wardenship

As houses of worship increased in number and improved in comfort, there were changes also in Galway's idiosyncratic form of religious administration. The Catholic wardenship became a diocese in 1831, while ten years later, the Municipal Corporations Act declared that the Protestant wardenship would end with the 'death, resignation, or removal' of the incumbent. Warden James Daly, however, did not oblige until 1864.[22]

Since 1485, Galway's religious affairs had been overseen by a warden (over the centuries, the wardenship also gained control over a number of rural parishes). The arrangement, whereby citizens were allowed to elect their own warden and vicars in the way that they elected their own mayor and aldermen, was not unusual in the mediaeval church. In seeking this privilege from Rome, Galway's civic leaders had emphasised the 'English' character of their religion, and their desire to be independent in religious matters from the barbarous natives. The position was complicated by the reformation, as the civil corporation became

Protestant and could not be permitted to appoint the Catholic clergy. The Collegiate church passed to the established church, but an underground Catholic corporation was formed to oversee the Catholic wardenship. This body become synonymous with the Catholic families constituting 'the tribes of Galway'. By 1800, Galway's religious arrangements were unique.[23]

The Catholic wardenship might have survived longer if its custodians had allowed it to reform itself, but the 'Tribes' were unwilling to see their privileges diluted. During the last decades of the institution's existence, the obstinacy of the privileged was a cause of constant conflict: between secular and regular clergy; between the 'Tribes' and 'non-Tribes'; between the warden and his clergy. There was also ongoing jurisdictional conflict between the wardenship and the Archbishops of Tuam, but the nature of this conflict changed with the appointment of Oliver Kelly in 1815.[24] The new archbishop was an opponent of arcane privilege; his very appointment was achieved in the face of indefatigable opposition from the gentry-connected old guard of Connacht bishops. Kelly had consolidated his advantage in the decrees of the Tuam Synod which, among other reforms, included several which severely clipped the wings of landed Catholics, including many who belonged to the Galway 'Tribes'. Having ended archaic privilege in one part of his diocese, Kelly had little sympathy for the claims of those who sought to retain equally archaic privileges in another.[25] Where Kelly differed from his predecessors, was that he did not covet either the territory or the income of the wardenship. He was convinced that the solution to the ongoing problems of Galway was its formal removal from his own jurisdiction and its acceptance of full diocesan status.

The curtain was raised for the final act of the Galway Catholic wardenship in 1806. The old age of Warden Bodkin drew attention to the succession, and it was realised that only the oldest of the vicars of the chapter — the group eligible for the higher office — bore the names of the 'Tribes'. To ensure that the office of warden remained within their group, the tribal corporation took the irregular step of electing three Dominican priests as vicars. It took four years for the necessary dispensation to be granted by Rome, and it was only granted because of a false assertion that there was a shortage of secular clergy in Galway. In 1812, Edmund Ffrench, O.P., was duly elected warden following the death of Warden Bodkin. Because the proceedings had deprived one of themselves of the position, the other vicars of the chapter refused for almost a year to 'institute' Ffrench, as was required before he could take office. Indeed, during the next eighteen years, Ffrench never gained the support of his clergy, something that hardly helped to reconcile the non-Tribal laity.[26]

The contemporaneous political struggle between the Protestant Corporation and the advocates of Catholic rights heightened the sense of democratic propriety, and the triennial elections for warden drew regular attention to the exclusivity of the wardenship franchise. One critic compared the corruption of the Protestant Daly political interest to behaviour of the Catholic 'Tribes' by pointing to 'the similarity of their natures':

> The Corporation excluded the people of the town from their
> elective franchise; the Tribes do so too. The Corporators are
> supported in their usurpation by non-residents; the tribes attempt
> to *force* their friends on the public by the same means.[27]

Among Galwegians there was particular disdain for the non-resident voters, the
descendants of merchant families who had left the town in centuries past, to
invest their wealth in land. Neither their association with the town, nor their
gentry status protected them from being derided as yokels, arriving back 'from
all the ambient villages, … from the tops of the Killeries, … even from far-
famed Crow Patrick', to cast their votes in wardenship elections. 'What a
system', one proponent of reform asked rhetorically, 'where one man born in
Ohio voted, another from Hindostan?' Soon', he concluded, 'Brahmins,
Cherokees and Laplanders would vote'. By the time the wardenship was wound
up, there were 281 eligible electors, of whom 61 lived in the town. Of those
actually voting close to half would have been resident.[28]

In the last decade of the wardenship, there was one singular success for the
'non-Tribal' interest. In 1823, Fr Peter Daly was elected a vicar, in succession
to Fr Lynch who was required to resign because of his public drunkenness. The
election was conducted in an atmosphere of public excitement, with electors,
in one instance, exchanging blows in church. Of wardenship contests,
generally, Oliver Kelly wrote: 'Canvassing, intrigue, abuse and upheavals
marked the elections; election day was one of a most unworthy spectacle'.[29]

The end of the wardenship was signalled in the following year, when Warden
Ffrench was appointed Bishop of Kilmacduagh and Kilfenora. Following the
appointment, Archbishop Oliver Kelly requested that Rome allow Ffrench to
continue in office in Galway, arguing that the income from his dioceses was too
low to decently support a bishop. With a bishop acting as warden, compromise
and lack of controversy were vital if the wardenship was to survive. The 'Tribes'
proved unwilling to make any meaningful concession, however, and many
among the 'non-Tribes' began to argue for the abolition of the institution,
rather than for its reform.

The last election of the wardenship was in 1828. The renewal of the warden's
mandate at the expiry of each three-year-term was normally a formality, but on
this occasion Ffrench was challenged by Peter Daly, who had the support of
most of the senior clergy. Acknowledging that forcing a contest was irregular,
Daly stated that he took the step only because he opposed plurality of benefices
—Ffrench could not be an effective warden in one district and an effective
bishop in another. Like the 1823 contest, the election was conducted in a
charged atmosphere. The town was placarded by both sides and there were
several turbulent meetings. The 'Tribes', however, rallied around their own
man, and the outcome was 109 to 35 in his favour.[30]

For Archbishop Kelly and for most of the hierarchy, the episode was evidence
that wardenship affairs were getting worse rather than better. It was bad enough

that there was an election among the laity to choose a holder of quasi-episcopal office, and that there was popular agitation for an extension of the franchise. But it was utterly intolerable that a bishop could be humiliated by being required to compete with one of his subordinates to retain his own office. In Rome, meanwhile, the regular petitions from a small town in the west of Ireland were increasingly seen as a nuisance. In February 1829, a petition from twenty Irish bishops asked that the wardenship be made a diocese. The Bishop of Dromore was sent to meet the various interested parties in this connection. To facilitate change, and to allow for the appointment of one with no involvement in the long-standing acrimony, Edmund Ffrench resigned as warden.

On 5 November 1831, 36-year-old George Browne, a priest of the Elphin diocese arrived in Galway to take over as bishop. According to one of his contemporaries, Browne had a 'conciliatory manner, wisdom and ability', necessary qualities, for one legacy of the wardenship was a lingering democratic spirit in church affairs in the town.[31]

Worship

Most of the visitors who published their impressions of religious practice in Galway in the pre-Famine period were Protestants, so their descriptions are more reliable for Protestant worship. In 1817, Trotter remarked that the Protestant congregation was 'very small'. The same point was made nearly two decades later by a visitor who liked the singing in the Collegiate Church but felt less 'fortunate in the minister whose turn it was to preach'. In 1835, de Tocqueville's impression was that the Protestant congregation was composed mainly of the rich and that this was reflected in the preaching. The topic of the day was the mooted Poor Law system, which the preacher opposed. Those who sought to bring about social equality by legislative means, he said, were 'senseless and perverse men' who would break 'the bond that establishes the kindness and gratitude between the rich and the poor'.[32]

In 1850, Asenath Nicholson joined the Presbyterian congregation, and found that most of those present were 'in military dress, with the weapons of death standing by their side'. She commented: 'the Christian Church has got a very supple kind of religion if these warlike principles can find a place within it'.[33]

Of the Catholic chapels, Trotter wrote that 'the numbers attending them at divine worship are very great indeed'. Inglis, in 1834, took a closer look, reporting: 'in the Catholic chapels, devotees are found at all hours of the day'.[34] The impression given by the reports of the 1842 tragedy was also of large Catholic congregations. It is probable, however, that Christmas morning was exceptional, and that congregations were smaller on Sundays.

All Catholics, save those excused by infirmity, were obliged to attend Mass on Sundays and holy days, but the evidence indicates that the obligation was unevenly observed in different parts of the country. The interpretation of figures from the 1835 *Report* of the Commissioners of Public Instruction has been a subject of debate, but several conclusions can be drawn from them:

church attendance was higher in urban than in rural areas; it was higher in the east than in the west; it was higher in English-speaking than in Irish-speaking areas.[35] What pattern should one expect in a town like Galway, located in the west and with a significant Irish-speaking population?

Reasons advanced for low church attendance include the following: a poor ratio of priests to people; dislocation and indiscipline in the aftermath of the penal laws; obstacles like distance, weather and bad roads. None of these applied to any extent in 1830s Galway, so one might expect to find attendances comparable to those of Dublin and Cork — up to three-quarters of all Catholics. The indications, however, are of much lower attendances in Galway, probably between a quarter and a third, comparable to rural parts of the west. In this regard, it may be significant that attendance at Galway's twelve churches were 'stationary' while, in other towns, most priests reported that they were 'rising'.*

So why were Galwegians relatively lax as regards church attendance? The answer can be no more than conjectural, but it would be reasonable to seek it in the town's unique form of church administration. Discipline was weak under the wardenship. Vicars were elected for life, and they regarded the warden as the first among equals rather than as a superior. They were elected by a portion of their parishioners and may have considered themselves answerable to their electorate rather than to the warden. Certainly, curates hoping for advancement to vicarships, and vicars who aspired to the wardenship had to be well-regarded by members of the Tribal corporation — an overwhelmingly middle- to upper-class body. Moreover, on all sides, it was accepted that the wardenship institutions were composed of an elite, and that this should continue. It was relevant also that the 'Tribes' had traditionally provided a large proportion of the priests — regular and secular.[36]

The close ties of the clergy to an elite pre-disposed them to serving that elite; the lack of discipline meant that it was difficult to re-direct their interest towards the working class. It has been shown that the general population in the pre-Famine period preferred to be catechised through Irish; yet many Galway priests did not speak Irish. There are other indications, too, of other shortcomings. Archbishop Dillon of Tuam — admittedly a hostile source — catalogued inappropriate clerical behaviour in Galway following his visitation of 1799: the warden had engaged in 'illicit' sexual relations and had gained his office by simony; nuns wore lay clothes and entertained lavishly; women lived and worked in the Augustinian and Franciscan convents; individual priests were friendly with apostate ex-priests and Freemasons. The general impression

---

* The calculation requires explanation: the returns indicate a congregation of 6,200 (19.9%) of a Catholic population of 31,201 in the parishes of St Nicholas and Rahoon. Following Corish (*Experience*, p. 167), and allowing that one fifth of the population was exempted — children, nursing mothers, the infirm — the 19.9% figure is increased to 24.83%. In the case of returns such as 'Augustinian friary, 800 to 1000', I took a mean figure — 900. The twelve churches and chapels were: St Nicholas R.C. chapel; Augustinian friary; Augustinian convent; Franciscan monastery; Franciscan convent; Dominican friary; Dominican convent; Bushy Park; Barna; Presentation convent; Presentation convent, Poulnaroona. (1835 *Report*, app.D, pp. 46-47).

257

given is of luxurious and decadent living, consistent maybe with what was witnessed by religious in noble and merchant households in European cities during their training, but very different from the experience of the majority of Galway Catholics.

The archbishop did emphasise that most priests were 'exemplary'. He noted, however, that many neglected their obligations to preach and to teach catechism, precisely the mechanisms through which the poor acquired their religious knowledge.[37] Almost thirty years after Dillon's visit — and not long before the *Report of the Commissioners of Public Instruction* — Warden Ffrench expressed concern about pastoral problems in Rahoon parish. Parish priest, Fr John Lowther, he stated, only celebrated a public mass on every second Sunday, while a second church in the parish lay idle, because Lowther refused to repair it. Rahoon people were dying without the sacraments, and were sometimes married before Confirmation, but the warden could do little about this, because Lowther was elected for life.[38]

Attendance at mass, of course, was not the only outlet for religious feeling. Manifestations of popular religion including 'pilgrimages, patterns, holy well penitentials, the observance of numerous holy days', thrived, according to Thomas McGrath, even where the precepts regarding regular Sunday mass-going could not be observed.[39] There is evidence of the persistence of such rustic mores in urban Galway. The people of the Claddagh, according to James Hardiman, venerated St Nicholas and celebrated his feast day with 'the strictest observance'. Other Catholic feast days too, to the chagrin of improvers, were

Worshipping at St. Augustine's Well, Lough Atalia. Note train in background and reversed image from *Illustrated London News*, 1880 (Brendan Laurence Glynn Collection).

observed by abstinence from work in the Claddagh and other communities. And there were numerous holy wells in the town and vicinity, which attracted pilgrims into the 20th century.[40]

It is likely that beliefs like those of the closely-studied Claddagh people were also held in other parts of the town. An 'ethnologist' reported in the 1850s:

> They believe in the actual presence of God amongst them, and they do everything in his name. It is worthy of remark that they never, by any chance, salute or speak to one another without the name of God ... They believe anything that has passed through fire is blessed — this must certainly be a remnant of the old fire worship ... When a boat comes in with fish, the boat-man gives a fish to every beggar who may be there to ask: it would be most unlucky, in their opinion, to refuse charity out of what God sent into the net.[41]

Church attendance increased after the end of the Catholic wardenship. Unfortunately, there exist no figures to chart the rate at which this occurred. There were some identifiable developments that encouraged devotional conformity, some of them facilitating those already disposed to attending church services, others creating such a disposition. In the former category was a improvement in clerical discipline. It was easier for a bishop than for a warden to ensure that recalcitrant priests did not neglect parish work. Moreover, the great improvement in the facilities for worship in the town from the 1830s meant that people might more easily attend services.

Significant too was the increase in religious personnel. According to census returns, there were just 14 priests in Galway in 1841. This had increased to 23 in 1871, and to 28 in 1911. In the context of a falling population there was a remarkable improvement in the ratio between resident priests and Catholic townspeople: from 1:1200 in 1841 to 1:460 in 1911. More dramatic still was the increase in the numbers of religious sisters and brothers. By 1911, if priests, brothers and nuns are taken together, there was one religious professional for every 60 Catholics in the town.[42]

Religious brothers and sisters had teaching, nursing and other responsibilities, but their role in encouraging devotional conformity was considerable. The descriptions of visitors, for example, make it clear that religion had the highest priority in the curriculum of religious-run schools.[43] And the impact of these brothers and sisters was felt outside the school as well as inside. The career of Patrician Brother, Paul O'Connor, who taught and proselytised in Galway during six decades of the 19th century, was exceptional, but his outlook and his approach may be regarded as representative. An examination of his writings shows that O'Connor considered education to be a means to religious ends.[44] Although the prominence of Catholic ritual and religious instruction in the curriculum of his school had to be lessened somewhat when his school came under the auspices of the National Board, it retained its importance for the headmaster. The Dominican preacher, Fr Tom Burke, who attended the Patrician Brothers school, recalled being questioned by Brother Paul as to when he had last received the sacraments. And pupils were encouraged to bring home religious publications from a small library in the school. In displaying their reading skills to members of their families, therefore, they were also introducing religious matters.[45] It is likely too that pupils were expected to influence their parents to attend religious ceremonies. That this was a preoccupation of Brother Paul is indicated in a letter to him from Fr Tom Burke in 1854: 'I was delighted to hear that things are looking up in Galway, and, above all, that the strayed sheep are returning to the embrace of the Good Shepherd. I almost envy you the joy you feel in witnessing it'.[46]

But Brother Paul O'Connor's capacity to influence his pupils (and through them the wider community) did not diminish when they left school. Through the Aloysian Society, which he established in 1830 — 'to save the youth of the city from the influence of bad example, and to render permanent the good that has been done'[47] — he kept a watchful eye over many of them as they grew into young men. And with the enthusiasm of his devotees in that society, he was enabled to introduce Galwegians to new practices associated with the so-called 'devotional revolution' of 19th century Irish Roman Catholicism, notably, the processions and meditations associated with the feast of Corpus Christi. According to his biographer, O'Connor 'was unwearied in his exertions to engage the members of the Aloysian Society, the pupils of the Monastery schools, and other pious youths in the city, to attend in solemn adoration during the octave [of Corpus Christi]'.[48] By 1854, if a report in the *Mercury* is an indication, his exertions had been rewarded:

> What sight then would be more consoling to the pious votary of our holy religion than that of seeing the Blessed Sacrament exhibited during the period alluded to, exposed on the tabernacle, and to behold the fervour, the piety and the veneration with which it was visited and honoured by the immense masses of the faithful … In those devotional duties, the members of the Society of St Aloysius gave a signal edification, relieving each other, by tens, hourly in the Church of St Nicholas …[49]

If 'strayed sheep', in the words of Fr Tom Burke, were encouraged by the piety of the 'masses of the faithful' to return to the Catholic fold, the tense religious climate of the 1850s and 1860s (described below) must also have reinforced Catholic devotional observance. By provoking riotous opposition to their efforts, the missionaries of the Protestant 'second Reformation' inadvertently encouraged non-observant, lapsed, and latent Catholics to return to practice.

Further encouragement to formal devotional practice was provided by parish missions. The desire to counteract the efforts of 'second reformation' proselytisers, led Bishop O'Donnell to invite the Vincentian Fathers to conduct a mission in Oughterard in 1852, but it was some time later before one was held in Galway itself. In introducing one of the earliest in September 1874, a Vincentian priest outlined the objectives of the mission, which were 'simply to keep alive in the hearts of the faithful a love of religion … and to show by the example of their lives that they were within the pale of the true church'. Penitence was the order of the day, for during the first week, homilies were given on the following topics: 'Penance and its Conditions', 'Conscience, Contrition, and its Qualities' and 'General Instructions as to the Manner of the Making of a Good Confession'. And to facilitate the penitent, confessions were heard for ten hours daily for the four-week duration of the mission. For one observer, the Vincentians' presence wrought great improvements in popular behaviour. Their 'pious labours … against the prevailing vices of the age', and in particular their 'eloquent denunciations' of drunkenness, had achieved 'marvellous results'.[50]

The temperance movement was undergoing a revival at that point, and one of its champions was Galway's Bishop MacEvilly. At the time of the mission, he was leading a campaign against Sunday drinking, and if the Vincentians were eloquent on the subject, it is likely that it was because of an explicit direction from the bishop.

MacEvilly, Galway's third bishop, had taken office in 1857. Previously a stern president of St Jarlath's College, Tuam, he became a close ally of Cardinal Cullen, the reforming archbishop of Dublin. By disposition, MacEvilly was a disciplinarian, a valued trait in the Cullen-dominated post-Famine Church. And Sunday drinkers were not the only group to arouse the bishop's displeasure.

MacEvilly was appalled by indiscipline among the Galway clergy, which, in writing to Cullen, he attributed to the experience of the wardenship:

> I must not … conceal from your Grace that we have much to contend with against the lax notions as regards episcopal governance and the blind obedience due to everything emanating from the See of Peter, which might to some extent be traced to the democratic or rather autocratic form of church government to which they had been long habituated.[51]

MacEvilly's strategy for eradicating clerical indiscipline was to single out the priest whose notions of episcopal governance were laxest of all. That was Fr Peter Daly, aspirant bishop, parish priest, town commission chairman, and entrepreneur. Daly's intemperate speeches, and his long-time neglect of his parishes, had been a cause of frustration to the previous bishop, Laurence O'Donnell. And although the struggle between MacEvilly and Daly did not end conclusively until the latter's death, the bishop's uncompromising handling of the affair served notice on anyone else who might be inclined to step out of line.[52]

Desecrating the Sabbath

Attendance at church was not the only aspect of Sunday behaviour that caused unease. Because exuberance on the streets was harder to ignore than not-quite-full churches, the 'profanation of the Sabbath' was a matter of greater concern. 'Respectable opinion' was unanimous that the Lord's Day should not be desecrated. There was not always agreement, however, as to what constituted desecration.

Sabbatarianism had a long tradition in England — one historian has suggested that it was 'the only important English contribution to the development of reformed theology'.[53] One legacy of this was a body of sporadically-invoked statute- and bye-law regulating public behaviour on Sundays. But Sabbatarians — who frowned on any activity other than worship on the Sabbath — were not the only ones eager to stamp out Sunday misbehaviour. Also concerned were adherents of 'Dominical' theology, orthodox among Catholics and held by many Episcopalians, which tolerated 'seemly' Sunday amusements provided they did not clash with church services. To a third group —neither necessarily Sabbatarian nor Dominical — belonged those who wished, in general terms, to reform the behaviour of the 'lower orders'. Because Sunday was the only non-working day of the week for many, it was the principal occasion of activities considered scandalous and demoralising.

The efforts of evangelical Sabbatarians in England resulted in significant legal changes in the later 18th century, but just as important was the effect of their campaigning on 'respectable' opinion throughout the two islands. The perception of what was 'proper' behaviour on Sundays altered, as the influential were cajoled, persuaded or embarrassed by evangelical propaganda. Certainly, by the 1780s, members of the Catholic hierarchy in Ireland were actively curbing excesses in their own communities — 'whether out of a desire to see the Sabbath observed in a decorous manner or out of disapproval of the amusements to which it was commonly devoted'.[54]

Sunday trading, public entertainment and intoxication were the principal infringements of the Sabbatarian ideal. All were features of the early 19th century Galway Sunday, but notwithstanding the tone of some contemporary commentary, abuses were not specific to Galway.* There was certainly an awareness of the laws on the matter and these were not too blatantly flouted. In the late 18th century, a French traveller remarked that Galway shops opened on Sundays — 'perhaps the whiskey shops more than the others' — but that shopkeepers coyly kept their shutters up, opening only their doors.[55]

Two decades later, an English visitor was dismayed to see Galway people on Sunday carrying out 'the household work most commonly allotted to Saturday'

---

* That Galway was unexceptional in this respect in the late 18th and early 19th centuries is indicated by the complaint that Cork had 'alehouses and dram shops constantly kept open for tippling and drunkenness, tobacconists vending their goods with as much industry as any other day, barbers exercising their trades and appearing openly in the streets in their work dress, furnished with curling tongs, &c. (Colman O'Mahony, *In the Shadows: Life in Cork, 1750-1930*, Cork 1997, p. 20).

and the adjacent peasantry 'at their accustomed labour'. Other sources contradict Curwen on the latter point, citing strong popular disapproval of 'unnecessary servile work' except in the direst circumstance. There is no disputing, however, his description of the streets of Galway: 'We found the inns and public houses filled with a great number of noisy people …and excepting the shops being shut there was nothing to indicate its being the Sabbath'.[56] Not long afterwards, James Hardiman — a pious but not a prim Catholic — complained that 'tippling houses' were 'most indecorously kept open during the hours of divine worship' and that the 'evening of the sacred day [was] not infrequently profaned by drunkenness and riot'. But Sundays had been even worse in Hardiman's memory: 'Several old and vulgar ceremonies, formerly in esteem, have long since disappeared. It is many years since the savage practice of bull-baiting has been laid aside … and the public cock-pit, formerly in such request, now lies deservedly neglected'.[57] Hardiman, one senses, would have been satisfied if the worst excesses were eliminated, and if publicans maintained decorum by remaining shut until after last mass.

Another middle-class Catholic, Bartley O'Flaherty of the *Connaught Journal* pontificated frequently on Sabbath abuses. In January 1823, he complained that all but a few grocery shops opened on Sundays. This was 'shameful', he argued, but it was also foolish. In Tuam and Loughrea, grocers closed on Sundays but lost no business, because their customers 'apply for their necessaries on the preceding evening'. This could be achieved in Galway, if one grocer circulated a resolution to the same effect among his colleagues, binding 'every man who signs it' and exposing backsliders to opprobrium.[58]

In the same year, the *Journal* drew attention to other abuses, congratulating magistrates for seizing the guns of Sunday sportsmen but pointing out that the 'ferocious sport' of badger-baiting still took place in the Square on Sundays. And corporation constables were chided for not intervening to bring an end to 'the regular practice of *cad-playing* in Eyre Square' on the Sabbath. The occasional injury to by-passers was not the worst evil associated with the game, for it was also the object of betting. Magistrates tolerated this 'traditional'

Commerce at every corner: the Galway Sunday (Hall's *Ireland*).

game, but O'Flaherty was not persuaded that 'a system of public gambling on the Sabbath is one of the privileges of the lower classes'.⁵⁹

And those who maintained an unofficial Sunday market were also cristicised:

> The very passage to the church is occupied at an early hour by women with baskets of vegetables, and more is absolutely sold on Sunday morning than on any other day of the week. This is doubly scandalous, first as a breach of the Sabbath, secondly as stopping up the most public streets of the town.⁶⁰

If the long-promised root market was opened, the *Journal* suggested, it would provide an out-of-the-way enclosure where the vegetable-sellers could be sent by constables. More significantly, for a newspaper that was critical of the temporal authority of the established church, the *Journal* then addressed itself to the Protestant church-wardens: they were legally empowered to prohibit commercial activity on Sundays; they should exercise these powers.

The *Journal's* campaign had an effect. A resolution circulated among grocers brought about the desired result for a period. But — 'in consequence of some having transgressed the rules then entered into, and disposed of their goods secretly, the old disgraceful system was again revived'. The newspaper acquired an ally in church-warden, John Lushington Reilly, who was advised that a 'few fines imposed, and rigorously exacted, will effectively accomplish this desirable object'. But, lacking the support of magistrates and constables, Reilly was forced to fall back on 'the inefficient business of coaxing'.⁶¹

Reilly's successor, one Smyth, eschewed coaxing and took decisive action himself. Visiting stalls and standings, he impounded stock, offering the seized meat and vegetables to the Mendicity Institute. However, for want of somebody to carry the forfeited articles, he was obliged to throw most of them over the bridge. The *Journal* reported Smyth's efforts but predicted that he would fail — until the Corporation was made accountable, no lasting improvement would be brought about.* If it was ironic that the pro-Catholic *Journal* was chiding the Protestant authorities for failing to maintain proper order among the Catholic 'lower orders', its attitude indicates that the issue was not a religiously-divisive one in the 1820s. But this would change as the evangelical movement gained influence in the established church.

The church-wardens persisted with their efforts to curb trade and boisterous behaviour an Sundays. It proved easier to dissuade the shopkeepers than the

---

* Smyth's approach was similar to that of a Lord Mayor of Dublin. Having 'commenced his perambulation of the city during Divine Service to see that the publicans, huxters and butchers kept their shops closed until two o'clock' he found a side of beef 'exposed for sale' in Cole St and was proceeding to seize it, when, 'the butcher to whom it belonged, brandishing his knife, swore that he would bone the first man who should attempt to deprive him of his goods on such cheap terms'. Unfazed, the Mayor produced 'a sort of whalebone wand, heavily leaded at one end' and 'threatened to fell him beneath the stall, if he offered further resistance'. This 'prompt style of despatching business had the desired effect' (*Connaught Journal*, 1 November 1827).

casual traders, but even the former tended to lapse back into the 'old system' if left unmolested for a while. In 1827, the Corporation took an interest in the matter, changing the market day from Saturday to Friday, so that unsold articles might be offered for sale on Saturday mornings rather than on Sundays. Habits were not easily altered, however, and there were further reported interventions by magistrates in 1829, 1830, 1831 and 1832.[62]

The *Journal* continued to report such efforts, but with diminishing enthusiasm. Significantly, in 1829, it insisted that, in drawing attention to Sunday abuses, it was 'not advocating *Puritanism*, which is mere hypocrisy, but public morality and social order'. This was the first indication that Sabbath observance was potentially a sectarian issue. Then, as if to emphasise that its attitude was a matter of 'social order' rather than of religion, the *Journal* drew attention to the 'poor shop boys' who suffered exploitation because of the public penchant for Sunday shopping. 'Grocer's Shopboy' was allowed to proclaim his 'suffering' because of 'the non-execution' of the law, threatening that if his complaint was ignored he would 'endeavour to get up a memorial to the Lord Lieutenant, for the appointment of some magistrate, who will not leave unexecuted the law of the realm'. The *Journal* commended the shopboy's appeal, but, a year later, when the Mayor did take action, argued that fines levied on publicans should be remitted provided they 'pledge themselves henceforward not to be guilty of the offence'.[63]

Probably because the issue became closely associated with the evangelical movement, Catholic sources were silent on the Sunday question from the early 1830s. Corporation, magistrates, even church-wardens, also lost interest. But the descriptions of visitors indicate that little had changed about the Galway Sunday. 'Tippling houses', continued to open, according to one who saw this as the persistence of 'the old Milesian habits of indolence'.[64]

Things became considerably quieter towards the end of the 1830s, with the rise of the temperance movement. The drastic fall in alcohol sales must have been particularly apparent on Sundays. Moreover, there are indications that the revivalist flavour of the movement persuaded many of the newly-abstemious to replace conviviality with devout practices.[65]

One indicator of change is provided by the tenor of criticism of Sabbath-breaking in the ultra-Protestant *Galway Advertiser* in the late 1830s and early 1840s. If there was public drunkenness, the *Advertiser's* readers would have been told about it. But episodes of Sabbath violation mentioned in the paper during this period related to games-playing rather than to inebriation. Boys, went one complaint, were 'at every high wall', playing ball on Sundays, and a report of the accidental death of a Sunday hurler in the county was fashioned into a moral tale, concluding 'so much for Sabbath breaking'.[66]

In the 1850s, Sabbath observance was a litmus test of Christianity for the proponents of the 'second reformation'. Catholicism was condemned insofar as it was considered to be tolerant of Sabbath violation. More than tolerant, indeed, for it countenanced the scandalous 'sale of Scapulars and Beads on our streets' on the Sabbath. Other complaints raised in the *Galway Express*, the mouthpiece of the evangelicals, were that the streets continued to be 'thronged and monopolised on the Sabbath by boys and women from the country — the latter with large baskets on their backs'. And shops, 'minor in character, but many in number', continued to open on the main streets. The introduction of Sunday afternoon steamboat excursions on the Corrib was also criticised, as was the age-old practice of 'maying' at Menlo.[67]

The assertive Catholicism of the Cullen era was not easily browbeaten by sabbatarian zealotry. Bishop MacEvilly regarded drunkenness as the only significant Sabbath abuse. He was determined to stamp it out, but he differed from evangelical supporters of the same cause in that he was willing to encourage the provision of alternative Sunday entertainment 'so as to make their withdrawal from the public houses less felt'.[68]

MacEvilly displayed his resolution in June 1874, when he ordered Catholic bar-owners in his diocese to shut their doors on Sundays. Most obeyed. Priests joined in the campaign, collecting signatures from publicans to a pledge, which was published with the list of signatories on placards throughout the town. Soon afterwards, however, the races 'rendered it necessary to some extent to break through the agreement', and, in October, MacEvilly returned to the offensive, declaring that the opening of a public house on Sunday was to be a reserved sin in the diocese, and encouraging 'respectable citizens' to object to the renewal of the licenses of those who broke the 'agreement'.[69] According to the *Vindicator*, results were immediate, and the number of cases at the Petty Sessions of 'assault, larceny and rioting … which originated mainly in Sunday drinking' was greatly diminished.[70] The changed atmosphere was described by an anonymous man who walked through the streets on Sunday, 25 October 1874; a man whose tone suggests that he may have gazed enviously through the open door of many a public house:

> No longer is heard the voice of the drunkard as he passes along the streets, desecrating the Lord's Day with impious oaths and foul expressions. No longer is witnessed those abominable scenes so frequently enacted in those dens of intoxication — men and women standing at counters singing improper songs, roaring like wild beasts, clamouring not for the food which God ordained for men, but for that which kills the soul and debilitates the body. No longer does the tap-room door open upon the ante-chambers of the infernal regions, where the very air is loathsome, where the unrestrained society of those of both sexes is permitted, where gambling is connived at, provided only that the price of man's eternal ruin finds its way into the pocket of the man with the seven day license.[71]

Catholics and Protestants

If many attended more assiduously at the taproom than at the tabernacle, this did not detract from their religious identity, and there is evidence of a stoutly-held sense of Catholicism among the common people. Ordinary Galwegians saw the Catholic religion as their birthright, and they were prepared to defend it whenever they felt that it was being attacked or subverted. And in defending it, they acted in many instances independently of their clergy.

Protestants were regarded as usurpers who had temporary ascendancy, an outlook reinforced by the existence, until the 1830s, of an alternative focus of authority in the unofficial Catholic corporation and wardenship. This attitude found its most frequent expression in relation to the Collegiate Church. On numerous occasions, popular triumphs were marked by the ringing of *Joybells* from the belfry of this Protestant place of worship.[72] Given the high levels of excitement which preceded the seizure of St Nicholas's on such occasions — food riots, strikes, elections — there was rarely opposition to the will of the people in the matter. In the 1880s, a defence of the practice was offered by town commissioner, Thomas O'Sullivan, when he argued that the bells were not the property of any church, but of the people, since they had been erected by the Corporation more than three centuries earlier.[73]

If there was a proprietorial attitude to the ancient church of the town, the same was the case with the Catholic priesthood. So-called 'pervert priests' who embraced Protestantism, were anathematised. This was consistent with the official Catholic position, not one that was always adhered to by the worldly clergymen of Galway, who shocked an archbishop of Tuam by maintaining friendly relations with an apostate Franciscan.[74] The more unforgiving popular attitude was summed up by one commentator:

> never in the eyes of the people can the apostate priest be cleansed from the foul sin of infidelity to his order, violation of his vows, and abjuration of his creed. His memory cannot outlive execration. No storied urn or pompous monument erected o'er the grave, where the mortal remains of the recreant priest await eternal judgement, can screen the dark deed from the knowledge of future generations.[75]

The reception accorded Rev. William Crotty, when he came to Galway in 1840 to preach in the Presbyterian kirk, was a case in point. Crotty was one of two clerical cousins who, following a dispute with the Catholic bishop of Killaloe, led Birr Catholics into schism in the late 1830s. Both eventually were forced to leave Birr, but not before the case became notorious. The policemen on duty during Crotty's Galway sermon, however, were unable to prevent the breaking of the kirk windows and, as for the preacher, he was forced to retire, 'lest the mob be inflamed'.[76] Because he was an ordained priest, Crotty's visit was considered particularly provocative, but anybody who sought to lure Catholics away from their religion — anybody who threatened the inviolability of the Catholic community — was met with suspicion.

The must vulnerable members of the Catholic community were orphans and foundlings — the latter almost certainly the children of Catholics. The legal position was that such children should be raised as Protestants, a cause of popular indignation. For breaking the law, Fr Peter Daly was controversially dismissed as workhouse chaplain in 1859, when he baptised a foundling.[77]

Before the 19th century, Protestants had undertaken little missionary work among the Catholic poor, but this changed under the influence of the evangelical movement. By 1823, Protestant missionaries were causing alarm in Catholic circles in Galway, alarm that was reflected in the founding of a (Catholic) Female Catechistical Society that clothed the girls who attended its classes. This was a response to reports that 'some poor [had] been relieved … some indigent children clothed, by the pious distributors of the Bible'.[78]

The following year, Fr Peter Daly won fame as a Catholic champion when he disrupted a Loughrea meeting of the London Hibernian Society, bringing him face-to-face with the Protestant Archbishop of Tuam, the leader of activist Protestantism in Ireland. The episode was celebrated in a Raftery poem.[79]

In 1826, conflict between evangelicals and Catholics in Ballinasloe provoked an 'indignation meeting' in Galway. Later in the same year, 'itinerant Theologues' of the London Hibernian Society appeared in the town. Their mission, according to the *Connaught Journal*, was 'to induce the poor to read the Bible, and to interpret it for themselves'.[80] Not long afterwards, there was a violent incident in the Collegiate Church, when 'a number of fellows' rushed into the church during service and began to 'shout, holloo and disturb the congregation', while striking the pews with large sticks. The warden was injured when he intervened. For Rev. John D'Arcy, who told magistrates that such incidents had become the 'constant practice,' it was all part of a plan to 'frighten people from Church going'.[81] If this was the case, the demonstration was probably directed at 'Biblemen', at their evangelically-minded supporters and, in particular, at any former Catholics attracted by their message.

Even the visibly sinful, evidently, were protected from those who would lure them away, and the female section of the town gaol was the scene of 'near riots' during 1827, when several imprisoned prostitutes converted to Methodism. The local paper took up the story, mocking Minister Freeland's motives for visiting the new members of his congregation, and calculating that his consequent eligibility for a gaol chaplainship was worth £50 a year. It would appear, however, that it was the prison matron, Mrs McCoy, who was the active Wesleyan Methodist in the institution. Her zeal earned her a rebuke from Rev. D'Arcy, who was also a local inspector of the gaol. But Catholic opinion was not satisfied. The matron should be dismissed, it was argued, for abusing her position, one of 'great influence over poor wretches', who were 'eager to please' those placed in authority over them.[82]

But popular hostility towards religious 'perverts' did not extend to the Catholic gentry, whose predicament was understood. Families like the Blakes of Menlo and the Martyns of Ballinahinch who conformed to protect property and position were readily forgiven. In some such instances, as shall be shown below, it was presumed that publicly-professed Protestantism was not genuine, and that converts and their families remained secretly Catholic.

If the provocative presence of would-be proselytisers intermittently stoked the animus against Protestants, some army regiments also kept the sectarian pot boiling. The behaviour of 'northern recruits' of the 43rd Depot in 1843 was considered so obnoxious that they were beset by groaning youths during their public appearances. Among the incidents complained of was the playing of 'Croppies lie down' from the barracks window in reply to the 'national airs' of the Mechanics' Institute band, the desecration of a Catholic prayer-book with 'the most blasphemous and obscene expressions', and the heckling of a priest by a group of off-duty soldiers at Salthill. Eventually, due to complaints from church and civic representatives, the 43rd was transferred to Limerick.[83]

The post-Famine period saw an intensification of evangelical activity in the west of Ireland, through Alexander Dallas's Irish Church Missions Society.[84] The town of Galway was not an important missionary field — more isolated and neglected communities were preferred — but ICMS efforts were inevitably felt in the principal town of the region. Dallas himself preached in Galway on several occasions, but his reception from local Protestants was lukewarm.[85] Catholics were actively hostile. At a Dallas sermon in February 1852, to which 'Catholics were affectionately invited', Patrick Connor was arrested for causing a disturbance. He was convicted, but magistrates sought only a guarantee of good behaviour.[86] Shortly afterwards, and probably provoked by Dallas's appearance there, a 'riotous mob' gathered outside the Collegiate Church, breaking 164 panes of glass. On this occasion, rioters were sentenced to a month in gaol, and the Chief Secretary offered £50 to anybody offering information which might lead to further convictions.[87]

If Dallas's *Missionary Herald* found evidence of Romish degeneracy in Galwegians' behaviour, the pro-Catholic press was just as keen to highlight evangelical shortcomings. In 1853, the *Galway Packet* gleefully reported a court case concerning damage to a house in Salthill. The house had been let to a prominent evangelical, Rev. Brownrigg, who had accommodated young street preachers in the house. The interior of the house was 'destroyed', and the *Packet* further alleged that the young men had been in the habit of entertaining 'girls', including one who found herself in 'an interesting condition'. The youthful exuberance of other preachers extended to annoying Poor Clare nuns by throwing biblical tracts over their convent wall.[88]

For the most part, however, complaints were about the 'nuisance' caused by excessive zeal on the part of street preachers and the undue provocation given to the simple faithful of the town. Particular exception was taken to the visit of a Father Gavazzi — an apostate Italian Catholic priest — in 1859.[89] A contributor to the *Galway Mercury* put the case forcefully:

> These religious firebrands must be put down; this rampant ruffianism cannot, will not, be any longer endured. Catholic Galway will no longer brook the insults of such clerical mountebanks. Jumpers, soupers and all that kind of folks … these

disturbers of the public peace must be taught that in a city where nineteen-twentieths of the population are Catholic, a mere fraction of the population, led on a small knot of designing and crafty knaves, must no longer run rampant and riotous, insulting the feelings and libelling the faith of the inhabitants. We will have no more of your Gavazzis.[90]

Given such encouragment, it is not surprising that Gavazzi was made unwelcome.

Gavazzi's first lecture dealt with 'The Character of Pio Nono'. For want of a larger venue, it took place in the mission schoolroom which, to accommodate the 'several hundred' who came, had its windows removed and its yard covered in canvas. As well as the several hundred, however, there arrived 'a large crowd of the blackguards and ragamuffins about the docks' who obstructed the entrance and, later, interrupted the lecturer with their 'coarse epithets and derisive cheers'. The following afternoon, for the second of three scheduled lectures — the third was not delivered — a hostile crowd assembled again. On this occasion, stones were showered on the building until the lecture finished, and those most prominently associated with the event were followed home, and pelted all the way with stones. Several were denied shelter by shopkeepers, and, even more outrageously in the opinion of the *Galway Express,* police refused to involve themselves. That night, several houses of Protestants were attacked. The greatest damage was to the home of Mrs Crotty, widow of Rev. William Crotty — there, 'eighty-four panes of glass, sashes, shutters and doors were smashed, and no watch-man, policeman or soldier to stay the avenging hand'.[91]

Rank-and-file policemen, of course, were predominantly Catholic and may have secretly sympathised with the protesters. A few years later, two 'respectable-aged' men who met outside the ICMS Ragged-school in Taylor's Hill were left in no doubt about the sympathies of one constable, when he interrupted their conversation 'on religious topics' and asked them to move on, threatening to summon them for obstructing the thoroughfare.[92]

During the 1850s and 1860s, there emerged a vibrant and assertively Protestant sub-culture in the town. Supported most actively by newcomers to the town, its principal features were a siege mentality, a middle-class outlook, and a disapproval of frivolity. The *Galway Express**— derisively referred to as the *Queen's College Gazette* in a rival publication — was its principal mouthpiece, but the sub-culture supported a variety of societies and fellowships, including

---

* The *Galway Express* was founded by John MacDougall in January 1853. MacDougall saw it as a 'weekly journal devoted to the maintenance of Protestantism, and to the advancement of the Commercial, Agricultural and Trading interests of Ireland; and which will particularly advocate unison of feeling between the landlord and tenant classes … The want of such a newspaper in the capital of the western province of Ireland', the prospectus went on, 'has been much felt by the intelligent portion of the community' since 'the existence of three radical papers in that city has exaggerated the evil and increased the difficulties by which those parties are met, who are engaged in the laudable and much needed work of inculcating the principles of pure Christianity, and promoting the appeal of useful knowledge among all classes'. The editor promised to 'labour for the extension and spread of those principles which have made the Province of Ulster as remarkable for industry, prosperity and happiness, as Connaught has been for poverty, wretchedness and misery …'.

a Galway Protestant Mutual Improvement Society, and a branch of the Benevolent Society of St Andrew. More specifically missionary in intent were branches of the Protestant Orphan Society and of the Army Scripture Readers & Soldiers Friend Society. Meetings, lectures, and sober social functions organised by these and kindred organisations took place in the Buckland Buildings* in Woodquay.[93] The general tenor of proceedings there was well conveyed in an 1873 lecture organised by the Mutual Improvement Society, when the topic — an untypically salacious one — was 'The Songs of the Street'. Having examined his topic under several headings, and having given especial emphasis to balladry's 'peculiar characteristics in this country', the lecturer concluded with the hope that 'this, as well as other departments of literature, would improve under the refining influence of a more general diffusion of education and knowledge'.[94]

One who was well placed to observe the evangelical sub-culture was D'Arcy Wentworth Thompson, an Anglican who became professor of Greek in the Queen's College in 1864. He published the following impression a year later:

> It is a melancholy fact that the city which has most disgraced itself by the perpetuation of religious animosities is the centre and nucleus of Scoto-Irish Presbyterianism [Belfast]. A Catholic city in the south [Galway] may be placed second in the discreditable list … Every single lay Protestant gentleman, and almost every Protestant clergyman with whose opinion on the subject I have become directly or indirectly conversant, views unfavourably the extreme measures adopted by that society. It was only of late that I was walking with two friends, whose attachment to our own communion is undoubted, but who have numerous friends attached to the older form of faith, when, at a turn in the street, we read on a large placard staring us in the face the following words: 'The hope of the Christian as contrasted with the hope of the Roman Catholic!' … If such a placard were posted up by the emissaries of a religious minority in the streets of Belfast, Aberdeen, Glasgow or Manchester, the posters would be fleet of foot indeed, if they escaped out of these towns with a sound head and a whole skin. It speaks well for the forbearance of the Catholic clergy, and the orderliness of our poorer population here, that the periodical appearance of such indecent manifestations here has never led to a disturbance of the peace.[95]

---

* The Buckland Buildings were located near the Town Hall (on the site now occupied by St Nicholas N.S.). They were named for the eccentric English naturalist, Frank Buckland, whose connection with Galway was short-lived, but who gave the inaugral lecture in the Buildings. Rev. John D'Arcy was so taken by what he heard on the night of 19 July 1864 that, while proposing the vote of thanks to the speaker, he announced that 'in future, the society's rooms would be known by the euphonious name of the Buckland Buildings'. (Timothy Collins, 'From Anatomy to Zoophagy: a Biographical Note on Frank Buckland, *JGAHS 55,* 2003, pp. 91-109).

Thompson's impressions can be assumed to reflect the attitude of liberal Galway Protestants, but he was not reliably informed about the attitude of the indigenous 'poorer population'. From a different Protestant perspective, John Lewis, Congregational clergyman, complained in 1866 that his church had been attacked six times in five years, observing that 'in the lower strata of society there are plenty who will do such things'.[96]

Much of the anti-Protestant violence was the result of provocation — actual or perceived. Given similar circumstances, as D'Arcy Thompson observed, any community might have responded in like manner. But leaving aside the disruption of proselytisers' meetings and the vandalising of their buildings, there are indications of a deep-rooted anti-Protestantism among working-class Catholic Galwegians. This was demonstrated in a variety of ways: in the occasional commandeering of the principal Protestant place of worship; in the extreme antipathy towards apostate priests; in the widespread belief in Protestant culpability for the 1842 Christmas disaster. To that list, one might add the evidence from disturbances at a number of 19th century funerals.

Mourning, Durkheim asserted in another context, 'is a duty imposed by the group … a ritual attitude' which the individual is 'forced to adopt out of respect for custom'.[97] Episodes of collective protest at funerals, therefore, might be considered to reflect the deep-rooted values of a community and, indeed, folklore offers examples from various parts of the country of attempts to assert the communal sense of propriety in respect to burial.* But, for several centuries in Ireland, the communal sense of propriety was circumscribed by the legal prohibition on Catholic ceremony in cemeteries. Contributing to controversy was the Catholic priesthood's penchant for death-bed conversions. The clergy's eagerness to receive ailing Protestants was a response to elite traffic in the opposite direction during the 18th century, bolstered by the popular belief that those who conformed to Protestantism did so only to protect position or property.[98] In the Catholic mind, a death-bed conversion undermined Protestantism by showing that an individual had adhered to it for temporal rather than religious reasons; in the Protestant mind, the same conversion underlined the devious nature of Catholicism, whose priests were prepared to bully the dying in order to claim a small sectarian success. The nature of the transaction meant that there was always room for doubt about both the actuality and the sincerity of a conversion, and doubt led to disagreements between relatives and between pastors. But disagreements would not have led to riots if it had not been for the popular suspicion that the established church

---

* Examples include: the disinterring of a Protestant corpse from a Catholic churchyard by Catholics in Cavan (Iml.815:292); the refusal of a Donegal community to permit the burial of a stranger in their churchyard (O.S. letters, Donegal, 1835, J. O'D, T.S., p.15, Ms, p. 32); the attempt to prevent the burial of an informer in a Cork churchyard (Iml.303:252). Consequences of the acceptance in the churchyard of a notorious corpse included the following: in Waterford, a neighbourhood was haunted for years by the ghost of the only Protestant interred in Rathcormack cemetery (O.S. letters, Waterford, 1841, T.S., p. 39, Ms. p. 72); all of the dead people were seen to leave a Cork graveyard rather than share it with an Englishman (Iml.107:571-72).

was as keen to appropriate the corpses of the dead as it was to claim the allegiance of the orphan children of Catholics.

The young Fr Peter Daly was the centre of controversy in 1822, when he came into conflict with the Protestant warden regarding the administration of the last rites to a Mr Hallyday. Following the disagreement, sheriffs were called to protect the Protestant clergyman from 'a mob'. A Protestant burial was completed but, that night, the 'mob' dug up the coffin and placed it outside the door of an urban official. For one local Protestant, the incident showed that 'our people [are] as ignorant as the Hottentots'.[99] There was a similar incident in May 1836 when a crowd gathered in the Collegiate churchyard to disinter the coffin of the Catholic wife of Scottish Presbyterian soldier and to remove it to Fort Hill cemetery, in accordance with the reputed wishes of the dead woman.[100]

Two disturbances during the 1870s won national notoriety. Both were sparked by the alleged death-bed conversions of popular members of the local elite.

In September 1873, the funeral of a former sub-sheriff and Protestant churchwarden, P. H. Cullen, was marred by an unseemly tussle for his coffin at the gates of the Collegiate Church. Cullen was a convert, but several of his relatives remained Catholic and, during his last days, these relatives brought a Jesuit priest to visit him. In one version of the story, the dying man asked to be received into the Catholic church; in another, the Catholic last rites were read over him as he lay unconscious. The rival sets of clergymen came to an agreement on how to handle the funeral: Catholic rites were held in the dead man's house; Catholic and Protestant clergyman walked together in the large cortege; the Catholic clergy withdrew at the church gates. Then, according to a Catholic source, as the pall-bearers were about to bring the coffin to the grave-side, 'an organised body of Protestant gentlemen seized the coffin and carried it into the church'.[101] The Protestant version was rather different:

> When the cortege reached the church-door, the coffin was laid hold of by a wild mob and dragged aside with a view, as it seemed, of preventing it being taken into the church. Several respectable gentlemen, including two J.P'.s intervened and helped to drive away the mob. During this time, the coffin was dragged about and jostled, and would have been trampled underfoot, or worse, if the courage and muscle of a few determined men had not rescued it and conveyed it into the church. During this scene, the crowd rushed to the rescue, and were it not that Mr Hill, R.M., gathered in some of the constabulary force, the contest would have lasted longer. The yells of the mob at this time, when there could not have been less than 500 or 600 present, were loud and ceaseless. The women were worse than the men ...[102]

More dramatic still were scenes, a little over a year later, during the burial of popular landlord, Sir Thomas Blake, at Menlo. His tenants believed that he was secretly Catholic, and that his request for a visit from a Catholic priest during his final illness had been denied by relatives. (For their part, the relatives believed that Sir Thomas had 'softening of the brain'.) Blake paternalism saw to it that the baronet was 'sent off in the grand old Irish style', but a four-day-long wake with bountiful refreshments did little to dispel the popular excitement. When the coffin — borne by Menlo tenants — reached the small graveyard, the crowd blocked the access of Protestant clergy and gentry. Violent scenes followed, but the tenants held firm, and themselves interred the remains of their landlord in the Blake vault. Sir Thomas's heirs were disposed to be conciliatory, but the affair had received extensive publicity, and it could not be overlooked. Several tenants served a month in prison for their involvement but, more remarkably, two middle-class Catholics were charged with — though not convicted of — having encouraged the Menlo people. *Vindicator* owner, Lewis Ferdinand, was no stranger to controversy, but the charging of magistrate E. C. Burke, just as he was about to hear the case against the Menlo men, caused consternation.[103]

If the Cullen and Blake disturbances raised more eyebrows than previous religiously-motivated riots, it was because such conflict was presumed to be a thing of the past by the 1870s. The Church of Ireland had been disestablished in 1869, while the evangelical movement had been losing impetus — and the capacity to provoke. Latent passions, however, had been aroused in the aftermath of the Nolan/Trench election campaign of 1872. The controversial judgement of Judge Keogh,[104] in particular, which was seen to scapegoat the Catholic clergy, rekindled the sectarian instincts of the people, making them sensitive to perceived slights on their religion and their community.

*

On Sunday evening, 12 December 1886, the Vincentian Fathers were due to end their mission in Galway's pro-Cathedral. By the time the missioners appeared, the building was extremely crowded, with many having to remain outside on the street. The *Galway Express* described what happened next:

> Just before the officiating clergyman came on the altar, a crash was heard in one of the galleries as if of the breaking of some timber, and simultaneously with the noise a quantity of mortar fell from the ceiling, which was the cause of creating a cry to the effect that the gallery was giving way, and immediately a rush was made for the doors, every person acting with the selfish desire of saving themselves. Some of those present jumped onto the altar, and there endeavoured to escape through the sacristy.[105]

Parish priest, Fr Peter Dooley, acted quickly. He ascended the pulpit and 'in a loud and firm voice' instructed the people to stay where they were, and warned them of the consequences of a rush towards the doors. Not everybody took heed, but the majority stayed put, and there were no serious injuries.

The similarities with the account of the 1842 disaster are startling, but the differences are important too. By comparison with their grand-parents, the Catholic worshippers of 1886 were orthodox, sober, and disciplined. But it was not just the Catholics who had changed. The *Express* was no less Protestant than it had ever been, but its fervour had dimmed. The *Standard* of 1842 was forthright — as the *Express* of the 1860s would have been — in identifying those flaws in Catholic practice which led to such a catastrophe. By contrast, the conclusion drawn by the *Express* of 1886 was restrained: 'We think this circumstance in itself should be a caution to those responsible against allowing the overcrowding of the galleries to such an extent in the future'.

NOTES

1. *Freeman's Journal.* 27 December 1842. See also James Mitchell, 'A Christmas Morning Tragedy' in *The Mantle,* vol. vii, no. 4, pp. 12-15.
2. *Galway Standard,* 30 December 1842.
3. *Galway Vindicator,* 28 December 1842.
4. ibid.
5. According to the *Vindicator* 'rumours are afloat, which require the most cautious investigation, and which, if proved to have any foundation in truth, must greatly tend to damage the good understanding that has hitherto subsisted in Galway between all classes of religionists' (28 December 1842).
6. ibid.
7. Henry Inglis, *A Journey Throughout Ireland during the Spring, Summer and Autumn of 1834*, London 1838 pp. 212, 217.
8. *First Report of the Commissioners of Public Instruction*, 1835, vol. xxxiii, p. 46d.
9. See D. H. Akenson, *Small Differences: Irish Catholics and Irish Protestants, 1815-1922,* Dublin 1988, passim.
10. *Freeman's Journal,* 8 July 1816.
11. *Connaught Journal,* 9 October 1823.
12. ibid., 30 December 1824.
13. ibid, 6 January 1825, 9 March 1826, 3 March 1828. Later purchases included 'a beautiful scripture painting' by 'Mr Haverty, the eminent artist' and 'a valuable lustre, which cost some thirty or forty guineas'.
14. Mitchell, 'Fr Daly', pp. 32, 43; *Connaught Journal,* 9 May, 7 July 1836; *Galway Packet,* 24 April 1852.
15. *Connaught Journal*, 16 February 1824.
16. J. Fleetwood Berry, *The Story of St Nicholas' Collegiate Church, Galway,* 1989 edn, Galway, pp. 85-6. Anon., *The Angler in Ireland, or an Englishman's ramble through Connaught & Munster,* London 1834, vol. i, pp. 80-81; Alexis de Tocqueville, *Journey in Ireland, July-August 1835,* 1970 edn, Shannon, p. 100.
17. *The Ecclesiologist,* 10 December 1861; *Galway Advertiser,* 24 February 1838, 10 August 1839; Berry, *St Nicholas,* p. 86.
18. *Irish Builder,* 1 November 1872.
19. Berry, *St Nicholas,* pp. 88-90.
20. *Connaught Journal,* 23 September 1834; *Galway Advertiser,* 12 May 1838.
21. *Galway Express,* 4 February, 19 May 1860, 20 July 1861, 4 July 1863. The Taylor's Hill building was occasionally referred to — without derogatory intent — as 'the Church of England' (ibid., 21 February 1863).
22. Berry, *St Nicholas,* pp. 43-44.
23. Rev. Fr Martin Coen, *The Wardenship of Galway,* Galway 1984, pp. 1-31.
24. ibid., pp. 75-117.
25. Rev. Fr Martin Coen, 'The choosing of Oliver Kelly' *JGAHS*, vol.xxxvi, 1977-78, pp.14-29; William J. Waldron. 'Archdiocese of Tuam, 1770-1817', unpublished M.A. thesis (minor), UCD 1993 pp. 54-59; John Cunningham *St Jarlath's College, Tuam: 1800-2000,* Tuam 1999, pp. 21-23, 26.
26. Coen, *Wardenship,* pp. 75-91.
27. *Connaught Journal,* 3 November 1823.

28. Coen, *Wardenship,* pp. 95, 106, 140.

29. ibid., p. 140.

30. ibid., pp. 118-35; Mitchell, 'Fr Daly', pp. 36-37.

31. Coen, *Wardenship,* pp. 136-71, 198. For democratic spirit, see T. P. Boland, *Thomas Carr: Archbishop of Melbourne,* pp. 61-62, 69-71

32. de Tocqueville, *Journey,* pp. 99-101; John Bernard Trotter, *Walks Through Ireland in the Years 1812, 1814, and 1817,* London 1819, p. 403; Anon., *The Angler,* p. 80.

33. Asenath Nicolson *The Bible in Ireland (Ireland's Welcome to the Stranger)* 1927 edn, New York, p. 116.

34. Trotter, *Walks,* p. 403; Inglis, *Journey,* p. 212.

35. See *Report from the Commissioners on Public Instruction in Ireland,* 1835, vol. xxxiii, app.D; D. W Miller, 'Irish Catholicism and the Great Famine' *Journal of Social History,* 1975, vol. ix, pp. 81-98; Emmet Larkin, 'The Devotional Revolution in Ireland, 1850-1875' in *American Historical Review,* vol. lxxvii (3), pp. 625-52; T. G. McGrath, 'The Tridentine Evolution of Irish Catholicism, 1653-1962' in R. Ó Muirí, ed., *Irish Church History Today,* Armagh, n.d., pp. 84-99; P. Corish, *The Irish Catholic Experience,* Dublin 1985, pp. 166-69.

36. Coen, *Wardenship,* passim.

37. ibid., p. 59-63. Warden Joyce was cleared of the sexual impropriety charge: it was accepted that this was the invention of a 'saucy' parishoner who had been financially assisted for a time by him.

38. ibid., pp. 136-37.

39. McGrath, 'Evolution', pp. 95-96.

40. Hardiman (*Galway,* p. 272n) mentioned seven holy wells in the town and its immediate vicinity, including three at Lough Atalia, dedicated respectively to St Augustine, St John the Baptist, and the Blessed Virgin. Evidently, the St Augustine pilgrimage was a survival of a Lúnasa tradition. Bridie Ó Flatharta (b.1910) recalled doing the traditional grotto devotions in Castlegar — 'walking to the village from Dominick Street for eighteen evenings of May' (*Galway Advertiser,* 2 March 2000).

41. J. McE, 'Fishermen of the Claddagh', pp. 164-65.

42. Census, 1841, 1871, 1911: Occupations of the people.

43. See Chapter Thirteen.

44. [Bro. John Lynch], *The Life of Brother Paul O'Connor,* Dublin 1887, pp. 34-58.

45. ibid., p.236; L.A. de Shiúbhlaí, 'Saothar Oideachais Bráithre Padraic in Éireann', unpublished M.A. thesis, UCG 1962, pp. 121-22.

46. Lynch, *O'Connor,* pp. 182-83.

47. ibid., p. 76. Other such societies in Galway included the Augustinian Society for Christian Doctrine and the Society for the Propagation of the Faith (*Galway Mercury,* 18 November 1854; *Irish Catholic Registry,* 1841).

48. Lynch, *O'Connor,* pp. 191-94, 245-46.

49. *Galway Mercury,* 24 June 1854.

50. James Mitchell, 'Fr. M.A. Kavanagh, 1812-64' in *The Mantle,* vol. ix, no. 4, pp. 18-25; *Galway Vindicator,* 23 September 1874, 7 October 1874.

51. Cited by Liam Bane, *The Bishop in Politics,* Westport 1993, p. 61.

52. ibid, pp. 60-73; Michell, 'Fr Daly', pp. 69-114.

53. M. M. Knappen, cited by J. Wigley in *The Rise and Fall of the Victorian Sunday,* Manchester 1980, pp. 6-7.

54. S. J. Connolly, *Priests and People in Pre-Famine Ireland,* Dublin, 1982, pp. 167-69; Corish, *Experience,* p. 177.

55. de Latocnaye, *A Frenchman's Walk through Ireland, 1796-97,* Belfast 1984, p. 148.

56. Curwen, *Observations,* vol. ii, p. 344; Desmond Keenan, *The Catholic Church in Nineteenth Century Ireland: a Sociological Study,* Dublin 1983, p. 100.

57. Hardiman, *Galway,* p. 315.

58. *Connaught Journal,* 13, 27 January 1823.

59. ibid., 27 January, 1 December 1823; 9 February 1826.

60. ibid., 22 May 1823.

61. ibid., 19 April, 18 May 1824, 16 May 1825.

62. *Connaught Journal,* 18 May 1829; 28 October 1830; 6 January 1831; 3, 6 February 1832.

63. ibid., 18 May 1829; 6 January 1831, 2, 6 February 1832. Wigley, *Victorian Sunday,* pp. 33-35.

64. Henry Heaney, ed., *The Irish Journals of Robert Graham of Redgorton, 1835-38.* Dublin 1999, p. 254.

65. Colm Kerrigan, 'Temperance and Politics in pre-Famine Galway', *JGAHS,* vol. xliii, pp. 82-94.

66. *Galway Advertiser,* 2 March, 4 May 1839; 2 January 1841.

67. *Galway Mercury*, 7 December 1850, 2 June 1855; *Galway Express*, 19 March 1859, 20 September 1862, 13 May 1865, 2 February 1867, 30 May 1868.

68. Malcolm, *Ireland Sober,* pp.183-86 Bane's *MacEvilly,* p. 79.

69. *Galway Vindicator,* 17 June, 7, 24 October, 1 November 1874; Bane's *MacEvilly,* p. 79.

70. *Galway Vindicator,* 1 November 1874.

71. ibid. The issue of the Sunday closing of pubs was a politically controversial one, which gave rise to several successful and unsuccessful parliamentary bills (Malcolm, *Ireland Sober,* pp. 238-50, 272-73).

72. *Connaught Journal*, 20 October 1836; National Archives, Outrage papers 1842, 11/11045; *Galway Mercury,* 2 June 1849, 2 September 1849. And, on at least one occasion, the ringing of the bells to mark a Protestant/Loyalist success provoked a riot (Outrage Papers 1847, 11/240).

73. *Galway Express,* 1 May 1886.

74. Coen, *Wardenship,* p. 59.

75. *Connaught Patriot,* 23 May 1863.

76. Ignatius Murphy in *The Diocese of Killaloe, 1800-1850,* pp. 100-133; National Archives, Outrage Papers, 11/16915, 26 September 1840.

77. Mitchell, 'Fr Daly, pp. 74-75.

78. *Connaught Journal,* 20 November 1823.

79. Desmond Bowen, *Protestant Crusade in Ireland, 1800-1870: a Study of Protestant-Catholic Relations between the Act of Union and Disestablishment,* Dublin 1978, pp. 71-74; Mitchell, 'Fr Daly' pp. 30-31.

80. *Connaught Journal,* 16 October, 6, 20 November 1826.

81. National Archives, State of the Country papers, 2832/1, letter from Tomkins Brew to Major Warburton, 1 January 1827.

82. *Connaught Journal,* 9 April, 21 June, 9 July 1827.

83. *Galway Vindicator,* 16, 30 September, 4 October 1843.

84. Bowen, *Protestant Crusade,* pp. 208-56.

85. *Galway Mercury,* 29 June, 13 July 1850.

86. ibid., 7 February 1852.

87. National Archives, Outrage Papers 1852, 11/108, letter from John Wynne to Chief Secretary, 22 March 1852.

88. *Galway Packet,* 12 November 1853, *Galway Mecury,* 8 April 1854.

89. *Galway Packet,* 12 June 1852; *Galway Mercury,* 18 March 1854, 16 June 1855. According to Bowen (*Crusade,* pp. 243, 273), Gavazzi was brought to Ireland by the evangelical Priests' Protection Society. His tour provoked opposition in several Irish cities.

90. Quoted in *Galway Express,* 9 April 1859.

91. ibid., 2 April 1859.

92. ibid., 27 December 1862..

93. See, for example, *Galway Express,* 16 August 1862, 10 January 1862, 4 January 1868, 4 December 1869, 6 February, 28 August 1875, 3 May 1879.

94. *Galway Express,* 15 February 1873.

95. D. W. Thompson, 'Galway: or the Citie of the Tribes' in *Macmillan's Magazine,* vol. xii, 1865, pp. 411-419.

96. *Galway Express* 7 April 1866. For other incidents, see ibid., 7 December 1861, 1 March 1862, 21 February 1863, 7 April 1866.

97. E. Durkheim, *The Elementary Forms of the Religious Life,* 1965 edn, p. 443.

98. Corish, *Experience,* p. 157; Liam Swords, *A Hidden Church: the Diocese of Achonry, 1689-1818,* Dublin 1997, pp. 155-57.

99. Letter from Henry Stratford Persse to his sons, 11 March 1822 in Pethica & Roy, *Persse's Letters,* pp. 72-73. Such incidents were not peculiar to Galway. For a 1779 incident in Co. Meath, see J. Brady, *Catholics in the 18th Century Press,* p. 197; for an 1838 incident in Tuam, see *Galway Advertiser,* 19, 26 May, 2 June 1838.

100. National Archives Outrage Papers, 1836, letter from Chief Constable Plunkett, 17 May 1836.

101. National Archives, CSORP 1874/14502; *Galway Vindicator,* 10 September 1873.

102. *Galway Express*, 6 September 1873.

103. Tomás de Bhaldraithe, *Seanchas Thomáis Laighléis,* Dublin 1977, pp. 45-47; *Galway Express,* 23 January 1875.

104. In the words of one local ballad of the period, Keogh 'insulted our clergy and likewise our bishop, / And scoffed at MacHale, the bright star of Mayo'.

105. *Galway Express,* 18 December 1886.

CHAPTER 12

'We do not condemn the frolic of mere urchins...'

LEISURE & ENTERTAINMENT

As I roved out through Galway town to seek for recreation
On the 17th of August, my mind was elevated,
There were multitudes assembled with their tickets at the station,
My eyes began to dazzle and they going to see the races
Agus fáim arís an crúisgín, is bíodh sé lán.

Grá mo chroí mo chrúisgín
Sláinte, geal mo vúirnín,
Is cuma liom, a cúilín, veh duv ná bán,
Má fháim arís an crúisgín, is bíodh sé lán.

It's there you'll see confectioners with sugarsticks and dainties,
The lozenges and oranges, the lemonade and raisins…
'The Sporting Races of Galway', composed *c*.1869,
NLI, MacLochlainn Ballad Collection.

At eight o'clock on a September evening in 1830, 'an amazing concourse of all ranks and classes' gathered in Eyre Square. And between the Square and the Six-mile-bush — a landmark at the occasional race-course near Derrydonnell — crowds of spectators lined the road. 'Even the ladies', it was observed, 'from the different windows', were completely absorbed. The objects of the unusual interest were John Kelly of the Newcastle Distillery and his black horse. Kelly had wagered 150 sovereigns that he could ride the return journey of twelve Irish miles between the Provincial Bank and the Six-mile-bush in less than an hour. Further thousands of pounds were wagered by spectators. As eight o'clock approached, every horse and carriage in the vicinity was borrowed or hired to better follow Kelly's progress. And Mr Stephens, watchmaker, was besieged by individuals seeking to borrow his 'detached patent lever time-keepers'. Most of Stephens's watches were returned with crystals broken or with hands lost, but nobody disputed the outcome. Despite delaying to retrieve a stirrup, Kelly completed the course in exactly fifty-eight minutes.[1]

The episode raises several questions. How was news of the challenge communicated to so many? Why did multitudes 'of all ranks and classes' congregate for the commonplace spectacle of a man riding a horse? How frequent were such gatherings? These questions have no definitive answers, but if one considers that the streets were the ordinary rendezvous of the inhabitants of the many deficient dwellings in the town — especially on fine evenings — it can be understood that exceptional commotion among the well-to-do would quickly attract a crowd. Nor should the attraction of gambling be underestimated — the prospect of seeing the rich losing fantastic sums, as much as the hope of winning a pittance oneself. In this chapter, it will be seen that betting was essential to many amusements in the 19th century town.

If the impromptu tournament described above was sufficiently unusual to gather a crowd, it was not unprecedented. In November 1827, a man 'rather of low stature' called Demsey, attracted crowds to the Square for an exhibition of 'Pedestrianism'.* Demsey's objective was, without leaving the Square, to walk a total of 105 Irish miles in twenty-four hours. Unhappily, his progress was interrupted after three hours and twenty-one miles by the Mayor, who feared that the display might provoke a riot.[2] Demsey, evidently, attracted a less fashionable following than Kelly would, but it can be inferred that his endeavour too was the subject of betting. Why, otherwise, would 'pedestrianism' have provoked such excitement that the Mayor feared a riot?

The difference in the fate of the two men — Kelly's triumphant entrance, Demsey's humiliating arrest — might be considered allegorical. Proletarian amusements were liable to be interrupted by magistrates, whereas officials rarely interfered in the recreations of the elite. The case should not be over-stated, however, because elite recreations often allowed for the participation of the poor. Events like race meetings and regattas depended for their atmosphere on mass participation — as had John Kelly's race against Mr Stephens's 'patent lever time-keepers'. Admission to enclosures and pavilions might be strictly controlled, but anybody could enjoy the spectacle from a lesser vantage point. And later, when habitués of pavilion and enclosure poured into the exclusive balls which invariably followed such events, hucksters, hawkers and trick o' the loops offered diversions for those excluded. The impression is that there was greater tolerance of proletarian exuberance during race meetings and the like than at ordinary times —that the carousing of the upper classes provided a degree of protection for the diversions of their social inferiors.

What about amusements that did not enjoy protection? Sabbatarians, it has been shown in Chapter Eleven, sought to suppress the Sunday recreations of the working-class. And such censoriousness, it has been argued, was part of a general phenomenon. Of England, one influential writer has argued that

---

* 'Pedestrianism', apparently, had been a fad of the Regency era. At Newmarket in 1809, a Captain Robert Barclay completed a walk of a thousand miles in a thousand hours for a wager of a thousand guineas (Mike Marquese, 'Boxing with John Bull', *Guardian*, 18 August 2001). Demsey's project more closely resembled that of another 'pedestrian', George Wilson of Newcastle, who had walked fifty miles in a period of twelve hours while in prison for debt.

'recreational customs were subjected to a multitude of direct attacks' from about the mid-18th century.[3] The needs of an industrialising society for a disciplined working-class dovetailed with the moral objectives of religiously-motivated reformers in the matter. A similar phenomenon has been detected in Ireland, although dated slightly later.[4]

But, arguably, it was always thus. Mary Donovan O'Sullivan has described attempts to suppress popular amusements in Galway between the 14th and 17th centuries.[5] Maybe Galway was exceptional — it was geographically isolated, and relatively immune to the predilections of both industrialists and Protestants. Certainly, it is by no means clear that 'recreational customs' were subject to more sustained, or more effective, onslaughts during the 19th century than in earlier periods. That is not to say that the character of working class amusements remained constant. Nor is it to deny that some activities were abandoned due to pressure from civil or religious authorities — Sunday drinking was curtailed by episcopal order; St John's Eve celebrations were ended by magisterial interest. Most changes in leisure activities, however, were due to other causes. Because of the commercialisation of entertainment during the 19th century, novel and spectacular amusements — the circus, for example — devalued many 'recreational customs' in people's own eyes. In the face of competition for people's interest from diverse sources, the age-old 'maying' at Menlo, for example, simply petered out.

It might be argued that the temperance movement represented a significant intervention in working class culture by the middle-class and the clergy. Unquestionably, drinking, and the fighting which invariably accompanied it, were vital elements of many proletarian amusements. Equally unquestionable is the extent to which the temperance movement — especially in its Mathewite phase — altered working-class behaviour. The 1840s, indeed, with Famine following immediately on mass pledge-taking, was the decade which saw the most significant fracture in the continuity in popular recreations. But that temperance was an elite-driven phenomenon is not clear-cut.

Galway was an early temperance stronghold, the home of three distinct temperance organisations — the Galway (Parent) Temperance Society, established in December 1836; a branch of the Cork Total Abstinence Society, founded early in 1839; and the recently-moribund Mechanics' Institute, which got a fresh lease of life after adding the words 'Total Abstinence and Mortality Society' to its title. The 'propensity to divide on every subject that has always been manifested in Galway', was the explanation offered for such division in the temperance forces. Each of these societies was led by a different Catholic priest and their efforts to rehabilitate habitual and occasional drunkards were led by committees of middle-class reformers.[6]

Records reveal that the movement developed slowly between 1836 and 1839, and that artisans were strongly represented in the ranks — thirty-two of the fifty-eight members of one society in 1838 were in that category. The same records indicate that a majority of early members soon lapsed, either because they were expelled, because they 'withdrew', or because they went 'out of town'. And an attempt at compulsion in the cause — a resolution to the Loan Fund committee asking that no money be advanced to 'any man who does not pledge himself to act in accordance with the rules of the Temperance Society' — did not yield any noticeable return.[7]

The pattern changed abruptly in December 1839, by which point the oldest of Galway's temperance societies had enrolled 188 members. At a public meeting on 4 December 1839, that society almost quadrupled its membership when 502 new members joined. This marked the beginning of an extraordinary period, when the people were seized by a frenzy of pledge-taking, transforming the character of the movement. Scholars have suggested that temperance, at this time, was driven by the millenarian impulses of the poor, rather than by the leadership skills of its directors.[8] People stopped drinking, not because they were told to or because they were individually persuaded, but because they wanted to stop drinking, because they came to invest all their personal hopes in abstinence. The revivalist tone of pro-temperance preaching, undoubtedly, helped to create the atmosphere for this, but it did not account for the extent of apparent irrationality and superstition among adherents in Galway.

To the person of Fr Mathew, and to objects like temperance medals, were attributed great supernatural powers. Late in 1839, it was reported:

> The Temperance Society is rapidly advancing. They hold their meetings on the evenings of Sundays and Tuesdays for the purpose of receiving members, and on Thursdays to distribute the medals and cards which they have received from the Reverend Mr Mathew. Mechanics and labourers are pouring into them in fifties a night.[9]

It was stated that 600 of the Claddagh people had taken the pledge, some of them having 'repaired to the apostle' — Fr Mathew — in Cork, an astonishing journey. And when the apostle himself came to Galway in March 1840, he was welcomed by crowds of would-be pledge-takers. Estimates for those attending at Clarke's Yard in Merchant's Road were between 60,000 and 100,000.[10]

The Protestant *Galway Advertiser* was awe-struck*: delighted by the new-found sobriety of the people; appalled by manifestations of superstition in the movement; indignant that priests were using compulsion in the cause; and alarmed at indications that the whole endeavour was infused by nationalism.[11]

---

* Sometimes the *Advertiser* was merely amused: 'There are 400 tee-totalers now in town with medals suspended from their necks, who had been the most incorrigible drunkards. The Mathewites ascribe something of the miraculous to their medals, and fancy if they violate their pledge, they will instantly go mad; and they really do. Their intemperate habits render drunkards necessarily more nervous than others, and consequently, any one of them who suddenly give up the use of ardent spirits is liable to hysterical fits bordering on delirium tremens. One or two of them broke out here and the next day, almost frantic retraced their steps to Cork, where the great necromancer succeeded in allaying the irritability of their distracted nerves.' (23 November 1839)

Increases in the numbers arrested for drunkenness between 1843 and 1845 indicate that temperance was waning. There were several revivals later in the century, but none had the mass character of the 1839-40 period. In 1849-50, St Patrick's Temperance Society claimed 200 members, a fraction of the numbers of a decade earlier. Thirty years later, in 1879, Father Peter Dooley was fund-raising for a 'Grand Temperance Building' to continue the 'great work of saving the working classes from the attractive and debasing influences of the public house'.[12]

At its height, the temperance movement was responsible for several innovations. Loan funds, and mortality societies provided alternatives to the publican's till for working men's wages, but people also needed alternative recreational outlets. Tea rooms and coffee parties played their part for a time, and the temperance bands of the early 1840s were the prototype for the many marching bands that graced Galway's streets during the following century.

Feast days and festivals

The traditional festival most affected by the temperance drive was St Patrick's Day. Almost two decades before the emergence of that movement, Hardiman described the Claddagh people's commemorations of the national holiday. Galway's historian considered them a 'singular' people but, as has been shown in relation to popular protest, it may be more appropriate to regard the Claddagh people as exemplars of popular preference rather than as members of a lost tribe with their own particular rites and ceremonies.

According to Hardiman, St Patrick's Day was a 'grand gala' which began with 'copious libations' and continued with 'plentiful repasts prepared at their favourite public houses'. In this manner, people continued 'for two or three days in one continued scene of merriment and ebriety'.[13] Such extravagant feasting had a negative aspect and, on St Patrick's Day 1836, before the establishment of the Galway Temperance Society, Rev. B. J. Roche concluded his homily with a graphic 'description of the intemperate liver' urging his congregation — for their physical as much as their spiritual welfare — to observe the saint's day in a sober fashion. A year later, 'a great decrease in intoxication' compared to former years was attributed to the 'friends of temperance'. In 1840, these gentlemen organised a St Patrick's Day 'Tea and Coffee Festival' in order to wean people from their favourite public houses.[14]

Later in the century, large numbers of country people spent the holiday in town, where they tended to become as drunk as the natives. In 1864, it was reported that fights broke out in the evening of the feast, the revellers having had their 'pugilistic feelings excited' by too much drink. Later in the 1860s, the *Express* noticed a general improvement in behaviour although it remarked that 'the influence of Double X was a little obvious on the country folks'. In 1869, thanks to the paternalistic interest of the management of the Clog Factory, an innovation was introduced to the celebrations:

> About mid-day, the band of the Clog Factory, under the eminent superintendence of Mr Ulla, dressed in a very neat uniform, marched through the town followed by admiring thousands, and played in excellent style the national anthem 'Patrick's Day', followed by 'Cheer Boys, Cheer', 'Long, Long Ago', and several other interesting and enlivening airs.[15]

Herr Ulla was still resident in 1877, when he was director of the revived temperance movement's 510-strong Temperance Band. In that year, band members spent the night before the feast parading and disturbing the sleeping with their cacophonous renditions of 'St Patrick's Day'. The Temperance Band set the tone for this and subsequent commemorations and, in 1880, a commentator was 'gratified' to notice the insignificant number of drunks among the great crowds in the streets.[16] But elements of the old and of the new could co-exist, as a description of the 1885 celebrations indicates:

> Scarcely had they time to allay their excitement at the martial strains of the Industrial School Band, than their ears were treated to the sound of the drum of the labourers' band … headed by Mr James O'Mara of Shop-street, who twirled a large switch he held in his hand in the manner of a drum major. He wore a green sash and rosette as president of the labourers' society and was looked on by the country people as a man in no way inferior to St Patrick himself … But with all of this excitement, it appears that the anniversary of our patron saint could not be carried out without a few rows, for at Henry-street, there was blood spilt, and a few noses broken in the latter part of the day. At Prospect Hill, there was a very brisk fight, and it is needless to say that Woodquay was not behind in this mode of celebration, for here a regular faction fight took place, in which the women joined and fought with a spirit that was astonishing. Sticks and stones were used, while those of the feminine gender who failed to get those implements of warfare, flung the gutter off the road into the faces of their antagonists.[17]

In 1903, the Gaelic League branch took responsibility for St Patrick's Day celebrations, and set the tone for 20th century celebrations of the feast. March 17 was not yet a public holiday, but the League took steps to ensure that it was truly 'national' holiday in Galway. To this end, a 'voluntary' closure of all businesses was enforced, contributing to the success of the several sporting events that were arranged and to the large crowds that turned out to cheer the procession of local organisations behind three marching bands.[18]

In the early 19th century, midsummer celebrations surpassed those of St Patrick's Day. St John's Eve had particular significance in the Claddagh, and the forms of celebration reflected the Claddagh people's sense of themselves as forming the fishermen's guild of the borough. Some of 'the peculiar kind of pageantry' of the occasion was clearly borrowed from earlier civic ceremonial:

> On the evening of that day, the young and old assemble at the head of the village; and their mayor, whose orders are decisive, adjusts the rank, order and precedence of this peculiar procession. They then set out, headed by a band of music, … through the principal streets and suburbs of the town; the young men all uniformly arrayed in short white jackets, with silken sashes, their hats ornamented with ribbons and flowers, … bearing long poles and standards with suitable devices, which are in general emblematic of their profession. To heighten the merriment of this festive scene, two of the stoutest disguised in masks, and entirely covered in party-covered rags, as 'merrymen', with many antic tricks and gambols, make way for the remainder. In the course of their progress they stop with loud cheerings and salutations opposite the houses of the principal inhabitants, from whom they generally receive money on the occasion. Having at length regained their village, they assemble in groups, dancing around and sometimes leaping through their bonfires, never forgetting to bring home part of the fire which they consider sacred; and thus the night ends as the day began, in one continuous scene of mirth and rejoicing.[19]

Hardiman thought he had witnessed 'the remnant of an ancient pagan rite' — suggested by the date and by the taking home of embers. However, the principal elements of the pageant — the band, the young men 'uniformly arrayed', the 'merrymen', even the collection from 'principal inhabitants' — were familiar to witnesses of urban carnival throughout Europe.

In 1823, news that this 'most innocent recreation of the lower orders' had been suppressed by the stipendary magistrate and the recorder of the town, was met with indignation. The announcement — delivered by the bell-man on the morning of 23 June — was ignored until constables were despatched to quench fires and to remove ricks of turf. 'Stones and brickbats' greeted the constables, so the magistrate deployed armed troops. This was sufficient to restore order.[20]

The context was one of agrarian disturbance in the vicinity of the town and, although they claimed to have been motivated only by the desire to suppress 'nuisance', it seems that the officials feared a riot. Subsequently defending their decision, they insisted that they had prohibited fires only in the main streets: 'where they might be considered as dangerous and public nuisances in the centre of so populous a place'. This justification, however, came after they had been reprimanded. At 1 pm on 24 June, an indignation meeting was held in the house of Edward Blake, J.P. Speakers were concerned to stress the 'loyalty' and the 'peaceability' of the 'lower orders': 'While Ribbonism surrounded us', according to one, 'the County of the Town of Galway remained exempt'. The damage done to Galway's reputation by the banning of a 'religious ceremony' concerned others, and an apology was sought from the stipendary magistrate. The sentiments of the meeting were conveyed to the Lord Lieutenant who later communicated his 'satisfaction' at this 'favourable report of the state of the the district'.[21]

Accounts of the controversy show that participation in the St John's Eve commemoration was general throughout the town, and not confined to the Claddagh people, as might be inferred from Hardiman. In reproaching those who had prohibited the celebrations, the *Connaught Journal* emphasised how broadly-based they were:

> Here in Galway these fires have been constantly lighted — the higher and middle classes of persons subscribing money towards the purchase of fuel for them. *No evil consequences have ever been attendant on them.* They have served as a most innocent recreation for the lower orders, who generally passed the evening dancing around them.[22]

Notwithstanding the indignation about the banning of the St John festival in 1823, it would seem that no further celebrations were held until 1840, when it was reported that the Claddagh fishermen — who had taken the pledge en masse — had 'revived their traditional festival' under Temperance aegis.[23] On that occasion, it was stated that John's Eve customs were 'abandoned many years since'. Given the officials' attitude in 1823, it is likely that the abandonment was due to their intervention — possibly on a few occasions — during the 1820s. And, given the participation of 'gentlemen of respectability' in the sanitised and short-lived revival of 1840, it is likely that the initiative on that occasion came from the middle-class leadership of the temperance movement — people familiar with Hardiman's description — rather than from the Claddagh.

> On Tuesday last, being the eve of St John, a very fine body of fishermen, members of the Temperance Societies in this town, presented a formidable and imposing appearance, decorated in a novel and curious manner, with a great profusion of ribbons, feathers and flowers in their hats, passed in procession through the several streets of the town, and visited at the country residences of many gentlemen in the vicinity whom they cordially greeted with cheers and acclamations.[24]

Some elements of the midsummer commemorations survived. During the 1860s, youngsters collecting money for fuel for a John's Eve bonfire were denounced as blackmailers. That this denunciation came four weeks before 23 June supports Caillois's observation that man lives 'in remembrance of one festival, and in expectation of the next'.[25] For their part, Galway's Freemasons continued to mark St John's Day with a celebratory banquet — 'a custom as old as Masonry itself'.[26]

A secular celebration, and one particular to Galway, was the annual 'Maying at Menlo', which took place on the first three Sundays of May. On those days, the patrician Blakes, leaders of the 'popular party' in borough politics, opened the grounds of their river-side demesne to their tenants and to the inhabitants of Galway. The origins of the celebration are uncertain, but 'May-games' were enjoyed by townspeople since the mediæval period,* and it is possible that the Menlo festivities derived, in some part, from these. Would it be fanciful to suggest that they were originally a concession to Blake tenants during the festive period in the town? And, that with the decay of the traditional 'May-games', outsiders were attracted to Menlo. Given the village's large population, and the *laissez-aller* attitude of generations of Blakes, outsiders might have been welcomed. If it had not happened before then, Valentine Blake's prominence in the political affairs of the town in the early 19th century would have made it expedient to formalise participation on the part of townspeople by means of a general invitation. Hardiman's failure to mention the Menlo amusements when referring to Patrick's Day and John's Eve festivities, while not conclusive, would indicate that the Menlo Sundays had not achieved their later prominence by the first two decades of the 19th century.

Townspeople travelled the two-odd miles to Menlo by boat from Woodquay and, once there, could and indulge in the 'hilarity of spirits and devil-may-care daring' for which the Menlo Sundays were renowned.[27] All classes participated, but there was an element of segregation. The gentry attended on the first Sunday only, while the middle-class and the 'respectable' working-class were more apparent on the second Sunday. On the third Sunday — 'Domhnach na dTincéirí' — the poor were predominant. The earliest description is from 1830, by which time the event was well established. Contrasting it with Dublin's Donnybrook Fair, the writer stressed Menlo's sylvan setting and the home-spun character of its amusements. In the process, and amidst much laborious punning, he told as much about Donnybrook as about Menlo. The principal difference, it would appear, was the absence of the travelling shows from England, who had put Donnybrook on their annual itineraries by this time.[28]

> There were no *merry-go-rounds* to set the heads of young gay and giddy, but there were substitutes in glasses going merrily round, cheering the heart and elevating the head until thousands became *hearty* and *heady*, but surely it is a pleasant thing to be going over

---

* Roderic O'Flaherty stated that it was to Blake's Hill 'whither the young men of Galway were wont to come the third of their May-game, and there dine between the hill and the castle of Barna'. Editing Flaherty's work in the 1840s, Hardiman added a note: 'The May games and other old customs, as "riding the ring", &c., formerly practiced here have long since fallen into disuse. The "young men" of the present day would be ashamed of those homely but manly amusements of their forefathers; although it is to be feared, that many of their modern pastimes are not altogether of so innocent a character' (*West or h-Iar Connaught*, 1846 edn, Dublin, p. 60).

to the *native*, when a glass of punch seems to be the *glass of fashion* … There were no booths at Menlo for puppets and mountebanks, but many a green *bank* was covered with a booth, where instead of *merry-Andrews* and *Punch-and-Judy*, Andrew and Judy passed the day not caring a farthing for *shew-men* or *tumblers*, while tumblers of punch were passing from hand to hand, and diffusing their *native* influence from heart to heart. Although there were no opera dancers to 'tip the light fantastic toe' … they seemed to be as handy about the feet as they had been careless about the heart … Although Bartholemew Fair and Donnybrook Fair surpassed Menlo in artificial amusement, Menlo has the advantage in pure and genuine Irish merriment.[29]

It was in the quality and pervasiveness of the singing that the differences with Donnybrook were most apparent:

How delightful to hear a sweet sentimental Irish song, when sung by an enamoured swain, endeavouring to convince his dear sweetheart that he more than loved her. We cannot forget the pleasure we felt when sitting amongst the trees, behind Mr Toomy's marquee, when we heard a young Menlonian sing *Nellogeen le ma anum hu* for a sweet smiling creature from Rahoon … How superior is this simple ditty of the Menlonian to 'Buy a broom', 'Cherry-ripe', or the other unsentimental songs of Donnybrook … The good old song *Go dhe shin go on ke shin* was sung over and over again at the close of evening.[30]

The occasional cancellation of festivities reminded people that their annual outing to Menlo was a privilege rather than a right. In 1837, the illness of the 'second Miss Blake' was the cause of disappointment and, in 1844, 'improper

'Paddy Conneely, The Galway Piper', depicted by Frederick William Burton (courtesy of National Gallery of Ireland).

conduct' — the theft of thirteen pet white rabbits, later discovered in a pawnbrokers' shop — led to the exemplary exclusion of 'the public at large', although the invitations issued to 'respectable persons' remained good.[31]

In 1844, 'improper conduct' had already been anticipated by a temperance society and, in line with its policy which was to 'discountenance the occasions of inebriety', it announced a rival 'Teetotal Festival' for its rooms in Middle-street. The announcement did not prove popular, however, so the society instead 'repaired to Menlo' itself, with guests from the Gort Temperance Band. Outside Menlo Castle, the band 'delighted' the people, guarding them 'from a violation of the Temperance pledge, or a frequenting of the numerous tents scattered among the trees and fields for the sale of intoxicating liquor'.[32]

If the temperance movement did not halt Menlo's 'maying', neither did the famine. A general invitation was issued by Sir Thomas Blake in 1847, although he prohibited the erection of tents and the sale of drink, but it seems that celebration lapsed in the following two years. It is inconceivable, certainly, that people could have been brought together during the cholera epidemic of 1849.[33]

In 1850, 'maying' was fully resumed and, in 1853, the Midland Great Western Railway ran a special train from Athlone for the first of the three Sundays. By then, the gathering was reported to have become 'quite fashionable'.[34]

The early 1850s marked the high-point of efforts to suppress Donnybrook Fair. Indeed, groups concerned to improve working-class behaviour brought an end to both Donnybrook and London's Old Bartlemy in 1855.[35] Why then were Menlo's attractions becoming 'quite fashionable' at the same time? It was hardly that drink was scarcer around the Blake demesne than elsewhere. Indeed, accounts from different periods mention that poteen was freely available. There was fighting too at Menlo, though perhaps less of it than at Donnybrook. The principal difference between Menlo and the suppressed proletarian gatherings of the period was Menlo's elite patronage. Blake interest ensured, at the very least, that drink tents were closed by evening, and that towspeople departed before dark. Moreover, unlike festivities associated with fairs, Menlo 'maying' did not encroach significantly on the working week.

There was a debate about Menlo, which was conducted in terms similar to that about Donnybrook. The difference was that opposition to Menlo was confined to a small minority, even of the improving middle-class. Persistent upper- and middle-class participation, greater regulation, the manifest 'respectability' of the Blakes, the fact that festivities did not greatly encroach on economic life all played their part in blunting opposition. Arguably, however, the source of the most forthright opposition in the post-Famine period was important in marshalling local middle-class support for Menlo.

Because it was an occasion of Sabbath-breaking, of drunkenness, and of gambling, evangelicals and their allies began to criticise Menlo during the 1850s. Responding in 1855 to one such, 'A Catholic' wondered why this 'rigid gentleman' should object that 'the hard-working man and the artisan — who is inhaling a poisonous atmosphere all week round — [should] get out to the open fields after the performance of Divine worship on Sunday, and refresh his body and soul by contemplating the beauties of nature'. Two years later some townspeople organised a collection to enhance the Menlo event by providing prizes for 'rural sports', which included pole-climbing, foot racing and sack-running. Even the police, it was reported, were invited to take part.[36] In 1860, prize-money for one rowing competition was collected in the town, while the prize for a four-oared boat race was put up by the young Valentine Blake. Such developments did not assuage Dublin's *Daily Express*:

> Maying at Menlo is one of the oldest customs known in this part of Ireland ... The grounds on which this shameful system is carried out is the property of Sir Thomas Blake, J.P., who is a Protestant, but it is presumed must be a nominal one ... From an early hour on Sunday morning, boats were employed in conveying persons up the lake to Menlo Castle, round which tents for the sale of drink are usually erected, and innumerable gambling tables are usually exhibited. As the day grows older, the scene changes from one of quiet to one of dissipation and blasphemy. Here may be seen a party consisting of the respectable shopkeepers accompanied by their wives or other females, dancing to the music of a German band, some of them in a state of intoxication. There you may discover in a crowd two or three pairs of low ruffians engaged in fighting, while their companions cheer and encourage them to the most brutal acts of pugilism ... The constabulary did not leave town for this Sabbath-breaking locality until six o'clock p.m, when they proceeded to Menlo for the purpose of pulling down tents and dispersing the drunken crowds, who as the night closed in, were finishing their revels in the established Irish fashion, with a fight. To their disgrace, be it stated that several Protestants were among the revellers.[37]

A view of Menlo Castle, *c.*1820 (from Hardiman Collection, courtesy of Galway County Library).

Sabbatarians continued to complain about intoxication and aggression at Menlo. Steps were taken to appease these critics and in 1885 it was reported that drink tents were not permitted inside Menlo's gates. However, the public house just outside the gates and the hawkers who sold liquor secretly ensured that the essential fuel of Menlo conviviality remained available.

Writers sympathetic to Menlo stressed activities other than drinking and fighting — the boat journey, the serenity of Menlo woods, the games and sports. An 1886 account described 'athletes in their shirt-sleeves competing for victory in the many practices of stone-throwing and jumping, while the juvenile portion of the male sex amused themselves at games of wrestling or leap-frog'. And the ambiance for young lovers during the 'maying' continued to be emphasised. If the 1830 witness had applauded the spectacle of Andrew and Judy getting pleasantly drunk together, later commentators focused on the tradition of lovers picking wildflowers in Menlo wood.* Significantly, there were few criticisms of Menlo maying as an occasion of sexual misbehaviour.

But if supporters of 'maying' stressed the variety of amusements, they did not deny that drinking took place. In fact, it would appear that despite the efforts of temperance advocates there were many who approved of drinking, and many who were amused — rather than scandalised — by quarrelling. This attitude was not reflected in the non-evangelical press, which ignored bacchanalian excesses rather than risk giving hostages to fortune. It was otherwise in popular balladry and if, for want of something more contiguous, we may take an example from Galway county, it is clear that there was an audience for material celebrating disorder. The Loughrea Donkey Races of the 1850s were similar to Menlo — with German bands and greasy poles — but one contemporary description gave far more attention to brawling than to programmed activities. The scenes described — and the indulgent attitude —were typical too of Menlo:

> There was Patsy Coyne and Johnny Lahy,
> Big 'Mad Bull' and quiet Tom Fahy,
> And Paddy Maginn and Jack Currahy
> With bloody broken faces.
> With Patcheen Madden and Tom Keogh,
> And ex-militiamen on the go,
> That dealt out many a sorry blow
> At the Loughrea Donkey Races
> For bones and backs and skulls were broken,
> With paving stones and cudgels oaken,
> Till the peelers by the self-same token,
> Marched off with hangmen's faces...[38]

---

* A poet of the 1890s described it thus: The Menlo Woods are blooming / All in the month of May; / To gather wild primroses / Or pluck the hawthorn spray / Do youths and maidens wander / As moving in a dream, / Along the road through Bohermore / Or by the Corrib stream. (R. Staunton-Cahill, cited by Maurice Semple in *Reflections on Lough Corrib*, p. 103.

Menlo Castle burned down in 1910, but it would seem that the building outlived the May festivities. In 1888, it was reported that, following custom, the Blakes had hoisted a flag at the castle, and that boat-races had taken place, but that 'there was an almost complete absence of the amusement and enthusiasm of former years'. In particular, the 'long-treasured custom' of boys and girls together picking flowers had been abandoned. Evidently, competing Sunday attractions were reducing attendances. Salthill had become popular among townspeople, especially since the opening of the tramway in 1879, while cheap railway excursions added further variety. And the increased numbers of sportsdays and football matches, even if they did not clash directly, must have dulled the appeal of the quaint Menlo amusements. For many of the would-be-fashionable, an outing with the cycling club established in April 1887 would have been more attractive than the familiar journey to Menlo.[39]

Around 1905, during Tomás Laighléis's childhood 'maying' died a natural death. Tomás recalled waiting one Sunday morning with several of his friends for the arrival of hawkers and showmen.[40] They did not appear. Two decades later, someone who had spent youthful Sundays at Menlo looked back:

> Boats from the Long Walk as well as the Borraholla boats were plying, and the shouting of the boatmen: 'Who's for Menlo? Twopence a head, children free', rent the air … It is a slow voyage, but no-one minds. Joe Banks, piper to the King, plays 'The Rakes of Mallow'. Joe Kelly is piping in another boat, which is occupied by the Mayor of Galway … Sweet vendors were working night and day preparing sugar-sticks and kiss-pipes which were sold in colours of red and white at a half-penny each … The cries of the different vendors of eatables and drinks rent the air: 'Cider a penny a glass — the real juice of the American apple; Guinness three-pence per pint and minerals twopence per bottle', is the shout … Puritans and temperance fanatics were unknown … The ladies in the enclosure, which was at this side of the Castle, with their sun-shades and costumes of mid-Victorian days, looked beautiful. The villagers and colleens with their shoulder-shawls and neat pinafores were a picture of neatness and comeliness. They were all dressed — not undressed as they are today. Lady Blake hands the prizes and cups to the successful crews. The Miss Blakes are chatting in good old Irish to Maureen, Shauneen and Paudeen.[41]

Theatre and performance

By the mid-18th century, the practice of touring theatre companies 'following the assizes' was established and Galway's playhouse — which existed by 1739 — was one of the stops on their itineraries. These companies depended on elite patronage but, in Dublin at any rate, their performances were attended also by other social classes — segregated from one another in boxes, pit, and gallery.[42]

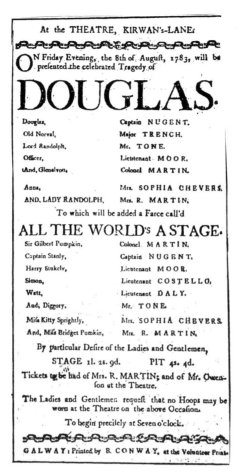

At the THEATRE, KIRWAN's-LANE.

ON Friday Evening, the 8th of August, 1783, will be presented the celebrated Tragedy of

DOUGLAS.

Douglas,	Captain NUGENT.
Old Norval,	Major TRENCH.
Lord Randolph,	Mr. TONE.
Officer,	Lieutenant MOOR.
And, Glenalvon,	Colonel MARTIN.
Anna,	Mrs. SOPHIA CHEVERS.
AND, LADY RANDOLPH,	Mrs. R. MARTIN.

To which will be added a Farce call'd

ALL THE WORLD's A STAGE.

Sir Gilbert Pumpkin,	Colonel MARTIN.
Captain Stanly,	Captain NUGENT.
Harry Stukely,	Lieutenant MOOR.
Simon,	Lieutenant COSTELLO.
Watt,	Lieutenant DALY.
And, Diggory,	Mr. TONE.
Miss Kitty Sprightly,	Mrs. SOPHIA CHEVERS.
And, Miss Bridget Pumkin,	Mrs. R. MARTIN.

By particular Desire of the Ladies and Gentlemen,

STAGE 1l. 2s. 9d.   PIT 4s. 4d.

Tickets to be had of Mrs. R. MARTIN; and of Mr. Owenson at the Theatre.

The Ladies and Gentlemen request that no Hoops may be worn at the Theatre on the above Occasion.

To begin precisely at Seven o'clock.

GALWAY: Printed by B. CONWAY, at the Volunteer Print.

Handbill for Kirwan's Lane Theatre, 1783. Actors listed include Wolfe Tone, 'Humanity Dick' Martin and Elizabeth Martin (courtesy of James Hardiman Library, NUI, Galway).

While it is likely that theatre in Galway was more exclusive than in Dublin, the late 18th century fashion for amateur theatricals — signalling the withdrawal of the genteel from the raucous and exuberant commercial theatres — spread to the western capital and, in 1783, a small theatre was established in Kirwan's Lane by Richard 'Humanity Dick' Martin. Robert Owenson — professional actor/impressario and father of novelist, Lady Morgan — was appointed manager, but Martin's main objective was to indulge his wife's amateur acting enthusiasm. Another enthusiasm of Elizabeth Martin's — for fellow amateur actor, Theobald Wolfe Tone — flourished for two years, but it was with an Englishman that Mrs Martin decamped in 1790.[43]

Richard Martin's interest did not survive his wife's departure, but his theatre proved resilient and, under various managements, it hosted the celebrated actors of the day. In 1792, new proprietor, Mr Macartney undertook extensive renovations: the building had its roof removed and had its walls raised by seven feet, to accommodate 'a regular gallery, an elegant circular set of boxes, a new pit, and a higher stage, with proper access to each place'.[44]

During the same period, plays were also put on in the Assembly Rooms, Middle-street. A local newspaper announced an imminent performance:

> Mrs Lynch returns her sincere thanks to the ladies and gentlemen of Galway for the kind patronage she has received from them for the years past. She now begs leave to inform them that there will be a drum in the Assembly Rooms on Saturday, being the last she means to trouble her friends…[45]

The proceeds of such benefits were essential to actors' livelihoods, with success being dependent on the popularity of the individual — and the approval of 'ladies' in the case of female actors. But because only one benefit could be held at the end of each run, they were a frequent cause of dispute among actors.

It would seem that the Assembly Rooms* were a particular resort of the well-to-do. According to Hardiman, it 'frequently displays an assemblage of native beauty, elegance and fashion, which would grace the drawing rooms of a court'. Touring spectacles and exhibitions, such as Maillardet's 'Mechanism' in June 1823, found a temporary home there. For an admission charge of 1s 8d — prohibitive for most people — the curious could marvel at a range of 'optical delusions' and other novelties. One visitor was impressed:

> During its operations the mind is kept continually in a state of the most pleasing anxiety … The principal figures (raised upon furniture of the most exquisite workmanship) on being, in succession, particularly introduced to notice by the motion of the features — and the grace and precision with which most difficult musical airs are executed, and other performances accomplished by them, strikes an adult with astonishment, whilst a juvenile spectator is kept in breathless extasy, the motions being so perfect as to produce a difficulty in believing, at the moment, you are witnessing the actions of real life — and wonder, if possible, is in a high degree excited by the delightful little mechanical animals which go alone through all the movements ascribed to the species they represent.[46]

Other notable attractions at the Assembly Rooms included travelling magician, Monsieur F. Testot — 'the *ne plus ultra* of the cabalistic art' — and astronomer, Mr Rodgers FSA, who flattered the indigenous intellect by by emphasising his

---

* According to de Latocnaye, who visited in 1796: 'There are Assemblies, with very moderate price of entry, nearly every day, sometimes full-dress, sometimes half-dress, sometimes undress, and called as they are one or the other — Assembly, Drum or Promenade. The price of entry varies with the name, but the thing itself is always the same. There is an air of merriment about these gatherings, and the Galway belles frequenting them could certainly teach their French sisters about coquetterie.It is to be expected that such a concourse of pretty women should attract a great number of young men…' (pp. 149-50).

talent of 'elucidating the subject, by which the the most abstruse department of Philosophy is brought down to the comprehension of the meanest capacity'. Possibly the greatest expectations of all were raised by a 'Professor of Mechanism and Metamorphist', Signor Blitz from Moravia, who invited 'admirers of Necromancy' to a performance of thaumaturgics, which would conclude with 'super-human feats in the occult sciences'.[47]

The Kirwan's Lane Theatre continued to provide more orthodox dramatic fare. Amateurs occasionally trod the boards there, as in 1792 when 'several gentlemen of rank' came together in a performance to 'alleviate the heavy loss' anticipated by proprietor, Mr Macartney. Twenty-five years later, the 'young gentlemen' of the town staged Sheridan's *The Rivals* to assist the building of the Catholic parish chapel. One critic was impressed 'to see the parts of females supplied with such elegance and propriety by gentlemen whose extreme youth adds to our wonder and their merit'.[48] In the same year — one of particular distress — the same amateurs performed for 'the benefit of the poor'. The £30 which remained after deducting expenses was handed to a committee of clergymen, and 'distributed to sick and indigent house-keepers'.[49]

Less well documented than performances for their benefit, were those attended by the indigent themselves. And when they did attract critical attention, it was for their nuisance value. One writer was 'aggravated' that

> a company of low players are permitted to occupy an empty store in Middle-street, and from eight o'clock at night till one or two in the morning, the entire neighbourhood is kept in perpetual alarm, and the better to congregate all the pick-pockets, loose women and ragamuffins of the town, those mountebanks send out a drummer and other fellows who keep up the loudest and most discordant noises, and we are really surprised at the uninterrupted continuance of the nuisance … every strolling vagabond may, with impunity, annoy the people of Galway.[50]

By 1808 — though still owned by Macartney — the Kirwan's Lane Theatre was managed by actor/impressario, Mr Clarke, who ran a chain of theatres. Clarke was still at the helm a decade later when James Hardiman declared that a new theatre 'in an open and central location appears necessary'. A few years later still, Clarke brought the most eminent actor of all, Edmund Kean, to Kirwan's Lane. Kean played Galway for six days, beginning on 6 September 1824 during an Irish tour. The theatre's ordinary arrangements were altered considerably — part of the pit was 'laid into boxes' — and to cover the 'very heavy expense', the price of admission were raised to 5s for the boxes and 2s 6d for the pit.[51]

Kean's programme was exhausting, but not untypical: on Monday, he played Richard III and appeared in 'a new Farce', called *The Spectre Bridegroom*; on Tuesday, he was Shylock in *The Merchant of Venice*; On Wednesday, he was Othello, on Thursday, he was Ruben Glenroy in *Town and Country;* on Friday, he was King Lear and, on Saturday, he was Sir Giles Overeach in the popular Jacobean comedy *A New Way to Pay Old Debts*.[52] Kean's performances aroused great enthusiasm, mingled with disappointment that 'Mr Clarke's engagements elsewhere prevented him from indulging the inhabitants of this place still longer'. There was regret also — that Kean had to take appear in 'our very limited, inconvenient and mis-named theatre — but optimism that the success of the Kean season would boost those advocating 'the building of our long-spoken-of theatre'.

Even had Clarke's diary allowed, Kean might have been reluctant to stay, for during his visit, the carriage of this 'gentleman of acknowledged talent, of mild and affable demeanour' was vandalised. Several 'highly respected gentlemen' offered a reward for information leading to the discovery of the 'unknown villain or villains' involved, but these were not apprehended.[53]

Kean's reception reflected well on Galway, commented the *Connaught Journal,* her people just as discerning as their contemporaries in larger centres:

> It has been remarked that they have never been mistaken in their good or bad opinion of the acting of any performer … Macready's performance drew (when his dramatic talents were first appearing) crowded houses in Galway and he is now the second performer of his day. Miss O'Neill, as an actress, was the greatest favourite that ever appeared before the people of Galway … We entreat of the play-going gentry to use their every exertion in forwarding this most desirable object — the erection of the new theatre.[54]

A new theatre would enhance cultural life, but also commercial life:

> The shopkeeper of almost every description would find his shop more fashionably attended, and his coffers more amply stored by those who have the means and inclination of frequenting the theatre, but who are prevented from gratifying their discernment by the inconvenience and awkward contrivance of the present one.[55]

Demands for the 'long-spoken-of theatre' were not satisfied by the conversion of 'a valuable plot in Shop-street' in 1827, nor by Mr Seymour's 'elegant and tasteful' modification of the ballroom at Kilroys' Hotel into a 'handsome little Theatre' in 1833.[56] It was not until 1835 that a new purpose-built theatre opened in Lombard-street, seventy shareholders having subscribed an average of £10 each. Mr Seymour was appointed manager, and he engaged a 'numerous and highly-talented company', which impressed with its first performance, an operatic play, *Rob Roy.*[57] The building itself, too, attracted admiration:

> The exterior of the theatre is extremely beautiful, the boxes are fitted up with peculiar taste and neatness, the panels of which are

ornamented with classic devices, and painted a bright salmon colour, the pit is commodious and capable of holding a great number of persons.[58]

An early favourite of New Theatre audiences was 'the celebrated African, Rocius', who visited Galway several times. On his first visit, one critic was agreeably surprised to find that Rocius's Othello was 'chaste' and 'judicious', that his 'reading of our divine bard [was] in strict keeping with the character'.[59]

Belatedly, the spacious new building democratised theatre-going in Galway. Although still out of reach of the majority, theatre became an affordable luxury for the lower middle-class and even for regularly-employed artisans. This tendency had been remarked-upon in more cosmopolitan places for more than half a century — it was considered responsible for the coarsening of dramatic content[60] — but it would seem that theatre in Galway remained elitist until the mid-1830s. Only the relatively wealthy could have afforded to sit in the Kirwan's Lane pit to see society beauty, Elizabeth Martin in 1783 or, for that matter, to appreciate the 'elegance and propriety' with which female parts were played by 'young gentlemen' in 1817. Tickets for professional productions were cheaper, but the cheapest ticket for Edmund Kean's 1824 performance cost 2s 6d — a day's pay for an artisan. In 1838, by contrast, 'the celebrated high comedian and dramatic ventriloquist', Mr Gallagher, could be seen by adults from the pit of the New Theatre for 1s, and cheaper still from the gallery, while children were admitted at half price. The practice of admitting late-comers, at a reduced tariff, during the interval of double-bill performances maximised box-office receipts and same time enabled the attendance of the not-so-wealthy.[61]

The democratisation of theatre was accompanied by increasing religious disapproval of it — probably the phenomena were connected. Evangelical disapproval, in particular, grew more severe and more widespread during the early and mid-19th century. In Galway, it was said that clergymen 'of both denominations' were opposed to drama in the mid-1820s.[62] This was hardly true of the Catholic clergy, who, a few years earlier, had accepted box-office proceeds for their new church and for poor parishioners. But, clearly, religious opposition was anticipated by the New Theatre's supporters, when they promoted their project as morally preferable to the 'wild mirth of the tavern, or the destructive pursuits of the gaming table.[63]

If Catholics, generally, were not hostile to drama in itself, they were sensitive to its subject matter. 'A Catholic and a Father', who attended *The Warden of Galway* in the New Theatre in 1842 was critical of the acting and the production — the curtain was raised, he wrote, after 'a preluding flourish from a *single violin!*' — but it was the script which gave greatest offence:

> Sir, the awful Sacrament of Confession is here made the subject of dramatic exhibition, and the mockery of a sacred institution ostentatiously paraded, as if to challenge our approbation. The

machinery of the plot appears to turn principally on revelations made in Confession … And not alone is the mockery represented, but the recital of guilt takes place in the presence of a third party, and is further revealed to others, thus proving an ignorance of the Sacrament thus disparaged. What would be said if the liturgy of the Church of England were recited on the stage by an actor in the dress of a clergyman? He would be very properly hooted off by the indignant spectators … But play-writers and actors think that they can take greater liberties with the Clergy and the doctrines of the Catholic Church.[64]

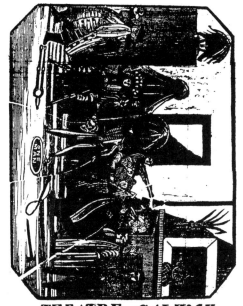

Notice for performance in New Theatre, Lombard Street. Note that woodcut illustration was placed on its side (*Galway Advertiser*, 18 August 1838).

The writer further complained that, having paid for a box, he found himself 'ensconced by the side of a private soldier — a class of persons, who however personally respectable, are not usually found in that part of any well-conducted theatre'. It was not surprising, he went on, that under 'such a system of management', few respectable people patronised the Theatre.

But entertainment was becoming ever less exclusive due to the growing scale of spectacles, and promoters had to appeal to all classes to make productions viable. The popularity of the circus was one example. Batty's Belfast-based Circus Royal presented a number of 'equestrian evenings' in Galway during 1841. The programme included a performance of *Valentine and Orson* and a 'pantomimic representation' of Queen Elizabeth's visit to Kenilworth, incorporating a 'display of the whole troop of male and female equestrians, and their steeds, gorgeously, but most appropriately clad and caparisoned'. The highpoint was a re-enactment of the Battle of Waterloo — 'in all its fearful reality' — beginning with a review of his army by the Duke of Wellington, and continuing with 'a splendid engagement between the English and French and the flight of Napoleon'. A range of admission prices segregated the audience, with tickets ranging from 3*s* 0*d* for front boxes to 6*d* for gallery seats. Children were admitted at half price. Two years after Batty's, Hughes's National Olympic Arena of Arts brought further equestrian displays, and the first Galway appearance of 'the stupendous male elephant of Africa'.[65]

Touring spectacles continued to visit Galway during the famine, but less frequently than formerly. Wombwell's Royal National Menagerie & Zoological School of Instruction exhibited 'lions, tigers and four hyenas' in Eyre Square in October 1846, alongside 'Mrs King, the Lion Queen' and 'The Great Gemian Marmont, or Savage of Ethiopia'. In October 1848, Mr Seymour — who also had theatrical interests elsewhere— brought a variety show to the Theatre, which included, 'Herr Kist and his infant son; Mademoiselle F. Camille, the celebrated dancer; Master Redwell, the young vocalist … and the dramatic drama of *Love in Humble Life*.[66]

In the immediate post-Famine period, the theatre was managed by a 'comic singer', Mr J. Ward. Despite his efforts, attendances were poor and, in 1851, the management was taken over by Mr H. May of London.[67] During this period, variety performances were popular, to the detriment of more traditional theatre. Audiences were beguiled, in particular, by the phenomenon of performers 'blacking-up' as American slave minstrels. For example, in early June 1850, the Galway public had a choice between 'The Female American Serenaders' — featuring 'a lady conductor' and musicians on banjo, bones, and tambourine — and a 'musical and comic treat' from Sandford's Ohio Minstrels.[68] Soon afterwards, another recent American innovation was seen on the Galway stage. During a performance by the gymnast Brothers Hutchinson, the dancer, Madamoiselle Rose, appeared in a pair of bloomers — 'that peculiar style of dress which the ladies on the other side of the Atlantic are said to patronise so liberally'. The *Galway Mercury* was not unduly concerned:

… we saw no ground whatsoever for the absurd clamour which has been raised against Bloomerism in England and elsewhere. Certainly, Mlle Rose did not appear to less advantage than when she wore the dress, and it materially added to her attraction as a *danseuse*. Whether it has found favour in the eyes of our fair friends generally, we are not able at present to determine, but we would seriously recommend its adoption to every lady who loves that *freedom* which the costume is known to indicate.[69]

There was rather different entertainment in the City Tavern in Mary-street. Proprietor, Mr J. Bermingham, announced in April 1853 that, 'in addition to his other vocalist', he had 'engaged the celebrated Bravura and Ballad singer', Mrs E. Williams, 'whose 'Irish and Scotch melodies give great delight'.[70]

Minstrel shows, variety shows, and circuses continued to attract crowds during the remainder of the century.

In the mid-1870s, there was renewed interest in amateur theatricals, but among a different class than heretofore. The 'commercial young gentlemen' — shop assistants — of the town gave performances in Black's Hotel, Eyre Square, in February 1874,[71] and again in March 1876. On the latter occasion, a rhyming prologue expressed the fading economic hopes of Galwegians

> … *Ere twelve months more had passed away*
> *We twine our hopes to see within our bay*
> *Galwegian commerce, with her flag unfurled,*
> *Connecting Europe with the western world —*
> *That world of freedom, where man's honest worth*
> *Is higher prized — more eager sought — than princely birth.*[72]

For the *Galway Express*, the most positive thing to be said about such performances was that that they kept shop assistants away from mischief:

> It is pleasing to see young men devote their leisure hours to their own improvement … even if they should not excel in the histrionic art, as it is certainly the means of keeping them agreeably employed, and estranging them from these vices of which idleness is the concomitant.[73]

The same paper was uncomplimentary too about the debut concert in the same venue in December 1875 of the Galway Choral Society. 'One always wishes to carry with them some after-pleasing recollection of an entertainment', remarked its critic, 'and the absence of it is the most decided proof of the absence of success'.[74] The new Temperance Building in Lombard-street, which was opened by Fr Peter Dooley in the second half of the 1870s, provided a headquarters for enthusiasts of both amateur drama and choral music.[75]

Visiting professional artistes, meanwhile, found a platform in Irvine's New Concert Hall in Victoria Place, which opened in July 1877.[76] By the 1890s, the Racket Court in Middle-street — which had been roofed by public subscription in the 1870s — was Galway's leading theatre and concert hall. It was during a variety show there in 1897 that 'the renowned Cinematographie, the most wonderful discovery of photography and electricity known' was first encountered by Galwegians. The *Galway Observer* gave a description:

> The first scene shown was of the departure of employees from a Manchester factory, followed by a picturesque view of Galway Bay, a regiment of cavalry on parade, a railway station in France, a comic scene in a barber's shop, and another amusing scene in which a gardener was seen watering flowers'.[77]

During the following decade or so, films gradually became part of variety fare in Galway until October 1911, when the proprietors of the Court Theatre began to show films nightly to packed houses. Particularly popular was Sidney Ollcot's adaptation of Boucicault's *Colleen Bawn* — a feature length film, strongly nationalist in tone, which was filmed on location in Kerry during 1911. The success of the new medium soon attracted others, and a 600-seat Galway Cinema Theatre — located off William-street at the rear of Alexander Moon's premises — opened for business on Easter Monday 1912. Later in 1912, the Town Hall, an established venue for dances, variety and boxing matches, began to show films regularly. In August 1915, the Victoria Cinema opened in Victoria Place.[78]

As the leading established venues were transforming themselves into cinemas, the popular taste for live performance did not disappear. Singers and musicians entertained in cinemas for the duration of the silent movie era, but amateur actors and variety artistes also continued to find audiences — often for benefit performances. The Augustinian fathers were particularly active as fundraisers in the early 20th century, especially during the priorship of the dynamic Fr Dennis Travers. An annual Augustinian excursion of this era brought as many as a thousand Galwegians to places including Killarney, Clifden, Cork and Dublin. And under Travers's stewardship, the Augustinian Hall (later An Taibhdhearc) was the venue of countless popular events — pantomimes, concerts, bazaars and religion-tinged entertainments.[79]

Sport and play

On arriving in Galway in 1834, Henry Inglis gazed at boys blithely 'exercising their juvenile propensities'.[80] The detail was left to the reader's imagination, but clearly a game was being played in the street. If Inglis was vague, at least — and unlike many of his contemporaries — he seemed well-disposed to games-playing. But, ironically, it was the critics who were more informative, and their complaints about the 'nuisance' value of the recreational activities of 'urchins' are the principal source of information about them.

If complainants often seemed severe and intolerant, they had their reasons. It may have been, as some historians assert, that such writers — invariably middle-class — were merely reflecting their class's mission of reforming the behaviour of the emerging working class, but there was much about proletarian amusements that caused inconvenience to those not engaged in them. Take, for example, complaints about snowball-throwing — only an occasional diversion in Galway's climate, and one which might be considered harmless. During a cold snap in 1827, one newspaper declared that it had no wish to interfere in 'the amusements of the lower orders' but, nonetheless, it was urging magistrates to act against snowballers, since they had forced shopkeepers to close their shutters.[81] Half a century later, and in similar terms, another editor condemned the same 'abominable habit':

> We do not condemn the frolic of mere urchins, or the sport indulged in by harmless playful young ladies, but when men — not of a very refined order either — band themselves together and mercilessly assail the young and old, men, women and children indiscriminately, we think steps should be taken to suppress such a dangerous nuisance. On last Sunday, it was at a great hazard that people of the town could venture to their respective places of worship, as every available corner was lined with a mixture of ragamuffin and well-to-do vagabond who, with malicious intent, unceasingly hurled snowballs of such firmness as to have seriously endangered the passers-by.[82]

Snowfalls inaugurated something like a period of carnival, during which it was permissible to assail one's elders — and evidently one's betters. And circumstances ensured that there were excesses. Most people lived in overcrowded smoky houses, uncomfortable places during waking hours. What was there for a young man to do, on a Sunday morning in 1873 when no pubs were open, except to keep warm by joining in a snowball fight? But for those who braved 'snowballs of such firmness' on their journey from drawing room to church, the scene would have seemed analagous to the Paris commune.

Snow was only occasionally available, but Galway's young did not depend on it for missiles. Until the 1840s, the single greatest source of complaint was the danger and inconvenience caused by sling-shots. In the Claddagh, according to an early anthropologist, skill with a sling was greatly-prized. Slings were used as weapons by the fishermen in conflicts with other seafarers; it is likely too that slinging at sea-birds occupied idle hours during fishing expeditions. According to the anthropologist, it was 'usual for them to have "slinging-matches"; and when a man was able to strike a shilling as far as it could be seen, he was considered a good shot'. By the 1850s, however, interest in this and other sports was said to be 'in abeyance'.[83] Pre-Famine complaints support this source. Most specifically referred to the Claddagh people in relation to sling-shots, but other communities were also mentioned. In 1826, it was the 'young fry of the Claddagh' who were making it impossible to walk along the quays. They had been amusing themselves by slinging stones across the river into the merchants yards. And a few years later, their fathers were blamed for preventing the unloading of the *Clyde*, when labourers and crew had to abandon the vessel because of the 'showers of stones' descending upon them from across the river. Two gunshots were fired before work could be resumed.[84] Was a 'slinging-match' taking place, or was there a grievance against either the ship-owner or the dock labourers.

With sling-shots as the weapons, mock-battles between youngsters from various parts of town were frequent. In 1830, it was observed that on Sundays and holidays, contests took place between the Rahoon boys and the Claddagh boys, who took up position on either side of the Rahoon road, to the danger of by-passers. This was no passing fad and, at Shantalla, seven years later 'upwards of 100 young men and boys' from two different parts of the town, were interrupted by policemen, having met 'by appointment' to sling stones at one another across the public road. In 1841, there was indignation at the 'large crowds of mischievous fellows which daily gather' in the area outside the Collegiate Church for sling-fights. Broken windows and 'personal injuries' were among the consequences.[85]

Later in the century, catapults replaced slings. The *Galway Express* objected:

> The introduction of these missiles now in common use throughout even the principal streets of the town is a dangerous innovation in the schedule of play toys, and it seems somewhat surprising to the public that not even the slightest notice is taken of them, nor any attempt made to prevent their use. A few days ago a countryman was struck by a stone thrown from one of them and severely cut. With a well-constructed one in the hands of a competent lad, one may be hit at some fifty yards and considerably hurt, but before you can lay hold of him, he has turned some corner or lane...[86]

A few years later, the same 'dangerous weapons' were still in the 'hands of street arabs who make a habit of firing at birds'. At the Square, meanwhile, it was observed that 'a similar practice was being carried on', but that the offenders belonged 'to that class whose parents ought to be made responsible'.[87]

If complaints are a source of information about the amusements of the people, reports of accidents are also informative. From this source, it would seem that the harbour, with its bustling ambiance, was a favourite play-ground of poor children. One who played there during 1871 was eleven-year-old Thomas Walsh of Middle-street. During August, Thomas spent a few days in the County Infirmary, where three of his fingers, which had been caught between a boat and the dock wall, were amputated. Hardly was he discharged than he was back again, this time after a serious accident. While shunting, with other boys, a wagon used in transferring cargo, he fell off. A wheel ran over his leg, 'smashing it to atoms'. Surgeon Browne doubted that he would survive.[88]

Evidently, midde-class children also played in the streets for, in 1837, the 'afflicted mother' of James Johnston Kearney had erected to her late eleven-year-old son, in the Collegiate Church, a commemorative plaque which concluded, poignantly: 'His death was occasioned by his top having fallen from him and, stooping to regain it, a car rolled on him in the street'.*

In Chapter Eleven are mentioned several amusements that were frowned upon because they took place on the Sabbath. In this context, Hardiman mentioned that bull-baiting no longer took place, and that cock-fighting was 'deservedly neglected'. Badger-baiting still took place in the 1820s, however, to the disgust of 'the respectable portion of the population', which frequented the Square on Sunday afternoons. The activity was funded by a levy of 'pence and half-pence from every person who was so cruelly curious as to witness the sport'.[89]

Blood-sports were condemned because of their cruelty, because they took place on Sundays, but also because they were an occasion of gambling. Cad† — a Sunday afternoon game of 'old-standing' which also took place in the Square — was likewise the subject of betting.[90] And gambling persisted in the vicinity of the Square, if the placing of a notice cautioning 'Toss' players at Higgins's Lane in the early 1870s is an indication. But their pastime was not the only offence given by the men who congregated there. Their habit of withdrawing to the lane to urinate — causing perpetual 'smells of pollution' — was considered by the *Galway Express* to be 'too vulgar even to name'.[91]

The fastidious also objected to swimming, a rare occasion of public nudity. In the 'rivers running through our streets … boys and even grown persons [were] committing indecencies … often in the immediate vicinity of houses, in which families of the first respectability reside'.[92] At Salthill, where the offenders were 'ignorant country fellows from various quarters', the same was happening, with calamitous results: 'In consequence of this most offensive practice, all visitors are driven from the delightful and beautiful promenade'.[93]

Concern about ball-playing was not new — the corporation had tried to ban it in 1527** — but the reasons for concern had changed. Civic leaders of the

---

* According to the *Galway Advertiser* (27 February 1837), this 'fine interesting child was the son of James Kearney Esq., Comptroller of Customs at the port'. The accident occurred while James 'was amusing himself with his top near his father's house in Back St'. Then, 'when the object of his amusement fell from him, and in his endeavour to take it up, a cart laden with timber… rolled over him… He lingered in excruciating pain till Wednesday morning last, when death put a period to his sufferings.' The tribute finished on an implausible note: 'In him the poor have lost a friend, for although he was young in years, he was old in charitableness…'

† Cad (caid in Irish) was the name given to a folk football game, but the context indicates that this is not what was meant here. Was it the 'Cad' game which was played in Annaghdown parish in the early 20th century, and which also involved betting? For that game, a short stick was raised between two stones, and hit by a player with a long stick. The winner was the player who propelled the short stick the farthest, the hitter being rendered 'out' by an opponent who caught the short stick in mid-air. (Information from Willie Cunningham, b.1917, formerly of Bun a' Tobar).

** The by-law included the following: 'what so ever man is found of what degree or condicion so ever he be of, plainge at choyttes or stonis, but only to shoot in long bowes, short crossboues and hurlige of dartes or speres, to lesse at every tyme so found in doing the same viiid., and also at no tyme to use ne occupye the horlinge of the littill balle with hockie sticks or staves, nor use no hande ball to play without the walles, but onely the great foote balle, on payn of the paynis above lymitted (M. D. O'Sullivan, *Old Galway*, pp. 441-42).

16th century had hoped to persuade young men to spend their spare time at archery; three centuries later, it was sabbath-breaking and the danger to by-passers which raised hackles. In 1791, Coquebert de Montbret noted that ball games were played against the town walls, just as they had been 260 years earlier. The demolition of the walls in the years after his visit meant that alternative arenas had to be found. Indeed, the 'nuisance' value of ball-playing as far as many newspapers writers were concerned, was the extent to which it interfered with walking, or promenading, a recreation of the genteel. In the late 18th century, the quay was the popular promenade but, by 1820, this had given way to the Square. By the 1830s, the Claddagh Quay had emerged 'as the only wholesome walk about Galway'.[94] Precisely the same open areas were the playgrounds of 'urchins' and 'vagabonds'.

From descriptions of ball-playing, it would seem that handball remained popular into the post-Famine period. In 1835, an injury to a boy who 'nearly had his eye knocked out' directed the attention of the police to the 'dangerous nuisance of ball-playing' on the road leading to the dock and 'other parts of the town'. A few years later, it was reported that there were boys playing ball 'at every high wall', and that they would not even stop 'to let the ladies pass'. Idle boys and even men' were criticised for ball-playing in the streets in 1854, while, in 1858, Peter Kelly, 'son of a poor widow woman', was injured while climbing a forty-foot wall to retrieve a ball lost while he and companions were playing against the wall of a roofless house in Middle-street.[95]

In the 1860s, there was a change in perceptions of ball-games — they still featured as 'nuisance' when played by 'urchins', but they began to be reported as sport when played by the 'respectable'. An account of a two-day match between Galway Cricket Club and a Clare XI in July 1860, was the first of many such reports during that decade. But something of the earlier attitude lingered. When Jesuit College boys, under their professors' supervision, began to use Eyre Square for cricket practice, there were objections on grounds of 'imminent danger to small children walking about under the charge of their nurses'.

Since the early 1840s, the Square had been enclosed, and those who wished to avail of it had to pay for a key, first getting the permission of the urban authority to use it for whatever purpose. 'Is any person who may purchase a key', wondered 'Argus' in a letter to the *Galway Express,* 'entitled to bring into the Square as many persons as he may think proper … [and] cut up the green?' It is possible that it was dislike of Jesuits which motivated those who chose to air their complaints in the *Express,* but a decade later, the propriety of playing cricket in the Square was raised again. This time, the boot was on the other foot, and it was the evangelical movement's cricket team which was seeking permission to use the Square. After a long discussion among Town Commissioners, it was decided to allow the request. However, it would seem that representatives divided along confessional lines, if a remark that 'the Scotch element has prevailed' is any indication. The popularity of cricket was not long confined to the middle-class, and 'urchins', according to one report, had adopted the game by the early 1870s. However, since they did not have the key to Eyre Square, their field of play was the churchyard of St Nicholas. Needless to say, their rendezvous attracted criticism.[96]

By 1887, 'urchins' had embraced hurling, which they played in Market-street and Lombard-street. But again it was the 'narrow escapes' of by-passers, rather than the skill of players which captured attention.[97] These 'urchins' were precocious in anticipating the popularity of hurling in the town. The game was played in the adjacent countryside, and there were GAA hurling clubs in Castlegar and in Oranmore before any were established in the town. Indeed, in February 1888, there was a complaint at a county GAA meeting that there was no 'Galway city' club affiliated, something which was attributed to the inactivity of local National League branches. Later in the year, several hurling clubs were functioning: St Nicholas's, the Temperance Club, St Patrick's, and Galway East. In November, a 'great hurling match' was reported between 'the Lemonade men' of the Temperance Club and St Patrick's. Such occasions were few during the 1890s, for organised hurling was a casualty of the decade's political divisions in the county, and a 'revival' did not begin until 1900. That the stronghold of the revived game was in the working class is indicated by the . addresses of those featuring in a 1905 Galway Town team photograph, and also by the four occupations given: 'foreman in Guinness's', 'worked in Guinness's yard'; 'worked in the Chemicals'; 'plasterer'.[98]

Queen's College students gave an impetus to sport among the middle-class, and also stimulated interest among the working class. Their annual sports attracted non-students as spectators, as this account from 1864 makes clear:

> An effort to obtain the beautiful grounds of Thos E. Blake of Menlo Castle failed, as the land was being prepared for meadow; but the Rev. Mr Hollowel very kindly agreed to give the students the use of a field at the back of Erasmus Smith's College … The gathering of sight-seers was very large, but we are sorry to say that roughs who thronged the place rendered portions of the proceedings anything but agreeable. Whenever the weight-throwing, pole-jumping, or vaulting began, a lot of fellows crowded round and all efforts to dislodge them failed. Of this portion of the sport (the weight-throwing &c.) few ladies saw anything, and as it occupied a good deal of time, many were quite wearied before the more exciting part of the programme, the racing, was resumed … The mile race was looked upon as the great contest of the day. Only two started, Messrs King and Mullins …[99]

The report is interesting for its cursory treatment of field events, which were evidently of interest to the 'roughs' among the spectators. The more refined track events, by contrast, which were eagerly anticipated by 'ladies', were more fully described. Some years later, Menlo was secured by the students' sports committee, when the 'lower classes' again joined them in a holiday. For the students, the holiday was an extended one and, over the previous weeks, 'many a lecture was sacrificed to … the half-mile, or the hurdle race'.[100] During the same period, Menlo was the venue for military sports*, where competitors were private soldiers, but spectators included 'the *elite* of the vicinity'.[101]

The university itself was the venue in 1865 for 'a match of football' which, although far from being the first played in Galway, was among the first to be dignified with a newspaper report. The teams, of twenty each, were drawn from the student body and from the recently established Corrib Rowing Club:

> The match began about one o'clock, and about half past two, the ball was after a hard struggle put into the goal by the College Club. This they succeeded in doing three times, and were accordingly declared winners. Much interest was taken in the match which we are glad to say terminated without any accidents.[102]

The report suggests that the match was played to rules resembling those of soccer. But reports of matches between university and Grammar School teams during the 1870s indicate that rugby became established soon after, being played as an alternative to cricket during winter.[103] For this, it is likely that Richard Biggs, an adherent of the vogue ideology of athleticism in education, was responsible. Biggs, who revitalised the Grammar School itself when he became headmaster in the mid-1870s, was a promoter of rugby, and became the first president of the Connacht branch of the Irish Rugby Football Union in 1885. Biggs's influence was also evident in the 'Old Galwegians' club, formed by Dublin-based Grammar School graduates, which took on Queen's College and Grammar School teams in 1883, and which played in Connaught Cup competitions after their inauguration in 1896. With an extremely narrow social base, however, rugby struggled to sink roots in Connacht and there were only five west of Ireland clubs in 1904: Galway Grammar, Old Galwegians, Queen's College Galway, Galway Town and St Ignatius' College, Galway.[104]

Races and regattas
Horse-racing was a securely-established sport in the county by the early 18th century, and the Galway gentry were prominent among those who established the Irish Turf Club late in that century.[105]

For several reasons — including the expense of breeding ever-faster horses — racing was an elite pursuit, but one which attracted the interest of other classes. The interest was not always appreciated, and occasional measures discouraged it. On the grounds that horse races encouraged 'idleness and

---

* The game of golf was popular among members of the military elite, and they were among those who established the Galway Golf Club in 1895. Army officers were also involved in the 'revival'of the Galway Hockey Club in 1911 (Michael McSweeney, *Galway Golf Club,* 1895-1995, pp. 11-12).

debauchery among the farmers, artificers and day labourers', an 1739 act of the Irish parliament made it illegal to wager less than £20 on a horse, or to attend a race for which the prize-money was less than £20. The measure did not succeed in its objective; it proved impossible to prevent the poor wagering their pennies, and 'idleness, drunkenness and riot' continued to be noticeable at race meetings. Legislation of 1791, directed at excluding the Dublin working class, prohibited the holding of race meetings within nine miles of Dublin Castle.[106]

No laws governed the matter in Galway, although it is possible that the desire to exclude the the urban populace was a consideration in having Galway race meetings held as far from the town as Six-mile-bush.* Only the doughtiest gamblers and idlers would have embarked upon the twenty-statute-mile return journey, but shorter distances were not prohibitive. In 1828, a German nobleman attended the race meeting at the Kiltulla course — four statute miles from Galway. Here he witnessed ferocious fighting involving hundreds of people, which did not cease with the end of the meeting, but continued on the journey home. According to his account, 'scores of drunkards' accompanied Pückler-Muskau's carriage on its journey back to Galway, fighting all the way.[107]

The Galway Races of 1833 were held over three days at Kiltulla, beginning on the Monday after the Assizes, thereby detaining grand jurors and their retinues for an additional week. It was a determinedly local affair with, for example, participation in the Galway Challenge Cup restricted to horses which were 'the property of residents of the county of the town', and entries in the Sweepstakes race confined to 'Hunters that have been fairly and regularly hunted last season with Mr St George's, Mr Daly's, Mr Blake's, Mr Nugent's, Mr Browne's, or the Eyrecourt hounds'. Afterwards, the social acquaintances of the same gentlemen entertained one another at exclusive balls in the town's hotel.[108] The 1834 meeting was held in August. Attendances on the first two days were disappointing, but the appearance of the sun transformed the picture:

> Every vehicle of high and low degree was wheeled off to the course and ... a most fashionable assembly was present — splendid equipages, pretty faces, gay hearts, elegant dresses. Full tents, empty bottles, pipers, fiddlers, and every other accompaniment of an Irish merry-making were present.[109]

Such scenes were infrequent, however and it was a cause of irritation that while 'Tuam proclaims its splendid plates' and that 'such comparatively small towns as ... Ballinasloe, Ballinrobe or Roscommon' could boast annual race meetings, they remained an occasional novelty in the western capital.[110] During the 1850s

---

* The relative merits of the available courses for Galway races were discussed as follows in the *Connaught Journal,* 9 August 1824: 'Two places are named as eligible for the race-course: Killeen and the Six-mile-bush. Killeen, on a confined scale, is an excellent course, but the one at the Six-mile-bush can admit of being enlarged to any extent necessary. It also possesses another desirable advantage: it commands a perfect view of the entire course. Killeen, however, is more contiguous to Galway, being distant only 3 miles, whilst the other course is 6 miles.

and 1860s, Kiltulla was used occasionally, but it was not until the course at nearby Ballybrit was settled upon in 1869 that the Galway Races became an annual event. The success of the new course was due to the MP for the town, Viscount St Lawrence — he became Earl of Howth in 1874 — who employed the leading racecourse designer of the period to make Ballybrit the finest course in the west and, just as importantly, secured the backing of the Midland Great Western Railway Co. — an 'unprecedented initiative', according to one writer — guaranteeing the success of the meeting. The railway company endowed a race, transported horses free, and laid on special trains to bring the crowds for which Ballybrit became renowned. The status of the meeting was secured within five years of its establishment, when it was authorised to award a royal plate — one of only seventeen in the country.[111]

Popular and secure they might have been, but the Races were also boisterous. Two hundred extra police were sent to the town in anticipation of trouble at the 1871 meeting and similar precautions were taken in 1872 and 1873. In 1882, the authorities considered banning the meeting when, due to the disturbed condition of the country they were unable to accede to the usual request for police reinforcements. However, because suspension might lead to the permanent loss of the prestigious royal plate, it was decided that the meeting should proceed. A detachment of 175 infantry was brought in to back up the police, and beer tents were obliged to close earlier than usual.

An illustrator's impression of the crowd heading for the Galway races at Ballybrit, 1879. From the *Illustrated Sporting and Dramatic News* (courtesy of Tom Kenny).

Precautions notwithstanding, the anticipated riot broke out when an arrested 'violent character' was rescued, and the police were assailed with a barrage of slates and bottles, necessitating the reading of the riot act.[112]

The evidence indicates that Galway race meetings were tumultuous and raucous throughout the 19th century. But, as with Menlo, commentators in the local press were silent on the matter, tending to welcome race meetings as unequivocally beneficial, as harmless outlets for the 'light, gay and national propensities'[113] of the people. Even the *Galway Express* which denounced every other occasion of proletarian merriment or delinquency, approached the inaugural 1869 meeting in Ballybrit in a spirit of bemused tolerance:

> Scarcely had we arrived at the entrance to the racecourse when the first salute we had from an old decrepid man was, 'commence well, and let ye give something for the poor of God, your honours'; and an old burly mendicant — minus both legs — hopped along, and exhibited his bodily defects with an appeal to humanity, while an old woman, blind and grey, roared out something for the 'poor orphan' … 'Trick-o'-the-loop' and all other trick fraternities were well represented; and if the fact of several gentlemen being eased of their time-pieces is any criterion of the presence of the light-fingered geniuses, truly they showed a fair share of their dexterity … Molly and Paddy were dancing away to the sounds of the bagpipes, while another chanted away 'Patrick's Day in the Morning' … we must confess the Irish are an original race, even in their short-comings and peculiarities.[114]

No doubt, the Races' contribution to the local economy, together with their patronage by the gentry, affected the attitude of the *Express,* allowing it to treat gambling and drinking at this particular festival as mere foibles, and causing it to avert its eyes whenever rioting threatened. The newspaper, however, did not conceal its evangelical opposition to blood-sports, and it conveyed its disapproval of an 1873 Race Week pigeon-shooting match — 'the first that has taken place in this part of the province, we trust it will be the last'.[115]

But the greatest threat to the Races lay, not in disorder, but in the overcharging of visitors. In 1870, horse owners threatened to withdraw from future meetings if the problem was not addressed. One editorial writer allowed that 'exceptional times, according to the laws of cause and effect, necessarily have exceptional prices' but argued that 'the spirit of morbid selfishness which on this, the last occasion, pervaded the entire mass of the lodging community' was contrary to the best interests of the town. The temptation to extract the maximum return from profligate race-goers during the busiest week of the year was not confined to providers of accommodation — jarveys succumbed too. But people kept coming back, well-warned that they would be fleeced. In 1912, Robert Lynd recorded that even the Salthill Tramway Co. — which carried passengers in the opposite direction to Ballybrit — raised its fares, displaying a notice which argued disingenuously: 'In order to prevent overcrowding in these trams, which is contrary to law, during the Galway Races there will be no fare which is less than 3d. By Order.[116]

Horse-racing was no more ancient an endeavour than boat-racing. But, as elite recreations, it was not until the second half of the 18th century that sailing and rowing became popular. As sports, the two had different origins. Recreational sailing emerged as a pursuit of aristocrats associated with the Royal Navy. Competitive rowing, by contrast, originated among watermen on the Thames and the Tyne, attracting crowds of spectators and gamblers. Having attracted the sponsorship of the well-to-do, some watermen became professional sportsmen; the amateur rowing clubs of 'gentlemen', although inspired by the watermen's spectacle, excluded professional and vocational oarsmen.[117]

The earliest Galway Bay Regatta, which included both sailing and rowing commenced on 15 August 1833. Lord Wallscourt, who had property on the southern side of the bay, was commodore of the event, which attracted an 'almost incredible' number of spectators, who 'lined the shore along Forthill, Renmore and Fairhill'. A more exclusive set was placed aboard a number of barges in the bay, viewing points that also became 'crowded to excess'. The sport over three days was varied: there were rowing competitions for gentlemen; sailing races for gentlemen — the *Connaught Journal* was unsure whether it was 'yatches' or 'yacths' that were employed; and rowing competitions between teams of coastguards. Significantly, there were also races for 'first class fishermen's hookers,' something which was attributable either to the democratic sympathies of Lord Wallscourt or to his desire to bring about improvements in local fishing practices.[118] The various social classes may have enjoyed the same spectacle, and been featured on the same racing programme, but there was strict segregation, as was shown by a minor controversy several years later, when a 'gentleman' oarsman sought the disqualification of a competitor whose team had included 'two common oarsmen'. Whether in response to such wrangling, or due to declining interest among the gentry, the 1839 regatta gave top billing to races featuring fishermen. Significant prizes were offered, sponsored evidently by Lord Wallscourt: £5 for first in the large sailing boat class; £1 for first in the four-oared herring boat class.[119]

The popularity of the early Galway Bay regattas prompted another group of 'gentleman' to organise the first 'Lake Corrib Regatta' in 1838. Although the distance from town prevented it becoming a spectacle on the scale of the bay event, there was popular involvement, in the shape of the Corrib turf boats. But of greater interest was a 'well-contested … match for gigs, pulled by women'. The good conduct of the spectators, on this occasion was attributed to 'the wholesome terror they have of the firmness and decision' of local magistrates.[120]

Regattas were held intermittently in the post-Famine decades. An event held in the bay in 1857 was attended by the Lord Lieutenant. In 1863, a 'Galway and Claddagh Regatta' was dominated by fishermen's races, while in 1868 there were hopes that a yacht race would be added to the programme of 'The Third Annual Galway Harbour Regatta'.[121] During the 1880s, when its organisation had become a function of the Royal Galway Yacht Club — established in 1882 — the Regatta continued to cater for the hookers and rowing boats of fishermen.[122]

For their part, Corrib regattas were resumed in the early 1850s. As has been shown, the Blakes of Menlo Castle supported these events and, indeed, sponsored rowing races during the annual May festivities. But it took the formation of the Corrib Rowing Club in 1864 to consolidate the sport. In 1868, shop assistants attempted to form a less exclusive club, but it was not until 1875 that the Commercial Rowing Club was successfully established. There followed a period of intense competition between the two clubs. Evidently, the social background of its membership conferred advantages on the Corrib club, and an 1880 victory by one of its crews in a race for four-oared outriggers was explained thus: 'they had a new boat with sliding seats whilst the Commercial had a very old boat, fixed seats, and weighed 50lbs more'.[123] Other rowing clubs followed, notably the St Patrick's Club, which was founded by Fr Peter Dooley among members of his Temperance Society in 1880, and the Galway Rowing Club which originated in 1908 as an off-shoot of the Ancient Order of Hibernians. This served to further broaden the social base of rowing in the town and vicinity. Arguably, the emergence as one of Ireland's leading clubs during the 1920s of the Menlo Emmetts Rowing Club — composed of the sons of former Blake tenants — indicated that this process was complete.[124]

NOTES

1. *Connaught Journal,* 20 September 1830.
2. ibid., 26 November 1827.
3. Robert Malcolmson, 'Popular recreations under attack, in Waites, Bennett, & Martin, *Popular Culture: Past and Present,* p. 20.
4. Fergus D'Arcy, 'The Decline and Fall of Donnybrook Fair' in *Saothar* 13, 1988, pp. 7-9; Séamus Ó Maitiú, *The Humours of Donnybrook,* pp. 36-37.
5. M.D. O'Sullivan, 'The Use of Leisure in Old Galway', *JGAHS,* vol.xviii, 1939, pp. 99-120.
6. Colm Kerrigan, 'Temperance & politics in pre-Famine Galway', *JGAHS* 43, 1991, pp. 82-83.
7. Galway Augustinian records, GA 2/2, 'The rules and constitution of the Galway Teetotal Society, 1836-39; The Rules and Constitution of the Galway Christian Temperance Society, 1837.
8. ibid.; Elizabeth Malcolm, *'Ireland Sober, Ireland Free': Drink and Temperance in Nineteenth Century Ireland,* pp. 147-50; Colm Kerrigan, *Father Mathew and the Irish Temperance Movement, 1838-1849,* pp. 132-52.
9. *Galway Advertiser,* 30 November 1839.
10. Kerrigan, 'Galway', pp. 83-84.
11. *Galway Advertiser,* 30 November 1839, 11 January 1840, 40, 15 February 1840; Kerrigan, 'Galway' p. 86.
12. *Galway Express,* 3 May 1879.
13. Hardiman, *Galway,* p. 295.
14. *Connaught Journal,* 17 March 1836, *Galway Patriot,* 21 March 1838, *Connaught Journal,* 19 March 1840.
15. *Galway Express,* 19 March 1864, 20 March 1869.
16. ibid., 17 March 1877, 20 March 1880.
17. ibid, 21 March 1885.
18. Peter Rabbitte, 'How the national feast day came into being in Galway', *City Tribune,* 14 March 2003.
19. Hardiman, *Galway,* p. 295.

20. *Connaught Journal,* 25 June 1823.
21. *Connaught Journal, 16,* 25, 30 June, 10 July 1823; State of the Country Papers, 1823, 2501/30.
22. ibid., 25 June 1823.
23. Kerrigan, 'Galway', p. 86.
24. *Connaught Journal,* 25 June 1840.
25. *Galway Express,* 27 May 1865; Callois cited by Peter Burke in *Popular Culture in Early Modern Europe,* p. 179.
26. *Galway Express,* 1 July 1876, 2 July 1881. For another masonic dinner, see *Connaught Journal,* 30 June 1836.
27. Tomás de Bhaldraithe, *Seanchas Thomáis Laighléis,* pp. 138-41.
28. ibid., p. 139; Ó Maitiú, *Donnybrook,* pp. 21-23.
29. *Connaught Journal,* 3 May 1830.
30. ibid.
31. *Galway Patriot,* 29 April 1837; *Galway Vindicator,* 15 May 1844.
32. *Galway Vindicator, 4,* 15 May 1844.
33. ibid., 28 April 1847.
34. *Galway Mercury,* 11 May 1850, 10 May 1851; *Galway Packet,* 27 April, 4, 11 May 1853.
35. D'Arcy, 'Donnybrook', pp.15-19; Ó Maitiú, *Donnybrook,* pp. 34-46.
36. *Galway Mercury,* 5 May 1855, 2 May 1857; *Galway Express,* 19 May 1860.
37. Cited in *Galway Express,* 12 May 1860.
38. National Library of Ireland, McCall Collection, vol. xii, p. 101
39. Semple, *Reflections,* p. 101; *Galway Express,* 8 September 1885, 10 December 1886, 23 April, 25 June 1887.
40. de Bhaldraithe, *Laighléis,* p. 140.
41. *Connacht Tribune,* 27 July 1926.
42. W. Clark, *The Irish Stage in the County Towns, 1720-1800,* pp. 3, 9; S. Connolly, '"Ag déanamh commanding": Elite responses to Popular Culture' in Donnelly, ed., *Irish Popular Culture, 1650-1850,* pp. 11-12.
43. ibid., pp. 11-14; Christopher Townley, 'Galway's Early Association with the Theatre' in *The Galway Reader,* iv, 1953, pp. 62-70; Richard J. Kelly, 'The old Galway theatres,' in *JRSAI,* xliv, 1914, pp. 358-364.
44. *Connaught Journal,* 23 April, 2 July 1892.
45. *Connaught Journal,* 23 April 1792.
46. ibid., 9 June 1823.
47. ibid., 13 October, 24 November 1825, 21 May 1832.
48. ibid., 17 April 1817.
49. ibid., 13, 24 February 1817.
50. *Galway Advertiser,* 2 March 1839.
51. *Connaught Journal,* 30 August 1824.
52. ibid.
53. ibid., 13 September 1824.
54. ibid.
55. ibid.
56. ibid., 18, 25 June 1827, 10 January 1833.
57. ibid., 16, 23 April, 25 June, 27 August 1835.
58. ibid., 27 August 1835.
59. ibid., 1 October 1835, 21 April 1836, *Galway Advertiser,* 10 August 1839.
60. Peter Kavanagh, *The Irish Theatre,* p. 395-98.
61. *Galway Advertiser,* 18 August 1835, 5 September 1840.
62. John Gray, 'Popular entertainment' in *Belfast: the Making of the City,* pp. 99-110; *Connaught Journal,* 13 September 1824.
63. *Connaught Journal,* 16 April 1835,
64. *Galway Vindicator,* 13 August 1842. The *Warden of Galway* dealt with the events that led to the legendary execution by Mayor Lynch of his only son.
65. ibid., 11, 14 August 1841, 28 October 1843.
66. ibid., 17 October 1846; *Galway Mercury,* 7, 21, 28 October 1848.
67. *Galway Mercury,* 5 January 1850, 16 August 1851.
68. ibid., 1 June 1850.

69. ibid., 22 November 1851.
70. *Galway Packet,* 2 April 1853.
71. *Galway Vindicator,* 28 January 1874.
72. *Galway Express,* 4 March 1876.
73. ibid.
74. ibid., 4 December 1875.
75. ibid., 28 October 1882, 8 January 1887. The Temperance Building opened 'five or six years ago' according to the *Galway Express* in October 1882.
76. ibid., 28 July, 4 August 1877.
77. *Galway Observer,* 24 April 1897.
78. Alan Brouder, 'The History of Cinema-going in Galway' in *Film West,* July 1995, pp. 20-22: Liam O'Leary, *Cinema Ireland, 1896-1950,* Dublin 1990, p. 12; Rockett, Gibbons, & Hill, *Cinema in Ireland,* New York, 1988, pp. 10, 31, 34.
79. Galway Augustinian Records, GA 2/5, Scrapbook, 1905-c.1918.
80. Henry Inglis, A *Journey Throughout Ireland during the Spring, Summer, and Autumn of 1834,* p. 213.
81. *Connaught Journal,* 4 January 1827.
82. *Galway Express,* 8 February 1873.
83. J. McE, 'Ethnological Sketches, No.1: The Fishermen of the Claddagh, at Galway', *Ulster Journal of Archaeology* 2, 1854, p. 163-64.
84. *Connaught Journal,* 28 December 1826; 6 February 1832
85. ibid., 22 March 1830; *Galway Patriot* 29 April 1837; *Galway Vindicator,* 30 October 1841.
86. *Galway Express,* 15 January 1876.
87. ibid., 17 January 1885.
88. ibid., 16 September 1871.
89. *Connaught Journal,* 9 February 1826.
90. ibid., 1 December 1823.
91. National Archives, CSORP 1871/10500, 29 May 1871; *Galway Express,* 20 May 1871.
92. *Galway Patriot,* 7 June 1837.
93. *Galway Vindicator,* 24 July 1841.
94. S. Ní Chinnéide, 'Coquebert de Montbret's Impressions of Galway City and County in the Year 1791, *JGAHS* 25, nos i & ii, 1952', p. 6; Hardiman, *Galway,* p. 316; *Galway Patriot,* 8 March 1837.
95. *Connaught Journal,* 4 June 1835; *Galway Advertiser,* 4 May 1839; *Galway Mercury,* 15 April 1854; *Galway Express,* 16 January 1858.
96. *Galway Express,* 13 October 1860, 22 April, 8 July 1871.
97. ibid., 12 November 1887.
98. Padraic Ó Laoi, *The Annals of the G.A.A. in Galway, 1884-1901,* Galway 1984, pp. 56-57, 72-75; Padraic Ó Laoi, *History of Castlegar Parish,* pp. 158-60; T. K[enny], 'Old Galway' in *Galway Advertiser,* 23 August 1984.
99. *Galway Express,* 23 April 1864.
100. ibid., 2 April 1870.
101. ibid., 29 September 1866.
102. *Galway Express,* 9 December 1865.
103. ibid.
104. ibid., 2 December 1876, 29 November 1879, 24 March 1883; Ralph O'Gorman, *Rugby in Connacht,* pp.11-13, 29-30; J. A. Mangan, *Athleticism in the Victorian and Edwardian Public School,* pp. 13-28.
105. Fergus D'Arcy, *Horses, Lords & Racing Men: the Turf Club, 1790-1990,* The Curragh c.1990, pp. 9-19; John Welcome, *Irish Horse-racing: an Illustrated History,* London 1982, pp.1-20.
106. D'Arcy's *Horses,* pp. 20-21.
107. Hermann Rasche, 'German Travellers in the West, 1828-58' in *JGAHS* 47, 1995, p. 90.
108. *Connaught Journal,* 10 June 1833.
109. ibid, 14 August 1838.
110. *Galway Vindicator,* 24 July 1841; *Galway Mercury,* 6 September 1851; *Galway Packet,* 30 April 1853.
111. D'Arcy, *Horses,* pp. 188-90.
112. National Archives, CSORP, 1873/10871, 1882/33264.
113. *Galway Mercury,* 12 August 1854.
114. *Galway Express,* 21 August 1869.
115. ibid., 9 August 1873.

116. ibid., 13 August 1870; Robert Lynd, *Galway of the Races: Selected essays*, pp. 58-87.

117. Richard Holt, *Sport & the British*, pp. 22-23, 108-09; Derek Birley, *Sport and the Making of Britain*, pp. 137-38.

118. *Connaught Journal,* 11 July, 19 August 1833. It is likely that the 1833 Regatta was prompted by an 1831 contest in the bay between the Northern and Western Yacht Clubs (ibid., 30 May 1831).

119. *Galway Advertiser,* 10 September 1838, 31 August 1839.

120. ibid., 1 September 1838.

121. *Galway Mercury,* 20 June 1857; *Galway Express,* 4 July 1863, 20 June 1868.

122. Semple, *Reflections,* p. 81.

123. *Galway Packet,* 10 August 1853; *Galway Mercury,* 9 September 1854; *Galway Express,* 25 June 1864, 22 May 1875; Semple's *Reflections,* p.81.

124. T. P. Boland, *Thomas Carr: Archbishop of Melbourne,* Melbourne, pp. 69-70; Semple, *Reflections,* pp. 75-85.

CHAPTER 13

'...to preserve the growing generation from the horrid prevailing vices'

LEARNING AND LITERACY

A gifted youth in his younger days,
He soon surpassed his teachers
And by Pius IX, he was pronounced
To be the prince of preachers...

With heavenly fire, his doctrine sound,
To us he did convey;
In thunderous voice he would impart
The terrors of the day...

From 'Elegaic Lines to the Memory of the
Very Rev. Fr Burke', 1883 (NLI, McCall Ballad Collection)

In 1771, Malachy Haneen was incarcerated in Galway gaol for attempting to rescue one Nicholas Haneen. The child was being conveyed to Dublin by the Incorporated Society of Charter Schools, in line with its policy of transferring pupils considered subject to Catholic influence to faraway schools. A Catholic, Nicholas was enrolled in the Galway Charter School, and it is clear that his move to Dublin was for religious rather than for educational reasons.[1]

A decade after the custody battle between Nicholas's family and his educators, Ireland's educational climate changed. Laws which prohibited Catholic education, and which caused some Catholic parents to send their children to Charter Schools, were eased in 1782. For a time, there was apparent harmony. But it did not last, and the Haneen case remained paradigmatic of educational circumstances. Education — regarded as being in the religious sphere of interest — was a source of continuing conflict, as Protestant and Catholic authorities fought for control of schools and of children, employing respectively the resources of the state and the mobilised community in their struggle. Suspicion was the instinctive response to every reform, as denominations and the state competed for control of the emerging system.[2]

Unlike most of their successors, the 1782 measures were welcomed by the Catholic hierarchy. But the penal restrictions which they lifted had not been rigorously enforced, and many Catholics had been educated in 'hedge schools' or classical schools. Others had attended Protestant institutions such as the Erasmus Smith School, established in 1666, and the Galway Charter School, which operated from 1755 to 1791.[3]

Most of Galway's 18th century Catholic-run schools left little trace. Total school attendance, however, may be estimated from the 1780s. Data on literacy levels, such as those based on the 1841 census returns, act as a guide to educational participation. Arguably, the proportion of an age group which declared itself 'able to read' or 'able to read and write', roughly corresponded with the proportion of that age group which had attended school.[4] Accordingly, variations in the responses of different decennial cohorts measure changes in educational participation during the half-century or so before their collection. And although the correspondence between literacy levels and earlier educational participation is not absolute, it is possible to trace the fortunes of elementary education in Galway from the 1780s.

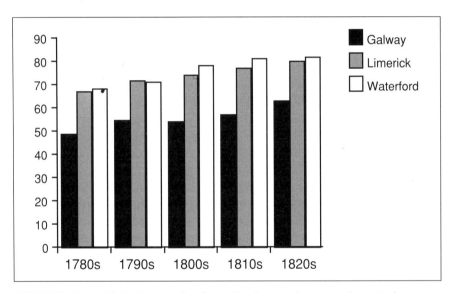

FIGURE 13.1: Male literacy for five school-age cohorts in three Irish towns, 1780s–1820s.
Source: 1841 Census. Note that data combines 'read & write' & 'read only' categories.

Of those surviving in the town of Galway in 1841 who reached the age of 5 during the 1780s, 49% of males declared themselves literate, and 25% of females. For both sexes, this was 20% lower than for the comparable towns of Limerick and Waterford [Figs 13.1 and 13.2]. No doubt, economic differences were partly responsible. For one thing, there were more obvious outlets for literacy and numeracy in the bustling southern ports than in stagnating Galway. For another, there were more regular artisan wages to pay the charges of pay-schools. But did the intra-Catholic disputes of Galway's wardenship also inhibit educational development?

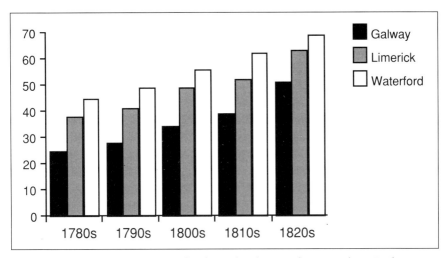

FIGURE 13.2: Female literacy for five school-age cohorts in three Irish towns, 1780s–1820s.
Source: 1841 Census. Note that data combines 'read & write' & 'read only' categories.

Crucial to understanding Galway's educational backwardness was language. Unlike most Munster towns, Galway had a significant population which was ignorant of English. 22% of females and 13.5% of males born in the first decade of the 19th century were monoglot speakers of Irish [See Fig. 13.3]. The chain of causality is elusive, but invariably places where Irish was strong had low literacy levels. It is true that education was rarely available through Irish, but that is hardly an explanation. Did the absence of education allow Irish to survive? Or did the strength of Irish inhibit the success of schools?

Free Schools
An early attempt to improve the educational position of the Catholic poor came five years after the 1782 legislation, when Warden Augustine Kirwan called on Galway's 'Catholic gentlemen' to establish a charity school. In response, several of them drafted an appeal 'To the Charitable and Humane'.[5] The document stressed that popular education was important to all classes:

> It being observed that the horrid vices of blasphemy, drunkenness and dishonesty are gaining ground among the lower class of people, and this being principally attributed to the want of early tuition, several respectable and benevolent persons have opened a subscription ... to establish a Charity School ... that some of the growing generation may be preserved from the general contagion, and hereafter become useful members of society.[6]

The response to the appeal was sufficient to permit the purchase of a building in Lower Abbeygate-street. Meanwhile, a management committee drafted ten rules for the new Charity School for boys, the first six dealing with finance, management, and regular inspection. Overall responsibility was entrusted to an annually-elected committee of laymen — a president, a treasurer, ten inspectors. Sensibly, it was anticipated that subscriptions would diminish, so practical procedures were adopted to ensure the school's survival. The clergy were not formally involved, but they took an active interest nonetheless. For his part, the warden was trustee of a fund devoted to the maintenance of the school, (part of which had previously supported seminarians in France).[7]

Rules 7-10 defined policy, which was shaped by Charter School practice — if that institution had not attracted pupils, it had informed public expectations regarding charity schools. Accordingly, it was emphasised that pupils would be 'supported and clothed' by their parents. But, following Charter School precedent, apprenticeships were offered to compliant boys. Significantly, 'moral' and 'Christian' objectives were stressed but, reflecting the need to elicit Protestant subscriptions, there was no reference to specifically 'Catholic' goals:

7. That as many boys from the age of eight to twelve as the funds will bear will be admitted, when previously recommended and approved of by the Committee. They are to be supported and clothed by their parents, and sent to school at appointed hours, washed, cleaned, and combed.

8. That they are to be instructed in reading, writing and arithmetic, and supplied with books, ink, pen and paper at the expense of the Society, and as emulation is the great spur to the infant mind, premiums will be distributed among the deserving, and such of them as shall pass three years at said school without breach of the moral duties shall be apprenticed …

9. That the master is to be a sober moral man …

10. That as the main end and design … is to preserve a few of the growing generation from the horrid prevailing vices … and by these means to give some useful members to society, the boys admitted to it are to be carefully instructed in their Christian principles.[8]

In 1792, shortly after its foundation, a report of an examination in the Charity School noted that there 'was much improvement since the last such'. 53 boys were examined — before the Committee and 'several other respectable gentlemen' — in 'spelling, reading, writing and Arithmetick'. Thirty years after its establishment, Hardiman reported that, through subscriptions and charity sermons, the school's trustees were 'enabled to afford daily instruction to 150 children, of whom 100 are annually clothed, and 12 apprenticed to useful trades'. In the town, he went on, there were 'many industrious tradesmen' who owed their education and apprenticeship to the school.[9]

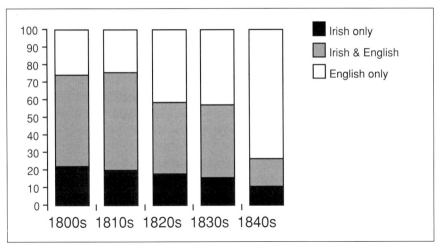

FIGURE 13.3a: Spoken language(s) of successive cohorts of Galway females, born 1800 to 1850.

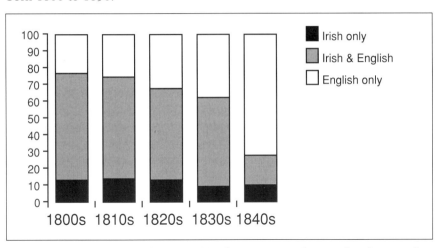

FIGURE 13.3b: Spoken language(s) of successive cohorts of Galway males, born 1800 to 1850.
Source: 1851 Census.

It was not until 1808 that a Female Charity School opened. Associated with an orphanage, it was managed by a committee of Catholic ladies, and operated by two sisters — 'the Misses Lynch of Nantes'. Their efforts, however, were considered inadequate. Warden Ffrench, indeed, came to the view that lay people were unsuited to the task of running schools for the poor — because they were 'mostly governed by mercenary views and temporal interests'. Accordingly, when it became possible, the Presentation Sisters were invited to undertake the education of the female poor. The order opened a school in Kirwan's Lane in 1815, moved to the Square in the following year and, in 1819, secured a sixty-year lease on the former Charter School in the western suburbs. 'The entire of this extensive concern', according to Hardiman, they 'thoroughly repaired and fitted up with convenient school-rooms'. By 1820, thirty female orphans were living in the building, with 'upwards of' 300 day scholars being 'instructed in useful needlework, reading, writing, the common rules of arithmetic, and the principles of religion'.[10] A few years later, an English visitor who examined first class pupils was unimpressed. Reading and spelling, he complained, were 'defective', and the girls had 'received no idea of what they are doing'. It would seem, however, that he did not allow for the fact that the language of instruction, not to mention the examiner's accent, was unfamiliar to many of the girls. As for the industrial department, he noted that 'plain work' was taught, and that 'straw platt was tried but was not successful'.[11]

But to what extent did the existence of two Charity Schools affect literacy in the town? Literacy levels increased significantly in the half-century after 1782, and these schools certainly had an effect, but the pattern of increase suggests that they were not the only agents responsible. Male literacy rose from 49% of the 1780s school-going cohort to 63% for the 1820s, but significantly, the gap with Limerick and Waterford did not close [Figs 13.1 and 13.2]. However, the gap between female and male literacy in Galway did close. In the same period, female literacy rose from 25% to 51%, but it reached 34% for the 1801-10 cohort, on whom the female charity school could have had little effect. This suggests growing enrolment of girls' in pay schools in the 1790s and 1800s. Significantly, as literacy increased, the use of Irish language declined. In 1820, Hardiman reported that 'all ranks, from the highest to the lowest, with very few individual exceptions, speak their vernacular language, the Irish, fluently'.[12] Fig 13.3 supports his observation. More than three-quarters of those who were in their teenage years in 1820 spoke Irish, and 18% of them spoke no English.

It is notable too that more females than males spoke Irish only. Indeed, almost as many of the women born in the first twenty years of the century grew up to be monoglot speakers of Irish as grew up to be monoglot speakers of English. A higher percentage of males than of females spoke Irish, but fewer depended upon it alone. The pattern indicates that Irish was the domestic language of half of Galway households before 1820, the males disproportionately acquiring English (and Irish in some cases) to conduct the family's business with the outside world. Education certainly played a part in the decline of Irish. Irish speakers learned English at school, making it unnecessary for those whose first language was English to learn Irish That the percentage of the bilingual declined more rapidly than the percentage of monoglot Irish speakers indicates that Irish speakers came to be concentrated in particular areas. One of these was the Claddagh where education made hardly any impression until the 1840s, despite the presence of a school there from the 1820s.

In the town, there were twice as many attending the female charity school as the male by the early 1820s. Since the size of the Abbeygate-street building precluded expansion in the provision for boys, the Lombard-street barracks were purchased by Warden Ffrench in 1823.[13] A school on two floors was envisaged, containing two 'well-ventilated' classrooms of 100 by 30 feet, and capable of accommodating over 1,000 pupils. However, disputes between the lay committee and the clergy delayed renovations. In particular, there were complaints that the warden encroached on the committee's domain. Conflict was rooted in the ongoing 'tribes'/'non-tribes' discord and, invariably, contentious matters — including the warden's resources — were aired in public:

> We should be glad to know how any further donations of money are absolutely necessary for the forwarding of this work? The estimate of the expenses handed in by Mr Clarke, a very intelligent architect, amounts only to £190, if we are rightly informed. The Male-Free-School can touch £500 at an hour's notice for more than £500 is lying by for this charity in very secure hands … It is advanced that this handsome sum should be left in the present hands in order to support the incidental expenses of the institution. The expenses of a well-regulated Lancastrian School are a trifle, when compared with those of other seminaries, and it is a strong impression on our minds that a few charity sermons through the year would fully answer those calls and perhaps leave a balance in favour of the establishment.[14]

Three years after the purchase of the premises, the 'Parochial School' opened in the autumn of 1826 — but only on its upper floor. In the meantime, Warden Ffrench's opinions on the relative merits of lay and religious teachers had been reinforced by the success of the Presentation Sisters. Before the end of the year, following representations from Ffrench to Bishop Doyle of Leighlin, Paul O'Connor of the Patrician Brothers' Tullow monastery arrived to take charge. He was joined by another brother and by a postulant.[15]

Enrolment increased rapidly after the Brothers' arrival, reaching 659 during 1827. Since the three men took charge of 220 pupils each, as well as of school administration, it is clear why Ffrench favoured religious over lay teachers with 'mercenary views and temporal interests'. And, it was fortunate that under the Lancastrian system then in vogue, senior pupils were enabled to act as monitors and, in fact, carried out most of the actual instruction in the school. The school timetable for 1828* shows the breadth of the curriculum, even if it does not

---

* 7.30   The School opens every morning throughout the year

8.00   Morning Prayer, and immediately after, Writing, Arithmetic, and Lecture on Book-keeping

8.30   Spelling and Reading Lessons in the Lower Room

9.00   All walk in regular order to the Chapel. Breakfast immediately after Mass. Whilst in the Chapel, some prudent boy is appointed to preside over the rest, to keep them in order, and to inform the Masters of any impropriety they may be guilty of.

10.30   School opens again, and the Scholars assemble

11.00   Writing, Arithmetic, and Lecture on Geometry, in the Upper Room. Stationery distributed for the day. In the Lower Room, all writing on slates

12.00   The "Angelus Domini" &c. Immediately after the rolls to be called and absent boys marked

12.15   Lecture on Geography, the Use of Globes or English Grammar. All other boys in the Upper Room at Arithmetic and in the Lower Room Spelling and Reading Lessons

reveal everything about school organisation. A striking aspect of the daily regime is how much time was spent on religion: morning and evening prayers; Angelus; Mass; Scripture History; Catechism; a Spiritual Lecture.[16] Otherwise, the emphasis was on the '3Rs'.

It would seem that the boys were divided into two large groups, and one small, with a teacher in charge of each. In the large upper and lower classrooms, a teacher supervised monitors who conducted repetitive exercises with twenty to thirty boys each — in accordance with the Lancastrian system. To facilitate this, seating was arranged around the walls and in the centre of the room. Older boys required a teacher to themselves, and it is likely that 'lectures' in the timetable — book keeping, geometry, etc. — were given to the small senior group, either in a section of a classroom or in a separate annexe.

A year after his arrival, Brother O'Connor placed his thoughts on education on the public record. His letters to the 'Children of the Poor of Galway' and to their parents, indicate that resistance — or at least indifference — met his efforts. The polemical letters first appeared in the local press, but they were later issued as a pamphlet, suggesting that their message was deemed important, persuasive, or both. They are worth examining in detail.

First addressing himself to parents, O'Connor warned that those who neglected their children's education, were answerable before God:

> Do not imagine that the salvation of your own souls should be the only object of your solicitude, the souls of your children are also committed to your care; and if you lose, through your own fault, any of those whom your Heavenly Father has given you, I know not what you will be able to answer when cited before the dire tribunal of a tremendous judge.[17]

But there were other reasons for giving boys the benefit of 'a good and virtuous' education — 'thus shall you render them the comfort of your old age'. And though their education was free, with 'all things necessary for their advancement in useful knowledge' being provided, it was in no way second-rate, for their sons would have teachers 'who will feel as much interest in the promotion of their literacy and moral improvement, as if they were to receive from you a considerable annual pension'. Some parents were not convinced of the benefits of education, others found it 'painful to their feelings' to have their children educated at a free school. Both groups O'Connor scolded:

1.00	Monitors Reading Lessons, and Scripture History
1.30	Spelling and Reading Lessons in both Rooms
2.00	Lecture on Mensuration, and General Classics of Practical Arithmetic
2.30	Catechism, and inspection of all the written Works of the day
3.00	Spiritual Lecture, to be read by one of the Boys, appointed each week, in turn, for that purpose. Evening prayer immediately after.
3.30	All dismissed for the day in the order of their respective classes
	*Catechistical Instructions at the School every Sunday morning throughout the year from 7 to 9 o'clock, principally designed as a preparation for Confession and Communion.

> If you have never tasted the sweets, or experienced the effects of a good education yourselves, shall you consider it no better than a useless lumber on their tender minds? Can you suppose that it is impossible for them to rise in the scale of Society, superior to your own present state of indigence? ... Or will you suffer them to grow up in ignorance and vice, whilst they have such a favourable opportunity of improving their minds and their morals? ... Were you, my friends, but a little versed in the history of mankind, you would discover many an eminent individual who rose to the highest summit of honour and power whose early education was that of a free scholar, who, in their youthful days, had as limited a prospect of promotion as your children now have.[18]

The ambition of Catholic educators had grown since the establishment of the male free school in 1787. Then, the object was to 'save a few from the prevailing vices'. For the Patrician Brothers in the 1820s, it was conceivable that every child be educated. And, rather than having to choose between trowel and spade, free scholars might aspire to clerical positions, from which they might climb to 'the highest summit of honour and power'.

In another respect, too, O'Connor's tone was very different to that of the 1787 committee. Reflecting the growth of Catholic confidence the letters were unabashedly confessional in tone, not confuting Catholic objectives with vaguely 'Christian' and 'moral' ones. Quite the reverse, for O'Connor exulted that the time was past 'when a Catholic schoolmaster would be loaded with chains'. The 'day-star of liberty' for Catholics, he wrote, was on the horizon.

His letter 'To the Children of the Poor of Galway' reiterated some of these points. The advice it contained was also intended to reassure parents:

> If your parents be peevish, bear with their infirmity, and do not suppose that their weakness is an excuse for your guilt. If age has weakened their understanding, and poverty wrinkled their brow, support them in the hour of affliction ... Reflect seriously on the many obligations that you lie under to those who brought you into life, who watched over your helpless infancy, who toil for your subsistence ...[19]

And a portion of the address to the children was intended also for the eyes of those who contributed money to the project:

> In your communication with the Deity, be not unmindful of your benefactors, who afforded you an opportunity of securing your present and future happiness ... They have dispelled the clouds of ignorance by which you were enveloped; they have baffled the puny efforts of canting proselytism, and emancipated you from the

fetters of mental destitution. They have opened at their own
expense, an establishment which in future generations will shed
lustre on their memory …[20]

If the importance of deference to social superiors and to parents was stressed,
so also were the virtues of diligence, and of obedience before authority:

> Let not a love of idleness deprive you of the blessings of education,
> or render you hereafter the pest of society … Apply to your
> teachers that they may clear up your doubts, and waste not your
> time in that thoughtless indolence for which too many schooldays
> are remarkable. Carefully shun the company and conversation of
> those as might lead you into sin, or nip the budding virtue of your
> heart, and fly with honour from those pestilential associations,
> where vice is held up in all its native deformity, and religion treated
> with ridicule and contempt. Look on every species of oath with the
> utmost abhorrence.[21]

Towards a National Education system

In their commitment to popular education, Brother O'Connor and Warden
Kirwan were men of their time. From the late 18th century, the issue had
preoccupied policy makers and philanthropists, pastors and philosophers. And
if the egalitarian spirit of the enlightenment was the stimulus for some such,
there were also pragmatic reasons for promoting literacy and numeracy. Adam
Smith had urged that states should encourage schooling, arguing that an
educated workforce was vital to an industrialising society. In Ireland, the need
to ensure that whatever system emerged was politically compliant provided the
state with a further reason to interest itself in education. Such interest is
indicated by the activity of a succession of educational commissions.

Education was of particular interest to religious organisations. Historically,
the established church was responsible for schools, while the Catholic church
had maintained an illegal system to prepare its clergy. From the late 18th
century, education became an arena of ardent religious competition. The
Catholic authorities were finally free to openly promote their own schools, and
new teaching orders emerged to join in the work. At the same time, adherents
of the evangelical movement within Protestantism saw that working through
schools could assist their project of converting the Catholic poor, and they
established a number of organisations, notably the London Hibernian Society
(1806) and the Irish Society for Promoting the Native Irish through the
Medium of their own Language (1818). It was a grievance of Catholics that
such bodies received state funding. While the lethargy displayed by the
management of Galway's charity school for boys up to the 1820s indicates that
it faced no challenge from this quarter, it may have been that it was the activity
of unidentified 'distributors of the bible' in 1823, and of agents of the London

Hibernian Society in 1826 which provided the stimuli for the purchase of the Lombard-street and for the invitation to the Patrician Brothers.[22]

As competing Catholic and evangelical bodies developed their educational networks, the philanthropists of the Kildare Place Society (1811) sought to establish a system, 'divested of all sectarian distinctions in Christianity'. Partly funded by the state and accepted for a time by the Catholic authorities, the Society was innovative in training teachers, in producing textbooks, and in overseeing a system of inspection. By the 1820s, its schools catered for 100,000. Further expansion was inhibited by Catholic opposition, arising principally from the Society's support for proselytising educational bodies, but also from misunderstandings between Protestant and Catholic members of the Society regarding the other groups' foibles in the matter of religious instruction. So, by the increasingly assertive Catholicism of the 1820s, the Kildare Place Society came to be pilloried as merely an untypically plausible proselytising agency.[23]

Notwithstanding the proliferation of educational agencies — Catholic, Protestant and ostensibly secular — the majority of school children in the 1820s attended unaffiliated 'pay-' or 'hedge-'schools. This was established by data collected for the education commissioners of the 1824-27 period, which showed that half-a-million pupils — 40% of those of school-going age — were enrolled in schools of some sort. Literacy statistics suggest that Galway school attendance was higher than the national average, but lower than the urban average. Returns to the Education Inquiry show that there were thirty-seven schools in the town and its immediate vicinity. The same returns included significant information about each: name and religion of the teacher; description of the building; religion and sex of the students.[24] Since, the data was gathered during 1826, it gives a useful picture of the educational situation in Galway on the eve of the arrival of the Patrician Brothers.

Several of the 37 schools in the town provided education for the children of middle class parents. Based on the low fees paid by pupils and the poor condition of school buildings, however, it is clear that there was a thriving hedge-school sector. Apart from the male and female free schools, at least 12 other schools catered to working class children in the town, and to the adjacent peasantry. Between them, they had an enrolment of more than 450 pupils, with boys accounting for almost three-quarters of that total. The largest of the schools was at Boherard, where William Smyth, a Catholic, charged 76 boys and 18 girls 3*d* each a week for classes in 'a room in a small cabin'. Between them Mary Smith, Mary Ruane, John Blake and Andrew Ruane, educated 97 boys and 49 girls in four schools in Bohermore; Mary Commons taught 13 boys and 13 girls in 'a small confined room' in Market-street; Thomas Smyth and Malachy O'Brien kept schools on the West-road; while John Cunningham charged 3 girls and 30 boys 2*d* each a week for lessons in Bushy Park Church. Just two schools received aid from the Kildare Place Society. One, with forty-eight Catholics enrolled, was in a substantial building at Merlin Park, recently built by the landlord. Mrs Blake, the landlord's wife, paid the salary of the Catholic teacher. The other was the Protestant parish school, which was also assisted by the London Hibernian Society but, as if to prove that Catholics had no monopoly on misery, the pupils — twenty-one Catholics, forty-five Protestants and one Presbyterian — attended classes in a building 'of the very worst description' in the grounds of the Collegiate Church.[25]

The Commissioners of 1824-27 gathered voluminous data, listened to various opinions, issued a total of nine reports, and recommended the establishment of a government board to take charge of elementary education. Despite thus acknowledging that Catholic opinion could not be reconciled with the otherwise-suitable Kildare Place Society, the Commissioners were unable to agree a satisfactory formula addressing the vexed questions of religious instruction and denominational influence. Consequently, it took several more years before a broadly acceptable arrangement could be announced. An 'undenominational' system was to be administered by a government-appointed and state-funded Board of Commissioners for National Education; many of its operational practices were borrowed from the Kildare Place Society.

Regulations favouring applications from denominationally-mixed local committees, and a policy of separating secular from religious education, underlined the government's 'undenominational' objectives. In time, however, the pliability of the regulations allowed advocates of religiously-segregated schooling to stake their claims throughout the country. With differing emphases, the religious groupings all favoured denominationally-managed (but state-funded) schooling. All of them, therefore, objected to the 'undenominational' character of the 1831 proposals. But, generally, the Catholic authorities were better-disposed to the system than their Anglican or Presbyterian counterparts. With the largest membership and the smallest resources, one can see why the Catholic bishops set scruples aside.[26]

National schools

Literacy increased rapidly during the remainder of the century, testifying to the effectiveness of the new system. Its provisions enabled the Education Commissioners to enforce standards and to influence schools' location. But transformation was gradual, and in the years after 1831, the Commissioners' task was to adapt a functioning system rather than to create a new one.

By 1833, more than 100,000 pupils had joined the system, but almost all of the national schools they attended had existed two years earlier. And as the system developed, more schools became 'connected' with the Board to reap the financial benefits offered by the connection. More fully integrated were 'vested' schools built after 1831 by local committees aided by the Commissioners. (Incidentally, the financial benefits were not sufficient to provide totally free education; fees were paid by parents considered able to afford them until the 1890s.) With schools of diverse origins, of several religious affiliations, and subject in varying degrees to central control, the national system emerged, according to one authority, as 'a sprawling structure, with all types of odd wings, tunnels and battlements'.[27]

In Galway, the free schools run by the Presentation Sisters and by the Patrician Brothers joined the system on the instruction of Bishop Browne. But not everybody was convinced that it was wise to trade independence for a relatively small annual income — £40 for the male free school, and £30 for the female. Later in the 1830s, schools in the archdiocese of Tuam cut their connection with the National Board, and in the ensuing conflict between archbishops MacHale and Murray, members of the hierarchy lined up on either side. One effect was that Rome pronounced against the system but, outside of Tuam, its progress was not significantly affected. In Galway, Brother Paul O'Connor disapproved of his school's connection with the National Board, but for Bishop Browne, the financial benefits were welcome.[28]

Insofar as they sought to extend education, the objectives of the Education Commissioners corresponded with those of Galway's teaching orders. Once resources were made available, it only remained to convince parents that it was worthwhile sending their children to school. And most were already persuaded, if the enrolment of 500,000 in the variously-funded and -endowed schools of the 1820s is an indication. But there was a section of the population that remained largely untouched by education. Paul O'Connor tried to reach this group with his letters of 1828, and increasing enrolment in the period following suggests that the endeavour evoked a response. Nonetheless, the children of the very poorest remained outside the system — excluded by their poverty, and requiring tangible rewards to prompt them to join it.

The provision of material encouragement was commonplace in early popular education. Apprenticeships, free clothes, and small prizes for examination success were offered in Galway's earliest free schools. But those who were not in a position to defer gratification to the end of their schooldays, or even to the end of term, would surely respond to a daily incentive in the form of food.

It was 'melancholy scenes … of children literally fainting in the school from want of food', which led Paul O'Connor to announce in April 1830 that an Orphans' Breakfast Institute was to be attached to his school. At first, the Institute catered for the small number of actual orphans on the rolls, but its facilities were soon extended to 'poor boys' generally. According to the charity's first annual report, fifty-four boys had been fed on occasion during the previous year. The parents of some were living, it was admitted, but such was 'the pitiable condition to which the hand of affliction [had] reduced themselves and their little offspring' that they could not be refused sustenance. In 1834, Henry Inglis commended the 'humane regulation' which allowed poor children 'a plentiful breakfast of stirabout and treacle' before their classes.[29]

Like other charities, the Breakfast Institute faced difficulties, and it was necessary on occasion to remind the charitable of the usefulness of its work.

Not only did it rehabilitate probable vagrants through education, but it saved citizens the annoyance of dealing daily with the entreaties of child beggars:

> … it affords a facility to the children of attending the school, and of thereby receiving food for the mind in connexion with their corporal sustenance, which could not possibly be the case were they obliged to receive from door to door the indispensible support of nature.[30]

Breakfast provision soon became an integral part of the education system. The Presentation Sisters followed Paul O'Connor's example, establishing a Female Breakfast Institute, which had grown to cater for 170 'destitute little ones' in 1844.[31] By then the Patrician Brothers facility had 187 names on its breakfast list, and an average daily complement of 142. And if these figures are remarkable in representing about a third of total enrolment in the two schools, they are remarkable also in indicating that breakfast was a real incentive to school attendance. Evidently, more than 75% of those on the breakfast list turned up for school, whereas the average of total enrolment marked 'present' in the district at that time hovered around 60%.[32]

Schools within the national system were visited by the Board's inspectors, but the intense interest in education of the period meant that schools were often also informally inspected by visitors — amateur educationalists, pious bigots, and the merely curious. Prevailing concepts regarding the accountability of teachers meant that such travellers were rarely denied admission to schools. Several visitors to the Presentation school during the 1830s and early 1840s left written accounts of their impressions. Henry Inglis was 'pleased' with the quality of instruction, but found no sign of the undenominational spirit of national education. The 'paraphernalia of Popery' was all over the school, he wrote.[33] More negative than Inglis was an anonymous 'lady' of evangelical outlook who was shown around during 1835. As far as she was concerned, the pupils were being brainwashed by teachers who were employing all of their 'arts' to 'induce the higher order of pupils to become nuns, whenever they have fortune sufficient to excite the cupidity of the superiors'. And although, it seems unlikely that many pupils in a charity school had fortunes of any consequence, she found that 'themes on virginity, priesthood and martyrdom' were emphasised unduly.[34] To James Johnson, however, who passed through in the early 1840s, 'the system of tuition appeared most excellent':

> I was present at several, examinations, and propounded questions to the girls myself — not without astonishment at the proficiency to which they had obtained. They had the history of the Bible, together with all the great events of the Jewish and Christian dispensations at their fingers' ends … They were not embarrassed in the slightest degree by various cross-questions put to them by

myself and others, proving that they were not crammed for the purpose of display, but well-grounded in the subjects of their study. But their knowledge of Geography, Astronomy, Statistics, etc., surprised me most of all. Over a very large chart of Europe, Miss O'Donnell [Sr. Maria de Pazzi] caused some of her pupils, not more than nine or ten years of age, to trace with a wand, the various kingdoms, states and cities, together with their population, religion, forms of government, etc..[35]

Jonathan Binns, too, who had previously 'entertained harsh and uncharitable opinions about the monastic life' was surprised at what he found. The operation of this 'admirable establishment', he wrote, made him realise that 'an entire withdrawal from what is called the world is compatible with a diligent and extensive exercise in philanthropy'.[36] The impressions of John Barrow were also positive. He found twenty-two nuns in the convent, and four hundred students who were taught needlework and the English language, and when sufficiently skilled in the former, were

> employed in making lace and tambour work, the materials for which are sent for the purpose in large quantities from Nottingham; and the girls paid, by those to whom the lace belongs, a certain sum for their labour, which assists their parents in clothing them and in the payment of their rent.[37]

The general impression is that both Presentation and Patrician schools were exemplary, something which was not the case with the third Galway school to join the national system, the 'small and inadequate' school in the Claddagh.

That there was a school at all in the Claddagh was a recent development. In 1820, James Hardiman wrote that 'a schoolmaster among them would be considered a phenomenon' and, a few years later, Hely Dutton, explained the Claddagh people's reluctance to send their children to school as being due to fears that having learnt English, the girls might be more easily seduced by soldiers and the boys enabled to join the Royal Navy.[38] Dutton might have noted that that Claddagh youngsters were economically active from an early age, in netmaking and in bait-gathering. He might also have discovered that, like their contemporaries in Bohermore, Claddagh people were prepared to have their children educated, but in a school within the community.

By all accounts, Patrick O'Brien's school in the Claddagh was scarcely worthy of the name. Nevertheless, it became a national school for a time, until this measure of recognition was withdrawn because of the incompetence of the master and the unsuitability of the premises. According to report, there was no glass in the windows and the approaches were 'so filthy that respectable people are deterred from visiting it or taking any interest whatsoever in it'. However, the school continued, and, in 1845, thirty girls were being taught there by 18-

year-old Bridget O'Brien — probably Patrick's daughter. But by then, the Dominican Fathers were in contact with the Education Commissioners, with a view to establishing 'such a well-conducted school as may impart the blessings of education to all the children of this increasing colony'. The result of these contacts was the Claddagh Piscatory School which opened on 1 August 1847.[39]

Elsewhere in the town also, the educational conquest by the religious orders proceeded apace. In 1842, the Presentation sisters were joined in their work of educating poor girls by the Mercy sisters.[40] Michael Lawler, schools superintendent, inspected the Mercy school in Newtownsmith in May 1845, following an application for funding. He reported that there were 201 girls on the rolls, that there had been an average attendance of 180 in the previous six months, and that there would be 100 more pupils if the school authorities could accept them. Six nuns were 'generally' engaged in teaching, but the application sought payment for only two — Catherine Lynch, 23, and Elizabeth Murphy, 17. Both were nuns and the superintendent judged them to be 'very clever'. In general, he considered the school to be 'a very fine one'.

A subsequent application from Newtownsmith sought payment for an 'Industrial teacher', Eliza Langley, 15, who had been trained by Carmelites in Kilkenny. It was stated that there was an average of twelve pupils in the industrial department of the school, who were taught plain sewing, embroidery, and lace work. The last was described as 'the chief object', since regular work was available from a Dublin firm. Proceeds from the contract went 'exclusively' to the twelve girls who were earning between 2*s* and 4*s* a week from this work, but it was anticipated that this would 'be increased by increased experience'. Recommending the Langley application, the inspector remarked that there was little work for females in Galway, that the lace work was 'of pecuniary importance' to those engaged in it, and that 'any effort to afford the means of employment' should be encouraged.[41] More generally, inspectors' reports show that the opportunity of acquiring needlework skills was the most powerful incentive to educational participation for poor girls.

On the outskirts of Galway, an 1842 report establishes the existence of schools in Menlo and in Bushy Park. In Menlo, there was an average daily attendance of twenty to thirty boys and of six to ten girls. The imbalance, however, was not because education was considered to be more important for boys, but because the Menlo school had just one teacher, a young male, and parents were reluctant to entrust their daughters to a male teacher. Across the river, in Bushy Park there was a similar situation, and in deference to popular preference, the Gortacleva female school was sanctioned in the early 1850s.[42]

National Schools during and after the famine
The steady advance of National education continued in the second half of the 19th century. Total enrolment peaked at almost 1.1m pupils in 1884, after the fall of the last significant bastion of opposition with the death of Archbishop MacHale of Tuam. Having weathered diverse challenges, the system had

become irrefutably 'national' in extent and in character by that point.

Even the Famine period was one of expansion. 1848, remarkably, was a record year which saw enrolment pass the half-million mark. Indeed, the national system was demonstrably strengthened by the Famine, its total enrolment in 1850 — in a much reduced population — being 20% higher than it had been in 1845.[43] This development was attributable, in large measure, to the provision of food through its schools during the crisis.

All of Galway's national schools provided food for significant numbers. At first, increased poverty put pressure on existing 'Breakfast Institutes', pressure which is evident in the ever-increasing desperation of public appeals. But new facilities were being established. In December 1846, for example, the Sisters of Mercy announced that they proposed providing 'a daily dinner' for a hundred pupils at Newtownsmith. Ingredients were collected using a specially-acquired horse and car: 'coarse meal' from millers; offal from butchers'; 'broken bread and crumbs' from bakers; sundry 'alms' from housekeepers.[44]

The value of such efforts was recognised by the Galway Relief Committee, which voted in January 1847 to assist them financially. And Quakers directed food from America to Paul O'Connor a few months later. Daily rations were still a bowl of 'good substantial stirabout', but it was rather different in character: oatmeal and treacle had given way to a compound of 'Indian Meal and Rice, with a fair allowance of slightly-diluted molasses as sauce'. The support meant that more children could be fed. From 4,319 in December 1846, the number of breakfasts served in Paul O'Connor's Institute grew to 13,360 in May 1847. And, as breakfast lists grew, so did pupil numbers. In the Patrician Brothers' school, enrolment increased from 883 in March 1847 to 1,139 in September 1847; in the Presentation school enrolment grew from 805 to 846.[45]

Further support from Quakers, and in the autumn of 1847 from the Vatican, enabled the several Institutes to remain in open, though with limited breakfast lists. But the announcement in November 1847 by the British Association for the Relief of Distress that it was giving food 'to all the Free Schools of the Union' allowed lists to be expanded. The announcement followed the Association's decision to distribute a daily ration of rye bread and broth to schoolchildren in all the distressed unions, a policy which would lead to national schools springing up 'like mushrooms' in parts of the west.[46] Inevitably, there were teething problems, giving rise to complications and controversy, notably when recipients of school breakfasts were struck off other relief lists, and when misunderstandings fuelled allegations that the Association was a proselytising agency.

Four Galway schools received British Association assistance and, by January 1848, almost two thousand children were receiving a daily breakfast. But the rations were insufficient to sustain life, and, in May 1848, it was recorded that 51 pupils of the Patrician Brothers' school had died in the previous twelve months.[47] Paul O'Connor described the scene in the school:

> Only look at our two great schoolrooms, each 100 ft. by 30, crammed to suffocation with famishing, emaciated little creatures, some of them striving to beguile the cravings of hunger by applications to the food of the mind, others pining away in listless inaction, and calculating as to when or where they may get a breakfast for today, or a crumb for tomorrow...[48]

In the circumstances, it is understandable that the distribution of food was given greater priority than education. Indeed, for a period during 1847, the Patrician Brothers' pupils were sent home directly after breakfast in order to reduce the spread of disease among them. In the system generally, it became clear to the Education Commissioners, that food distribution was interfering 'with the discipline and efficiency of the schools'. Accordingly, new rules were devised: all children receiving food were required to attend classes; at least four hours of the day was to be devoted to instruction; attendance was to remain 'limited to the accommodation provided, allowing six square feet per child'. The British Association's efforts, which prompted these regulations, ended in November 1848, but breakfast provision in Galway schools continued on a reduced scale, and without any regular source of funding.[49]

The national school where enrolment was most dramatically boosted by the Famine was that attached to the workhouse. In March 1846, it had 218 pupils; by March 1847 it had 482. Pressure of space forced the Vice-Guardians to relocate the school to a riverside site at Dangan — recently an Ursuline boarding school.[50] When Sidney Godolphin Osborne visited, there were a thousand inmates. Osborne, who was critical of other Galway Poor Law facilities, praised Dangan, especially for preparing its charges for useful employment:

> 150 of them work on the farm, under the superintendence and tutelage of an Agricultural instructor ... 50 are employed in cooking, mending the roads and other miscellaneous labour ... There is a paid master tailor who has a staff of lads to instruct in his trade, and to whom is entrusted the repair of the clothing of the establishment. There are also a schoolmaster and assistant schoolmaster, and a matron. We found the farm very highly worked, and the crops coming up remarkably ... The whole is cultivated by the hand ... These boys look far healthier and happier in every way than any I saw in any other Union ....[51]

Preparation for work was also the objective of new schools established in the Claddagh during the Famine. The process was set in train in 1844 when an application from Fr Thomas Rushe, was supported by schools' superintendent, Michael Lawler, on the grounds that the Dominicans had 'such an influence with the Claddagh people that they will induce them, though naturally averse to education, or to anything that might alter their primitive habits, to send their children to school'. By September 1847, the list of national schools included the Claddagh male with 80 pupils; the Claddagh female with 36; the Claddagh male piscatory with 69. All of these schools were located in the new Dominican building, on which construction work had begun in February 1846. The schools grew rapidly, with average daily attendance reaching 400 in early 1848. Virtually all of the pupils in the Claddagh — as against two-thirds of those attending the Patrician Brothers' school — received the British Association breakfast during 1848.[52] It is tempting to conclude, therefore, that broth and rye bread were more powerful factors in overcoming indifference to education in the Claddagh than the influence of the Dominicans, or the promise of a relevantly piscatorial education. It is probable, however, that the breakdown of the Claddagh's traditional economy would soon have persuaded sceptics to send their children to school in any case.

One writer has shown that the education in the Claddagh, even in the male piscatory school, was never notably nautical. It may be that supporters of the project did not make adequate preparations — certainly, the times were not favourable for detailed planning. For their part, the Education Commissioners saw the project as a prototype on the lines of agricultural and industrial national schools, and issued a textbook for the Claddagh in 1847, 'especially adapted to schools situated on the sea-coast, and which … will contain a brief history of the different species of fish, the best modes of catching and curing it, and of the various kinds of articles required by fishermen.[53]

As well as overseeing the Claddagh schools, Fr Rushe had other educational interests. In February 1848, he applied to the National Board. for funding for the 'Ladies of the Dominican Nunnery' at Taylor's Hill. The application was supported by schools superintendent, William Savage, who noted that the Board's textbooks were being used by the 200 girls present on the day of inspection. The school had developed initially to cater to the educational needs of children attending a soup kitchen run by the Dominican Sisters.[54]

If the Famine years saw an expansion in national education, some gaps remained. One was in Menlo, where a school, under the patronage of Thomas E. Blake, had opened in 1842. Teacher, Patrick Crean was dismissed for 'continued neglect and inattention', and the school closed in 1849. Blake paid little attention to his tenants' educational needs for more than a decade, and it was not until 1861 that a fresh application was made — in response to the 'wants of a popolous village and district, hitherto totally neglected by all parties, and from its peculiar position cut off from all means of education'.[55]

Another notably neglected quarter was Bohermore. In the 1820s, four pay-schools there had a combined attendance of almost 150 pupils, yet no national school was established. In December 1852, the parish priest, Fr B. J. Roche, sought recognition for a recently-opened school in the community. The schools inspector reported that the school was 'situated in one of the most thickly populated districts' and that 'residents, who are mostly of the lower classes, are most anxious that schools in connexion with the board should be established in their locality'. Existing national schools were felt to be 'at a considerable distance', but more significantly, they were described as being 'in a different quarter of town'. The Bohermore school operated satisfactorily for several years, until it was handed over to the Sisters of Mercy in 1859 as an 'auxiliary school'. Recognition was then withdrawn by the Education Commissioners, prompting the withdrawal of the nuns — with the female pupils — to their main school in Newtownsmith. A fresh application for a boys' school was received in 1864, with an inspector's recommendation remarking on the continued existence of 'three "hedge" or venture schools' in the community. A new national school, he was certain, would not compete with other national schools, but would drive hedge-schools out of business.[56]

It may have been the fact that the Mercy Sisters had extended their influence in several directions that prompted the Board to keep them out of Bohermore. In the early 1850s, they won recognition for their school in Gortacleva, and they were called in to re-open the Claddagh female school, when it proved impossible to find a replacement for an incompetent lay teacher. Concerning the nun's proposal to provide three hours a day of industrial instruction for the Claddagh girls, one official commented that this 'circumstance' would recommend the school to the parents of the children. They appreciated 'the advantages of combining industrial and literary instruction', he went on, since they knew that their daughters 'must eventually turn their hands to manual labour'.[57]

Industrial training made schooling attractive to parents who were not convinced of the utility of a literary education, but this brought with it some disadvantages. Of the Presentation School in the 1850s, it was reported:

> The Nuns complain with much reason, that the introduction of fancy needlework amongst the poorer classes has produced a remarkable distaste for literary instruction; that it is with greatest difficulty the girls ... can be persuaded even one hour in the day to any occupation except embroidery or muslin work, and that, consequently, as soon as they acquire at school, even a slight degree of expertness, they finally discontinue their attendance, in order to give up their entire time to the work in their own houses.[58]

For Schools Inspector John E. Sheridan, this was an 'evil of great magnitude':

> It bids fair to the progress of intellectual and moral cultivation amongst the females of the lower class, by inducing them ... to devote their time to a mere manual occupation, from which, after all, it would seem there is not the least likelihood of their ever being able to earn anything like a decent subsistence.[59]

Primary education in the late 19th century

By the late 1850s, National Education had entered its mature phase, and the priority of Board officials was to improve the system rather than to extend it. Issues of teachers' proficiency and pupils' attendance came to dominate reports from the field. And although inspectors must have known that the 'undenominational' horse had bolted, blatant infringements continued to be reported. Hence, the manager of the Newtownsmith school was warned in 1858 that *The Ursuline History of England* could not be used for 'ordinary instruction', but only for religious instruction, and that '*medals* worn by children as badges of good behaviour and bearing sectarian mottoes', should not be worn during ordinary instruction'.[60]

Particular inspectorial attention during the 1860s was given to the capabilities of monitors. The unsatisfactory situation regarding teacher training resulting from the Catholic hierarchy's opposition to model schools (see below) meant that monitorial experience was the principal route into teaching in Catholic-run schools until the agreement on religious-run training colleges in the early 1880s. Given the irritation of the National Board at the bishop's attitude, it is likely there was an element of inspectorial pique in the repeated rejection of monitors for 'bad answering' in the Board's examinations, such as in the Presentation school in the 1869-71 period. And the problem of inadequate training was not one that could be easily solved in a system responsible for 8000 schools. Indeed into the 1890s, more than two-thirds of teachers in the Galway district were considered to be 'untrained'.[61]

The so-called 'untrained' were former monitors who had passed Board examinations and inspections, thereby becoming recognised, but officials disapproved of that route into teaching. In 1891, an inspector reported that the schools in the Galway district where 'instruction [was] carried out in an intelligent fashion' were, invariably, those staffed by training colleges graduates. Exceptions were the 'convent and monastery schools' within his jurisdiction, which he also considered to be exemplary.[62] Since such schools accounted for a large proportion of total enrolment in Galway itself, it can be inferred that the quality of elementary education in the town was satisfactory. The impression is confirmed by inspection reports from the period 1860-1900, but there was one significant (and consistent) black spot. That was the Claddagh, where there were ongoing problems in both male and female schools. The worse situation was in the male school.

In 1860, it would appear, the National Board still aspired to providing a piscatorial education for Claddagh boys. In that year, it was discovered that teacher John Ryan's knowledge of mathematics was 'entirely below the average requirement' but, because 'he [knew] the definitions of nautical astronomy, and the practical solutions of some of the principal problems of general navigation', he was considered to be qualified for his position. Later in the year, Ryan lost a premium due to the 'low condition of classes', while in 1862 he was demoted to second class teacher, 'his school being in a low and most unsatisfactory state'. But, despite continuing to be 'admonished' and 'reprimanded' by inspectors, Ryan was restored to his former status before his departure in 1869.[63] Ryan's successor Patrick Shaughnessy survived reprimands for almost a decade before being dismissed in 1878. His replacement, James Quoyle, was no improvement. Quoyle was admonished and reprimanded during his first decade in the school, but things deteriorated markedly during the 1890s, when the school passed from Dominican to diocesan management. But despite incurring 'severe' and 'serious' reprimands, Quoyle was allowed to take on his son John — a chip off the old block — as an assistant in 1894. Into the new century, father and son continued to attract unfavourable attention. Complaints about the 'filthy state' of the premises and about general neglect indicate that standards in the Claddagh in 1900 were little different to those maintained by Malachy O'Brien in the 1830s.[64]

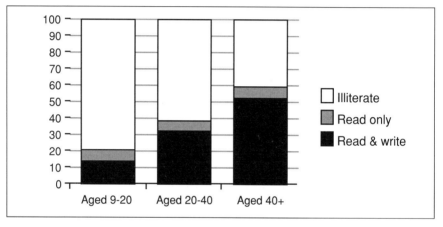

FIGURE 13.4: Literacy in three age groups, 1891.
Source: 1891 Census.

As well as particular problems with individual schools and teachers, Board officials were concerned with the general problem of poor attendance. As enrolment in the national system went up — from half-a million in 1849 to a million, almost every single child on the island, by the mid-1870s — attendance failed to keep pace. From 282,575 — 52% of those enrolled — in 1852, average daily attendance reached 395,390 — 39% of those enrolled — in 1874. And schools in Galway town struggled to reach the national average. Average daily attendance in the Patrician Brothers' school in 1874 was 326 (34%); in Bohermore, it was only 45 (29.8%). Schools for girls fared somewhat better, but daily attendance was only 40.7% in Newtownsmith. The following decades saw improvement. According to an 1891 report on the 130 schools in the Galway district, pupils in the town attended more regularly than those in the countryside. The reporting official was disappointed that 'the disparity between the average number on rolls and the average attendance' was 35%, but there had been a marked improvement in this regard since the 1870s. By the time that school attendance became compulsory — during the 1890s

— it was almost universal. A short time after attendance legislation was put into force in Galway, the district schools' inspector reported that he had 'casually' learnt that 'the accustomed scarcity of "caddies" upon the local golf-links is attributable to this cause', but that, otherwise, there was no discernible change.[65]

Sources for the history of education tended to focus on lacunae and on problems; competent teachers and regularly-attending pupils attracted little comment. The reports of the National Board are rich in subjective accounts from the field, as well as in data on enrolment and attendance, but Census statistics on literacy are more revealing of the system's progress than any other. In 1891, on the eve of compulsory education, the majority (52%) of over-40s in Galway town declared themselves illiterate, but less than a third (32%) of those in the 20-40 age group were in this category, and less than 14% of those under 20. The bare statistics might have exaggerated the rate of progress — a comparison with Figs 13.1 and 13.2 shows that literacy levels were higher before the Famine than among the over-40s in 1891. But the discrepancy may be explained by Galway's declining population and by the pattern of migration — literate people may have been more likely to leave. If the post-Famine educational transformation was not as dramatic as indicated by Fig. 13.4, it was remarkable nonetheless.

Education of the middle-class

By the late 19th century, Irish education had taken the shape it would retain over most of the island until the 1960s. There were the National schools — denominationally-managed but state-supervised — which provided a free (or nearly free) elementary education to children of all social classes. And there was the fee-paying second-level or intermediate sector, consisting of privately-owned schools and colleges, generally under religious control, and catering almost exclusively for the middle-class. After 1878, second-level schools participated in state examinations and accepted the associated financial rewards, but they did not become markedly less exclusive. That Irish education assumed this shape was due to the success of the National system, which satisfied the parents of middle-class children as well as those of the working-class and tenantry. But for most of the 19th century, the division in education was not between primary and secondary sectors, but between schools serving the poorer parts of society on the one hand, and those catering for the middle-class on the other.[66] The national system grew out of the 'free-' and 'hedge-school' milieu; the intermediate sector developed from academies offering, in the words of one observer, education that was 'partly elementary and partly academical'.[67]

There were certainly 'popish school-masters' in 18th century Galway catering to the Catholic middle-class, and competing with the long-established Erasmus Smith school which, by softening its Protestant ethos, attracted some Catholics.[68] But alternatives to Smith were not readily available, even after penal restrictions were eased, and even to those prepared to pay 'very liberal' fees. The following advertisement was placed in 1792:

> A School Master wanted by a number of the inhabitants of Galway, who will engage to send thirty scholars to any School Master of good morals and competent abilities on the first day he should open school in the said town. A person whose character and conduct will bear strict enquiry and who is capable of teaching mathematics, writing and the English language grammatically may apply to the printer hereof and be assured of very liberal terms.[69]

The situation had improved by the 1820s. At least 18 schools catering for the children of people of some means can be identified in the returns to the Irish Education Enquiry. The level of fees is a guide to the status of a school, but aspirations to 'respectability' are also indicated by the fact that they were charged on a quarterly rather than on a weekly basis. Thus, the school operated by Thomas Smyth in a one-roomed cabin on the West Road, and charging 2*d* a week, can be considered typical of schools oriented towards the working-class, while that taught by Nicholas Smyth in 'a good room' in William-street, and charging 11*s* 4*d* per quarter, can be considered typical of those available to the middle-class. But, depending on aspirations and means, a 'respectable' education might be purchased for as little as 4*s* 4*d* per quarter from Patt O'Brien in Quay-street, or as much as 4 guineas a year (25 guineas for boarders) from Mr & Mrs Nicholais in Middle-street.[70]

As for the curriculum of middle-class schools, there were differences between schools charging a pound a year and those charging four guineas. At the lower end, there was an emphasis on clerical and commercial skills, while the more expensive offered a classical education to boys, or a range of accomplishments to girls. Newspaper advertisements provided details of individual schools. For example, in O'Grady's School in Church Lane, instruction at 'moderate terms' was available in Algebra, Arithmetic, Geometry, Mensuration, Book-keeping, Reading, Writing, Spelling, English Grammar, Globes, Geography and Catechism. By contrast, Mr Kearns Academy in Flood-street — with fifty boys, and fees of four guineas a year — emphasised the Classics. Subjects examined there in 1827 were Greek, Latin, French, Grecian History, Roman History, English History, Geography, Writing, Arithmetic, Catechism, and Sacred History. And a school for girls established in 1817 by Mrs Haverty in Flood-street, and oriented also towards the upper middle-class, advertised a different programme. A 'limited number of pupils' were instructed in 'French and English grammatically; History, Biography, Astronomy & Geography; The Use of Globes; Plain and Fancy Work, &c.' In addition, 'the most approved Masters' gave classes in music, writing, and drawing'.[71]

If the extent of advertising is an indication, competition was keen among girls' schools: Miss Kelly's Galway Boarding School in Back-street; Mrs Verdon's Seminary in High-street; Miss Coppinger's Boarding and Day School; Mrs Donelan's Galway Seminary in Middle-street; Mrs O'Connor's Boarding and Day School in Dominick-street; the Misses Berry's School in Middle-street; Mrs Campbell's Boarding and Day School in High-street; Miss Maxey's Seminary in Back-street; Mrs Duffy's School and the Misses Fahy's Seminary in Back-street, actively sought female pupils during the late 1820s and 1830s.[72]

All of these schools were independently-owned by educational entrepreneurs seeking to make a profit by catering to the needs and foibles of the middle-class; many of them were extremely short-lived; none of them were accountable except to the parents of their students. Rather different in these respects was the Erasmus Smith school, which was owned by a philanthropic foundation, which had existed since the 17th century, and which was subject to inspection by the public authorities. The school was one of five established in Ireland by a Cromwellian adventurer but, given its resources — the endowment included over a thousand acres in and around the town — the school might have contributed more to Galway education than it did. Children of tenants on the estate were entitled by the founding charter to free schooling, but not many availed of the offer. Those who did during the 18th century included numbers of Catholics. There might have been more, but for a usually concealed school objective, indiscreetly admitted by Headmaster Campbell in 1788 — the 'readiness' of many Catholics to entrust their children to his care, he said, meant that they might 'be brought over' to the Established Church.[73]

In 1809, 44 boys were attending the school which was located over a shop in High-street. Since this was considered an unsuitable location for boarders, a new school building was erected at a cost of £8,000 on a spacious site in College Road in 1812. If the ensuing fall in enrolment is a guide, the move was not a success. According to the Education Inquiry of the 1820s, the school had only 20 students, 15 Protestants and 5 Catholics. There was something of a revival in the 1830s, but by the mid-1850s, enrolment was back again to only 20 students. Subsequent years saw things get worse, for the headmaster was reported to have allowed the premises 'to fall into a state of disrepair'. It was not until the appointment of Dr Biggs in 1875 that the situation improved. Biggs had previously operated a school in Parsonstown (Birr), and he brought the boarders from that school with him to Galway. When examined for the Commissioners for Endowed Schools in 1880, the school, by then known as the Grammar School, was thriving, with 70 boarders and 25 day students.[74]

During the first four decades of the 19th century, there was little Catholic concern about middle-class education. The Erasmus Smith school avoided ostracisation during its expansionary phase in the 1830s by employing a Catholic assistant teacher. Elsewhere, too, outside 'free-schools' and 'hedge schools', education was religiously-mixed — a pattern evident also, to give one example, in pre-Famine Derry. And the more expensive the school, the more religiously-mixed it was likely to be. The exclusive school run by Roman Catholics, Mr & Mrs Nicholais, in Middle-street had 31 Catholics and 30 Protestants in the mid-1820s. And even religiously-connected schools operated by Catholics catered to pupils of all denominations. Take, for example, the Kearns establishment, which claimed to prepare candidates for Maynooth.

According to the Irish Education Inquiry, it had 42 Catholics and 8 Protestants on its rolls. And the Galway Seminary for Young Ladies, which claimed the patronage of two Catholic bishops, had 21 Protestants and 44 Catholics.[75]

The publication by schools in the 1830s of material testifying to their religious scrupulosity suggests that there may have been some concern about the religious question in middle-class schools. Likewise with the opening of a new Back-street seminary in 1832. Miss Maxey, the headmistress, promised that her system would be 'precisely similar to that followed at Winchester Convent in Hampshire', where she has been educated. In welcoming the arrival of a 'respectable young lady connected with Galway, who has been educated at one of the first Catholic seminaries in England', a local paper argued that a school such as Miss Maxey's 'which embraces more particularly the English system of education' had 'long been a desideratum' in Galway. In fact, the published curriculum differed little from that offered by Mrs Haverty in 1817 and, indeed, by most of the academies and seminaries for girls that had advertised in the intervening years.[76]

Protestations such as those of Kearns, Maxey, and the Misses Golding of the Galway Seminary may have satisfied some, but they did not indefinitely postpone the intervention of Catholic religious in middle-class education. The late 1830s and early 1840s saw the establishment of two schools under immediate religious control.

'Troubles' in their Ennis convent and community caused the Ursuline Sisters to enter the crowded market in Galway in 1839, with a short-lived boarding school in the countryside at Dangan. Their curriculum was similar to that of the other institutions mentioned but, in 'the various branches of ornamental knowledge' — 'botany, conchology, minerology, heraldry, &c.' — the Ursulines had an edge. Moreover, students at Dangan whose parents were willing to pay extra might enjoy 'sea bathing, warm baths, or car exercise'. The persistence of 'troubles' in their community, however, led the Ursulines to leave Dangan and to follow their patron, Bishop Browne, to the diocese of Elphin in 1844.[77]

In 1843, shortly before his departure from Galway, Bishop Browne announced that the Augustinian Fathers were preparing to open a seminary for boys. The plan did not proceed very far, for in the same year, Fr John P. O'Toole, Galway-born professor of metaphysics at the Irish College in Paris, returned to open a school. Suitable premises became available in Helen-street in 1844, and, in 1846, Browne's successor, Laurence O'Donnell, declared the institution to be the diocesan college. This had implications for the attendance, requiring that 'all candidates for the Sacred Ministry in this diocese are henceforth to make their preparatory studies at St Mary's College of this town'.[78] But, like other diocesan colleges, St Mary's accepted non-ecclesiastical students. Indeed, ecclesiastics were a minority of students, and publicity emphasised that the College provided an education and an ambiance suitable for 'gentlemen':

> A constant and active superintendence is exercised over the pupils;
> they are never left alone, and thus the infractions of discipline are

prevented rather than repressed ... The course of instruction embraces the Latin and Greek classics, English Literature, the French and Italian Languages (universally acknowledged in this age of travelling to be an indispensable complement of a gentleman's education).[81]

Within a year of the College's establishment, there were fifty on the rolls, day students and boarders. At £30 a year, boarding fees were high but knowledge appropriate to the 'age of travelling' could hardly be provided cheaply.

These initiatives represented a fresh orientation of the local Catholic church towards middle-class education. In the previous period, the fear of proselytism had concentrated the attention of Catholic educationalists on elementary schooling. If this was changing in the early 1840s, the publication of the Queen's Colleges legislation in 1845 shifted the focus unequivocally onto the education of the middle-class.

The University legislation was part of a package of Irish reforms undertaken by Peel's government. As they were designed to assuage both Catholic and Protestant misgivings, the proposals might easily have been accepted. The Catholic bishops — in line with their position on the National system — sought denominationally-controlled colleges but, as in the former instance, there were many among them prepared to accept arrangements which fell short of the ideal. The ranks of the diehards, however, had been reinforced since the early 1830s, and their sense of purpose fortified. Moreover, they were able to win the backing of the Pope, as well as that of Vatican-insider, Paul Cullen who, crucially, was appointed to the See of Armagh in 1849.[80]

Galway's bishop, Laurence O'Donnell, was one of those who expressed reservations about the University legislation. But it would seem that he did so as part of a negotiating ploy, and that, privately, he was prepared to accept the 'Godless Colleges'. For their part, leading local Catholics lobbied that one of the Colleges be located in Galway. Another clergyman, engaged in a delicate negotiating process was Oughterard parish priest, J. W. Kirwan, who having preached against the colleges generally, applied for the presidency of Queen's College Galway. His application was successful — over other priests, including Fr O'Toole of St Mary's College. Kirwan died in 1849, two months after the first University students registered in Galway. He was succeeded by Vice-President, Berwick, but, since it was considered important that a Catholic occupy a senior post, Dr O'Toole's dusted-down application was sufficient to gain him the vice-presidency. Bishop O'Donnell approved his decision to accept.[81]

One casualty of all of this was St Mary's College. O'Toole closed it down, suggesting that the building be used as a Catholic university residence. Then, months after O'Toole's appointment, Cardinal Cullen won approval at the Synod of Thurles for a resolution insisting that Catholic priests break all connections with the 'Godless Colleges', and that the Catholic laity avoid them. Dr O'Toole had little choice but to resign, and accept a ministry in England.[82]

At that point, the future of Queen's College Galway seemed little brighter than that of St Mary's. Numbers in all three Queen's College were low from the beginning, with Galway's lowest of all. Situated in the poorest, the most emigration-ridden, the most Catholic part of Ireland, the mere survival of the Galway College was an accomplishment in itself. Numbers went up slowly in the early years, from 68 in 1849-50 to 85 in 1854-55. Enrolment reached its 19th century peak — 208 — in 1880-81, but the repeal of the rule requiring that students attend lectures brought about a disastrous reduction. There were less than a hundred students in 1885-86, and numbers did not recover substantially during the remainder of the century. Were it not for the influx of Ulster Presbyterians — they were the largest religious group in the 1880s — the College would hardly have survived attempts to close it.[83]

If Queen's College Galway was marginal to Irish education in the 19th century, it made a certain impression in its host city. Its construction and maintenance provided employment; its staff and their families boosted attendance at society events and minority church services; several of its professors strained themselves to enhance the intellectual and economic life of the town. Students too were a conspicuous if not a pervasive presence. During the quiet winter months, they were about 1% of the urban population, occupying — and occasionally vandalising — houses in Salthill which were let to visitors during the summer. For most Galwegians, the College was a place apart, its under-employed professors the secular equivalents of ministers of the established church. There was more contact with students whose teams, as was

In architectural style, Queen's College, Galway displays the influence of Christ Church College, Oxford (courtesy of NUI, Galway).

shown in Chapter Twelve, provided opposition for the nascent sports clubs of the late 19th century.*

If the controversy surrounding their establishment damaged the Queen's Colleges, it also had wider effects on Irish education. Caught in crossfire almost immediately was the National Board's plan to open a model school in each school district. Staffed by 'teachers of superior attainment', these schools would provide training for teachers, since male and female model schools in Dublin were unable to train enough teachers for the expanding system. But, since the network was under the direct control of the Board, it had the same defects in the eyes of the bishops as the 'Godless Colleges'. Two years before the Galway school opened in 1852, the project was condemned at the Synod of Thurles.

Nonetheless, the Galway Model School was an immediate success. No religious-run schools provided for the middle-class since the closure of the St Mary's and Ursuline seminaries, and the new school filled the vacuum. In its first year, there were 300 pupils, and enrolment reached almost 400 in 1862. A report from W.H. Newell, Head Inspector of National Schools, indicates what made the school attractive. 'It would be difficult to find', he wrote, 'a better elementary English school'. Bishop O'Donnell did not seriously oppose the school, and any expression of his reservations would have been negated by the manifest approval of Fr Peter Daly for the institution. The latter clergyman, more prominent in the 1850s than his bishop, acted for a time as an examiner in the school.[84] However, the appointment of Cardinal Cullen's close ally, John MacEvilly, to succeed O'Donnell in 1857, changed the local climate.

A few years elapsed before MacEvilly addressed the Model School issue. Then he acted decisively. He directed the Patrician Brothers and Mercy Sisters to open new schools to serve 'the middle-class of society', and instructed Catholic parents to withdraw their children from the school. Inspector Newell's report of February 1863 referred to the 'great blow' consequent to this announcement — the departure of 199 pupils and the resignation of Catholic monitresses. A year later, MacEvilly made attendance at the Model School a 'reserved sin' (which had to be confessed to the bishop in person) in the diocese. The school never recovered. Only half of the Catholic students left in 1863, but few were willing to face MacEvilly with a reserved sin to confess. By 1872, only 19 of the 133 pupils in the Model School were Catholics.[85]

Just as the Mercy Sisters and the Patrician Brothers joined battle against the Model School, two other religious orders took up the work of educating the middle-class. The Dominican Sisters opened a day school 'for Young Ladies' in Taylor's Hill in 1858 and, in 1859, the Jesuits returned to Galway after an

---

* Students' extra-curricular activities also impressed upon other aspects of town life: when a new police station was located in Salthill in the early 1860s, the nocturnal 'outrages' of College students in the area was cited as the principal factor making it necessary; when Town Commissioners lobbied the Lord Lieutenant to require President Berwick to live in the College a few years later, they were prompted by a series of disorderly episodes, which had culminated in the imprisonment (with hard labour) of five students for smashing window panes (National Archives, CSORP 1865/3644).

absence of almost a century, opening St Ignatius College — for 'boys of the upper classes', according to MacEvilly — in the following year. From the beginning, St Ignatius's had a strongly academic emphasis, and distinguished itself in the examinations run by Newman's Catholic University.[86]

But despite the efforts of Jesuits and others, the numbers receiving a 'Superior' education remained modest in Galway (A 'Superior' education was defined as one which included at least one subject of the range: Latin, Greek, Modern Languages, Mathematics). In 1871, only 288 pupils — 51 Protestant boys, 98 Catholic boys, and 139 Catholic girls — were in this category, with the provision of French as an 'accomplishment' explaining the strong female showing.[87]

A desire to improve standards and participation levels post-primary led to the introduction of Intermediate examinations in 1879. The examinations were the device used to reform the sector — 'intermediate' because of its position between elementary schools and universities. Based on the system in the Catholic colony of Trinidad, Intermediate Education was introduced uncontroversially because — in line with Catholic demands — it was state-funded but allowed for denominational control. Schools, and students, were rewarded according to their performance in state examinations but were not subject to inspection. 80 boys and 34 girls sat the first examinations in Galway. Early results were discouraging and the number of candidates declined in subsequent years. In 1882, for example, 42 boys sat the examinations in the Grammar School, 32 boys in St Ignatius's, and 25 girls at the examination centre in Mack's Hotel Room. The results premiums paid show that only the Grammar School profited from the system, and that Galway's Catholic schools performed poorly. In 1892, two Galway schools won results premiums: the Grammar school received £175.17.6 and St Ignatius's £1.17.0. Elsewhere in the county, to give one example, St Jarlath's of Tuam got £111.8.6. And, reflecting the emphasis on 'accomplishment' rather than on academic achievement, no girls' schools between Ballymote, Co. Sligo, and Ennis won a premium.[88]

Some reasons for the poor Catholic performance in Intermediate examinations were provided by Brother John Lynch, founding superior of the Patrician Brothers seminary (the Bishop's school, or simply 'the Bish'), a witness before the Education Endowments Commissioners in 1888. His school was a recognised National School, but a quarter of the hundred-odd students were receiving a 'Superior' education. For several years, however, none of the 'Bish' boys had taken Intermediate examinations. The Commissioners were curious about this, especially since 'the Christian Brothers taught almost 40% of all the boys' who had passed these exams. Lynch considered the comparison between his order and the Christian Brothers to be unfair. His school was small, whereas, in Dublin and Cork, it was possible for the Christian Brothers to 'select from all their schools the pupils who are suited for a certain class', and to appoint 'masters who pay special attention to that class'. Moreover, he did not have the resources to equip his school with the apparatus for Natural Philosophy, and many of his boys could not afford Intermediate texts.

Lynch expressed severe reservations about the system, arguing that some boys who had done well in Intermediate exams were 'completely ignorant of other matters that were actually essential' for their future careers. (Other western schools complained that their students were disadvantaged because they started school at too late an age and were ineligible to compete in the Intermediate grade appropriate to their schooling.) But notwithstanding his defensiveness under questioning, Lynch had in fact reconsidered his attitude and was, even then, preparing a class for the forthcoming Intermediate examinations.[89]

In 1900, 'the Bish' capitulated fully to the demands of the intermediate system when it divided itself in two, an elementary school — still distinct from the Patrician's elementary school for poorer boys — and a secondary school. Thereafter, 'Bish' students excelled in the Intermediate system. Something of the early 20th century atmosphere in the school — and perhaps of other schools — was conveyed in a former pupil's description of one of his teachers:

> Red-faced and low-sized, stout within his green sash; given to headaches in the morning and (extraordinary cure) wearing when so afflicted a handkerchief rolled and tightly knotted about his brow; full of aphorisms; wise in the knowledge of the farmyard; a persistent and resourceful teacher with a threatening cane and a heart of pure gold … He dominated that room that no longer exists — that room of glazed folding doors, brown tongued-and-grooved sheeting and pictures of a Viking raid and Shane O'Neill at the court of Elizabeth on the walls — dominated it like a hanging judge, or a benevolent despot, or a father of his family.[90]

Mechanics' Institute

The establishment of a Galway Mechanics' Institute was announced in August 1826. It was anticipated that the provision of instruction and of appropriate reading materials for Galway artisans would be of great benefit, both to the artisans themselves and to the town:

> While the tradesman feels its effect in a moral point of view, he finds his mind enlightened, and becomes acquainted with the politics of the day, and how various matters connected with his welfare and prosperity as an Operative and as a Citizen are ordered elsewhere.[91]

The initiative came from a committee, which included the mayor, James Hardiman Burke; James O'Hara, M.P; Lord Wallscourt; and Robert Martin of Ross, who offered the Institute the use of the ballroom above the Corn Exchange. Such patronage was characteristic of the Mechanics' Institutes movement, which was inaugurated in London in 1823, and introduced to Ireland with the foundation of Dublin's Institute in 1825. Middle- and upper-class patrons became involved for various reasons: some were philanthropists;

others were employers seeking to provide counter-attraction to tradesmen's combinations; yet others were entrepreneurs eager to enhance the skills of the local artisanate. Predictably, the differing perspective of middle-class and of mechanic members was a source of early conflict in many Institutes.[92]

Such motives were not absent among the Galway patrons, but the main difference between them and artisans was political. The Institute's founders were supporters of the Daly interest, while existing trades 'guilds' had been hostile to the Dalys who had opposed extending the franchise to Catholic freemen. There were suspicions that the initiative was an attempt to win over artisans in advance of their inevitable enfranchisement. This was denied: the Institute was 'totally unconnected with Politics', one apologist asserted, its purpose was to disseminate 'knowledge of Mechanics, the Arts and Sciences, Philosophy, &c.'[93]

By 1828, a spokesman for the Institute insisted that great progress had been made. A 'scientific library' was in place, and the local tradesmen had 'evinced more than ordinary enthusiasm' in availing of this facility. Indeed, some of them — improbably — had been 'initiated in the mysteries of science in a few days'. In just two years, it was claimed, the Institute had already reached a position where it was possible to consider withdrawing newspapers from its library. These had been 'introduced to attract people initially', but it was felt that 'light reading is not suitable to the purpose of the Mechanics' Institute'.[94]

The possession of scientific knowledge boosted the confidence of younger tradesmen, leading some of them to challenge their masters and to ignore established procedures. At one point, in response to this unwelcome tendency, master operatives withdrew in a body from the Institute.[95]

And politically-rooted suspicion also persisted. This was adverted to in the Institute's own publicity, which claimed that local tradesmen were entirely committed to the Institute, 'with the exception of a few of the minor orders of mechanics who seceded from feelings of stupid ignorance, or untoward prejudice'. For many, the partisanship of the Institute was confirmed by presentations and addresses during 1829 to two benefactors, the Rev. John D'Arcy, and the evangelical Protestant Archbishop of Tuam, le Poer Trench. The latter gesture prompted condemnatory resolutions from several trades guilds, and, apparently, led the landlord of the Mechanics' premises to reclaim the building and its contents.[96]

Potential patrons were also alienated. An anonymous 'Mechanic' complained in 1830 of a 'shameful falling off' of many subscribers' including 'those, who at its formation, seemed most desirous for the establishment of such an Institute'. He went on to outline the potential benefits of the movement, before acknowledging the failure of its local manifestation:

> Here the mechanic has a resting place after his day's labour, where,
> in place of going to the public house to spend at night perhaps
> what was earned in the day, he is induced by a well-selected library,

composed of the works of all the mechanics who have gone before and wrote for his improvement, to come and enlarge his ideas … I cannot, Mr Editor, but lament that our Galway Mechanics' Institute does not receive such support as should enable it to confer all of these advantages.[97]

'Mechanic' was convinced that the situation was more favourable elsewhere, but the truth was that Mechanics' Institutes throughout Ireland declined after the commotion surrounding their establishment abated. This has been attributed to the unrealistic expectations aroused by the movement's early propaganda, to opposition from employers who feared that education would render their workforce less malleable, and to the alternative focus of interest provided by the O'Connellite politics.[98]

Facing these challenges, Galway's Institute did not help matters by associating with a brand of politics unpopular among its target membership. Before the 1830 general election, it placed an advertisement detailing the virtues of James O'Hara, M.P. (although it did not break its own rules by canvassing votes for him). In the same election, the tradesmen's guilds were unanimous in supporting O'Hara's opponent, Valentine Blake.[99] The indications are that the bitterness aroused by this contest was the final nail in the coffin of the ailing Institute. Certainly, its affairs, if any, were no longer reported.

A revival of the Mechanics' Institutes in Ireland took place in the mid-1830s, but Galway lagged behind. By the time the movement was re-established, its promoters preferred to forget the earlier initiative. A history of the Institute in Galway was compiled in 1844 by its secretary, Patrick Field, who traced the story 'from its first foundation in a small room in Shop-street in the year 1840 up to the present period, which attests its more vigorous existence in a new and beautiful structure in Middle-street'.[100] In its second incarnation, the Galway Institute was an arm of the temperance movement, and membership was restricted to those who had taken the pledge. As in the 1820s, politics were renounced. 'On no account', according to the rules, 'shall politics, religious controversy, or other irritating subjects be introduced'. In 1844, the rules were amended to admit 'sober and well-conducted mechanics who may not as yet have taken the pledge', but those 'teetotal members' who violated their pledge remained liable to expulsion. For those satisfying these conditions, the rules defined two categories of membership, collective and individual:

Fourth — that the payment of 10*s*, to be paid quarterly by the Trades, members of this Institute, shall constitute the yearly subscription, and entitle each member to a free place during the annual course of lectures to be delivered at the Institute by a Professor from the Royal Dublin Society.

Fifth — that in order to extend more widely the benefit of a well conducted Mechanics' Institute, as well as to secure for it the encouragement and sanction which Mechanics' Institutes have met with in the sister country, from every situation and class, all professional gentlemen, as well as those in trade or business, may, in accordance with these rules, become members of this Institute for the annual subscription of £1 ...[101]

The approach to recruitment indicates that the promoters of the revived Institute had far-reaching objectives for the artisans. By enrolling them through the affiliation of their trades unions, by educating them, by bringing them into contact with shopkeepers and professionals, it was anticipated that both the social position and the general outlook of artisans would be affected. But, as the decision to admit the 'sober' alongside the teetotal shows, the reality on the ground sometimes meant that procedures had to be adjusted.

If the admission policy was demanding of members, so was the educational programme. Take, for example, the course of twelve lectures given by Dr Robert Kane in 1844. The advertised topics of the first lecture were as follows: 'Objects and Advantages of the Study of Natural Philosophy; Laws of Motion; Inertia, Action, and Reaction; Composition and Resolution of Forces; Parallel Forces; Angular Forces'. As the weeks passed, more complex material was introduced, until the final weeks, when the latest technologies were explained: Lecture Eleventh: Construction of the Double Acting Condensing Steam Engine; Of the Cylinder and its Valves; The Eccentric; Of the Beam and Parallel Motion; Nature of the Crank Apparatus for Condensation; Steam Gauges; Squirt Cock and hot water Pump; Cold water Pump; Governor and Throttle Pump.[102]

It was an ambitious programme, and one wonders whether tradesmen who were admitted free, or even the middle-class men who paid ten shillings, derived much benefit from them. In fairness to Kane, a keen supporter of Mechanics' Institutes, he was aware that his lectures went over most heads and, at the Dublin Institute in 1844, he proposed that tutorial support be provided, so that people might benefit more from libraries and lectures.[103]

Kane's expertise found another outlet in 1845 — he was appointed to the government's commission inquiring into potato blight — and events also cut across the ordinary work of the Institutes. In January 1846, the Institute's secretary drew attention to the 'alarming state' of Galway tradesmen and, for a number of years, the matter of survival took precedence over self-improvement. When the fortunes of local tradesmen improved with the beginning of major building projects late in the 1840s, the Mechanics Institute acted as the headquarters of several of their trade unions (see Chapter Four).

It was not until August 1849, by which time there were solid indications of recovery, that lectures were resumed with a series on 'Universal History' by Rev. D. W. Cahill. More focused, and more topical, in the following year was the series on 'Political Economy' given by the new Professor of Logic and Metaphysics at Queen's College Galway, Thomas Moffett.* The Committee might have been gratified that Moffett's lectures attracted the 'notice of every grade and class', but the tone of the Institute was becoming too bourgeois for some, and, in 1850, the *Galway Mercury* urged members to attend the annual meeting to ensure that 'proper working men' were elected to positions.[104]

Some re-orientation was attempted in 1851 when it was resolved to follow the example of the Limerick Institute in providing night classes for the children of tradesmen 'who may be prevented by their occupations from attending the ordinary daily schools'. Classes in Limerick were attracting large numbers.[105]

Progress was inhibited by financial problems — to the discredit, it was said, of 'tradesmen who've been getting ample wages during the last four years' — and the building closed completely in November 1853. The crisis forced a merger with St Patrick's Temperance Society and, with the benefit of a soiree and a number of donations, activities resumed.[106] Occasional public lectures were reported, but the Institute operated at a low key for some years, until the night school issue was re-visited in 1870. Welcoming the extension of working class education, the *Galway Express* commented that the only 'wonder was that such extension was not made long before this'. As far as the youth of that class were concerned, the paper went on:

> The long interval which usually elapses from the cessation of school-going till the completion of the apprenticeship to business or trades is, generally, as regards the improvement of the intellect, unprofitably spent; nay, do we not know that many of the leisure hours of that portion of the life are unfortunately spent in demoralising or debasing pleasures, which, as a matter of course, bring on their usual train of sad consequences.[107]

The project was supported by the National Board, but success was limited. In 1874, by official return, there were 210 on the rolls but average nightly attendance was only 23.[108]

The night classes of the 1850s and 1870s were an attempt by the Institute to reach the 'mechanic' class for which it was founded. Otherwise, its facilities increasingly catered to the relatively educated, and there was little difference between lectures organised by the scholarly Royal Galway Institution and those of the Institute. There is an indication of the post-Famine membership profile in the occupations given for nine new members admitted in August 1863: civil engineer, bank official, 'gentleman', two grocers, two masons, fitter and turner, tailor. Of lecture series during the same era, it was noted that they were always

---

* Cahill was an unsuccessful applicant for the presidency of QCG in 1845. Moffett, for his part, was a keen political economist, who lectured widely throughout Ireland to Mechanics' Institutes and kindred bodies (Foley & Bateman, 'English, History and Philosophy' in Foley, ed., *From Queen's College*, p. 395).

well-attended at the beginning, but that few persisted with them. Tradesmen, one critic argued, derived 'little benefit' from lectures because preliminary reading — or preliminary knowledge — was required to understand them.[109]

This might have changed in the mid-1870s, when evangelicals identified the Institute as an arena for their work. A number of controversial topics were considered under the auspices of a Mechanics' Institute Literary and Debating Society, and plans were made to run 'Penny readings'. The initiative was soon abandoned, however.[110] A decade later, prompted by the renovation of its Middle-street premises, a local newspaper commented on the ambiance and traditions of the Institute. Its remarks might equally have been applied to the County Club:

> The Institution, which is one of the oldest established in Galway, has a most magnificent library, which contains many rare works of inestimable value. The number of members is very large, and comprises the most learned and respectable gentlemen in the community, amongst which all branches of science and all grades and professions are represented.[111]

During the Land League era, there are indications of change in the political tone of the Institute — change that was not to the taste of all members. Subscriptions to conservative and English periodicals were allowed to lapse (London's *Times,* for example, was discontinued in September 1880), to be replaced by Irish publications. Significantly also, Parnell was honoured by the Institute in 1880, while Michael Davitt delivered a lecture to members and guests in 1884. There were efforts, meanwhile, to preserve the Institute's social tone. Committee resolutions urged silence in the reading room, and members were occasionally disciplined — but rarely expelled — for 'ungentlemanly language', and for 'disorderly conduct'. Occasional initiatives of a loosely educational character aimed at satisfying the generally lower middle-class membership rather than at 'improving' the mechanic class as a whole. A literary society, launched in 1886, was one such and it enabled members to present short papers on pet topics to small numbers of their colleagues. Events under the auspices of the excursions committee of the Institute, which was established two decades later, attracted rather more interest.[112]

'…every article in the stationery and bookselling way'
In the 1830s, some thousands of Galwegians could read, yet one visitor was disappointed that reading seemed to be little valued: 'Not only is there no literary institution', he complained, 'but not even a bookseller's shop'. Henry Inglis's remark became the conventional wisdom on the subject when it was quoted by two separate witnesses before a select committee on education in Ireland.[113] Thackeray, a few years later, also failed to find a 'regular book-shop', but he found some books: 'A man who sells hunting whips, gunpowder, guns, fishing tackle, and brass and iron ware, has a few books on his counter, and a

lady in a bye-street, who carries on the profession of a milliner, eked out her stock in a similar way'.[114] Neither of the distinguished travellers were knowledgeable on the operation of Ireland's provincial book trade, for only in the cities of Dublin, Belfast and Cork were there specialist bookshops. Outside of these major centres, books were sold by stationers and such traders. There certainly existed in Galway book-sellers somewhat more 'regular' than Thackeray's milliner and gunsmith. As early as the 1790s, George Hynes, a grocer and auctioneer of High-street, ran a circulating library and claimed to stock 'every article in the stationery and bookselling way'.[115] And in the second decade of the 19th century, bookbinder Caleb Conolly advertised a selection of books in his shop at the New Buildings, High-street, at 'from 25 to 50 per Cent. under the usual prices'. These included the twelve volumes of Gibbon's History of Rome, as well as 'Catholic and Protestant Bibles at various sizes'.

Conolly also stocked popular titles, notably *Six Weeks at Long's, Tales of My Landlord,* and Lady Morgan's *France.* Galway had several circulating libraries, and one writer has shown that several of them at did a brisk trade. Caleb Conolly's relative, George Conolly, publisher of the *Galway Advertiser* and *Galway Independent,* ran a library for four decades after 1800, which had over 1,000 volumes which were let out to subscribers for as little as three-halfpence a night.[116] Almost anybody, therefore, might have afforded to read a book. Scandalous predilections were catered for, and in the early 19th century, there were locally-generated examples of the popular 'Crim. Con.' genre — transcripts of proceedings from the civil courts — some of which had a circulation far beyond the town. Under the heading 'Crim. Con.', Caleb Conolly brought a recent publication to the attention of the public in 1817:

> A full, factual, and impartial report of that curious, extraordinary and interesting trial with the speeches of Counsel, and judge's charge, in the case wherein Mark Browne, Esq., was Plaintiff, and Martin J. Blake, Esq., defendant in an action for damages for Crim. Con. with the plaintiff's wife.[117]

A neighbour of Conolly's in Galway's literary quarter of High-street was John Clayton, who was promoting his wares in 1823.* By the mid-1830s, this business had passed to P. Clayton, whose enterprise should have been noticed by Henry Inglis. Clayton, who also sold luxury toiletries and perfumes, had an extensive list of novels and improving works, as well as a stock of 'Periodicals, Reviews and Magazines', which included *The Quarterly Review, The Westminster Review,* and *The Dublin University Magazine.*[118]

The tone of his announcement and the titles of his periodicals, indicate that Clayton catered to an upper- and middle-class clientele. And as for locally-

---

* Pigott's *Directory* of 1821 listed six 'Booksellers & Stationers' as follows: 'Clayton Matthew, (perfumer and general fancy warehouse) High-st; Conolly, Caleb, High-st; Connolly, George, High-st; Ians Christians, High-st; Macartney Saint George, Shop-st; O'Flaherty John, Cross-st'.

published newspapers, their insignificant circulation points in a similar direction. In 1822 — sixty-eight years after its establishment — the *Connaught Journal* claimed a circulation of only 192 copies, Conolly's *Galway Weekly Advertiser* claimed 145, while in the period following its foundation in 1825, the *Galway Independent* claimed less than a hundred. And to achieve these figures, editors found it necessary to include material appealing to well-to-do readers throughout the county and beyond.[119] (Publishers, it should be noted, sometimes under-stated true circulation in order to avoid stamp duty.)

Before George Conolly died in 1839, his 'printing, book-binding and circulating library establishment' passed to his son, Thomas. There may, at the same time, have been a decline in the enterprise's ethical standard, for Thomas came to the attention of magistrates soon afterwards. Having ceased publishing the ultra-Protestant *Galway Advertiser* in 1843, he had turned his efforts to a slim and scurrilous periodical entitled *Will O' the Wisp: Galway Weekly Visitor,* costing just a penny and aimed at a popular readership. A humorous publication, two of its pages were taken up with articles lifted from English magazines. Of greater interest was the local gossip in the other two pages, of which the following, headed 'Cross-street', is illustrative:

> We caution a certain widow residing in Cross-street, to drop from this forth her ingenious devies in severing the ties of conjugal comfort by coveting the society of a certain gentleman, and causing him to lavish money that would otherwise be applied for domestic comfort. We trust this shameful conduct will be discontinued, if not we shall have recourse to strong personal language.[120]

Conolly was not satisfied to merely circulate scandal, but he also boosted circulation by approaching those he proposed featuring in forthcoming issues for subscriptions. For a mere 2*s* 6*d*, subscribers might excise any unfavourable references to themselves in *Will O' the Wisp.* It was this clumsy attempt at blackmail rather than the contents of the periodical that attracted the authorities' attention.[121] Surviving examples of ephemeral reading material are rare: a solitary sample of Thomas Conolly's paper survives, but only because it was a vehicle for its editor's criminality. As far as its readership was concerned, it can be hazarded that it was greater than that of the other Conolly family weeklies, the *Advertiser* and the *Independent.*

It is possible that working-class readers enjoyed reading about the shenanigans of their social superiors in *Will O' the Wisp;* it is possible too that they patronised one or more of the circulating libraries in the town. The impression, however, is that their reading habits were different from the middle- and upper-classes, and that their reading material was acquired in different circumstances. Much of it was not purchased in bookshops, 'regular' or otherwise, but in the streets, from itinerant peddlars, chapmen, and ballad-singers. And, as more people of the working and peasant classes learned to read, there was growing concern about the content of their reading, popular books like Cosgrave's *Irish Rogues* being considered subversive insofar as they exculpated criminality. Nevertheless, according to Archbishop Kelly of Tuam, such books were employed as texts in West of Ireland schools in the 1820s.[122]

Considered subversive also were the ballad-slips sold by ballad singers at fairs, elections, and executions. Headed by woodcut illustrations so as to appeal to non-literate people, the words of street ballads tended to reflect popular sentiment and prejudice. Sometimes, this meant that they were romantic or humorous, but often it meant that they articulated sectarian or seditious attitudes. One ballad which drew unwanted attention to its singer was the following, supporting Martin Blake, O'Connellite candidate for Galway county in 1835. It is not known whether it was published by Blake's campaign team, but in indicting indifferent electors as apostates in league with 'priest hunters', it may have played a part in consolidating support for the candidate:

> Martin Blake he will stand for the city election
> And craves of poor Erin for dearest protection
> The vengeance of heaven I'm sure will prevail
> On any apostate that will turn tail
> To join those priest hunters who are sworn to grind you
> So vote for Martin Blake and Shela na Guire

Galway Advertiser and *Will O' the Wisp*: two very different publications from the Conolly Press in High Street.

The surviving copy of the printed ballad, located in a secret intelligence file, had an explanatory hand-written note on the back:

> Galway. 12 January 1835. The person who was singing these ballads was by order of the Mayor arrested and brought to the police barracks. Immediately after M. Blake attended at the barracks and ordered the police to release the prisoner, which was complied with.[123]

Other surviving ballad slips from the 19th century were prompted by political tumult such as the Nolan/Trench election of 1872, by public executions such as that of the Maamtrasna Martyrs in 1882, and by the funeral of the Dominican preacher, Fr Tom Burke, in 1883 — all events which mobilised large crowds. But whether ballads inspired by such public events were as popular than those in praise of 'Eileen Dheelish of Athenry' or of 'The Maid of Ardrahan' can only be guessed at. However, the survival of a number of ballad-slips celebrating the Galway packet station project of the 1850s indicates that it captured the popular imagination for a time, and at least one of them entered the oral tradition.[124] Such publications represented an intermediate stage between an oral and a literate culture, and between an Irish and an English one. Sometimes macaronic — with alternate verses or familiar Irish language refrains rendered in English orthography and phonology — they functioned more as *aides memoires* than as texts.

Also representing an intermediate stage between the oral and the literate were the so-called 'Penny Readings' of the 1870s and 1880s, organised by *bienfaisant* groupings concerned to shape the tastes of tentative readers.[125] Such concern, indeed, developed in step with the growth in literacy levels and, already, Paul O'Connor had established a library to save his pupils from being corrupted by their education. In 1856, he urged former pupils to join the library attached to his Aloysian Society, which had 'nearly one thousand select volumes, affording wholesome food for your minds, and an antidote to the poisonous literature of the world'.[126] In the era of universal literacy, the censorious impulse would become almost hysterical, culminating in campaigns against 'evil literature' — especially English newspapers — in the early 20th century.

But a less formal manuscript and oral tradition continued to exist in the era of the printed ballad and the 'penny dreadful', as the following news item, headlined 'An Unlucky Poet' indicates:

> On Sunday night last a young fellow named Walsh, a painter by trade, was arrested for having indulged too freely in the essence of the barleycorn, and when searched in the police station, as is the custom when a victim of intemperance falls into the hands of the constabulary, a piece of paper was found in his pocket, which was read by the police, and turned out to be a production of the most

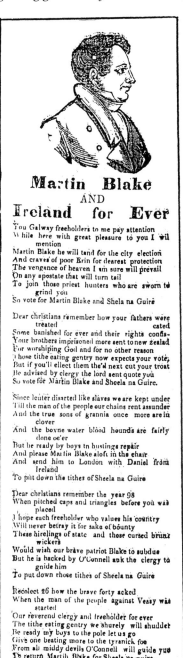

Ballad slip issued during Galway town election of 1835 (NAI).

contemptible doggerel ever … The effusion was nothing less than a description of the reception which Mayor Clifford Lloyd would meet with should he honour the 'Citie of the Tribes' with a visit.[127]

Walsh denied having written the offending verses, whereupon the spotlight turned upon his drinking companion, one Carr. The police went to that man's home in Buttermilk-lane — 'one of the last places in town where a person might expect to find an admirer of the muses' — and took him to the barracks:

> After searching every nook and corner of his residence for anything that might give a clue to his connection with some desperate plot, such as revolvers, gun-cotton, dynamite, or infernal machines, but without effect, for nothing could be got other than a copy-book in which the poet was in the habit of practising his penmanship, and this the constabulary thought bore some resemblance to the writing found in Walsh's pocket … It is stated that Carr, who is a young man bearing a good character, has a propensity for making verses … and this being known to the police, and the fact that he had been last in the company of Walsh, induced them to connect him with this 'mountain in labour'.[128]

The *Express* writer's mocking tone was a response to the topic of Carr's verses — Loyalist hero, Clifford Lloyd, had to be defended. But there was an undertone of more general disapproval in the report. The idea that a tradesman might be 'an admirer of the muses' was ridiculed and, with it, any suggestion that popular balladry could have merit. Despite disapproval, however, 'songs of the street' retained their popularity in the era of universal literacy.

NOTES

1. John Brady, *Catholics and Catholicism in the Eighteenth Century Press,* Maynooth 1965, p. 145; Kenneth Milne, *The Irish Charter Schools, 1730-1830,* Dublin 1997, pp. 11-33.
2. See D. H Akenson, *The Irish Education Experiment: the National System of Education in the Nineteenth Century,* London 1970; John Coolahan, *Irish Education: History and Structure,* Dublin 1981.
3. Akenson, *Experiment,* pp.17-59; Milne's *Charter Schools,* passim.; James Hardiman, *History of Galway,* Galway 1820, p. 176n, 305-06, 310-12.
4. For several reasons, especially that they were based on self-assessment, census returns are defective guides to literacy; they are a guide nonetheless. See John Logan, 'Sufficient to their needs: literacy and elementary schooling in the 19th century' in Daly & Dickson, eds, *Origins of Popular literacy,* Dublin 1990, pp. 113-38.
5. K. P. Hackett, 'Phases of education in Galway City', unpublished M.A. thesis, UCG 1935, pp. 6-19.
6. ibid., pp. 7-8.
7. ibid., pp. 6-11.
8. ibid., p. 9.
9. *Burke's Connaught Journal,* 19 January 1792; Hardiman's *Galway,* p. 306.
10. Hackett, 'Phases', p. 65; Hardiman, *Galway,* p. 278. The Charter School site is in the modern Presentation Rd.
11. James Glassford, *Notes of Three Tours in Ireland in 1824 and 1826,* Bristol 1832, p. 280.
12. Hardiman, *Galway,* p. 313n. For language shift, see M. Ó Murchú, *Language and Community,* passim, G. B. Adams. 'The 1851 language census in the north of Ireland' in *Ulster Folklife,* 20, 1974, pp. 65-70, and 'Aspects of monoglottism in Ulster, *Ulster Folklife* 22, 1976, pp. 76-87; G. Fitzgerald, 'Estimates for baronies of minimum levels of Irish-speaking' in *Proceedings of the R.I.A,* sect. C, vol. 84, no. 3, Dublin 1984; M. E. Daly 'Literacy and Language Change' in Daly & Dickson, eds, *The Origins of Popular Literacy in Ireland,* Dublin 1990, pp. 153-66.

13. L. A. de Shiubhlaí, 'Saothar Oideachais Bráithre Padraic in Éireann, 1808-1878' unpublished M.A. thesis, UCG 1962, pp. 116-17.
14. *Connaught Journal,* 16 February 1824. See also ibid., 29 January, 12 February 1824.
15. de Shiubhlaí, 'Bráithre Padraic', pp.116-7; Sr M. Fahy, *Education in the Diocese of Kilmacduagh,* pp. 100-1.
16. de Shiubhlaí, 'Bráithre Padraic', p. 117-19; *Connaught Journal,* 29 January 1828.
17. *Connaught Journal,* 29 January 1828.
18. ibid.
19. ibid.
20. ibid.
21. ibid.
22. Akenson, *Experiment,* pp.17-80; *Connaught Journal,* 20 November 1823, 16 October, 6, 20 November 1826.
23. Akenson, *Experiment,* pp. 86-96.
24. *Appendix to 2nd report of Commissioners of Irish Education Inquiry,* 1826-7 xii, pp1222-29. Information was provided by Catholic and Protestant authorities. In some details they disagree, and where this is the case, the Catholic information is relied upon.
25. ibid.
26. Akenson, *Experiment,* pp. 94-122.
27. ibid., p. 156.
28. ibid., pp. 206-13; John P. Lynch, *Life of Brother Paul O'Connor,* Dublin 1886, pp. 162-68; *Connaught Journal,* 5 February, 9 April 1835.
29. *Connaught Journal,* 15 April 1830, 5 May 1831, 15 January 1835; Henry Inglis, *A Journey Throughout Ireland during the Spring, Summer, and Autumn of 1834,* London 1838, p. 216.
30. *Connaught Journal,* 15 January 1835
31. *Galway Advertiser,* 24 March 1838; *Galway Vindicator,* 20 March 1844.
32. *Galway Vindicator,* 8 July 1844; *Appendices to National Education Report* 1864, xix, pt. ii, p. 161.
33. Inglis, *Journey,* p. 216.
34. John Barrow, *A Tour Around Ireland Through the Sea-coast Counties,* Appendix 1, pp. 12-13.
35. Cited in *Presentation Convent, Galway, 1815-1965,* Galway 1965, p. 59.
36. Jonathon Binns, *The Miseries and Beauties of Ireland,* London 1837, p. 407.
37. Barrow, *Tour,* pp. 266-67.
38. Hardiman, *Galway,* p. 294n; Dutton, *Galway,* p. 410. Incidentally, Hely Dutton's attitude to the place is indicated by his translation of 'Claddagh' as 'dirty place' rather than as 'stony shore'.
39. Alf MacLochlainn, 'The Claddagh Piscatory School', pp. 7-11; ED1/34, Claddagh.
40. M. P. Cryan, 'The Sisters of Mercy in Connaught, 1840-70', M.A. thesis, U.C.G., 1963, p. 48.
41. ED1/34; ED1/35, Newtownsmith.
42. EDI/34, Menlo, Bushypark.
43. *15th National Education Report,* 1849 xxiii, pp. 3-4; Akenson, *Experiment,* pp. 140, 321, 346.
44. Linus H. Walker, *One Man's Famine,* pp. 12-15; *Galway Vindicator,* 18 March , 23 December 1846.
45. Walker, *One Man's Famine,* pp. 23-25, 31; *Appendix to 14th National Education Report* 1847-8 xxix, p. 132.
46. Walker, *One Man's Famine,* p. 58; C. Kinealy, *This Great Calamity,* pp. 207-09; *15th Report of Education Commssioners,* 1849 xxiii, pp. 3-4.
47. Walker, *One Man's Famine,* pp. 23-25, 31, 80.
48. ibid., p. 37.
49. *15th National Education Report,,* 1849 xxiii, pp. 3-4; Walker, *One Man's Famine,* pp. 104.
50. *Appendix to 13th National Education Report,* 1847 xvii, pp. 112-13; *Appendix to 14th National Education Report,* 1847-48 xxix, pp. 131-33; *Papers relating to … relief of distress, 6th series,* 1847-48 lvi, pp. 141-43, 147.
51. Hon. & Rev. Sidney Godolphn Osborne, *Gleanings in the West of Ireland,* London 1850, pp. 55-57.
52. Walker, *One Man's Famine,* p. 61
53. Alf MacLochlainn, 'Claddagh Piscatory School', pp15-18; *14th National Education Report,* 1847-8 xxix, p. 15.
54. ED1/34, Taylor's Hill Convent School; Sr Rose O'Neill, *A Rich Inheritance,* pp. 51-52.
55. ED1/35, No. 34; ED18/NO. 84, Menlo.
56. ED1/35, Bohermore.
57. ED1/34, 143, Gortacleva, 152, Claddagh Female.
58. ED 18/75, Rahoon Female.

59. ibid.
60. ED2/136, Newtownsmith school.
61. ED2/136, Rahoon female; *Appendix to 58th National Education Report,* 1892 xxx, p. 280.
62. ibid.
63. ED 2/136, Claddagh Male
64. ibid.; Eustás Ó Héideáin, O.P. (ed.), *The Dominicans in Galway, 1241-1991,* Galway 1991, p. 17-18.
65. Akenson, *Experiment,* pp. 276, 321. *Appendices to 41st National Education Report,* 1875 xxv, p. 245-46, *to 58th National Education Report,* 1892 xxx, p.278, *to 66th National Education Report* 1900 xxxiii, p. 102.
66. Coolahan, *Irish education,* pp. 52-83; An Roinn Oideachais,*Tuarascáil na Comhairle Oideachais: curaclam na meánscoile,* 1962, pp. 28-50.
67. *Select Committee on Foundation Schools,* 1837-38 vii, p. 15.
68. Hardiman, *Galway,* pp. 176n, 310, 311n; *Endowed Schools Commission,* 1857-58 xxii, p. 69.
69. *Burke's Connaught Journal,* 30 July 1792.
70. *Appendix to 2nd report of Commissioners of Irish Education Inquiry,* 1826-7 xii, pp. 1222-29.
71. *Connaught Journal,* 24 February 1817, 20 December 1827, 22 December 1831.
72. ibid., 31 March, 5 May 1828, 5, 12 January, 23 March 1829, 6 September 1830, 17 July, 15 December 1831, 10 July 1834, 23 April 1835.
73. Hardiman, *Galway,* p. 311n
74. *Endowed Schools Commission,* 1857-58 xxii pt 1, pp. 69-70; *Endowed Schools Commission,* 1881 xxxv, p. 80.
75. *Appendix to 2nd Report of Commissioners of Irish Education Inquiry,* 1826-7 xii, pp. 1222-29. ibid.; *Connaught Journal,* 22 December 1831, 23 April 1835; John Hume, *Derry: Beyond the Walls,* Belfast 2002, pp. 98-101.
76. *Connaught Journal,* 15 December 1831.
77. *Catholic Registry,* 1844, pp. 422-23; Anon,'The Ursuline Nuns in Galway, 1839-44' in *The Mantle,* vol ii, no. 1, pp. 22-24; Sr. M. Kelly, *The Sligo Ursulines,* pp. 157-58; Caitriona Clear, *Nuns in Nineteenth Century Ireland*, Dublin 1987, p. 44.
78. *Galway Vindicator,* 5 April 1843; James Mitchell, 'The First St Mary's in *The Mantle,* vol. v, no. 3, pp. 27-32.
79. ibid., p. 28.
80. Gearóid Ó Tuathaigh, 'The Establishment of the Queen's Colleges' in T. Foley, ed., *From Queen's College to National University,* pp. 1-15.
81. James Mitchell, 'The Appointment of Revd J. W. Kirwan', *JGAHS* li, 1999, pp. 1-23.
82. Mitchell, 'St Mary's', pp. 31-32.
83. *Report of QCG President,* 1864 xix pt 1, pp. 3-8; *Appendix to Report of QCG President* 1900 xxx, p. 11; *Galway Mercury,* 23 December 1854.
84. *Appendix to 27th National Education Report,* 1861 xx, pp. 74-75; James Mitchell, 'Fr Peter Daly', in *JGAHS* 39, 1983-84, p. 81; *Galway Express,* 10 November 1860.
85. Liam Bane, *The Bishop in Politics,* Westport 1993, pp.87-88; *Appendices to 30th National Education Report,* 1864 xix, pt II. pp. 109-11; *Appendices to £1st National Education Report,* 1865 xix, pp. 100-01; *Appendices to 40th National Education Report,* 1874 xxx, pp. 148-50.
86. O'Neill, *Rich Inheritance,* pp. 84-86; F. Finegan, 'The Jesuit tradition in Galway, 1620-1963' in *Jesuit Year Book,* 1964, pp. 77-92; *Freemans' Journal,* 9 January 1863.
87. *1871 Census (Education),* 1876 lxxxi, pp. 178-83; Clear, *Nuns,* pp. 120-25.
88. Coolahan, *Irish Education,* pp. 61-65; Seán Farragher, *Pere Leman,* Dublin 1988, pp. 388-416; *Reports of the Intermediate Education Board for Ireland,* 1880, xxiii, pp. 8-9; 1883 xxvi, pp. 10-13; 1893-4 xxvii, pp. 56-58.
89. *Educational Endowments Commission,* 1889 xxx, pp.44-46; Cunningham, *St Jarlath's College,* pp. 138-39.
90. G. A. Hayes-McCoy, 'Emotion recollected' in *The Centenary Record,* pp. 37-40.
91. *Connaught Journal,* 17 August 1826.
92. ibid., 13 November 1826; K. Byrne, 'Mechanics' Institutes in Ireland, 1825-50', *Proceedings of the Educational Studies Assn of Ireland Conference, Dublin 1979,* Galway 1979; M. J. McGuinness, 'The Londonderry Mechanics' Institute, 1829-30', *Templemore: Jnl. of the North West Archaeological and Historical Society,* vol. i, 1984-85, pp. 61-68; E. P. Thompson, *The Making of the English Working Class,* 1968 edn, Aylesbury, pp. 516-18; D'Arcy & Hannigan, *Workers in Union,* p. 75.
93. *Connaught Journal,* 24 August 1826.
94. ibid., 12 June 1828.
95 . K. R. Byrne, 'Mechanics' Institutes in Ireland before 1855', unpublished MA thesis, UCC 1976, pp. 120-21.

96. ibid., pp.122-24; *Connaught Journal,* 9 March, 12 June, 5 July, 2 August 1829.
97. ibid., 1 April 1830. 'Support', in the shape of books for the library had come from James O' Hara, M.P. and also from James Hardiman who in 1828 gave 'a very valuable donation comprising upwards of forty publications on various subjects connected with science and the fine arts, together with a series of maps, rare catalogues, &c., &c.' (ibid., 25 February 1828).
98. Byrne, 'Mechanic's Institutes', 1979, p. 39.
99. *Connaught Journal,* 6, 17 May, 12 July 1830.
100. *Galway Vindicator,* 16 November 1844.
101. ibid.
102. ibid., 10 August 1844.
103. Byrne, 'Mechanics Institutes', 1979, p. 43.
104. *Galway Mercury,* 11 August 1849, 12 January 1850.
105. *Galway Mercury,* 25 October 1851.
106. *Galway Packet,* 2, 23 November, 28 December 1853, 18 March 1854.
107. *Galway Express,* 8 January 1870.
108. *Appendices to 41st National Education Report,* 1875 xxv, p. 246.
109. Galway Mechanics Institute Records, Minute Book, 1863-68, 25 August 1863; *Galway Mercury,* 12 May 1855.
110. *Galway Express,* 6 February 1875, 15 January 1876.
111. ibid., 30 April 1887.
112. Galway Mechanics Institute Records, Minute Book, 1863-68, 29 January, 13 September 1863, Minute Book, 1880-94, 20 August, 10 September, 10 October 1880, 24 October 1884, 19 December 1884, 3 March 1885, Literary Society Minute Book, passim, Excursion Committee Minute Book, passim.
113. Inglis, *Journey,* p. 217; *Select Committee on Education in Ireland, minutes of evidence,* 1836 xiii, par. 218, par. 6621. The population figures are for the county of the town.
114. W. M. Thackeray, *The Irish Sketchbook,* p. 180-81.
115. Vincent Kinnane, 'The Early Book Trade in Galway' in *Books beyond the Pale: Aspects of the Provincial Book Trade in Ireland before 1850,* Dublin 1996, p. 55.
116. *Connaught Journal,* 27 March 1817; Kinnane, 'Early Book Trade', pp. 67-68.
117. *Connaught Journal,* 21 July 1817.
118. *Connaught Journal,* 13 January 1823. 10 April 1836.
119. Kinnane, 'Early Book Trade', pp. 55.
120. National Archives, Outrage papers, 1844, 11/3701, containing material sent to Dublin Castle by magistrate T. E. Blake: a blackmailing letter; information sworn by informants; 18th issue of *Will O' the Wisp,* 16 February 1844.
121. ibid.
122. George-Denis Zimmerman, *Songs of Irish Rebellion: Political Street Ballads and Rebel Songs 1780-1900,* Dublin 1967, pp. 20-24; V. E. Neuberg, 'The literature of the streets' in Dyos & Wolff, eds, *The Victorian City: Image and Reality,* vol. i, London 1973, pp. 191-209; Niall Ó Ciosáin, 'The Irish Rogues' in James S. Donnelly, ed., *Irish Popular Culture, 1650-1850,* Dublin 1998; R. Loeber & M. Stouthammer Loeber, 'Fiction available to and written for cottagers and their children' in Cunningham & Kennedy, eds, *The Experience of Reading: Irish Historical Perspectives,* Dublin 1999, pp. 124-72; Appendix to *First Report of Commissioners of Irish Education,* 1825.
123. National Archives, CSORP, Private index, 1835/130, pp. 1-5.
124. National Library of Ireland: examples from MacLochlain ballad collection and McCall papers; *Tuam Herald,* 4 January 1913.
125. *Galway Express,* 24 February 1872, 25 December 1880.
126. Lynch, *Brother Paul O'Connor,* p. 195.
127. *Galway Express,* 15 July 1882.
128. ibid.

Epilogue

A 'most interesting encampment...'

If you'd fish or fowl in,
Or save your soul in,
Any place on earth.
Then this is your ground.
Of if drink, or fighting,
You take delight in,
Troth, a place like it
Cannot be found.

>   From 'Down in Galway' by O'Flanagan O'Flaherty.[1]

Writing in 1912, the essayist Robert Lynd described Galway as 'a grey city set among abounding waters', exuding an air of 'stony permanence that refuses to be destroyed'. The impression, a century earlier, of the visitor who encountered 'an old town, gloomy and massive', had not been very different.[2]

Lynd arrived on the eve of the Galway Races amidst tumult and, in his own words, 'scenes of indiscipline which are common in a country where people are not allowed to make law and order for themselves, and therefore seem to look on law and order as a foreign and superfluous thing'.[3] For Lynd, Galway was something less than a city, but also something more:

> … amid the solid ruins of this city, amid this scene of abandoned greatness, the Irish have found their most interesting encampment on a large scale. Galway is Irish in a sense in which Dublin and Belfast and Cork and Derry are not Irish but cosmopolitan. Its people, their speech, their black hair, their eyes like blue flames, excite the imagination with curious surmises. Galway city — technically, it is only a town — is to the discoverer of Ireland something like what Chapman's *Homer* was to Keats.[4]

Countless travellers before Lynd had found Galway and its inhabitants to be exotic, something they had fancifully attributed to residual Spanish or 'Milesian' legacies.[5] Like Lynd, they had been excited to discover a 'wild, fierce, and most original town' on the far fringe of Europe.[6] But, it may be asked, were Galway and its people still as different as all that in 1912?

Most of the evidence would suggest that they were not. The fishing community of the Claddagh, guardian of plebeian cultural distinctiveness in pre-Famine Galway, was shrunken and demoralised by the early 20th century. Irish was still spoken in the streets, but it was the language of country people coming to market, and not that of the townspeople as it had been in the early 19th century. The demeanour and appearance of country people was changing too. For one thing, the 'characteristic red flannel petticoat' of the women, described at length by 'M' in 1887, was giving way to shop-bought clothing.[7] Certainly, 'scenes of indiscipline', such as those witnessed by Lynd, were becoming unusual outside of race week. Otherwise, during the early 20th century, popular commotion was confined to the serious labour disputes of 1912 and 1913, and to four parliamentary elections. Of his own experience of the town, Stephen Gwynn M.P. remarked that 'enough primitive spirit survives to make the occasion joyous for everyone but the candidates'.[8] But as far as most aspects of life were concerned, the 'primitive spirit' of working-class Galwegians had been tamed in the course of the 19th century. The 'devil-may-care daring' of the Menlo May Sundays had given way to somewhat more disciplined team games, while circuses and amateur dramatics in the Temperance Hall had replaced entertainments such as those provided by transient companies 'of low players' in the pre-Famine decades. In an era of which it has been contended that there was an 'end of deference' in rural Ireland, the majority of Galway people were becoming more conformist, more deferential, before secular and religious authority. The contrast between the assertive pre-Poor Law food-rioters and the respectful deputations of the labouring poor who petitioned late 19th century Boards of Guardians was but one example of this.

The religious identity of Galway Catholics was never really in question, but their religious orthodoxy was. The activity of proselytising Protestant missionaries reinforced the former, while the efforts of new religious orders after 1815, the reform of church structures in the 1830s, and the rigour of Bishop MacEvilly — Cardinal Cullen's 'man in the west', according to one historian[9] — from the late 1850s, combined to make them fully-'practicing' Catholics before the end of the 19th century. The same religious protagonists were active in influencing an increasing number of parents to enrol their children in schools and, eventually, in persuading them to attend classes regularly. And, nothwithstanding Lynd's impression that the law seemed a 'foreign and superfluous thing' to Galwegians, the compulsory school attendance legislation of the 1890s secured the compliance of those not previously persuaded.

Lynd's characterisation of Galway as a 'most interesting encampment' was intriguing, suggesting that Galwegians did not fully inhabit their town. And indeed, apart from the ruins from the city's 16th century heyday, there were many empty and under-utilised buildings, monuments to Galway's more recent bleak economic history. The abandoned mills and warehouses built in the late 18th and early 19th centuries testified to the decline of the flour industry. More starkly, the under-utilised infrastructural developments of the mid-19th century — when grandiose ambition briefly coincided with political opportunity — sustained faint hopes that Galway could yet be the 'Liverpool of Ireland'. For one influential writer of the early 20th century, however, prospects were not bright. 'Galway drags on an existence', wrote William Bulfin, having gone 'to the bad when its ocean trade was killed'. Bulfin certainly did not foresee Galway's revival. Rather he dismissed the possibility on the grounds that 'there was no popolous and fertile land near enough to be a support to business'.[10]

However, the regeneration of Galway was part of a larger discussion of the early 20th century regarding the general condition of and prospects for the Irish economy under the new structures promised in some version of Home Rule. Nationalists claimed that under self-government those aspects of Irish demographic decline and economic stagnation of which they complained would be addressed and put on a healthier path. The fate of Galway, and indeed of other Irish towns which had not prospered in the post-Famine decades, was to be discussed in the context of the regenerative potential of Irish self-government. Only time would tell whether the new dawn would be as bright as nationalists claimed it would be.

NOTES

1. From 'Down in Galway' by O'Flanagan O'Flaherty, cited by Timothy Collins, in 'The Galway Line in Context, pt.ii, in *JGAHS* 47, 1995, p. 81.
2. Robert Lynd, *Galway of the Races: Selected Essays*, Dublin 1990, p. 58; [T. Walford], *The Scientific Tourist through Ireland, in which the Traveller is Directed to the Principal Objects, Antiquity, Art, Science and the Picturesque, by an Irish Gentleman, Aided with the Communication of Friends*, London 1818.
3. Lynd's *Galway*, p. 60
4. ibid., p. 58.
5. For example, Edgeworth's *Tour*, (early 1830s), p. 15; Barrow's *Tour*, 1836, p. 264; Graham's *Irish Journals*, (1836); p. 254; Inglis's *Journey*, 1838, p. 212; Preston White's *Tour*, 1849, pp. 2-3; Ashworth's *Saxon*, 1851, p. 16; Anon., *Irish Tourists' Illustrated Handbook*, 1852, pp. 120-21; Head's *Fortnight*, 1852, p. 216; Coyne & Bartlett's *Scenery*, vol. i, (1850s) pp. 95-96; Marmion's *Maritime Ports*, 1858, pp. 454-55.
6. Lynd's *Galway*, p. 60.
7. Chris Day, *Problems of Poverty in the Congested Districts, 1890-1914*, unpublished M.A. thesis, U.C.G. 1986, pp. 27-34.
8. Stephen Gwynn, *The Famous Cities of Ireland*, Dublin 1915, p. 96.
9. T. P. Boland, *Thomas Carr: Bishop of Melbourne*, Melbourne 1997, p. 60.
10. William Bulfin, *Rambles in Eirinn*, Dublin 1907, p. 24.

Bibliography

ARCHIVAL MATERIAL

NATIONAL ARCHIVES OF IRELAND
Rebellion papers.
State of the country papers, 1800-32.
Chief Secretary's office registered papers: outrage papers, 1832-49.
Chief Secretary's office registered papers: outrage papers, private index.
Chief Secretary's office registered papers, 1850-1900.
National education, reports on individual schools.

NATIONAL LIBARY OF IRELAND
Bradshaw ballad collection (microfilm).
McCall papers.
MacLochlainn ballad collection.

GALWAY COUNTY LIBRARY
Board of Guardians minute books.
Mechanics Institute records.

JAMES HARDIMAN LIBRARY, NUI, GALWAY
Galway Harbour Commissioners records (microfilm).
Roinn Bhéaloideas Éireann (UCD) folklore collection (microfilm).
Galway Corporation papers.
Journal of the committee of ladies visiting the Grace Asylum, 1867-1900
    (microfilm).

ST NICHOLAS'S COLLEGIATE CHURCH, GALWAY
Select Vestry records, 1805-1909.

AUGUSTINIAN ARCHIVE, BALLYBODEN, DUBLIN
Records of the Galway Augustinian Order.

PARLIAMENTARY PAPERS
*First report from the select committee on the state of disease and condition of the
    labouring poor in Ireland,* 1819, viii.
First report from the commissioners of Irish education inquiry, 1825, xii.
*Report from the select committee on the Galway election, together with the special
    report from the said committee, and also the minutes of evidence taken before
    them,* 1826-27, iv.

Second report from the commissioners of Irish education inquiry, 1826-7, xii.

A Return of the corporations in the counties and the counties of cities and towns in Ireland instituted for the relief of the poor and for punishing vagabonds and sturdy beggars in pursuance of acts ii and iii, Geo.3, c.30, 1828, xxviii.

Census of population of Ireland: abstract of answers and returns; comparative abstract, 1821 and 1831, 1833, xxxix.

Reports from the commissioners on the municipal corporations of Ireland, 1835, xxvii.

First report from His Majesty's commissioners for inquiry into the condition of the poorer classes with appendix (A) and supplement, 1835, xxxii, pt.i.

Appendix B to first report from His Majesty's commissioners for inquiry into the condition of the poorer classes, containing general reports upon the existing system of public medical relief in Ireland, 1835, xxxii, pt.ii.

First report from the commissioners of public instruction in Ireland, 1835, xxxiii.

Report from the select committee on education in Ireland, with the minutes of evidence, 1836, xiii.

Third report of the commissioners for inquiring into the condition of the poorer classes in Ireland, 1836, xxx.

First report of the commissioners of inquiry into the state of the Irish fisheries, minutes of evidence, and appendix, 1837, xxii.

Report from the select committee on foundation schools and education in Ireland, 1837-38, vii.

Report from the select committee on pawnbroking in Ireland, together with the minutes of evidence, 1837-8, xvii.

Second report of the commissioners appointed to consider and recommend a general system of railways in Ireland, 1837-8, xxxv.

Second report of George Nicholls, Esq., to Her Majesty's principal secretary on the poor laws, Ireland, 1837-8, xxxviii.

Copy of a memorial submitted to the Lord Lieutenant of Ireland in the month of December 1839, respecting the present state of the fisheries in the bay of Galway; with the reply of the Chief Secretary of Ireland thereto, 1840, xlvii.

Report of the poor law commissioners on medical charities in Ireland, 1841, xi.

Report of the commissioners appointed to take the census in Ireland for the year 1841, 1843, xxiv.

Select committee on the laws relating to relief of the destitute poor in Ireland, 1846, xi, pt.i.

13th report of the commissioners of national education in Ireland, with appendix, 1847, xvii.

Correspondence from July 1846 to January 1847, relative to the measures adopted for the relief of distress in Ireland (Board of Works series), 1847, l.

Correspondence from January to March 1847, relative to the measures adopted for the relief of distress in Ireland (Board of Works), second part, 1847, l.

Correspondence from July 1846 to January 1847, relating to the measures adopted for the relief of distress (Commissariat series), 1847, li.

Correspondence from January to March 1847, relating to the measures adopted for the relief of distress (Commissariat series), second part, 1847, lii.

Fifth, sixth, and seventh reports from the relief commissioners constituted under the Act 10 Vic. cap.7, with appendices, 1847-8, xxix.

14th report of the commissioners of national education in Ireland, with appendix, 1847-48, xxix.

Papers relating to proceedings for the relief of distress, and state of the unions and workhouses in Ireland, eighth series, 1848, 1849, xlviii.

Papers relating to proceedings for the relief of distress, and state of the unions and workhouses in Ireland, fourth series, 1847, 1847-8, liv.

Papers relating to proceedings for the relief of distress, and state of the unions and workhouses in Ireland, seventh series, 1848, 1847-8, liv.

Papers relating to proceedings for the relief of distress, and state of the unions and workhouses in Ireland, fifth series, 1848, 1847-8, lv.

Papers relating to proceedings for the relief of distress, and state of the unions and workhouses in Ireland, sixth series, 1848, 1847-8, lvi.

Fifteenth report of the commissioners of national education in Ireland, 1848, 1849, xxiii.

Returns of the numbers of persons who were receiving relief on the last day of February 1850, distinguishing the unions, the in-door from the out-door paupers..., 1850, l.

A return showing the financial state of each union in Ireland where paid guardians have been appointed ... and copies of all reports and resolutions made by boards of guardians... in those unions, 1850, l.

Copies of the correspondence between the poor law commissioners of Ireland and their inspectors, relative to the statements contained in an extract from a book, entitled 'Gleanings in the west of Ireland', 1851, xlix.

The census of Ireland for the year 1851, pt.i, showing the area, population and number of houses, vol.iv: Connaught, 1852-53, xcii.

The census of Ireland for the year 1851, pt.v, tables of deaths. vol.i, containing the report, tables of pestilences, and analysis of the tables of deaths, 1856, xxix.

The census of Ireland for the year 1851 (general report), 1856, xxxi.

Report of the commissioners appointed to enquire into the existence of corrupt practices in elections of members to serve in parliament for the county of the town of Galway, together with the minutes of evidence, 1857-58, xii.

Report of Her Majesty's commissioners appointed to inquire into the actual condition of all schools endowed for the purpose of education in Ireland, 1857-58, xxii.

Report from the select committee on poor relief (Ireland), together with the proceedings of the committee, minutes of evidence, and appendix, 1861, x.

Appendix to the 27th report of the national education commissioners in Ireland, 1861, xx.

The census of Ireland for the year 1861, pt.iv, reports and tables relating to the religious profession, education, and occupations of the people, 1863, lx.

Appendices to the 30th report of the national education commissioners in Ireland, 1864, xix, pt.ii.

Appendices to the 31st report of the national education commissioners in Ireland, 1864, xix.

The report of the president of Queen's College, Galway, for the academic year 1862-63, 1864, xix, pt.i.

The report of the president of Queen's College, Galway, for the academic year 1863-64, 1865, xviii.

Appendices to the 31st report of the commissioners of national education in Ireland, 1865, xix.

Minutes of evidence taken before the select committee on the Galway town election petitions, with the proceedings of the committee, 1866, x.

Report from the select committee on the fisheries (Ireland) bill; with the proceedings, minutes of evidence, appendix, and index, 1867, xiv.

Report of the special commissioners for Irish fisheries for 1867, 1867-8, xix.

Report of the deep sea and coast fishery commissioners, Ireland, for 1868, 1868-9, xv.

Report of the royal commission of inquiry into primary education in Ireland, with minutes of evidence, 1870, xxviii.

Appendices to the 40th report of the commissioners of national education in Ireland, 1874, xix.

The census of Ireland for the year 1871, pt.iv, reports and tables relating to the religious profession, education, and occupations of the people, vol.iv, province of Connaught, 1874, lxxiv, pt.ii.

Appendices to 41st report of the national education commissioners in Ireland, 1875, xxv.

The census of Ireland for the year 1871, pt.iii, general report, with illustrative maps and diagrams, summary tables and appendix, 1876, lxxxi.

Report of the inspectors of Irish fisheries on the sea and inland fisheries of Ireland for 1879, 1880, xiv.

Report of the intermediate education board for Ireland, 1880, xxiii.

Report of the commissioners appointed to inquire into the endowments, funds, and actual condition of all schools endowed for the purposes of education, 1881, xxxv.

Report of the inspectors of Irish fisheries on the sea and inland fisheries of Ireland for 1881, 1882, xvii.

Report of the intermediate education board for Ireland, 1883, xxvi.

Report from the select committee on Industries (Ireland) together with the proceedings of the committee, minutes of evidence, and appendix, 1884-5, ix.

Appendices to the 51st report of the commissioners of national education in Ireland, 1884-85, xxiv.

Report of the inspectors of Irish fisheries on the sea and inland fisheries of Ireland for 1885, 1886, xv.

Poor relief (Ireland) inquiry commission, report of evidence, with appendices, 1887, xxxviii.

Educational endowments commission: annual report of the commissioners for the year 1888-89, together with minutes of evidence and appendices, 1889, xxx.

Census of Ireland, 1891: area, population and number of houses; occupations, religion and education, vol.iv, province of Connaught, 1892, xciii.

Appendices to the 58th report of the commissioners of national education in Ireland, 1892, xxx.

Report of the intermediate education board for Ireland — appendix, 1893-94, xxvii.

Report of the intermediate education board for Ireland, 1899, xxiv.

The report of the president of Queen's College, Galway, for the session 1895-96, 1896, xxviii.

Appendix to the 66th report of the commissioners of national education in Ireland for the year 1899-1900, section one, 1900, xxxiii.

The report of the president of Queen's College, Galway, for the session 1899-1900, 1900, xxiii.

An Roinn Oideachais, *Tuarascáil na comhairle oideachais: curaclam na meánscoile,* 1962.

NEWSPAPERS

Connaught Journal, 1817, 1823-1836.
Connacht Tribune, 1909-14.
Galway Advertiser, 1838-41.
Galway Express, 1856-1889.
Galway Mercury, 1847-52, 1854-57.
Galway Observer, 1889-1909.
Galway Packet, 1852-53.
Galway Patriot. 1837.
Galway Vindicator, 1842-47, 1874-75.

DIRECTORIES

Pigott's *City of Dublin and Hibernian provincial directory: directory for 1821.*
Pigot's *City of Dublin and Hibernian provincial directory for 1824.*
Irish Catholic registry, 1841.
Irish Catholic registry, 1844.
Slater's *National commercial directory of Ireland for 1846.*
Thom's *Official directory of the United Kingdom and Ireland for the year 1889.*
Galway year book and directory, 1905.
Galway year book and directory, 1907.
Porter's *Guide to the manufacturers and shippers of Ireland, containing the names and addresses of persons interested in the make or sale of Irish manufactures or products throughout the four provinces of Ireland,* Belfast *c.*1908.

OTHER CONTEMPORARY WRITINGS

Anon., *The Irish tourists' illustrated handbook for visitors to Ireland,* London 1852.

Anon., *The angler in Ireland, or an Englishman's ramble through Connaught and Munster during the summer of 1833,* London 1834.

John Hervey Ashworth, *The Saxon in Ireland: or, the rambles of an Englishman in search of a settlement in the west of Ireland,* London 1851.

Mary Banim *Here and there through Ireland,* 2 vols, Dublin, 1891-1892.

John Barrow, *A tour around Ireland, through the sea-coast counties in the autumn of 1835,* London 1836.

Jonathan Binns, *The miseries and beauties of Ireland,* London 1837.

Helen Blackburn, *Handy book of reference for Irishwomen,* London 1888.

The Misses Blake, *Letters from the Irish highlands of Cunnemara,* London 1825.

Matthias O'Donnell Bodkin, 'Judge Bodkin remembers' in John A. Claffey (ed.) *Glimpses of Tuam since the famine,* Tuam 1997, pp. 17-22.

Thomas Carlyle, *Reminiscences of my Irish journey in 1849,* London 1882.

[M. A. Carroll], *Leaves from the Annals of the Sisters of Mercy in Ireland,* 1998 edn, London.

James Connolly, *Labour in Irish history,* 1973 edn, Dublin.

Joseph Stirling Coyne & W. H. Bartlett, *The scenery and antiquities of Ireland,* 2 vols, London 1841.

J. C. Curwen, *Observations on the state of Ireland, principally directed to its agriculture and rural population,* 2 vols, London 1818.

Tomás de Bhaldraithe, ed, *Seanchas Thomáis Laighléis,* Dublin 1977.

Marie-Anne de Bovet, *Trois mois en Irlande,* Paris 1891.

M. de Latocnaye, *A Frenchman's walk through Ireland, 1796-97,* Belfast 1984.

Alexis de Tocqueville, *Journey in Ireland, July-August 1835,* Washington 1990.

Daniel Dewar, *Observations on the characater, customs, and superstitions of the Irish, and on some of the causes which have retarded the moral and political improvement of Ireland,* 2 vols, London 1812.

Hely Dutton, *A statistical and agricultural survey of the County of Galway,* Dublin 1824.

Maria Edgeworth, *Tour in Connemara, and the Martins of Ballinahinch,* 1950 edn, London.

Thomas Campbell Foster, *Letters on the condition of the people of Ireland,* London 1846.

James Glassford, *Notes of three tours in Ireland in 1824 and 1826,* Bristol 1832.

Stephen Gwynn, *The famous cities of Ireland,* Dublin 1915.

— *Experiences of a literary man,* London, 1926.

— 'A Galway merchant', *Memories of enjoyment,* Tralee 1946, pp. 96-99.

Mr and Mrs Samuel Carter Hall, *Ireland, its scenery, character, &c.,* 3 vols, London 1841-1843.

James Hardiman, *The history of the town and county of the town of Galway,* Dublin 1820.

G. A. Hayes-McCoy, 'Emotion recollected', *The centenary record of St Joseph's College, Galway (Patrician Brothers), 1862-1962.* Galway 1962, pp. 37-40.

Sir Francis Head, *A fortnight in Ireland.* London 1852.

Henry Heaney ed., *A Scottish Whig in Ireland, 1835-38: The Irish journals of Robert Graham of Redgorton.* Dublin 1999.

Samuel Reynolds Hole (an Oxonian), *A little tour in Ireland, being a visit to Dublin, Galway, Connamara, Athlone, Limerick, Killarney, Glengarriff, Cork, &c., &c., &c.,* London 1859.

Douglas Hyde, *Religious songs of Connacht,* 2 vols, Dublin, c.1975.

Henry Inglis, *A journey throughout Ireland during the spring, summer, and autumn of 1834,* London 1838.

Samuel Lewis, *A topographical dictionary of Ireland,* 2 vols, London 1837.

Arthur Lynch, *My life story,* London 1924.

John P. Lynch, *The life of Brother Paul J. O'Connor,* Dublin 1886.

Robert Lynd, *Galway of the races: selected essays,* Dublin 1990.

Anthony Marmion, *The ancient and modern history of the maritime ports of Ireland,* 3rd edn, London 1858.

Michael McCarthy, *Priests and people in Ireland,* Dublin 1902.

J. McE., 'Ethnological sketches. — no. 1: The fishermen of the Claddagh, at Galway' (*Ulster Journal of Archaeology* 2, 1854, pp. 160-67.

Asenath Nicolson, *The bible in Ireland (Ireland's welcome to the stranger), or excursions through Ireland in 1844 and 1845 for the purpose of personally investigating the condition of the poor.* 1927 edn, New York.
— *Lights and shades of Ireland in three parts,* London 1850.

T. P. O'Connor, M.P., *Memoirs of an old parliamentarian,* 2 vols, London 1929.

Brian Ó Dálaigh, ed., *The Corporation book of Ennis,* Dublin 1990.

Liam O'Flaherty, *House of gold,* London 1929.

Hon. & Rev. S. Godolphin Osborne, *Gleanings in the west of Ireland,* London, 1850.

Thomas Colville Scott, *Connemara after the famine: journal of a survey of the Martin estate, 1853,* Dublin 1995.

Society of Friends, central relief committee, *Transactions of the central relief committee of the Society of Friends during the famine in Ireland in 1846 and 1847,* Dublin 1852.

Thomas Edward Symonds, *Observations on the fisheries of the west coast of Ireland, having reference more particularly to the operations of London and West of Ireland Fishing Company,* London 1855.

William Makepeace Thackeray, *The Irish sketchbook 1842, with numerous engravings on wood drawn by the author,* 1990 edn, Sutton.

Henry David Thoreau, *Cape Cod,* 1983 edn, Princeton.

D. W. Thompson, 'Galway: or the Citie of the Tribes' in *Macmillan's Magazine,* vol. xii, 1865, pp. 411-419.

John Bernard Trotter, *Walks through Ireland in the years 1812, 1814, and 1817,* London 1819.

Edward Wakefield, *An account of Ireland, statistical and political,* 2 vols, London 1812.

[T. Walford], *The scientific tourist through Ireland, in which the traveller is directed to the principal objects, antiquity, art, science and the picturesque, by an Irish gentleman, aided with the communication of friends,* London 1818.

Charles R. Weld, *Vacations in Ireland,* London 1857.

George Preston White, *A tour in Connemara, with remarks on its great physical capabilities,* London 1849.

Arthur Young, *A tour in Ireland, 1776-79,* 1970 edn, Shannon.

LATER WRITINGS
a) Books and pamphlets

Anon *Presentation Convent, Galway, 1815-1965: sesquicentenary souvenir,* Galway 1965.

Donald Harman Akenson, *The Irish education experiment: the national system of education in the nineteenth century,* London 1970.

— *Small differences: Irish Catholics and Irish Protestants, 1815-1922, an international perspective,* Dublin 1991.

Liam Bane, *The bishop in politics — loyal friend, bitter foe — life and career of John MacEvilly, bishop of Galway 1857-81, archbishop of Tuam, 1881-1902,* Westport 1993.

J. Fleetwood Berry, *The story of St Nicholas' Collegiate Church,* 1989 edn, Galway.

Andy Bielenberg, *Cork's industrial revolution, 1780-1880: development or decline?,* Cork 1991.

Derek Birley, *Sport and the making of Britain,* Manchester 1993.

John Bohstedt, *Riots and community politics in England and Wales, 1790-1910,* Harvard 1983.

T. P. Boland, *Thomas Carr: Archbishop of Melbourne,* Melbourne 1997.

Desmond Bowen, *The Protestant crusade in Ireland, 1800-1870: a study of Catholic-Protestant relations between the Act of Union and disestablishment,* Dublin 1978.

John Boyle, *The Irish labor movement in the nineteenth century,* Washington 1988.

John Brady, *Catholics and Catholicism in the eighteenth century press,* Maynooth 1965.

Helen Burke, *The people and the poor law in nineteenth century Ireland,* Littlehampton 1987.

Peter Burke, *Popular culture in early modern Europe,* 1994 edn, Aldershot.

Art Byrne, and Seán McMahon, *Faces of the west: a record of life in the west of Ireland,* Belfast 1977.

James Casserly, *An open door: A history of the Society of St Vincent de Paul in Galway, 1849-1999,* Galway 1999.

Peter Clark, ed., *The Cambridge urban history of Britain,* vol. ii, Cambridge 2000.

Samuel Clark, *Social origins of the Irish land war,* Princeton 1979.

William Smith Clark, *The Irish stage in the county towns, 1720-1800,* Oxford 1965.

Howard B. Clarke, ed., *Irish cities,* Cork 1995.

J. D. Clarkson, *Labour and nationalism in Ireland,* 1970 edn, New York.

Caitríona Clear, *Nuns in nineteenth century Ireland,* Dublin 1987.

Rev. Fr. Martin Coen, *The wardenship of Galway,* Galway 1984.

R. V. Comerford, *The Fenians in context: Irish politics and Irish society, 1848-82,* 1998 edn, Dublin.

S. J. Connolly, *Priests and people in pre-famine Ireland,* Dublin, 1982.

— (ed.) *The Oxford companion to Irish history,* Oxford 1998.

John Coolahan, *Irish education: history and structure,* Dublin 1981.

Patrick Corish, *The Irish Catholic experience: a historical survey,* Dublin 1985.

Maura Cronin, *Country, class or craft? The politicisation of the skilled artisan in nineteenth century Cork,* Cork 1994.

Mike Cronin, *Sport and nationalism in Ireland: Gaelic games, soccer, and Irish identity since 1884,* Dublin, 1999.

Virginia Crossman, *Local government in nineteenth century Ireland,* Belfast 1994, — *Politics, law and order in nineteenth-century Ireland,* Dublin 1996.

Raymond Crotty, *Irish agricultural production: its volume and structure,* Cork 1966.

Louis M. Cullen, *An economic history of Ireland since 1660,* London 1972.

— *The emergence of modern Ireland, 1600-1900,* 1983 edn, Dublin.

— ed., *The formation of the Irish economy,* Cork 1969.

John Cunningham, *St Jarlath's College, Tuam: 1800-2000,* Tuam 1999.

— *Labour in the west of Ireland: working life and struggle, 1890-1914,* Belfast 1995.

Mary E. Daly, *Social and economic history of Ireland since 1800,* Dublin 1981.

— *Dublin, the deposed capital: an economic and social history, 1860-1914,* Cork 1984

— *The famine in Ireland,* Dundalk 1986.

— and David Dickson, eds, *The origins of popular literacy in Ireland: language change and educational development, 1700-1920,* Dublin 1990.

Fergus D'Arcy, *Horses, lords and racing men: the Turf Club, 1790-1990,* The Curragh, *c.*1990.

— and Ken Hannigan, eds, *Workers in union: documents and commentaries on the history of Irish labour,* Dublin 1988.

David Dickson, *Arctic Ireland,* Belfast 1997.

John de Courcey Ireland, *Ireland's sea fisheries: a history,* Dublin 1981.

James S. Donnelly Jr, ed., *Irish popular culture, 1650-1850,* Dublin 1998.

David Englander, *Poverty and poor law reform in nineteenth century Britain, 1834-1914.* London 1998.

Seán Farragher, *Pere Leman: educator and missionary,* Dublin 1988.

Mary de Lourdes Fahy, *Education in the diocese of Kilmacduagh in the nineteenth century,* Gort 1973.

Hugh Fenning, *The Irish Dominican province,* Dublin 1990.

Raymond Gillespie and Myrtle Hill, *Doing Irish local history: pursuit and practice,* Belfast 1998.

Raymond Gillespie and Gerard Moran, *'A various country': essays in Mayo history,* Westport 1987.

Brian J. Graham and Lindsay J. Proudfoot, eds, *An historical geography of Ireland,* London 1993.

— *Urban improvement in provincial Ireland,* Kilkenny 1994.

Peter Gray, *Famine, land and politics, British government and Irish society, 1843-1850,* Dublin 1999.

Karen J. Harvey, *The Bellews of Mountbellew: A Catholic gentry family in eighteenth century Ireland,* Dublin 1998.

Helen E. Hatton, *The largest amount of good: Quaker relief in Ireland, 1654-1921,* Montreal 1993.

P.J. Henry, *Sligo: medical care in the past, 1800-1965,* Sligo 1995.

Judith Hill, *The building of Limerick,* Cork 1991.

Eric Hobsbawm, *Primitive rebels: studies in archaic forms of social movements in the nineteenth and twentieth centuries,* 1978 edn, Manchester.

Richard Holt, *Sport and the British: a modern history,* Oxford 1989.

K. Theodore Hoppen, *Ireland since 1800: conflict and conformity,* Harlow, 1989.

— *Elections, politics and society in Ireland, 1832-1885,* Oxford 1984.

Tom Inglis, *Moral monopoly: the Catholic church in modern Irish society,* Dublin 1987.

Donald E. Jordan, *Land and popular politics in Ireland: County Mayo from the plantation to the land war,* Cambridge 1994.

Peter Jupp, *British and Irish elections, 1784-1831,* Newton Abbot, 1973.

Peter Kavanagh, *The Irish theatre: being a history of the drama in Ireland from the earliest period up to the present day,* Tralee 1946.

Desmond Keenan, *The Catholic church in nineteenth century Ireland: a sociological study,* Dublin 1983.

Sr. M. Kelly, *The Sligo Ursulines,* Sligo, n.d.

Dermot Keogh, *The rise of the Irish working class: the Dublin trade union movement and labour leadership, 1890-1914,* Belfast 1982.

Donal Kerr, *The Catholic church and the famine,* Dublin 1996.

— *A nation of beggars?: priests, people, and politics in famine Ireland, 1846-1852,* Oxford 1994.

Colm Kerrigan, *Father Mathew and the Irish temperance movement, 1838-1849,* Cork 1992.

Christine Kinealy, *This great calamity: the Irish famine, 1845-52,* Dublin 1994.

Maureen Langan-Egan, *Galway women in the nineteenth century,* Dublin 1999.

Emmet Larkin, *The historical dimensions of Irish Catholicism,* Dublin, 1997 edn.

— *The consolidation of the Roman Catholic church in Ireland, 1860-1870,* Chapel Hill 1987.

Joseph Lee, *Irish historiography, 1970-79,* Cork 1991

Marie Louise Legg, *Newspapers and nationalism: the Irish provincial press, 1850-1892,* Dublin 1999.

Catherina Lis and Hugo Soly, *Poverty and capitalism in pre-industrial Europe,* Brighton 1979.

Shevawn Lynam, *Humanity Dick Martin: 'King of Connemara', 1754-1834,* 1989 edn, Dublin.

Oliver MacDonagh, *O'Connell: the Life of Daniel O'Connell, 1775-1847,* London 1991.

Thomas J. McElligott, *Secondary education in Ireland, 1870-1921,* Dublin 1981.

E.B. McGuire, *Irish whiskey: a history of Irish distilling, the spirit trade, and excise controls in Ireland,* Dublin 1973.

Ned McHugh, *Drogheda before the famine: urban poverty in the shadow of privilege,* Dublin 1998.

Michael McSweeney, *Galway Golf Club, 1895-1995,* Galway 1995.

Helen Maher, *Galway authors: a contribution towards a biographical and bibliographical index, with an essay on the history of literature in Galway,* Galway 1996.

Elizabeth Malcolm, *Ireland sober, Ireland free: drink and temperance in nineteenth century Ireland,* Dublin 1986.

Patrick Maume, *The long gestation: Irish nationalist life, 1891-1918,* Dublin 1999.

Kenneth Milne, *The Irish charter schools, 1730-1830,* Dublin 1997.

Joel Mokyr, *Why Ireland starved: a quantitive and analytical history of the Irish economy, 1800-1850,* London 1983.

Gerard Moran, ed., *Galway, history and society: interdisciplinary essays on the history of an Irish county,* Dublin 1996.
  — *A radical priest in Mayo. Fr Patrick Lavelle: the rise and fall of an Irish nationalist, 1825-86,* Dublin 1994, pp.136-41.

Michael Mulcahy and Marie Fitzgibbon, *The voice of the people: songs and history of Ireland,* Dublin 1982.

Ignatius Murphy, *The diocese of Killaloe, 1800-1850,* Dublin 1992.
  — *Before the famine struck: life in west Clare, 1834-1845,* Dublin 1996.

James P. Murray, *Galway: a medico-social history,* Galway, n.d.

William Nolan and Anngret Simms, eds, *Irish towns: a guide to sources,* Dublin 1998.

Diarmuid Ó Cearbhaill, ed., *Galway: town and gown, 1484-1984,* Dublin 1984.

Emmet O'Connor, *A labour history of Ireland, 1824-1960,* Dublin 1992.

Gabriel O'Connor, *A history of Galway County Council,* Galway 1999.

John O'Connor, O.S.A. *The Galway Augustinians,* Dublin, n.d.

Seán O'Donnell, *Clonmel, 1840-1900: anatomy of an Irish town,* Dublin 1999.

Peadar O'Dowd, *Down by the Claddagh,* Galway 1993.
  — *In from the west — the McDonogh dynasty,* Galway 2002.

Roderic O'Flaherty, *A choreographical description of west or h-iar Connaught,* Dublin 1846.

Ralph O'Gorman, *Rugby in Connacht,* Galway 1996.

Cormac Ó Gráda, *Ireland: a new economic history, 1780-1939,* Oxford 1994.
— *An drochshaol: béaloideas agus amhráin,* Baile Átha Cliath, 1994.

Eustás Ó Héideáin, O.P. (ed.), *The Dominicans in Galway, 1241-1991,* Galway 1991.

Padraic Ó Laoi, *Nora Barnacle Joyce: a portrait,* Galway 1982.
— *The annals of the G.A.A. in Galway, 1884-1901,* Galway 1984.
— *History of Castlegar parish,* Galway 1998.

Colman O'Mahony, *In the shadows: life in Cork, 1750-1930,* Cork 1997.

Séamus Ó Maitiú, *The humours of Donnybrook: Dublin's famous fair and its suppression,* Dublin 1995.

Máirtín Ó Murchú, *Language and community* (Comhairle na Gaeilge occasional paper no. 1), Dublin, n.d.

Sr Rose O'Neill, *A rich inheritance: Galway Dominican nuns, 1644-1994,* Galway 1994.

Gearóid Ó Tuathaigh, *Ireland before the famine, 1798-1848,* 1990 edn, Dublin.

M. D. O'Sullivan, *Old Galway: the history of a Norman colony in Ireland,* Cambridge 1942.

J. L. Pethica and J. C. Roy, *Henry Stratford Persse's letters from Galway to America, 1821-1832,* Cork 1998.

John Dexter Post, *The last great subsistence crisis in the western world,* Baltimore 1977.

F. W. Powell, *The politics of Irish social policy, 1600-1990,* Lewiston 1992.

Thomas P. Power, *Land, politics and society in eighteenth century Tipperary,* Oxford 1993.
— and Kevin Whelan (eds) *Endurance and emergence: Catholics in Ireland in the eighteenth century,* Dublin 1990.

Jacinta Prunty, *Dublin slums: a study in urban geography,* Dublin 1998.

Joseph Robins, *The miasma: epidemic and panic in nineteenth century Ireland,* Dublin 1995.

Tim Robinson *Stones of Aran: pilgrimage,* Mullingar 1986.

George Rudé, *The crowd in history: a study of popular disturbances in France and England,* 1995 edn, London.

Richard J. Scott, *The Galway hookers: working sailboats of Galway bay,* Dublin 1983.

Maurice Semple, *Reflections on Lough Corrib,* 2nd edn, Galway 1989.
— *By the Corribside,* 2nd edn, Galway 1984.
— *Some Galway memories: a pictorial record,* Galway 1973.

Amartya Sen, *Poverty and famines: an essay on entitlement and deprivation,* 1982 edn, Oxford.

Seán Spellissy, *The history of Galway: city and county,* Limerick 1999.

Liam Swords, *A hidden church: diocese of Achonry, 1689-1818,* Dublin 1997.

Laurence Taylor, *Occasions of faith: an anthropology of Irish Catholics,* 1997 edn, Dublin.

E. P. Thompson, *Customs in common*, London 1991.

— *The making of the English working class*, 1968 edn, Harmondsworth.

John Towner, *An historical geography of recreation and tourism in the western world, 1540-1940*, Chichester 1996.

Kathleen Villiers-Tuthill, *Beyond the twelve bens: a history of Clifden and district*, Galway 1986.

Linus H. Walker, *One man's famine: one man's tribute to Bro. Paul James O'Connor on his centenary, 17 April 1978*, Galway 1978.

Paul Walsh, *Discover Galway*, Dublin 2001.

James Walvin, *Beside the seaside: a social history of the popular seaside holiday*, London 1978.

— *English urban life: 1776-1851*, London 1984.

— *Victorian values*, London 1987.

John Welcome, *Irish horse-racing: an illustrated history*, London 1982.

John Wigley, *The rise and fall of the Victorian Sunday*, Manchester 1980.

Michael Winstanley, *The shopkeeper's world, 1830-1914*, Manchester 1983.

Cecil Woodham Smith, *The great hunger: Ireland, 1845-49*, 1977 edn, Sevenoaks.

Kieran Woodman, *Tribes to tigers: a history of Galway Chamber of Commerce and Industry*, Galway 2001.

— *The annals of the Galway harbour commissioners, 1830-1997*, Galway 2000.

Maud Wynne, *An Irishman and his family: Lord Morris and Killanin*, London 1937.

George Dennis Zimmerman, *Songs of Irish rebellion: political street ballads and rebel songs, 1780-1960*, Dublin 1967.

b) Scholarly articles

(n.b., *Journal of the Galway Archaeological and Historical Society* is listed as *JGAHS*)

Anon, 'The Ursuline nuns in Galway, 1839-44', *The mantle* (Galway R.C. diocesan periodical) vol. ii, no. 1, 1958-59, pp. 22-24.

G. B. Adams. 'The 1851 language census in the north of Ireland', *Ulster folklife*, 20, 1974, pp. 65-70.

— 'Aspects of monoglottism in Ulster, *Ulster folklife* 22, 1976, pp. 76-87.

Thomas Bartlett, 'An end to moral economy: the Irish militia disturbances of 1793', *Past and present* 99, 1983, pp. 41-64.

— 'A Galway election squib of 1783', *JGAHS* 37, 1979-80, pp. 85-89.

Francois Béderida, 'The growth of urban history in France: some methodological trends' in H. J. Dyos, ed., *The study of urban history*, London 1968.

John Bohstedt, 'Gender, household and community politics: women in English riots 1790-1810', *Past and present* 120, 1988, pp. 88-122.

Kieran Byrne, 'Mechanics' Institutes in Ireland, 1825-50', *Proceedings of the Educational Studies Association of Ireland conference, Dublin 1979*, Galway 1979.

Mary Clancy, '…it was our joy to keep the flag flying': a study of the women's suffrage campaign in County Galway', *U.C.G. Women's Studies Centre review,* vol. iii, 1995, pp. 91-104.

A. W. Coats, 'Contrary moralities: plebs, paternalists and political economists', *Past and present* 54, 1972, pp. 130-33.

Rev. Fr. Martin Coen, 'The choosing of Oliver Kelly', *JGAHS* 36, 1977-78, pp. 14-29.

Timothy Collins, 'The Galway Line in context', pt.1, *JGAHS* 46, 1994, pp. 1-42.

— The Galway Line in context', pt. 2, *JGAHS* 47, 1995, pp. 36-86.

— 'From anatomy to zoophagy: a biographical note on Frank Buckland', *JGAHS* 55, 2003, pp. 91-109.

Janette Condon, 'Children's books in nineteenth century Ireland', Valerie Coghlan and Celia Keenan, eds, *The big guide 2: Irish children's books,* Dublin 2000, pp. 53-59.

S. J. Connolly, 'The "blessed turf": cholera and popular panic in Ireland, June 1832', in *Irish historical studies,* vol. xxiii, May 1983, pp. 215-31.

— '"Ag déanamh commanding": elite responses to popular culture', J. S. Donnelly, *Irish popular culture, 1650-1850,* Dublin 1998.

Des Cowman, 'Trade and society in Waterford city, 1800-1840', William Nolan and Thomas Power, eds, *Waterford, history and society: interdisciplinary essays on the history of an Irish county,* Dublin 1992, pp. 427-58.

Virginia Crossman, 'The army and law and order in the nineteenth century'.

Thomas Bartlett and Keith Jeffrey, eds, *A military history of Ireland,* Cambridge 1996.

Louis M. Cullen: see Lughaidh Ó Cuileáin.

John Cunningham, 'Lord Wallscourt, 1787-1849: an early Irish socialist', *JGAHS* 56, 2005.

— 'Galway shopworkers and trades unionism — the early years', MANDATE conference programme, 2000.

— 'Padraic Ó Conaire's socialism', *Red banner: a magazine of socialist ideas* 18, March 2004, pp. 35-42.

— 'Waiting for the promised money: trade unions in County Galway, 1890-1914', Gerard Moran, ed., *Galway, history and society: interdisciplinary essays on the history of an Irish county,* Dublin 1996, pp. 521-55.

— 'A glimpse of the Galway Workers and Labourers' Union, 1913', *Saothar: journal of the Irish Labour History Society* 15, 1990, pp. 109-12.

— 'The "soviet at Galway" and the downfall of Dunkellin', *Cathair na Mart* 10, 1990, pp. 115-33.

Martin Cunningham, 'Dabhach Cuana', *Kilcoona grapevine,* Kilcoona 1997, p. 24.

Mary E. Daly, 'The operations of famine relief, 1845-47', Cathal Póirtéir, ed., *The great Irish famine,* Cork 1995, pp. 123-34.

— Literacy and language change', Mary Daly and David Dickson, eds, *The origins of popular literacy in Ireland: language change and educational development, 1700-1920,* Dublin 1990, pp. 153-66.

— 'Dublin in the nineteenth century Irish economy', Paul Butel and Louis M. Cullen, eds, *Cities and merchants: French and Irish perspectives on urban development, 1500-1900,* Dublin 1986, pp. 53-65.

Fergus D'Arcy, 'The artisans of Dublin and Daniel O'Connell: an unquiet liaison', *Irish historical studies,* vol.xvii, 1970-71, pp. 221-43.

— The decline and fall of Donnybrook Fair: moral reform and social control in nineteenth century Dublin', *Saothar: journal of the Irish Labour History Society* 13, 1988, pp. 7-21.

David Dickson, 'In search of the old Irish poor law', Rosalind Mitchenson and Peter Roebuck, eds, *Economy and Society in Scotland and Ireland, 1500-1939,* Edinburgh 1988, pp. 149-59.

J. N. Dillon, 'The Lords of Dunsandle', *Kiltullagh/Killimordaly: a history from 1500 to 1900,* Kiltullagh 2000, pp. 49-51.

James S. Donnelly Jr, 'Irish property must pay for Irish poverty: British public opinion and the great Irish famine', Chris Morash and Richard Hayes, eds, *Fearful realities: new perspectives on the famine,* Dublin 1996, pp. 60-76.

— 'Famine and the government response, 1845-46', W. E. Vaughan, ed., *A new history of Ireland, v: Ireland under the Union, 1, 1800-1870,* Oxford 1989, pp. 272-85.

H. J. Dyos and D. A. Reeder, 'Slums and suburbs', H. J. Dyos and Michael Wolff, eds, *The Victorian city: images and realities,* vol. 1, London 1973.

Rev. Patrick K. Egan, 'Progress and suppression of the United Irishmen in the western counties, 1798-99', *JGAHS* 25, pt. iii and iv, 1953-54, pp. 104-34.

Andrés Eiríksson, 'Food supply and food riots', Cormac Ó Gráda, ed., *Famine 150: commemorative lecture series,* Dublin 1997, pp. 67-93.

Angela Fahy, 'Residence, workplace and patterns of change: Cork 1787-1863',

Paul Butel and Louis M.Cullen, eds, *Cities and merchants: French and Irish perspectives on urban development, 1500-1900,* Dublin 1986.

F. Finegan, 'The Jesuit tradition in Galway', *Jesuit Year Book* 1964, pp. 77-92.

Garret Fitzgerald, 'Estimates for baronies of minimum levels of Irish-speaking', proceedings *of the Royal Irish Academy,* section C, vol. 84, no. 3, Dublin 1984.

Tadhg Foley and Fiona Bateman, 'English, history and philosophy', Tadhg Foley, ed., *From Queen's College to National University: essays towards an academic history of QCG/UCG/NUI, Galway,* Dublin 1999, pp. 384-420.

John Foster, 'Nineteenth century towns: a class dimension', H. J. Dyos, ed., *The study of urban history,* London 1968, pp. 281-99.

William Fraher, 'The Dungarvan disturbances of 1846 and sequels', Des Cowman and Donald Brady, eds, *The famine in Waterford, 1845-50,* Dublin 1995.

Peter Froggatt, 'Industrialisation and health in Belfast in the early nineteenth century', D. Harkness and M. O'Dowd, eds, *The town in Ireland,* Belfast 1981, pp. 155-85.

—'The census of Ireland, 1813-15', *Irish historical studies* vol. xiv, 55, March 1965, pp. 227-35.

Manfred Gailus, 'Food riots in Germany in the late 1840s', *Past and present*, 145, 1994, pp. 157-93.

B. J. Graham and Susan Hood, 'Town tenant protest in late nineteenth- and early twentieth-century Ireland', *Irish Economic and Social History Society journal* 21, 1994, pp. 39-57.

John Gray, 'Popular entertainment', J. C. Beckett, *Belfast: the making of a city,* 1988 edn, Belfast, pp. 99-110.

Peter Gray, 'Ideology and the Famine', Cathal Póirtéir, ed., *The great Irish famine,* Cork, pp. 86-103.

Robert Herbert, 'The Lax Weir and Fishers Stent of Limerick', *North Munster Antiquarian Journal,* 5 (ii) (iii), 1946-47.

Michael D. Higgins, 'The "gombeenman" in fact and fiction', *Etudes Irlandaises,* 10, 1985, pp. 31-52.

Jacqueline Hill, 'Corporatist ideology and practice in Ireland', S. J. Connolly, ed., *Political ideas in eighteenth century Ireland,* Dublin 2000, pp. 64-82.

Gertrude Himmelfarb, 'The culture of poverty', H. J. Dyos and Michael Wolfe, eds, *The Victorian city: images and reality,* vol. 2, London 1973, pp. 707-36.

K. Theodore Hoppen, 'The franchise and electoral politics in England and Ireland, 1832-1885', *History* 70, 1985, pp. 202-17.

Michael Hurst, 'Ireland and the ballot act of 1872', Alan O'Day, ed., *Reactions to Irish nationalism,* London 1987, pp. 33-59.

J. H. Johnson, 'The "two Irelands" at the beginning of the nineteenth century', Nicholas Stephens and Robin E. Glasscock, eds, *Irish geographical studies in honour of E. Estyn Evans,* Belfast 1970.

Donald E. Jordan, 'John O'Connor Power, Charles Stewart Parnell and the centralisation of popular politics in Ireland', *Irish historical studies,* vol. xxx, 1986, pp. 46-66.

Toby Joyce, 'The *Galway American*, 1862-63', pt. 2, *JGAHS* 48, 1996, pp. 104-36.

Peter Jupp, 'Urban Politics in Ireland', D. Harkness and M. O'Dowd, eds, *The town in Ireland,* Belfast 1981, pp. 103-23.

James Kelly, 'The Politics of Protestant ascendancy', Gerard Moran, ed., *Galway, history and society: interdisciplinary essays on the history of an Irish county,* Dublin 1996, pp. 229-70.

R. J. Kelly, 'The Old Galway theatres', *Journal of the Royal Society of Antiquaries of Ireland* 44, 1914, pp. 358-364.

Patrick J. Kennedy, 'The county of the town of Galway, its establishment, extent, and function', *JGAHS* 30 (iii, iv) 1963, pp. 90-101.

Colm Kerrigan, 'Temperance and politics in pre-famine Galway', *JGAHS* 43, 1991, pp. 82-94.

Vincent Kinnane, 'The early book trade in Galway', Gerard Long, ed., *Books beyond the Pale: aspects of the provincial book trade in Ireland before 1850,* Dublin 1996, pp. 51-73.

Rolf Loeber and Magda Stouthammer Loeber, 'Fiction available to and written for cottagers and their children', Bernadette Cunningham and Maire Kennedy, eds, *The experience of reading: Irish historical perspectives,* Dublin 1999, pp. 124-72.

John Logan, 'Sufficient to their needs: literacy and elementary schooling in the nineteenth century', Mary Daly and David Dickson, eds, *The origins of popular literacy in Ireland: language change and educational development, 1700-1920,* Dublin 1990, pp. 113-38.

James Loughlin, 'Constructing the political spectacle: Parnell, the press, and national leadership, 1879-1886', David George Boyce and Alan O'Day, eds, *Parnell in Perspective,* London 1991, pp. 221-41.

F. S. L. Lyons, 'Parnell and the Galway by-election of 1886', *Irish historical studies,* vol. ix, March 1955, pp. 319-38.

P. B. Lysaght, 'The house of industry: a register, 1774-1793', *North Munster Antiquarian Journal,* xxx, 1990, pp. 70-74.

Desmond McCabe, 'Social order and the ghost of moral economy in pre-famine Mayo', Raymond Gillespie and Gerard Moran, eds, *A various country: essays in Mayo history, 1500-1900,* Westport 1987, pp. 91-112.

Oliver McDonagh, Ideas and institutions, 1830-45', W. E. Vaughan, ed., *A new history of Ireland, v: Ireland under the union, 1, 1800-1870,* Oxford 1989, pp. 1-23.

Seán Mac Giollarnáth (and Seán Ó Cuinneagáin, Bun a' Tobar), 'Frank Ó Ciardhubháin as Cluain Lionnáin', *Béaloideas* 17, 1947, vols. i and ii, pp. 116-18.

T. G. McGrath's 'The tridentine evolution of Irish Catholicism, 1653-1962', Reamonn Ó Muirí, ed., *Irish church history today,* Armagh, n.d.

M. J. McGuinness, 'The Londonderry Mechanics' Institute, 1829-30', *Templemore: journal of the North West Archaeological and Historical Society,* vol. i, 1984-85, pp. 61-68.

Alf MacLochlainn, 'Foreword: the personality of Galway', Gerard Moran, ed., *Galway, history and society: interdisciplinary essays on the history of an Irish county,* Dublin 1996, pp. xxvi-xxx.

— 'The Claddagh piscatory school', *Two Galway schools,* Galway 1993, pp. 5-20.

Fidelma Maddock, 'The cot fishermen of the River Nore', William Nolan and Kevin Whelan, eds, *Kilkenny, history and society: interdisciplinary essays on the history of an Irish county,* Dublin 1990, pp. 541-65.

Elizabeth Malcolm, 'Popular recreation in nineteenth century Ireland', MacDonagh, Mandle and Travers, eds, *Irish culture and nationalism, 1750-1950,* Canberra 1983, pp. 40-55.

Robert Malcolmson, 'Popular recreations under attack', Bernard Waites, Tony Bennett, and Graham Martin, *Popular culture past and present: a reader,* London 1982, pp. 20-46.

Peter Mandler, 'Poverty and charity in the nineteenth century metropolis', Peter Mandler, ed., *The uses of charity: the poor on relief in the nineteenth century metropolis,* Philadephia, 1990, pp. 1-37.

D. W Miller, 'Irish Catholicism and the great famine', *Journal of social history,* 1975, vol. ix, pp. 81-98.

James Mitchell 'The appointment of Revd J. W. Kirwan as first president of Queen's College, Galway, and his years in office', *JGAHS* 51, 1999, pp. 1-23.

— 'Father Peter Daly (*c.*1788-1868)', *JGAHS* 39, 1983-84, pp. 27-114.

— 'The first St Mary's', *The mantle* (Galway R.C. diocesan periodical), vol. v, no. 3, 1962, pp. 27-32.

— 'A Christmas Morning Tragedy', *The mantle* (Galway R.C. diocesan periodical), vol. vii, no. 4, 1964, pp. 12-15.

Gerard Moran, 'The land war, urban destitution, and town tenant protests, 1879-1882', *Saothar: journal of the Irish Labour History Society* 20, 1995, pp. 17-30.

F. Darrell Munsell, 'Charles Edward Trevelyan and the Peelite Irish famine policy, 1845-1846', *Societas — a review of social history,* I, iv, 1971, pp. 299-315.

Maura Murphy, 'The economic and social structure of nineteenth century Cork', D. Harkness and M. O'Dowd, eds, *The town in Ireland,* Belfast 1981, pp. 125-54.

— 'The ballad singer and the role of the seditious ballad in nineteenth century Ireland — Dublin Castle's view', *Ulster folklife* 25, 1979, pp. 79-102.

— 'Fenianism, Parnellism, and the Cork trades' in *Saothar: journal of the Irish Labour History Society* 5, 1979, pp. 27-38.

Síle Ní Chinnéide, 'Coquebert de Montbret's impressions of Galway city and county in the year 1791', *JGAHS* 25, 1952, pp. 1-14.

Victor E. Neuberg, 'The literature of the streets', H. J. Dyos and Michael Wolff, eds, *The Victorian city: image and reality,* vol. i, London 1973, pp. 191-209.

Kevin P. Nowlan, 'The political background', R. Dudley Edwards and T. Desmond Williams, *The great famine: studies in Irish history, 1845-52,* 1994 edn, Dublin, pp. 131-206.

Gerard O'Brien, 'The establishment of poor law unions in Ireland, 1838-43', *Irish historical studies,* vol. xxiii, no. 90, November 1982, pp. 1-24.

John B. O'Brien, 'Merchants in Cork before the famine' in Paul Butel and Louis M. Cullen, eds, *Cities and merchants: French and Irish perspectives on urban development, 1500-1900,* Dublin 1986, pp. 221-30.

Niall Ó Ciosáin, 'Boccoughs and God's poor: deserving and undeserving poor in Irish popular culture', Tadhg Foley and Sean Ryder, eds, *Ideology and Ireland in the nineteenth century,* Dublin 1998, pp.93-99.

— 'The Irish rogues', Kirby Miller and J. S. Donnelly, ed., *Irish popular culture, 1650-1850,* Dublin 1998, pp. 78-96.

Lughaidh Ó Cuileáin, 'Tráchtáil idir iarthar na hÉireann is an Fhrainc, 1660-1800', *Galvia: irisleabhar chumann seandáluíochta is staire na Gaillimhe* 4, 1957, pp. 27-48.

— 'Tráchtáil is baincéaracht i nGaillimh san 18ú Céad', *Galvia: irisleabhar chumann seandáluíochta is staire na Gaillimhe* 5, 1958, pp. 43-65.

— 'Galway merchants and the outside world, 1650-1800', Diarmuid Ó Cearbhaill, ed., *Galway: town and gown, 1484-1984,* Dublin 1984, pp. 62-89.

— 'Eighteenth century flour milling in Ireland', *Irish Economic and Social History Society journal* 4, 1977, pp. 5-25.

Greagóir Ó Dúghaill, 'Galway in the first famine winter', *Saothar: journal of the Irish Labour History Society* '1, 1975, pp. 63-67.

Philip O'Gorman, 'The labour court is not new,' *The Galway reader* 2 (i, ii), 1949-50, pp. 100-101.

Thomas P. O'Neill 'The organisation and administration of relief, 1845-52', R. Dudley Edwards and T. Desmond Williams, *The great famine: studies in Irish history, 1845-52,* 1994 edn, Dublin, pp. 209-259.

— 'Freemen and voters', *Galway roots, clanna na Gaillimhe: journal of the Galway Family History Society,* vol. 1, 1993, pp. 38-9.

Timothy O'Neill, 'Irish trade banners', C. Ó Danchair, ed., *Folk and farm,* Dublin 1976, pp. 177-99.

— 'Poverty in Ireland, 1815-45', *Folk life* xi, 1973, pp. 22-33.

— 'The Catholic church and the relief of the poor, 1815-45', *Archivium Hibernicum* xxxi, 1973, pp. 132-45.

— 'Minor famines and relief in County Galway, 1815-1925', Gerard Moran, ed., *Galway, history and society: interdisciplinary essays on the history of an Irish county,,* Dublin 1996, pp. 445-85.

— 'Seán Mac Héil agus bochtaineacht an iarthair', Áine Ní Cheanáin, ed., *Leon an iarthair: aistí ar Sheáin Mac Héil,* Dublin 1983, pp. 25-35.

Gearóid Ó Tuathaigh 'The establishment of the Queen's Colleges', Tadhg Foley, ed., *From Queen's College to National University: essays towards an academic history of QCG/UCG/NUI, Galway,* Dublin 1999, pp. 1-15.

— 'the air of a place of importance': aspects of nineteenth century Galway', Diarmuid Ó Cearbhaill, ed., *Galway: town and gown, 1484-1984,* Dublin 1984, pp. 129-47.

— 'Galway in the modern period: survival and revival', H. B. Clarke, ed., *Irish cities,* Cork 1995, pp. 136-49.

— 'Gaelic Ireland, popular politics, and Daniel O'Connell', *JGAHS* 34, 1974-75, pp. 21-34.

— 'Nineteenth century Irish politics: the case for normalcy', *Anglo-Irish studies,* vol. i, 1975, pp. 71-81.

M. D. O'Sullivan, 'The use of leisure in old Galway', *JGAHS* 28, 1939, pp. 99-120.

Peter Rabbitte, 'How the national feast day came into being in Galway', *City Tribune,* 14 March 2003.

Hermann Rasche, 'German travellers in the west, 1828-1858', *JGAHS* 47, 1995, pp. 87-107.

Raymond James Raymond, 'Pawnbrokers and pawnbroking in Dublin, 1830-1870', *Dublin historical record,* vol. xxxii(1), 1978, pp. 15-26.

Tony Regan, 'The Salthill industrial school', *Two Galway schools,* Galway 1993, pp. 21-36.

Richard Rodger, 'Urban history: prospect and retrospect', *Urban History* 19, pt.i, 1992, pp. 1-22.

Stephen Royle, 'Industrialisation, urbanisation, and urban society in post-famine Ireland, *c.*1850-1914', Brian J. Graham and Lindsay J. Proudfoot, eds, *An historical geography of Ireland,* London 1993, pp. 259-92.

Michael Ryan, 'Municipal dignity?: a controversy in Galway', *JGAHS* 43, 1991, pp. 139-55.

Walter S. Sanderlin, 'Galway as a trans-Atlantic port in the nineteenth century', *Éire-Ireland* 5, 1970, no. iii, pp. 15-31.

Sr M. Colombiere Scully, PhD, 'The great famine and the role of the Presentation sisters', (Galway) *City Tribune,* 31 May 1991.

J. G. Simms, 'Connacht in the eighteenth century', *Irish historical studies,* vol.xi, no. 42, 1959, pp. 116-33.

Christopher Townley, 'Galway's early association with the theatre', *The Galway reader,* iv, 1953, pp. 62-70.

Marco H. D. van Leeuwen, 'Logic of charity: poor relief in pre-industrial Europe' *Journal of interdisciplinary history* xxiv:4, 1994, pp. 589-613.

Patrick Wallace, 'The organisation of pre-railway public transport in Counties Limerick and Clare', *North Munster Antiquarian Journal,* vol. xv, 1972, pp. 34-58.

Paul Walsh, 'The topography of medieval and early modern Galway', Gerard Moran, ed., *Galway, history and society: interdisciplinary essays on the history of an Irish county,,* Dublin 1996, pp. 27-96.

Roger Wells 'The Irish famine of 1799-1801: market culture, moral economies and social protest', Adrian Randall and Andrew Charlesworth, *Markets, market culture, and popular protest in eighteenth century Britain and Ireland,* Liverpool 1996.

Kevin Whelan, 'The regional impact of Irish Catholicism, 1700-1850', William J. Smyth and Kevin Whelan, *Common Ground: essays on the historical geography of Ireland,* 1988, pp. 252-277.

c) Academic theses

Mary P. Cryan, 'The Sisters of Mercy in Connaught, 1840-70', M.A., University College Galway, 1963.

John Cunningham, 'Patterns of social change in a provincial capital: Galway, *c.*1800-1914,' Ph.D., NUI, Galway, 2001.

— 'Labour and labour organisation in Connacht, 1890-1914', M.A., University College Galway, 1993.

Chris Day, 'Problems of poverty in the congested districts, 1890-1914', (M.A., University College Galway, 1986.

L. A. de Shiubhlaí, 'Saothar oideachais Bráithre Padraic in Éireann, 1808-1878', M.A., University College Galway, 1962.

Padraic Flynn, 'A study of local government in Galway in the early nineteenth century', M.A. thesis, University College Galway, 1981.

K. P. Hackett, 'Phases of education in Galway city', M.A., University College Galway, 1935.

P. M Hogan, 'Civil unrest in the province of Connacht, 1793-98', M.Ed., University College Galway, 1976.

Patricia Kelly, 'From workhouse to hospital: the role of the Irish workhouse in medical relief, to 1921', M.A., University College Galway, 1972.

Tim Kelly, 'Ennis in the nineteenth century', M.A., University College Galway, 1971.

Columba Leahy 'The Galway sea fishing industry from the union to the famine', M.A., University College Galway, 1964.

Anne M.A. Mannion, 'The social geography of the British army in nineteenth century Ireland with specific reference to Galway', (M.A., University College Galway, 1994.

Thomas Murtagh, 'Power and politics in Galway, 1770-1830', (M.A., University College Galway, 1982.

Neasa Ní Chinnéide, 'Patrúin comhchruinnithe daonra: cás na Gaillimhe', M.A., University College Galway, 1975.

N. P. T. O'Donnellan, 'Manufacturing industry in Galway, 1911-1957', M.A., University College Galway, 1979.

Padraic Ó Tuairisg, 'Ábhar a bhaineann le ard-dheoise Thuama sa 19ú aois i gcartlann Choláiste na nGael sa Róimh', M.A., University College Galway, 1982.

John Solan, 'Religion and society in the ecclesiastical province of Tuam before the famine', M.A., University College Galway, 1989.

W. J. Waldron. 'Archdiocese of Tuam, 1770-1817', M.A., University College Dublin, 1993.

General Index

abandoned infants, 62

Abbeygate-street, 54, 55, 59, 117, 178, 211, 250, 322

Aberdeen, 271

Achill Missionary Herald, 269

Act of Union, 15, 105, 106, 107

Adriatic, 178

advertising, 33, 34, 61, 340, 341

Advice, The, 97

Advocate, The, 225

Ainslie, Captain, 131

All For Ireland League, 224

All Saints Day, 85

All-Ireland Congress of Trades, 239

All-Red Route, 7

Aloysian Society, 260, 356

Amalgamated Building Trades Society, 239

Amalgamated Society of Carpenters and Joiners, 240

Amalgamated Society of Tailors, 239

Amos, Walter, 146

Ancient Order of Hibernians, 312

Andrews, Mr, 179

Angliham, 22, 24

Annaghdown, 107, 137, 154, 304

Anti-Tory Association, 120

Appleyard, Thomas, 23, 24, 86

apprentices, 74, 94

Árainn, 180, 229, 231

Ardfry, 26, 145, 148

fisheries disturbances, 232

Argo, The, 176

Armagh, 38, 343

army, 34, 82, 92, 115, 167, 209, 252, 269, 307, 331
  barracks, 34, 131
  Connaught Rangers, 128, 132
  military ball, 150
  military sports, 307
  43rd Depot, 269
  6th Dragoons, 135

Army Scripture Readers & Soldiers Friend Society, 201, 271

artisans (see tradesmen)

Ashe, Tom, 219

Assembly Rooms, Middle-street, 294

assizes, 55, 137, 232, 292, 308

Athenry, 222

Athlone, 24, 88, 89, 167, 289

Atlantic Royal Mail Steam Navigation Company, 174

Augustinian Friars, 111, 150, 257, 342

Augustinian Hall, 301

Aylwood, Mr, 133

Back-street, 38, 87, 117, 140, 341, 342

badger-baiting, 263, 304

Bag Factory, 179, 181-82, 185, 188, 189

bakers and bakeries, 5, 32, 75, 78, 112, 117, 200, 210, 211, 239, 333
  County Galway Bakers' Society, 239

ballad-singers, 355

Ballinasloe, 24, 221, 268, 308

Ballindine, 131

Ballinrobe, 308

Ballymoney, 218

ball-playing, 304

Ballybrit, 309- 11

Ballymote, Co. Sligo, 346

Ballynacourty, 81

Baltimore, Maryland, 178

Banim, Mary, 236

Bank of Ireland, 23, 184

banks, 22, 23, 54, 179, 184

Barclay, Robert (Capt.), 280

Barna (see Bearna)

Barnacle Michael, 78

Barnacle, Nora, 61, 78

Barnicle, Thomas, 61

Barrow, John, 331

Bartlett, Thomas, 98

Barton, Mr, 168-69, 177
Battle of Waterloo, 299
Beard and Partridge, Messrs, 178
Bearna, 7, 26, 135, 143, 153, 208
begging, 43-44, 47-50, 52, 57, 68-
  69, 96, 194-96
Belfast, 38, 58, 89, 149, 172, 179,
  183, 237, 353, 365, 367
Benevolent Society of St Andrew, 271
Bermingham, Mr J., 300
Berry, the Misses
Berwick, Edward, 343, 345
Biggar, Joseph, 217
Biggs, Richard, 307, 341
Binns, Jonathan, 19, 331
Birmingham, 78
Birr, 267
Black's Hotel, Eyre Square, 215, 300
blackleg, 78
Blackrock, 65, 130, 135, 168
Blackrock House, 30
blacksmiths, 200, 221
Blake, Edward, J.P., 285
Blake, Dr, 62
Blake, John, 327
Blake, John (Lieutenant Colonel),
  39, 119
Blake, Martin J., 118, 149, 206, 207-
  210, 355, 356
Blake, Mrs Georgina, 62
Blakes of Menlo, 268, 287, 312
  Blake, John, 115
  Misses, 19, 292
  Sir Thomas, 131, 273, 274, 289,
    290, 30-6, 335
  Sir Valentine, 15, 16, 107, 109-11,
    114, 116-18, 206, 287, 349
Blake's Hill, 287
Blennerhasset, Sir Rowland, 212, 214
Blitz, Signor, 295
blood-sports, 304, 310
bludgeon men (& batyeen boys) 113-
  14, 209, 212, 224
Blue Manufactory, 22
Board of Town Commissioners, 36,
  37, 38

Board of Trade, 242
Board of Works, 35, 36, 79, 127,
  128, 131, 135, 139, 170, 232
boat-races, 292, 311-12
Bodkin, John J., 117, 120
Bodkin, Warden, 254
Boherard, 327
Boherbeg, 134
Bohermore, 60, 64, 251, 327, 331,
  335, 336, 338
Boston, 233
Boucicault, Dion, 301
Brady, building contractor, 79
Breakfast Institutes, 202, 333
Brereton, Major-General, 86, 92
brewing, 22-23
bricklayers, 112
Bright, Henry, 248
Bright, Mrs, 248
Bristol, 110
British and American Intercourse
  Company, 165
British Association for the Relief of
  Distress, 333-35
British Relief Association, 146
Brodie Dr, 197, 199
Brophy, John, 234, 235
Browne, trawler owner, 229, 231
Browne, Bishop, 329, 342
Browne, George, 256
Browne, James Valentine, 210-11
Browne, Surgeon, 304
Brownrigg, Rev., 269
brush factory, 3, 185
brushmakers, 221
Buckland Buildings, 271
Bulfin, William, 367
bull-baiting, 304
Burke, John, 248
Burke, Sir John, 117, 119
Burke, Mary, 156
Burke, Michael, 156
Burke, Dr Stephen, 56, 58
Burke, Thomas, 76
Burke, Sir Thomas, 116
Burke, Fr Tom, 260, 356

Bushy Park, 251, 327, 332
butchers, 20-21, 113, 196, 200, 209-11, 264, 333
Buttermilk-lane, 358

cad-playing, 263, 304
Cahill, Rev. D. W., 351
Campbell, Headmaster, 341
Campbell, James, JP, 180
Campbell, Mrs, 341
canal (see Eglinton Canal)
Carlisle, Earl of, 232
Carlyle, Thomas, 84
Carmelites, 332
carpenters, 21, 76-77, 79, 112, 129, 150, 200, 221, 237, 239, 240
Carr's Hotel, 236
Carty, Anthony, 144
Castlegar, 306
catapults, 303
Catholic Association, 111
Catholic Emancipation, 35, 111, 116
Catholic enfranchisement, 106, 108
Catholic / Protestant conflict, 266-75
Cavan, 272n
Ceantar na nOileáin, 187
Census, (1812) 18, (1821) 18, (1831) 18, 21, 32, (1841) 18, (1851) 154, (1891) 338, 339, (1911) 1
Chamber of Commerce, 4, 35
chandler, 200
chapmen, 355
Chard, Arthur, 85
Charitable Pawn Office, 61
charity, 18, 35, 43-49, 52, 54, 65, 66, 87, 194, 196, 201-04, 259, 319, 320, 322, 323
    Mercy Sisters, 202, 204
Charity Schools, 319, 320-22, 326, 329-30, 341
Charter School, 317-18, 320-21
cholera, 35, 52, 58-59, 149, 180, 289
Choral Society, 300
Christian Brothers, 202, 346, 347
Church of England, 298

Church of Ireland, 44, 59, 63, 250, 262, 274
    vestry cess, 35, 44, 46, 62, 63, 252
Cinema 301
circus, 281, 299
City Tavern, 300
Claddagh, 25-28, 73-74, 79-85, 90-91, 94-97, 112, 122, 127, 131, 165, 170, 178-179, 194, 218, 222, 224, 229, 231-36, 258-59, 282-84, 286, 302, 303, 305, 331, 334, 335, 337, 338, 366
    basin, 147
    mayor, admiral or 'king' of, 83
    Regatta, 311
    schools, 331-32, 335-37
Clanmorris, Lord, 169
Clanricarde, Earl of, 110, 111, 116, 119, 180, 207-08, 214
Clare, 4, 27, 88, 151, 155, 156, 209, 217, 222
Claregalway, 89
Clarinbridge, 218
Clarke, Mr (impressario), 295,
Clarke, Mr (architect), 323
Clarke's Yard, Merchant's Road, 282
Clayton, John, 33, 353
Clayton, Oliver, 23
Clayton, P., 353-54
Clements, Mr (surveyor), 130
Clifden, 114, 120, 184, 301
Clog Factory, 181, 283, 284
Clonmel, 52
Clush, 143
Clyde, The, 303
cock-fighting, 304
Coghlan, Pat, 143
Coghlan, Matron
Cohasset, Massachussets, 156
Coleman, James, 199
College Club, 307
College House, 251
College-road, 47, 64, 203, 341
Collegiate Church, (see St Nicholas)
Collins, Timothy, 173, 271
Colonial Buildings, 171

Combination Acts, 75
Comerford, Henry, 155-56
Comerford, Marie, 187
Commercial Rowing Club, 312
Commissioners for Endowed
    Schools, 341
Commons, Fr. George, 127
Commons, Mary, 327
Conamara, 7, 22, 80, 95, 157, 168,
    187, 188
confectioners, 200, 279
Cong, 135
Congregationalist Church, 253
Congress (Trade Union) Reception
    Committee, 240
Connacht Tribune, 225
Connaught Champion, 224, 225
Connaught Cup, 307
Connaught Journal, 21, 22, 30, 33,
    45, 47, 58, 61, 73, 81, 106, 110,
    115, 117, 119, 251, 263, 264, 268,
    286, 296, 308, 311, 354
Connaught Lunatic Asylum
    (Ballinasloe), 193
Connemara (see Conamara)
Connolly, Stephen, 76
Connor, Catherine, 231
Connor, John, 211
Conolly, George, 353-54
Conolly, Thomas, 354
contagion, 43, 47, 53, 57, 147, 319
Coolough, 131
Coombe, Mary, 157
Coppinger, Mrs, 341
Corcoran, Pat, 156
Cork, 4, 5, 13, 17, 28, 56, 79, 154,
    182, 237, 257, 262, 272, 282, 301,
    347, 353, 365
    Foundling Hospital, 63
    Total Abstinence Society, 281
Corn Exchange, 348
Corporation, 14-16, 21, 35, 36, 37,
    39, 52-56, 80, 106, 108-09, 111,
    116, 122, 173, 201, 253, 264, 265,
    267, 304

Corrib Regatta, 311
Corrib Rowing Club, 307, 312
Corrib/Mask canal, 170
Corrib/Mask drainage, 79
Corrigan, Dr, 63
Corrupt Practices Act (1883), 205
County Club, 215
County Infirmary (see Infirmary)
County of the town, 14,-15, 18, 107,
    122, 128, 143, 308
Court Theatre, 301
Courthouse, 21, 127
Coyne, Mrs, 156
Cricket Club, 305
Crimean war, 173, 179
Cromwell's Fort, 240
Crookanabrucky, 19
Cross-street, 37, 76, 353-54
Crotty, Rev. William, 267
Crotty, Mrs, 270
Cullen, Paul (Cardinal), 201, 213,
    261, 343-45, 366
Cullen, Louis, 17
Cullen, P. H., 273-74
Cullinane, William, 88-89
Cummings, 156
Cunningham, John, 327
Cunningham, Willie, 304n
Curwen, John C., 43, 263
Cusack, Thomas, 76
Cuthbert, E., 201
cycling club, 292

d'Arcy, John (Clifden), 114, 120
d'Arcy, Rev. John, 35-39, 48, 50, 52-
    53, 59, 61, 78, 85, 91, 137, 140,
    165, 167, 187, 268, 348
Daily Express, 290
Dalkey, 169
Dallas, Alexander, 269
Daly, James (Warden), 133, 253
Daly, Fr Peter, 30, 45, 61, 65, 120,
    133, 150, 166, 172-74, 176, 181,
    187, 189, 201, 212-13, 255, 261,
    268, 273, 345

Daly political connection, 14, 15-16, 24, 39, 54, 74, 87, 107-09, 208, 348
  Denis 120
  Denis Bowes, 106
  Hyacinth, 109
  James, 13, 14, 15, 106-09, 111-12, 116-17, 119-20, 181
  Richard (Mayor), 15, 93
  St George, 15
Dalyston, 107
Dangan, 130, 147, 151, 334
Davis, Mr, 75
Davitt, Michael, 352
de Latocnaye, 294
de Montbret, Coquebert, 28, 305
De Pazzi, Sr Mary, 146, 331
de Tocqueville, Alexis, 67, 256
De Wets (Athenry), 222
Delaney, Peggy, 231
Demsey, 280
Deposit Fund, 61
Derrydonnell, 279
Development Association, 4, 223
Devlin, Charles, 223
Dillon, Edward (Archbishop), 257
disease, 30, 43, 47, 52, 57, 58, 59, 61, 149, 157, 197, 334
Dispensary, 43, 47, 54-60, 69, 194
distilling, 3, 22-23, 183
Docks and Canal Bill, 35
dock labourers, 239, 240, 242
docks (see harbour)
Dombrain, Sir James, 180
Domhnach na dTincéirí, 287
Dominical theology, 262
Dominican Friars, 32, 83, 85, 140, 254, 257, 334-35
Dominican Sisters, 335, 346
Dominick-street, 20, 22, 62, 64, 81, 87, 110, 341
Donegal, 272
Donnellan, Mrs, 341
Donnybrook Fair, 289
Donovan O'Sullivan, Mary, 281
Dooley Fr Peter, 5, 189, 219, 220, 274, 283, 300, 312

Dooras, 65
Doyle, Moll, 109, 118
Doyle, Mr, 58
dressmaker, 200
Dublin, 1, 15, 18, 24, 34, 37, 48, 50, 56, 58, 60, 63, 67, 75, 78, 80, 87-89, 118, 125, 142, 165, 167, 172, 181-84, 197, 217-19, 232, 237, 239, 240, 252, 257, 261, 264, 287, 292, 293, 301, 317, 332, 345, 347-48, 353, 365
  Foundling Hospital, 63
  Lying-in Hospital, 62
  'Liberty boys', 114
Donnybrook Fair, 287
Dublin Evening Post, 58
Duffy, Mrs, 341
Dunkellin, Lord, 207-08, 210, 213
Dunmore, Co. Galway, 252
Dunraven, Lord, 224
Dunsandle, 13, 107, 108, 110
Durkheim, Emile, 272
Dutton, Hely, 20, 21, 22, 23, 24, 26, 331
dysentery, 58, 60

Earl's Island, 28, 181
Early Closing Association, 236
East Anglia, 89
Ecclesiastical Commissioners, 252
Ecclesiastical Titles Bill, 207
Education Endowments Commissioners, 346
Education Enquiry, 340-42
Egan, Butcher, 195-96
Eglinton Baths, 171
Eglinton Buildings, 171
Eglinton Canal, 24, 35, 79, 116, 131, 147, 170-173, 179, 180, 231
Eglinton Cricket Club, 171
Eglinton, Earl of, 170-71
Eglinton Hotel, 171
Eglinton Racquet Court, 171
Eglinton Scutch Mill, 179
Eglinton-street, 171
Egypt, 58

Elections, 14, 61, 67, 83, 106, 108, 103-22, 117, 175, 205-25, 255, 267, 355, 366
  'bludgeon men', 212
  bribery, 103, 211-12
  Enfranchisement Bill, 35, 116, 117
  enquiries, 112-13, 206-10
  'inducements', 121
  personation, 113, 115
  treating, 119
  Secret Ballot Act 1872, 212
  violence, 103, 111-14, 117
Elphin, 256, 342
emigration, 235-37
Employers' Federation, 241
employment, 13, 21-25, 34, 44-45, 64, 78, 91, 177-78, 185, 189, 196-97, 199, 208-09, 332, 334, 344
Encumbered Estates court, 168, 183
Ennis, 47, 342, 346
Enniskillen, 86, 89
epidemic disease, 43-44, 52, 56- 59, 149, 150, 289
Episcopalians (see Church of Ireland)
equestrian display, 299
Erasmus Smith Foundation and Schools, 54, 171, 306-07, 318, 339, 341, 346,
ethnographers, 84
Eureka Stockade, 221
European continent, 14, 56, 58, 89, 151, 165, 168, 172, 285, 300, 331, 366
excise officers, 34
exports, 2, 17, 25, 34, 97, 172, 182-83
Eyre charity, 201
Eyre Square, 78, 114-15, 137, 187, 197, 240, 252, 263, 279, 299, 305-06
Eyre, Giles, 106
Eyrecourt hounds, 308

Faherty, Bridget, 231
Fahy, Fr, 32
Fahy, the Misses, 340

fairs, 32
Fairhill, 32, 311
Fallon, Mary, 231
Fallon, Mr & Mrs, 107
Famine
  beggars, 143, 144, 151, 157
  Board of Works, 127, 129, 130, 131, 135, 139
  by-election, 139
  Calcutta Relief Committee, 130
  children, 146-47
  cholera, 146, 149-50
  Claddagh, 134-35
  clergy, 127-28, 140-41
  coffin ships, 155-57
  contagion, 157
  cornstores, 127
  Corrib/Mask scheme, 127, 131
  corruption, 136
  Dominican Fathers, 126
  emigration, 154-55
  employment, 127, 133, 135, 137, 147, 150, 156
  food convoys attacked, 131, 134, 135, 140-41, 157
  food exports, 126, 127, 128, 157
  food preparation, 129
  food prices, 126, 130, 135, 136
  food rioters, 126-28, 134
  forestallers, 130, 133
  Gregory Clause, 142, 157
  imports, 129, 134
  jail, 144
  laissez faire policy, 132
  landlords, 143, 146
  Liberal Party (See Whig)
  Liverpool, 126
  London, 126
  magistrates, 126, 128, 131, 134, 141, 143-44, 146
  Mechanics Institute, 129, 150
  merchants, 127, 129-30, 134-35
  O'Connell, Daniel, 132
  outdoor relief, 141, 146-49, 152
  Poor Law Amendment, 142
  Poor Law Commissioners, 147

poor law union, 139-40, 143
poor rates, 143, 144, 145, 146,
    149, 157
potato failure, 125, 133
Presentation Sisters, 146
proselytising, 146
protests, 127, 135-36, 141
Relief Committee, 128, 130, 133,
    135, 137, 140
relief schemes, 126, 128, 130, 131,
    136, 139
Scientific Commission, 126
soup kitchens, 139-43
theatre, 138
Tories, 132
Town commissioners, 126-27, 129,
    131, 133, 134
tradesmen, 139
Treasury, 126, 132, 133, 147
wages, 128, 147
Whig policy, 132, 133, 142
workhouse, 126, 131, 136-38,
    142-44, 146-47, 149-52, 158
'workhouse test', 148
farmers, 16, 45, 80, 171, 178, 184,
    205, 217, 225, 308
Farquarson & Moon, 171
Female Catechistical Society, 268
Fenians, 213, 217
Fenton's coach factory, 238
Ferdinand, Lewis, 274
Festivals, 283-92
fever epidemic, 47, 68
Fever Hospital, 43, 47, 56, 57, 58,
    59, 60, 69
Ffrench, Edmund (Warden), 254-56,
    258, 321-23
Ffrench's Bank, 23
Field, Patrick, 349
Fisher, Robert, 85
fisheries disturbances, 73, 80-85,
    229-32, 234
fishermen, 26-28, 73, 80-85, 88, 91,
    95, 97, 112, 122, 178, 232, 234,
    235, 285, 286, 302, 311, 312, 335
fishing industry, 178

Flood-street, 62, 340
Flour and grain trade, 24-25, 86-89,
    92
Fogarty, 78, 156
Folan, Fr, 126
food prices, 25, 43, 60
food rioting, 43, 73, 76, 78, 86-98,
    229, 236, 267, 366
football, 292, 307
forestallers, 73, 88, 90, 92, 97
Forthill, 311
Foster, Thomas C., 19
Foster, W. E., 85
Foundlings, 47, 62, 63
Franciscan community, 251, 257
Francis-street, 187
Franklin, Mr, 78
free schools (see Charity Schools)
freeholders, 14, 15, 104, 106, 109,
    112-13, 115-16,
Freeland, Minister, 268
Freeman's Journal, 86, 247
Freemasons, 257, 287
freemen, 14-16, 74, 80, 106, 108-09,
    116-18, 121-22, 206-12, 221, 237
French revolution, 44, 106
French, Colonel, 206-07
Fry, Elizabeth, 56
funerals, 59, 272
Fynn, Fr Mark, 49, 53, 64, 65
Gaelic Athletic Association, 222,
    306
Gaelic League, 284
Gale, Parnell, 87, 89
Gallagher, M., 297
Galway Act (1717), 16, 116
Galway Advertiser, 47, 54, 95, 97,
    211, 265, 282, 304, 353, 354
Galway Express, 167, 203, 212, 215,
    217, 253, 265, 270, 274, 275, 300,
    303, 304, 305, 310, 351
    profile, 270
Galway Independent, 214, 353, 354
Galway Independents, 13-15, 106-11,
    116, 118, 214
Galway Line, 173-77

Galway Mercury, 236, 269, 299, 351
Galway Observer, 78, 301
Galway Packet, 169, 170, 269
Galway Patriot, 31
Galway Races, 3, 150, 280, 307-09, 311, 365-66
Galway Standard, 78, 247, 248, 249, 275
Galway Subsidy, 73
Galway time, 167
Galway Vindicator, 92, 122, 131, 134, 136, 140, 141, 142, 219, 235, 248, 249, 266, 274
Galway Workers and General Labourers Union, 2, 240-41
Galway Vindicator, 155
gambling, 304, 308
Gas Company, 37-39, 167, 170
Gavazzi, Fr, 269, 270
Geoghegan, John, 156
George IV, 116
German band, 290
Germany, 181
Gillen, Constable, 231
Glasgow, 38, 271
Glassford, Mr, 180
Godolphin Osborne, Sidney, 151, 334
golf, 307
Good, John, 232
Gort, 75, 289
Gortacleva female school, 332
Gortrevagh, 143
Grace Asylum, 201
Grain exporters (see flour and grain trade)
Grammar School (see Erasmus Smith)
Grand Jury, 52-54, 58
Granite Company, 4
Gray, Surgeon, 62
Greaney, Patrick, 211
Gregory, Lady Augusta, 6, 142
Gregory, Sir William, 142
Gripe, The, 234
Grocers' assistants (see shop assistants)

Guinness brewing family, 201
Gwynn, Stephen, 3, 6, 223, 224, 225, 242, 366

Haidee, The, 157
Halifax, 7, 172, 174
Hall, Jonathan, 151, 153
Hallet, T. G. P., 217, 221
Hamburg, 58
handball, 305
Haneen, Malachy, 317
Haneen, Nicholas, 317
Hannon, Patrick J., 4
harbour, 2, 7, 14-17, 24-25, 28-29, 35, 36-36, 39, 107, 116, 141, 151, 165, 167, 172-73, 177, 183-84,m 240-41, 304
Harbour Commissioners, Board of, 3, 35, 36, 39, 167, 170, 173, 177, 180, 197, 199, 367
Hardiman, James, 13, 14, 16, 18, 20, 24, 25, 26, 27, 28, 48, 55, 56, 80, 84, 93, 106, 107, 108, 258, 263, 283, 285, 286, 287, 294, 295, 304, 320, 322, 331
Hardiman Burke, James, 348
Harper's Weekly, 157
Harrison, John, 197
hawkers, 26, 33, 94, 280, 291, 292
Headford, 75
Healy, Tim, 217
hedge schools, 318, 327, 336, 341
Hellard, Captain, 140, 144, 145
Hennessy, Constable, 231
Henry-street, 1, 284
Herbert, Robert, 80
Hickey, Kate, 231
hides, 177
Higgins's Lane, 304
High-street, 23, 33, 187, 341, 353
Hill, Resident Magistrate, 273
Hobsbawm, Eric, 93, 94
Hollowel, Rev., 306
holy wells, 258-59
hookers, 170, 188, 311-12
Hoppen, Theodore, 114

Horse, Cattle and Carriage Repository, 178
horse-racing (see Galway Races)
House League, 225
House of Commons, 16, 67, 108, 112, 116, 237
House of Lords, 36
House of Mercy, 202, 203
Houses of Industry, 44, 47
housing, 1, 19, 43, 54, 189, 225
Howard, John, 54, 55
hucksters, 33, 280
Hughes, Fr Patrick, 84
Hurd, Mrs, 64
Hutchinson Brothers, 299
Hynes, Bartley, 83

illegitimacy, 63
Illustrated London News, 90
Improvements Bill, 37
Incorporated Society of Charter Schools, 317
Indian Empire, The, 173, 174
Industrial School, 202, 284
industry, 3, 5-8, 15, 19, 22, 26, 28-29, 66, 176-79, 181, 183, 185, 188-89, 208, 262, 270, 367
infanticide and abandonment, 63-64
Infirmary, 20, 47, 54-57, 68, 91, 193-94, 204, 303
Inglis, Henry, 30, 249, 301, 329, 330, 353, 354
Inis Oírr, 231
Intermediate Education, 346-47
Ireland, John, 24, 91, 128, 133, 137
Irish Church Missions Society, 269-70
Irish Drapers' Assistants Association, 239
Irish Industrial Development Association, 6
Irish Iodine & Marine Salts Company, 179, 180
Irish language, 31, 319, 322
Irish Manufacture Movement, 179
Irish National Bakers' Federal Trade Union, 239

Irish parliament, 24, 44, 218, 308
Irish People, 103
Irish Reform Association, 224
Irish Reform bill, 118
Irish Rugby Football Union, 307
Irish Society for Promoting the Native Irish through the Medium of their own Language, 326
Irish Trades Union Congress, 240
Irish Turf Club, 307
Irvine's New Concert Hall, 301
jails, 144, 154, 203, 268, 317
Jesuit community, 305, 346
Johnson, James, 330
Jones, Owen, 83
Jordan, Donald C., 98
Joybells, 91, 139, 150, 267
Joyce & Lynch, 23
Joyce, Patrick, 183
Joyce, Pierce, 198
Joyces of Merview, 23
Jute Spinning Company (see Bag Factory)

Kane, Dr Robert, 350
Kavanagh, Fr, 141-42, 149
Kean, Edmund, 296-97
Kearney, James Johnston, 304
Kearn's Academy, 340
Keedy, Bartholomew, 130
Kelly, Oliver (Archbishop), 254-55, 355
Kelly, Bridget, 134
Kelly, John, 279, 280
Kelly, Miss, 340
Kelly, Peter, 305
Kennedy, Michael and John, 78-79
Kenyon, Lord Chief Justice, 93
Keogh, Judge, 214, 216
Kerins, A. B., 202
Kernan, John, Resident Magistrate, 128, 135, 144, 231-32
Kildare Place Society, 327-28
Kilkenny, 332
Killala, 106
Killaloe, Catholic bishop of, 267

Killanin, Lord (see Morris)
Killarney, 301
Killeen, 308
Killian & Co., 171
Killiney, 169
Kilroy's Hotel, 115, 296
Kiltulla, 308, 309
King & Mullins, Messrs, 306
King, James, 89
King, Mrs, 236
King, Padge, 233
King's Bench, 109
Kingston, 169
Kinsale, 15
Kinvarra, 95
Kirwan, Augustine (Warden) 319, 326
Kirwan, Francis (Captain), 107
Kirwan, Denis, 78
Kirwan, J. W., 343
Kirwan, John, 211
Kirwan's Lane, 321
Kirwan's Lane Theatre, 293, 295-97
Knocknacarra, 81, 143
Kruger, General, 222

Labour (also see trade unionism)
Labour councillors, 225, 242
Labour Electoral Association, 221
Labour Party (British), 221
Labourer's Society, 239,
Lackagh, 141, 154
Ladies' Association, 28, 60
Laighléis, Tomás, 292
Lambert, James Staunton, 110-14, 117
Lambert, Thomas, 115
Lancashire Clog Sole Manufacturing Company, 181
Lancastrian system, 323, 324
Land Act of 1903, 223
Land League, 352
Langley, Eliza, 332
Larkin, Jim, 240-41
Latty, Mrs, 62
Lawler, Michael, 332, 334
Lawson, Judge, 216

le Poer Trench, Power (Archbishop), 348
le Poer Trench, William, 73, 89
le Poer Trench, William (Captain), 214
Leahy, Columba, 83
Leamy, Edmund, 220, 221
leather-cutter, 206, 211
Lenaboy, 181
Lever, Charles, 103, 104
Lever, John Orrel, 173, 175-76, 212, 213, 217
Lewis, John, 272
Liberal (see Whig)
Liberal Trades Club, 118
libraries, 353, 356
Limerick, 6, 18, 19, 26, 47, 52, 60, 78, 80, 116, 154, 182, 203, 237, 240, 269, 318, 322, 351
linen, 22, 28-29, 32, 113, 179
literacy, 317-19, 338
Liverpool, 2, 151, 242
Lloyd, Clifford, 358
Loan Fund, 61, 282
Local Government Act, 221
Local Government Board, 199
Lombard-street, 31, 65, 187, 203, 296, 306, 322, 327
London, 18-19, 28, 60, 84, 88-89, 113, 115, 126, 129, 165, 216, 223, 236, 268, 328, 348
London & Leeds Woollen-Hall, 28
London Hibernian Society, 268, 326, 327, 328
London Tavern Committee, 58, 60, 65
London & West of Ireland Fishing & Fish Manure Company, 178
Long Walk, 180, 292
Lord Lieutenant, 84, 89, 133, 135, 140, 151, 171, 265, 286, 311, 345
Lough Carra, 170
Lough Corrib (see also Corrib), 35, 170, 186
Lough Mask, 170
Loughrea, 15-16, 117, 263, 268, 291
Louis XVI, 106

Lower Abbeygate-street, 320
Lowther, Fr John, 258
Luddism, 86
Lushington Reilly, John, 48, 264
Lushington Reilly, Mrs, 29
Lyddle, Mr, 38
Lying-in Hospital, 54, 61-63
Lynch, Andrew, 117-18, 121, 126
Lynch, Arthur, 220-23
Lynch, Fr, 255
Lynch, Michael, 217-19
Lynch, Mr, 199
Lynch, Mrs, 65, 294
Lynch, Nicholas (of Bearna), 135-36, 143, 153, 208
Lynch, John (Brother), 202
Lynch, Patrick & James, 23
Lynch, Patrick Mark, 122
Lynch, Richard Mark, 68-69
Lynch, 'the Misses', 65, 202, 321
Lynd, Robert, 310, 365
Lyons, F. S., 217

Maamtrasna Martyrs, 356
McArdle & Bullock's iodine factory, 179
McArdle, James Smith, 180
McArdle, Patrick, 171
McAuley, Catherine, 202, 193
Macartney, Saint George, 353n
Macartney, Mr, 293, 295
McBride, John, 222
McCaul, Mr, 179
McCormack, Bishop, 189, 220
McCoy, Mrs, 268
MacDonagh, Thomas, 76
McDonogh, Honoria, 187
McDonogh, Máirtín Mór, 3, 4, 7, 187-88, 241-42
McDonogh, Michael, 187
McDonogh, Monica, 187
McDonogh, Thomas, 187
McDonogh, Thomas & Sons, 3, 4, 7
McDonogh & Comerford, 187
McDougall, Alexander (Constable), 231

MacDougall, John, 253, 270
McDowell, Robert, 34
MacEvilly, John (Bishop), 197, 213-14, 216, 261, 266, 345-46, 366
McGrath, Thomas, 258
MacHale, John (Archbishop), 67, 214, 332
Mackie, John, 24
McKie, Major Patrick, 145, 149
MacLachlan, Lachlan, 84, 118, 140, 150
McNally, Maria, Bridget and Michael, 231
McSweeney, Michael, 307
Mack's Hotel Room, 346

Magdalen Asylum, 43, 47, 54, 65, 150, 202-03
Magdeburg, 181
magistrates, 47, 57, 87, 90, 93, 97, 107, 115, 128, 167, 195, 231-32, 263-65, 268-69, 280, 302, 311, 354
Mainguard-street, 20, 31, 75, 210
Malthus, Robert, 44
Manchester, 173, 271, 301
Mansion House Committee, 60, 125
marble, 2, 22, 24, 177, 185
Marie Antoinette, 106
Marine Salts Company, 180
market jury, 31, 32, 93
markets, 27, 31, 91-95, 187
Market-street, 24, 185, 187, 306, 327
Martin, Elizabeth, 293, 297
Martin, Harriet, 104
Martin, P. K. & Co., 34
Martin, Richard 'Humanity', 49, 104, 107, 110, 112-14, 116, 214, 268, 293
Martin, Robert of Ross, 348
Martin, Thomas, 119-20
Martyn, Mr, 146
masons, 21, 78, 79, 129, 150, 200, 221, 352
maternity hospital, (see Lying-in Hospital)
Mathew, Fr, 282

Maxey, Miss, 341-42
May, Mr H., 299
May games, 287
'maying' at Menlo, 287-92, 290
Maynooth, 342
Mayo, 98, 106, 154, 155, 173, 215
mechanics (see tradesmen)
Mechanics' Institute, 5, 150, 249,
  269, 281, 347-52
Medical Dispensaries Act, 193
Mediterranean, 58, 134
Melbourne, Viscount, 66
Melville, Alexander (Professor), 253
Mendicity Institute, 46-47, 193, 264
Menlo, 15, 19, 24, 62, 107, 114-15,
  121, 131, 135, 215, 237, 266, 273,
  274, 287-92, 306-07, 310, 332
Menlo Castle, 15, 107, 115, 121,
  289-92, 306
Menlo Emmetts Rowing Club, 312
Menlo National School, 332, 335
merchants, 3, 5, 8, 15, 17-18, 23, 28,
  33, 35, 74, 87- 89, 93, 97-98, 106-
  07, 175, 178-79, 182, 187, 240-
  41, 303
Merchants Road, 141
Mercy Sisters, 66, 140, 149, 202-04,
  251, 332-33, 336, 345-46
  National School, 193, 332,
Merlin Park, 22, 62, 327
Merville, 30
Methodism, 250, 252, 268
Meyrick, General, 20, 21
Meyrick's Square, 20
Midas, The, 156
Middle-street, 62, 250, 289, 295,
  301, 303, 305, 340, 341, 342, 349,
  352
Mill-street, 62, 171
Miller, John, 253
millers and milling, 2-3, 22-24, 32,
  86, 91, 112, 128, 177-78, 182,
  333, 367
missions, 260-61
Model School, 345-46
Moffett, Thomas, 351

Monaghan (Co.), 180
Monahan, J. H., 139
Montpellier Hotel, 30
Moon, Alexander, 253
Moore, John, 87
Moran, Dr, 61
Morgan, Lady, 104, 293
Morisey, John, 112-13
Morning Chronicle, 129
Morris, Captain, 81, 84
Morris, George, 214
Morris, James, 22
Morris, Martin, 221-22
Morris, Michael, 213
Mortality Society, 61
Mountbellew, 181, 184
Moycullen, 89, 146
Municipal Reform Act of 1840, 35,
  253
Munster-Connacht Exhibition, 6
Munster-lane, 2
Murray, Timothy, 211
Murray, Archbishop, 146, 329
Murray, Mary, 242
musicians, 200
Muslin, 179

Na Forbacha, 26
nailers, 75, 112
Nantes, 65-66, 202, 321
National Association, 213
National Bank, 23, 184
National Coast & Deep-Sea Fishery
  Company, 84
National Education, Board of
  Commissioners, 328-29, 329, 334-
  35, 337, 339, 345, 351,
National Education system, 326
National Schools (see individual
  schools)
National Union of Dock Labourers,
  241
Navy Reserve, 236
New Baths, 30
New Buildings, 353
New Orleans, 154

New Road, 171
New Theatre, 297
New York, 7, 154, 155, 172, 174, 178
New York & Galway Steamship
    Company, 172
Newcastle, 22, 135
Newcastle Distillery, 279
Newcastle-road, 68
Newell, W. H., 345
Newmarket, 280
Newry, 29
Newtownsmith, 21-22, 171, 189,
    203, 332-33, 336-38
Nicholls, George, 66, 67, 68
Nicholson, Asenath, 152, 256
Nile Lodge, 135
Nimmo, Alexander, 170
Nolan, John Philip, M.P., 214, 356
Nottingham, 331
Nun's Island, 3, 24, 61, 64, 183, 201,
    252
Nuttall, Thomas, 75

O'Brien, Bridget, 332
O'Brien, Malachy, 327
O'Brien, Patrick, 331
O'Brien, Patt, 340
O'Brien, William, 224
O'Connell, Daniel, 39, 67, 117-18,
    208
    in Galway, 110-11, 120, 239
O'Connor, Michael, 113
O'Connor, Mrs, 341
O'Connor, Paul (Brother) 259-60,
    32-26, 329-30, 333, 356
O'Connor, T. P., 216-18
O'Donnell, Frank Hugh,
O'Donnell, Laurence (Bishop), 61,
    212, 213, 216, 261, 342-45
O'Flaherty, Anthony, 139, 150, 166,
    197, 206-08, 214
O'Flaherty, Bartley, 263-64
O'Flaherty, Liam, 4
O'Flaherty, Martin, 214
O'Flaherty, Roderic, 287

O'Gorman, Philip, 4, 6
O'Grady's school, 340
O'Halloran, Andrew, 78
O'Halloran, William, 240
O'Hara, James (Colonel), 181-84, 187
O'Hara, James (M.P.), 111-13, 116,
    117, 348-49
O'Mahony, Colman, 262
O'Maley, Thomas (Dr), 58
O'Malley, Charles, 103
O'Malley, Godfrey, 104
O'Meara, James, 219, 284
O'Neill, Eliza (actress), 296
O'Neill, Kitty, 29
O'Neill, Mary Devenport, 1
O'Reilly, Police Sub-inspector, 197
O'Riordan, Mr, 5
O'Rourke, John (Canon), 138
O'Shea, Captain William, 217-19
O'Shea, Katherine, 217
O'Sullivan, Dennis, 115
O'Sullivan, Jeremiah, 115
O'Sullivan, Thomas, 267
O'Toole, Fr John P., 342-44
O'Dea, Mary, 231

'Old Bartlemy', 289
Old Galwegians, 307
Oliver, John, 210
Ollcot, Sidney, 301
Oranmore, 131, 154, 232, 236, 306
Orphans, 43, 47, 64, 65
Orphans' Breakfast Institute, 329-30,
    333-34
Oughterard, 143, 261, 343
Ouseley, Gideon, 252
outdoor relief, 67, 202
Overend, Mr, 179
Owen, Robert, 44
Owenson, Robert, 293

Palestine, 58
Pankhurst, Christabel, 225
Parnell, Charles Stewart, 87, 216-21,
    239, 352

Parochial School, 323
Parsonstown (Birr), 341
Patrician Brothers, 140, 251, 260, 325, 327, 329-30, 333-35, 338, 345-47
paupers, 44, 49, 51-54, 62, 63, 68, 149, 200, 237
pawnbrokers, 45, 60, 85, 211, 289
Peace Preservation Act, 87
peddlars, 33, 355
Pedestrianism, 280
Peel, Robert, 126, 132-33, 343
penal laws, 257
Penny Readings, 356
Persse, Dudley, 111, 113
Persse, Thomas Moore, 183
Persse's Distillery, 183
Peru, 181
philanthropy, 48, 85, 331
piece-work, 76, 79, 182, 185
pilgrimages, 258
Pinkerton, John, 218-20, 222
Piscatory School, 83, 235
Plunkett, Horace, 223
police, 35-36, 63, 90-91, 95-97, 103, 114-15, 196-97, 215, 231, 242, 267, 270, 290, 305, 309-10, 356-58
Ponsonby, Frederick, 108
Poor Clare community, 269
Poor Law, generally, 35, 44-45, 53-54, 60, 66-67, 126, 152, 193-94, 197, 199, 201, 203-04, 236, 256
    Commissioners, 67, 68, 145, 151 193, 194, 197, 199, 203
    Board of Guardians, 1, 36, 67, 76, 138, 148, 153-54, 194, 197, 199, 202, 334, 366
    Poor Inquiry, 19, 45, 56, 59, 61, 63
Pope Pius IX, 270
population, 1, 18, 165
port, (see harbour)
Port Manton Island, Nova Scotia, 156
post office, 174
Postmaster General, 172
potato market, 90, 93, 96, 186

Pouleeny, 143
poverty, 19, 43-45, 48, 53, 60, 66, 89, 109, 143, 178, 185, 198-99, 242, 251, 270, 325, 329, 333
Presbyterians, 256, 256
Presentation Sisters, 202, 251, 257, 321, 323, 329-30, 332, 336
pro-Cathedral (Catholic), 247-50, 257n, 274
proselytising, 269, 272, 327, 333, 366
Prospect Hill, 54-55, 284
protest, 13, 39, 73-74, 79, 86, 87, 89-90, 92-98, 113, 117, 199, 121, 198, 218, 223, 229, 231-32, 238, 240, 263, 272, 280, 283, 285, 308, 310
Protestant Mutual Improvement Society, 271
Protestant Orphan Society, 271
Provincial Bank, 23, 184, 279
Pückler-Muskau, Fürst, 308

Quakers, 85, 229, 333
Quay-street, 141
Quebec, 154
Queen Elizabeth 1, 110
Queen Victoria, 127
Queen's College, 4, 79, 131, 147, 169, 181, 204, 210, 216, 343-45, 271, 306-07, 343, 344, 351
'Queen's College Gazette' (Galway Express), 270

Raftery, Anthony, 268
Rahoon, 19, 73, 146, 166, 250, 257, 258, 288, 303
railway, 5, 6, 150-51, 165-73, 183-84, 239, 292, 309
    MGWR, 172, 173, 178, 183, 184, 289, 309
Railway Hotel, 169, 171, 217, 218, 219
ratepayers, 68-69, 143, 153, 203
Redington, Charles Talbot, 218
Redington, Sir Thomas, 135, 176
Redmond, John, 222
Regan, Mr, 24

regattas, 311-12
regraters, 73, 92
Renmore, 131, 157, 311
Renville, 26
Renvyle, 19
Repeal, 67, 118
Repeal Rock, Shantalla, 239
retailing, 31-34
Ribbonism, 79, 285
riot (see protest),
Roberts, Samuel, 79
Roche, B. J., Fr, 127, 146, 283, 335
Roche, John, Fr, 134
Rochford, John, 76
Rome, 253-56, 329
Roscommon, 69, 141, 308
Rose, Madamoiselle, 299
Rosmuc, 113
rowing, 290, 312
Royal College of Surgeons of Ireland, 59, 61
Royal Dublin Society, 350
Royal Galway Institute, 91, 179, 352
Royal Galway Yacht Club, 312
Royal Irish Agricultural Society, 171
Royal Navy, 233, 235, 311, 331
RSPCA, 104
Ruane, Andrew, 327
Ruane, Mary, 327
rugby, 307
Rush & Palmer, Messrs, 128, 134, 135
Rush, Thomas, OP, 83-85, 179, 334
Russell, Lord John, 132, 133
Russia, 129
Rutledge, Mr, 169

Sabbatarianism, 262-66, 280, 290-91
Salthill, 30-31, 130, 136, 150, 168, 169, 171, 177, 215, 253, 269, 292, 304, 345
Salthill Industrial School, 185, 202
Salthill Tramway Co, 310
Sarah Milledge, The, 155-56
Savage, William, 335
sawyers, 76, 78, 112, 117, 237

Scottish Benevolent Society of St Andrew, 201
Sea Road, 253
Seapoint, 130, 168, 169
seaweed, 27, 95, 128, 180
Second Reformation Protestantism, 201, 260
Secret Ballot Act, 122, 205
sectarian tensions, 34, 247-50, 230-31, 266-74
Semple, John, 210
Sen, Amartya, 157
servants, 30, 60, 65-66, 200, 203, 248
sexual mores and behaviour, 63, 291
Seymour, Mr, 296
Shawe-Taylor, Captain John, 4, 6, 223-24
Sheridan, John E., 336
sheriff, 73, 82, 91, 115, 197, 213
Shipping Federation of Great Britain, 242
shipwrights, 112, 200
shoemakers, 33, 75-76, 79, 112, 117, 120, 211, 221, 237-38
shop assistants, 5, 236-37, 239
shopkeepers, 6, 7, 26, 33, 200, 209, 237-39, 262, 264, 270, 290, 296, 302, 350
Shop-street, 23, 31, 34, 196, 253, 284, 296, 349
Sinn Fein, 225
Six-mile-bush, 279, 308
Skilling, Thomas, 148
slaters, 112, 129, 221
Sligo, 18, 19, 23, 26, 48, 154, 239
sling-fights, 302-03
smallpox, 60, 194
Smith, Adam, 93, 326
Smith, Mary, 327
Smyth, Charles, 34
Smyth, Nicholas, 340
Smyth, Thomas, 327, 320
Smyth, William, 327
smiths, 112
snowball-throwing, 302
soldiers, (see army)

soup kitchens, 96
spinners, 29
sport, 292, 301-12
Spring Rice, Thomas, 116
St George, Christopher, 143, 157
St Ignatius College, 307, 346
St Jarlath's College, Tuam, 261, 346
St John's Eve / Day, 83, 89, 281, 284, 286-87
St Joseph's (the 'Bish'), 347
St Lawrence, Lord, 214, 309
St Magdalen Society, 65
St Mary's College, 2, 343-45
St Nicholas Collegiate Church, 14, 76, 91, 117, 139, 150, 166, 250-52, 254- 60, 267-69, 267, 273, 303-04, 306, 328
St Nicholas R.C. Church, (see pro-Cathedral)
St Nicholas East, 141
St Nicholas N.S., 271
St Patrick's GAA Club, 306
St Patrick's Rowing Club, 312
St Patrick's Day, 202, 283-84
St Patrick's Day 'Tea and Coffee Festival', 283
St Patrick's Temperance Society, 283, 351
St Vincent de Paul Society, 201, 202
St. Johns, Newfoundland, 154
St. John, The, 156
Staunton-Cahill, R., 291
Stephens, Thomas, 78, 133, 279-80
Stephens's Foundry, 38
Stitt, Captain, 156
stockings, 19, 28, 176-77
stonecutter, 200
stone-throwing, 291
straw bottle envelope industry, 185
Straw Lodge, 149
street preachers, 269
strikes, 5, 74-76, 198, 242, 302
  Bag Factory, 182
  bakers, 78
  carpenters, 77
  Connacht Laundry, 240

dock labourers, 239, 241
labourers, 79
labourers at Franklin's quarry, 237
labourers building Clifden line, 239
newsboys, 240
sawyers, 76
shoemakers, 76, 79
shop assistants at Moon's, 239
university students, 240
Sullivan, Mrs., 46
Sullivan, Tom, 219
Sundays, 262-66
Swan, John, 248, 249
Sweeney, Patt, 79
swimming, 304
Symmonds, Thomas Edward, 233
Synge, Francis, 229-30
Synge, John Millington, 6, 229
Synge, Rev. Alexander, 230
Synod of Thurles, 344, 345

tailor, 5, 33, 79, 112, 128, 200, 221, 334, 352
tanners, 112
Tarpey, Hugh, 216
Tatton, Mr, 177
taxation populaire, 89, 95
Taylor's Hill, 148, 253
teachers, 182, 200, 323-27, 330, 337-39, 345, 347
Teetotal Festival, 289
telegraph, 170-71
Temperance movement, 61, 219, 261, 265, 281-84, 286, 289, 300, 306, 349
tenant farmers, 67, 132, 146, 208
Tenant League, 207
Terryland, 180, 208
Testot, Monsieur, 294
textile manufacturing, 28-29
Thackeray, William M., 32, 353
Theatre, 292-301
Tholsel, 88-89
Thompson, D'Arcy Wentworth, 271, 272
Thompson, Edward P., 92, 98, 236

Thompson, Thomas H., 180
Thonabrucky, 19, 131
Times, The, 352
Todhunter, William, 82
Tories (Conservatives) 35, 119, 213
toss, game of, 304
tourism and tourists, 14, 24, 29-31, 69, 169, 177, 194
Town Commissioners (and Urban Council), 3, 35, 36-39, 78, 91, 127, 129, 167, 173, 181, 182, 197, 219, 261, 305, 345
Town Hall, 5-6, 7, 38, 117, 125, 197, 271, 301,
Town Tenants League, 225
Townshend, The, 81, 84
trade, 2-5, 13-14, 16-18, 22-25, 28-29, 33, 49, 74-75, 78-79, 86-87, 93, 108, 122, 132, 165, 167, 169, 176-79, 181, 185, 187, 194, 221, 225, 232, 240, 264, 334, 350-53, 357, 367
trades guilds, 73-74, 80, 108, 110, 117-18, 150, 348-349
trade unionism, 5, 74-79, 225, 236-42
tradesmen, 21, 26, 33, 45, 60-61, 73-79, 106-09, 111, 113, 116-118, 122, 196-97, 206, 208, 229, 238, 348-49, 281, 297, 347-48, 350
Trades and Labour Council, 225, 240
Trades Political Union, 118
Trades, Union of, 76, 109, 110
transportation, 107
Travers, Fr Dennis, 4, 5
trawling, 28, 84-85, 229-36
Traynor, Mr, 76
Trench, Wilbraham Fitz-John, 4
Trevelyan, Charles, 132-33, 142
'Tribes of Galway', 17, 23, 106, 254-55, 257
and 'non-tribes', 254-55
trick o' the loops, 280
Trinidad, 346
Trotter, John Bernard, 43, 256

Tuam, 67, 134, 138, 184, 214, 217, 222, 263, 267, 308, 329, 332, 340, 355
Tuam Herald, 240
Tuam Synod, 254
Tullow, 323
typhus, 56-58, 180
Typographical Association, 239
Tyrone, 95

Ulla, Herr, 284
Ulster, 22, 29, 44, 107, 179, 218, 252, 270, 344
Ulster Bank, 184
Ulster Railway Company, 179
unemployment, 43, 229, 237
Unionist, 221, 224
Unionist Party, 6
United Irishman, 220
United Irishmen, 107
United Kingdom, 151
United States, 154-55, 177, 151, 180, 183, 235, 251,
Ursuline Sisters, 332, 334-35

vagrants, 93, 330
Vatican, 333
Veitch, Dr Andrew James, 56
Veitch, Dr James, 56
Verdon, Mrs, 341
Viceroy, The, 172
Victoria Cinema, 301
Vincentian Fathers, 261, 274
Vixen, The, 97

wages, 61, 74-75, 151, 169, 179, 182-83, 198, 237, 239, 241, 283, 318, 351
wakes, 59
Wallscourt, Lord, 81, 145, 148, 311, 348
Walsh, Thomas, 75, 303
War
First World War, 4, 7, 205, 225
Napoleonic Wars, 22, 28, 43

Warburton, George (Major), 64, 114, 115
Ward, Georgy, 171
Ward, Michael, 216
Ward, Mr J., 299
Ward, Robert E, 340
Warden of Galway, 253-56
Waterford, 17, 19, 52, 154, 272, 318, 322
weavers, 29, 46, 95, 179, 200
weight-throwing, 306
Welsh language, 31
Wesley, John, 90
West Bridge, 82
West Indies, 18
'West, the', 1, 2, 29
Westport, 26, 98
West-road, 327
Whigs, 35, 119-20, 132, 176, 207, 214
whiskey, 3, 26, 139, 177, 183, 262
Whistler, Dr, 59
Whiteboyism, 73
Widows' and Orphans' Asylum, 54, 63, 64, 203
Will o' the Wisp, 354
Williams, Mrs E., 300

Williamsgate-street, 20, 238
William-street, 28, 301, 340
Wilson, George, 280
Winchester Convent, Hampshire, 342
Wolfe Tone, Theobald, 293
Wombwell's Royal National Menagerie, 137, 299
Wood, Charles, 133
Woodlawn, 184
Woodquay, 47, 53, 114, 171, 187, 271, 284, 287
wool / woollen industry, 2, 17, 28-29, 48, 177
Woollen Mills, 2-4, 189
workhouse, 47, 48, 62, 66-69, 76, 96, 97, 142, 145, 147, 154, 193-202, 203, 204, 234, 268, 334
Wyndham, George (Chief Secretary), 223

Xenophon, 33

Yeats, William Butler, 6
yeomanry, 107
Youghal, 15
Young Ireland Hall, 217
Young, Arthur, 44